As students, you are on a journey to gain the knowledge and skills needed to work with children who have exceptional learning needs, their families, and others who are concerned with their education and wellbeing. As part of this journey, you are joining a group of practitioners who have dedicated themselves to making the world a better place for individuals with exceptionalities. You are, in short, joining the profession of special education. Like most professions, special education has defined a body of information, standards for the field, that prepare practitioners for their work and has established a code of ethics. This information provides the foundation for what each practitioner needs to know and how to carry out these duties.

This information has been drawn from the **Council for Exceptional Children (www.cec.sped.org)**, the largest professional organization in special education. This information is continued on the back inside cover of this book so that you will have easy access to it as you move through the chapters.

You will find:

1. A description of CEC
2. A summary of how these standards have been used within this text and accompanying materials
3. The CEC Code of Ethics
4. A list of the primary standards for special educators

We welcome you to the world of special education where working together we can make a difference in the lives of children with exceptionalities.

Council for Exceptional Children

The Council for Exceptional Children (CEC) is the largest international professional organization dedicated to improving educational outcomes for individuals with exceptionalities, students with disabilities, and the gifted. CEC advocates for appropriate governmental policies, sets professional standards, provides continual professional development, advocates for newly and historically underserved individuals with exceptionalities, and helps professionals obtain conditions and resources necessary for effective professional practice.

How the CEC Standards Relate to This Text

As you read this text you will notice that the content and information directly relate to the standards. This is no accident! In addition to the foundational information in Chapters 1 and 2, each subsequent chapter reflects on historical roots; looks carefully at the characteristics of children and their learning differences; examines the child's overall development (language, social, etc.); presents information on instructional planning and methods and strategies; addresses the assessment needs of children; and discusses the role of collaboration and ethical practice. As an introductory text, we do not expect that all of the knowledge and skills needed for a practicing special education teacher will be mastered with this one text and course—but we do hope that a solid foundation will be built for future learning. In addition to using the standards as guidelines as we wrote the text, here are other ways that they are incorporated:

- The test bank of questions provided with the text has been designed to look at the knowledge identified for each standard;
- Activities that accompany each chapter are set up to facilitate the development of the skills needed within each standard;
- Your professor may request a portfolio as part of your assessment (or you may choose to create one for your own use). Suggestions have been given on how to show your accomplishments within the standards;
- We have also developed a self-reflections log based on the CEC Standards (see the student website) to help you monitor your learning.

As you grow professionally you will continue to draw on the standards for the field, expanding your knowledge and skills and enhancing your ability to meet the needs of your students. We encourage you to connect with other professionals who share your same commitment as a first step in your journey toward professionalism.

THIRTEENTH
EDITION

Educating Exceptional Children

Samuel Kirk

Late of University of Arizona

James J. Gallagher

University of North Carolina at Chapel Hill

Mary Ruth Coleman

University of North Carolina at Chapel Hill

Nick Anastasiow

Emeritus, Hunter College, City University of New York

WADSWORTH
CENGAGE Learning

Australia • Brazil • Japan • Korea • Mexico • Singapore • Spain • United Kingdom • United States

FL

Educating Exceptional Children,
Thirteenth Edition
Samuel Kirk, James Gallagher, Mary Ruth Coleman, and Nick Anastasiow

Executive Editor, Education: Mark Kerr

Developmental Editor: Beth Kaufman

Assistant Editor: Caitlin Cox

Editorial Assistant: Genevieve Allen

Media Editor: Ashley Cronin

Marketing Manager: Kara Kindstrom Parsons

Marketing Assistant: Dimitri Hagnere

Marketing Communications Manager: Tami Strang

Sr. Content Project Manager: Tanya Nigh

Design Director: Rob Hugel

Art Director: Maria Epes

Print Buyer: Judy Inouye

Rights Acquisitions Specialist: Don Schlotman

Production Service: Integra Software Services, Inc.

Text Designer: Diane Beasley

Photo Researcher: Scott Rosen, Bill Smith Group

Text Researcher: Sue Brekka

Cover Designer: Bartay Studio

Cover Image: Thomas Balsamo

Compositor: Integra Software Services, Inc.

Library of Congress Control Number: 2010936948

Student Edition:
ISBN-13: 978-0-495-91360-3
ISBN-10: 0-495-91360-X

Loose-leaf Edition:
ISBN-13: 978-1-111-35611-8
ISBN-10: 1-111-35611-4

Wadsworth
20 Davis Drive
Belmont, CA 94002-3098
USA

Cengage Learning is a leading provider of customized learning solutions with office locations around the globe, including Singapore, the United Kingdom, Australia, Mexico, Brazil, and Japan. Locate your local office at: **www.cengage.com/global.**

Cengage Learning products are represented in Canada by Nelson Education, Ltd.

To learn more about Wadsworth, visit **www.cengage.com/wadsworth**

Purchase any of our products at your local college store or at our preferred online store **www.cengagebrain.com.**

Printed in Canada
1 2 3 4 5 6 7 14 13 12 11 10

11/7/11

Dedication

The authors wish to dedicate this 13th edition of *Educating Exceptional Children* to the memory of a tireless advocate for children with special needs, Eunice Kennedy Shriver. The world is a better place for her having been among us.

James J. Gallagher
Mary Ruth Coleman
Nick Anastasiow

From *The Washington Post* August 11, 2009:

"Eunice Kennedy Shriver, a sister of President John F. Kennedy and Senators Robert F. Kennedy and Edward M. Kennedy, was credited with playing a major role in changing the perception of mental retardation. When she began her work in the field half a century ago, it was common for mentally disabled people to be placed in institutions that did little more than warehouse them. Through her programs and hands-on efforts, she demonstrated that with appropriate help, most developmentally disabled people can lead productive and useful lives.

In a statement, her family said, 'She set out to change the world and to change us, and she did that and more. She founded the movement that became Special Olympics, the largest movement for acceptance and inclusion for people with intellectual disabilities in the history of the world. Her work transformed the lives of hundreds of millions of people across the globe, and they in turn are her living legacy.'"

Brief Contents

Contents

PART ONE Introduction, History, and Social Forces in Special Education 1

1 Children with Exceptionalities and Their Families 2

2 Children with Exceptionalities and Social Institutions: Government, Schools, and the Courts 31

PART TWO
. . . .

4 Children with Learning Disabilities   106

5 Children with Autism Spectrum Disorders   146

6 Children with Intellectual and Developmental Disabilities   177

7 Children with Emotional and Behavior Disorders   212

8 Children with Communication, Language, and Speech Disorders   247

9 Children Who Have Special Gifts and Talents 280

PART THREE
. . . .

10 Children Who Are Deaf or Hard of Hearing   316

11 Children with Visual Impairments

12 Children with Physical Disabilities, Health Impairments, and Multiple Disabilities 393

Preface

More than forty years ago, Sam Kirk, a brilliant scientist and educator, penned the first edition of *Educating Exceptional Children*. Since that time, monumental changes have taken place in our knowledge of these special children and in the educational strategies needed to help them achieve and prosper.

When the first edition of this text was published in the 1960s, the future for children with exceptional learning needs was just beginning to change. Still a decade ahead was the key legislation that promised children with disabilities a "free and appropriate public education" (FAPE). Still further ahead were the numerous court decisions that solidified the educational rights of these children with exceptionalities.

In the first edition of this book, there was no mention of "inclusion" or "positive behavior supports" or "mirror neurons" or "DNA." The brain, so central a concern of ours today, was treated as a "black box" where stimuli went in and responses came out. We had little understanding of what went on inside. The predominant educational strategy for children with serious losses in hearing, vision, or intellect was to isolate them in large residential institutions far away from family and ordinary schools.

We have learned a great deal since that time. As we learn more, we write new editions of this textbook (this is our 13th!) that reflect the most current theory and research about special education, the increased sophistication of our educational strategies, and the most recent changes in public policies for exceptional students.

What's New in the 13th Edition?

As our knowledge about children with exceptionalities, their families, and their schooling expands, we add new emphases to each new edition of the text. In this 13th edition, we will emphasize several areas worthy of additional consideration due to the progress that has been made in these special fields:

The Information Processing Model

We are excited to present, for the first time, an information processing model (IPM) related to the education of exceptional children (see next page). Our IPM visually illustrates how each area of exceptionality impacts an individual's ability to learn. In each chapter, the information processing model graphically outlines the key elements of information reception (input), thinking (central processing), and expression (output), as well as showing how the executive function interacts with each of these—all within the context of emotion. Understanding how a child processes information allows educators to adapt learning environments, teaching strategies, and curriculum to address the child's strengths and needs. Further, the IPM describes how decision making takes place through what we call the executive function. The executive function determines what we attend to, what mental processes are used to solve problems, and which of the many ways we have of acting on information. Executive function helps us decide whether to add, subtract, or multiply when solving a math problem and how to react (should we run or laugh or shake hands?) when faced with a new social situation. Finally, the IPM includes an emotional context that may color how we take in

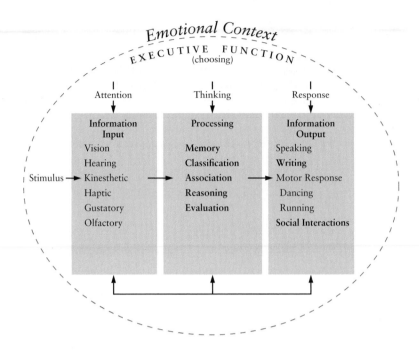

information, think about it, and act on it. For more detailed information about the information processing model, please notice its appearance and context in each chapter of the text.

Special Coverage of Neurology and Genetics

Two rapidly developing scientific fields, neurology and genetics, have dramatically changed our understanding of the development of children with special needs. Tools such as magnetic resonance imaging (MRI) and the results of the Human Genome Project have allowed us to peer into the brain's function and begin to understand the very building blocks of life: our genes and chromosomes. There have probably been more discoveries regarding brain function in the past two decades than in all previous history put together. We no longer think it unusual to ask the neurologist what is going on in the brain when a child solves the simple problem $2 + 2 = 4$ or when a child imitates an adult bouncing a ball or mimics her mother in saying "MaMa."

For many children and families, it is more important to understand what is happening neurologically when the child is *unable* to imitate the behaviors of others easily, as is the case for some children with autism. Our understanding of neurology can help us learn how we can counteract these difficulties. A special boxed feature in each chapter will bring readers up to date on current neurological findings related to children with exceptionalities.

Great advances have also been made in the science of genetics. While we have long been aware of how children physically resemble their parents, now we can begin to develop a portrait of their genetic similarities. Looking at the relationship of genetics to exceptionalities, we can see the impact of genetic differences, and we can counsel parents regarding potential risk factors.

While we know that genetics does not predetermine the future of children and adults, we are nevertheless aware that genes can influence a child's development in various ways. Genetics can influence tendencies towards aggressiveness, hyperactivity, or social isolation. The progressive and sequential interactions between genetic traits and the environmental envelope surrounding the child remain a rich field to explore. In each chapter, we summarize key genetic information for each of the various exceptionalities under discussion. In each chapter, look for the special heading with the double helix icon to see where genetics is discussed.

Focus on Early Childhood and Early Intervention

In the not-too-distant past, we became aware of special developmental problems in children only when children appeared at the schoolhouse door at age five or six. While this age may seem young to us, it is actually quite late in children's development if we wish to enhance their chances for optimal educational success. Early intervention and support, beginning at birth, can significantly improve the success of a child with special needs. Conversely, a failure to respond in the early years can extend major difficulties—as when a child with serious hearing problems has difficulty in language development or a child with special learning disabilities is prevented from learning the phonics necessary for her to read.

The early years are so important to the development of exceptional children that we have not only devoted a full chapter to early intervention (Chapter 3), but we also include information on the early years of children with behavior problems, on the early development of children with autism, and on children who seem to blossom early and become prodigies. Each chapter takes a closer look at the years from birth onward that are crucial educational opportunities where progress can be made more rapidly if we intervene with appropriate supports and services.

Integrated Coverage of Attention Deficit Disorder and Attention Deficit Hyperactivity Disorder (ADD/ADHD)

As we will learn within this book, ADD/ADHD is a neurological condition that can and does appear with a variety of other exceptionalities such as learning disabilities, autism, behavior disorders, and intellectual disabilities. It also affects a child's ability to effectively process information. Because of this, ADD/ADHD is addressed within each of the chapters wherever it is relevant. A more comprehensive discussion of ADD/ADHD is also presented in Chapter 4. A marginal icon appears each time ADD/ADHD is discussed within the text.

ADD/ADHD

Coverage of Inclusion in Every Chapter

One of the consistent themes of modern special education is the desire to address the needs of children with exceptionalities within the general education classroom and school. Inclusion rests on the firm belief that children with exceptionalities should be *a part of,* not *apart from,* the general population. A discussion of strategies needed for full inclusion of children with exceptionalities is now part of each chapter. We also realize that for some children, the least restrictive environment means that a different therapeutic approach may be needed, and so we discuss a continuum of supports and services.

Emphasis on the RTI Model

One educational strategy that intersects general and special education and emphasizes inclusion is the response to intervention (RTI) model. The illusion of two separate groups of children ("regular" and "special") has been created by laws designed to aid children with exceptionalities. The unintended consequence of these laws has been creating too much concern about group eligibility for special services rather than focusing on meeting children's individual needs through educational problem solving. Obviously, many children have trouble learning in school but do not officially qualify for special education. RTI—a three-tiered approach to supports and services focusing on the children who fall between general and special education but who still need support—is necessary for a comprehensive educational approach. RTI plays a major role in our discussions throughout this text—especially in looking at how we address the strengths and needs of children with exceptionalities. A special introduction to the RTI model follows this Preface so that students can begin to understand the model and see how it is changing the way we meet the needs of children with exceptionalities.

Throughout the text, when RTI is discussed, you will see the triangular RTI icon in the margin.

Increased Coverage of Assistive Technology

Human beings are toolmakers. Whenever there is a particular need (e.g., for creating a means of transportation, preparing meals, educating the young), we devise special tools to make the tasks easier. The education of children with exceptionalities presents special challenges, and these challenges have brought forth a variety of tools. Hearing aids and magnifiers, for example, are two tools that help to minimize the impact of sensory disabilities.

The major tools of recent decades, however, have been computers, the Internet, and other communication devices. While the computer can make tasks easier for some, it also introduces problems for other children who need adaptations so that they, too, can access this tool. Assistive technologies that support children with exceptionalities are discussed in each chapter of the text and also within a special boxed feature.

Emphasis on Current Educational Methods and Strategies

In this new edition, we aim to include an overview of the current and best educational practices for different populations of exceptional students. The updated Educational Responses sections in Chapters 3 through 12 spotlight these current educational methodologies and strategies. For example, in the new edition, we cover new ways of addressing disruptive behavior that have emerged through such approaches as functional behavior assessment and positive behavior supports. We also discuss new ways of presenting curriculum using Universal Design for Learning and problem-based learning approaches. You will find these special Educational Responses sections on special shaded pages in the middle of these chapters. They provide a useful overview for preservice educators and clinicians, and individuals already practicing in the field.

Text Coverage of Diversity Issues and Disproportionate Representation

Disproportionate representation of different subgroups within special and gifted education is a complex and persistent challenge. While we must make sure that every child who needs supports and services receives them, we also must also be sure that children's strengths and needs are appropriately identified. Throughout this text, we have examined the patterns of representation across areas of exceptionality. Within each chapter, we address the specific issues related to appropriate identification, and services to address children's needs:

- Chapters 1 and 2 look at families and the social impact of culture, language, and poverty.

- Chapter 3 examines family centered interventions and culturally resonant practice.

- Chapter 4 explores the increasing identification of Latina youth as learning disabled and raises questions about the impact of language differences on identification.

- Chapter 5 discusses the dramatic increase of identification with regard to gender differences — four times as many boys are identified with Autism Spectrum Disorder (as compared with girls).

- Chapter 6 explores the social implication of identification for children with Intellectual and Developmental Disabilities, along with a discussion of the use of measurement data in decision making.

- Chapter 7 examines the role of cultural perspectives in defining emotional and behavioral disorders, and the importance of cultural competence for appropriate identification and support.

- In Chapter 8, we discuss the critical importance of understanding a child's cultural and linguistic background in assessing communication, language and speech disorders, along with typical language development patterns for bilingual children.

- Chapter 9 addresses the disproportionate underrepresentation of children of color and poverty in services for gifted learners, and offers examples of programs that have addressed these challenges.

- Chapter 10 explores the impact of Deaf culture on children and families, and the need for bilingual/bicultural approaches to understanding the needs of children with hearing impairments.

- Chapter 11 addresses the multicultural needs of children with visual impairments and their families.

- In Chapter 12, we focus on honoring differences while recognizing the shared nature of humanity as we address the needs of children with physical, health, and multiple disabilities.

Throughout the text, we also focus on the RTI approach to addressing students' needs. We believe that this multitiered model holds promise for providing early supports to address children's diverse strengths and needs, and pathways for success that may allow for more appropriate identification of exceptionalities.

Organization of the Thirteenth Edition

This book is divided into three major sections. Part One provides the history and foundations of special education.

Part Two deals with high-incidence exceptionalities (those experienced by more than 1 percent of the population). Part Three addresses low-incidence exceptionalities—those experienced by students who make up less than 1 percent of the general population. And though they will appear more rarely in the general classroom, their needs may be even more pressing and demanding of the attention of school personnel. Please reference the detailed Contents for more information about text and chapter organization.

 # Student Learning Features

In each chapter of the 13th edition, we have included new and proven pedagogical features that are designed to help students master course content. It is our hope that these special text features will also enhance student learning:

- **Chapter-opening focus questions** provide an overview of the key issues within each chapter. These questions guide readers as they work their way through the chapter. If students can give thoughtful answers to the focus questions, they are well on their way to understanding the needs of children with exceptionalities and their families.

- **Exceptional Lives, Exceptional Stories** boxes offer first-person pieces about exceptional children and their families. These special stories share the insights, perceptions, and wisdom of individuals with exceptionalities and their families, capturing the joys and sometimes the frustrations faced in everyday life.

- **Video Connection boxes** provide a brief description of an accompanying video clip (which can be found on the Education Coursemate website) and reflective questions to guide student viewing. These action videos illustrate the ideas discussed in each chapter and show teachers, parents, and students in a variety of learning contexts.

- **Neurology and Brain Development boxes** describe how the brain is impacted by the exceptionalities discussed in each chapter. These boxes spotlight recent scientific research findings that help us understand the neurological implications for children's learning.

- **Marginal features** such as summary notes, websites, and icons alert the reader to special information throughout the chapter. These marginal features include key chapter points, relevant websites where the interested reader can find additional information, and icons indicating specific content on RTI or ADD/ADHD.

- **Educational Responses sections** (located within Chapters 3 through 12) offer practical guidance for future teachers and multidisciplinary teams. These sections address teaching and learning strategies across grade levels for each area of exceptionality.

- **Assistive Technology boxes** provide information on technologies that can be used to support exceptional individuals with learning and daily life skills. Relevant websites are often included in these boxes because the area of assistive technology is ever emerging!

- **Moral Dilemma boxes** at the very end of each chapter's narrative are brief case studies that offer students a chance to reflect on their own values and beliefs and explore how these will influence them in their work with exceptional children and their families.

- **Chapter-ending summaries** are provided to highlight key themes addressed within the chapter. These summaries should help the reader anchor learning by recapping the major points covered in each chapter.

- **Future Challenges sections** discuss the areas we are still wrestling with as the field of special education continues to evolve. These are areas that students may wish to follow up on in future work as they grow professionally. They can also be used by professors for classroom discussion.

- **Relevant Resources** (such as journals, books, and websites) are provided at the end of each chapter to support further learning, and to help students who wish to pursue an area of interest in more depth.

 # Specific Chapter Revisions in the 13th Edition

We have revised and updated each of the chapters in this 13th edition. Here are the highlights of these chapters:

Chapter 1: Children with Exceptionalities and Their Families.

Explored in this chapter are the definition of exceptionalities and the influence of family and siblings on the child with exceptionalities. We also introduce the information processing model, which describes the effect of the exceptionality on the child's learning and adaptation potential, as well as the RTI model, which is a key response of the schools to the student with special needs.

Chapter 2: Children with Exceptionalities and Social Institutions: Government, Schools, and Courts.

This chapter presents the social and cultural influences on children with exceptionalities. The predominant influences from society come from the institutions of government, the courts, and the schools. Legislation such as No Child Left Behind is analyzed for its influence on children with exceptionalities, and the latest actions of the courts are noted as well. The influence of schools (and the rules and standards they set) is described so that the reader can gain a perspective on the impact these entities have on children with exceptionalities.

Chapter 3: Early Intervention Supports and Services.

Early intervention has seen the rapid development of preschool programs for both exceptional children and children of typical development. It is now widely accepted by both professionals and the general public that education in the early years is needed for subsequent development. This chapter addresses how early intervention supports and services can meet the needs of young children and their families. Early childhood mental health and inclusion within an RTI framework are new focus areas for the chapter.

Chapter 4: Children with Learning Disabilities.

The largest group of children in special education consists of those with learning disabilities. The distinctive nature of the individual's needs creates educational challenges for the teacher. The RTI model stressed in this text emerged out of concern for children with learning disabilities and the shortcomings of historical definitions. The RTI model also serves as a guide to planning effective educational responses to meet the needs of students with learning difficulties. The information processing model presents a method to review the student's needs and to determine strategies to meet these needs. An expanded section addresses the needs of children with attention deficit disorders with and without hyperactivity.

Chapter 5: Children with Autism Spectrum Disorders.

Autism is the fastest growing disorder in the population of children with special needs. This chapter presents the social and communicative needs of these children. It also details the many recent advances in diagnosis and the array of methods designed to cope with the special social, motor, and learning challenges faced by these students. The reasons for the rapid increase in prevalence are noted together with a major emphasis on early intervention approaches. Also presented are the positive results obtained from many different perspectives.

Chapter 6: Children with Intellectual and Developmental Disabilities (IDD).

This chapter explores the special needs of students in the intellectual and adaptive behavior domains. It also explains reasons for changing the terminology from *mental retardation* to *intellectual and developmental disabilities*. Special attention is presented as to how the response to intervention model can be used to cope with the educational and social challenges these students face, and special emphasis is given to the transition stage from school to community.

Chapter 7: Children with Emotional and Behavior Disorders.

Children with pervasive interpersonal challenges and children with deep anxieties and depression are described separately with regard to their identification and treatments. The roles played by positive behavior supports and functional behavioral assessments are emphasized, and the information processing and response to intervention models are presented to show the developmental areas of special concern, as well as new ways of helping these students cope with the challenges of the general classroom.

Chapter 8: Children with Communication, Language, and Speech Disorders.

This chapter addresses the needs of children who have communication, language, and speech disorders. In it we discuss typical development of language and examine how the needs of children can be addressed through collaboration within an RTI framework. Special emphasis is given to children with language differences and to children who are bilingual.

Chapter 9: Children Who Have Special Gifts and Talents.

The reasons why these students have substantially been ignored in the educational system are laid out in the debate between equity and excellence as educational goals. The major societal contributions that some of these students make in adulthood is discussed, along with the difficulty and importance of finding students with gifts and talents from economically depressed environments. A variety of methods, such as educational acceleration and special curriculum interventions (e.g., International Baccalaureate), is analyzed.

Chapter 10: Children Who Are Deaf or Hard of Hearing.

The special problems of early linguistic development are discussed together with the challenges for parents and teachers in communicating with young children who are deaf or hard of hearing. New medical and technological advances with cochlear implants are presented along with the need for multiple supports and services. Attention is also devoted to the Deaf culture and to the need for family support. Strategies for supporting academic development and reading have been expanded.

Chapter 11: Children with Visual Impairments.

Students with visual impairments are separated into two groups: those who can use visual enhancement techniques to learn and those whose exceptionality requires the introduction of Braille, mobility training, and specially trained teachers to respond to their educational challenges. The Universal Design for Learning is presented as a major teaching strategy along with the advanced technology available for both of these groups of students. The RTI model is a useful approach to the various levels of visual challenges faced by these students.

Chapter 12: Children with Physical Disabilities, Health Impairments, and Multiple Disabilities.

This chapter provides students with an opportunity to reflect on all they have learned about other areas of disability as they focus on students with some of the most intense challenges. Addressing the needs of children with physical, health, and multiple disabilities requires a multidisciplinary team; how this team works collaboratively is the focus of much of the chapter. An expanded discussion of the needs of children who are deafblind has been added.

Supplemental Materials to Aid Teaching and Learning

This edition offers an expanded and enhanced package of support material for instructors and students:

Instructor's Resource Manual with Test Bank

This is an all-purpose tool for reference and ideas when teaching this book. This manual, offered on the instructor website, provides chapter-by-chapter resources that include chapter learning objectives, focus questions, key terms, PowerPoint lecture outlines, class activities and exercises, student take-home activities, and student handouts. The test bank has been thoroughly revised. Assessment materials include both multiple choice and essay questions.

PowerLecture with ExamView

This one-stop digital library and presentation tool includes preassembled Microsoft® PowerPoint® lecture slides. In addition to a full Instructor's Manual and Test Bank, PowerLecture includes ExamView® testing software, with all the test items from the Test Bank in electronic format, enabling you to create customized tests in print or online and all of your media resources in one place including an image library with graphics from the book itself and TeachSource Video Connections.

Student and Instructor Websites

For students, Cengage Learning's Education Coursemate brings course concepts to life with interactive learning, study, and exam preparation tools that support the printed textbook. Access an integrated eBook and chapter-specific learning tools including flashcards, TeachSource Video Connections, links to related sites for each chapter of the text, tutorial quizzes, interactive glossary flashcards, portfolio resources, reflection and critical thinking activities, information about standards in the United States and Canada, and more. Some content is password protected. Go to CengageBrain.com to register access codes or purchase access. For instructors, EngagementTracker is a first-of-its-kind tool that monitors student engagement in the course. The accompanying instructor website offers access to password-protected resources such as an electronic version of the instructor's manual with a test bank, model syllabi, and PowerPoint® slides. Access instructor resources at login.cengage.com.

TeachSource Video Cases

Available online, each "case" is a 4- to 6-minute module consisting of video and audio files presenting actual classroom scenarios that depict the complex problems and opportunities teachers face every day. The video and audio clips are accompanied by "artifacts" to provide background information and allow preservice teachers to experience true classroom applications in their multiple dimensions. Access these videos on the Education Coursemate website.

WebTutor on Blackboard and WebCT

Jumpstart your course with customizable, rich, text-specific content within your Course Management System. Whether you want to Web-enable your class or put an entire course online, WebTutor™ delivers. WebTutor™ offers a wide array of resources including media assets, quizzes, Web links, exercises, and more. Visit webtutor.cengage.com to learn more.

 # Acknowledgments

The authors would like to acknowledge the following individuals for their support with this work:

First, we would like to thank our spouses, Rani Gallagher and Phil Coleman, for their strong support during this work and for their willingness to endure our absences and the neglect they have suffered because of our focus on this work.

Second, we thank the team here at FPG. Thanks to Sam Odom, director of the Frank Porter Graham Child Development Institute, whose generous allotments of time, facilities, and space made the production of this edition possible. Thanks to Jennifer Job for her constant attention to details and her steady focus on getting things right. Jennifer kept the project moving forward, taking on the role of an assistant editor to help us with all aspects of the work from the smallest to the largest. We owe her a huge debt of gratitude! We also thank Allison Dennis who helped with the final polishing of the book to ensure it would be its best.

We thank Beth Kaufman, development editor, for her dedicated editing of the many drafts and her feedback, which was thoughtful, insightful, and supportive. We appreciate all that you brought to the ideas as they developed.

We also wish to thank the entire Cengage book team Tanya Nigh, Maria Epes, Kara Kindstrom, Don Schlotman, Latoya Oliver, Linda Stewart, Genevieve Allen, Ashley Cronin, Caitlin Cox, Linda Schreiber, and Mark Kerr—for all of their care and attention to this book and for their patience with us as authors. The strong commitment to excellence that this team showed was a joy to see, and the personal support you offered us was very helpful.

We also wish to express special appreciation for the dedicated work of Dr. Doreen Fairbank of Meredith College for her careful work in shaping the ancillary materials that accompany this text. Her attention to detail and dedication to supporting learning are very much appreciated.

A special thanks to photographer Thomas Balsamo for allowing us to use his incredible photographs on the cover and throughout the book. Your work is an inspiration to all of us!

We owe a special debt to the individuals who provided in-depth reviews for each of the chapters. These outstanding professionals gave of their time, their ideas, and their expertise to help shape the revision and bring the content up to date. Much of what you see in this 13th edition was shaped by their feedback and wisdom:

Tamara Ashton, California State University at Northridge

Beverley Barkon, Carlow College

Rocio Delgado, Trinity University

Gloria Hayes, Mississippi State University

Joann Migyanka, Indiana University of Pennsylvania

Kimberley Nettleton, Morehead State University

Linda Revay, University of Akron

Tami Stephenson, Otero Junior College

Mal Ward, Fayetteville State University

Cheryl Zaccagnini, West Virginia University at Morgantown.

A special thank you to our amazing advisory board of expert reviewers (see page xxxvii).

Finally, we would like to acknowledge the senior author of this text, Dr. Samuel A. Kirk. His vision for this book and for the field of special education continues to guide us. Sam was a true giant in the field of education. He was a scholar, teacher, writer, mentor, policymaker, colleague, and friend. Thousands of children and families who never knew his name have benefited from his work.

In this text, we attempt to capture the changing views of the child with exceptionalities, our changing bodies of knowledge, and the changing education scene. We welcome your comments as this text continues to grow along with the field.

James G. Gallagher
Mary Ruth Coleman
Nicholas J. Anastasiow

It's your first day teaching. As you look out at your new class, you are nervous and excited to see who your students are. You know that it may take some time to get to know your students as individuals, but you have already started to learn about their needs. In preparation for today, when you would see them for the first time, you reviewed each student's folder. This was helpful because you learned that five of your students have disabilities, and you know that they will need special attention. Another four of your students have been identified as gifted and talented. You also have three children who are English language learners, and you are grateful that you speak a little Spanish so that you can help them feel comfortable in the class. The other eighteen students do not have any specific identification, but you are certain that they will have their own special needs as well.

You have already heard that two of your students were considered for retention last year, and they will certainly need extra support. You also know that one of your students has just lost her mother to cancer—and thinking of this breaks your heart. With all of these needs, it is hard not to wonder how the year will go.

During teacher orientation, you met the special education teachers, the gifted education specialist, the English as a second language teacher, the reading support teacher, the guidance counselor, and—most importantly—your mentor teacher. You know that you have the support of this team to help you meet your students' needs. The orientation director kept reminding the new teachers that with the RTI approach used in their schools, teams of teachers collaborate to meet students' needs. She asked the new teachers to remember this and even had them repeat together, "I'm not expected to do this alone."

Now facing your class for the first time, you find yourself silently repeating the mantra that you heard during your teacher orientation: "I'm not expected to do this alone!"

Introducing the Response to Intervention Model (RTI)

One of the major challenges teachers face in schools today is meeting the wide range of student needs. In any given classroom, teachers will have students who struggle to learn sitting beside students who learn easily. Most classes will have students who have been formally diagnosed with disabilities and other students who just seem to need more support in order to achieve success. Some students will have emotional difficulties and behavior problems, while others may have social adjustment needs. The range of students' needs can feel overwhelming to a teacher. But the good news is that in today's schools teachers are not expected to do the job alone. Teams of teachers can work collaboratively to address their students' strengths and needs. In fact this collaborative approach is catching on across the country through a movement called **RTI**.

RTI is a multitiered framework designed to meet the needs of all students. It brings together important information about each child (e.g., data on the child's strengths and challenges) with evidence-based instructional approaches so that teachers and related service providers can recognize and respond to the student's needs (Brown-Chidsey & Steege, 2005; Fuchs & Fuchs, 2006; Division for Learning Disabilities, 2007; Bradley, Danielson, & Doolittle, 2007).

RTI is the approach used throughout this text to describe supports and services for children with exceptionalities. We have chosen RTI as the anchor for

this text because it reflects our belief in the collaborative approach needed to meet the needs of today's students (Gallagher, 2006). RTI approaches are being implemented in a variety of ways in school districts across the country (Berkeley, Bender, Peaster, & Saunders, 2009). While we believe that RTI holds promise for the future, we know that it must continue to evolve through further research and experience in the coming years, and we look forward to this evolution.

RTI Coverage Within This Text

Throughout this text, when RTI is discussed, you will find a small RTI triangle icon in the margin.

RTI

Each time you see this icon, you may wish to refer back to this introduction to remind yourself what RTI is and to refresh your understanding of the key components of the RTI approach.

Why RTI?

It can be difficult to support children who are struggling to learn but who do not qualify for special education service.

In the past, we often created two groups of children: the "regular education children" and the "special education children." This is an artificial dichotomy; there are not two groups of children. There are just children, and many of the children we teach will have special needs. Two major difficulties are created when we divide children into distinct groups:

- Teachers get assigned to one or the other group and often do not pool their expertise to meet the needs of all children;

- The children who are struggling with some aspect of learning, *but who do not meet the eligibility criteria for special education,* often fall through the cracks, getting very little extra help to be successful. (Conversely children who are advanced but do not qualify for gifted education services often get little to address their strengths.)

Does this mean that we should do away with general and special education? Of course not. What we need to do away with is the artificial structure that keeps us from working together collaboratively, combining resources and expertise to meet the needs of children. The tiered approach to services that RTI offers (see figure) provides the structure needed to support the collaboration between general and special education. Tiered supports and services provide a framework for addressing the strengths and needs of children. Using this framework, we can provide extra support for children who do not need the intense and full services we provide through special education. We can also provide additional enhancements for children who need them. Tiered supports and services allow us to match the child's strengths and needs with appropriate interventions.

We believe that RTI represents an educational approach that moves us toward a better future. A future where children's needs are addressed by *multidisciplinary teams* (professionals from various domains such as special education, speech pathology, occupational therapy, etc.) working collaboratively to address children's special needs (Gallagher, 2006). Resources are focused on meeting children's needs, and families work in partnership with professionals (Kame'enui, 2007).

Key Components of RTI

RTI can be implemented in many ways, but all RTI approaches share some key components:

- a tiered hierarchy of supports and services;

- comprehensive assessments and progress monitoring used to make informed decisions about a child's strengths and needs;

- standard protocols, drawn from evidence-based practices, for intervention when children need more support; and

- problem-solving approaches that include parents to plan supports and services. The following figure (see this also in Chapter 2 on page 43) shows the RTI approach visually, using three tiers.

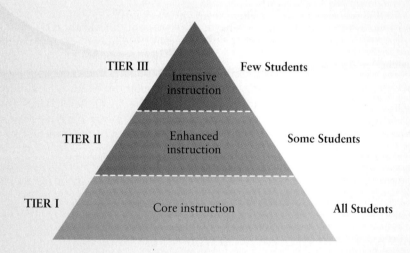

Explaining the RTI Model

This visual representation of the RTI shows the relationships between each of the key components. As you look at the RTI triangle carefully, you will see that the shading deepens as you move from the bottom to the top. This shading indicates that the supports and services offered at each tier increase in intensity—with Tier III being the most intense level of service. The RTI triangle shows that as the intensity of the child's strengths and needs increase, our response to these strengths and needs also increases in intensity.

Tier I: Universal supports and services are typically provided in a general education setting for all children. This tier incorporates universal screening to detect if children need any additional support or enhancement to meet with success and progress monitoring to ensure that the support being provided is appropriate for the child (you will learn more about progress monitoring in Chapters 3 and 4). Screening and progress monitoring are ways to collect data on students' strengths and needs, provide appropriate instruction, and document the progress the students are making. Progress monitoring is critical because it allows educators to see very quickly when a child needs additional supports and enhancements to achieve success. For children who need more support, we can move to Tier II.

Tier II: Targeted supports and services are provided collaboratively, drawing on general and special educational resources, and additional resource personnel when needed. A full implementation of Tier II will likely require additional personnel. In Tier II, the supports and enhancements become more targeted, and they are based on the documented strengths and needs of the children. These services may include more intensive and explicit instruction or more rigorous and challenging curriculum provided in smaller groups, and they will often involve more frequent progress monitoring to make sure that learning stays on track. Some children will need even more intensive supports and enhancements to meet with success, and for these children Tier III should be considered.

Tier III: Intensive supports and services are provided to address specific student strengths and needs. These supports and services may include the formal identification of students for special and or gifted education (Council for Exceptional Children, 2007). Supports and services provided at Tier III are tailored specifically to the child's strengths and needs and typically require individualized educational programming. Most of the children you will meet in this text receive supports and services at the Tier III level.

You may also notice, as you examine the RTI triangle, that there are dashed lines between each tier. The dashed lines are important because as children develop and their strengths and needs change, our educational services must also change. The dashed lines also show that each child may have needs at all three tiers, simultaneously. You will meet several children in this text and learn through them that our educational supports and services must remain flexible in order to meet the ever-changing strengths and needs of our students. It is also important to note that children at Tier III with intense needs may be referred for the services provided from the other tiers at any time.

Two Additional Components of RTI

Two important components of RTI that are not reflected in the figure are the use of standard protocols for instruction and the problem-solving approach to collaborative planning. Standard protocols for instruction are designed to help the teacher provide additional support for students who are struggling to master the material presented and or additional enhancements for students who need more advanced learning opportunities. Standard protocols are used at Tier II to guide the instruction and are developed from evidence-based practices. These practices have a documented track record of success that comes from research, practitioners' experience or wisdom, and an acceptance of the practice by the families and community. For evidence-based practice to work, we must reflect on instructional methods and curriculum choices to make sure that these are working well for our students. For a student who is struggling with reading, for example, a standard protocol might include targeted small-group instruction and practice with phonics, matching letters and sounds. On the other hand, for a student who is advanced in reading, our standard protocol may include the seminar approach to guide discussions about an advanced book in combination with asking the student to keep a reflective reading log. These standard protocols are evidence-based because they are supported by research (teachers have used them successfully), and they are acceptable to families and the community. Specific protocols must be created to meet the strengths and needs of students in each content area and across each grade level. Standard protocols for instruction are useful because they provide the teacher with clear guidelines in supporting children who are struggling and enhance the education for children who need further opportunities, but there is no guarantee that the standard protocol will be effective for all children.

The use of a collaborative planning process must also be part of an RTI approach because this allows the members of a multidisciplinary team to work together to address the child's needs (usually through his individual education plan). This team should include teachers, related service providers, and parents. Throughout the text, the importance of the multidisciplinary team will be discussed. The importance of the parents or caregivers as members of the multidisciplinary team, described as the family-centered approach, is a cornerstone of special education and is critical to RTI. Throughout this text you will learn more about all of these ideas.

Major innovations like the RTI model always bring with them a series of questions in the school system's attempt to implement them. How will the RTI program be administered, and who will be responsible for hiring staff and monitoring the program? This is especially true for Tier II, which is an addition to existing operations. Also, who will pay for the costs of the RTI model, which will likely go beyond existing funding? There are many hardworking educators who are addressing this issue right now, and some form of collaboration between general education and special education is expected. The recognition of the need for such a model to assist students with exceptionalities is almost universal, and we expect the next decade to be one of expanding the existing RTI services.

Taken as a whole, the RTI approach attempts to bring together the best of general and special education to create a bright future for children with exceptionalities.

Resources for RTI

References of Special Interest

Bender, W., & Shores, C. (2007). *Response to intervention: A practical guide for every teacher.* Arlington, VA: Joint Publication Council for Exceptional Children; Thousand Oaks, CA: Corwin Press. This is a comprehensive guide for the implementation of RTI in the classroom. Examples of RTI in action for a variety of grade levels and content areas are given. This book also contains several lists of resources and validated curriculum that can be used for interventions with students who are struggling.

Berkeley, Bebder, Peaster, & Saunders (2009). Implementation of response to intervention: A snapshot of progress. *Journal of Learning Disabilities, 42*(1), 85–95.

Council for Exceptional Children (2008). *CEC's positions on response to intervention (RTI): The unique role of special education and special educators.* Arlington, VA: Council for Exceptional Children.

Division for Learning Disabilities. (2007). *Thinking about response to intervention and learning disabilities: A teacher's guide.* Arlington, VA: Author. This publication of the Council for Exceptional Children's Division for Learning Disabilities is a brief, user-friendly guide to how the RTI approach can be used with students who have learning disabilities. It provides an excellent overview for teachers who will be working to implement RTI in their schools and classrooms.

Fuchs & Fuchs (2006). A framework for building capacity for responsiveness to intervention. *School Psychology Review, 35*(4), 621–626.

Professional Organizations

The Division for Learning Disabilities, Council for Exceptional Children
www.TeachLD.org
National Center for Learning Disabilities RTI Action Network
www.ncld.org
Learning Disabilities Association (LDA)
www.ldanatl.org
RTI Action Network
www.RTINetwork.org

About the Authors

Samuel Kirk, Ph.D., is the founding author of *Educating Exceptional Children*. He earned his doctorate in clinical psychology from the University of Michigan in 1935, which led to 60 years of work and research. He developed the term "learning disabilities" in the 1960s after years of observation during work with teenagers with IDD in Chicago and a training school in Ann Arbor. President Kennedy named him as the director of the Federal Office of Education's Division of Handicapped Children, and Dr. Kirk was instrumental in convincing the government to provide funding for training teachers to work with students with special needs. He was also the founding director of the Institute for Research on Exceptional Children at the University of Illinois. He ended his career at the University of Arizona.

James J. Gallagher, Ph.D., is a senior scientist emeritus and former director of FPG Child Development Institute, which he has been affiliated with since 1970. Dr. Gallagher served on Governor James B. Hunt's planning team to develop the North Carolina School for Science and Mathematics. Prior to joining FPG, Dr. Gallagher was the first Chief of the Bureau of Education for the Handicapped in the U.S. Office of Education. He oversaw a wide range of new legislation representing the first major thrust by the federal government to help children with disabilities. The Bureau was the leader in helping to implement laws that provided funds for research, personnel preparation, technical assistance, regional resource centers, centers for media development, and state grants to help with the education of children with disabilities. He was promoted to Deputy Assistant Secretary for Planning, Research, and Evaluation during the tenure of Commissioner Jim Allen. Dr. Gallagher also served as the assistant director of the Institute for Research on Exceptional Children at the University of Illinois at Champaign–Urbana. Dr. Gallagher has produced over two hundred articles in a wide range of professional journals. He has also authored and edited a number of book chapters and books.

Mary Ruth Coleman, Ph.D., is a senior scientist at the FPG Child Development Institute at the University of North Carolina at Chapel Hill and a research associate professor in the School of Education. She directed Project U-STARS~PLUS (Using Science, Talents and Abilities to Recognize Students~Promoting Learning in Under-served Students), and Project ACCESS (Achievement in Content and Curriculum for Every Student's Success). She was the coprincipal investigator for the Early Learning Disabilities Initiative sponsored by the Emily Hall Tremaine Foundation. She has served three terms on the board of directors for The Association for the Gifted (TAG), one of which she was president; three terms on the board of the National Association for Gifted Children (NAGC); and two terms on the board of directors for the Council for Exceptional Children (CEC). She was president of the Council in 2007.

Nicholas Anastasiow, Ph.D., received his degrees from the University of California at Berkeley and Stanford University, along with postdoctoral courses in neurology at Columbia University. He has been an elementary school teacher, school principal, and director of the Institute for Child Study at Indiana University. He is the author of several books including *Development and Disability: A Psychobiological Analysis for Special Educators,* as well as collections of presentations in Israel on the at-risk infant. At Hunter College in New York City, he was a professor of special education, and he was a professor of educational psychology at The Graduate Center of the City University of New York (CUNY). Dr. Anastasiow served as a consultant to the Assistant Secretary on Human Development, the White House Conferences on the Handicapped, and the President's Council for Exceptional Children. He has researched classes of children with disabilities in the former Soviet Union and participated in several conferences in Israel.

Expert Reviewers

Jan Blacher Jan Blacher is Professor of Education in the Graduate School of Education, and Founding Director of the SEARCH Family Autism Resource Center at the University of California, Riverside. Dr. Blacher's NIH-funded research focuses on the family context of children and adolescents with and without developmental disabilities, family coping in Anglo and Latino families, and student-teacher relationships, including those for children with autism spectrum disorders.

Dr. Blacher serves as Consulting Editor for several journals, and is the North American Editor and Associate Editor of the international *Journal of Intellectual Disability Research*. She was recently appointed to the National Research Council of The National Academy of Sciences, and the Johnson & Johnson/Rosalynn Carter Institute Caregivers Program. She contributes a column for EP, Exceptional Parent Magazine (www.eparent.com). She is a Fellow of the American Association for the Advancement of Science (AAAS).

Donald Deshler Donald Deshler, Ph.D., is the Director of the University of Kansas Center for Research on Learning. He is also the Williamson Family Distinguished Professor of Special Education at the University of Kansas, as well as the Gene A. Budig Teaching Professor of Special Education. Deshler serves as an advisor on adolescent achievement to several organizations including the Carnegie Corporation of New York, the National Governor's Association, the Alliance for Excellent Education, the Council on Families and Literacy, and the U. S. State Department. He has presented on matters of educational policy regarding adolescent literacy to the nation's governors at the James B. Hunt Institute for Educational Leadership and Policy and has testified in Congress and several state legislatures on secondary school reform. Through the Aspen Institute, he has worked with members of Congress to shape policies addressing the challenges of high school reform.

Thomas Farmer Thomas Farmer, Ph.D. is an Associate Professor of Education at Penn State University. He teaches courses in the etiology and characteristics of students with disabilities, practices and research issues in the education and treatment of students with behavioral disorders, and the social development of students with disabilities. His primary research interests are in the prevention and treatment of aggression and antisocial behavior, social development of students with disabilities, bullying and classroom social dynamics, and rural education. Dr. Farmer has written extensively on interpersonal competence and relationships of students. He is the director of the National Research Center on Rural Education Support and is on the faculty of the Children, Youth and Families Consortium at Penn State.

Susan Fowler Susan Fowler is a professor in Special Education at the University of Illinois. Her research has focused on the lives of young children and their families between birth and age 8. She looks at programmatic and policy factors that influence family involvement in the delivery of services to their young children who are at risk for disabilities or identified as disabled and examines factors that influence professionals in their delivery and coordination of services. Her research fits three clusters: research and development of intervention strategies to enhance language, social and cognitive development in young children; development of guidelines and practices to help communities and programs coordinate delivery of services to young children and families, particularly as they leave one service system for another; and, increasing practitioners' understanding of the roles that cultural and linguistic diversity may play in family's participation in services.

Janet Lerner Janet Lerner, Ph.D., notes that it has been a pleasure to contribute to the classic book, *Educating Exceptional Children*. Her book, *Learning Disabilities and Related Mild Disabilities*, 12th ed, by Janet Lerner and Beverley Johns is published by Cengage Learning. Janet W. Lerner is Professor Emeritus of Northeastern Illinois University, and she is an adjunct instructor in the PACE program at National-Louis University. She is a recipient of the Romaine P. Mackie Award. Pioneers Division of CEC, 2009, the J.E. Wallace Wallin Lifetime Achievement Award, Council for Exceptional Children, 2004, and the Pi Lambda Theta Award, Outstanding Book of the Year, for *Children with Learning Disabilities*.

John Luckner Dr. John Luckner is a professor and the coordinator of the Deaf Education teacher preparation program in the School of Special Education and the Director of Research for the Bresnahan/Halstead Center at the University of Northern Colorado. Dr. Luckner was a classroom teacher of students who are deaf or hard of hearing for nine years. His current research interests include literacy, teacher preparation, social-emotional development and the provision of appropriate services for students who are deaf or hard of hearing and their families.

Gary Mesibov Dr. Gary B. Mesibov is a Professor of Psychology in the Departments of Psychiatry and Psychology at the University of North Carolina at Chapel Hill, where he has served on the faculty for the past 35 years. He was the Director of Division TEACCH at the University of North Carolina from 1992 until 2010. This internationally recognized statewide program is one of a kind in its pioneering approaches to service, treatment, training, research and the education of individuals with Autism Spectrum Disorders. Dr. Mesibov has received degrees from Stanford University (A.B.), The University of Michigan (M.A.), Brandeis University (Ph.D.), and the University of North Carolina at Chapel Hill (Postdoctoral Fellowship). Dr. Mesibov is a licensed psychologist in the state of North Carolina.

Dr. Mesibov's editorial appointments include: Editor of the Journal of Autism and Developmental Disorders for 10 years and membership on the Editorial Boards of the Journal of Clinical Child Psychology and the Journal of Pediatric Psychology. He has written numerous books, journal articles, book reviews, editorials, chapters and research papers dealing with all aspects of autism and developmental disabilities and has been recognized with numerous local, national and international awards for his work.

Froma Roth Froma P. Roth, Ph.D., is a Professor in the Department of Hearing and Speech Sciences at the University of Maryland. Her current research program is directed at specifying the developmental relationships between oral language, emergent and early literacy, and clarifying the language skills and background factors that underlie the development of phonological awareness and early reading skills. She has developed the Promoting Awareness of Sounds in Speech (PASS) program, which the U.S. Department of Education has implemented as a component of an Early Reading First project. Dr. Roth was a member of the Committee on Early Intervention formed by the American Speech, Language, and Hearing Association (ASHA) and serves as ASHA's liaison to the National Joint Council on Learning Disabilities. She is the co-author of a basic textbook on speech and language intervention entitled *Treatment Resource Manual for Speech-Language Pathology* (Thomson Delmar Learning, 2005)

Martin Schwartzman Dr. Schwartzman is a board certified pediatrician who specializes in pulmonary diseases. He has been involved with Cystic Fibrosis since 1963. Presently, he is the medical director of the Cystic Fibrosis Center that is affiliated with the Joe DiMaggio Children's Hospital at Memorial Regional Hospital in Hollywood, Florida. Dr. Schwartzman, whose previous experience includes working as a private practitioner for 40 years, was a medical consultant for the Health Rehabilitative Service Agency, Dade County, Florida. His responsibilities included caring for infants, children, and adolescents with chronic disease, such as neurological disorders, muscular disease and myopathies and chronic pulmonary diseases. He was also involved with the care and treatment of children with special needs who resided in various group homes.

In addition, he serves as medical director for a prescribed pediatric extended care facility for children with medical and physical impairments and has served on many advisory boards, medical boards, and boards of directors, including the American Lung Association of South Florida and the American Lung Associate of the State of Florida. Dr. Schwartzman was also a former member of the executive committee of the Joe DiMaggio Children's Hospital. He was past president of the medical staff as well as past Chief of Pediatrics at Miami Children's Hospital, Miami, Florida. Dr. Schwartzman has lectured to students at local universities and to civic groups and professional organizations. Currently, he is the asthma consultant for the Asthma Improvement Management Program for the Broward County Public School System in Broward County, Florida. He has co-authored several text books and publisher articles in various medical journals. His interest lies in creating new avenues to improve the care for children and adolescents with medical needs and physical and mental impairments.

Introduction, History, and Social Forces in Special Education

THE MAIN GOAL OF this book is to introduce you to children with exceptional educational needs. Throughout the chapters, you will come to know and understand many children, learning the most effective ways to support and educate them. Whether you plan to teach in general education, teach in special education, or specialize in speech pathology, school psychology, or educational administration, you will meet children with exceptionalities every day.

In this first section, we begin with a look at who **children with exceptionalities** are. We will review the rich history of special education over the past five decades, and we will learn about the social forces that have played a significant role in establishing special education in the schools. In Chapter 1, we focus on children with exceptionalities, their families, and the social environments that surround them. In Chapter 2, we explore the impact of three major social institutions on children with exceptionalities: the government, the courts, and the public schools.

© Thomas Balsamo

Children with Exceptionalities and Their Families

Focus Questions

▶ Who are the children with exceptionalities that we will learn about in this book?

▶ What is the role played by intraindividual and interindividual differences in special education?

▶ Why is early identification of children with exceptionalities so important?

▶ How does the Information Processing Model help us understand how children learn?

▶ What are some of the major causes of exceptionalities?

▶ How many children with exceptionalities are there?

▶ What is the ecological model and why is it important?

▶ How does the child with exceptionalities affect the immediate family—the parents and the siblings?

▶ How do cultural differences in families affect children with exceptionalities?

Courtesy of Cengage Learning

I t's not easy being different. We have all felt the sting of not belonging, of not feeling a part of the group. We have all felt overwhelmed when asked to do things beyond our skills and capabilities, and bored when asked to do simple things that do not challenge us. Of course, being different is not always negative: It is what makes us interesting people.

But it also means we may have to adapt to social expectations that are often designed for the person who is "typical." When being different means that a child is not able to receive information through the normal senses; is not able to express thoughts, needs, and feelings; or processes information differently, special adaptations in the education program are necessary. All children need and deserve an educational environment where they belong and where their differences are addressed and honored. This book will provide you with important information about how schools and communities can support individuals with special needs across a variety of environments to ensure that being different does not mean being left out!

> We consider a child to be exceptional when his or her differences or disabilities occur to such a degree that school practices must be modified to serve the child's needs.

 ## The Child with Exceptionalities: An Overview

Who is the child with exceptionalities? The term *exceptional* is generally used to include both the child with developmental disabilities and the child with gifts or talents. Here we define a child with exceptionalities as a child who differs from the typical child in (1) mental characteristics, (2) sensory abilities, (3) communication abilities, (4) behavior and emotional development, and/ or (5) physical characteristics (these areas of difference are fully explained in Table 1.1. In an exceptional child, these differences occur to such an extent that he or she requires either a modification of school practices or special educational services to develop his or her unique capabilities.

Of course, this definition is general and raises several questions. What do we mean by "the *typical* child"? How extensive must the differences be for the child to require a special education? What is special education? What role does the environment play in supporting the child? We ask these questions in different forms throughout this text as we discuss each group or category of children with exceptionalities.

Individuals with exceptionalities help us better understand human development. Variation is a natural part of human development; by studying and teaching children who are remarkably different from the norm, we learn about the many ways in which children develop and learn. Through this knowledge, we inform ourselves more thoroughly about the developmental processes of all children. In this way, we develop our teaching skills and strategies for all students. Throughout this book we will meet many children and their families, and we will glimpse a small part of the life they lead. We also come to understand that while an area of difference makes the child unique, the child with exceptionalities is a child first and so shares the same needs as all children.

Educational Areas of Exceptionalities

If we define a child with exceptionalities as one who differs in some way from a group norm, then many children are exceptional. A child with red hair is "exceptional" if all the other children in the class have black, brown, or blond hair. A child who is a foot taller than his or her peers is "exceptional." But these differences, though interesting to a geneticist, are of little concern to the teacher.

TABLE 1.1
Definitions of Disabilities—Areas Covered by Law

Autism	Developmental disability that significantly affects verbal and nonverbal communication and social interaction, generally evident before age 3, and that adversely affects a child's educational performance
Communication Impairment	Significantly limited, impaired, or delayed capacity to use expressive and/or receptive language, exhibited by difficulties in one or more of the following areas: speech, such as articulation and/or voice; conveying, understanding, or using spoken, written, or symbolic language
Developmental Delay	Significantly limited, impaired, or delayed learning capacity of a young child (3–9 years old), exhibited by difficulties in one or more of the following areas: receptive and/or expressive language cognitive abilities; physical functioning; social, emotional, or adaptive functioning; and/or self-help skills
Emotional Impairment	One or more of the following characteristics exhibited over a long period of time and to such a marked degree that it adversely affects educational performance: an inability to learn that cannot be explained by intellectual, sensory, or health factors; an inability to build or maintain satisfactory interpersonal relationships with peers and teachers; inappropriate types of behavior or feelings under normal circumstances; a general pervasive mood of unhappiness or depression; or a tendency to develop physical symptoms or fears associated with personal or school problems
Health Impairment	Chronic or acute health problems such that the physiological capacity to function is significantly limited or impaired and that results in limited strength, vitality, or alertness, including a heightened alertness to environmental stimuli, resulting in limited alertness with respect to the educational environment
Intellectual Impairment	Significant limitation or impairment in the permanent capacity for performing cognitive tasks, functions, or problem solving, exhibited by more than one of the following: a slower rate of learning, disorganized patterns of learning, difficulty with adaptive behavior, and/or difficulty understanding abstract concepts
Neurological Impairment	Limitation or impairment in the capacity of the nervous system, with difficulties exhibited in one or more of the following areas: the use of memory, the control and use of cognitive functioning, sensory and motor skills, skills in speech and language, organizational skills, information processing, affect, social skills, or basic life functions
Physical Impairment	Significant limitation, impairment, or delay in physical capacity to move, coordinate actions, or perform physical activities, exhibited by difficulties in one or more of the following areas: physical and motor tasks, independent movement, performing basic life functions. The term shall include severe orthopedic impairments or impairments caused by congenital anomaly, cerebral palsy, amputations, and fractures if such impairment adversely affects a student's educational performance.
Sensory Impairment	1. *Hearing.* Limitation, impairment, or absence of the capacity to hear with amplification, resulting in one or more of the following: reduced performance in hearing acuity tasks, difficulty with oral communication, and/or difficulty in understanding auditorially presented information in the education environment. The term includes students who are deaf and students with significant hearing loss. 2. *Vision.* Limitation, impairment, or absence of capacity to see after correction, resulting in one or more of the following: reduced performance in visual acuity tasks, difficulty with written communication, and/or difficulty with understanding information presented visually in the education environment. The term includes students who are blind and students with limited vision.

	3. *Deafblind.* Concomitant hearing and visual impairments, the combination of which causes severe communication and other developmental and educational needs.
Specific Learning Disability	Disorder in one or more of the basic psychological processes involved in understanding or in using language, spoken or written, that may manifest itself in an imperfect ability to listen, think, speak, read, write, spell, or do mathematical calculations, including conditions such as perceptual disabilities, brain injury, minimal brain dysfunction, dyslexia, and developmental aphasia. *Disorders not included in learning disabilities:* Learning problems that are primarily the result of visual, hearing, or motor disabilities, of intellectual or developmental delay, of emotional disturbance, or of environmental, cultural, or economic disadvantage.

Source: www.doe.mass.edu/sped/definitions.html

Educationally speaking, students are not considered "exceptional" unless the educational program needs to be modified to help them be successful. If a child's exceptionalities mean he needs additional support to read or to master learning, or if he is so far ahead that he is bored by what is being taught, or he is unable to adjust to the social needs of the classroom, then special educational methods become necessary.

The standard groupings or categories of differences in children with exceptionalities are the following:

- *intellectual differences,* including children who are intellectually advanced (gifted) and children who learn more slowly (with intellectual and developmental disabilities)

- *communication differences,* including children with speech and language disabilities and disabilities like autism, in which communication is delayed or impaired

- *learning disabilities,* including children with problems learning and attending in the classroom

- *sensory differences,* including children with hearing or visual impairments

- *behavioral differences,* including children who are emotionally or socially challenged

- *multiple and severe disabilities,* including children with combinations of impairments (such as cerebral palsy and intellectual and developmental disabilities, or deafness and blindness together)

- *physical differences,* including children with nonsensory impairments that impede mobility, health, and physical vitality

A child with disabilities can be eligible for special education services in thirteen different legal categories, as shown in Table 1.1. These categories are outlined in the Individuals with Disabilities Education Act (IDEA, 2004), an important piece of federal legislation (discussed in detail in Chapter 2). The definitions in the table are given in technical language, but they are the best descriptors that we have of these areas of exceptionalities. Through case studies and vignettes in the chapters ahead, we will meet students who live with these disabilities. We will also come to see how we can support each child's success.

Socialization and collaboration are two important goals in special education.
(© Ellen Senisi)

You may have noticed that children with special gifts and talents are not included in Table 1.1. This is because federal legislation, which generated this list, does not address children with special gifts and talents. These children do, however, have special needs. They need to escape boredom from the typical curriculum and be motivated to use their talents to the fullest. Every child has the right to reach his or her potential; for children with special gifts and talents, it is also important to society that we support their unique contributions.

Interindividual and Intraindividual Differences

Children with exceptionalities are different in some ways from other children of the same life age. These differences between children are called **interindividual differences**, and they can present educators with many challenges. What sometimes goes unnoticed is that some students also show substantial intraindividual differences. **Intraindividual differences,** or differences that occur within a single child, such as a gap between motor skills needed for writing and cognitive abilities, must also be taken into account when planning for the child. For example, Jason, who is 9, has the intelligence of an 11-year-old but the social behavior of a 6-year-old, and so both interindividual and intraindividual differences must be addressed.

Intraindividual differences can show up in any area: intellectual, emotional, physical, or social. A child may be very bright but may have a hearing loss. A child's physical development might be on target, but he might be unable to relate socially to his agemates. It is just as important for teachers to know the child's unique pattern of strengths and challenges as it is to know how the child compares with other children. Understanding a child's intraindividual differences can help us develop individualized approaches to instruction. These approaches are tailored to the strengths and needs of the individual child. Individualized approaches do not necessarily consider how that child compares with other children; the focus is on the specific child. One reason for the development of the **individualized education program (IEP)**—we will discuss IEPs throughout the text—is that these intraindividual differences can pose unique patterns of needs that educators must address.

The Story of Max: A Historical Case Study

Let us now gain some historical perspective about society's treatment of children with special needs. Consider the story of Max, a short, stocky 8-year-old boy who has been diagnosed with autism, a condition that seriously affects his ability to communicate and form relationships with others. He is receiving special services to strengthen his social skills and build his academic achievement. An interesting question, though, is this: What would have happened to Max if he had been born in 1850 or 1900 or 1925 or 1950 or 1975?

In 1850, only a smattering of physicians were interested in children like Max. Two doctors, Jean-Marc Itard and Edouard Seguin, were the first known individuals who tried to teach children with intellectual and developmental delays (which is likely how Max would have been viewed). In all likelihood, Max would have dropped out of school early, if he had had any schooling at all. At this same point in history, several individuals were interested in helping children who were deaf. Thomas Gallaudet and others were experimenting with various models of communication for children with hearing loss. However, this would not have been much help to Max.

In 1900, there were some isolated stirrings within urban communities focused on starting classes for children with disabilities. These, however, would have been unlikely to help Max, who would probably have been called "mentally deficient" if he had received any attention at all.

In 1922, the Council for Exceptional Children (CEC) was founded in order to organize teachers who were working to help children with exceptionalities. A few classes had begun in urban settings, but these still would not have been much help to Max.

In 1950, the post–World War II era saw the beginnings of special programs for children with exceptionalities (in states such as California and Illinois). If Max had been in the right place, he might have received some help in one of these special classrooms.

Dr. Sam Kirk—a key figure in the beginnings and organization of special education; original author of this text, and director of the Institute for Research on Exceptional Children at the University of Illinois 1948–1966.
(Photo 0003318 Courtesy of the University of Illinois Archives)

> The increase in early childhood programs means increases in school budgets, which necessarily delay program growth.

By 1975, the federal government had enacted legislation designed to provide real help for children like Max. The courts were validating parents' claims to a free and appropriate education. Still, autism was not a well-known disorder, and any well-meaning efforts might not have been sufficient for Max's needs.

Today, in the first part of the twenty-first century, there is a greater likelihood that Max would be seen by a multidisciplinary team of specialists (neurologists, psychologists, speech pathologists, etc.) who would be aware of his condition and the special adaptations needed to maximize Max's strengths and abilities. The good news is that today, Max's opportunities to meet with educational success have greatly increased.

This brief historical overview featuring Max reveals, however, that intentional, organized, and multidisciplinary efforts are a relatively new development for children with disabilities. For good reasons, the medical profession was the first to become interested in the children with exceptionalities. Many children with exceptionalities had physical and health problems that brought them to the attention of physicians. The early terminology relating to these exceptionalities was dominated by medical labels, such as *phenylketonuria, Down syndrome, mental deficiency, blindness,* and *deafness.*

The medical community is still deeply involved in the prevention and discovery of causes related to exceptionality. However, even though a disability might have a medical cause, we in education have gradually realized that we are the key professionals who must address the needs created by the unusual and atypical development of children with exceptionalities. Teachers work with and spend the most time with the child every day. Further, enhancing developmental patterns is usually the province of educators, social scientists, and therapists rather than of medical practitioners. For these reasons, educators have become the key professionals responsible for supporting the child with exceptionalities.

The field of special education received a good amount of attention at the beginning of the twenty-first century. This is due to the fact that during the 1970s, a strong state and federal legislative base for special education was established. A history of favorable court decisions supporting a "free and appropriate public education" (FAPE) for all citizens also resulted in the establishment of special education practices (see Chapter 2 for more details about FAPE). This interest of the government, the courts, and schools in children with exceptionalities is a clear indication of the general support of larger society. This support is critical as programs for children with exceptionalities continue to evolve.

In public education today, a new approach used by teams of school professionals is the **response to intervention (RTI).** As noted in the preface of this book, the RTI model has three layers or tiers of intervention: I—classroom-wide changes to incorporate children with exceptionalities into regular programs (such as classroom discipline rules and procedures), II—targeted intervention for small groups of students requiring special instruction (such as special reading groups), and III—individualized programming for children with very special needs. This new model provides educational strategies for special education to collaborate with general education to meet the needs of children who need help but who may not need special education services. Each chapter of this text will spotlight different aspects of the RTI model.

RTI

▶❚❚ TeachSource VIDEO CONNECTION

Inclusion: Grouping Strategies for the Classroom

Visit the Education CourseMate website to access this Video Case. In this case, you will see a fifth grade classroom where a teacher uses small groups to provide appropriate learning opportunities for typical children and for children with special needs. The teacher collaborates with specialists to individualize the lessons focused on a shared topic.

As you watch this video, what do you notice about the collaboration between these teachers? How is the lesson enhanced by having specialists involved?

Early Identification of Children with Exceptionalities

Identification of students with exceptionalities (defined in Table 1.1) is taken quite seriously by educators because this identification is often the first step to successful interventions. Appropriate identification is important so that we can match supports and services, or interventions, to the child's specific needs. If we know, for example, that a child has a learning disability in reading, we know what interventions should be put in place to support the child. There is also an economic reason for appropriate identification. Children who are formally identified as having disabilities (as defined in Table 1.1) are eligible for services and can receive support from specialized personnel. These supports and services are provided through funds from the federal and state governments. Because of this, identification becomes a policy and economic issue—as well as an educational issue.

Until recently, the American public school system was not involved with the education and care of young, preschool-age children. Given their extensive K–12 responsibilities, there was some resistance to public schools taking on the additional responsibilities of prekindergarten programs. Because of this, the needs of the child from birth to 5 years have historically been in the hands of a wide variety of persons representing a variety of disciplines. Early childhood programs take many forms including family day care, center-based care, Head Start, and Title I (Improving the Academic Achievement of the Disadvantaged). Many of these entities can offer early intervention programs to help families who have young children with special developmental problems or disabilities (Cryer & Clifford, 2003).

All of the professions that serve children with exceptionalities (e.g., medicine, education, social work, psychology, speech pathology, etc.) agree on one major proposition: The earlier the intervention in the developmental sequence of the child, the better. In the case of early intervention, *better* means more significant positive outcomes with less effort (Gallagher, 2006). Public preschools and early childhood programs are beginning to emerge with increasing pressure to begin treatment as soon as a disability is discovered, which means support for some children begins at birth—well before kindergarten or even prekindergarten.

In the past decade, the *prekindergarten movement* has emerged, and thirty-eight states now have some state-supported provisions for helping young children develop. This shift in attention and support to young children is due to new understandings about the early years of a child's development.

We know the following:

1. The brain develops through interaction with the environment; therefore, it is essential that there are optimal early environments for learning (Plomin, Defries, Craig & McGuffin, 2003).

A disability is not always easily observed by teachers or by peers.
(© Elizabeth Crews Photography)

2. What happens to the infant and toddler casts long shadows ahead in his or her development; if a child is abused or neglected, the impact is great and it takes a significant effort to counteract the negative effects later (Thompson, 2005).

3. The rapid increase of mothers in the workforce has made it especially important to have positive early childcare (Haskins, 2007).

A flurry of activity and interest now surrounds the preschool child, often from birth on, and over $4.6 billion is currently spent on pre-K state programs (Barnett et al., 2006). Chapter 3 in this text is devoted to young children with exceptionalities, and we will also comment in each chapter on the special issues that involve the preschool child because we too believe that the earlier the intervention begins, the better!

The Information Processing Model

One way of thinking about how children learn is by using the **information processing model (IPM).** We will be using an IPM (Figure 1.1) throughout this text to explore the various components of information processing that are impacted by the presence of a disability or exceptionality. Information processing explains how students interact with and respond to the world around them and describes the learning process. First, children receive information from their senses through input (visual, hearing, etc.). Next, they process this information through memory classification and reasoning abilities. Finally, they respond to information through output (i.e., speaking, writing, or acting). Students are aided in this processing of information by their *executive function,* or the ability to decide which information to attend to, how to interpret the information, and which option to use in response. Information processing takes place within an *emotional context* that influences every aspect of the system: input, processing, output, and executive function.

For example, Gloria may hear from her teacher (hearing) about an assignment of a report due on Friday. The assignment is also written on the teacher's handout (visual). Gloria remembers (memory) what happened the last time she missed an assignment and decides to use her *reasoning* and *evaluative* abilities to create a report. She will go to the library (motor) and prepare to give an oral report (speaking). Finishing the report tends to reduce Gloria's anxiety about her school performance (emotional context).

Special education is often required when a student is unable to process information effectively. The

Emotional Context

EXECUTIVE FUNCTION
(choosing)

Attention   Thinking   Response

Information Input	Processing	Information Output
Vision	Memory	Speaking
Hearing	Classification	Writing
Kinesthetic	Association	Motor Response
Haptic	Reasoning	Dancing
Gustatory	Evaluation	Running
Olfactory		Social Interactions

Stimulus →

key
Primary
Associated

FIGURE 1.1
The Information Processing Model

problems of the student may be in the *input* of information (visual, hearing, or other) or the internal *processing* of that information (using memory, reasoning, or evaluation) or in the *output* or response to the information. The *executive function* is the decision-making aspect of the model that helps the student attend to the input by choosing what thinking processes he or she should call upon and deciding how to react. Imagine what happens when the executive function doesn't respond well.

All of this information processing is done within an *emotional context,* which can help or scramble the other components of the model under conditions of stress, anxiety, or calm and confidence. In each of the following chapters, we will present the information processing model and show which elements are impacted by the exceptionality under discussion.

Causation of Exceptionalities

Each succeeding chapter devotes some space to the many potential causes of the exceptionality discussed. The role of *neurology* and *genetics* is so important to the discussion of causation that it will have a special section within each of the chapters. A discussion of the roles of heredity and environment is central to understanding causation of various kinds of exceptionality.

> It is important to consider the values of the culture and community as a major factor in how the child with exceptionalities will be identified and will adapt to education.

The Interaction of Heredity and Environment

Few topics stimulate more fascination than the question of how we become who and what we are. What forces shape our development and sequentially build a confident and complex adult from an apparently helpless infant? For many decades, we have been aware of the effects that both heredity and environment have on the developing child. Because it is the role of educators to change the environment of the child through instruction, we have often ignored the role of heredity.

But the recent dramatic progress in the field of genetics makes heredity impossible to ignore. Historically, we have been through three major stages in our belief systems about the relative influence of heredity and environment, and each stage has had a profound effect on how we have behaved as educators. Up until about 1960, it was strongly believed that heredity drove and determined various conditions related to intelligence, such as *mild* intellectual disability, giftedness, or mental illness. Our beliefs about the potency of heredity led us to consider it more or less impossible to change a child's condition, and the role of educators was seen as helping individuals adapt as well as possible to their hereditary roll of the dice (Plomin & Petrill, 1997).

Starting around 1960, there was a major movement to discover the important role played by *environment,* which suggested that many exceptionalities can be created or intensified by various environmental conditions. Researchers reasoned that mild developmental disabilities could be caused by lack of early stimulation or that special gifts and talents emerged only because the environment for some children was incredibly favorable. Educators were encouraged to try to find ways to reverse unfavorable environmental effects and to accentuate favorable outcomes through education.

Around 1990, a similar shift in the view of the relative roles of heredity and environment took place. The emphasis was placed on the progressive *interaction of heredity and environment* and the resulting effects of those interactions. Gottlieb (1997) proposed that by changing the environmental conditions of early childhood, we can activate different patterns of genes, which then can result in behavioral changes.

The growing sophistication of genetic research has made it clear that many conditions that lead to exceptionality are linked to an intertwining of genetics and environment. Conditions such as fragile X syndrome, intellectual and developmental disabilities (IDD), attention-deficit hyperactivity disorder (ADHD), and dyslexia all seem to have strong genetic components (McGuffin, Riley, & Plomin, 2001), yet all can be positively influenced by favorable environments.

One of the most dramatic recent scientific breakthroughs has been made by the Human Genome Project (see Figure 1.2: Human Genome). The goals of this international project were to determine the complete sequence of the three billion DNA subunits (bases) and to identify all human genes and make them accessible for further biological study (Tartaglia, Hansen, & Hagerman, 2007). The U.S. Department of Energy and the National Institutes of Health were the U.S. sponsors. The initial goals of determining the entire Human Genome were reached in 2003. The many research projects fanning out from these basic discoveries include a number that relate to children with exceptionalities. The results are reported for individual disability categories throughout the rest of the book.

As our ability to identify genes has increased, we have become interested in **gene-environment interaction.** Some of the earlier questions have been oversimplified (i.e., which gene causes which condition), but we now have a better view of reality reflected in the following understandings:

Human Genome Project
www.ornl.gov/hgm

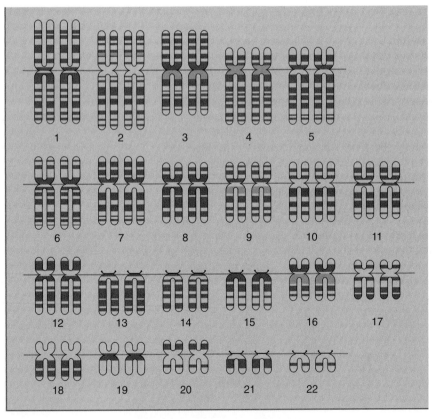

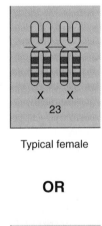

Typical female

OR

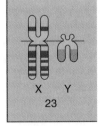

Typical male

Typical human females and males have
22 chromosome pairs in common.

The 23rd pair, the sex
chromosomes, differentiates
between females and males.

FIGURE 1.2
The Human Genome
Source: Freberg, L. (2006). *Discovering biological psychology,* p. 121. Used by permission of Cengage Learning.

a. Genes do not control behavior directly.

b. Almost all behavioral traits emerge from complex interactions between multiple genes and environments.

c. The causes of personality and ability are found across complex neural networks—not in a single location in the brain (with the exception of extreme causes of focal brain lesions) (Beauchaine et al., 2008, p. 746).

In short, we cannot say that genes cause depression or ADHD, but rather that the complex mix of environments and multiple genes can result in some unfavorable outcomes. Since we can do little about the genes, we continue to concentrate on intervening within the environment to improve educational and social outcomes for children (Rutter, 2007).

Prevalence: How Many Children with Exceptionalities Are There?

Educational policy makers—those who make the decisions about how we should spend societal resources on education—want to know just how many children with exceptionalities there are in the United States. These numbers tell us how big an issue this is and how much we, as a society, will have to invest in education.

The general public appears to look on these categories of exceptional children as "present or absent." One either has the condition (autism or learning disability or emotional disturbance) or one does not. In reality, things are not that simple. For example, why do some professionals say that 1 percent of the school population has emotional disturbances while others say that actually 20 percent of the population does? This is a difference of thousands of children (Cullinan, 2004). The answer is that there is a gradual shading (as the colors of the rainbow blend into one another) within every category of exceptionality. The category itself has been formed by establishing an arbitrary cutoff point determined by medical, educational, and psychological professionals who diagnose children with exceptionalities. The children on either side of this arbitrary cutoff point, however, are very similar to one another. This is one important reason for using the RTI approach (described in the Preface) that recognizes that some children falling just outside the line demarcating identification for "special education" services still need additional supports to perform successfully in academic settings. The tiered approach to supports and services used in RTI can address the needs of children who miss the "cut-off points" for formal identification but who still need some supports.

RTI

A reasonable estimate is that more than six million children in the United States can be classified across the categories of exceptionality. This estimate is obtained by aggregating the reports from the fifty states. This means that approximately one out of about every ten children is *exceptional* (using the definitions in Table 1.1). This is one reason for the extensive attention given to children with exceptionality in our school systems today.

Children with disabilities are not distributed equally across the defined categories—far from it. Figure 1.3 gives a breakdown of the six high-incidence categories of disabilities. The term **high-incidence disabilities** include the categories of disability that are most prevalent—composing at least 1 percent of the school population. The prevalence of children in the gifted category is not included here because special gifts and talents are not included in the federal legislation from which these figures are derived.

Figure 1.3 represents the number of children reported who are served by the U.S. Department of Education, drawing on reports from the fifty states (Twenty-Eighth Annual Report to Congress, 2008). Note that these are the

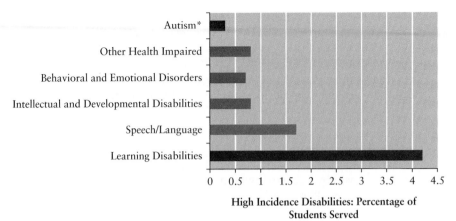

FIGURE 1.3
High Incidence Disabilities: Percentages of Students Served by Category
* These figures have sharply increased since data was collected in 2006.
Source: U.S. Department of Education. (2008). *Twenty-Eighth Annual Report to Congress*. Washington, D.C.: Office of Special Education Programs.

numbers of children *receiving service*—not necessarily *all* of the children in each specific category. There are a number of children with disabilities who are undiagnosed. By far, the largest category is that of learning disabilities—4.2 percent. (Chapter 4 will discuss these figures and their implications.)

About 1.7% of children are found in the Speech and Language category, while close to one percent of children are either identified as having an Intellectual or Developmental Disorder or a Behavioral and Emotional Disorder. The one data point that seems incorrect or out of place is the .3% of children with Autism. The actual figure as of 2010 is closer to 1%. In fact, Autism is the only disability category that has increased greatly over the last few years. This increase in Autism Spectrum diagnoses has received substantial media attention, and it will be discussed in greater detail in Chapter 5.

Figure 1.4 provides estimates of prevalence of **low-incidence disabilities.** These are categories that make up less than 1 percent of the school population.

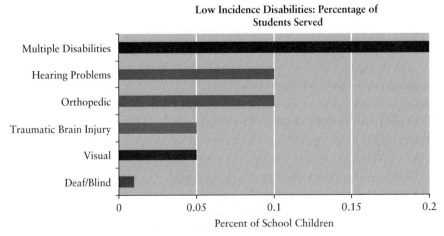

FIGURE 1.4
Low Incidence Disabilities: Percentages of Students Served
Source: U.S. Department of Education. (2008). *Twenty-Eighth Annual Report to Congress*. Washington, D.C.: Office of Special Education Programs.

Children with these exceptionalities show up only rarely in the general education classroom. Multiple disabilities is the largest of these categories. The reason for the small percentage (less than .5 percent) for visual problems is that although many children wear glasses, this figure only includes children with "uncorrected" vision problems that can interfere with learning. The traumatic brain injury category makes up only one half of one percent of children. Furthermore, while it a serious condition, deafblindness in children is extremely rare (only one in a thousand).

As researchers learn more about children and various conditions, they have a tendency to establish more categories. Children with ADHD, for example, are not included in the tables presented here. Children with ADHD have many similarities with other groups of exceptional children—notably children with learning disabilities or behavior disorders—and therefore are included in discussions of these exceptionalities in a number of chapters within this text.

ADD/ADHD

As the ADHD term implies, these students have difficulty in attending to importing information and recording it in the memory. The overactive nature of children with ADHD adds to the lack of attention span (see the Information Processing Model, Figure 1.1) and the student not only doesn't learn essential information, but is often a source of disruption in the classroom.

Disproportionate Representation of Culturally/ Linguistically Diverse Children in Special Education

One specific way in which culture interacts with educational decisions is the overrepresentation of some culturally and linguistically diverse students assigned to special education. The issue of disproportionate representation came to the attention of the Office of Civil Rights (OCR) in the U.S. Department of Education, and OCR mounted a major national survey to determine whether these patterns were valid (Donovan & Cross, 2002).

Figure 1.5 shows the risk percentage or the likelihood of finding a child of a particular racial or ethnic background in special education programs. For example, black students may be twice as likely as white students to find themselves identified for a program serving students with intellectual and developmental disabilities. Note that there are still likely to be more white students in these programs than black students because the base figures of each population in American schools are so different.

Similarly, Asian students may be one-third as likely to find themselves in a learning disabilities program as black students, as seen in Figure 1.5. And Hispanic students would have about half the chance of being identified for a program serving students who are emotionally disturbed as white students. These risk figures are upsetting to many observers who see racial discrimination at work. While discrimination undoubtedly does occur, an alternative explanation stems from the data presented in Figure 1.6, showing the results of fourth grade students' reading proficiency on the National Assessment for Educational Progress (NAPE).

The NAPE results show that 50 percent of black and Latino

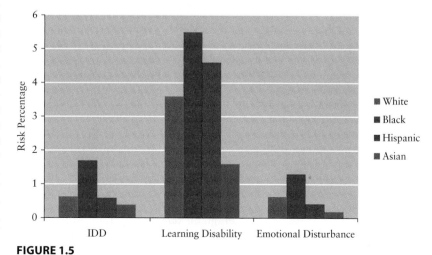

FIGURE 1.5
National Special Education Risk Percentages by Race/Ethnicity
Source: Reschley, D. (2009). Minority special education disproportionality findings and misconceptions. *Minorities in Special Education.* U.S. Commission on Civil Rights.

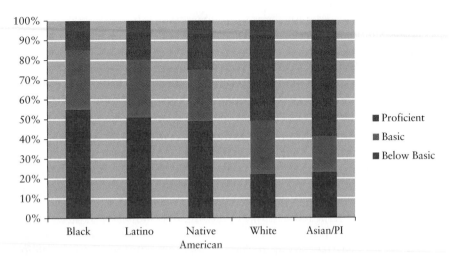

FIGURE 1.6
Reading Proficiency Percentages by Race/Ethnicity
Source: The Nation's Report Card: Reading 2007. NAEP, US Department of Education,
Table A-9.

students are falling below basic skills in reading, while only 20 percent of white students are falling below. When a teacher finds a student remarkably below standard in reading, she is likely to call for help, and this call may lead to a special education placement. In the RTI model, as we begin to strengthen Tier I support for all children and to provide targeted support (Tier II) for children who need it, we hope to see a change in this pattern.

RTI

 ## The Ecological Approach and the Importance of Family

As you will learn throughout this text, families, peers, and communities play an important role in the lives of exceptional children. In this section, we will briefly discuss both the positive and challenging components of the family's role.

The Ecological Approach

Perhaps one of the most dramatic changes in educators' views of how to teach young children has resulted from the adoption of the ecological approach to child development. With this recognition of the role of the environment, the field moved from a **medical model** of exceptionality, which assumes that a physical condition or disease exists within a patient, to an **ecological model**, in which we see the child with exceptionalities in complex interaction with many environmental forces.

The ecological approach tries not only to modify the exceptional child's learning and behavior but also to improve the environment surrounding the child, including the family and the neighborhood—the entire context of the child's life. This ecological approach became the strategy of Head Start and other programs targeted at children from economically disadvantaged families. Head Start pays much attention to the family, in addition to the child (Zigler & Styfco, 2004). The ecological model also helps us understand what we can realistically expect to accomplish through intervention programs.

Increasingly, the approach that educators use to support the child who has milder forms of exceptionalities is to try to aid the child's adjustment by modifying

> The ecological approach seeks to modify the child's behavior directly by improving the context in which the child lives, learns, and plays.

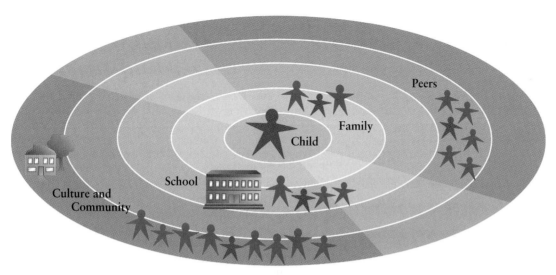

FIGURE 1.7
The Context/Ecology of the Exceptional Child
Source: U.S. Department of Education (2003). *Twenty-fourth Annual Report to Congress.*
Washington, DC: Office of Special Education Programs.

the life circles around the child (see Figure 1.7), in addition to directly addressing the child's developmental delays and other exceptionalities (Gallagher, 2006).

The Family System

One of the major forces that influences the child with exceptionalities, as well as any child, is the family system. Because it is a system, we expect that anything that happens to one member of that family will have an impact on all the other members of the family (Cox & Paley, 1997). If we expect to be effective in special education, we need to interact with the members of the family in which the child lives—not just with the child. The trend toward early intervention (before the age of 5) increases the importance of the family. Much of the intervention with young children is directed toward supporting the family environment and preparing the parent(s) or caretakers to care for and teach children with disabilities. At the very least, intervention tries to support constructive parent-child interactions. (Chapter 3 focuses specifically on early childhood intervention from a variety of perspectives.) Years of experience and study have led to the following principles regarding the family:

1. Children and families are inextricably intertwined. Intentional or not, intervention with children almost invariably influences families; likewise, intervention and support with families almost invariably influence children.

2. Involving and supporting families is likely to be a more powerful intervention than one that focuses exclusively on the children.

3. Family members should be able to choose their level of involvement in program planning, decision making, and service delivery.

Families of exceptional children play an important role in early intervention. Parents can teach their children some of the skills and learning tools that will later be reinforced in a school setting.

(© Peter Hvizdak/The Image Works)

A Day in the Life of Roger's Family

The responsibilities of two-parent working families are difficult enough without adding the special needs of a child with disabilities. Roger is a 10-year-old boy with cerebral palsy and developmental delay. Roger's father and mother are awakened at 6:30 in the morning by the cries of Roger's younger sister, Anna. Roger has to be washed and dressed, a task of considerable difficulty because of his cerebral palsy. Meanwhile, Roger's mother is setting out breakfast and beginning to think about her own workday as a teacher at a local school.

Roger's father gets Roger washed and dressed and down to the breakfast table and then begins to think about a shower and shave before going to the construction company where he works. Before work, he takes Roger to the developmental day-care program, where he is in an integrated program with his same-age peers. The family is fortunate in that Roger's sister goes to the school where her mother teaches, so one transportation problem is solved.

Breakfast is often a chaotic affair with no one sitting down at the same time. Roger needs extra help eating because he has difficulty directing the spoon full of cereal and milk to his mouth. Mom puts the breakfast dishes in the dishwasher, and Dad is off with Roger while Mom helps Anna find her bookbag so they can also head off.

In the late afternoon and evening, the same procedure is reversed. This time Mom picks up Roger because Dad is at a construction site on the other side of town. She is delayed by the teacher, who describes an incident that involved Roger's conflict with another child over possession of some toy. There is still dinner to prepare, baths to be given, and stories to read before the children are tucked in. Is it any wonder that the parents are weary at the end of the day? Tomorrow will be even more challenging because Roger has a medical checkup in addition to the normal daily activities, and it still needs to be determined who will take him to the doctor.

When both parents share responsibility for the family tasks, there is *family harmony*. The important factor in family harmony is that parents understand the roles and responsibilities that each will fulfill to meet the family's needs so that each parent feels supported.

Imagine what would happen if the parents cannot agree about responsibilities or if there are tensions between them regarding discipline, finances, or expectations for the children. It is easy to see that the family relationships are key to a positive context for the exceptional child.

When considering basic family responsibilities, it is important to realize the enormous diversity of families. There has been a substantial increase in the number of single-parent families. Because many single mothers live in poverty, their children are less likely to receive good prenatal and postnatal care, and this increases the chances of a child having physical, academic, and emotional problems. It is difficult to imagine the added stress single mothers face in meeting the needs of their children.

> Parents of a child with serious disabilities must face two crises: the symbolic death at birth of the child who could have been and the difficulty of providing daily care for the child who is.

There are many stresses in the lives of families who have children with disabilities, but their lives also can be filled with joy, laughter, and fun. Children can light up parents' hearts with a smile, and parents of children with disabilities, just like other parents, have their favorite stories of their child's adventures and antics. As a parent, your child is always your child first, and their exceptionality comes second.

Pivotal Issues

- In what ways does the routine of Roger's family seem typical, just like any family?

- How is the routine different?

- What kinds of external support would help Roger's family meet his needs and reduce their stress?

- Imagine what may happen in the family if one of Roger's parents gets sick?

4. Family members should be able to choose their level of involvement in program planning, decision making, and service delivery.

5. Professionals should attend to family priorities for goals and services, even when those priorities differ substantially from professional priorities (Turnbull & Turnbull, 2004).

Family Response to a Child with a Disability

The response to the information that they, the parents, have a child with disabilities is remarkably varied and personal. The family response is critical because it may well determine the success of intervention and school programming for the exceptional child. In the family that is attentive and optimistic, the child can respond positively to educational stimulation. If parents are "in denial" about their child's learning or developmental challenges, the child may not receive important early interventions that are critical for his or her future success (Blacher & Hatton, 2007).

Most parents who have a child with serious disabilities face two major crises. The first is the "symbolic death" of the child who was to be. When their child is first diagnosed as having a serious disability, most parents feel shock and then denial, guilt, anger, and sadness before they finally adjust. A few parents react with severe depression. Support groups composed of parents of children with similar disabilities can be quite effective in helping new parents by sharing ways in which they have faced similar challenges in their own families.

The second, quite different, crisis that many parents of a child with exceptionalities face is the problem of providing daily care for the child. A child who has cerebral palsy or is emotionally disturbed is often difficult to feed, dress, and put to bed. It is the continual, day-to-day responsibilities and care that often exhaust families (see the Exceptional Lives, Exceptional Stories box). The realization that their child may not go through a normal developmental process, and may never gain independence as an adult, often causes parents to worry about their child's future. Parents and family members therefore require support and empathetic professional attention.

> Environment, or ecology, plays a major role in the initial development of an exceptional child. Some atypical behaviors can be a response to the reactions of family and friends rather than genetics or pathology.

Family-Professional Relationships

Over the past few decades, the relationship between professionals and families in the field of exceptional children has changed. Originally, the professional's role was to explain the special needs of the child to the parents and give them directions and training for the proper care and treatment of the child. The mother was the traditional contact, and other family members played a lesser role. Today all family members are encouraged to play a significant role in the life of the child with disabilities, and supports are provided to help families meet the needs of their child. Professionals work in partnership with families, and interventions are centered on the families' needs.

Turnbull and Turnbull (2002) describe the **family-centered model** in this way:

First, the family-centered model primarily attempted to honor family choice by changing the power relationship between professionals and families.

Second, the family-centered model abandoned a pathology orientation and adopted a strengths orientation.

Third, the entire family has become the unit of support—not just the child with a disability and the child's mother (p. 92).

These three principles center the relationship between the family and professional on family needs, motivating special educators to look for the strengths in the child and family rather than focusing on the deficits. The purpose of this **family-focused** (or family-centered) **approach** is to help parents become autonomous and confident in their abilities to meet the needs of their child.

The change from an almost exclusive emphasis on the child to an emphasis on the family has placed a lot of professionals in unfamiliar territory. Many

> Teachers need practice in their roles as members of a team, just like athletes do.

teachers, psychologists, occupational therapists, and others are more accustomed to the old "treat the child" model. But the family-focused approach is essential to establishing the supports needed for the wellbeing of the child.

Emotional Development and the Family

The emotional repertoire of the child is not only the natural manifestation of his or her constitutional makeup, but it is also socially constructed through learning and experience (Shonkoff & Phillips, 2000). When a child is not able to understand and interpret the behaviors and communications of others, there are long-term social consequences (Flavell & Miller, 1998). The emotional repertoire of the child is, in part, socially constructed so it can be socially modified. Helping the child develop a healthy social and emotional repertoire is one of the major objectives of special education.

Because the social and emotional wellbeing of the child is closely tied to the quality of family life, researchers have begun to look at these issues. An effort to examine family quality of life has been led by Ann and Rud Turnbull at the Beach Center on Disability at the University of Kansas. They developed their Family Quality of Life Scale (FQOL), provided in Table 1.2, by questioning many parents and professionals about what is "important for families to have a good life together." By defining and measuring a family's quality of life, we can see how and where additional supports would be helpful.

This scale can be used to reflect the current quality of the family's life, to document progress as a result of family support programs, and to inform planning for specific families of children with exceptionalities. The scale includes the emotional well-being of the family and the key elements of parenting, and captures the degree of help provided to support the child with disabilities. You might want to fill out the scale for your own family to see how it works in identifying quality of life needs.

Family support is one of the most important strengths for a child with disabilities.
(© Ellen Senisi)

Culturally and Linguistically Diverse Families

Families are unique and complex. Each family has its own perspectives, but families who share cultural orientations often have similar values and beliefs. These values and beliefs influence child rearing practices. Respect for the breadwinner, religious beliefs, child disciplinary practices, and even attitudes toward professional support may reflect the values of the family's cultural group. Because cultural values play a critical role in shaping the child's world, it is critical that these are understood and honored by professionals working with the child and family.

Here are some examples of how cultural values might affect the child with special needs: If a family's **culture** emphasizes a dominant masculine role, how will the father of a child with disabilities respond to a female professional working with his child? Will he reject her advice and suggestions in order to maintain a strong masculine self-image? And what does he feel about his son who has disabilities that are so serious that the father despairs about the boy ever being able to fulfill a masculine role? These issues of core values are not easy to discuss, but they can rest at the heart of parental concerns for many years.

TABLE 1.2
Family Quality of Life Scale: Scoring and Items

Items	The FQOL Scale uses satisfaction as the primary response format. The anchors of the items rated on satisfaction are rated on a 5-point scale, where 1 = *very dissatisfied*, 3 = *neither satisfied nor dissatisfied*, and 5 = *very satisfied*. There are 25 items in the FQOL Scale. Below are the items keyed to each of the subscale domains:
Family Interaction	• My family enjoys spending time together. • My family members talk openly with each other. • My family solves problems together. • My family members support each other to accomplish goals. • My family members show that they love and care for each other.
Parenting	• My family is able to handle life's ups and downs. • Family members help the children learn to be independent. • Family members help the children with schoolwork and activities. • Family members teach the children how to get along with others. • Adults in my family teach the children to make good decisions. • Adults in my family know other people in the children's lives (i.e., friends, teachers). • Adults in my family have time to take care of the individual needs of every child.
Emotional Well-being	• My family has the support we need to relieve stress. • My family members have friends or others who provide support. • My family members have some time to pursue their own interests. • My family has outside help available to us to take care of special needs of all family members.
Physical/Material Well-being	• My family members have transportation to get to the places they need to be. • My family gets dental care when needed. • My family gets medical care when needed. • My family has a way to take care of our expenses. • My family feels safe at home, work, school, and in our neighborhood.
Disability-Related Support	• My family member with special needs has support to make progress at school or work. • My family member with special needs has support to make progress at home. • My family member with special needs has support to make friends. • My family has a good relationship with the service providers who work with our family member with a disability.

Source: www.beachcenter.org/resource_library/beach_resource_detail_1.brain_page. Reprinted by permission of Beach Center on Disability, University of Kansas.

One of the first challenges educators face is how to correctly identify children with exceptionalities from culturally and linguistically diverse families. Clearly, giving a child who does not speak English an IQ test in English is a bad idea. But the issue is more complicated than that. For children who are bilingual, language develops differently (see full discussion in Chapter 7). This makes it difficult to determine if a child has a learning disability or just a normal delay as he masters two language systems. All too often, culturally/linguistically diverse children are inappropriately referred to special education services when, in fact, they need a very different set of experiences to support their success.

RTI

This again is where the RTI model is helpful. Because the needs of many children from culturally and linguistically diverse families fall in between the general education and the special education services, RTI offers a collaborative level of support (Harry, 2007). It is in Tier II, targeted support, where many students' needs will be addressed, because while they may not need special education services, they may well need some type of supplementary supports in order to meet with success in the education system.

The needs of children from culturally and linguistically diverse families may be further impacted by issues related to poverty. The overlays of race and poverty of children with disabilities have led many to wonder if overrepresentation is related to two separate categories of special education students. The first involves neurological and biological problems (for example, children with Down syndrome, cerebral palsy, autism, and so forth). The second involves socially constructed conditions or outcomes such as mild intellectual and developmental disabilities (IDD), emotional disturbance, and learning disabilities that may come as a result of environmental factors such as poverty. As Harry (2007) points out, special education should reconceptualize struggling learners on a continuum of instruction rather than requiring that they be defined as "disabled." We believe that the RTI approach may help us by focusing on the child's needs rather than the program options.

Alternative Families

Once upon a time the word *family* evoked an image of a mother, a father, and two or more children. Today's families, however, are more varied. In fact, the National Institute of Mental Health defines "family" as merely "a network of mutual commitment" (2010). Today many families are headed by a single parent. One of the clear consequences of the single-parent family is reduced economic circumstances. Many families exist at or near the poverty line, a circumstance that makes expensive care for children with special needs extremely difficult. This may mean that during the early developmental period when a child needs special help, he or she is less likely to receive it. The recent public policy movement toward welfare reform (Haskins, 2007) has forced many mothers into the work force again, but it does not provide an answer for children with special needs. Often, policy reform to address one issue creates unintended consequences.

However, positive forces in the larger society are trying to cope with these problems. The establishment of prekindergarten programs in public schools allows children with special needs to be identified at age 3 or 4 and to receive important care earlier. Also, a wide variety of child-care and day-care options have been established to try to meet the needs of children whose parents work outside the home. It is important that these programs are of high quality so that children with disabilities can be appropriately cared for. Some current evidence shows that all too often the quality of child care in the United States is not high enough (Early et al., 2007). The result of uneven care for young children is that

To help empower parents, teachers might refer parents to any one of the many parent support groups for children with disabilities.

too many children enter kindergarten unprepared for the experience, and the consequences for increased school failure become predictable (Lee & Burkam, 2002). An investment in early childhood education and support for families of young children may be one of our society's greatest policy needs.

Siblings of Children with Exceptionalities

We now know enough about the family environment to dismiss the proposition that two children experience the *same* environment when they are growing up— merely because they live in the same household. Obviously the home environment is not the same for a child with disabilities as it is for his or her nondisabled sibling, or for an older daughter as it is for a younger son.

Assumptions are often made about families with a child with a disability— that the nondisabled sibling is inevitably neglected because the parents must pay so much attention to the child with disabilities and that, as a result, the sibling becomes resentful of the child with disabilities. It is now clear that although this set of events may happen, it certainly does not have to happen, particularly when the parents are sensitive to natural sibling rivalry and the needs for equivalent attention to each child.

Siblings of the child with a disability can spend at least the same amount of time with their mother and receive the same type of discipline that their brother or sister with disabilities receives. Siblings may perform a greater amount of household tasks. The sibling who may be vulnerable to special adjustment problems is the older sibling if the parents have given her or him additional child-care responsibilities. As in other family situations, it is not so much the actions of the parents that count as how the sibling interprets those actions. If the sibling is sure of being loved and cared for by the parent, then being given additional responsibilities for the child with disabilities does not seem to cause a negative reaction (Gallagher, Powell, & Rhodes, 2006).

Still, however, parents often worry about the effect that the child with disabilities has on his or her siblings. Will they grow resentful of the child with special needs or of the attention that the parents inevitably have to spend on him or her? When the parents grow old and are no longer able to take care of the child (then an adult) with disabilities, will the siblings pitch in and help meet their brother or sister's needs? Although each situation is different, there does not seem to be any evidence that the siblings of children with disabilities are more stressed or face greater adjustment problems than siblings of children without disabilities. The goal of most American parents is for their child with disabilities to become an independent and self-sufficient adult living away from home, and many siblings appear willing to assume the role of protector if that is necessary (Krauss, Seltzer, Gordon, & Friedman, 1996).

Answering the siblings' questions to help them understand their brother or sister's needs is an important part of the parents' responsibilities. For example, consider the following

A child's siblings can be invaluable for helping adjust to a new learning style or environment.
(© Ellen Senisi)

questions, which are examples of concerns a sibling may have but feel uncomfortable sharing:

- Why does he behave so strangely?
- Can she grow out of this?
- Will other brothers and sisters also have disabilities?
- Will he ever be able to live on his own?
- Will I be expected to take care of her as an adult?
- Am I loved as much as my brother?
- How can I tell my best friends about my sister?
- What am I supposed to do when other children tease my brother?
- Will my own children be more likely to have a disability?

The fact that a sibling may not verbalize fears and questions does not mean that he or she is not thinking about them. It is the parents' responsibility to try to answer even unverbalized questions and anxieties that the brother or sister may have about the sibling with disabilities and the family.

The number of questions that siblings have does not diminish over time. The concerns evident in the questions will reflect developmental changes. For example, an illness or death of one of the parents may heighten the siblings' concern about their own responsibilities. If the parents are gone or are no longer able to care for the sibling with disabilities, will they be expected to share in the care of their sibling throughout his or her lifetime? Each family has to answer these questions in its own way, but the answers must be clear and unambiguous for all family members. You may want to think about the kinds of questions you would have if your brother or sister had a disability. Would your questions change if you had a disability?

Also available to siblings of exceptional children are Sibshops, which are designed as workshops for siblings of children with special needs (Meyer & Vadasy, 2007). These Sibshops have been conducted in over 200 communities and eight countries, which are an indication of their popularity and usefulness. Originally designed by Don Meyer for children ages 8 to 13 who have siblings with special needs, these workshops are presented as having goals such as learning "how others handle situations commonly experienced by siblings with special needs" (Sibling Support, 2010).

These Sibshops are commonly facilitated by a team of service providers who have been trained in the process of Sibshops—such as social workers, special education teachers, and psychologists. Comments from participants are positive, but no formal evaluation has been done on the effectiveness of these workshops.

Efforts are increasing to provide more organized help for siblings, such as, for example, The Sibling Support Project, which conducts workshops for parents and professionals and peer support (The Kindering Center, Bellevue, Washington).

Family as Advocate: The Power of Parents

The recognition that society and the community at large, as well as schools, have a responsibility for caring for exceptional children stemmed in large measure from the activities of parents. Years ago, parents who were unable to get help for their children from local governments created their own programs in church basements, vacant stores, or any place that would house them. These informal groups, loosely formed around the common needs of the children, often provided important information to new parents struggling to find help for their children with disabilities. They were also a source of emotional support for parents—a means of sharing and solving the problems of accepting and living with exceptional children.

These parent groups quickly realized that fundamental changes were needed in the allocation of educational resources at local, state, and federal levels. A casual, haphazard approach was not going to provide the kind of help or support that parents or their children with exceptionalities needed. Accordingly, large parents' groups, such as the National Association of Retarded Children (now the Association of Retarded Citizens, ARC); the United Cerebral Palsy Association in the 1940s and 1950s; and the Association for Children with Learning Disabilities in the 1960s (now the Learning Disabilities Association of America, LDA) began to form. Parents of children with Down syndrome, autism (Autism Society of America), and other specific conditions have also formed groups to advocate for their children's special needs. These parent organizations have successfully stimulated legislation at the state and federal levels that has provided additional trained personnel, research, and equipment. To a large extent we can thank parents for the gains we have made as a society in the inclusion of individuals with disabilities.

Organized parents' groups for children who are gifted have not yet had the same political influence as the national organizations for children with disabilities. Still, these groups are helping the parents of children who are gifted cope with the problems of precocious development (Gallagher, 2002).

Assessment of Family Programs

Although concern for the families of children with special needs has been around for decades, there are still limited evaluations of the effectiveness of interventions with the family. The task is made more difficult because the "interventions" take so many different forms in content, length, and intensity.

The authors of a review of twenty-six different articles (Friend, Summers, & Turnbull, 2009) tried to draw some generalizations from the diverse attempts to help families:

> Intervention research suggests that parent training programs improved parenting skills and relieved parental stress. ... General family-centered practice offering an array of support, improved family cohesion and parental well-being ... respite care has short term effects on reducing parent stress. (p. 468)

In short, almost any sustained approach to the family by professionals appears to pay off in improved parental quality of life—particularly when the child is of prekindergarten age.

 # The Influence of Culture and Community

Culture refers to the attitudes, values, customs, and languages that family and friends transmit to children. These attitudes, values, customs, and languages have been passed down from generations of ancestors and have formed an identifiable pattern or heritage. The child is embedded in the family, its habits, and its traditions; this is as true for the child with special needs as for one who does not have special needs. Although the child may be only slightly aware of these

Cultural differences are often apparent in religious views, child rearing practices, and attitudes toward authority.

cultural influences, it makes a world of difference to the child's experiences if his or her family is fourth-generation American or first-generation Irish, Mexican, Italian, Nigerian, or Taiwanese.

Families' religious beliefs, child-rearing practices, attitudes toward authority, and so forth, can often be traced to their cultural identity. Therefore, the schools must understand and honor that cultural background in order to form positive relationships with the families. Children from diverse cultural backgrounds often may encounter conflicting expectations and values in the home and in the school. We can easily assume that the differences between school and family are due to family idiosyncrasies, when in fact they reflect the long history of that family in the cultural background of parents and grandparents. Teachers can help children by becoming aware of the wide range of norms represented in their classrooms and communities. When values fostered by the school, such as competitiveness and willingness to work at a desk with a minimum of talking, conflict with a cultural preference for cooperation and for lively discussion, tensions may arise between families and school expectations. Such tensions may increase with the additional concerns for a child with disabilities. Cultural awareness and understanding can help families and schools work together to address the child's needs.

In order to be more culturally aware, we often must become more self-aware (Turnbull & Turnbull, 2002). Teachers need to be aware of what factors shape their own cultural views and values. This builds an understanding that although personal cultural beliefs and traditions may work well for them, these may not necessarily work for others. The child's cultural context and the family's beliefs and values must be honored, and this starts with identifying the strengths of the culture and family. Whatever the immediate problems the family and the exceptional child may have, they also have many strengths. Their ability to make the child feel loved and accepted, a willingness to seek support from friends and counselors, a strong religious faith, and a caring extended family (Turnbull & Turnbull, 2002) are strengths that should be respected as a foundation for building a support system for the child.

It is important for teachers to identify the strengths of students and their families who are from diverse cultures.

The impact of environmental forces varies as the child grows: initially the family is predominant in caring for the child and acts as a link between the child and the larger environment (see Figure 1.7 on page 17: Context/Ecology of the Child). The support of the family continues to be important but is joined by other factors as the child enters school.

Lifespan Issues

As the child grows older, the peer group becomes a major force. Adolescence, with its focus on social development and career orientation, is a special challenge for the child with exceptionalities. Potential rejection or bullying by the peer group can have a powerful influence on the adaptation of the child with disabilities or the child with special talents (as it can on any vulnerable and self-conscious adolescent).

Finally, society, which includes the culture and community along with the work environment, influences the student who is trying to make the transition from school to a relatively independent lifestyle. Throughout their lives, many adults with exceptionalities will be in contact with a support system that includes advocates, educators, friends, and service providers. In addition, representatives of the larger society (such as government leaders) often make rules that determine whether the exceptional person receives needed resources or is given an opportunity to succeed at some level of independence. (We discuss these environments further in Chapter 2.) All these forces contribute to the full picture of the individual with exceptionalities.

Community Resources

The type and number of resources available within your own community to assist families who have a child with a disability are often quite extensive but are usually hidden from the casual observer. Suppose you have been approached by a neighbor whose 3-year-old has just been diagnosed with autism. She now asks you—as the person who knows about special education and related subjects—where she can go to get some help.

Track down and report on all of the currently available community agencies or individuals who might be able to provide some help for your neighbor and his family. Be sure and note the techniques (e.g., Internet) that you used in your search.

Moral Dilemmas in Special Education

The presence of exceptional children in our families and our communities can raise any number of moral and ethical questions. We present for your consideration one of these in each chapter.

moral dilemma

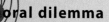

The Cost of Educating Children with Disabilities

The education of children with disabilities inevitably costs more than the education of children without disabilities. This is true because of the need for smaller teacher-student ratios in many cases, more support personnel, and technology to meet the needs of these students. This extra expenditure is a point of contention with some parents and citizens. Their views may be summed up one or more of these ways:

1. Why should the school be spending more tax dollars for these students when my own child has many unmet needs?

2. Why spend this extra money on students who will have to struggle to maintain themselves in society and may never be able to contribute to society?

3. Why not spend the money on the brightest students? They will be the leaders who will discover new cures for diseases or improve our economy. How would you respond to these questions from the perspective of (a) a school board member responsible for the education budget, (b) a tax-paying citizen, and (c) the parent of a child with disabilities?

To answer these questions online, visit the Education CourseMate website.

 Summary

▶ The major categories of exceptionality include children with intellectual differences, communication differences, learning disabilities, sensory differences, behavioral differences, multiple and severe disabilities, physical and health differences, ADHD, and autism.

▶ Exceptional children show both interindividual (among children) and intra-individual (within themselves) differences. Both kinds of differences require special adaptation by the teacher at school.

▶ Early identification of exceptionalities is critical for providing appropriate interventions.

▶ The special needs of children can be described through an information processing model involving input, central processing, output, executive functioning, and emotional context.

▶ There is a disproportionate number of culturally diverse children in special education requiring special program efforts.

▶ The RTI model provides three layers of intervention depending on the degree of severity of the needs.

▶ The adjustment of siblings of children with disabilities can be improved through programs of intervention.

▶ **Family empowerment** gives parents more influence on the special programs established for their children and requires rethinking of the traditional roles played by professionals and parents.

▶ Cultural attitudes, values, customs, and language are often embedded in families and must be taken into account when educators and other professionals work with exceptional children from a variety of cultural backgrounds.

▶ Families from diverse cultures may have differing values and child-rearing practices, which compound the issues of adaptation for children with special needs.

Future Challenges

Every generation leaves, as its legacy to the next generation, certain problems for which solutions have not been found. There are many issues in the field of special education that today's professionals have been unable to resolve. The end-of-chapter sections titled "Future Challenges" briefly describe widely debated topics as a beginning agenda for the current generation of students, who will face these issues in their professional or private lives.

1 Who is identified as exceptional?

The boundary line separating children with exceptionalities from nonexceptional children has become blurred where children with mild disabilities are concerned. Yet legislation and the courts call for eligibility standards to clearly separate children who should receive special education from those who should not. How do we distinguish, for example, between the child who is emotionally disturbed and the child who is experiencing a temporary behavior problem? The RTI model may help with students who are having difficulties but who do not require special educational placement or services, but how will we appropriately use these tiers of support?

2 *What is the impact of the family on children with special needs?*

For many years, special educators focused on the child with exceptionalities. Increasingly, we have become aware that the child is only one component in a complex family and ecological system. We understand that many elements within that system can have a positive or negative impact on the child. How can special education incorporate this understanding into our personnel preparation and educational programs to help us build constructive relationships with the family?

3 *How should a student's cultural and linguistic needs be honored in the educational approach to children with special needs?*

We have only begun to consider how a child's cultural background will influence an appropriate education. With the increase of multicultural and multilingual students within our schools, this is becoming even more important. With few bilingual and bicultural teachers available who also have training in special education, we face a continuing challenge to build cultural awareness. How can we recruit a more diverse workforce for special education?

Key Terms

children with exceptionalities p. 1

culture p. 20

ecological model p. 16

family-centered model p. 19

family empowerment p. 28

family-focused approach p. 19

gene-environment interaction p. 12

high-incidence disabilities p. 13

individualized education program (IEP) p. 7

information processing model (IPM) p. 10

interindividual differences p. 6

intraindividual differences p. 6

low-incidence disabilities p. 14

medical model p. 16

response to intervention (RTI) p. 8

Resources

References of Special Interest

Donovan, M., & Cross, C. (2002). *Minority students in special and gifted education.* Washington, D.C.: National Research Council. A report from a special panel brought together by the National Academy of Sciences to address the disproportionate numbers of minority students in special education programs for children with disabilities and also for children who are gifted. The panel explores whether such disproportions in fact exist and, if they do, why they exist and what can be done about this issue. The panel concludes that such disproportions do exist and proposes better integrated general education and special education programs, increased teacher training in sensitivity to cultural differences, high-quality early childhood intervention programs, and increased research.

Florian, L. (Ed.) (2007). *The SAGE handbook of special education.* London: Sage Publications. A comprehensive review of current special education progress through forty chapters with major sections on inclusion, knowledge production, teacher strategies, and approaches and future directions for research and practice. It includes a number of authors and references from the European field of special education.

Odom, S., Horner, R., Snell, M., & Blacher, J. (Eds.) (2007). *Handbook of developmental disabilities.* New York: Guilford Press. A collection of experts from multidisciplinary backgrounds have assembled a synthesis of current research on developmental disabilities as a prelude to more effective action. The topics range from infancy to adulthood and from education to genetics. This is a valuable sourcebook for those working in this field.

Salvia, J., Ysseldyke, J., & Bolt S. (2010). *Assessment in special and inclusive education* (11th ed.). Boston: Houghton Mifflin. One of the problems in identifying children with special needs is the lack of knowledge about acceptable measuring instruments. This volume provides a wide variety of informal and formal methods of assessment and several chapters discussing the broad topic of general assessment itself. The authors include developmental appraisals of infants, toddlers, and preschoolers. Also included is a chapter on outcomes-based accountability assessment, which is a topic of growing interest in education.

Shonkoff, J., & Phillips, D. (Eds.) (2000). *From neurons to neighborhoods.* Washington, D.C.: National Academy Press. An update from the National Academy of Sciences on the current state of the science of early childhood development by a distinguished multidisciplinary panel. The book includes the latest information on nature versus nurture, the developing brain, and the latest trend toward studying the ecology of the developing child. A series of recommendations for scientists and public policy makers is provided based on current knowledge.

Turnbull, A., & Turnbull, H. R. (2006). *Families, professionals and exceptionality: A special partnership* (4th ed.). Upper Saddle River, NJ: Pearson/Merrill-Prentice Hall. A comprehensive portrait of the relationship of families to professionals in the tasks of helping children with disabilities reach levels of self-determination. The authors argue that there should be a true partnership between parents and professionals in planning and executing special education plans for children with special developmental problems.

Journals

Exceptional Children Council for Exceptional Children (CEC)
www.cec.sped.org

Journal of Special Education
www.proedinc.com

Teaching Exceptional Children
www.cec.sped.org

Professional Organizations

Council for Exceptional Children (CEC)
www.cec.sped.org

 Visit the Education CourseMate website for additional TeachSource Video Cases, information about CEC standards, study tools, and much more.

Children with Exceptionalities and Social Institutions: Government, Schools, and the Courts

 Focus Questions

▶ How has society at large responded to children with exceptionalities over the years?

▶ What government legislation supports and protects students with disabilities?

▶ How have the courts influenced the development of educational services for children with disabilities?

▶ What are some ways in which schools can modify programs for children with special needs?

▶ How does the individualized education program (IEP) shape special education practice?

▶ How do inclusion policies impact children with disabilities and their classmates and classrooms?

▶ How does technology augment the educational programming for children with exceptionalities?

▶ What is universal design for learning (UDL), and how does it affect children with exceptionalities?

© Susie Fitzhugh

In Chapter 1, we discussed the nature of children with exceptionalities and their surrounding ecology of family, peers, and culture. In this chapter, we look at the responses of three major social institutions—government, courts, and schools—to the needs of children with exceptionalities. How a society feels about its diverse membership, particularly about citizens who are different, is expressed through such institutions. See Figure 2.1, which briefly explains the impact of each social institution on children with exceptionalities.

Each of the social institutions depicted in Figure 2.1 has its own rules and traditions that influence how decisions are made and how conclusions are reached. This chapter touches briefly on how each of them affects the child who is exceptional in our society. Take, for example, Sam.

Sam is a 5-year-old with Down syndrome, a genetic but not hereditary condition that will affect his entire life. He has developmental disabilities and other problems caused by this genetic accident. Yet how Sam will fare in life will depend to a large degree on the environmental circumstances around him—family, school, community, and other societal forces such as government and legislation.

Will Sam do better in a loving family? In a neighborhood with some comfort and resources? In a school program that recognizes his needs and adapts the program to meet his needs? Of course!

No matter what the degree of exceptionality, how the child will eventually adapt to life is determined in large measure by how the environmental forces outside the child facilitate or inhibit his or her development. That is why we spend so much time studying these outside forces, which we refer to as the **ecology of the child**, or the **context of the child**.

How the child with exceptionalities will adjust to adulthood is determined in large measure by his or her interactions with these social institutions and the way in which they are mediated by family and by the child's unique characteristics. It is difficult, if not impossible, to predict the outcome of special education services for a specific individual because of the range of each child's response and potential and the differing environments in which they may be placed.

We begin this chapter with an overview of society's attitudes toward the education of individuals with exceptionalities so that we can better understand how schools work to address their needs.

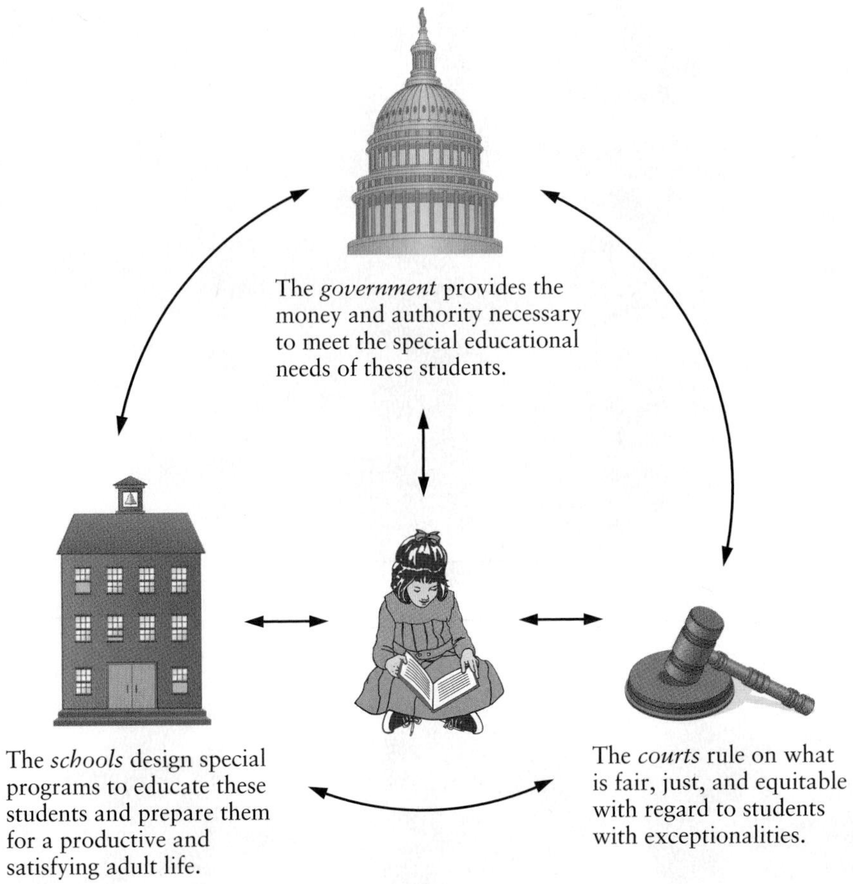

Council for Exceptional Children
www.cec.sped.org

The *government* provides the money and authority necessary to meet the special educational needs of these students.

The *schools* design special programs to educate these students and prepare them for a productive and satisfying adult life.

The *courts* rule on what is fair, just, and equitable with regard to students with exceptionalities.

FIGURE 2.1
The Exceptional Child and Social Institutions

Societal Responses to Children with Exceptionalities

During the past century, enormous changes have taken place in the way society treats children with exceptionalities, moving from rejection, to the charitable isolation of children with disabilities, to the acceptance of them as contributing members of society. The current level of acceptance has few precedents, representing a much more enlightened view than was evident even in the immediate past. The notion of educating *every* child to achieve his or her greatest potential is a relatively new idea.

After World War II, individual states became involved in a limited way in subsidizing programs in public schools for children with sensory disabilities (blindness, deafness) and physical impairments. Some states helped organize and support classes for children who had intellectual and developmental disabilities or behavioral problems. After World War II, many states expanded their involvement, providing financial support for special classes and services to local schools for children with all types of disability. This expansion caused two problems that many believed could only be solved by federal legislation.

First, these new and larger programs created a personnel scarcity in the late 1940s and early 1950s. Professional special educators were in short supply, and the field of special education was not firmly established. Second, because not all states expanded their involvement in special education, organized parents' groups began asking why children with disabilities and their parents should be penalized because they lived in a particular state or a particular region of a state. Were not U.S. citizens (in this case, the parents of children with disabilities) entitled to equal treatment anywhere in the United States? Should parents, in addition to the challenges of having children with special needs, be forced to move their families to a community in which special education resources were available because no local resources existed? The blatant unfairness of the situation called for attention at the federal level.

> The government, courts and schools are special institutions that have a major impact on the education of children with special needs.

The Role of Government

For more than 150 years, we have relied on our public school systems to educate about 89 percent of our school-age children (National Center for Educational Statistics, 2009). Public schools have been supported by the nation's taxpayers as a commitment to the future of our society ("Public Education in the United States," *Microsoft® Encarta® Online Encyclopedia, 2007*).

Major social institutions that have had a long-lasting effect on the education of children with exceptionalities have been the state and federal governments. The executive branches and the legislatures have the responsibility to create policies, draft laws, and find the necessary money for the special services and extra expenses involved in educating children with exceptionalities. Legislation as a vehicle for change (Gallagher, 2006) has a way of shortening discussions and disputes. If you, as an educator, do not perform as the legislation states, you are no longer just showing your disagreement, you are breaking the law!

Federal legislation clearly was needed, both to bring qualified people into special education and to equalize educational opportunities across the country. But that legislation was not easy to obtain. It violated the strong American tradition of education as a state and local responsibility. In spite of this, organized parents'

The Education for All Handicapped Children Act ensured a free and appropriate education for all children. President Gerald Ford, seen here greeting a child with disabilities, was instrumental in supporting this legislation.
(© From the United Cerebral Palsy Association Inc., Courtesy of the Museum of Disability)

groups, with the support of other interested citizens, convinced Congress that they needed help. This help was finally granted through a series of laws, summarized in the following pages.

A Summary of Special Education Legislation

Public Law 88–164

In 1963, Public Law (PL) **88–164** authorized funds for training professionals to work with children with special needs and for research and demonstration (the illustration of best practices) for students with intellectual and developmental disabilities and deafness. The law represented a strong initiative by President John F. Kennedy, whose interest was heightened by his sister's intellectual and developmental disabilities. These first efforts were followed by many others, and from that small beginning emerged thirty years of legislation to ensure that all children with disabilities have access to an appropriate education.

That flood of legislation served notice that the federal government accepted responsibility for providing support and resources for children with disabilities and for encouraging the states to carry out their basic responsibilities.

Public Law 94–142

In 1975, Congress passed **PL 94–142**, the Education for All Handicapped Children Act. The measure, which took effect in 1977, was designed "to assure that all handicapped children have available to them a free appropriate public education which emphasizes special education and related services designed to meet their unique needs" (U.S. House of Representatives, 1975, p. 35). See Table 2.1, "Six Key Provisions of the Education for All Handicapped Children Act" for the key provisions of this legislation.

To carry out the provisions of this law, the federal government authorized the spending of up to $3 billion by 1982, promising much larger sums of money to aid the states than had previously been provided. However, by 1990, the government was only spending about $1 billion a year. In return for this aid, states were required to show evidence that they were doing their best to help children with disabilities receive needed services. Specific provisions in the law placed substantial pressure on public school systems, demanding more in the way of **assessment**, parental contact, and student evaluation than most school systems had been accustomed to providing.

Not surprisingly, many educators protested the burden that these new laws placed on them. But this law has become part of the educational landscape. In the past three decades, the federal government moved from little involvement in special education to becoming a major partner in local and state programs for students who have disabilities, expanding the reach of PL 94–142 through additional legislation.

> These provisions form the heart of special education policy.

TABLE 2.1
Six Key Provisions of the Education for All Handicapped Children Act (1975)

Six key principles at the heart of PL 94–142 have shaped special as well as general education during the past three decades:

- **Zero reject.** All children with disabilities must be provided a free and appropriate public education.

- **Nondiscriminatory evaluation.** Each student must receive a full individual examination before being placed in a special education program, with tests appropriate to the child's cultural and linguistic background.

- **Individualized education program.** An individualized education program (IEP) must be written for every student with a disability who is receiving special education. The IEP must describe the child's current performance and goals for the school year, the particular special education services to be delivered, and the procedures by which outcomes are evaluated.

- **Least restrictive environment.** As much as possible, children who have disabilities must be educated with children who are not handicapped.

- **Due process.** Due process is a set of legal procedures to ensure the fairness of educational decisions and the accountability of both professionals and parents in making those decisions.

- **Parental participation.** Parents are to be included in the development of the IEP, and they have the right to access their child's educational records.

Public Law 99–457

The Education for All Handicapped Children Act (PL 94–142) was, in fact, misnamed. It was not meant for all children of *all ages*. It became increasingly evident that early intervention was important, both for the children with exceptionalities and for their families, and pressure increased for the law to include younger children.

PL 99–457 (Education of the Handicapped Act Amendments of 1986) provided that opportunity by allocating federal funds for the states to develop plans and programs for children and their families *from birth on*. The title of the Education of the Handicapped Act was changed to the **Individuals with Disabilities Education Act,** or **IDEA.** The impact of IDEA is discussed throughout the text.

Individuals with Disabilities Education Act 2004 (IDEA)

IDEA 2004 is the reauthorization of the original legislation (Education for All Handicapped Children Act PL 94–142) designed to strengthen and improve earlier versions. Some of the major changes in IDEA 2004 involve the following:

- *Quality of personnel.* Special education specialists must hold full state certification as special education

Federal legislation insures that young children with special needs receive the intervention they need.
(Courtesy of Cengage Learning)

teachers and have a license to teach. They must demonstrate subject-matter competence in the academic programs they teach.

- *IEP standards (section 1400).* IEPs (see more discussion later in the chapter) must reflect scientifically based instructional practices, cognitive behavioral interventions, and early intervention services, as appropriate. They must include plans for the use of **assistive technology** and short-term objectives for children with disabilities who take alternative assessments.

- *Transition services.* A transition plan must be included in all IEPs for students at age 16 and for younger students if appropriate. **Transition services** must include instruction, community experiences, development of employment, and other postschool adult-living objectives.

Two other important pieces of legislation play a role in the life of children with disabilities.

Section 504 of the Rehabilitation Act of 1973 (PL 93–112)

This legislation has been brought into play when the rights of individuals with disabilities have been denied or interfered with. The key provision of the act says that it is illegal to deny participation in activities or programs solely because of a disability. Individuals with disabilities must have equal access to programs and services. One of its advantages is that children who might not meet the stringent criteria for IDEA may still be judged eligible for services under Section 504.

RTI

Problems such as failing grades, a pattern of suspensions, and chronic behavior problems may qualify a child for additional support under Section 504. This law can act as a bridge between general and special education and may be a first step to the response to intervention (RTI) model, mentioned in Chapter 1, so that the three-tier RTI model of support can be brought into play for children who don't quite meet the qualifications for special education.

Americans with Disabilities Act of 1992

The Americans with Disabilities Act of 1992 (PL 101–336) extends civil rights to persons with disabilities. These rights are guaranteed without regard to race, color, national origin, gender, or religion through the Civil Rights Act of 1964.

These three pieces of legislation—IDEA 2004, Section 504 of the Rehabilitation Act, and the Americans with Disabilities Act—make clear that American society is determined to see that children with disabilities have equal access to educational resources and cannot be discriminated against solely on the basis of their disabilities.

Public Law 107–110: No Child Left Behind Act of 2001

> One limitation of NCLB is that it places all the responsibility on the child and her school, and none on the society in which they are embedded.

Sometimes a piece of legislation is so important that it affects children with disabilities even if they were not the target of the legislation. The No Child Left Behind (NCLB) Act of 2001 has had an impact on all schoolchildren and a special impact on children with disabilities. It was the major education legislation in the George W. Bush administration, and its purpose was to hold schools and educators responsible for bringing students to a minimum level of competency.

The NCLB Act requires schools to present test data to prove their effectiveness. This causes problems for some children with disabilities, who have a difficult time gaining a year academically for every year spent in school, and for their teachers, who must deal with such unrealistic expectations.

Imagine a rule that says that every child at a school should be able to run the 100-yard dash in 14 seconds or less. If the school is unable to meet the standards, and if more children every year do not meet the standards, the school will be disciplined and have its funds removed. We know that there are children who, for a variety of reasons, will never be able to run the 100-yard dash in 14 seconds, no matter what the physical education department does. What will happen when the school doesn't meet the standards and its funds are removed?

You may well imagine what happened with NCLB when the standard of 100 percent proficiency on the part of students and schools was proposed. Some students with disabilities could not meet the standards no matter how hard they tried. A number of attempts have been made to provide alternative assessments for children with disabilities (about 2 percent of children enrolled) so that students with disabilities can participate in the overall assessment in meaningful and appropriate ways.

NCLB created a different problem for students with special gifts and talents in that the tests create no challenge, and the standards can usually be reached with little or no effort (see Chapter 9). In addition, because the classroom teachers must focus more time on helping other students reach basic standards, they often do not have time to stimulate students with special gifts and talents through unique projects or assignments.

TeachSource VIDEO CONNECTION

Aligning Instruction with Federal Legislation

Visit the Education CourseMate website to access this Video Case. A principal, teachers, and a student intern discuss modifying instruction to take federal legislation into account. Questions about the impacts of IDEA and No Child Left Behind are raised by the new intern, and other general education teachers and special education teachers chime in with their viewpoints. After listening to this discussion, reflect on how federal legislation impacts education practice. What are the pros and cons of federal educational legislation like IDEA?

American Recovery and Reinvestment Act

One of the clear results of the 2009 recession was the passage of the American Recovery and Reinvestment Act in that same year, whose goal was to stimulate economic activity in a number of areas, including financial and social institutions, and education, to ensure the long-time economic health of our nation. This resulted in large funds provided to the states under IDEA on a one-time basis to improve the delivery of quality of early intervention services. Infants and toddlers with disabilities from birth to age 2 received $500 million in federal funds, and children ages 3 to 5 were provided $400 million in federal funds.

Because these were one-time funds, they were directed to activities such as Child Find—a data system to track children, improve delivery of services, and establish accountability standards for young children with disabilities. As of the publication of this book, states have not yet acted on these opportunities, but it is important to note that children with disabilities were included in the omnibus effort of the federal government to strengthen the health and economy of our nation. Find out what your state has done with these funds and whether or not you disagree with the decisions that have been made.

Federal Actions for Students Who Are Gifted

Except for a brief period in the 1970s, there has been little movement at the federal legislative level to provide resources for the education of children who are gifted.

Programs for gifted are long-term issues, not short-time crises, which results in little support from legislators.

President Barack Obama signed the America Recovery and
Reinvestment Act which provided millions of dollars in funding
for early intervention services
(AFP PHOTO / Saul LOEB / Newscom)

The Javits Act (PL 100–297)—named
after New York senator Jacob Javits, who
showed early interest and support—
provided a small sum of money to
support research and demonstration programs that focused on the special needs
of gifted students from economically disadvantaged circumstances, from culturally or linguistically diverse families, or
with disabilities (twice-exceptional). The
Javits programs have helped with the
development of alternative identification
methods designed to measure intellectual ability in special populations more
adequately (see Chapter 9 for a discussion of this movement).

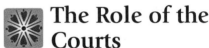

The Role of the Courts

Another of society's social institutions,
the court system, has played a significant role in the lives of children with
exceptionalities and their families. It is the duty of the courts to rule on the
interpretation of the laws and regulations generated by the executive and
legislative branches. If the law says that every child is entitled to a "free and
appropriate public education," how does that translate at the community
level? Does that mean that a school cannot expel a child with disabilities?
Many important court decisions have formed the foundation for special
education.

> Courts have affirmed the right of children with special needs to a free and appropriate public education (FAPE).

The basic issue here is that children with special needs deserve a **free and
appropriate public education** (FAPE), just as do all children in the United States.
If that right is being abridged, or if other inequities are being created, citizens can
appeal to the courts for justice and equity. During the past four decades, a series
of legal cases solidified the rights of children with exceptionalities and their guaranteed right to FAPE.

A landmark case (1972) that began a series of court decisions in favor of
children with exceptionalities and their right to FAPE was the Pennsylvania
Association for Retarded Children (PARC) v. Commonwealth of Pennsylvania
lawsuit and decision. In this case, the court decided that children with intellectual and developmental disabilities could not be excluded from school and did
have a right to FAPE and that when the state constitution said "*all* children are
entitled to a free public education," the term *all* did, in fact, refer to *all* children,
including children with disabilities.

This movement toward judicial action was, in part, a recognition of the
success of the Civil Rights movement in using the courts to establish their
educational rights. In 1954, with the classic school desegregation case Brown
v. Board of Education, the courts began to reaffirm the rights of minority citizens in a wide variety of settings. If court decisions could protect the rights
of one group of citizens, they could do the same for another group: those
with disabilities. Soon, supporters of people with disabilities were working

> ### TABLE 2.2
> ### Court Cases Affirming the Rights of Children with Disabilities
>
> - A child with disabilities cannot be excluded from school without careful due process, and it is the responsibility of the schools to provide appropriate programs for children who are different (Pennsylvania Association for Retarded Children v. Commonwealth of Pennsylvania, 1972; Goss v. Lopez, 1974; Hairston v. Drosick, 1974).
>
> - The presumed absence of funds is not an excuse for failing to provide educational services to children with exceptionalities. If sufficient funds are not available, then all programs should be cut back (Mills v. Board of Education, 1972).
>
> - Children with disabilities who are committed to state institutions must be provided a meaningful education in that setting or their incarceration is considered unlawful detention (Wyatt v. Stickney, 1972).
>
> - Children should not be labeled "handicapped" or placed into special education without adequate diagnosis that takes into account different cultural and linguistic backgrounds (Larry P. v. Riles, 1979).
>
> - Bilingual children with exceptionalities need identification, evaluation, and educational procedures that reflect and respect their dual-language backgrounds (Jose P. v. Ambach, 1979).
>
> - An individual with learning disabilities has a right to services whatever his or her age (Frederick L. v. Thomas, 1980).
>
> - A child with disabilities is entitled to an appropriate, not an optimum, education (Board of Education v. Rowley, 1982). The Rowley decision was the first court decision that suggested that there was a limit to the resources that children with exceptionalities could expect.
>
> - A subsequent case to the Rowley decision made it clear that such services, though not optimal, must be more than *de minimus*—that is, must provide sufficient support so the child with disabilities can benefit educationally (Polk v. Central Susquehanna Intermediate Unit 16, 1988).

to translate abstract legal rights into tangible social action through the judicial system.

Class action suits have been influential in changing the status of children with disabilities in the United States. A *class action suit* provides that legal action taken as part of the suit applies not only to the individual who brings the particular case to court but also to all members of the class to which that individual belongs. That means the rights of all people with disabilities can be reaffirmed by a single case involving just one child. The rulings in several court cases have reaffirmed the rights of individuals with disabilities and have defined the limits of those rights (see Table 2.2).

Inclusion and Funding Issues

After establishing the basic rights of children with disabilities to a free and appropriate public education, the courts then turned to the issues of *inclusion* (bring children with exceptionalities into regular classrooms) and *least restrictive environment* and to what an appropriate program for children with exceptionalities should be. The results are a mixture of rulings, some supporting a strong version of inclusion and some supporting a continuum of services (McCarthy, 1994):

- A child with a hearing disability was allowed to attend a school several miles from home instead of a neighborhood school because the centralized program at the special school better met the child's needs (Barnett v. Fairfax County Board of Education, 1991).

- A child with Down syndrome was placed in a general education program rather than in a special education class because of the presumed priority of inclusion in IDEA (Greer v. Rome City School District, 1991).

- A court ruled that it is the responsibility of the school district to demonstrate that the child's disabilities are so severe that he or she will receive little benefit from inclusion or will be so disruptive as to keep other classmates from learning (Oberti v. Board of Education of the Borough of Clementon School District, 1993).

Clearly, these rulings reflect the specifics of each individual case and the interpretation of local or district courts. It may take a Supreme Court decision to provide more general guidance on the issue of what appropriate means for education of children with exceptionalities. Nevertheless, when the courts speak, people listen, because court decisions represent the law as we currently know it and must be obeyed.

The late 1990s saw an increased number of court cases concerning the provision of services for children with autism, with parents battling the schools for additional services for their children (Lord, 2001). The results of these court cases depended on local circumstances, with both sides (parent or school) prevailing depending on the facts of the case.

Appropriate Special Education Services

In the last few years, the questions raised in court cases have focused on whether the services recommended by the student's IEP committees were adequate or appropriate, or implemented appropriately. There were a few cases of *predetermination* (the school system had already made up its mind as to what it was going to do before meeting with the parents—a violation of proper procedure). They include the following:

- In a court case in Maine, a child with Asperger's syndrome (a form of autism discussed in Chapter 5) was denied special education services because she was performing well academically. She had attempted suicide and was determined by a psychiatrist to be depressed. The court determined that she should have special education. (L.I. v. Maine School Administrative District, No. 55, 480 F 3rd [1st Cir. 2007]).

- A child with autism was awarded reimbursement for private school costs because the judge found that the public school system knowingly and repeatedly failed to provide an appropriate educational program (Henrico County School Board v. R.T. 20 U.S.C. 1400 [c] [4]).

- A child who never received services from a public school was nevertheless awarded reimbursement for private school services on the grounds that the school district failed to provide a free and appropriate public education plan (Forest Grove School District v. T.A. 129 St. Ct. 2484 [2009]).

Just as laws have to be enforced and money has to be appropriated, so court decisions have to be executed. The court decisions noted in the previous list created the expectation that something would be done, but they did not guarantee it. Closing down state institutions, reorganizing public schools, and providing special services to all children with disabilities were substantial and costly changes. They raised a serious problem for program administrators: Where would the money come from for implementation? Ultimately, school and local leaders turned to Washington, pressuring Congress to appropriate funds to help pay for the changes that the courts were demanding. Even with federal assistance, implementation has come slowly.

The Children with Exceptionalities and the School

Most of us consider ourselves experts on the schools. After all, haven't we spent twelve or more years of our lives in them? Unfortunately, as students, our contact with the schools, in most instances, was limited to specific teachers and classrooms. Sometimes there was a principal to administer "corrective action" if our behavior got out of hand. We were only dimly aware of policies or standards that were influencing the teacher and her or his behavior.

Certainly the schools are one of the most significant of all our social institutions. Schools in large measure are a mirror of our society as a whole. Most of the values taught there reflect the values of the dominant sectors of society. Many of the problems encountered in the schools, such as lack of motivation, drug use, and violence, are part of the larger societal fabric.

In the last part of the twentieth century, there was constant discussion within the education field as to *where* the children with exceptionalities should be placed and what relationship should exist between general education and special education. The struggle for special services and special programming for children with exceptionalities consumed much of the attention of special educators during that time.

The changing social environment of children with exceptionalities has spawned a new and different vocabulary. Two terms that are in common use today are *inclusion* and *continuum of services*. These terms reflect the interest of society in trying to integrate children and adults with exceptionalities more effectively into the school and community at large.

- **Inclusion** is the process of bringing all, or nearly all, children with exceptionalities into the general classroom for their education, with special educational support.

- **Continuum of services** refers to the range of placements that may constitute the "least restrictive environment" in which the child with exceptionalities learns best.

Our discussion of schools as institutions focuses on the policies that influenced teachers, in particular, of children with disabilities and children who are gifted. Four major tasks face the schools:

1. Finding the child with special needs

2. Identifying and specifying these needs in individual cases

3. Organizing special planning to meet these needs

4. Proving that the special planning works

In most instances, the policies and standards that are followed to accomplish those four goals are made collaboratively, with many persons involved, including the classroom teacher and the child's parents. Sometimes these rules are made in the state capitals or the executive branch of the federal government.

Also, children with exceptionalities are affected by major trends in the general field of education, as are all other students. The trend toward *accountability*, a term used to determine whether educators have done what they said they would do for their students, has forced special education to demonstrate not only that children with exceptionalities are receiving special services, but also whether the students have profited from a special program as expected.

The emphasis on accountability has raised the question regarding which of two seemingly contradictory purposes should be emphasized. The IDEA of 2004 proposed the need for specially designed instruction (meaning shaping or creating lessons to meet the special needs of the individual who has those needs), which is to be spelled out in the IEP. However, IDEA *also* wishes to ensure the children with exceptionalities have access to the general curriculum. This would mean that the exceptional child will be included in regular class activities to the extent that he or she can master the basic facts and knowledge that all students are expected to master. The fact that the vast majority of children with exceptionalities are to be included in statewide testing programs (only a small percentage are allowed to take alternative assessments) indicates that the schools are expected to attain *both* of these desirable goals—individual plans and access to general curriculum—and that it is the responsibility of the schools to achieve these results in individual circumstances.

Finding the Child with Special Needs

A child may be referred for special education services for any of a variety of reasons; most often referrals are made on the basis of observations by school staff that this child differs from his peers in a significant way that is affecting his or her learning in school.

Sometimes the school will administer screening tests in reading or arithmetic in the early grades in an effort to discover children who need special help before they have identified themselves to their teachers through either failure or extraordinary success in school. For example, Paul, age 8, has been referred for special education services because his third-grade teacher, Mrs. Parker, claims he is insolent, talks back to her, is not mastering his reading and math skills, and is constantly disturbing the other children. Maybe Paul acts this way because he has a serious learning disability or behavioral disorder; but maybe he and the teacher have just started off on the wrong foot. He may be reacting in a predictable way to his inability to do the schoolwork (which may seem uninteresting to him anyway), and Mrs. Parker may not know how to cope with Paul's frustrations.

In such a situation, many school systems establish a *prereferral committee*, or a child-study committee, to find ways of coping with a child's behavior short of a referral for special education services (Buck, Polloway, Smith-Thomas, & Cook, 2003). In this case, the assistant principal, a master teacher, and a psychologist meet with Mrs. Parker to see what she might be able to do to help Paul adjust. Not every child having trouble adjusting to school is a candidate for special education. In Paul's case, several weeks go by with no appreciable improvement in his behavior despite the modifications his teacher has made, so a formal referral is made, calling for a comprehensive assessment of Paul and consideration for special education. Even if Paul is not eligible for special education services, he may still need educational help—perhaps in Tier II of the RTI model.

Assessment

One of the major tasks of special education is to assess both individual students and the effectiveness of the special programs. Student assessment is designed to capture the strengths and weaknesses of individual students and to determine whether the student is eligible for special education services or support through the RTI model approach (see Figure 2.2). This is another reason why we need a team of specialists to make proper assessments.

Assessment is a major part of the RTI model presented here. In Tier I there is universal screening of children in the early grades to find those students who may need special help. There is then a diagnostic assessment of those students who have been identified by the screening to enable the schools to plan an appropriate program for those students. In addition, there is periodic monitoring of students in Tier II and Tier III to measure progress and to determine if the students are receiving appropriate support. Finally, there is the use of assessment to determine if expected gains are achieved by groups of children as well as the individual children with special programs.

The task of determining how an individual child is different, and along a variety of dimensions, has become a major step in identifying and educating children with exceptionalities. Teachers and other team members can use five general approaches to provide an assessment of a child: norm-referenced tests, diagnostic achievement tests, interviews, observations, and informal assessments. Table 2.3 summarizes these approaches. Generally, a combination of assessments and procedures is used to detect and thoroughly evaluate a child's interindividual and intraindividual differences. Each method has advantages and disadvantages.

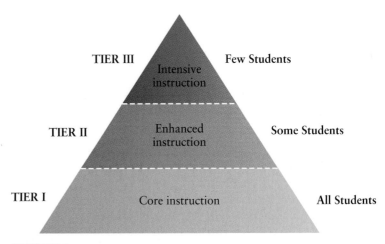

FIGURE 2.2
Response to Intervention (RTI) Model
Source: Salvia, J., Ysseldyke, J. & Bolt, S. (2007). *Assessment: In special and inclusive education.*

Interindividual Differences

As we learned in Chapter 1, **interindividual differences** are substantial differences among children of a similar life age along key dimensions of development. Special educators and school psychologists assess interindividual differences along key dimensions such as academic aptitude, academic performance, language development, psychomotor skills, and psychosocial development. These key areas provide critical information on the child's strengths and needs and can help us plan for the child.

Academic Aptitude

One area in which interindividual differences appear is **academic aptitude.** The measure of children's aptitudes can tell teachers and schools a great deal about their student population and how students are performing in relationship to their potential.

For decades, one standard measure of academic aptitude has been intelligence tests. IQ tests measure the development of memory, association, reasoning, evaluation, and classification, which are the mental operations so

Intelligence tests are not pure measures of intellectual potential; rather they are valuable predictors of academic ability and performance.

Inclusion for Caryn

Caryn is a 13-year-old girl who has been diagnosed with mild autism. She attends seventh grade in a midwestern suburban public school. Caryn's parents can be considered middle to upper middle class, and both have university degrees. Both she and her only sibling, a younger brother, have been identified as having autism. Both have received special education services throughout their public school education. Caryn is fully included in the classroom and receives speech and language services as well as the services of a special education teacher. Her brother has more intensive needs and requires greater accommodations and services.

Unlike many children with autism, Caryn does not demonstrate intellectual or developmental disabilities. Testing has revealed that Caryn's intellectual ability and academic achievement are in the average range. She can be described as a solitary child who enjoys horseback riding. Caryn has often told her parents, "I'm a loner. I like to be with animals more than people." While an interest in horses can be typical for a child of her age, her range of interests is restricted, and she will "get stuck" on the topic of horses and their care.

The social requirements of family get-togethers are also difficult for her. She will greet everyone only if promised she can go to her room afterward. Caryn does not seek social interactions and will often avoid situations in which she must interact with others. Until the second grade, Caryn never entered the classroom nor went to her seat directly. In an effort to avoid peer interactions, she would circle the room along the wall until she reached her seat. Up until age 10 or so, she observed others and played in parallel. It has only been within the last two years that she has started to initiate social interaction with her peers.

Used with permission of Council For Exceptional Children, from "Strategies for increasing positive social interactions in children with autism: a case study," by Welton et al, from Teaching Exceptional Children, 37(1) 40-41, copyright (c) 2004 by Council For Exceptional Children (VA); permission conveyed through Copyright Clearance Center, Inc.

Pivotal Issues

- How might Caryn's social interactions be enhanced in the classroom?

- What special services does Carol need?

important to school performance. In fact, intelligence tests are accurate predictors of academic performance: Those who score high on intelligence tests generally do well in school; those who score low generally do poorly (Salvia & Ysseldyke, & Bolt, 2007).

Any serious developmental delay in the student's mental operations can create major difficulties in school. However, intelligence tests assume a common experience base for most children (and the desire of the child to do well). We must be cautious in our interpretation of test results for individuals whose language or experience or both differ from those of the normative and majority culture.

In addition, some students have special talents in art, while others seem to actually enjoy mathematics. One example of this diversity in aptitude is Howard Gardner's theory of **multiple intelligences**, in which he proposed in 1983 and extended later that there is more than a "general intelligence" that needs to be measured and taken into account in curriculum (Gardner, 2000, 2006). He has identified the various intelligences shown in Table 2.4.

While people disagree as to the separate existence of these nine intelligences and debate whether they all represent aspects of a more general intelligence, Gardner's ideas have impacted education because he has linked his ideas to curriculum planning, as well as shown the consequences of these separate intelligences and designed ways to pay particular attention to children who lack or have an abundance of some of them.

TABLE 2.3
Assessment Strategies: Strengths and Weaknesses

Strategy	Advantages	Disadvantages
Norm-referenced test	It provides a comparison of a particular child's performance against the performance of a reference group of children.	It does not provide reasons for the results; for culturally diverse children, the reference groups used for comparison may be inappropriate.
Diagnostic achievement test	It is designed to provide a profile of strengths and weaknesses, analyses of errors, etc., in arithmetic or reading.	The scores generated by these instruments often have limited or suspect reliability.
Interview	Information from the child, parent, teacher, or others can provide insight into the reasons for the child's current performance.	All interviewees see the child through personal perspectives that may be limited by experience, personal bias, etc.
Observation	It can provide information based on the child's spontaneous behavior in natural settings and a basis for intervention planning.	The child may not reveal significant behaviors during the observation; the meaning of the child's behavior may be unclear.
Informal assessment	It uses information from teacher-made tests, particular language samples, or descriptions of significant events in the life of the child.	It is rarely possible to match a particular child's performance with the performance of others on these measures or observations.
Portfolio assessment	The student collects items of quality from his or her work. This allows a more direct assessment of student performance.	A problem of rater bias is possible: Did the student create the work included? Also, portfolio assessment is labor-intensive.

TABLE 2.4
Gardner's Theory of Multiple Intelligences

Linguistic: Ability to understand and use spoken and written communication. Ideal vocation: poet.

Logical-mathematical: Ability to understand and use logic and numerical symbols and operations. Ideal vocation: computer programmer.

Musical: Ability to understand and use such concepts as rhythm, pitch, melody, and harmony. Ideal vocation: composer.

Spatial: Ability to orient and manipulate three-dimensional space. Ideal vocation: architect.

Bodily-kinesthetic: Ability to coordinate physical movement. Ideal vocation: athlete.

Naturalistic: Ability to distinguish and categorize objects or phenomena in nature. Ideal vocation: zoologist.

Interpersonal: Ability to understand and interact well with other people. Ideal vocation: politician; salesperson.

Intrapersonal: Ability to understand and use one's thoughts, feelings, preferences, and interests. Ideal vocation: autobiographer; entrepreneur. (Although high intrapersonal intelligence should help in almost any job because of its role in self-regulation, few paid positions reward a person solely for knowing himself or herself well.)

Existential: Ability to contemplate phenomena or questions beyond sensory data, such as the infinite and infinitesimal. Ideal vocation: cosmologist; philosopher.

Source: Moran, S., Kornhaber, M., & Gardner, H. (2006). Orchestrating multiple intelligences. Educational Leadership, 64(1), 22–27. Copyright (c) 2006 by the Association for Supervision & Curriculum Development. Reprinted by permission. The Association for Supervision and Curriculum Development is a worldwide community of educators advocating sound policies and sharing best practices to achieve the success of each learner. To learn more, visit ASCD at www.ascd.com.

Academic Performance

Two well-accepted approaches to describing interindividual differences in academic performance are **standard (norm-referenced) achievement tests** and **diagnostic achievement tests** (see Table 2.3).

As currently constructed, standard achievement tests do not adequately measure the attainments of many children with exceptionalities. The child with intellectual and developmental disabilities (IDD) may be learning many practical sets of skills and knowledge that are not covered by the standard curriculum and standard tests, and the abilities and attainments of the child with special gifts and talents will surely be underestimated because of the lack of depth and conceptual complexity of most of these measures.

The norm-referenced tests compare the student's knowledge of a content field with others of similar age and grade. The diagnostic tests are designed to reveal the process by which a student attacks a subject such as reading or arithmetic and whether the student reveals a poorly developed or incorrect approach.

Cultural and Language Diversity and Assessment

As the student population becomes more diverse, the schools have a special responsibility to appropriately assess students who come from culturally or linguistically diverse families. Special attention should be paid to the possible test biases caused by the assumption that the student has had a set of standard experiences in the mainstream culture (Klingner, Blanchett, & Harry, 2007).

As the number of children from Latino families rapidly increases, so does concern about the appropriate referral of these students to special education services. As pointed out by Klingner and Harry (2006), the RTI three-tier model may have the potential for more appropriate placement and planning.

Assessment and Culture

Each of the succeeding chapters contains a discussion of how a child who has disabilities *and* who comes from another culture can be properly assessed. It is easy to understand that a child who does not have English as a first language can be poorly assessed with an achievement test written in English. What are we testing in such a situation—the child's vocabulary or his or her cultural experience (Salvia & Ysseldyke, & Bolt, 2007)?

A number of attempts have been made to promote a nonbiased assessment for children from different cultures, including the use of interpreters, "culture fair" tests, separate norms, and so on—all of which have their drawbacks. Trends have been toward replacing standardized tests with alternative assessments, informal procedures, or the use of a mix of formal and informal measures to try to capture the child's range of abilities. The real problem may lie not in the tests themselves but in their interpretations (McLaughlin & Lewis, 2001; Salvia & Ysseldyke, & Bolt, 2007).

Consider Jorge, a 10-year-old Hispanic child with learning disabilities that prevent him from grasping the reading process. Jorge comes from a rich tradition of a close-knit family with common interests and loyalty. The family is wary about the Anglo school Jorge is attending. When teachers and psychologists who are of a culture different from that of the family tell the family that something is wrong with Jorge's approach to school, are they reflecting a prejudice against Jorge because of his Hispanic background and his bilingual family? Are they going to help Jorge, or is this a way to prevent Jorge from getting a proper education? Will Jorge's father, misunderstanding the school's message, put even *more* pressure on Jorge to do well in school, assuming that his son is not giving proper effort to his school lessons? The opportunities for misunderstanding from one culture to another are great and can substantially complicate the original learning problems faced by the exceptional child.

 # Organizing Special Planning to Meet Needs

The Information Processing Model in Identifying Needs

The information processing model introduced in Chapter 1 can be used to identify special areas needing educational attention, such as children with visual problems or children with learning disabilities. It also could be used to highlight the issues for individual children like Dianne.

Dianne is a second grader who has performed poorly in the first grade for no obvious reason. As a candidate for special education, Dianne was given a variety of tests and observed in the classroom. Her first grade teacher was also interviewed. The intent was to rule out possible causes for her poor academic performance.

As Figure 2.3 indicates, Dianne's vision and hearing test results were normal. She was not judged as having emotional difficulties—although her frustration was growing about her inability to do her work. Her general academic aptitude fell into the normal range, so the planning team was left wondering why Dianne couldn't read. The central problem (revealed by diagnostic tests and observation) is her inability to translate visual symbols from print to understanding, which would indicate a learning disability. Dianne's learning disability requires special attention and tutoring to help her translate these important visual symbols into meaning.

As Figure 2.3 illustrates, Diane's central problem of processing information can lead to secondary problems. If she is having trouble reading, this will obviously impact her writing and perhaps her peer relations (social interactions) and may even cause her to feel depressed and unhappy (emotional context). So one problem in the information processing model (IPM) can easily lead to others unless they are contained or remediated.

In Diane's case, but not necessarily with other children with the same exceptionality, she may lose her ability to make good decisions in school executive function. This is why school systems need support services to back up the general education teacher.

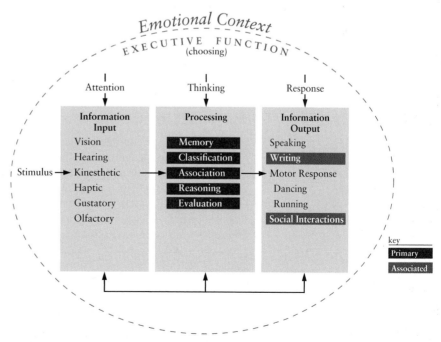

FIGURE 2.3
Dianne's Information Processing Model

Instruction can be adapted to the differences found in exceptional children in several ways—by varying the learning environment, the content of lessons, and the skills being taught, and by introducing technology that can meet special needs.

(© Bob Daemmrich/ The Image Works)

Most of the attention of special educators in the latter part of the twentieth century was devoted to bringing a specially prepared teacher into direct contact with the child with special needs so that the child could receive an appropriate educational experience. In the past decades, we have increasingly recognized that quality education requires more than just well-prepared teachers. A series of support services are needed to help these students with special needs (Gallagher, 2006; Mainzer, Deshler, Coleman, Kozleski, & Rodriguez-Walling, 2003).

Support Services

In many ways these support services resemble the well-organized system supporting the medical practitioner. Think about how limited your own physician would be without laboratories and x-ray technicians to help with diagnosis, active pharmaceutical enterprises producing new effective drugs, hospitals where special treatments can be applied, or medical schools that do important research on new techniques and produce new generations of qualified physicians. So when some say, "I have a really good doctor," they actually mean "I have a good health-care system."

If we do not provide that hard-working general education or special education teacher with a similar collection of support services, then we are placing our teacher in the same situation the physician would be in if deprived of his or her supports. One version of a quality support system consists of the components listed in Table 2.5.

The Need for Collaboration

It has long been recognized that the nature of children with exceptionalities requires the knowledge and skills of a large number of disciplines to devise a comprehensive plan for a particular child. In medicine alone, pediatricians, geneticists, orthopedists, neurologists, and many other specialists may be helpful in individual cases. Then there are educators, psychologists, sociologists, social workers, special educators, speech/language therapists, occupational therapists, and others who may have needed knowledge and skills to add to a plan. Think of Larry, who has a mild physical impairment with suspected brain injury, a hearing loss, and a communication problem, and who is not learning at his age level. How will we meet his needs except in some form of collaborative services?

It has always been difficult to bring all of these various specialists together to chart out a plan, such as an IEP, because they work in different areas and institutions—hospitals, schools, universities, and so forth. But the need for collaborative services is made clear throughout this text, and many persons

TABLE 2.5 Special Education Support Systems	
Personnel preparation	The importance of programs designed to prepare specialists cannot be overestimated, and many institutions of higher education have cooperated in providing such programming.
Technical assistance	Continued support for the classroom teacher has been achieved through such organizations as regional resource centers and the National Early Childhood Technical Assistance Center (NECTAC).
Research and program evaluation	There is a continual need to develop better techniques for diagnosing children with special needs and evaluate programs of effectiveness.
Communication	With the growing use of the Internet, websites can help disseminate information. Selected Internet websites have been placed in the margins throughout this book.
Demonstration	Sometimes it is important for teachers and administrators to actually see new ideas and practices in action. There is a series of demonstration centers for children with disabilities that offer programs illustrating techniques for teachers and administrators.
Data systems	An often-overlooked aid is a system of data collection that provides information about the availability of specialists, the number and types of students needing special assistance, and program effectiveness.
Comprehensive planning	The need for long-range state planning has been well accepted. The issue is how to coordinate the various support elements so that educational resources are available in the right place and at the right time.

Source: Adapted from Gallagher, J., & Clifford, R. (2000). The missing support infrastructure in early childhood. *Early Childhood Research and Practices, 2*(1), 1–24.

are seeking strategies to bring teams together to make use of the totality of special skills that no one person could possibly master. A similar challenge exists with the individual family service plan (IFSP) designed for preschool-age children with disabilities. The family plays an even stronger role in IFSPs (Dunst, 2007).

With a growing number of students with exceptionalities being included in general education classrooms, the roles and responsibilities of teachers have changed. General education teachers find themselves faced with students with exceptionalities who have a range of needs and who require program modifications. Special education teachers are now expected to collaborate with general education teachers in planning and implementing lessons for students with exceptionalities in the general education classroom.

Introducing the Team Approach

Similar to the multidisciplinary approach described in the previous section, we endorse the view that education of children with exceptionalities is a *team game*. Professional collaboration becomes critical as the vehicle for bringing quality educational services to children with special needs. While we can have some feelings of nostalgia for a picture of thirty students and a fourth grade teacher, no one should really expect one general education teacher to cope with the needs of thirty children, three of whom will likely need special education services, and five or six more who will need adaptations to support them in the regular education curriculum and some who may be advanced several years in some academic areas.

What we really need to ask is whether the education professionals and paraprofessionals (trained aides who assist teachers) have been prepared to play the roles necessary for good teamwork. Most of the general education teachers at work now have been prepared to act independently, with little team experience. Even with the development of the IEP, the emphasis is often on limited professional interaction.

We don't expect college professors to teach one course in English, another in nuclear physics, and another in African geography. In this light, our demands on elementary and middle school teachers to handle multiple content and process areas seem far from reasonable. If we hope to meet the needs of all children, then we must expect teachers to become used to working collaboratively with their colleagues, each of whom brings something special to the table for planning for children with exceptional needs.

It has become increasingly apparent that collaborative work is important in special education, not only for individual professionals but for organizations as well. The Office of Special Education Programs (OSEP) in the U.S. Department of Education has funded the Technical Assistance Alliance for Parent Centers, which is an innovative partnership of one national and six regional parent technical assistance centers. This nationwide system of centers in turn provides help for over 100 Parent Training and Information Centers (PTIs) and Community Parent Resource Centers (OSEP, 2009).

This alliance provides up-to-date information for parents in addition to high-quality resources and materials, holds national conferences and institutes, and provides management expertise. The parent centers provide training and information to parents of infants, toddlers, children, and youth with disabilities and to the professionals who work with them. Many of these centers are staffed by parents of children with disabilities or by adults who have disabilities themselves, making them uniquely qualified to provide counsel and advice for parents.

Proving That Special Programs Work: Accountability

Proper assessment of special education often needs special measures developed for that purpose.

The word *accountability* throws a mild chill into every educator. The general public tells us that we are to be held responsible for the students whom we release from the educational system. No longer will the general public take the educator's word about what progress is being made in education; it wants to be shown. The public wants proof that education and special education produce good results, and it does not react well when told how difficult it is to produce that proof, however valid the reasons (Gallagher, 2006).

In the field of educating children with exceptionalities, the goals of IEPs might be quite different from one child to another, and so aggregating results into a total report on the special education program may be difficult. For example, if Mary is trying to achieve social acceptance goals and Sam is working on spelling, it would be hard to assess Sam's progress with a social acceptance scale or Mary's progress with a spelling test, and it is inappropriate to add up all the scores of the special students on these measures as a way of judging progress.

> Special education provides special services and support not usually available in general education.

Special education exists to provide children with exceptionalities with services not available to them in the typical education program. It's important to realize that the reason special education exists is *not* that regular education has failed. Classroom teachers and general educational programs simply cannot respond fully to the special needs of children with exceptionalities without a substantial change in the structure, program, and staffing of the typical classroom. Estimates of state, federal, and local expenditures for special education approach $70 billion for 2008–2009, clearly indicating the extent of the financial commitment made by society on behalf of children with exceptionalities and their families.

Instruction can be adapted to the interindividual and intraindividual differences found in children with exceptionalities in several ways: We can (1) adapt the learning environment to create an appropriate setting in which to learn, (2) change the actual content of lessons or the specific knowledge being taught, (3) adapt teaching strategies, and (4) introduce technology that meets the special needs of students with exceptionalities. All subsequent chapters include a special Educational Responses section that is organized around the four areas listed in Table 2.6.

Within the school environment, all of the many forces acting on children with exceptionalities interact and influence each other. Laws regulate who receives services; courts interpret those laws and apply them to specific circumstances; and families support children's efforts and provide goals, values, and expectations that generally reflect their cultural backgrounds. The school is particularly important for children with exceptionalities who may need very special kinds of help to become productive adults.

Building on Developmental Strengths

Children with learning problems used to be presented as having widely varying developmental weaknesses, and those weaknesses became the focal point of special education efforts to try to make the children's developmental patterns more even. The focus was largely on correcting the deficit or fixing what was "wrong with the child." So if a child who was deaf and missing oral language were approached, an enormous effort was made to help him or her to talk, and other developmental areas, such as cognition and social processes, were often ignored or downplayed.

TABLE 2.6 Educational Adaptations	
Adapting the learning environment	One can change the physical setting in which special services are delivered to make the instruction more likely to be effective.
Adapting the curriculum	It is often necessary to modify the curriculum content of the lessons to meet the needs of children with exceptionalities who are performing markedly below or above the rest of the class. Special additional curricula are necessary for some students with exceptionalities. Some examples of these specialized approaches are Braille, sign language, and mobility education. Special curricular adaptations may be needed for children with special gifts and talents.
Adapting teaching strategies	Special strategies are needed for coping with attentional problems and for organizing and presenting content to meet the needs of the student with exceptionalities.
Adapting assistive and instructional technology	Special assistive technology devices help students with exceptionalities to communicate and receive information; instructional technology devices aid them in mastering necessary knowledge and skills.

We now realize that it can be more effective to analyze a child's *strengths* and to focus a therapeutic program around these strengths. Therefore, now increased efforts are being made to find and support the child's and family's strengths so that these can help mitigate the areas of challenge.

Adapting the Learning Environment

Often, a special learning environment is necessary to help some children with exceptionalities master particular content and skills. Making changes in the learning environment, however, has repercussions throughout the entire educational system. This may be one reason environmental modifications are the subject of greater controversy than are changes in either content or skills.

The Inclusion Movement

Inclusion has been the most significant movement in special education over the past three decades. As an educational philosophy, it essentially says that children with exceptionalities should be *a part of, not apart from,* general education. The question that still bothers both special educators and general educators is how the philosophy of inclusion can be made operational in so many different schools in so many different communities. Additional questions include:

● Does inclusion mean that the child with exceptionalities is always to be placed in the general education classroom?

● Does inclusion mean that the essential responsibility for the education of the children with exceptionalities is in the hands of the general classroom teacher?

The concept of **least-restrictive environment** means that teachers attempt to educate a child in the environmental setting that maximizes the chances that the child with exceptionalities will respond successfully to the educational goals and objectives set for him or her. It should not be imagined, however, that the emphasis on inclusion has brought all children with exceptionalities back into the general education classroom.

Group discussion in an inclusive classroom.
(© Ellen Senisi/ The Image Works)

There are still great disparities among students who are included and those who are not. Students with speech and language disorders are in the regular classroom almost universally. On the other hand, many students with intellectual and developmental disabilities or autism or multiple handicaps often may spend more than 60 percent of their day in other educational settings outside the regular classroom. The legislation and court cases supporting inclusion have clearly had an effect. If the existing trends are maintained, even more students will likely receive supports and services in inclusive classrooms than today. Our challenge will be to provide the special services and support needed to educate children with exceptionalities in those inclusive classrooms.

▲ Inclusion in Context

Part of the inclusion process depends on what resources will be available to help general education classroom teachers. Will special education teachers be available in the classroom with the general education teacher for a significant amount of time to help with special instruction? Will paraprofessionals be present to provide necessary assistance to the children with special needs, particularly students with physical disabilities? Will general educators receive personnel preparation for their new roles in working with children with special needs?

Those who support inclusion generally believe that supportive resources will be available for the general education teacher, whereas critics point to many situations in which the support forces are not there (Hunt & McDonnell, 2007). An alternative to full inclusion emphasizes providing a continuum of services based on each child's individual needs. The RTI approach, with its tiers of service, can help provide this continuum of services.

Adapting Content

One of the systematic ways for adapting content and teacher strategy has been the IEP. The **individualized education program (IEP)** was developed to address concerns about what was happening in the newly formed special classes for children with disabilities. Although these students had been removed from the inappropriate regular classroom curriculum, concerns arose about what they were getting in its stead in the special classroom. Was it just what the special teacher was able to come up with from her or his own experience?

To counteract this vagueness, Gallagher (1972) proposed a special education contract for each student that stated specific goals for each student, parental participation in the plan, and a means of determining whether the goals had been met. These procedures were codified in the Education for All Handicapped Children Act (1975), which required that each child must have an individual plan to meet his or her needs.

The IEP process remains controversial to this day because of the amount of professional time it takes to produce these plans and concern about the degree to which they have been implemented successfully. Extensive regulations have been written to determine who makes the plans, who carries out the plans, and who determines the success of the plans.

One of the unique features of the IEP is not only the plan itself for each individual student with disabilities but also how the plan is constructed. The members of the team, as prescribed by law, include:

1. Parent or guardian of the child

2. One regular educator with responsibility for implementing the plan

3. A special educator with responsibility for implementing the plan

4. A principal or administrator who takes responsibility for seeing to it that the plan is implemented

5. Other personnel whose specialized knowledge can be helpful in constructing a plan (e.g., school psychologist, social worker, and so on; see Figure 2.4)

The required presence of the parent or guardian is a clear sign that the IEP is expected to take into account the wishes and feelings of the family of the student, as well as the educators involved.

Table 2.7 outlines the major parts of the IEP as provided by the U. S. Department of Education (2004). As a specific example, an IEP sequence for a child who has a reading disability might be as follows:

1. *Present level of performance (PLOP):* Reads first-grade material at 20 to 30 words per minute with between 5 and 10 errors; guesses at all unknown words.

2. *Service to be provided:* One-to-one tutoring in highly structured reading program; five sessions weekly, 45 minutes each; provided in private, quiet setting.

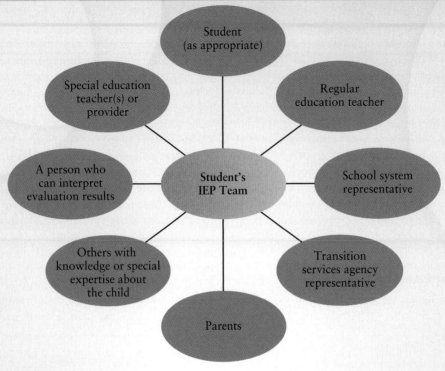

FIGURE 2.4
A Student's IEP Team

3. *Annual goal:* Given a 500-word story at third-grade reading level, student will read 80 to 100 words per minute with 0 to 2 errors.

The text website contains several full IEP samples.

IEPs and Transition

> The IEP is a key tool in special education and, like all tools, needs practice and experience to perform well.

Recent surveys have shown a number of former special education students having problems adjusting to adulthood in the community (see U.S. Department of Education, 2004). Because of these difficulties, a section has been added to the IEP for students 16 years and older that addresses *transition planning.* This plan should be in effect *when the child turns 16, or younger if determined appropriate by the IEP Team,* and updated annually thereafter. The IEP must include the following: appropriate measurable postsecondary goals based upon age-appropriate transition assessments related to training, education, employment, and, where appropriate, independent living skills. The transition services (including courses of study) needed to assist the child in reaching those goals need to be specifically provided.

Another addition that can be made to the standard IEP is a *behavior intervention plan* (BIP) for those students who have been excluded from school for more than ten days for disciplinary reasons. Students with these intense behavioral needs should have a *functional behavior assessment* that considers events preceding the precipitating cause. The BIP must include positive behavior intervention and strategies to help the student back into the academic community. It should also include a clear statement of the targeted behaviors to be increased (e.g., time on task), the intervention strategies to be used, and the quantitative outcomes to be achieved (Bateman & Linden, 2006). IEPs are particularly useful in cataloging the range of positive behavior strategies and the hopeful consequences of those strategies.

TABLE 2.7
Individualized Education Program

The IEP is a written document that is developed for each eligible child with a disability. It includes:

- A statement of the child's present levels of academic achievement and functional performance, including:
  - How the child's disability affects the child's involvement and progress in the general education curriculum (i.e., the same curriculum given to nondisabled children) or for preschool children

- A statement of measurable annual goals, including academic and functional goals designed to:
  - Meet the child's needs that result from the child's disability to enable the child to be involved in and make progress in the general education curriculum
  - Meet each of the child's other educational needs that result from the child's disability

- A description of how the child's progress toward meeting the annual goals will be measured

- A statement of the *special education and related services* and *supplementary aids and services,* based on peer-reviewed research to the extent practicable, that are to be provided to the child, or on behalf of the child, and *a statement of the program modifications or supports* for school personnel that will be provided to enable the child:
  - To advance appropriately toward attaining the annual goals
  - To be involved in and make progress in the general education curriculum and to participate in extracurricular and other nonacademic activities
  - To be educated and participate with other children with disabilities and nondisabled children in extracurricular and other nonacademic activities

- An explanation of the extent, if any, to which the child will *not* participate with nondisabled children in the regular classroom and in extracurricular and other nonacademic activities

- If the IEP team determines that the child must take an alternate assessment instead of a particular regular state or district-wide assessment of student achievement, a statement of why:
  - The child cannot participate in the regular assessment, and
  - The particular alternate assessment selected is appropriate for the child

- The projected date for the beginning of the services and modifications and the anticipated frequency, location, and duration of *special education and related services* and *supplementary aids and services* and *modifications and supports*

Source: Office of Special Education Programs, U.S. Department of Education, 2004.

A number of attempts have been made to bring together "access to the general education curriculum" and the "meeting of individual needs" in inclusive settings for children with disabilities. For example, a junior high science program in an inner-city neighborhood was designed to include students with disabilities by establishing teams of special education and general education teachers and constructing a variety of hands-on materials and tasks to aid in comprehension. Crucial to the programs was a 100-hour training program for 15 three-person teams to prepare them for team activities in the classrooms and to aid in bonding personnel to a common purpose and common curriculum. Fifteen students with a diagnosis of severe emotional and behavior disturbances (E/BDs) or serious learning disabilities (LDs) were included in the 114 students involved.

The results indicated that the students with disabilities had the same passing rate (69 percent) as the general education students (from a neighborhood school in a poverty setting), and the social adjustment during the program was good, with discipline referrals and attendance figures within acceptable limits (Cawley, Hayden, Cade, & Baker-Kroczynski, 2002).

▲ Social Relationships in the Inclusive Classroom

The formation of social relationships is an overarching goal for those supporting the inclusion movement, in addition to mastery of certain academic and technical skills. This is the position of The Association for Persons with Severe Handicaps (TASH), which advocates for inclusion. The policy of full inclusion follows this path of reasoning: If we are to have, as a major goal, the *social integration* of persons with disabilities into adult society, then the school environment should foster the development of social skills, personal friendships, and relationships among children with and without disabilities. These skills are available to nondisabled persons in the natural course of their educational experiences.

Reflect on your own youth. Did you always form friendships with peers with whom your parents wished you to be friends in the hope that they would be good role models for you? Or were your parents occasionally horrified to see whom you brought home and which friends stirred in you some bond of interest or some common feeling about the school or world around you?

Adapting Teacher Strategies

Much of the preparation of special educators deals with adapting instruction to the needs and levels of the students. This need for teacher flexibility is exemplified by the **universal design for learning (UDL)** approach.

▲ Universal Design for Learning (UDL)

One teaching strategy is to build flexibility into the instruction so that the products and environments can be usable by the largest possible number of students. This is called universal design for learning. UDL promises three crucial steps to be taken to make inclusion work:

1. Provide multiple ways to access information, including text, audio clips, and video.

2. Provide multiple methods that allow students to interact with new information and develop new

skills through text, audio, video, technology, and so forth.

3. Provide multiple methods for students to communicate their understanding of a given topic or acquisition of a particular skill through multiple ways (Russell, Hoffmann, & Higgins, 2009).

It was soon recognized that considerable help was going to be required to translate these principles into workable classroom reality and transform the print-bound materials that have formed the basis for the usual education curriculum. The Office of Special Education Programs (OSEP) funded the Center for Applied Special Technology (CAST), whose task was to develop technology to provide diverse means of delivering information.

CAST, in turn, established the National Instructional Materials Accessibility Standard (NIMAS), whose purpose was to produce alternative presentations of materials that could be received by students with a wide variety of individual needs. One of the major strategies was to digitize textbooks to make them accessible through text-to-speech technology, Braille, or other visual means for those who cannot learn through the standard print methods (Rose & Meyer, 2002).

But the next task was to alert special education teachers and curriculum specialists about how they could utilize these new materials and methods. A major technical assistance program for states, disability experts, and publishers was undertaken in an effort to provide training and information to a growing number of educators about this new technology. NIMAS guides the production and electronic distribution of digital versions of textbooks and other instructional materials, as well as conducts workshops and technical assistance for special and general educators across the country. The activities of institutes such as CAST and NIMAS will make the future a more productive one for children with special needs.

In universal design, the assistive supports are built in rather than added as an afterthought. One of the key examples of UDL flexibility is *closed captioning*, standard on most TV sets, so that persons with hearing problems can read the text at the bottom of the screen. The same message is being delivered through two separate channels—visual and auditory. UDL also allows flexibility in student expression. Instead of giving a paper-and-pencil answer, a student may use drawings or illustrations or respond through a computer.

A careful analysis of four secondary schools in four different states illustrates the new UDL approach (Wallace, Anderson, Bartholomay, & Hupp, 2002). As part of the Beacons of Excellence project, they were chosen from a roster of 114 schools nominated by a national advisory panel for their successful inclusion programs. The Beacons of Excellence project was funded by the Office of Special Education Programs in the U.S. Department of Education to increase the understanding of how schools can improve learning results for students with disabilities within the context of efforts to achieve exemplary results for all children. After extensive observations of general education students and special education students, the authors reached the following conclusions:

- Merely including students with disabilities in the general education classroom is not enough to ensure their success.

- The school administration in each of the schools must support team teaching with special and general education teachers.

- A significant amount of time must be spent guiding students in their preparation for learning and teaching them directly, using a variety of strategies, including technology.

- Teachers must know a variety of instructional strategies in order to address the diverse learning needs of students, and they need to know how to work with each other to effectively implement the strategies (p. 357).

In short, success in UDL is neither an accident nor attributable to good luck. It requires extensive planning, preparation, and teamwork. These plans may be made in Tier I of the RTI model for all classroom students and will also be incorporated in Tiers II and III for students with more intense needs.

Adapting Technology

Special education has often led the way in the acceptance and use of technology in education. That achievement may well be due to the unique challenges that special educators face. Because they are educating children with special needs, they have

New technologies in the classroom can both assist and instruct students with special needs.

been willing to try new devices, such as computers adapted to special needs, hearing aids, print magnifiers, and machines that trace eye movements as the student reads.

There are two quite different uses of technology for children with disabilities: assistive and instructional uses.

▲ Assistive technology

Assistive technology is designed primarily to allow the child with special needs to gain access to information. For the person who is blind, it provides Braille readers and typewriters; for the person who is deaf, hearing aids; for the person who cannot speak, communication boards for pointing to and composing messages. Assistive technology can be as sophisticated as a device that translates print into oral language or as simple as a headband and a pointer that allow students who have cerebral palsy to point to text or communication boards. Such devices have dramatically improved individual children's ability to receive and transmit information effectively and are most often used with children with moderate to severe disabilities that create major barriers to communication. Many of the subsequent chapters include examples of the uses of assistive technology. We often think of assistive technology as being sophisticated, complicated, or computer-driven, but this is not always the case. Assistive technology devices, in fact, can be classified as low-, middle-, or high-tech.

- Low-tech devices may include nonelectronic devices like pencil grips, adaptive spoon handles, and picture boards (these may not involve technology at all!).

- Middle-tech devices include things like audio books, word-processing computers, tape recorders, and other uncomplicated mechanical devices.

- High-tech assistive devices are usually specifically designed to support an individual's needs and may include speech recognition software, electronic communication devices, and mobility technologies for guiding wheel chairs.

With the support of assistive technology, individuals with

The National Assistive Technology Research Institute: http://natri.uky.edu

disabilities can often participate fully in many activities (Technology and Media Division of the Council for Exceptional Children, 2007).

The National Assistive Technology Research Institute suggests that when considering what kind of assistive technology would be useful we:

- Identify the environments where the student lives, works, and plays.

- Determine the functional areas where support would be helpful.

- Select the assistive technology device that can be used across all settings to maximize functioning (Bausch, Ault, & Hasselbring, 2006).

It is also important to remember that the best device is not always the most high-tech. Sometimes a lower-tech option like a communication picture board is more useful than a sophisticated communication device. The selection of the right device also depends on the demands of the environment in combination with the developmental level of the individual (Campbell, Milborne, Dugan, & Wilcox, 2006). As the child grows and/or the demands change, the assistive technology support must

Technology and Media Division of the Council for Exceptional Children
www.tamcec.org

be adapted and modified as well. When assistive technology is needed, the child's IEP should describe what and how this is to be provided and include a plan for periodically reviewing the appropriateness of the device.

Each chapter of this text includes a discussion of how assistive technology can be used to enhance the lives of individuals with special needs.

Instructional technology is developed primarily as a means to deliver content and instruction in an appropriate manner to children with exceptionalities. Table 2.8 provides a sample list of assistive and instructional technology devices.

Major attempts are being made to go beyond the traditional transmission of knowledge and to use technology as a means to aid children with exceptionalities in thinking and problem solving. Hasselbring (2001) points out that a student may understand how the special characteristics of a camel may help the animal survive desert sandstorms yet fail to understand that this survival illustrates the phenomenon of *adaptation*. When asked about the concept of adaptation, the student may not realize that his or her knowledge of camels is relevant or is a good illustration of the term.
www.abledata.com

There is good reason to believe that concept instruction is much more likely than fact-oriented instruction to produce transferable knowledge. That

TABLE 2.8
Uses of Technology

Assistive Technology	Instructional Technology
Tools for enhancing the routine functioning of people who have physical or sensory disabilities	Computers and related technology for the delivery and support of instruction
- Communication boards	- Computers and software programs
- Computer-screen readers	- Phone/fax
- Braille printers	- Internet
- Head pointers	- Data compression
- Kurzweil reading devices for the visually impaired	- CD-ROM
	- DVDs

Source: Adapted from T. Hasselbring, *Florida's Future in Special Education: Applications of Technology.* Vision 2000 Conference, University of South Florida, Tampa. Reprinted with the permission of the author.

The effective use of technology is one important goal for instruction.

(© Purestock/Getty Images)

is the reason major efforts are being made to use technology not just to master specific information but also as a tool to help in problem solving. It is especially important for teachers who work with children with exceptionalities to learn how to apply technology to their instruction. For the most part, teachers have been left on their own to learn as best they can, or they have been given short-term training introducing them to the technology but rarely allowing them sufficient time to explore the full potential of these new tools.

Now, legislation (IDEA, 2004) mandates the mastery of technology on the part of special education teachers, and so teachers must now consider the appropriateness of assistive technology as a tool for intervention (Lahm & Nichels, 1999). It can provide access to data and other programs. Even more important, computers allow children to learn at their own rate and provide immediate feedback and reinforcement. The child's learning becomes more active and self-directed.

For resources, see the book *Computer and Web Resources for People with Disabilities: A Guide to Exploring Today's Assistive Technology;* **www.hunterhouse.com**

The increasing use of **high-stakes testing** has created special problems for children with exceptionalities because important decisions are based on the results of such tests—decisions as to whether the student receives a diploma or passes from one grade to the next. The Council for Exceptional Children, the major professional association for children with special needs, wants policies that hold programs for children with exceptionalities accountable, as long as the measures used are appropriate:

a. All students with exceptional learning needs shall be included in all assessment and accountability systems and shall have available the opportunity to participate in general assessments.

b. Only assessment processes and instruments that have been developed and validated on student samples that included students who have exceptionalities and that validly demonstrate their performance shall be used (Council for Exceptional Children, 2003, sec. 4, pt. 3, p. 137).

A number of people and institutions have struggled over how to ensure that Jerry, with his cerebral palsy, or Paula, with her limited vision, can be adequately assessed. A series of accommodations such as reading test questions aloud or giving students with special needs more time have been suggested (Lazarus, Thurlow, Lail, & Christensen, 2009). While there is wide variation from one state to another, there is general agreement in extending time limits and seeking tests that meet the Universal Design Model. Some new approaches have appeared to supplement the standard achievement tests. They bear such names as *performance assessment, authentic assessment,* and *real-life assessment.* Because performance is knowledge put to use, **performance assessment** is a measure of the applications of knowledge. If a student is asked to write an essay on a particular topic, that essay can be the basis for a performance assessment. Similarly, if a student is asked to conduct a research project or produce an oral presentation on a topic, that assignment could be the basis for a performance assessment.

Authentic assessment involves the typical classroom performance of the student, rather than a contrived task. Quite typically, it might be an examination of a student portfolio providing evidence of student performance over time. In this way, we have an assessment in real time, using classroom work and assignments as the basis for evaluation.

These forms of evaluation still leave the task of determining just what level of performance is acceptable or outstanding. Often such judgments are rather crude 3-point or 4-point scales ranging from *excellent* to *unacceptable.* Added to that would be a substantive critique of writing style or scientific procedures revealed through the authentic assessment.

Student Expectations

One of the sources of tensions between No Child Left Behind and IDEA involves student expectations. If special education has done a good job, then what should we expect in student performance? NCLB seems to expect all or nearly all children with disabilities to be performing at grade level. It seems like a reasonable expectation, but is it?

We can take the case of Jim, who is typical of a large number of students with mild disabilities. Jim, at age 12, has been falling progressively farther behind each year of school until now—he is performing at a third-grade level while in the sixth grade. Is it reasonable to expect that next year, with the help of special education, a miracle drug, or any other intervention, Jim will be performing at the sixth or seventh grade level?

To show this kind of growth, Jim would have to leap three grades in one year after years of inefficient learning and consequent low motivation. If he doesn't make such a gain, does that mean that the special education program has failed? We do have a responsibility to reverse the negative trends that Jim has shown and we must find ways to support his growth and performance. These positive gains would be a highly desired outcome and one we would be proud of.

Special education, as well as general education, should be held accountable for student performance. But the goals should be in line with what we have learned about developmental patterns and the various forces at work that influence educational performance.

RTI

RTI Model and Culturally/Linguistically Diverse Students

Many students for whom English is a second language have difficulty learning in American schools and may be referred to special education as a result. The RTI model Tier II, which allows for additional support for learning, short of referral to special education, should be effective in this situation. The major problem, according to Klingner and Harry (2006), is the assumption that instruction is being adequately provided in Tiers I and II. Their qualitative study of 12 schools through observation in the classroom and in child study teams (CST) did not confirm that good instruction was provided in either tier; consequently, some of these children were referred to special education anyway.

There has been such concern about the assessment of culturally or linguistically diverse students that a panel was established by the National Academy of Sciences to answer key questions of assessment (Donovan & Cross, 2002).

1. *Is there a higher incidence of children with special needs or giftedness among some racial and ethnic groups?* Yes. Disproportionate numbers of minority students are living in poverty. Major differences in measured aptitude between groups are documented at kindergarten entry.

2. *Does schooling contribute to these differences found in racial and ethnic groups?* Yes. Schools with higher concentrations of low-income minority students have fewer well-trained teachers and fewer resources.

3. *Does the current referral and assessment process reliably identify students with special needs and gifts, or is it biased by race and ethnicity?* The answer to this is not clear, although it does seem that minority status increases likelihood that the scores on assessment measures may be depressed.

4. *Is placement in special education a benefit or a risk? Is that outcome different by race or ethnic group?* There are insufficient data for answering the question, but there are substantial data that show that early identification and intervention are more effective than later identification and intervention.

The report clearly calls the current policy of "wait to fail" before referring the student for help unwise. Screening mechanisms exist for early identification of children at risk for reading and behavior problems and should be used to help place students in the proper tier or placement.

We address this issue of ethnic and racial groups and their interaction with special education in many of the subsequent chapters concerning individual categories of children with special needs.

Transition from School to Work or Advanced Education

The number of graduates from special education services who are unable to gain employment has sensitized professionals to the need for more direct services to bridge the gap between school and community adjustment. Specially trained personnel now have direct responsibility for helping students during this period.

As noted earlier, IEPs for older teenagers must include a plan for transition services. The following case example provides one illustration of the use of transition services to help Jim get a driver's license, critical for many jobs that he is capable of doing. His reading difficulties may cause setbacks on the state exam for the license, and thus special tutoring and sample exams will need to be provided with the necessary practice to give him the confidence to pass. In this case, accountability is fairly direct. If he passes the exam, the transition plan will be successful.

Other transition planning may involve direct collaboration with potential employers to prepare students for transition or with vocational schools to help with postsecondary training.

Case Example: Transition Planning Goals for Jim's IEP

Jim, who has a continuing reading disability, has special concerns about getting a driver's license, which is necessary to his employment. Therefore, the following transition plans will be added to his IEP:

Present Level of Performance (PLOP): Jim has been driving on a learner's permit but worries about passing the written test needed for his license.

Special Education: Jim will seek from the Division of Motor Vehicles any accommodations made for students with disabilities and will take special instruction in map reading and route highlighting.

Goal: By March 1, Jim will be given a practice exam and will score 70 percent or better. Given a city map, Jim will highlight common routes he follows to work and routes to the mall, downtown, and so forth. By March 15th, Jim will take the licensing exam.

moral dilemma
The Inclusive Classroom

Two parents are discussing the merits of inclusion (keeping children with disabilities in the regular classroom with their age group). The first parent says, "It is the right thing to do. They should be with their same-age peers. If they are separated, they will get an inferior education. No one will really care what happens to them, and they will feel that they are being segregated and will have bad feelings about themselves as a result."

The second parent nods her head and then says, "Yes, but if they are in the regular class, they will demand the attention of the classroom teacher, who won't be able to give her attention to the other students, and they may well be a disruptive force in the classroom that will downgrade the education of all. We know the schools will say they have special personnel to help, but we all know it won't be enough."

Write a paragraph on your views on the matter.

Go to the Education CourseMate website to share your thoughts on this dilemma and email your responses to your instructor.

✳ *Summary*

- The social institutions of government, schools, and the courts all have important roles to play in the education of children with special needs.

- Legislation is the vehicle for providing additional resources for children with special needs and also creates the structure that educators must use.

- Court decisions have validated the rights of children with developmental disabilities.

- Courts now require school systems to have strong documentation before moving a child with disabilities from the general education classroom.

- Instruction can be adapted to the individual needs of students with exceptionalities in several ways: We can vary the learning environment, change the presentation of the curriculum, adapt teaching strategies, and utilize technology.

- There is a clear trend for more children with disabilities to be placed in the general education classroom now than there was ten years ago.

- *Inclusion* refers to educational situations in which children with disabilities are educated with same-age peers; one major goal is social integration.

- The response to intervention (RTI) approach, which provides three levels of service rather than two (special education and general education), seems to provide a more effective model for aiding children in need of help in the academic setting.

▶ An individualized education program (IEP) defines the nature of a child's academic situation, the program's long-term goals and short-term objectives, needed services, and criteria for evaluation.

▶ In addition to well-prepared teachers, a support system of educational services is needed to provide continued assistance for those teachers.

▶ Technology can serve two separate purposes for children with disabilities. Assistive technology enhances routine functioning and communication. Instructional technology aids in the delivery and support of instruction.

▶ Universal design for learning (UDL) provides alternative pathways for instruction for children with special needs.

▶ Program assessment is an important part of special education programs.

▶ The special needs of culturally and linguistically diverse children in special education require specific attention.

Future Challenges

1 *What is the future role of the courts in protecting the rights of children with exceptionalities?*

During the last part of the twentieth century, the courts played a significant role in affirming the rights of children with exceptionalities to a free and appropriate education. But who is to determine what is "appropriate"? Now that the courts have ruled, in the *Rowley* case, that it is sufficient for the schools to give reasonable help, clarification is needed as to how much is enough. It is unlikely that the courts have the professional knowledge to make such decisions.

2 *How can we build an educational infrastructure that will support education of children with exceptionalities?*

Since education in the United States has grown from local to state to federal levels, there has not been the opportunity to insert many systemic components into the educational enterprise, such as technical assistance or program evaluation or personnel preparation. These are all necessities for children with exceptionalities. We recognize the importance of an educational infrastructure just as we accept the need for infrastructure in medicine and transportation. But how will it be institutionalized in education: through legislation, court decisions, or administrative actions?

3 *How do we meet the requirements of No Child Left Behind and the vocational needs of children with disabilities?*

There seems to be great value in planning a vocational job-oriented program for children with disabilities in the secondary schools, perhaps even beginning in the middle school. This requires a different curriculum and activities. But the requirements of NCLB to receive the common curriculum and be tested on it is in conflict with the needs of these students. How will the schools reconcile these differing objectives?

Key Terms

academic aptitude p. 43

assessment p. 34

assistive technology p. 36

authentic assessment p. 60

context of the child p. 32

continuum of services p. 41

diagnostic achievement tests p. 46

ecology of the child p. 32

high-stakes testing p. 60

Individuals with Disabilities Education Act (IDEA) p. 35

inclusion p. 41

individualized education program (IEP) p. 53

instructional technology p. 58

interindividual differences p. 43

least-restrictive environment p. 52

multiple intelligences p. 44

performance assessment p. 60

PL 88-64 p. 34

PL 94-142 p. 34

PL 99-457 p. 35

standard (norm-referenced) achievement tests p. 46

transition services p. 36

universal design for learning (UDL) p. 56

Resources

References of Special Interest

Eisenman, L., & Ferretti, R. (Eds.) (2010). Special issue: Changing conceptions of special education. *Exceptional Children, 76*(3). An entire issue of the journal is devoted to changing views of special education that has emerged through federal legislation and educational experience. In particular, it focuses on the tension created by laws such as No Child Left Behind and the special needs of children with exceptionalities. The special role played by the response to intervention (RTI) model is also discussed, including its role in the blurring of the lines of special education. An important reference for reviewing current policies.

Gallagher, J. (2006). *Driving change in special education.* Baltimore: Brookes. An attempt to supply a new approach to providing services through special education. The focus is on the necessary infrastructure of support services needed for quality programs. The author uses the engines of change, legislation, court decisions, administrative changes, and professional and parent initiatives as the vehicles for the discussion of needed change.

Grzywacz, P. (Ed.) (2001). *Students with disabilities and special education* (18th ed.). Birmingham, AL: Oakstone Legal and Business Publishing. A valuable resource book that presents major legislation dealing with special education, synthesizes legal cases, and provides a detailed accounting of the federal regulations implementing IDEA. Legal cases dealing with placement, school liability, related services, and discrimination are included.

Iris Resource Locator http://iris.peabody.vanderbilt.edu/resources.html Vanderbilt University's IRIS Center gives high quality resources about students with disabilities by providing free, online, interactive training enhancements that translate research about the education of students with disabilities into practice. The IRIS Resource Locator is an interactive, Flash-based database of teaching modules, case studies, activities, information briefs, and podcasts covering a range of topics from RTI to Learning Strategies for Disabilities. Each module is easy to follow, and the information briefs are excellent resources for both parents and educators alike. The Resource Locator is an excellent source seamlessly combining technology, research, and best practice.

National Research Council (2002). *Minority students in special and gifted education.* Washington, DC: National Academy Press. A comprehensive report examining issues that lead to the disproportionately high representation of culturally and linguistically diverse students in special education and to their disproportionately low representation in gifted education. Complex factors that create additional risk for children living in poverty are presented. These risk factors are discussed in terms of their impact on students' achievement and behavior in school settings. Recommendations for policy and practice are offered.

Salvia, J., Ysseldyke, J., & Bolt, S. (2010). *Assessment* (11th ed.). Boston: Cengage Learning. A comprehensive book that covers all aspects of assessment, including both formal and informal measures, and that provides a basic discussion of measurement and its various problems. A special chapter is provided on how to adapt tests to accommodate children with disabilities. Special chapters are devoted to the assessment of perceptual-motor skills, socioemotional behavior, and adaptive behavior.

Turnbull, H., Stowe, M., Turnbull, A., & Schrandt., M. (2007). A 35-year retrospective and a 5-year prospective based on the core concepts of disability policy. In Odom, S., Horner, R., Snell, M., & Blacher, J. *Handbook of developmental disabilities.* New York: The Guilford Press. A comprehensive review of the core concepts in public policy for children with developmental disabilities as revealed through legislative actions and judicial decisions. Eighteen core concepts are considered, including freedom, inclusion, integration, family-centered services, and accountability, and their development through public policy.

Journals

Teaching Exceptional Children
   www.cec.sped.org/bk/abtec.htm/

Remedial and Special Education
   www.proedinc.com/journals.htm/

Journal of Special Education
   www.proedinc.com

Educational Leadership
   www.ascd.org

Exceptional Children
   www.cec.sped.org

Journal of Special Education Technology
   jset.univ.edu

Professional Organizations

Council for Exceptional Children
   www.cec.sped.org

 Visit the Education CourseMate website for additional TeachSource Video Cases, information about CEC standards, study tools, and much more.

High-Incidence Exceptionalities

© Thomas Balsamo

THE SEVEN CHAPTERS in Part 2 are devoted to children who make up between 8 and 9 percent of the population of school-age children in the United States. Chapter 3 looks at the needs of young children and early intervention, while Chapters 4 through 9 focus on children identified with learning disabilities, autism spectrum disorders, intellectual and developmental delays, emotional and behavior disorders, communication disorders, and gifts and talents. The high numbers of children with these exceptionalities reinforces the critical need for the supports and services that are described in these chapters.

Early Intervention Supports and Services

Focus Questions

▸ In what ways did research change historical beliefs about child development and set the stage for early intervention?

▸ What is early intervention, and why is it so important for infants and toddlers with disabilities?

▸ How do we identify children who are in need of early intervention shortly after birth and during their toddler years?

▸ What are the five developmental domains that states use to define developmental delays in young children?

▸ Why is family involvement so critical to the health and well-being of the child, and what are family-centered early intervention and the individual family service plan (IFSP)?

▸ What do we mean by "inclusion" and "natural environments," and what are the benefits to providing supports and services in these settings?

▸ How can we ensure the quality of early childhood programs, and why is quality important?

▸ What kinds of supports are needed to help families navigate the transitions in services for young children?

The birth of a child is a wondrous event. It is a time filled with expectation, anticipation, and excitement. It can also be an overwhelming time for parents as they learn how to meet the needs of their newborn child. The challenges of feeding, changing, and calming a newborn can feel daunting, especially when parents are trying to manage all of this in a sleep-deprived state. Under the best of circumstances, the anxiety of caring for a newborn can be intense (Nugent, Keefer, Minear, Johnson, & Blanchard, 2007a).

Newborns enter the world with a vast array of skills and abilities that will help them negotiate their early lives. The newborn prefers visual stimuli with clearly contrasting patterns; orients early to the mother's face and voice, recognizing these as distinct from a stranger's; and is biologically wired to seek social contact (Nugent et al., 2007). These early skills and abilities help the newborn and the mother form a bond that is critical to both during the first few weeks of life. The mother and father learn together how to communicate with and respond to the needs of the infant. During this process, the mother gains confidence when her baby is happy, calm, and responsive, and the baby begins to thrive within this supportive environment (Quesenberry, Ostrosky, & Corso, 2007). All of this takes place in the greater context of the family and the environmental circumstances within which the family lives.

The newborn and the mother, family, and environment form a set of complex relationships that are an interdependent system and that facilitate the optimal development of the child (Fox, Carta, Strain, Dunlap, & Hemmeter, 2010; Center on the Social and Emotional Foundations for Early Learning [CSEFELb], 2010); Dunst, 2007; Guralnick, 2005; Reis, D., 2003). When challenges exist within any of these components (the child, the mother and family, or the environment), they can affect the health and well-being of the baby (Fox et al., 2010; CSEFELb, 2010; Dunst, 2007; Guralnick, 2005; Reis, D., 2003). The purpose of **early intervention** is to provide necessary supports and services to optimize the child's development as early as possible. Each of the chapters that follow also briefly addresses young children with specific disabilities and/or talents, but because early development is so important, we have devoted this chapter to young children. In this chapter, we explore the world of early intervention, looking at the supports and services that are available to help ensure that each family has what is needed for the optimal development of their child. We look at what it takes to support the development of physically and mentally healthy young children who can explore and learn with confidence (CSEFELa, 2010). We review the history of early intervention, look at early childhood as a developmental period, explore the risk factors and stressors that can lead to difficulties, and examine the roles of families and professionals working together to meet the needs of young children.

> The purpose of early intervention is to provide necessary supports and services needed for optimizing the child's development as early as possible.

History of Early Intervention

Although the benefits of early intervention are widely accepted today, this has not always been the case. Early intervention supports and services are a logical extension of early childhood programs, which have a long history in the United States, beginning in the late 1930s (Noonan & McCormick, 2006). Historically, programs known as nursery schools or preschools were an outgrowth of psychologists' concerns for children's mental health (Cairns, 1983), which psychologists believed was fostered by positive child-rearing practices during the first years of life (Anastasiow & Nucci, 1994). Children with disabilities, however, were excluded from most of these programs (until the 1960s). The prevailing opinion was that little could be done for a child with disabilities because intelligence and abilities were fixed at birth and therefore could not be changed. As a result of this

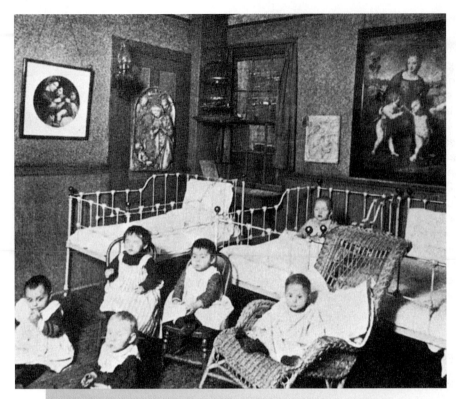

In the early 1900s, the belief that a person's abilities were fixed at birth and could not be changed resulted in many children with disabilities being placed in institutions.

(© The Granger Collection, NY)

belief, parents were encouraged to place children with disabilities in institutions and orphanages, where they often received only custodial care (see nearby photo). Special schools for children with sensory disabilities (hearing and vision) were beginning to emerge at this time as well and we will learn more about these in subsequent chapters.

In the 1930s, the belief that nothing could be done to improve outcomes for children with disabilities was dramatically challenged when Drs. Harold Skeels and Harold Dye performed a seminal research study (Noonan & McCormick, 2006). These researchers found that children who were placed in foster homes or who were adopted fared much better than did a comparable group of children who remained in an orphanage (Skeels & Dye, 1939). The fostered-adopted group achieved normal intelligence, whereas many of the institutionalized children were classified as mentally retarded.

Amazingly, these gains seemed to hold for the fostered-adopted group into adulthood (Skeels, 1966). Samuel Kirk, lead author of this text (1950), further demonstrated that preschool experience could increase the rate of mental development and the social skills of children who were classified as mentally retarded. The belief that children's potential was fixed at birth was beginning to give way to the exciting idea that, with the right supports and services provided early on, we could significantly improve outcomes for children who were "at risk."

> The belief that children's potential is fixed at birth has given way to the exciting idea that we can significantly improve developmental outcomes for children who are "at risk."

A major longitudinal study looking at the impact of early intervention, the High/Scope Perry Preschool Study expanded our understanding of the need for early intervention (Schweinhart et al., 2005). In this study, 123 African American children, born in poverty and identified as at risk for school failure, were assigned at ages 3 and 4 to either an intervention or control group (these assignments were primarily random, however some children attended their neighborhood child-care center). The intervention group received the High/Scope participatory learning approach in preschool, whereas the other half received normal preschool services. The long-term outcomes—looking at these individuals as adults at age 40—showed positive gains for the group that attended preschool (Schweinhart et al., 2005). The reported positive gains included 19 percent fewer arrests, 20 percent more high school graduations, and 20 percent higher earnings for the group who attended preschool (Schweinhart et al., 2005).

One of the longest running studies of the importance of early intervention is the Abecedarian Study that began in 1972 and continues through today (Campbell & Ramey, 1995; Campbell, Ramey, Pungello, Miller-Johnson, & Sparling, 2002; Winton & Buysse, 2006). The Abecedarian study randomly assigned infants (4.4 months on average) into two groups in order to examine the impact of quality early child care on children from economically disadvantaged families (Winton & Buysse, 2006). One of the groups of children received enriched high-quality child care through the preschool years, and included some special curricular opportunities (Sparling, 2007). The second group of children received their traditional child care. Both groups of children have been followed into adulthood. This seminal study showed that early intervention can have long-term positive benefits.

As young adults, the enriched group earned reading scores 1.8 grade levels higher and math scores 1.3 grade levels higher than the control group. They were more than twice as likely to enroll in a four-year college or university (36 percent to 14 percent) and were less likely to have their first child at age 18 or younger (26 percent versus 45 percent) (Campbell & Ramey, 1995; Campbell, Ramey, Pungello, Miller-Johnson, & Sparling, 2002; Winton & Buysse, 2006). A follow-up study of the groups as adults showed the experimental group was less likely to report depressive symptoms (McLauglin, Campbell, Pungello, & Skinner, 2007). However, unlike the High/Scope Perry Preschool project findings, follow-up studies of adult crime rates for the Abecedarian project showed little to no differences for the two groups (Clarke & Campbell, 1998). One of the best sources of how caregiver practices can influence child development is the Kauai Longitudinal Study, conducted from 1952 to 2000 (Werner & Smith, 1992; 2001). The study followed individuals from their prenatal care through age 40 and demonstrated that many children who were at risk for developmental delays could achieve success (Werner, 2000). The study showed that child-rearing practices, such as providing a home environment of psychological warmth, low physical punishment, responsiveness, verbalness, and intentional encouragement for development, can help at-risk children achieve normal milestones (Werner, 2004). These child-rearing practices help ameliorate the negative effects of a difficult or abnormal birth (Kolvin, Miller, Scott, Gatzanis, & Fleeting, 1990; Rutter, 2000; Werner, 2000). These seminal studies paved the way for the acceptance of early intervention as critical for improving outcomes for children with disabilities.

Why Is Early Intervention So Important?

The first years of life are a critical developmental time, laying the foundation for all that is to come. From birth to the age of 3, the brain develops rapidly (Sandman & Kemp, 2007; Shonkoff & Phillips 2000). Information from the environment is stored in pathways in the brain that are ready to receive it. During this period, the basic "self" emerges through a dynamic relationship with the caregivers and the environment, and this provides the foundation for autonomous emotional functioning (Guralnick, 2005). Language emerges during these early years, and during this time the child learns how to cope with the world. The infant is learning at a staggeringly fast rate, and the rapid development of the brain in these early years sets the stage for all further learning. If information is not provided through experience, the brain's neural pathways are unused; conversely, if enriched experiences are provided, they actually help to build a more efficient brain (Freberg, 2006; Sandman & Kemp, 2007; Shonkoff & Phillips 2000).

Neurology and Brain Development
Information Related to Infancy and Young Children

During fetal development, the brain grows at an amazingly rapid rate, estimated to be 50,000 to 100,000 neurons per second, creating an extensive network that forms a system for learning (Given, 2002). Around half of these nearly 200 billion neurons will die off during the fifth month of gestation, ensuring that only neurons that have made connections are preserved (Sousa, 2001). At birth, the infant immediately begins to use this learning system to make sense of the world (Smith, 2005; Sousa, 2001). From the moment they are born, babies tend to show a preference for humans. They respond to faces, voices, and smells and have a special preference for their mother (Nugent et al., 2007a). Newborn babies get bored and look away when visual stimulus repeats too often. Very early on, infants learn to imitate the facial expressions and gestures of their caregivers (Smith, 2005).

> The brain grows and develops through experiences, as well as maturation.

The brain is preset for learning, and each experience the infant has reinforces this predisposition. One area that the brain seems to be hardwired for is the learning of language (Given, 2002). Language develops spontaneously and naturally for most children. With little formal instruction, a child learns to understand and imitate the sounds of the language she hears each day (Given, 2002). But language learning, like all areas of brain development, can be enhanced by favorable environments where caregivers talk with the child and offer lots of positive reinforcement to the baby (Sousa, 2001; Smith, 2005; Wolfe & Brandt, 1998). One of the reasons that early intervention to support children with disabilities is so important is that during the early years, birth though age 6, there are "windows of opportunity" or sensitive time periods where learning in a particular area is optimal (Sousa, 2001). These sensitive time periods are not rigid, and the brain does have a significant amount of plasticity (i.e., the ability to reorganize itself and shift learning functions from one area to another). Mastery of key learning is easiest if done within the optimal window (Sousa, 2001). Figure 3.1 show the windows of opportunity for learning as the child's brain matures.

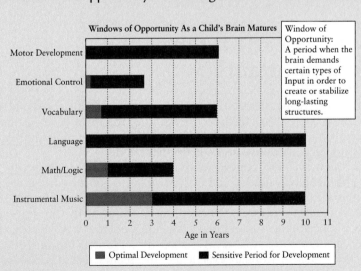

FIGURE 3.1
The Development of the Brain
Adapted with permission of Corwin Press, from How the Brain Learns by David A. Sousa, copyright © 2005; permission conveyed through Copyright Clearwater Center, Inc.

Throughout this text, we will be using the information processing model (IPM) to describe how the brain works as the child learns by taking in information (input), working with this information (processing), and sharing information through a variety of means of communication (output). Information processing also involves the executive function, or the decision-making role of learning. In addition, all of this takes place within the context of emotions (see page 74 for the information processing model as it is applied to our story of Tyron).

We can see, for example, the dramatic impact of early intervention with children who are deaf. Children who are deaf are more successful academically if they learn sign language by age 2 than if they wait until age 6 (Moeller, 2000). The early use of sign language allows children who are deaf to communicate, and this allows them to develop relationships, expand their thinking, and build their self-confidence (Goldin-Meadow, 1998; Moeller, 2000). The ability to communicate one's needs, fears, and desires reduces the frustration a child experiences, and so early sign language instruction also helps prevent secondary social and emotional problems that might develop for the child (Odom, Rogers, McDougle, Hume, & McGee, 2007). We may see a similarly dramatic effect of early intervention with many children who have speech difficulties. When interventions are activated by age 3, many children with speech difficulties are problem free by age 5 (Roth, Troia, Worthington, & Handy, 2006). The first step in early intervention is identifying children who need additional supports and services.

Profiles of Two Children Who Need Early Intervention Supports and Services

Children can need early intervention supports for a wide variety of reasons. We look at two children, Jennifer and Tyron, to see how needs for early intervention can differ from child to child.

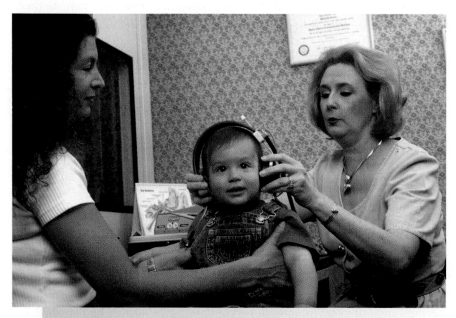

Assessing the child's strengths and needs is essential to planning appropriate interventions.

(© Robin Sachs/Photo Edit)

Jennifer: Jennifer was born at 28 weeks' gestation and is a preterm infant. Her parents were told that she would need to spend her first few months in the hospital's neonatal care unit with oxygen support because her respiratory system was immature. Jennifer's early birth and prolonged hospital stay were very stressful for her mother, Sandra, and her father, Tony. Sandra and Tony knew that the pregnancy was considered to be high risk because of Sandra's age and health (Sandra is 38 and has type 2 diabetes), and so they had prepared early for their daughter's birth; but no prior knowledge could prepare them for the anxiety and worry they faced as they watched their tiny daughter fight for her life. Sandra and Tony felt helpless, knowing there was little they could do for Jennifer. They visited the hospital every day, and the neonatal care nurses encouraged them to hold and feed Jennifer on these visits. In the early weeks, Sandra often left the hospital in tears, feeling that she had let Jennifer and Tony down by not being able to carry the pregnancy to full term. When they finally were able to take Jennifer home, both parents were concerned that they would not be able to meet her needs. The family was referred to the local early intervention program, and home visits were set up through the visiting nurse's agency. These supports were critical to building Sandra and Tony's confidence in their parenting. We will meet Jennifer again later in the chapter to see how she is doing on page 85.

Tyron: Tyron's need for early intervention was not recognized until several months after his birth. He had been carried full term, and there were no complications. His early development seemed relatively normal, and, because Tyron was their first child, Michael and Laura were not really sure what to expect. Laura had gone back to work when Tyron was 3 months old, and things had settled down in the family routine. When Tyron was 10 months old, however, Laura started to feel uneasy. Tyron seemed different from some of the other babies in the child-care center. When Laura would go to pick him up he was fine, but he did not seem to know her in the same way the other babies recognized their mothers. She watched as other mothers called out their children's names when they entered the room and she saw how their children's faces brightened at the sight of their mothers. She also noticed that the other babies responded to their mothers' voices with smiles and "baby talk." Tyron was calm but seemed not to realize that she was there to pick him up. At first Laura kept her worries to herself, reassuring herself that Tyron seemed content and was just quieter than other children. Because Laura had had mixed feelings about going back to work, she also felt that maybe it was somehow her fault that Tyron did not seem to recognize her. When she finally shared these worries with Michael, he reassured her that Tyron seemed fine to him. But Laura continued to feel that something was not right. To reassure her, Michael agreed that they should talk with Tyron's pediatrician, Dr. Nolan, on their next visit, his one-year well-baby checkpoint.

In preparation for this visit, Laura made a list of her concerns about Tyron: "He does not recognize his name when I call to him; he does not seem to know me when I come to get him; unless he is upset, when his tantrums can be fierce, he's so quiet. And he does not seem to want to play with us; he seems not to hear us when we talk to him—could he be deaf?" As she reviewed her list, she felt that she might be being silly, and she hoped the pediatrician would tell her not to worry. Tyron's health checkup went well. He had gained some weight, and everything seemed normal. Dr. Nolan was surprised when Laura burst into tears when she asked if there were any concerns. Laura was also surprised by the intensity of her feelings as she described her fears about her son's behavior. Dr. Nolan listened carefully and jotted down notes into Tyron's file. When Laura had finished, Dr. Nolan shook her head and said, "Well, this is probably all normal, and Tyron is likely just fine, but, Laura, I think we would all feel better if we looked into your concerns a bit further." After an initial screening showed some problems, Dr. Nolan recommended that a full assessment for possible developmental delays be completed with Tyron (See Figure 3.2, Tyron's Information Processing Model.). Laura left feeling both relieved that her concerns had been validated and that something would be done and more worried that something might be wrong with her son. Laura and Michael met with a **multidisciplinary team** to help with the assessment. The results from this assessment showed that Tyron did in fact have some developmental delays, confirming Laura's worst fears. The team also recommended that a follow-up assessment be completed

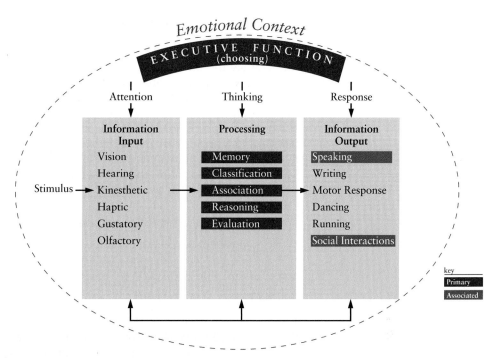

FIGURE 3.2
Tyron's Information Processing Model

when Tyron was 2 years old. The family immediately began working with the multidisciplinary team to develop an **individualized family service plan (IFSP)** to meet Tyron's needs. We will learn more about the multidisciplinary team and the plan they developed for Tyron later in the chapter on page 92.

As we can see from Jennifer and Tyron's stories, the needs for early intervention can vary widely from child to child. The shared theme, however, is that the child and family need additional supports to help them thrive. Later in the chapter we will learn about these supports and how they can be delivered.

Defining Early Intervention

Early intervention consists of sustained and systematic efforts to provide support to the family—as well as caregivers—and to the child in order to promote optimal development for children who have developmental delays and/or disabilities during their early childhood years (Noonan & McCormick, 2006). In some states the definition of "early childhood" extends to children through age 7, and first and second graders are included within this population. In this chapter, however, we focus on children's earliest years—from conception through age 5. Early intervention supports and services may address the needs of the child and the child's family during pregnancy, infancy, and the prekindergarten years (Rous & Hallam, 2006). A critical component of early intervention is strengthening the parents' capacity to meet their child's needs (Campbell, Sawyer, & Muhlenhaupt, 2009; Dunst, 2007; Turnbull & Turnbull, 1997). **Family-centered early intervention** means working to ensure that the parents or caregivers are able to meet the child's needs. This is critical because the parents or caregivers are central to the well-being of the child (Friend, Summers, & Turnbull, 2009; Campbell, Sawyer, & Muhlenhaupt, 2009; Dunst, 2007; Turnbull & Turnbull, 1997).

Center of the Social and Emotional Foundations for Early Learning
http://www.vanderbilt.edu/csefel/

Supporting parents as they learn to care for their newborn and toddler is a critical part of ensuring the child's mental health (Fox et al., 2010; Sopko, 2009). Early responsive relationships that form positive attachments with the primary caregiver are the foundation for the infant and toddler's social and emotional well-being and mental health (CSEFELb, 2010). The non-profit organization Zero to Three defines infant mental health as "the developing capacity of the child from birth to age three to: experience, regulate, and express emotions; form close and secure relationships; and explore the environment and learn all in the context of family community and cultural expectations for young children. Infant mental health is synonymous with healthy social and emotional development." (2009). We will learn more about early mental health and how to support families and children later in the chapter.

The Family-Centered Approach and Cultural Diversity

When it comes to successful early intervention, our current understanding is that the family needs to be placed at the center and the family members' goals and opinions addressed and honored (Parette & Petch-Hogan, 2000; Turnbull & Turnbull, 1997). Gaining the family's trust is essential as professionals work to encourage parents to accept proven practices for their child (Dunst, 2007; Banks, Milagros, & Roof, 2003; Barrere, 2000; Harry, Rueda, & Kalyanpur, 1999). Centering the intervention within the family is essential because the family is fundamental to the development of any child, with or without disabilities (Dunst, 2007; Osofsky, & Thompson, 2000). The key to success is the ability of the parents or caregivers to relate to the child and to provide a responsive, caring environment. Most parents will provide the kind of environment their children need, and if a child is disabled, the parents will seek out professionals and learn desired methods of facilitating growth from them. As professionals, it is our job to make sure that we get to know each family's unique and culturally specific beliefs about their child and what their child needs to thrive.

Cultural responsiveness is essential when working with families (Fowler, Ostrosky, & Yates, 2007; Garcia & Magnuson, 2000). Exploring the following questions is an important part of assessing the appropriateness of services for children and families from a variety of cultural backgrounds:

National Parent Information Network
www.npin.org

1. What is the child's primary language, and how is it used in the home?

2. What are the parents' expectations as to the use of language to communicate? How is language use valued in the home?

3. What are the preferred strategies of learning: verbal, nonverbal, observation, imitation?

4. To what degree is the family acculturated? Do they agree or disagree about cultural values and mores?

5. What goals does the family have for the child?

Teachers may find the Culturally and Linguistically Appropriate Services (CLAS) website helpful for locating culturally and linguistically appropriate instructional material (Corso, Santos, & Roof, 2002). Through effective collaboration, families and professionals can provide optimal support for young children with disabilities and help them thrive.

Culturally and Linguistically
Appropriate Services (CLAS)
http://clas.uiuc.edu

Legislation on Early Intervention

Legislative support for young children with disabilities began in 1968, when Congress passed the Handicapped Children's Early Education Assistance Act

(HCEEAA; Gallagher, 2000). This act set up twenty model programs, including Head Start, across the United States to demonstrate how working with children with disabilities could improve their lives. During the 1970s and 1980s the legal rights of young children with disabilities were addressed in legislation. With the passage of PL 99-457, federal funding was extended to support children with disabilities and their families from birth on (Noonan & McCormick, 2006). You may want to look back at Chapter 2 as you think about the legislation for young children in the context of other laws.

Today, the needs of young children are addressed in two sections of the 2004 Individuals with Disabilities Education Act (IDEA). Infants and toddlers (children from birth to age 2) with disabilities and/or developmental delays are addressed in IDEA, Part C, which encourages states to develop comprehensive, coordinated, multidisciplinary early intervention systems (Council for Exceptional Children, 2007; Guralnick, 2005). Part C also stipulates that early interventions should be provided, to the maximum extent possible, in **natural environments**, or settings that are typical for children who do not have disabilities (Noonan & McCormick, 2006).

Natural environments for young children can include the home, church or temple, parks, playgrounds, grocery stores, child-care centers, and preschools (Campbell, Sawyer, & Muhlenhaupt, 2009). These settings provide an authentic context for learning and practicing the child's targeted skills (e.g. self feeding, pulling-up to walk, vocabulary building) (Stremel & Campbell, 2007). Providing early intervention support within the child's natural environments (e.g. home, neighborhood, or community) is also critical to building strong family partnerships. When interventions are provided in the home, for example, they can become part of the family's daily routines and activities (Trivette & Dunst, 2010; Campbell & Sawyer, 2007). Supporting the family as the family members provide for the child with special needs is essential to family-centered early intervention (Basu, Salisbury, & Thorkildsen, 2010). Seven key principles for practicing within natural environments (see Table 3.1) have been identified by the Office for Special Education Programs Technical Assistance Workgroup on Principles and Practices in Natural Environments (2009).

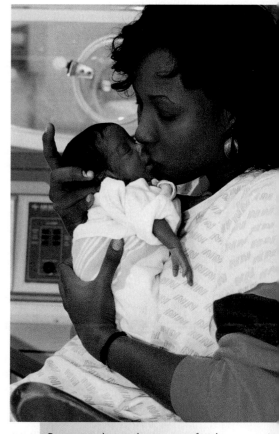

Parents are key to the success of early interventions for the child

(© Annie Griffiths Belt/CORBIS)

 National Early Childhood Technical Assistance Center **http://www.nectac.org/ default.asp**

Children with disabilities age 3 through 5 are addressed in Part B of IDEA, which provides funds for states to ensure that all preschool-age children with disabilities receive special education and related services (Council for Exceptional Children, 2007) The 2004 reauthorization of IDEA further emphasizes the need to provide services to all members of the family, recognizing the importance of the family in the child's development (Council for Exceptional Children, 2007; Cryer & Clifford, 2003). IDEA 2004 requires transition planning across the early years, because services for children from birth through age 2 and for children ages 3 through 5 are addressed in different ways, and thus families often have to navigate complex networks of agencies as their children move across the age span of early childhood (National Center for Learning Disabilities, 2007; Rous & Hallam, 2006). Navigating these complex networks is essential, however, because securing the services and supports needed for the family and child can be critical for a child's optimal development.

The needs of young children are addressed in the Individuals with Disabilities Education Act (IDEA) of 2004.

Early Childhood and RTI

IDEA is also influencing our thinking about how we meet the needs of young children with disabilities and developmental delays in early childhood through the use of response to intervention (RTI) approaches. The philosophy of early

TABLE 3.1
Seven Key Principles for Working in Natural Environments

1. Infants and toddlers learn best through everyday experiences and interactions with familiar people in familiar contexts

Key Concepts	• Learning activities and opportunities must be functional, based on child and family interest and enjoyment • Learning is relationship-based • Learning should provide opportunities to practice and build upon previously mastered skills • Learning occurs through participation in a variety of enjoyable activities

2. All families, with the necessary supports and resources, can enhance children's learning and development

Key Concepts	• All means ALL (income levels, racial and cultural backgrounds, educational levels, skill levels, living with varied levels of stress and resources) • The consistent adults in a child's life have the greatest influence on learning and development—not early intervention (EI) providers • All families have strengths and capabilities that can be used to help their child • All families are resourceful, but all families do not have equal access to resources • Supports (informal and formal) need to build on strengths and reduce stressors so families are able to engage with their children in mutually enjoyable interactions and activities

3. The primary role of the service provider in early intervention is to work with and support the family members and caregivers in a child's life

Key Concepts	• EI providers engage with the adults to enhance confidence and competence in their inherent role as the people who teach and foster the child's development • Families are equal partners in the relationship with service providers • Mutual trust, respect, honesty, and open communication characterize the family-provider relationship

4. The early intervention process, from initial contacts through transition, must be dynamic and individualized to reflect the child's and family members' preferences, learning styles, and cultural beliefs

Key Concepts	• Families are active participants in all aspects of services • Families are the ultimate decision makers in the amount and type of assistance and support they receive • Child and family needs, interests, and skills change; the individual family service plan (IFSP) must be fluid, and revised accordingly • The adults in a child's life each have their own preferred learning styles; interactions must be sensitive and responsive to individuals • Each family's culture, spiritual beliefs and activities, values, and traditions will be different from the service provider's (even if from a seemingly similar culture); service providers should seek to understand, not judge • Family "ways" are more important than provider comfort and beliefs (short of abuse/neglect)

5. IFSP outcomes must be functional and based on children's and families' needs and priorities

Key Concepts	• Functional outcomes improve participation in meaningful activities • Functional outcomes build on natural motivations to learn and do; fit what's important to families; strengthen naturally occurring routines; enhance natural learning opportunities • The family understands that strategies are worth working on because they lead to practical improvements in child and family life • Functional outcomes keep the team focused on what's meaningful to the family in its day-to-day activities

6. The family's priorities, needs, and interests are addressed most appropriately by a primary provider who represents and receives team and community support.	
Key Concepts	• The team can include friends, relatives, and community support people, as well as specialized service providers • Good teaming practices are used • One consistent person needs to understand and keep abreast of the changing circumstances, needs, interests, strengths, and demands in a family's life • The primary provider brings in other services and supports as needed, assuring outcomes, activities, and advice are compatible with family life and won't overwhelm or confuse family members
7. Interventions with young children and family members must be based on explicit principles, validated practices, best available research and relevant laws and regulations.	
Key Concepts	• Practices must be based on and consistent with explicit principles • Providers should be able to provide a rationale for practice decisions • Research is ongoing and informs evolving practices • Practice decisions must be data-based and ongoing evaluation is essential • Practices must fit with relevant laws and regulations • As research and practice evolve, laws and regulations must be amended accordingly

Source: Workgroup on Principles and Practices in Natural Environments (February, 2008) *Seven key principles: looks like/doesn't look like.* OSEP TA Community of Practice-Part C Settings. Work group members: Susan Addision, Betsy Ayankoya, Mary Beth Bruder, Carl Dunst, Larry Edlerman, Andy Gomm, Barbara Hanft, Cori Hill, Joicey Hurth, Grace Kelley, Anne Lucase, Robin McWilliam, Stephanie Moss, Lynda Pletcher, Dathan Rush, M'Lisa Shelden, Mary Steenberg, Judy Swett, Nora Thompson, Julianne Woods, Naomie Younggern.

intervention is central to the RTI approaches being used with school-age children, and we are now seeing adaptations of RTI for preschool children (Coleman, Roth, & West, 2009; Barnett et al., 2006; Coleman, Buysse, & Neitzel, 2006a). RTI models for pre-K focus on universal screening and progress monitoring data to look at the child's needs, on the use of **evidence-based practices** to respond to these needs, and on working with the family to help the child become successful (Hojnoski, Caskie, Gischlar, Key, Barry, & Hughes, 2009; Hojnoski, Gischlar, Missall, 2009; Coleman, Buysse, & Neitzel, 2006b). Later in this chapter, we will see how Tyron's teachers collect and use data on his class participation and his use of words to ask for things in order to help them target support and monitor his progress.

Pre-K RTI approaches that are most compatible with early intervention for preschool children include a focus on providing a high-quality learning environment, an emphasis on providing supports to children as soon as a difficulty emerges rather than waiting for a formal label, tailoring instruction to meet the child's needs, and working with parents to provide the support (Coleman, Roth, & West, 2009; Coleman et al., 2006a). The use of intervening hierarchies, or tiered service delivery, is also compatible with current early childhood approaches (Fox, Carta, Strain, Dunlap, & Hemmeter, 2010; Coleman, Roth, & West, 2009; VanDerHeyden & Snyder, 2006; Fox, Dunlap, Hemmeter, Joseph, & Strain, 2003; Brown, Odom, & Conroy, 2001). Later in the chapter we will look at how early intervention services and support can be provided for young children within the RTI multitiered framework (see page 96).

The age span addressed by early intervention typically includes children from birth through age 5, and, as we saw with Jennifer and Tyron, the need for early intervention can be identified at any point during this time. Some disabilities are recognized very early on—at the birth of the child or even prenatally—whereas other needs do not become apparent until later. For more information on the prenatal identification of possible disabilities, please visit the Education CourseMate website that accompanies this text.

RTI

http://www.rtinetwork.org/
Pre-K

Detecting Potential Problems Shortly After Birth

Can a physician or other professional tell whether an infant has a disability or is at risk for a disabling condition within the first few minutes of the child's birth? When a child is born, the physician administers the first screening test to determine whether the infant has any identifiable problems or abnormalities (Nugent et al., 2007). Screening tests are simple tests that are easy to administer and that separate infants without serious developmental problems from those who have a disability or are suspected of being at risk for a disabling condition (Anastasiow, Frankenburg, & Fandall, 1982). The first infant screening is done in the hospital at one minute and five minutes after birth. It is known as the **Apgar test**, after Virginia Apgar, who developed it in 1952. When a child is born, the physician administers the Apgar test to determine whether the infant has any identifiable problems or abnormalities.

In administering the Apgar test, the physician examines the infant's heart rate, respiratory effort, muscle tone, and general physical state, including skin color. A blue cast to the skin, for example, may indicate breathing or heart problems. Jaundice at birth is indicated by a yellow cast to the skin and eyes. A serious disorder, jaundice reflects the failure of the liver to process adequately because of its immaturity; as a result, bilirubin can accumulate. Many infants with jaundice recover in about a week. In more serious cases, the infant is placed under fluorescent lights for a day or two. This light treatment helps the infant process the bilirubin until the liver can function normally (Batshaw & Perret, 2002).

An infant with a below-average Apgar score at one minute or five minutes after birth is monitored by the physician to determine whether a disability or medical problem exists and whether medical intervention is needed. Lower than average Apgar scores are not necessarily predictive of disabilities, but they do serve to alert the physician that the infant may have special needs.

Because hearing impairments should be detected as soon as possible in order for the child to make desired developmental progress, universal hearing assessment is recommended at birth.

		Score	
Characteristic	0	1	2
Heart rate	Absent	Slow (fewer than 100 beats per minute)	Over 100 beats per minute
Respiratory effort	Absent	Slow or irregular	Good; baby is crying
Muscle tone	Flaccid, limp	Weak, some flexion	Strong, active motion
Color	Blue or pale	Body pink, extremities blue	Completely pink
Reflect irritability	No response	Frown, grimace, or weak cry	Vigorous cries, coughs, sneezes

Note: Letters in Apgar are an acronym for the test's five criteria: A = Appearance, P = Pulse, G = Grimace, A = Activity level, R = Respiratory effort.

FIGURE 3.3
The Apgar Test
Source: From Shaffer/Kipp. Developmental Psychology, 8E. © 2010 Wadsworth, a part of Cengage Learning, Inc. Reproduced by permission. www.cengage.com/permissions.

More recently the newborn behavioral observations (NBO) approach is being introduced to help parents and professionals understand the preferences and vulnerabilities of the newly born infant (Nugent et al., 2007). The NBO approach can be used in a variety of settings and helps sensitize parents to the competencies and needs of their baby. This approach builds on naturalistic observations of the caregiver and infant to help create an optimal support system for both the family and the child (Nugent, Blanchard, & Stewart, 2007). Using the NBO, the clinician partners with the parent to understand the infant and models strategies to help the parent gain confidence and parenting skills (Nugent & Blanchard, 2006). Through a series of observations, an understanding is formed of the infant's unique traits and temperament, and this knowledge allows the parents to better respond to their baby's needs. The patterns revealed by the NBO approach can also help parents and clinicians decide whether further developmental assessments are needed (Levine, 2006). A sample NBO is included in Figure 3.4.

> Using the newborn behavioral observations approach, professionals and parents can learn together how the infant communicates his or her needs.

Newborn Behavioral Observations (NBO) System
RECORDING FORM

Name of infant _____ Gender _____ Date of birth _____

Today's date _____

Gestational age _____ Weight _____ APGAR _____ Parity _____

Type of feeding _____ Setting _____

Others present _____ Practitioner _____

| | OBSERVATION RECORD | | | ANTICIPATORY GUIDANCE |
BEHAVIOR	3	2	1	CHECKLIST*
1. Habituation to light (flashlight)	with ease	with some diffiuculty	with great difficulty	☐ Sleep patterns
2. Habituation to sound (rattle)	with ease	with some diffiuculty	with great difficulty	☐ Sleep protection
3. Muscle tone: legs and arms	strong	fairly strong	very high/very low	☐ Muscle tone
4. Rooting	strong	fairly strong	weak	☐ Feeding cues
5. Sucking	strong	fairly strong	weak	☐ Feeding cues
6. Hand grasp	strong	fairly strong	weak	☐ Touch and contact
7. Shoulder and neck tone (pull-to-sit)	strong	fairly strong	weak	☐ Muscle tone
8. Crawling response	strong	fairly strong	weak	☐ Sleep position and safety

FIGURE 3.4
Sample Newborn Observation Form

(continued)

Source: Newborn Behavioral Observations (NBO) system recording form. Copyright 2007 Children's Hospital Boston, from Understanding Newborn Behavior and Early Relationships: The Newborn Behavioral Observations (NBO) System Handbook, by J. Kevin Nugent, Constance, H. Keefer, Susan Minear, Lise C. Johnson and Yvette Blanchard. Copyright 2007 Paul H. Brookes Publishing Co. All rights reserved.

BEHAVIOR	OBSERVATION RECORD 3	2	1	ANTICIPATORY GUIDANCE CHECKLIST*
9. Response to face and voice	very responsive	moderately responsive	not responsive	☐ Social interaction
10. Visual response (to face)	very responsive	moderately responsive	not responsive	☐ Vision
11. Orientation to voice	very responsive	moderately responsive	not responsive	☐ Hearing
12. Orientation to sound (rattle)	very responsive	moderately responsive	not responsive	☐ Hearing
13. Visual tracking (red ball)	very responsive	moderately responsive	not responsive	☐ Communication cues
14. Crying	very little	occasionally	a lot	☐ Crying and soothability
15. Soothability	soothes easily	soothes with some difficulty	soothes with great difficulty	☐ Self-soothing
16. State regulation	well-organized	somewhat organized	not organized	☐ State regulation
17. Response to stress: color changes, tremors, startles	not stressed	moderately stressed	very stressed	☐ Stimulation threshold
18. Activity level	optimal	moderate	very high/ very low	☐ Needs support

SUMMARY PROFILE AND RECOMMENDATIONS

Strengths _____

_____

_____

_____

Challenges/areas in need of support _____

_____

_____

_____

Additional comments _____

_____

_____

_____

* Use the checklist to specify areas that may require discussion, guidance, or continued follow-up.

Child Find for Children Who Need Early Intervention

Not all disabilities can be recognized prenatally or at birth, and so most states have developed extensive **Child Find** networks to help locate young children who may need additional supports in their early years.

Child Find is a critical component of the law. IDEA 2004 requires that states identify, locate, and evaluate all children from birth to age 21 who are in need of early intervention services or special education (U.S. Department of Education Child Find Project, 2007). Some state Child Find programs involve a continuous process of building public awareness to increase the referral and identification of children and families in need of early intervention supports. Child Find programs include the following elements (U.S. Department of Education Child Find Project, 2007):

The parent and professional work together to observe the infant's strengths and learn how the infant communicates.

(© Bob Daemmrich/The Image Works)

- Definition of target population(s)—how the State defines "development delays" will determine which children are eligible for services

- Public awareness campaigns—outreach to parents, caregivers, and the community is essential to finding children who may need additional support

- Referral and intake processes—each state has a system to manage this process

- Screening and identification procedures—these will vary from state to state

- Eligibility determination criteria—these policies guide decision making about which children will receive services

- Tracking and monitoring services—evaluating the system of service providers is key to ensuring that it is successful

- Interagency coordination—because Child Find services often involve multiple agencies (e.g., Head Start, public schools, child mental health, etc.), it is essential that these organizations work together to address child and families needs

FIGURE 3.5
The Five Critical Domains of Development
Source: a. Jordygraph/Dreamstime b. Brebca/Dreamstime c. Pavla Zakova/Dreamstime d. Noam Armonn/Dreamstime e. Orangeline/Dreamstime

Child Find services are coordinated at the state level with services for infants and toddlers covered under Part C of IDEA and with services for preschool children who require special education covered under Part B. This means that in some states two agencies have responsibilities for services as the child progresses from birth through preschool. Once a child is "found," the next step is to determine whether he or she is eligible for early intervention services.

Eligibility requires that a child receive a comprehensive individual evaluation *and* that this evaluation be conducted in the child's primary language (Council for Exceptional Children, 2007). In addition to the services for young children with identified disabilities, early intervention may be provided for children from birth through age 2 who have developmental delays. **Developmental delays** are defined by each state and can occur in any of the five critical domains: cognitive, communicative, social-emotional, motor, and adaptive development (see Figure 3.5). The purpose of early support for children who may have developmental delays is twofold: first, to optimize early development; and, second, to prevent secondary problems from emerging.

> Developmental delays are defined by each state and can occur in any of the five critical domains: cognitive, communicative, social-emotional, motor, and adaptive development.

 ## Children with Developmental Delays

Infants develop at varying rates. Some sit at 6 months of age, others at 4 months, and still others at 8 months (Lundy, 2003). Some walk early, and some walk late. These variations are the major reason for being cautious when deciding whether an infant or toddler has developmental delays. Further, cultural beliefs about child rearing will influence when children hit certain developmental milestones. Families have differing thoughts about the child's independence versus dependence, and these beliefs will shape expectations for walking, self-feeding, safe boundaries for independent exploration of the environment, and time needed for self-regulation before intervening when the child is distressed (CSEFELb). Understanding and honoring these beliefs is essential for successful family-centered interventions (Trivette & Dunst, 2010; Unger, Tressell, Jones, & Park, 2004).

Delays in development are identified by comparing a child's development in the five key domains (see Fig. 3.5) with the development of other same-age children. The average ages of a task's accomplishment are put together in a **developmental profile.** If, for example, a child does not sit, stand, walk, or speak within the age range at which most children in his or her culture have acquired these skills, a disability or developmental delay is suspected. So what are some typical developmental milestones? Figure 3.6 shows some milestones for typical development that can serve as benchmarks for concerns regarding a child's development.

Although understanding typical developmental milestones is helpful when we are learning about children with special needs, a chart such as the one in Figure 3.6 can make things seem rather simplistic and static. We must remember that the early development of a child is anything but simplistic and is certainly not static.

Children develop through a series of interactions with their family and other caregivers and with their environment (Guralnick, 2005). These constant interactions shape who the child is and who he or she is becoming. When the early care and environment are optimal, the child's development is enhanced. This is the reason why early intervention is family-centered and works to enhance the capacity of the family to meet the child's needs (Dunst, 2007). When stress enters these dynamic relationships in any way, the child's development may be compromised (CSEFELb). Figure 3.7 shows how stressors can affect these relationships, jeopardizing the optimal development of the child (Guralnick, 2005).

> When the family is highly stressed, the caregiving relationship with the child is more likely to be fragile, and the child is more likely to be neglected or abused.

In Figure 3.7, we can see that stressors may include inherent challenges for the child. Remember Jennifer and the challenges she faced as a preterm infant? Jennifer's challenges were not over when she was finally discharged to go home. At home she continued to have difficulty with feeding, and her sleep patterns seemed to be reversed. She was most alert and wakeful at night when things were quiet and seemed to be drowsy and fussy during the day. Jennifer also cried a great deal and it was very difficult to calm her down. Her mother, Sandra, felt like nothing she did for Jennifer seemed to be right,

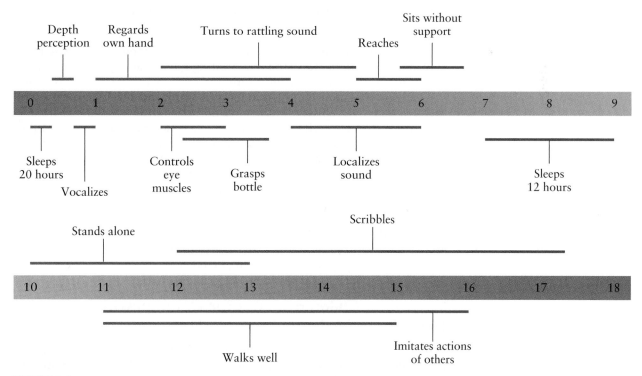

FIGURE 3.6
Typical Developmental Milestones (in Months)
Source: From www.brainconnection.com/topics/?main=fa/child-brain. © Posit Science Corporation. Reprinted by permission.

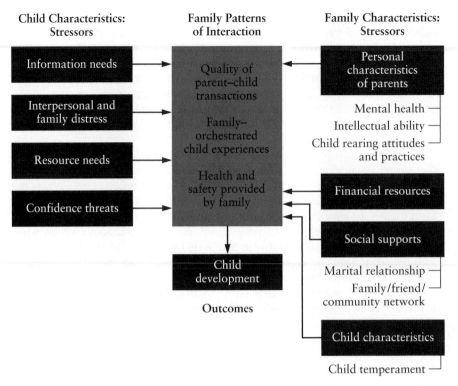

FIGURE 3.7
Potential Stressors That Affect Optimal Early Childhood Development
Source: Guralnick, M. J. (2005). The developmental systems approach to early intervention (pp. 11 Fig. 1.1 and 14 Fig. 1.2). Baltmore: Brookes. Reprinted by permission.

and this growing feeling of incompetence made her wonder whether Jennifer may have come home too soon. The visiting nurse, Tammy, was well versed in the newborn behavioral observation system (Nugent et al., 2007), and she was able to remind Sandra that Jennifer's physical development was still catching up to her full-term birth date and that Jennifer was likely to become overstimulated very easily. Tammy also helped Sandra understand that during Jennifer's earliest weeks of life she was in a busy, noisy, neonatal unit and that this activity actually helped Jennifer sleep. Sandra used this information to begin adapting the environment to gradually allow Jennifer to sleep with less external stimulation. Throughout this process, Sandra's confidence began to grow. For Jennifer and her family, her preterm birth and early complications placed her at risk for developmental delays and added stress to the system, making the early parenting patterns more complicated. Stress can also be added to the system in other ways, through a variety of factors that can put the child at risk for developmental delays.

What Puts Children at Risk for Developmental Delays?

Infants are considered as being at risk for developmental delays because of low birth weight, prematurity, or the presence of serious medical complications (March of Dimes, 2008). Researchers have identified three general categories of conditions that put children at risk: genetic disorders, events occurring during pregnancy and birth, and environmental stressors (Batshaw, 2002).

Genetic Disorders

Genetics is one of the most exciting areas in which new knowledge is increasing our understanding of human development. Chapter 1 discusses emerging genetics knowledge in detail. The Human Genome Project has led the way in helping us understand the role of genes in human variation, including how and why cognitive disabilities occur (Tartaglia, Hansen, & Hagerman, 2007).

The first opportunity to detect potential genetic disorders actually occurs before conception, in **genetic counseling.** A counselor interviews the prospective parents about their families' histories of disabilities and analyzes samples of the clients' blood to determine whether they carry any problematic genes that might be passed on to their children. Individuals may choose to receive this counseling before a child is conceived. A genetic counselor can calculate the probability or odds of a couple's having a child with a disabling condition or a genetic disorder (March of Dimes, 2008), *but the counselor cannot confirm whether the child will be born with or without disabilities.* If the parents have a high probability of having a child with disabilities, the expectant mother may choose to have additional testing to determine whether the child she is carrying may have a disability. Because genetic counseling is relatively new, we have yet to explore all the ethical issues that knowledge of genetic problems can create for individuals and for society.

Events During Pregnancy and Birth

The second broad category of conditions that may put infants at risk are events that occur during pregnancy or during the birth. The health and well-being of the mother are critical to the prenatal development of the infant. Under optimal conditions the fetus will develop normally during the gestation period. If the mother becomes ill, is malnourished, or consumes harmful substances, the health of the fetus can be jeopardized. Prenatal care is critical because it alerts mothers to the potential dangers of certain drugs and diseases (Schonberg & Tifft, 2002). If the mother contracts German measles or chicken pox during pregnancy, for example, this can damage the fetus. Fortunately these diseases can be prevented by currently available vaccines. The most common maternal illness that causes difficulties with fetal development is diabetes. Controlling diabetes during pregnancy can prevent the occurrence of many disabilities (March of Dimes, 2008). Doctors may also limit the use of some over-the-counter and prescription medications during pregnancy to prevent complications for the fetus.

Substance abuse by the mother or father can be linked to behavior problems and disabilities in children. The use of alcohol during pregnancy may result in the infant having **fetal alcohol spectrum disorder** (Brown, Olson, & Croninger, 2010). Children with fetal alcohol spectrum disorder have facial abnormalities, droopy eyelids, and heart defects; are often small in size; and usually have some degree of intellectual disability (Wunsch, Conlon, & Scheidt, 2002). At nine months, delayed social and motor development has been identified for infants whose mothers had one to three drinks per week (Brown, Olson, & Croninger, 2010). Expectant mothers who use heroin may give birth to premature or low-birth-weight infants. These infants may exhibit severe drug withdrawal symptoms and will likely be at risk for disabilities. Heroin and cocaine appear not to cause disabilities in utero, but they often lead to premature births, and the problems associated with low birth weight and prematurity may lead to physical or behavioral irregularities as these children mature (Eichenwald & Stark, 2008). In addition, children whose mothers use drugs tend to be more emotionally and developmentally delayed than the children of nonusers (Krauss et al., 2000). If the expectant mother smokes two packs or more of cigarettes a day, she risks giving birth prematurely or having a low-birth-weight infant. Major national campaigns have been mounted to discourage pregnant women from smoking and using substances that may harm their fetuses (March of Dimes, 2008). In Chapter 6 you will learn more about children with developmental delays.

Environmental Risks

Environmental risk factors, the third area for concerns, are conditions and occurrences in the life of the child and the child's family that interfere with the child's development. Environmental risk factors are the major cause of disabilities for young children. Two well-known environmental factors that interfere with development are poverty and child abuse (March of Dimes, 2008).

Poverty can increase the risk factors for a child in many ways. Women who live in poverty are likely to have insufficient medical care (including prenatal care), poor housing, and inadequate nutrition. In the absence of prenatal care, potential disorders that a physician could detect and treat are missed. Single mothers are at greater risk for living in poverty because they do not have the financial support of the father. If the expectant mother is a teenager living in poverty, she is at great risk of having a premature or low-birth-weight infant, who is in turn at great risk for a variety of disabilities. Young parents who are unaware of the child-rearing strategies that facilitate development face particular risks in rearing low-birth-weight or premature babies because of the complications connected to their infant's needs. Other risks occur when family resources are too limited to provide adequate nutrition, medical care, and housing (Unger, Tressell, Jones, & Park, 2004). These social conditions can, however, be addressed, and preliminary studies have shown that teenage mothers who live in economically advantaged homes, have good prenatal care, and receive emotional support from their spouses or families are more likely to give birth to healthy infants (Anastasiow, 1982; March of Dimes, 2008).

If you think back to Guralnick's system of interactive components that affect the child's development (Figure 3.7), you will remember that a lack of financial resources is one of the major stressors that can jeopardize the family's ability to meet the child's needs. When the family is stressed, the caregiving relationship with the child is more likely to be fragile, and the child is more likely to be neglected or abused (CSEFELa, 2010; Dunlap et al., 2006; Friend, Summers, & Turnbull, 2009).

Many of us may find it hard to understand the existence of child abuse. How can an adult physically harm a baby or a young child, particularly one with disabilities? Yet most of us cannot imagine the stress that parents of children with disabilities face. Imagine a child who cries constantly and is inconsolable. For hours during the night, the parents try everything they can think of to calm him. They walk him, feed him, and bounce him, but nothing works. Throw into the equation a difficult marriage, pressures at work, and no prospect that tomorrow will be any better than today, and you have the potential for child abuse.

As many as three to ten million children are abused or neglected, and 20 percent of these children have diagnosable disorders (Sameroff & Feise, 2000). Research suggests that children with disabilities are abused more often than other children (Cosmos, 2001). Physical punishment is strongly associated with child abuse, and Zigler, Finn-Stevenson, and Hall (2003) report that 60 percent of cases of child abuse evolved from situations in which parents were attempting to discipline their children physically. When

Welcome to Holland

I am often asked to describe the experience of raising a child with a disability—to try to help people who have not shared that unique experience to understand it, to imagine how it would feel. It's like this....

When you're going to have a baby, it's like planning a fabulous vacation trip to Italy. You buy a bunch of guide-books and make your wonderful plans. The Coliseum. Michelangelo's David. The gondolas in Venice. You may even learn some handy phrases in Italian. It's all very exciting.

After months of eager anticipation, the day finally arrives. You pack your bags and off you go. Several hours later the plane lands. The stewardess comes in and says, "Welcome to Holland."

"Holland?" you say. "What do you mean Holland? I signed up for Italy. I'm supposed to be in Italy. All my life I've dreamed of going to Italy."

But there's been a change in the flight plan. They've landed in Holland, and there you must stay.

The important thing is that they haven't taken you to a horrible, disgusting, filthy place, full of pestilence, famine and disease. It's just a different place.

So you must go out and buy new guidebooks. And you must learn a whole new language. And you will meet a whole new group of people you would never have met.

It's just a different place. It's slower-paced than Italy, less flashy than Italy. But after you've been there for a while and you catch your breath, you look around and you begin to notice that Holland has windmills, Holland has tulips. Holland even has Rembrandts.

But everyone you know is busy coming and going from Italy, and they're all bragging about what a wonderful time they had there. And for the rest of your life, you will say "Yes, that's where I was supposed to go. That's what I had planned."

And the pain of that will never, ever, ever go away, because the loss of that dream is a very significant loss.

But if you spend your life mourning the fact that you didn't get to Italy, you may never be free to enjoy the very special, the very lovely things about Holland.

Pivotal Issues

- How can we support parents as they struggle to understand and accept the special needs of their child with exceptionalities?

- What positive things emerge as the family learns how to cope with disappointments?

the circumstances of the family are very stressful, life is a challenge. These environmental risk factors are some of the most difficult stressors for a family to cope with, and they often feel overwhelming and insurmountable. Supporting vulnerable families to help them meet the needs of their child is central to the child's optimal development and mental health (Unger, Tressell, Jones, & Park, 2004).

As we learn more about mental health, we understand how critical the early years are to the child's overall well-being and future success (CSEFELb, 2010). Young children's mental health is critical for school readiness and positive long-term outcomes (Thompson & Raikes, 2007; Dunlap et al., 2006; Kauffman Early Education Exchange, 2002). Because of the critical role mental health plays in children's success, many early childhood programs are implementing programs that target the social and emotional development of young children. One model that is widely used to support social and emotional development of young children is the Pyramid Model (Hemmeter, Fox, Jack, & Broyles 2007). We will learn more about this in the Educational Responses section later in this chapter. Optimal child development is dependent on how several factors come together to create a dynamic system (remember Figure 3.7) that either supports or inhibits children's well-being.

> Optimal child development is dependent on how several factors come together to create a dynamic system that supports the child's well-being.

The National Early Childhood
Technical Assistance Center
www.nectac.org

These factors include the child, the caregiver/family, and the environmental circumstances. Stressors can enter this system at any point and can make the child and family more vulnerable. Because optimal child development must be viewed in light of this system, the supports and services provided to enhance a child's development must address each component of the system. This is why one goal of family-centered early intervention in natural settings is to support the family with knowledge and skills that help them draw on their strengths as caregivers (Campbell, Sawyer, & Muhlenhaupt, 2009; Dunst, 2007). One organization with a 37-year history of providing support to children and families is The National Early Childhood Technical Assistance Center (NECTAC, at the FPG Child Development Institute, University of North Carolina at Chapel Hill), whose mission is: to strengthen service systems to ensure that children with disabilities (birth through 5 years) and their families receive and benefit from high-quality, culturally appropriate, and family-centered supports and services. You may wish to visit the NECTAC website to learn more about how these support systems are organized.

Quality of Early Child Care Services and Developmentally Appropriate Practice

High-quality child care and early intervention classrooms aid cognitive and language development.

As prekindergarten becomes universal and as an increasing number of children enter school earlier, more children with developmental delays and disabilities will gain access to the supports and services they need (Pianta, 2007). Many states have already increased their commitments to early childhood education, and currently 38 states provide some type of publicly funded prekindergarten services (Ritchie, Maxwell, & Clifford, 2007). These services, however, do not reach all children with developmental delays and/or disabilities, and even inclusive child-care settings may not provide the supports and services needed; thus, full and meaningful inclusion has not been accomplished for many children (Grisham-Brown et al., 2005).

Children with disabilities need a program that focuses on all of their developmental needs. Most children with disabilities are, in other ways, like children without disabilities, and they have similar needs (Buysse, Skinner, & Grant, 2001; Guralnick, 2001). This makes inclusion an even more important service option, particularly if the inclusive classroom is high in quality.

Parents Helping Parents
http://www.php.com/

The overall quality of the preschool classroom is clearly linked to successful outcomes for children (Gallagher & Lambert, 2006; Pianta, Howes, Burchinal, Bryant, Clifford, Early, & Barbarin, 2005). Factors typically associated with high quality include low child-to-teacher ratios, high education levels for teachers, positive social interactions, and appropriate academic stimulation. In other words, a high-quality classroom provides a safe and nurturing emotional environment with rich and stimulating opportunities for learning. Research from child-care studies suggests that the curriculum in high-quality programs is associated with cognitive and language gains, as well as gains in social and emotional development (Love et al., 2003). Lower levels of aggression and fewer problem behaviors occur among children in high-quality programs. The curricula of these programs focus on children's self-determination, choice making, and initiative taking (Erwin & Brown, 2003), thereby encouraging them to interact with the environment (people and objects) in appropriate ways.

In this section, we look at how services and supports can be provided to children and their families. Some conditions can be prevented and others remediated, but many can be neither prevented nor remediated entirely. With most disabilities and developmental delays, however, improved outcomes for children can be achieved through carefully planned and implemented intervention programs. The goal of all early intervention supports and services is to help the young child develop to his or her full potential. Ideally, early intervention takes place within an environment that is both inclusive and naturalistic. As noted earlier in this chapter, family centered practices that engage parents and caregivers within the home setting provide support for the child's development using typical activities and routines (Campbell & Sawyer, 2007; Sandall, Hemmeter, Smith, & McLean, 2005; Trivette & Dunst, 2010).

The Individualized Family Services Plan

Finding the right combination of supports and services for each child and his or her family is critical, and this process involves the development of an individualized family service plan (IFSP) (Xu, 2008). The IFSP is similar to the individual education plan (IEP) that is developed for older children (see Chapter 2). Because preschool children with disabilities can be found in different settings (e.g. private child-care centers, Head Start programs, and public prekindergarten classrooms) it can be difficult to tell who is responsible for developing and carrying out the IFSP. A service coordinator is key to helping the family access and navigate the system of support that is available. The service coordinator oversees the development and implementation of the IFSP.

Part C of IDEA requires that an IFSP be developed for each child from birth through 2 years of age who is diagnosed as disabled, developmentally delayed, or at risk for delays. When the child qualifies for early childhood special education services, such as Early Head Start, at 3 years of age, an IEP generally takes the place of the IFSP.

- IDEA, Part C: Legal Requirements of the IFSP

IDEA, Part C, requires that IFSPs be constructed to include the following:

- A statement of the infant's or toddler's present levels of physical development, cognitive development, communication development, social-emotional development, and adaptive development, based on objective criteria

- A statement of the family's resources, priorities, and concerns relating to enhancing the development of the family's infant or toddler with a disability

- A statement of the major outcomes expected to be achieved for the infant or toddler and the family, and the criteria, procedures, and timelines used to determine the degree to which progress toward achieving the outcomes is being made and whether modifications or revisions of the outcomes or services are necessary

- A statement of specific early intervention services necessary to meet the unique needs of the infant or toddler and the family, including the frequency, intensity, and method of delivering services

- A statement of the natural environments in which early intervention services shall appropriately be provided, including a justification of the extent, if any, to which the services will not be provided in a natural environment

- The projected dates for initiation of services and the anticipated duration of the services

- The identification of the service coordinator from the profession most immediately relevant to the infant's/toddler's or family's needs (or who is otherwise qualified to carry out all applicable responsibilities under Part C) who will be responsible for the implementation of the plan and coordination with other agencies and persons

- The steps to be taken to support the transition of the toddler with a disability to preschool or other appropriate services (Council for Exceptional Children, 2007)

The focus on the *family* is an important outgrowth of the findings of early childhood intervention programs: a child with disabilities is a child in a family, and family members may need educational, financial, or emotional support to be able to provide the best setting, support, security, and stimulation to help the child with disabilities or developmental delays achieve his or

Qualification for Services

Tyron has been identified with significant developmental delays with possible autism; the team will reassess Tyron within six months to determine progress and additional needs.

Family's Concerns and Desired Priorities

- Tyron's lack of recognition and greeting Mom when she picks him up from preschool
- Tyron's inability to play and engage with others (adults and other children)
- Inability to use words to communicate needs, to avoid frustrations and "melt downs"
- Mom wants more time with Tyron, feels she is working too much and that this is interfering with her ability to meet Tyron's needs
- Dad is concerned about Tyron's ability to get along with others and play

Child and Family's Strengths

- Tyron is a contented child who can entertain himself for long periods of time
- Both parents enjoy Tyron and are committed to meeting his needs. The family also includes grandparents, aunts, uncles, and cousins who love and support the parents & Tyron

Child's Present Levels of Development

- 12-months health check showed no difficulties with Tyron's vision, hearing, and overall health. Tyron's cognitive abilities also seem to be on target; however, these are more difficult to assess because of delays in communication and social engagement.
- Tyron shows significant delays in his expressive language (i.e., his use of words to express his thoughts, needs, and wants). Tyron's receptive language (his understanding of what others say to him) is difficult to gauge because he does not engage socially with others.
- Tyron's self-help skills seem to be on target; he feeds himself when finger food is prepared, he holds the sippie cup to drink, and he can help with dressing. However, parents say they are usually in a hurry and just dress him themselves.
- Tyron's fine and gross motor skills are not significantly delayed.

Goal/Outcome

1. Tyron will engage in more social-play with parents, family, and other children (increase from baseline of 1 to 4 exchanges per-day as documented by parents and teachers).
2. Tyron will show a 20% increase his use of words to express thoughts, needs, and wants.

FIGURE 3.8
Tyron's Individual Family Service Plan

her potential (Trivette & Dunst, 2010; Xu, 2008; Dunst, 2007; Sandall et al., 2005). The family may need help in locating, obtaining, and implementing the services specified in the IFSP; in fact, the family will need access to a multidisciplinary team of specialists who can help meet the needs of the child. Examples of family service plans can be found on Nebraska's Family Service Planning website. You may wish to visit this site to see how these plans are created.

Nebraska's Individual Family Service Plan
www.ifspweb.org

Collaboration and the Multidisciplinary Team

The law also recognizes that families who have children with disabilities need more than friendly neighbors or relatives to help them. They may need a variety of services from specialists and a service coordinator who can help them locate, obtain, and implement the services specified in the IFSP. Children who qualify for services under IDEA must have been identified, screened, and diagnosed by a multidisciplinary team as having a disability known to be associated with developmental delays or as being at risk for the occurrence of developmental delays. Under the guidance of a service coordinator the term multidisciplinary means that we must draws from the knowledge and skills of more than one professional in working with the family and child. The child may need physical therapy to improve motor function, speech-language therapy to assist control of the muscles involved in speech, and educational programming to support cognitive development. Thus, a multidisciplinary team working in an early intervention program might include a member of each of these professions. The team always includes a parent or guardian as a key member who helps to inform the team of the child's and family's needs and helps to shape the service plan so that it will meet these needs. Individuals who may serve on the multidisciplinary team working with infants and young children with disabilities are listed in Table 3.2. Each team will comprise the specific individuals needed to address the child's unique needs. In most cases the child will receive between one and three services (NEILS Study, 2003). Putting the multidisciplinary team together can be challenging given the variety of child-care settings for young children (e.g., family-based, center-based, Head Start, and public schools), and the role of the service coordinator is critical.

> No one professional can be expected to perform all of the necessary tasks required to support a child with exceptionalities.

Ideally the team works together to gather and review information about the child's and family's needs so that a comprehensive and workable plan can be developed to address these needs (Banks, Milagros, & Roof, 2003). Let's look at how this process worked for Tyron and his family when he was first diagnosed with developmental delays. His teacher, after consultation with Tyron's parents, contacted the state coordinator for Child Find to initiate the formation of the team. (You may want to locate the Child Find services website for your state to see how you could secure support for a child like Tyron if you were his teacher.)

TABLE 3.2
Possible Multidisciplinary Team Members

Parent(s)/guardian(s)	Share knowledge of the child and the family culture/values
Audiologist	Determines hearing abilities
Ophthalmologist	Determines vision abilities
Early childhood special educator	Plans and administers educational services and coordinates special therapies and supports
Physician	Determines whether biological or health problems exist and plans treatment
Nurse	Provides a plan for adequate health care
Occupational therapist	Promotes individual development of self-help skills, play, and autonomy; provides needed therapies
Physical therapist	Enhances motor development and suggests prostheses and positioning strategies; provides needed therapies
Psychologist	Provides a comprehensive document of the child's strengths and weaknesses and helps the family deal with the stress of having a child with disabilities
Social worker	Assists the family in implementing appropriate child-rearing strategies and helps families locate services as needed
Speech and language pathologist	Provides necessary assessment plan for needed therapies and delivers services to facilitate communication skills

You may remember that Tyron's mother, Laura, was the first one to become concerned about his behavior. She was worried that he did not seem as responsive as other children his age that she had seen at the child-care center. Tyron's pediatrician, Dr. Nolan, listened to her and suggested that Tyron have a comprehensive assessment to determine what was going on. This assessment required the involvement of a multidisciplinary team. Tyron's hearing and vision were tested; his motor control, self-help skills, and sensory integration were assessed; and his overall communication and social skills were reviewed. Tyron's parents filled out a lengthy questionnaire, and his teachers completed some observational notes documenting Tyron's behavior under a variety of circumstances. A special education teacher with extensive experience working with children with developmental delays and possible autism observed Tyron at his child-care center and at home. When all of this information had been gathered, the team met to review Tyron's needs. The team confirmed Laura's worries and determined that Tyron was indeed showing some delays; it diagnosed Tyron with developmental delays in communication and social-emotional domains. The team agreed that his progress should be followed closely and monitored

for possible autism spectrum disorders (Boyd, Odom, Humphreys, & Sam, 2010). Identifying Tyron's needs, however, was just the first step for the team. The most important work was yet to come.

Once Tyron's needs had been formally identified, the team's next step was to determine what interventions should be put into place to meet these needs. Because Tyron was only 1½ years old, he still qualified under part C of IDEA for an IFSP. The team worked to create an IFSP that would meet the family's needs, agreeing that Tyron's plan would focus on communication and social skills (see Figure 3.8). Tyron's parents met with a speech-language therapist to learn ways that they could prompt and facilitate Tyron's communications. Tyron would receive support for speech-language three times per week, and his preschool teacher would make sure to focus on language and communication with Tyron during the class activities and routines. Tyron's parents would set up more play times and would encourage his use of words to communicate. The team agreed to monitor Tyron's progress and to reevaluate his needs within six months. Using data to chart progress is critical for decision making (Hojnoski, Gischlar, & Missall, 2009; Luze & Hughes, 2008).

Individual Growth and Development Indicators (IDGIs)
www.igdi.ku.edu

Tyron's progress monitoring chart (Figure 3.9) shows how his teachers collected and used data on his use of words and his participation in class activities. Using the Individual Growth and Development Indicators (IGDIs), the team first established a baseline for

Early childhood programs are essential for kids with special needs.

(Courtesy of Cengage Learning)

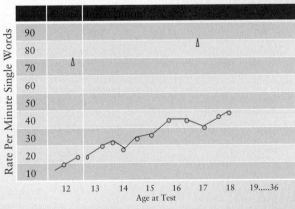

▲ Peer Level of Function

FIGURE 3.9
Tyron's Progress Monitoring chart

Tyron and then worked to support his use of language during daily routines. You can see that while Tyron's use of language increased over time, he still needs more support for this and for his participation in class activities. The progress-monitoring chart will help Tyron's teachers and parents see how things are going when they meet.

Tyron's needs, like those of most children, will best be met through inclusion in his preschool and supports in his home.

▲ Inclusion and Natural Learning Environments

Early intervention laws are designed to promote inclusion in the broadest sense. Inclusion takes many forms and varies as to whether the child spends the total day or a portion of the day with typically developing youngsters, but what is critical is that the child is meaningfully engaged with nondisabled peers (Grisham-Brown, Hemmeter, Pretti-Frontczak, 2005; Casey & McWilliam, 2008). Inclusion is primarily designed to promote social relationships between children with disabilities and those without disabilities and to facilitate optimal access to learning opportunities. The use of **blended practices** that draw from general early childhood and early childhood special education allows the teacher in the inclusive classroom to meet the needs of all of his or her children (Grisham-Brown et al., 2005).

Activity: Discovery table   Date: Week of November 1st

Group: Tyron, Kehla, Alex, & Marcy

Content Area	Broad Outcomes	Individually Targeted Behaviors
Language and literacy	"Read" environmental signs that are part of "map"	Use symbols to communicate wants and needs (Tyron)
Mathematics	Sequence objects/materials in sand	Sequence events in day (discovery table comes after breakfast) (Kehla)
Science	Investigate basic concepts (properties of objects/materials)	Show knowledge of object use (cup is for pouring) (Alex)
Social studies	Use symbols to mark locations on a "map"	Use symbols to communicate wants and needs (Tyron)
Approach to learning	Attempt more than one solution to solve a problem	Engage and attend to activity (Marcy)

FIGURE 3.10
Planning to Meet Individual Student Needs by Embedding Specific Goals Within Class Activities
Source: Grisham-Brown, J., Hemmeter, M. L., & Pretti-Frontczak, K. (2005). *Blended practices for teaching young children in inclusive settings* (p. 160). Baltimore: Brookes. Reprinted by permission.

Figure 3.10 shows how teachers plan to meet the needs of their children by embedding specific goals within the classroom activities. In this case, we see that the teacher is focusing on helping Tyron—who is now almost 4 years old—develop a variety of communication strategies. She is helping him use symbols to express his thoughts and will also be prompting Tyron with words. The use of **embedded instruction** (i.e. the use of a child's daily activities to teach and reinforce key skills) helps us meet the needs of children with disabilities in the context of the inclusive classroom. Activity-based, embedded approaches are particularly useful in promoting and enhancing young children's social competence (Squires & Bricker, 2007).

RTI approaches for preschool children use a three-tiered framework for meeting needs. Each tier is described in Table 3.3. As the needs of children increase and/or become more complex, the responses made to meet these needs must become more explicit and more intense.

TABLE 3.3
Levels of Support Provided in Tiers I, II, & III Within an RTI Framework

	Definition	Focus	Goals	Roles of Parents and Professionals	Assessment Strategies
Universal **Tier I:** Effective core curriculum and intentional teaching	*Curriculum and instruction* that is focused on all domains of learning and development, and is guided by observation and assessment	*All* children need a supportive and enriched learning experience	Provide **high-quality early-childhood instruction** to meet the academic and behavioral needs of all children in the classroom	*Classroom teachers and staff* plan and implement core curriculum and instruction; collaborating and communicating with families	Universal screening *three times each year* (e.g., fall, winter, spring)
Targeted **Tier II:** Group and embedded instruction	*Explicit instruction*: content-specific curricula (e.g., math, literacy, phonic awareness) and instructional approaches (dialogic reading) **Embedded instruction:** environmental arrangement, curricular modifications, peer support	*Some* children identified on the basis of universal and periodic screening need additional support to achieve success	Provide **targeted instruction** through additional supports and opportunities to practice skills within small groups, or as part of daily routines and for additional enrichment for learning	*Specialists* assist **teachers**; *parents* receive progress reports and engage in a collaborative problem-solving process with early childhood staff	Progress monitoring to ensure adequate progress and learning *every 8–10 weeks*
Intensive **Tier III:** Intensive and individualized instruction	*Individualized instructional strategies:* prompting, modeling, physical assistance, giving a directive and waiting for a response, combined with *explicit and embedded approaches*	A *few* children need additional intensive support or enrichment to achieve success	Provide **intensive instruction** through individualized instructional strategies to support or enrich learning	*Expanded team of professionals and parents* develop more intensive plans for individual children and make decisions about referral for further evaluation; parents receive more frequent reports and engage in the collaborative problem-solving process with teachers and other professionals	Progress monitoring to ensure adequate process and learning *every 4–6 weeks* **Referral** for further evaluation if needed

Within the Universal support level, Tier I, high-quality learning environments are in place; universal screening is done to look at all children's needs; and periodic progress monitoring is used to see how each child is doing. When a child is not thriving within this environment, he or she may need more support to help him or her learn.

At the Targeted support level, Tier II, we begin to see teachers using more embedded activities, such as those for Tyron, and more explicit instruction. In Tyron's case, the speech-language teacher has suggested a variety of activities that can be done within the day to promote communication and enhance Tyron's learning. One activity, called "turn taking," is being used during story time. The teacher gives four children two cards each. Each child's cards are a different color. The teacher reads a story and prompts the children to take turns with their comments. After each child has talked, he or she places one of his or her cards in the center. The child must then wait until at least two other children have taken their turn to talk and have placed their cards in the center before he or she can talk again. With Tyron, the teacher also prompts him with a specific question about the story.

Because Tyron has significant language delays, he also receives services at the Intensive level, Tier III. The speech-language therapist works with Tyron three times per week. Sometimes she works with a small group of children in Tyron's class, sometimes she models strategies to enhance communication during daily routines, and sometimes she provides intensive individualized activities. Tyron's parents have also been given strategies to enhance his communication in the home and other naturalistic environments.

Tiered approaches to supports are also used when the primary need of the child falls within the area of behavior.

> The Pyramid Model at Vanderbilt University
> **http://www.vanderbilt.edu/csefel/**

Behavioral Support Models for Inclusive Environments

The Pyramid Model, a multitiered approach to supports that aligns with an RTI framework, helps teachers establish a positive nurturing environment for all children while providing additional support for any child whose behaviors continue to be challenging (Fox et al., 2003, 2010). A nurturing environment that fosters positive relationships combined with classroom practices that minimize or prevent the need for disruptive behaviors (i.e., children feel safe and know that their needs will be attended to and adult–child relationships support and nurture prosocial interactions) is the foundation for all children (Hemmeter, Fox, Jack, & Broyles, 2007). When children need additional support to overcome challenging behavior, teachers and parents work together to create a **behavioral support plan** (Squired & Bricker, 2007). The key to behavioral support planning is understanding the ABCs of a child's behavior: "A," the **A**ntecedent (e.g., event or circumstance) that triggers the child's difficult behavior; "B," the **B**ehavior that is causing problems; and "C," the **C**onsequences of the behavior for the child, the adults, and others who are impacted by the behavior (Squires & Bricker, 2007).

Through an analysis of the child's behavior, the adults look at the antecedents or trigger(s) for the challenging behavior; what, when, and how the behavior is initiated (the context) and an examination of the behavior itself; the purpose for the behavior; what the child is trying to achieve or communicate; what the child needs; why the child is acting in this way. Finally, the adults look at the consequences of the child's behavior. They identify strategies to minimize the triggers (e.g., plan for transitions and give five-minute warnings to children so that they know what is coming next) and to teach replacement behaviors so that children have positive ways to express their needs (e.g., asking with words when they want a toy instead of grabbing it). Through the use of this careful planning, teachers and parents can structure the environment to minimize challenging behavior and promote positive interactions.

Because of Tyron's language delays, he does not use words to ask for toys and things that he wants and often just grabs these away from other children. As you can imagine, this gets him into difficulty when other children become upset! Tyron's teachers and parents worked together to examine this behavior so they could plan to support Tyron as he learns to use words to ask for what he needs and wants). This level of support falls within Tier III of RTI.   **RTI**

Naturalistic Environments

IDEA 2004 encourages educating young children in natural environments—that is, settings that are normal for children of that age who do not have disabilities (Campbell, Sawyer, & Muhlenhaupt, 2009; Carta & Kong, 2007; Noonan & McCormick, 2006). The intent is to facilitate learning through naturally occurring experiences in daily activities and routines (mealtimes, out-of-home shopping, and so on). The early childhood special educator provides parents with strategies to maximize their child's learning in their daily activities and routines and helps to identify learning opportunities in the home and community (Trivette & Dunst, 2010; Jung, 2003; Sandall & Ostrosky, 2000).

Therapists, teachers, and other interventionists often provide services in the home for a number of reasons (Campbell & Sawyer, 2007). A common belief among many educators is that education should take place in the setting in which the skills will be used; hence, the home is the functional setting for very young children. Infants spend most of their time sleeping, and it is not practical to take them to an early intervention program that offers educational and therapeutic practice. In addition, parents who are going through the process of accepting their child's disability may be most comfortable in their own home setting (Trivette & Dunst, 2007; Basu, Salisbury, & Thorkildsen, 2010). In some rural areas, early childhood special education centers may be a long way from the home, and parents would spend much valuable time traveling instead of interacting with and caring for their child. Furthermore, the caregivers' primary responsibility is to establish in-the-home routines that will facilitate the child's development.

The first person to visit the home may be a home health nurse who works with the caregivers to help them understand their child's disability, child development in general, and parenting practices. The home health nurse may also help the parents coordinate other therapies and may help to identify a curriculum for the child and family (Nugent & Blanchard, 2006). In the process, the home visitor provides emotional support for and contact with the family. Earlier in the chapter we described the home health nurse, Tammy, who visited Sandra and Tony, Jennifer's parents, during her first few months at home. You might want to look back at this section and think about the critical supports that were provided to help Sandra and Tony meet Jennifer's needs. The home visitor can also act as a service coordinator and help the parents apply for additional services for the child or the family.

Some additional services may be provided by occupational or physical therapists, who visit the home once or twice a week to teach the caregivers to position, carry, sit, bathe, feed, and generally care for the child. Promoting a child's competence through family routines and community activities also facilitates his or her movement into child-care programs (Bruder & Dunst, 2000; Dunst, 2007). The teacher can facilitate learning through the embedded material in the routine activities of the classroom, such as snack time, bathroom use, entering, and leaving (Carta & Kong, 2007; Kaiser & Hancock, 2003; McWilliam & Casey, 2008).

Importance of Learning Through Play

We have known for some time that the natural manner in which all children learn is through play (DiCarlo & Vagianos, 2009; Lerner, 1986). It is particularly crucial for young children, who are innately curious, to look at objects, manipulate (for example, shake or rattle) them to see what they will do, and then play with them. Play is used in most early childhood programs (Buchanan & Cooney, 2000; Linder, 1993). Play has long been known to involve children's thinking, their motivation, and their socioemotional development. Many young children with disabilities will tend to spend time observing rather than interacting (McWilliam & Casey, 2008). They engage in more solitary or isolated play, which is functional and on a low sensory level, rather than in higher-level dramatic or constructive play (Kim et al., 2003). In encouraging higher-level learning, the importance of toys and play activities cannot be overemphasized.

> Play is how children interact and learn about their environments.

Early studies have concluded that children with disabilities tend to be less active (more passive) and less curious about the world around them; they have fewer coping skills with which to respond to environmental demands; therefore, an interventionist may have to teach a child with disabilities how to play so the child can use play to learn (Anastasiow, 1996; Field, 1989; Zeitlin & Williamson, 1994). Many positive social outcomes result from providing children with toys, allowing them to choose toys, and encouraging them to play with other children, with or without disabilities (Erwin & Brown, 2003). Engaging children through play enhances their interactions with each other and promotes communication (McWilliam & Casey, 2008).

Higher-level social play can be encouraged by providing dress-up clothes, a housekeeping corner, blocks, and puppets, as well as encouraging group block play. The National Parent Network on Disabilities catalog has toys that have been specifically adapted for children with disabilities. A high-quality learning environment will provide plenty of developmentally appropriate experiences for the child.

What is clear is that most effective programs are child centered, include developmentally appropriate practices, and are intensive in nature (Halpern, 2000). Two useful scales have been used to assess quality care: the Infant/Toddler Environmental Rating Scale (for birth through age 5; Harms & Clifford, 1980) and the Early Childhood Environmental Rating Scale (ECERS) (Harms, Cryer, & Clifford, 1990). These scales assess the appropriateness of classroom practices, the quality of teacher-child interactions, and the general classroom environment.

High-quality child care and early intervention classrooms result in positive cognitive and language development (Burchinal, Peisner-Feinberg, Pianta, & Howes, 2002; Burchinal et al., 2000; Love et al., 2003). Evidence indicates that children who enter a well-planned, intensively structured program during the first five years of life and stay in that program for a long period of time make the greatest gains and suffer the least loss (Guralnick, 1998). High-quality child care draws on what we consider to be developmentally appropriate practices.

Children learn through play and develop through interactions with their environment.

(© Bob Daemmrich/The Image Works Need)

Concern over the education of young children led the National Association for the Education of Young Children (NAEYC) to publish guidelines for **developmentally appropriate practice (DAP)** (NAEYC, 2009). Developmentally appropriate practices meet the child where he or she is, responding to the child's needs with appropriate supports and enhancements so that the he or she can thrive (NAEYC, 2009). This means that teachers must get to know each child so that meaningful learning experiences can be planned that are both challenging and achievable. The use of multiple forms of data is critical to getting to know the child and planning to meet the child's needs (Hojnoski et al., 2009). All five of the developmental domains must be considered in planning for the child's needs.

Although special educators agree with the goals of DAP, their list of suggested practices includes more teacher-directed suggestions. For example, the activity-based intervention program (Bricker & Cripes, 1992; Carta & Kong, 2007), though consistent with the goals of DAP, looks for opportunities to embed the teaching of specific skills that the child has not mastered (Grisham-Brown et al., 2005). The major difference between the approaches resides in how one engages the child (McWilliam & Casey, 2008). Child engagement is defined as the amount of time the child spends interacting within the environment in a way that is developmentally and contextually appropriate (McWilliam & Bailey, 1992; McWilliam & Casey, 2008). Special educators recognize that children with disabilities do not always readily engage and often have to be taught to do so (Casey & McWilliam, 2007). Figure 3.11 shows a classroom planning matrix designed to increase children's engagement in activities. In this you will note that the teacher is targeting Tyron's engagement during several of the class activities to provide him with additional supports. All of these supports are part of Tier II, targeted supports within RTI.

RTI

Planning consideration	Arrival	Circle/Story	Art	Snack	Outside	Centers	Free Play	Toileting	Dance/Music	Dress-up	Sand and Water	Transition
Materials accessible?	*	*	*			*	*				*	
Which child?	Tyron	Tyron	Jane		Tyron	Tyron	Tyron					Jane
Incidental teaching?	*		*	*	*	*	*		*		*	
Which child?	Tyron		Jane	Tyron	David	Tyron	Leon		Jane		Tyron	
Interesting activity?		*			*	*			*			
Which child?		Tyron			Tyron	Jane			Leon			
Challenge?		*				*			*		*	
Which child?		Leon			David				Jane		David	
Address persistence?						*	*	*			*	
Which child?						Jane	Leon	David			Jane	
Obvious goal?			*			*				*		*
Which child?			Jane			Tyron				David		Jane

FIGURE 3.11
Activity Planning for Encouraging Engagement
Source: McWilliam, R.A. (2005). *Activity Planning Matrix for Encouraging Engagement (APMEE).* Center for Child Development, Vanderbilt University Medical Center, Nashville, TN.

 ## Assistive Technology for Young Children

Assistive technology (AT) includes any item or device that helps the child participate more fully and function more independently within the environment (Mistrett, Ruffino, Lane, Robinson, Reed, & Milbourne, 2006). Often we think of computers when we hear "technology," and while computers may be one aspect of assistive technology, there are many other forms that AT can take—ranging from low-tech to high-tech (Bausch, Ault, & Hasselbring, 2006). The following are various forms of AT:

- Low-tech AT items can include nonelectronic devices like a specialized spoon grip and cup to help a child with self feeding or story boards with pictures and words to help a child learn key concepts for early literacy.

- Medium-tech AT options may include easy-to-operate mechanical devices like switch-operated toys and manual wheel chairs.

- High-tech supports can be very sophisticated electronic devices such as voice recognition programs and communication supports.

Finding the right level of AT support for each child is important—especially given the cost associated with many high-tech devices. Families and teachers work together to analyze which tasks and skills the child needs help with, and select an appropriate support device to meet the child's level of functioning and needs (Castellani & Warger, 2009). As part of Tyron's support for communication, the speech pathologist uses pictures with words on them to help him express what he wants and needs in the classroom. His parents also use these to support his communication at home. These picture boards are an example of low-tech assistive technology that can support a child's communication.

 # Navigating Transitions in Early Childhood

Navigating the change of service providers for early intervention may be a daunting task for families as they work to maintain supports for their child (Rous & Hallam, 2006). During the early years families may need to shift service providers three or four times as their child moves from hospital to early intervention to preschool and eventually to kindergarten (Rosenkoetter, Hains, & Fowler, 1994; Rous, Myers, & Stricklin, 2007). Transitions are a time of change, and even at their best they can be stressful (Pianta, Cox, & Snow, 2007). For a family with a child who has disabilities, this stress is likely to be greatly intensified, as their fears about their child's well-being may make changes even more worrisome (Rous & Hallam, 2006). IDEA requires the development of a transition plan to support families during these changes and to ensure that children receive uninterrupted services as they move through their early years (Rous & Hallam, 2006).

Remember when Jennifer (the preterm infant presented earlier in the chapter) was finally ready to go home from the hospital? After weeks of worry, her parents, Sandra and Tony, had mixed feelings about finally taking Jennifer home. They worried that they would be unable to meet her needs and keep her safe. The first phase of intervention, the initial medical support, was ending, and the second phase started with home visits and home-based support. This support was provided through the state's Part C coordinator (remember that in IDEA, Part C is the section of the law that covers children from birth through age 2). This first transition was successful, and over the first two years of Jennifer's life, Sandra and Tony learned to trust their home-health nurse and the members of the multidisciplinary team they worked with as they struggled to meet Jennifer's needs. They were very comfortable with the family service plan that had guided the support they had received. So their concerns were natural when Jennifer was about to turn 3 and they had to change her services. Fortunately, a plan was developed to help create a smooth transition from Part C to Part B services (for preschool children).

Under Part B, Jennifer qualified for an IEP because she was still showing developmental delays in motor functioning and cognitive abilities. The multidisciplinary team recommended continued physical and occupational therapies and helped the family identify the inclusion prekindergarten programs close to their home. Although kindergarten is a long way off for Jennifer, her parents are already thinking about this fourth transition.

The transition to formal schooling in kindergarten is recognized as a landmark event by millions of families across the country (Pianta, Cox, & Snow, 2007; NCLD, 2007). This normal developmental milestone may be more difficult for children with disabilities and their families. A smooth transition depends on several factors coming together. Moving from early child care to kindergarten is a critical step for young children, and carefully formulated transition plans can facilitate their adjustment and success in school (Pianta & Kraft-Sayre, 2003). Successful transition requires communication among the preschool teacher, the parents, and the kindergarten teacher, preferably before the child enters the class. It should be a collaborative process in which past experiences are linked to future goals.

The readiness of the child, as discussed earlier, is critical, but the readiness of the school to receive the child is just as important (Pianta & Kraft-Sayre, 2003). School strategies

▶❙❙ TeachSource VIDEO CONNECTION

Best Practices for Assistive Technology

Visit the Education CourseMate website to access this ABC News video. Jamie uses a variety of assistive technology supports to help her learn and communicate. As you watch the video, think about the following questions: What kinds of low- and high-tech supports does Jamie use, and how does each help her learn and communicate? How does the use of assistive technologies impact the teacher, the other children, and the curriculum being taught?

What would be some examples of assistive technologies you might use to help Jamie learn about one-to-one correspondence in math (e.g., five children get one cookie; how many cookies will you need)?

Transitions are a time of change and can be stressful to a child and family.

▶❙❙ TeachSource VIDEO CONNECTION

Preschool IEP and Transition Meeting

Visit the Education CourseMate website to watch this ABC News video. Mark is getting ready to make the big move from preschool to kindergarten! His teachers and parents are meeting to look at his needs and plan for a smooth transition. As you watch the video, think about the following questions: How did Mark's teacher, Ann, set a positive tone for the meeting and why is this so important? What questions might Ann ask of Mark's parents to make sure that their concerns are addressed and that their ideas are incorporated into the planning?

This was a multidisciplinary team meeting; who was involved and what roles did they fulfill in helping to plan for Mark's needs?

that can facilitate this transition include sending letters home to parents, holding open-house visits, calling parents, and making home visits (Pianta & Cox, 2002). One difficulty is that families who need support during this transition (those who live in poverty, those who reside in urban and rural communities, and those who have children with disabilities) may in fact receive fewer services (Rosenkoetter, Whaley, Hains, & Pierce, 2001). Transition planning for children with disabilities who are receiving early intervention is essential. These children and their families should have a transition plan that is developed and implemented by a team (Pianta, Cox, Early, & Taylor, 1999; Rous & Hallam, 2006). Transition planning for a smooth entry into school is key to ensuring that gains made by early intervention are not lost.

moral dilemma
Using Genetic Counseling

Shelia and Shea had been married for two years and were beginning to talk about starting a family. Although they wanted to have children, both of them were concerned that they might have some complications. Shea's family had a history of sickle cell anemia. They wondered whether they might pass this on to their own children. They decided to go for genetic counseling. During the session, the counselor asked for family histories and then reviewed the results from the blood work they had completed prior to the visit. The counselor explained that the information she could share with them could *not* tell them whether they would have a child with disabilities and that it could only give them an idea about the likelihood of problems. The counselor told Shelia and Shea that they both had "sickle cell trait," which meant that they were carriers of the sickle cell gene. Because they both carried the problematic gene, the counselor told them they had a 25 percent chance of having a child with sickle cell anemia. Shea asked about the likelihood of his sister carrying the sickle cell gene, because he knew that she and her husband were also thinking about having children. The counselor said that it was possible that Shea's sister also carried the gene. Shelia and Shea had been given a lot to think about, but the first thing Shea wanted to do when they got home was to call his sister and share their news with her. Shelia was not certain that he should let his sister know that she might also carry the sickle cell gene.

Should Shea inform his sister that she might be a carrier? What problems could having this information create for her (personal, social, health insurance, and so forth)? Is it better to know or not to know? If Shea decides to tell his sister, what should he say?

Go to the Education CourseMate website to share your thoughts on this dilemma and email your responses to your instructor.

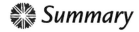 Summary

▶ Early intervention is now widely accepted as essential to improving outcomes for children with disabilities and developmental delays.

▶ Early intervention consists of sustained and systemic efforts to provide support to the family, caregivers, and child to promote optimal development for the child.

▶ Early intervention may begin before pregnancy with the mother-to-be receiving appropriate medical care and support.

▶ At birth, physicians will check for the infant's overall functioning and health and will initiate any supports needed based on the results of the initial tests.

▶ Family-centered approaches are key to the success of early interventions because the parent or caregiver is critical to the child's well-being.

▶ Supports and services for children and families must address all components of the child's needs and must be culturally responsive to the families.

▶ Child Find is a critical component of the early intervention system as it helps to locate children and families who need support.

▶ A multidisciplinary team helps to identify the child's needs and develops a plan to respond to these needs: an IFSP for children from birth to 3 years; an IEP for children age 3 and older.

▶ Inclusion and naturalistic environments are key components of how and where early intervention services are provided.

▶ The RTI approach for young children focused on the use of data to plan developmental appropriate supports and enhancements to ensure that learning is both challenging and achievable.

▶ Supporting children and families during transitions is essential to ensuring a smooth delivery of supports and services.

Future Challenges

1 *What will be the impact of universal child and maternal health care?*

Primary prevention through prenatal care is not available to all expectant mothers, particularly those who live in poverty. However, in the fall of 2010, the Obama administration's Affordable Care Act directs all health plans, including Medicaid, to provide prenatal screening and counseling for expectant mothers. But even when it is available, some individuals do not take advantage of it. If prenatal care were provided universally, it could markedly reduce the number of premature and low-birthweight children who are at risk for disabilities. Is the new policy enough to ensure the most healthy pregnancies possible? What strategies would we need to employ to ensure access to these services for all mothers-to-be?

2 *How can we provide appropriate supports and services for families of children with disabilities?*

Having a child with disabilities has a profound impact on the family system. The additional stress, need for resources, and time spent in caregiving can all take a toll on the family's ability to meet the needs of the child. How can we support the family to help them be successful? What are the health care/insurance, social support, and education needs of families? How can these be provided in ways that address families' cultural values?

3 *How can we increase the quality of early child care in the United States?*
Increasing numbers of children are receiving early child care, and a number of these children require early intervention supports and services. How can we ensure that all children have access to high-quality child care and early intervention if they need additional supports? How would universal prekindergarten affect the well-being of children?

Key Terms

Apgar test p. 80

behavioral support plan p. 97

blended practices p. 95

Child Find p. 83

developmental delays p. 84

developmental profile p. 84

developmentally appropriate practice (DAP) p. 99

early intervention p. 69

embedded instruction p. 96

evidence-based practice p. 79

family-centered early intervention p. 75

fetal alcohol spectrum disorder p. 87

genetic counseling p. 87

individualized family service plan (IFSP) p. 75

multidisciplinary team p. 75

natural environments p. 77

Resources

References of Special Interest

Odom, S. L., Horner, R. H., Snell, M. E., & Blancher, J. (Eds.) (2007). *Handbook of developmental disabilities.* New York: Guilford Press. This is a comprehensive reference on research related to children with disabilities. It reviews our current understanding of the field of study for developmental disabilities: the health, neuroscience and genetics, and practice related to meeting the needs of children and families.

Krajicek, M., Steinke, T., Hertzdeng, D., Anastasiow, N., & Skandel, S. (Eds.) (2003). *Handbook for the care of infants and toddlers with disabilities and chronic conditions; Instructor's guide for the handbook for the care of infants and toddlers with disabilities and chronic conditions.* Austin, TX: PRO-ED. These materials cover a wide range of disabilities, providing information about conditions as well as techniques (such as positioning) for treating them. They were prepared under the leadership of Marilyn Krajicek, Ed.D., R.N., at the University of Colorado School of Nursing.

Guralnick, M. (Ed.) (2005). *The developmental systems approach to early intervention.* Baltimore: Brookes. The systems approach to early intervention describes supports and services for young children and their families. As early intervention becomes more univer-

sally available, the quality and coordination of services remain critical challenges. This book offers comprehensive thinking about how we can meet these challenges.

Sandall, S., Hemmeter, M. L, Smith, B. J., & McLean, M. E. (2005). *DEC recommended practices: A comprehensive guide for practical application in early intervention/early childhood special education.* Missoula, MT: Council for Exceptional Children, Division for Early Childhood. The Division for Early Childhood of the Council for Exceptional Children gives clear guidelines for best practices for young children with disabilities. This book is an important handbook for all those who work with young children and their families.

Technical Assistance Center on Social and Emotional Intervention (2007). *Practical Strategies for Teaching Social Emotional Skills-DVD.* Can be found at www.challengingbehavior.org. This 28-minute DVD highlights many practical strategies and approaches that early childhood personnel and families can use to systematically target social emotional supports that build young children's skills in making friends, problem solving, asking for help, talking about feelings, and managing their emotions. The strategies rely on a three-stage approach to supporting young children's social-emotional development by (1) introducing and practicing a skill, (2) building fluency and competency with a skill, and (3) ensuring there is maintenance of a skill.

Young Exceptional Children Monograph Series. Missoula, MT: Council for Exceptional Children, Division for Early Childhood. These topical monographs cover all the essential areas related to services for young children with disabilities. These are essential references for practitioners and families.

Journals

Journal of Early Intervention
www.dec-sped.org.

Young Exceptional Children
www.dec-sped.org.

Early Developments
www.fpg.unc.edu

Professional Organizations

FPG Child Development Institute
www.fpg.unc.edu

Center for Response to Intervention in Early Childhood
www.crtiec.org

The Beach Center on Disability
www.beachcenter.org

Division for Early Childhood of the Council for Exceptional Children
www.dec-sped.org

March of Dimes Resource Center Birth Defects Foundation
www.modimes.org

National Center for Early Development and Learning (NCEDL)
www.fpg.unc.edu/ncedl/

National Information Center for Children and Youth with Disabilities
www.nichcy.org

Parents Helping Parents Resource Center
www.php.com

Head Start
www.nhsa.org

 Visit the Education CourseMate website for additional TeachSource Video Cases, information about CEC standards, study tools, and much more.

Children with Learning Disabilities

Focus Questions

▶ What is the history of the learning disabilities field?

▶ What are some characteristics of children with learning disabilities?

▶ How are learning disabilities, dyslexia, and attention deficits defined?

▶ What are some causes of learning disabilities?

▶ Why is recognizing early indications of a learning disability so important?

▶ What challenges do we face in working to identify appropriately students whose primary language is not English?

▶ How is RTI changing the field of learning disabilities?

▶ How does the information processing model help us understand learning disabilities?

▶ What teaching and learning strategies work well for students with learning disabilities?

▶ What technology is available to support academic learning?

▶ How does a child with learning disabilities impact the family?

▶ What kind of supports will students with learning disabilities need to be successful in college, in the work place, and in adult life?

David Roth/Getty Images

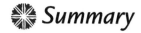 **Summary**

▶ Early intervention is now widely accepted as essential to improving outcomes for children with disabilities and developmental delays.

▶ Early intervention consists of sustained and systemic efforts to provide support to the family, caregivers, and child to promote optimal development for the child.

▶ Early intervention may begin before pregnancy with the mother-to-be receiving appropriate medical care and support.

▶ At birth, physicians will check for the infant's overall functioning and health and will initiate any supports needed based on the results of the initial tests.

▶ Family-centered approaches are key to the success of early interventions because the parent or caregiver is critical to the child's well-being.

▶ Supports and services for children and families must address all components of the child's needs and must be culturally responsive to the families.

▶ Child Find is a critical component of the early intervention system as it helps to locate children and families who need support.

▶ A multidisciplinary team helps to identify the child's needs and develops a plan to respond to these needs: an IFSP for children from birth to 3 years; an IEP for children age 3 and older.

▶ Inclusion and naturalistic environments are key components of how and where early intervention services are provided.

▶ The RTI approach for young children focused on the use of data to plan developmental appropriate supports and enhancements to ensure that learning is both challenging and achievable.

▶ Supporting children and families during transitions is essential to ensuring a smooth delivery of supports and services.

Future Challenges

1 *What will be the impact of universal child and maternal health care?*

Primary prevention through prenatal care is not available to all expectant mothers, particularly those who live in poverty. However, in the fall of 2010, the Obama administration's Affordable Care Act directs all health plans, including Medicaid, to provide prenatal screening and counseling for expectant mothers. But even when it is available, some individuals do not take advantage of it. If prenatal care were provided universally, it could markedly reduce the number of premature and low-birthweight children who are at risk for disabilities. Is the new policy enough to ensure the most healthy pregnancies possible? What strategies would we need to employ to ensure access to these services for all mothers-to-be?

2 *How can we provide appropriate supports and services for families of children with disabilities?*

Having a child with disabilities has a profound impact on the family system. The additional stress, need for resources, and time spent in caregiving can all take a toll on the family's ability to meet the needs of the child. How can we support the family to help them be successful? What are the health care/insurance, social support, and education needs of families? How can these be provided in ways that address families' cultural values?

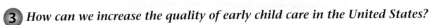 **How can we increase the quality of early child care in the United States?**

Increasing numbers of children are receiving early child care, and a number of these children require early intervention supports and services. How can we ensure that all children have access to high-quality child care and early intervention if they need additional supports? How would universal prekindergarten affect the well-being of children?

Key Terms

Apgar test p. 80

behavioral support plan p. 97

blended practices p. 95

Child Find p. 83

developmental delays p. 84

developmental profile p. 84

developmentally appropriate practice (DAP) p. 99

early intervention p. 69

embedded instruction p. 96

evidence-based practice p. 79

family-centered early intervention p. 75

fetal alcohol spectrum disorder p. 87

genetic counseling p. 87

individualized family service plan (IFSP) p. 75

multidisciplinary team p. 75

natural environments p. 77

Resources

References of Special Interest

Odom, S. L., Horner, R. H., Snell, M. E., & Blancher, J. (Eds.) (2007). *Handbook of developmental disabilities.* New York: Guilford Press. This is a comprehensive reference on research related to children with disabilities. It reviews our current understanding of the field of study for developmental disabilities: the health, neuroscience and genetics, and practice related to meeting the needs of children and families.

Krajicek, M., Steinke, T., Hertzdeng, D., Anastasiow, N., & Skandel, S. (Eds.) (2003). *Handbook for the care of infants and toddlers with disabilities and chronic conditions; Instructor's guide for the handbook for the care of infants and toddlers with disabilities and chronic conditions.* Austin, TX: PRO-ED. These materials cover a wide range of disabilities, providing information about conditions as well as techniques (such as positioning) for treating them. They were prepared under the leadership of Marilyn Krajicek, Ed.D., R.N., at the University of Colorado School of Nursing.

Guralnick, M. (Ed.) (2005). *The developmental systems approach to early intervention.* Baltimore: Brookes. The systems approach to early intervention describes supports and services for young children and their families. As early intervention becomes more univer-

sally available, the quality and coordination of services remain critical challenges. This book offers comprehensive thinking about how we can meet these challenges.

Sandall, S., Hemmeter, M. L, Smith, B. J., & McLean, M. E. (2005). *DEC recommended practices: A comprehensive guide for practical application in early intervention/early childhood special education.* Missoula, MT: Council for Exceptional Children, Division for Early Childhood. The Division for Early Childhood of the Council for Exceptional Children gives clear guidelines for best practices for young children with disabilities. This book is an important handbook for all those who work with young children and their families.

Technical Assistance Center on Social and Emotional Intervention (2007). *Practical Strategies for Teaching Social Emotional Skills-DVD.* Can be found at www.challengingbehavior.org. This 28-minute DVD highlights many practical strategies and approaches that early childhood personnel and families can use to systematically target social emotional supports that build young children's skills in making friends, problem solving, asking for help, talking about feelings, and managing their emotions. The strategies rely on a three-stage approach to supporting young children's social-emotional

Children with learning disabilities are both puzzling and paradoxical. In spite of near-average or higher-than-average intelligence, students with learning disabilities often find school to be very difficult. Just as the term *learning disabilities* implies, these children struggle to learn and often need additional supports to help them succeed in school. Andrew, for example, is a bright and talkative third grader who loves to socialize with his friends. When books are read to him he understands and remembers all the details and often asks intriguing questions. His teacher noticed this and felt that Andrew should be a very capable student, yet his independent reading level was barely at the first-grade level. At first his teacher assumed that he was just being lazy, but when she saw how frustrated he was becoming with reading, she decided there might be more to it, and indeed there was: Andrew has a learning disability.

The reasons that children with learning disabilities do not do well in school have fascinated and baffled researchers and practitioners in the fields of reading, cognition, speech and hearing, neurology, learning, vision, audition, and education. Not all children with learning disabilities have the same set of challenges. Most have difficulty learning to read, spell, and write. Others have trouble with math or with attending to information and completing tasks. Some have difficulty with all academic areas. In this chapter, we look at the history of learning disabilities, how learning disabilities are defined, and how the school and family can work together to create a climate of success for individuals with learning disabilities.

A Brief Historical Overview of Learning Disabilities

The phrase *learning disability* was coined in 1962 by Samuel Kirk, the first author of this text. It came to life during discussions at a 1963 conference with concerned parents and professionals that focused on students who in spite of average or above-average intelligence seemed to be encountering substantial difficulties in school. Prior to 1962, these students had been labeled with terms such as *minimal brain dysfunction, Strauss syndrome*, and *brain injured* (Lerner & Johns, 2009; Swanson, Harris, & Graham, 2003). From Kirk's perspective, students with learning disabilities were a heterogeneous group who shared one commonality: All had a neurologically based problem that affected learning in various ways (Hallahan & Mercer, 2002; Hallahan & Mock, 2003; Cortiella, 2009).

The assumption that a learning disability has a neurological basis is sound, but it is hard for teachers to use "neurological anomalies" as evidence when they are trying to decide whether or not a student has a learning disability. There may come a time in the not too distant future when brain studies will be part of the identification process, but currently we must rely on a student's behavior and performance to help us determine the presence of a learning disability (Galaburda, 2005; Miller, Sanchez, & Hynd, 2003; Sternberg, 2008; Chandrasekaran, Hornichel, Skoe, Nicol, & Kraus, 2009). Because of this limitation, the students we currently identify as having learning disabilities are a very diverse group: They include those with assumed neurologically based learning problems (the group that Samuel Kirk was focused on) *and* students who are not performing well for other reasons (e.g., poor motivation, problems at home, teacher–student personality conflicts, and so forth). This situation has made the category of learning disabilities a "catch-all" for students who need additional support in school. Many of these students do *not* have an underlying neurological base for their difficulties. This group of students has been identified as learning disabled because of **unexplained underachievement.** We explore this further when we discuss how we define learning disabilities (Fuchs, Fuchs, Mathes, Lipsey, & Roberts, 2002).

Characteristics of Children with Learning Disabilities

Children with learning disabilities are like snowflakes; each has his or her own unique structure, combining strengths and needs to form an individual pattern. Children with specific learning disabilities vary in their academic, personal, and social characteristics. Students Jason and Ray (discussed in the following paragraphs) show the variation that children with learning disabilities often exhibit.

Children with learning disabilities face a variety of challenges that include difficulty in learning to read, spell, write, and use math, or trouble with receiving information and completing tasks.

Jason: Jason is a fifth grader with a measured IQ score of 135. Although this score places him in the gifted range intellectually, he still struggles with many academic tasks. Jason is a **twice-exceptional** (2e) learner. He is a solid reader but a very poor speller. Jason also has difficulty with handwriting, and so, although he can talk in great detail about subjects of interest, he has a very hard time writing about them. Jason also struggles with organizing his thoughts and his written products are very hard to follow. Even when he seems to be committed to a writing project, like his report on the NASA space program (Jason would like to be an astronaut), he refuses to revise his work to strengthen it. Because of these challenges, he often tries to distract the class with antics when he becomes frustrated. This disruptive behavior has led to some social isolation, as Jason's classmates do not want to get into trouble because of his behavior. Jason's teacher is frustrated with him; she sees how bright he is when he is participating in discussions and wonders why he can't apply himself more diligently when he is writing. She is also puzzled by his disruptive behavior and feels that he might need more discipline—both at school and at home. Later in the chapter we explore how specific writing strategies, computers, and assistive technology can be used to help Jason become more successful.

Students with learning disabilities are a heterogeneous group.

Ray: Ray looks very different from Jason. Ray has average intelligence but encounters extreme problems with reading, spelling, and writing (sometimes called **dyslexia**). He has a hard time organizing his ideas and is frequently distracted. His reading problems are so severe that he is almost a nonreader. Because of his poor academic performance, his classmates believe he is "stupid." In spite of these academic problems, Ray excels in one area: art. Ray is very creative and loves hands-on building projects. In fact, he happily volunteers for all art projects. His teacher feels that he needs a great deal of support for learning and is grateful for the resource teacher's help with Ray. The resource teacher has expertise in working with students with special needs. She works with Ray and a small group of students with similar needs for an hour each day, and she also helps Ray's general classroom teacher adapt her lessons to provide more support for Ray. Together, both of Ray's teachers are looking for ways to use his strength in art to bolster his self-esteem and build more social support for him with his peers.

The way in which a child responds to evidence-based interventions can be used as one part of a comprehensive assessment of the child's strengths and challenges.

Both Jason and Ray have learning disabilities, and yet each is unique in his combination of strengths and challenges. Students with learning disabilities have difficulties with processing information, and this can lead

TABLE 4.1
Sample Characteristics of Students with Learning Disabilities

- Language Development
  Delays in learning to speak
  Difficulties with naming objects and word retrieval
  Voice modulation (loud/soft; tone) may be problematic
  Limited vocabulary and word usage

- Reading
  Delays and difficulties with skills (i.e., phonemic awareness, word recognition, comprehension)
  May have stronger listening comprehension
  Slow reading rate
  Substitutes words or leaves out words when reading

- Written Language
  Avoids or dislikes writing and copying tasks
  Reverses letters and words
  Uneven and poorly spaced/shaped penmanship
  Poor spelling

- Math
  Difficulty with arithmetic facts and skills
  Challenges with telling and estimating time
  Problems with memorizing information
  Difficulty with interpreting graphs and charts

- Social and Emotional
  Difficulty interpreting and understanding others' moods/feelings
  Problems with self-control and impulsivity
  Difficulty with realistic goal setting
  Challenges understanding peer and group expectations

- Gross and Fine Motor Skills
  May be awkward or clumsy
  Difficulty with buttons, hooks, snaps, zippers, shoe laces
  Awkward pencil grasp
  Dislikes and avoids games with balls, bats, moving parts

Horowitz, S., & Stecker, D. *Checklist for Learning Disabilities.* © 2010 National Center for Learning Disabilities, Inc. All rights reserved. Adapted with permission. For more information, visit LD.org.

to problems across several areas including language development, academic learning, motor coordination, social and emotional self-regulation, and focusing attention (Horowitz & Stecker, 2007). Table 4.1 shows some of the major characteristics that students with learning disabilities often share. In looking at these characteristics, it is important to remember that individuals with learning disabilities will have their own unique combination of strengths and challenges.

Because of these differences, each student with a learning disability will need either an individualized educational program (IEP) or a 504 plan, as discussed in Chapter 2 to support his or her success in school. Later in this chapter, we will explore how teachers and parents can work together with the child to promote success, but first we take a look at how learning disabilities are defined by law.

Defining Learning Disabilities

More than forty-five years have passed since Samuel Kirk used the term *learning disabilities* to describe children who, despite average or above average intelligence, seemed to be encountering problems with school (Coleman, Buysse, & Neitzel, 2006a). At that time Kirk believed that these children would likely be a very small subset of children with disabilities. Little did we know that children with learning disabilities would become the largest group of students served by our special education programs. Current estimations indicate that 4.2 percent of the school-age children who receive special education are categorized as learning disabled (U.S. Department of Education, 2010). While the numbers of children identified as learning disabled is going down, this is still the largest category within special education (Cortiella, 2009). One possible explanation for the high numbers is the way we have defined learning disabilities. The U.S. Department of Education (2004) gives us the following definition:

SEC. 602. DEFINITIONS.
(29) SPECIFIC LEARNING DISABILTIY.

(A) IN GENERAL. The term "specific learning disability" means a disorder in 1 or more of the basic psychological processes involved in understanding or in using language, spoken or written, which disorder may manifest itself in the imperfect ability to listen, think, speak, write, spell, or do mathematical calculations....

(B) DISORDERS INCLUDE. Such term includes such conditions as perceptual disabilities, brain injury, minimal brain dysfunction, dyslexia, and developmental aphasia....

(C) DISORDERS NOT INCLUDED. Such term does not include a learning problem that is primarily the result of visual, hearing, or motor disabilities, of mental retardation, of emotional disturbance, or of environmental, cultural, or economic disadvantage.

This is a theoretical definition and must be "operationalized" to help us actually identify students with learning disabilities (Herr & Bateman, 2003). To operationalize this definition, most states developed formulas that hinged on the discrepancies between intellectual abilities (IQ) and achievement and/or performance. The magnitude of these discrepancies was thought to indicate the degree of underlying disability affecting a child's psychological processing. Each state set up its own formulas for determining the degree of the discrepancy. Jason, for example, is a bright young man who is doing poorly in school. His poor performance may be due to a learning disability, or it may be due to any number of other things (for example, a lack of interest in school, teachers who are inexperienced, or even problems with home and family). Some educators believe that the use of discrepancy models to identify students with learning disabilities has broadened the category to include any child who experiences problems with learning. Many students have been labeled because they are underachieving in school and there is no apparent reason for their lack of success (Conyers, Reynolds, & Ou, 2003; Fuchs, Mock, Morgan, & Young, 2003; Gerber et al., 2004; Kavale, Holdnack, & Mostert, 2005). Partly because of this, the category has remained large as the "learning disability" label has been given to any student whom teachers feel would benefit from some level of systematic support (MacMillan & Siperstein, 2002).

The following concerns highlight several problems with the discrepancy model as it is used to identify children with learning disabilities:

1. Discrepancies between IQ and achievement/performance are often difficult to measure with children in pre-K through third grade.

2. Discrepancies between IQ and achievement/performance may exist for any number of reasons; thus, this approach is really just helping us find children with "unexplained underachievement" that may or may *not* be due to a learning disability.

3. To find discrepancies we must wait until the gap between IQ and achievement/performance is wide enough to measure, and this means that we must wait until the child has experienced substantial failure with learning.

4. The "wait-to-fail" model creates a situation in which the primary problems a child is experiencing get worse and are frequently compounded by secondary problems with behavior, self-concept, and academic readiness (Coleman, Buysse, & Neitzel, 2006b).

Because of these problems with the discrepancy model, many educators maintain that the ways we identify and serve students with learning disabilities within both general and special education are not working (Fuchs & Fuchs, 2006; Vellutino et al., 1996). These educators believe that it will take a major paradigm shift to get back on track so that the needs of students with learning disabilities can be met (National Association of State Directors of Special Education [NASDSE], 2005; Fletcher, Denton, & Francis, 2005). The response to intervention (RTI) approach, described in Chapters 1, 2, and 3, was initially conceived as a way to help us identify and serve children with learning disabilities (NASDSE, 2005).

Students with learning disabilities often experience difficulties with classwork.

(© Courtesy of Cengage Learning)

Learning Disabilities: The Paradigm Shift to RTI

The recent reauthorization of the Individuals with Disabilities Education Act (IDEA; reauthorized as the Individuals with Disabilities Education Improvement Act, 2004) reflects this change in thinking about how we define and serve students with learning disabilities. IDEA 2004 includes an RTI approach as one option that schools can use to identify students with learning disabilities. The new language is part of Section 614, the section that addresses evaluations, eligibility determinations, individualized education programs, and educational placements:

RTI

(b) EVALUATION PROCEDURES.
(6) SPECIFIC LEARNING DISABILITIES.

(A) IN GENERAL. Notwithstanding section 607 (b0, . . . when determining whether a child has a specific learning disability as defined in section 602 (29), a local educational agency shall not be required to take into consideration whether a child has a severe discrepancy between achievement and intellectual ability in oral expression, listening comprehension, written expression, basic reading skill, reading comprehension, mathematical calculation, or mathematical reasoning. . . .

(B) ADDITIONAL AUTHORITY. In determining whether a child has a specific learning disability, a local educational agency may use a process that determines if the child responds to evidence-based intervention as a part of the evaluation procedures described in paragraphs (2) and (3) (IDEA, 2004).

It is important to note that the language of the law does *not* preclude a review of the student's strengths and challenges as part of a comprehensive educational evaluation of the student's needs (Fuchs & Fuchs, 2007). This section allows the use of information that shows how a child has responded to **evidence-based interventions** *as one part of a comprehensive evaluation of students' needs* (Kame'enui, 2007). This approach is called *response to intervention*. The need for comprehensive evaluations assessing students' needs is even more important within an RTI approach because understanding *why* a child is unable to learn is key to reshaping our educational supports to help him succeed. In addition to being comprehensive, a recent Supreme Court decision emphasizes that the evaluation of the student's needs must be done in a timely manner to ensure that supports and services can be put in place as early as possible (Forest Grove School District vs. T.A., 08-305, 2009).

The RTI model focuses on prereferral prevention and intervention and on recognizing the needs of students so that we can deliver appropriate supports and services through a collaborative approach (President's Commission on Excellence in Special Education, 2002). While RTI began as an alternative route for identifying students with learning disabilities, it has grown into a movement focused on building collaborative approaches to meeting students needs (Whitten, Esteves, & Woodrow, 2009).

RTI

The RTI approach allows early and intensive interventions based on students' needs without waiting for children to "fail" in the third grade (Whitten, Esteves, & Woodrow, 2009; Gersten, Compton, Conner, Dimino, Santoro, Linan-Thompson, & Tilly, 2008; Fuchs & Fuchs, 2007; Fuchs, Fuchs, Mathes, Lipsey, & Roberts, 2002; Fuchs, Mock, Morgan, & Young, 2003; Jenkins & O'Connor, 2002; Vaughn & Fuchs, 2003).

If we think about Ray's experience in school, we can see how the RTI approach would have been useful. Ray, as you may recall, is a fifth grader who is struggling in school and has severe problems with reading, spelling, and writing. In the early grades Ray's teachers hoped that he would catch up to grade level if he worked a little harder. They did not refer Ray for an educational assessment to initiate special education services because, although he was falling behind, his teachers did not yet see an acute discrepancy between his abilities IQ (which is average) and his performance (somewhat below average). It was not until Ray was in the third grade that he qualified for learning disabilities services, at which point he was finally failing. With the RTI approach, Ray's teachers would have been able to activate supports and services as soon as they noticed that Ray was encountering difficulties; they would not have had to wait for a formal label of learning disabilities (Gersten et al., 2008). Ray would have had more intensive instruction provided in small groups, as Tier II interventions, early on, and his teachers would have initiated formal assessments and **progress monitoring** as soon as they realized that Ray was continuing to fall behind. Ray's learning disability would have been identified, but he would not have had to fail in third grade in order to get the help he needed. To help us get a fuller picture of Ray's learning disabilities, let's look at two related areas: dyslexia and **attention-deficit hyperactivity disorders.**

Dyslexia

Currently, dyslexia is accepted as a disorder within the learning disability population, and it is defined by the International Dyslexia Association as follows:

Dyslexia is characterized by difficulties with accurate or/and fluent word recognition and by poor spelling and decoding abilities. These difficulties typically result from a deficit in the phonological component of language that is often unexpected in relation to other cognitive abilities and the provision of effective classroom instruction. Secondary consequences may include problems in reading comprehension and reduced reading experience that can impede growth of vocabulary and background knowledge. (Adopted by the IDA Board of Directors, Nov. 12, 2002). This definition is also used by the National Institute of Child Health and Human Development [NICHD] [http://www.interdys.org/FAQWhatIs.htm; April 15, 2010]).

International Dyslexia Association
www.interdys.org

The major conclusion is that children with dyslexia have brains that operate differently from the brains of children without dyslexia (Maisog, Einbinder, Flowers, Turkeltaub, & Eden, et al., 2008; Shaywitz & Shaywitz, 2008; Miller et al, 2003; Rourke, 1991; Willingham, 2008; Willis, 2008). Although persons with dyslexia have difficulties in language-based tasks (reading, spelling, writing, and phonological awareness), many have well-developed abilities in visual, spatial, motor, and nonverbal problem solving (Dickman, 1996). Ray's problems with learning could be called *dyslexia* because his specific learning disabilities are in the language area. It is important to remember that not all children with learning disabilities have dyslexia and that dyslexia is often considered a medical term, whereas *specific learning disability* is used in educational settings. Ray also has a great deal of difficulty with paying attention in school, and his mind often seems to wander, which causes difficulties for him in school and is a source of frustration to his teachers. Ray's difficulties are extreme enough that his teachers feel he may also have an attention-deficit disorder. Many individuals with learning difficulties will also have attention-deficit disorders (Silver, 2010).

Researchers recently have focused on analyzing what children must learn and on identifying the problems that children with learning disabilities have in mastering the material.

(© Courtesy of Cengage Learning)

Attention-Deficit Hyperactivity Disorder

Attention-deficit hyperactivity disorders (ADHD) are specific information processing problems related to an individual's inability to attend to or focus on a given task. We have chosen to introduce ADHD within this chapter because of its neurological basis and because many of the educational strategies we use to respond to the needs of students with ADHD are similar to the supports we use with children who have other forms of learning disabilities (Cutting & Denckla, 2003). Because issues related to attention are often associated with other areas of exceptionality, we will also discuss attention-deficit disorder (ADD) and ADHD within many of the chapters that follow. If you want to locate information on ADD and ADHD in each chapter, you can look for the following icon in the margin, which will show where this is being discussed.

The organization for Children and Adults with Attention-Deficit Hyperactivity Disorder (CHADD) defines ADHD as follows: "Attention-deficit hyperactivity disorder (ADHD) is a condition affecting children and adults that is characterized by problems with attention, impulsivity, and overactivity" (CHADD, 2008).

ADD/ADHD

The symptoms of ADHD are also typical of many children with autism, intellectual and developmental disabilities, and emotional and behavior disorders.

Children and Adults with
Attention-Deficit Hyperactivity
Disorder
http://www.chadd.org

Angelina has ADHD. She is easily distracted and often distracts other students. Angelina makes careless mistakes in her work and seems to daydream much of the time. It is hard for her to concentrate in school, and her teacher refers to her as a "wiggle worm." Angelina's parents feel that she is impulsive, and they find it frustrating that she cannot follow through with simple household chores, such as setting the table, unless she is prompted several times. Her parents feel that they have become "nags" and that Angelina is changing from their fun-loving little girl into an angry and unhappy child. As you review the indicators of ADHD in Table 4.2, from the *Diagnostic and Statistical*

TABLE 4.2
Symptoms of Attention-Deficit Hyperactivity Disorder

Note: All of the symptoms of inattention, hyperactivity, and impulsivity must have persisted for at least six months to a degree that is maladaptive and inconsistent with the developmental level of the child.

Inattention

- Fails to give close attention to details or makes careless mistakes in schoolwork, work, or other activities
- Has difficulty sustaining attention in tasks or play activities
- Does not seem to listen when spoken to directly
- Does not follow through on instructions and fails to finish schoolwork, chores, or duties in the workplace (not due to oppositional behavior or failure to understand instructions)
- Has difficulty organizing tasks and activities
- Avoids, dislikes, or is reluctant to engage in tasks that require sustained mental effort (such as schoolwork or homework)
- Loses things necessary for tasks or activities (for example, toys, school assignments, pencils, books, or tools)
- Is easily distracted by extraneous stimuli
- Is forgetful in daily activities

Hyperactivity

- Fidgets with hands or feet or squirms in seat
- Leaves seat in classroom or in other situations in which remaining seated is expected
- Runs about or climbs excessively in situations in which it is inappropriate
- Has difficulty playing or engaging in leisure activities quietly
- Is often "on the go" or acts as if "driven by a motor"
- Talks excessively

Impulsivity

- Blurts out answers before questions have been completed
- Has difficulty awaiting turn
- Interrupts or intrudes on others (for example, butts into conversations or games)

Source: Used with permission of American Psychiatric Association, from *Diagnostic and Statistical Manual of Mental Disorders* 4th ed., TR; permission conveyed through Copyright Clearance Center, Inc.

Manual of Mental Disorders IV, you will see that Angelina has several of the symptoms listed.

Although many children encounter periodic problems with attention and follow-through, individuals with ADHD face lifelong challenges and need a variety of supports to help them be successful. Many individuals with ADHD may benefit from medications to help them focus and sustain their attention.

 # Causes of Learning Disabilities

No one has discovered a single cause of learning disabilities. Studies that focus on subgroups within the larger population of children with learning disabilities have identified some neurological differences associated with their learning problems (Hynd, 1992; Lyon, 1995; Rourke, 1994).

Although no one is quite sure what causes learning disabilities, some evidence indicates that learning disabilities may be genetic, as they seem to "run in families."

 ## Genetics of Learning Disabilities

Genetic patterns for children with learning disabilities have been noted in family relationships and chances are good that their parents, grandparents, aunts and uncles, and/or other relatives will also have learning difficulties (Paracchini, Scerri, & Monaco, 2007). Studies are currently working to isolate the genetic markers for learning disabilities, and these may help us better understand the link between biology and learning (Cope, Harold, Hill, Maskvina, Stevenson, Holmans et al., 2005). All learning disabilities, however, cannot be attributed to genetic causes. Some learning disabilities may stem from environmental factors and/or from inadequate prenatal health care which may influence brain development.

 ### Neurology and Brain Development
The Brain and Learning Disabilities

The brain is hardwired for learning, so what happens when an individual has a learning disability? Neurologists believe that the organization of the brain is different when a learning disability is present (Hoeft, et.al., 2006; Masiog, et, al, 2008; Shaywitz & Shaywitz, 2008). Remember that while the brain functions as a whole, each area of the brain takes on specialized tasks (Freberg, 2006). Recent studies using imaging technology have found differences in brain structure among students who have reading problems, attention deficits, and auditory processing difficulties (Jensen, 2000; Castellanos et al., 2002; Willingham, 2008; Willis, 2008). We still do not understand how these structural anomalies impact information processing. In these studies, the brain scans show different patterns of activity for children with dyslexia compared to children with no reading difficulties during reading tasks (McCandliss & Noble, 2003; Hoeft, 2006). One encouraging finding is the emerging evidence that when children are given explicit and intense instruction on reading skills (i.e., phonological awareness, decoding, etc.), their brain scans show similarities in how their brains process information to the scans of their nondisabled peers (McCandliss & Noble, 2003). Although there is significant evidence of brain abnormalities for children with dyslexia, we still do not know the specific impact and causal link of these differences with learning problems (Hoeft et al., 2006).

Prevalence of Learning Disabilities

Although learning disabilities have an impact at all ages, we focus our discussion of prevalence on school-age individuals, from 6 to 21 years old. The *28th Annual Report to Congress on the Implementation of the Individuals with Disabilities Education Act, 2006,* reports that 4.2 percent of individuals ages 6 to 21 are receiving special education and/or related services because of specific learning disabilities, and, as noted earlier, the learning disabilities category makes up approximately 44 percent of all students with disabilities (U.S. Department of Education, 2010). While learning disabilities remains the largest category of children with disabilities, the numbers of identified children has declined, and during the last decade the number has dropped by 7 percent (Cortiella, 2009). This decline is likely due to several factors including early interventions to support children as they learn to read, changes in definitions and identification practices, and the use of research-based instructional methods (Cortiella, 2009).

> We must continue to review identification procedures to ensure that we do not inadvertently over-identify children from some racial groups.

In spite of these declines, learning disabilities remain the largest category of disability among all racial and ethnic groups; however, there are differences in identification patterns across groups. The *28th Annual Report* indicates that American Indians/Alaska Natives, black non-Hispanic, and Hispanic students are somewhat more likely to be identified as having learning disabilities, whereas identification is somewhat lower for white non-Hispanic and Asian/Pacific Islanders. These patterns continue to remind us that the identification process we use must be fair and equitable so that we do not inadvertently over-identify children from some racial and ethnic groups.

Appropriate Identification of Bilingual Children

Appropriate identification of children with learning disabilities whose first language is not English presents a special challenge (Spear-Swerling, 2006). The National Longitudinal Transition Studies found an increase in learning disabilities identification, from 1.3 percent in 1987 to 15.4 percent in 2001, for students ages 15 to 17 whose primary language was not English (Cortiella, 2009). This increase may represent the demands faced by students who must communicate in two or more languages and likely contributes to the disproportionate representation of Hispanic students with learning disabilities (Ortiz, 2001; Spear-Swerling, 2006). Because mastering more than one language is difficult in and of itself, bilingual assessments of the child's abilities and skills are critical to understanding if learning disabilities are present. The dual language demands faced by children who are bilingual will be examined in depth in Chapter 7, but the following example of Juan illustrates some of the challenges we have been discussing:

RTI

Juan is a high school student whose primary language is Spanish. While he is a hard worker and seems to like school, he is struggling with the demands of reading in the academic subjects. His teachers are concerned about this and feel that he may have a learning disability. They are reluctant to refer him for special education because they also feel that his reading problems may stem from his dual language usage. More and more students like Juan are being supported by being taught specific strategies for reading in the content areas within Tier II of the RTI model to help them meet with success (Deshler, Schumaker, Lenz, Bulgren, Hock, Knight, & Ehren, 2001). Juan's teachers decide to intensify support for him using embedded vocabulary development opportunities (Ortiz, 2001); specific guidance on paraphrasing key readings to build understanding (Deshler et al., 2001); and instruction on writing using the self-regulated strategy (e.g., reading back and reflecting on meaning) development approach to guide and model the writing process (Graham & Harris, 2009). The decision to provide this extra support for Juan was made by a team of teachers including the English language learners specialist, the special education teacher, and his general education teachers. In the meeting, Juan requested additional support with his homework, and the team agreed that he should participate in the student support program offered either before school, during lunch hours, and after school through the RTI services. Because Juan relies on the school bus and has after-school responsibilities to his family, Juan decided to attend the lunch hour support session. He also planned to talk a few of his friends into going with him so he would have a small group to eat with during the lessons.

Where Are Students with Learning Disabilities Served?

Figure 4.1 shows how the services for students with learning disabilities are provided across both general and special educational settings. The majority of students with learning disabilities (52 percent) spend most of their time in general education classes. Thirty-five percent of students with learning disabilities receive services in other settings for between one and one-half and three and one-half hours a day. A much smaller percentage of students with learning disabilities (12 percent) spend over half of their school day in settings other than the general classroom, and 1 percent receive services in a different environment (U.S. Department of Education, 2010).

As you can see from Figure 4.1, the vast majority of students with learning disabilities receive all or most of their education within the general education setting. There is a continuing trend toward full inclusion for students with learning disabilities with an increasing number of students spending most of their time in general education classrooms. Students with learning disabilities

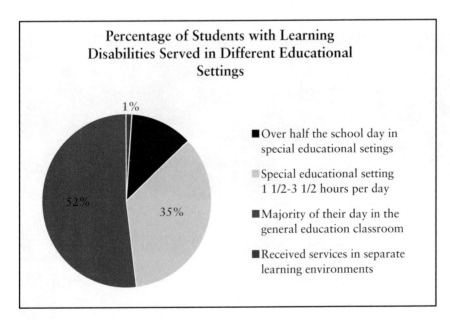

FIGURE 4.1
Percentage of Students with Learning Disabilities Served in Different Educational Settings
Source: US Department of Education, (2008). *Twenty-Eighth Annual Report to Congress.* Washington, D.C.: Office of Special Educational Programs.

typically participate in the same learning activities and assessments alongside their nondisabled peers; however, skilled teachers use a variety of strategies to support students with success (Cortiella & Baurnette, 2008).

Children with Learning Disabilities in Early Childhood

Recognizing young children who may show early indications of learning disabilities is important so that support can be provided for their development (Coleman, Roth, & West, 2006). The National Joint Council on Learning Disabilities (2006) states that "the purpose of early identification is to determine which children have developmental problems that may be obstacles to learning or that place children at risk." They further recommend systematic observations of a child's behavior and abilities over time as an important way to document possible early learning disabilities.

One observation tool that is being developed to help with this is the Early Learning Observation & Rating Scale (ELORS) (Coleman, West, & Gillis, 2010). The ELORS is a concerns-based tool that helps teachers and parents gather and share information about young children who may have learning disabilities (Gillis, West, & Coleman, 2010a) Using the ELORS, teachers and parents can systematically rate their concerns from 1 (little or no concern) to 4 (great concern) across seven developmental domains. The seven areas of development are perceptual and motor, self-management, social and emotional, early math, early literacy, receptive language, and expressive language (Gillis, West, & Coleman, 2010b). Ten examples of typical developmental tasks are provided for each domain, and teachers and parents use these to rate their levels of concern. Table 4.3 shows a sample of the items for each domain.

Because reading and arithmetic are similar in many ways (for example, numbers and words stand for concepts), a child with language difficulty is likely to have difficulty in learning to calculate.

(© Monika Graff/The Image Works)

TABLE 4.3
Sample: Early Learning Observation and Rating Scale (ELORS)

Teacher-Individual Child Form	4 (great concern) 1 (little or no concern)			
Domain of Learning: Perceptual and Motor				
Eye-hand coordination	1	2	3	4
Large muscle coordination	1	2	3	4
Holding a pencil or spoon	1	2	3	4
Drawing simple shapes (e.g., circle, square)	1	2	3	4
Dressing skills (e.g., zippers, buttons, shoes, socks)	1	2	3	4
Domain of Learning: Self-Management				
Adjusting to changes in routine	1	2	3	4
Transitioning from one activity to another	1	2	3	4
Understanding the consequences of behaviors	1	2	3	4
Using words to solve problems with peers	1	2	3	4
Concentrating for brief periods	1	2	3	4
Domain of Learning: Social and Emotional				
Playing cooperatively with other children	1	2	3	4
Participating in social activities	1	2	3	4
Expressing frustration appropriately	1	2	3	4
Maintaining friendships	1	2	3	4
Showing a range of emotions (e.g., happy, worried, sad)	1	2	3	4
Domain of Learning: Early Math				
Naming numbers	1	2	3	4
Showing understanding of one-to-one correspondence	1	2	3	4
Determining which of two groups of objects has more	1	2	3	4
Showing understanding of basic time sequences	1	2	3	4
Domain of Learning: Early Literacy				
Interest in reading activities	1	2	3	4
Identifying words (e.g., "STOP" on a stop sign)	1	2	3	4
Remembering names of letters	1	2	3	4
Learning letter sounds	1	2	3	4
Showing an understanding of which words rhyme	1	2	3	4
Domain of Learning: Receptive Language				
Paying attention to speech in the presence of background noise	1	2	3	4
Responding to verbal requests	1	2	3	4
Following simple 3-step directions	1	2	3	4
Requiring modeling or demonstration	1	2	3	4
Completing sound or word patterns (e.g., in repetitive books)	1	2	3	4
Domain of Learning: Expressive Language				
Expressing wants, needs, and thoughts verbally	1	2	3	4
Size of vocabulary	1	2	3	4
Length of typical sentences	1	2	3	4
Retelling details of a story	1	2	3	4
Using appropriate words rather than filler words (e.g., that "thing")	1	2	3	4

This ELORS focuses on seven areas of development that are associated with children who have learning disabilities. Significant difficulties for a young child within any of these seven areas should be a cause for concern to parents and teachers. Social validity studies with the ELORS teacher and parent versions showed that it is perceived as very helpful and that it may be used during the **collaborative problem-solving** discussions within the RTI approach (Gillis, West, Coleman, 2010b).

 # Information Processing Model

As discussed in earlier chapters, the **information processing model (IPM)** is useful in helping us understand the impact that a learning disability can have on a student's ability to take in, think about, and share things that he or she is learning (Willis, 2008; Wong, Harris, Graham, & Butler, 2003; Dai & Sternberg, 2004). This model describes learning as a series of components that involve sensory stimulation/input, processing/thinking, and output, or sharing what has been learned. In this chapter, we focus on the impact that a learning disability has on one's ability to process information; in later chapters we address how sensory impairments and other disabilities can be viewed using the IPM.

> Using the IPM helps us to understand the components of learning and plan a remedial program.

Overarching each of these components is the **executive function** that serves as the system's decision maker. In learning, we sometimes call this aspect of the IPM **metacognition**. We have added a surrounding emotional context for information processing because this emotional context is a critical mediator in the way students with learning disabilities process information (Cutting & Denckla, 2003; Jensen, 2000; Lewis & Stieben, 2004; Linnenbrink & Pintrich, 2004; Immordino-Yang & Damasio, 2007; Willis, 2008). The IPM is not the only way to describe learning, but it is a useful way to think about learning in the presence of a learning disability (Sternberg & Grigorenko, 2002; Willingham, 2008). Because learning disabilities can impact any area of processing, it is difficult to portray a "typical" child with learning disabilities. Figure 4.2 shows us that Ray, the student we met earlier in the chapter, has difficulties involving **executive processing**, understanding auditory input (e.g., hearing letter sounds, following directions given orally), memory (especially for things he hears), and both speaking and writing as ways to share his ideas. The secondary areas that cause difficulties for Ray are more generalized. Because of his challenges with both memory and focus or attending, he struggles with all of the deeper processing areas (classification, association, reasoning, and evaluation). He also has had

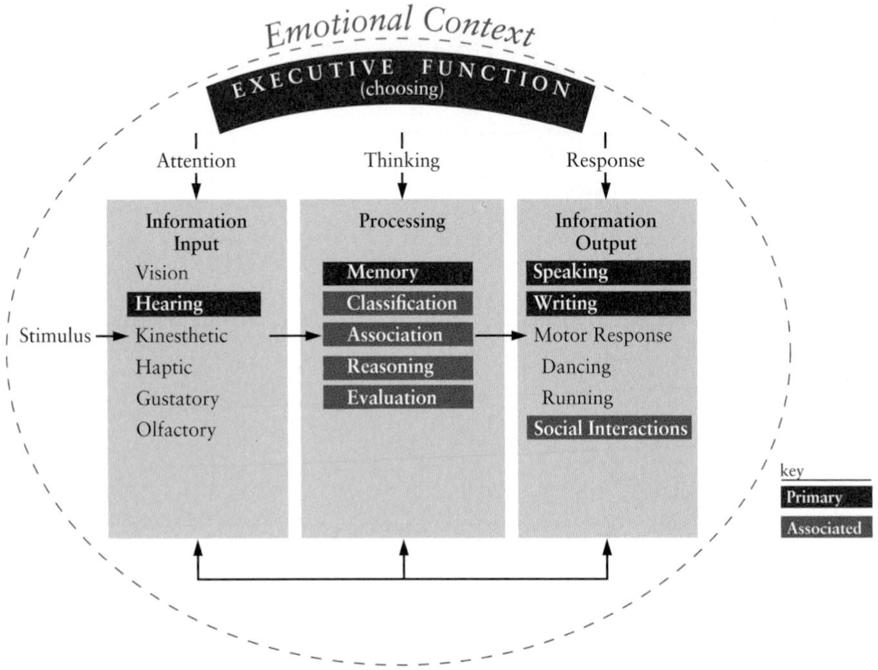

FIGURE 4.2
The Information Processing Model

difficulties with social interactions that require processing a lot of auditory information (e.g., tone of voice, inferential intent of words, and emotional content of the message). As you can see in Figure 4.2, Ray's challenges are pretty pervasive. The good news is that he has strong visual and kinesthetic skills, and these are what help him with his art.

The IPM shows the components of learning and how they are impacted by a learning disability. The IPM also gives us direct insight into strategies we can use to support student learning. The four major components (input, processing, output, and executive function) operate in the context of an emotional environment that influences the processing of information (Immordino-Yang & Damasio, 2007). Each component carries out an important function related to learning, and optimum learning takes place when the components function smoothly as one system. A learning disability can be explained as a glitch in this system. Let's look at each component and explore what the glitches mean for students.

Problems with Input

When the learning difficulty occurs because of input glitches, a sensory perceptual problem exists. Unlike sensory acuity problems, perceptual problems cannot be corrected with glasses or hearing aids. Those with **visual perception** problems can experience figure-ground (seeing an object against the background), closure (completion of a figure), and spatial relationship problems. Any one of these problems can make learning very difficult. If they are combined with auditory perceptional difficulties—figure-ground auditory problems (hearing speech against background noise) or difficulties in sound

Technology can be used to support children's learning when they have visual or auditory perception difficulties

(© Jim West/Photo Edit)

discriminations and/or sound recognition—then learning becomes even more difficult (Lerner & Johns, 2009). Andrew, the first child we met in this chapter, has visual perceptual problems that make reading very difficult. His **auditory perception,** however, is strong, so he can understand information that is read to him. Ray, as noted earlier, has the opposite pattern: strong visual perception with weak auditory perception.

In addition to perceptual problems, some individuals with learning disabilities experience sensory integration difficulties. **Sensory integration** involves the ability to use two or more senses simultaneously and smoothly (Lerner & Johns, 2009). A student's inability to listen and take notes during class is an example of a sensory integration dysfunction because this task requires blending auditory perception and tactile or **proprioceptive** (an awareness of where your body is in relation to the space around it) actions.

A final area of concern with this component is oversensitivity to sensory input; this may mirror the difficulties faced by some children with autism (see Chapter 5). Lights, sounds, smells, and tastes may become overwhelming. When this **heightened sensitivity** affects the sense of touch, it is called **tactile defensiveness,** in which touch can trigger acute discomfort (Packer, 2004). For individuals who are tactually defensive, a light or soft touch seems to be more uncomfortable than firm contact. In a typical busy classroom, it is easy to see how a student with these sensory sensitivities would experience difficulties.

Problems with Processing or Thinking

When problems with learning primarily affect processing or thinking, we see difficulties with memory and with organizing ideas or thoughts in meaningful ways. Problems in these areas can be especially frustrating for students and their teachers. Although Ray's problems occur in several areas, the most difficult of them involves his inability to organize his thoughts and ideas. This inability creates great challenges across most school tasks, and it is only when he can be creative in the arts that he feels truly at home. Jason, on the other hand, excels in his thinking. He seems to thrive in the world of ideas, and he has a great memory. His struggle, as we see later, comes when he must write his ideas down. Let's look at glitches that affect memory and information retrieval and then at the problems with organizing thoughts.

The division of memory into sensory, short-term, and long-term memory helps us understand how students process different tasks (Bender, 2001; Swanson & Sáez, 2003). See Figure 4.3 for an information processing model of how memory

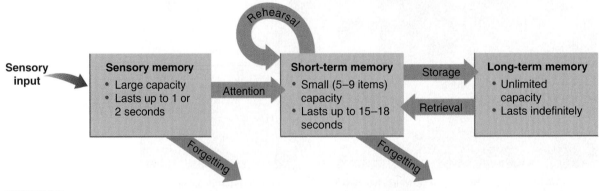

FIGURE 4.3
The Atkinson-Shiffrin Model of Memory
Source: From Freberg, L. (2006). *Discovering biological psychology* (p. 354). Used by permission of Cengage Learning.

works. Our **sensory memory** can hold large amounts of information for a very short period of time (2 to 3 seconds). We use **short-term memory** to remember the directions and steps for solving a math problem while simultaneously doing the calculations. **Long-term memory** stores information that we have made our own to draw on for future use. Problems with any of these forms of memory lead to major learning difficulties (Swanson, Zheng, & Jerman, 2009). However, the greatest impact occurs when students struggle with long-term memory storage and retrieval.

Another way to view memory is to consider how the information is stored. We typically store information in three kinds of memory: semantic, episodic, and physical/motor (Lerner & Johns, 2009).

- **Semantic memory** stores concepts, words, symbols, and generalizations. This is the most frequently used form of memory in school.

- **Episodic memory** is our ability to recall whole scenes or episodes from our past. When we experience episodic memory, we feel we are "right back there" with all senses engaged. Often episodic memories are triggered by smells. When you smell lavender perfume like your grandmother wore, you are immediately transported back to the times she read to you while you sat on her lap. Episodic memories are often associated with strong emotions that can be either positive or negative.

- **Motor memory** is our ability to program our body movements. Our bodies learn patterns and retain them for future use. We learn to ride a bicycle, play the piano, or write our names. Some motor memories seem to last after we no longer use them—thus the expression "It's like riding a bike."

When an individual has a learning disability that affects memory in any form, school can be a challenging place.

In addition to memory, the processing component includes thinking. Students work with the information to interpret and combine it with prior knowledge as they create meaning for themselves by constructing their own understandings. Original ideas are born in this stage that allow the learner to move beyond the known into new areas of thought. It is in this component of the IPM that real learning takes place.

When problems occur in thinking, they are likely to stem from an inability to organize thoughts in meaningful ways (i.e., classifying, forming associations, and using reasoning abilities). In other words, ideas remain fragmented and disconnected so that patterns and relationships across ideas never jell into useful concepts. Interestingly, when information is stored in memory as isolated bits and pieces, it is more difficult to retrieve and is less useful for thinking (Coleman, 2005). Structuring teaching around concepts and big ideas is useful in helping our students reduce retrieval problems (this is discussed further later in the chapter) (Ellis, Farmer, & Newman, 2005).

Learning, according to the IPM, is a function of how well an individual processes the information. Deep processing is necessary to understanding information so that it can be used in meaningful ways. Deep processing occurs when we transform the information to make it ours (Willis, 2008). Such processing might include forming categories where new information is linked with existing information. It also includes analytical and evaluative thinking. The ultimate transformation occurs when we use the information to create new ways of thinking and share these new understandings with others. Ray, for example, has a hard time getting new information to "stick." In preparation for an upcoming social studies test, his mother spent several nights helping him study by quizzing him on vocabulary and dates. During the study sessions he seemed to be getting the information, and everyone was discouraged

> When information is stored in memory as isolated bits and pieces, it is more difficult to retrieve and is harder to use in meaningful ways. By structuring our teaching around concepts and big ideas, we can help students remember what they learn.

when he all but failed the actual test. Ray had not processed the information deeply during his study time, and so he was not able to apply his learning when it came to the test. On the other hand, after he completed his social studies project—a topographical map of his state showing its different regions, populations, and products—he was able to remember and discuss everything he had learned in great detail. For Ray, this hands-on art-related project helped him process the information more deeply so that he could remember and use what he had learned. Sharing information, or using what you have learned, is represented in the output component of the IPM.

Problems with Output

For some individuals with learning disabilities, the problem is primarily output, or the expression of ideas and thoughts, that can take several forms.

When output problems affect speech, they may be called *developmental aphasia* because the symptoms mirror those of a stroke patient with speech difficulties. These problems include word retrieval and speech fluency, which can make communication difficult.

A second form of an output glitch involves the motor mechanics of handwriting (Berninger & Amtmann, 2003). The easiest way to understand this is to imagine that the connection between the brain and the hand is not efficient. There is "static on the line," which makes it difficult for the hand to know what to do and for the brain to understand what the hand has done. If you think back to Jason's profile, you will remember that this was one of his challenges. Difficulties with handwriting are sometimes called dysgraphia, which literally means *bad writing*. To produce legible products, these students have to "draw" their letters and form them into words. This process is very taxing and cannot be sustained for general work. When **dysgraphia** is combined with visual and auditory perceptual problems or sensory integration difficulties, note taking during lectures and copying from the board are virtually impossible.

Another form that output learning disabilities can take is an inability to both understand and produce gestures and facial expressions that correspond with feelings and emotions. In this case, individuals have difficulty interpreting emotional nuances that are communicated through facial expressions and body language. Because a tremendous amount of information is communicated nonverbally through looks and body positions, an individual who does not "read" these clues is at a distinct disadvantage when communication is required.

Individuals with these problems may also have a flat affect (an absence of expression on the face) that can limit their ability to express needs and wants, thus making communication more problematic. Social situations can be quite painful for these individuals, creating an early pattern of social avoidance.

Problems with Executive Functions

As we discussed earlier, the executive function, or metacognition, is the decision-making component of this model. Decisions are made about

- What input to notice or screen out
- What strategies to use to store information or whether the information needs to be stored

- How useful the information is

- How ideas and understandings will be expressed

Metacognition also includes **self-regulatory skills** (Wery & Nietfeld, 2010; Hidi & Ainley, 2008). We monitor ourselves so that we can continuously adapt our thoughts, speech, and actions to accomplish our goals. Self-regulatory skills help us adapt to the environment, and they are essential (Wong, 2004; Zimmerman, 2002; Zimmerman, 2008). Self-regulation implies that an individual is in control of and responsible for his or her own actions. In addition to its importance for learning, self-control is also a key ingredient in social success. Impulsivity can lead to disastrous results: essentially leaping before looking. In learning, self-regulation allows us to monitor our understanding. Good readers, for example, continuously monitor their comprehension and work to make sense of their reading (Pierangelo & Giuliani, 2006). When something is not clear, good readers loop back and reread the passage. Poor readers, on the other hand, often fail to recognize that something does not make sense. Even when they do recognize the problem, they often fail to initiate a strategy such as rereading to help them make sense of the text (Williams, 2003; Wery & Nietfeld, 2010).

In addition to problems with self-regulation, difficulties with the executive function can show up as ADHD (Cutting & Denckla, 2003). With an attention disorder, as noted earlier, individuals may have difficulty maintaining their focus and can easily be distracted. This distractibility occurs because they are unable to screen out stimuli that are irrelevant to the present task. Therefore, all stimuli are given equal weight, and the information-processing system can be overwhelmed with input. Imagine being in a store with forty-five televisions tuned to forty-five different channels. Trying to watch only one program would be difficult because all the TVs are producing sound and visual images that are competing for your attention. This is the experience that individuals with ADHD have when environmental stimulation is abundant. For an individual with ADHD, such as Angelina, introduced earlier in the chapter, a typical busy classroom may be challenging due to its numerous distractions. This is the world as she knows it, and it is no wonder that she finds it overwhelming at times.

ADD/ADHD

For an individual with ADHD, the activities of a typical busy classroom may be full of distractions.

Emotional Context of Information Processing

Emotional context is critical to our understanding of how students learn (Immordino-Yang & Damasio, 2007; Campos, Frankel & Camras, 2004). The IPM usually describes learning as a purely cognitive activity, but this is not how learning really takes place (Jensen, 2000, 2008). Both one's emotional environment and internal emotional state have a dramatic impact on one's ability to learn (Shattell, Bartlett, & Rowe, 2008; Willis, 2008). When the emotional environment is harsh or we perceive it as dangerous, our internal emotional states become acutely stressed and defensive. Neither this environment nor the internal state it produces is optimal for learning. Think for a moment of a time when you were trying to learn something new or to perform a task under a great deal of pressure and stress. Perhaps you were taking an exam, or maybe you were learning to drive. Take yourself back to that time and try to remember how you felt. Can you see how strong emotions can affect our ability to learn and to perform with success? In fact, strong negative emotions have an impact on all aspects of our ability to process information, coloring our perceptions,

A Painful Situation

A bad year
Without bad people really
No one exactly to blame
Just a sequence of events
A class that didn't belong to me
And I not belonging to it
The round peg in the square whole [*sic*]
So slowly I faded out
At first just the field trips and their ilk
Then for part of the day
And finally completely
As words sprang and papers vanished
I became more and more lost and confused
And most of all sad
So the round peg
Found a round whole
And so the story ends
At least it was without villains

(unpublished poem, by Shane Wilder 2004)

Shane was born in 1992 and has lived in Albuquerque his whole life. He began writing in the second grade, when he won the New Mexico PTA Reflections Fair. Years later one of his stories, *To Top It All Off*, about his experience of having a learning disability, was placed in the Library of Congress. In 2005 and 2006 Shane was recognized as an All-American Scholar. But in spite of these academic successes, Shane's early life was filled with struggles in school. His parents captured Shane's dilemma this way: "In the early elementary school grades, Shane experienced profound failure and, in our view, a lack of understanding that a student could have a substantial learning disability and also be intellectually gifted. This was especially confusing for some teachers because his primary area of disability identified was in reading and written language, and yet these are also the primary areas of his giftedness." Like other students who are *twice exceptional*, Shane

is gifted in several areas, but these strengths are combined with areas of great challenge. In Shane's case, he has a specific learning disability that affects reading. In fact, through fourth grade, Shane was essentially a nonreader, and he describes his difficulties this way: "It all began in the second grade. That was when I realized that I couldn't read, write, or keep track of things like other kids could. Thus I sort of fell out of regular education, first into a special education class at my school and eventually into Mr. Higgins's twice-exceptional class."

Shane Wilder
(Courtesy of Author)

scrambling our thinking, interrupting our ability to communicate, and, perhaps most important, clouding our judgment or executive functioning (Lewis & Stieben, 2004). As our understanding of neurology develops, we see that emotions and cognition are interwoven and cannot be viewed separately (Zimmerman & Schunk, 2008).

Individuals with learning disabilities may be even more vulnerable to toxic emotional environments than other students because their internal

Shane kept his love of language and learning alive by getting his books on tape. According to his parents, "Shane continued to be a motivated learner, but he became very discouraged about his daily failure at school. At home he discovered books on tape, which greatly helped his mental state as he was able to read the books he loved independently and continue to learn new words and ideas that were so important to him." One of Shane's teachers in middle school said, "Shane's passion for language would be remarkable in any teenager but is astounding when coupled with the severe learning disability that made reading 'with his eyes' a struggle at best and, for most of his elementary years, an impossibility. How could a boy who faced years of failure—and at times stinging humiliation—maintain his love of books? Thank heavens for books on tape!" The books on tape allowed Shane to use his strong listening comprehension, his outstanding ability to think, and his natural curiosity about life to continue learning.

Shane was also fortunate because the Albuquerque Public Schools has one of the finest programs for students who are twice exceptional. As Shane's struggles in school increased, his parents sought out ways to help him:

> We were so very fortunate at that time to meet Dr. Dennis Higgins. Shane was eventually transferred to the school where Dr. Higgins was teaching a model elementary school classroom for students who were identified as both gifted and having an area of disability. Shane felt "at home" from the moment he stepped into this classroom and, with the love and guidance, became willing to try again to be a "successful" student.

Shane talks about his journey back to school success this way:

> It began with learning to accept school again once I got to Mr. Higgins's class. This occurred by beginning my time in Mr. Higgins's class with very little work and a lot of support for those few things. In Mr. Higgins's class I slowly learned, one, to catch up in skills that I have missed and, two,

to persist in things that were hard. As well, I had a series of reading teachers who had varying levels of success, until the final one who taught the Wilson Program, which was exceedingly dull and boring, but it had its desired effect. By working two hours a week one-on-one with the teacher, I finally learned to read in the fifth grade.

> I am currently doing well in the ninth grade, where I take honors English, analytical biology, and a "gifted" health class but also study skills (a.k.a. resource room special education support). The most important support for being successful in challenging academic classes at this point are my IEP modifications, especially those that allow a teacher to accept my work based on content that might otherwise be disqualified because of spelling and/or conventions of writing. Books on tape are and always will be the most important adaptation for me because, even though I can now read at an expected level, it is still slow and less effective; therefore, I rely on audio books for most of my reading. The final modification of great relevance is the ability to either use voice activation software (which is new to me) or dictation for long written work.

He added that although he does not have any "sage" advice, he would suggest that others who struggle with twice exceptionalities should "find Dr. Higgins or his clone!"

Pivotal Issues

- Students who are twice exceptional have complex needs. What should we be doing to recognize and respond to these needs?

- How can teachers help their students develop the persistence in the face of difficulty that Shane describes?

- How do you think Shane's elementary school years might have been changed if his school had used an RTI approach?

emotional states are often less secure (Shattell, et al., 2008). Repeated experiences of failure and frustration can lead to **anticipatory anxiety** in the face of new situations, even when the situation is not particularly stressful (Bender, 2001; Levine, 2003). This anticipatory anxiety can sabotage success by undermining self-confidence at the start of a new experience. Anticipatory anxiety can also lead to heightened sensitivity and defensiveness, which further erode an individual's ability to respond to new situations and opportunities.

> The emotional environment and our internal emotional states have a dramatic impact on information processing.

Thus far we have discussed the impact of the emotional context on cognition, but the emotional context also affects social situations. When an individual has a learning disability that affects his or her ability to read and understand social cues, social situations can feel threatening because people are often very unpredictable. The individual may have difficulty reading and understanding social cues due to this unpredictability.

In a classroom, a student's success is directly related to his or her skills in understanding and interpreting the teacher's expectations. Most students know when they are about to "cross the line" with a teacher and pull back enough to prevent negative consequences. Students who have learning disabilities that affect their understanding of social cues and who have difficulty with self-regulation may often find themselves in trouble. This tendency further exacerbates the anxiety response in the face of similar situations. When you are fairly certain that you will get in trouble and you don't know how to prevent it, you can become anxious when anticipating the future.

Put yourself in the shoes of Andrew, Jason, Ray, or Angelina for a moment and think about how their frustrations, fears, and anxieties compound their difficulties and make learning even harder for them. The importance of a positive emotional climate for learning is discussed later in the chapter.

The Information Processing Model as a System

Although each part of the IPM has been discussed separately, the components work together as a system. Each component influences and is influenced by others in a continuous feedback loop. An anomaly or problem in one area will have an impact on other components.

For example, a student with a visual processing problem that affects *closure* will have a difficult time recognizing the differences between the letter pairs *a/u, n/h, a/d, h/b, a/g, c/o, a/q, c/d, t/f, i/l, i/j, o/p, r/n,* and *v/y.* If he or she has a problem with *visual rotations* and *mirror images,* then the following letter pairs will become difficult: *b/d, q/p, q/g, u/n, h/y, m/w,* and *g/p.* With these moderate perceptual difficulties, reading becomes a struggle. The

The appropriate instruction is based on the child's individual needs.
(© Courtesy of Cengage Learning)

Throughout this chapter we have looked at the multiple ways that a learning disability can affect a student's ability to learn. We have noted that the category of learning disabilities includes individuals with widely different kinds of strengths and needs. Because of these unique needs, an IEP or 504 plan that links educational interventions and supports to the specific needs of each student is essential. The following section on educational adaptations gives general suggestions and strategies for meeting the needs of students with learning disabilities, understanding that as teachers we must match these to the individual student's needs. In this section we use the RTI model to look at the three tiers of the intervening hierarchy and think about how students' needs are addressed at each level. We will also refer back to the information processing model (Figure 4.2) to present a variety of strategies that can support students with problems in each of the processing areas (input, processing, output, executive functions, and self-regulation of emotional states) for the content areas of reading, math, and writing.

Adapting the Learning Environment

The RTI approach to meeting students' needs builds on collaboration between general and special education across the intervention hierarchy, or tiers of support. The **intervening hierarchy,** used to deliver supports and services to students with learning problems, shows how the needs of students can be addressed in a variety of settings within the school (see Figure 4.4). At each tier teachers work to match instruction to the learning needs of the student through systematic progress monitoring (Bush & Reschly, 2007). Students receive support at the different tiers based on the intensity of their needs, and movement across the tiers is determined by the students' responses to the supports offered.

▲ Tier I: "Universal"—The General Education Classroom

The general education classroom is the primary prevention and intervention site for all students. Effective teaching using evidence-based curriculum and pedagogy creates a high-quality learning environment in which most students should be successful. Teachers intentionally plan for their students, responding to their needs. The general classroom teacher uses universal screening and periodic progress monitoring to check on the needs of her or his students (Compton, Fuchs, Fuchs, & Bryant, 2006). Progress monitoring at Tier I helps the teacher to determine whether her or his students are making appropriate gains in their

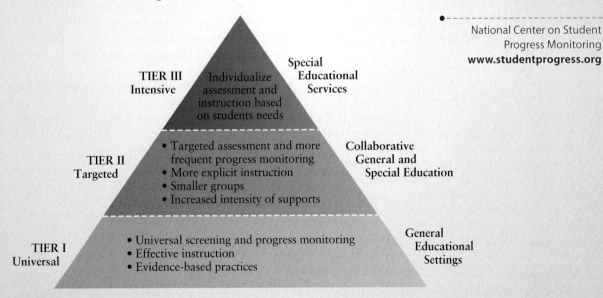

National Center on Student Progress Monitoring
www.studentprogress.org

FIGURE 4.4
Intervening Hierarchy for RTI
Adapted from www.nasdse.org/projects.cfm? page projectid=23. Reprinted by permission of National Association of State Directors of Special Education.

learning. Teachers may use performance outcome measures that align the overall learning goals (these are often called curriculum-based measures) to monitor progress, or they may use work sampling, in which tasks are drawn directly from the learning activities and are used as evidence of a student's mastery or needs.

When we first met Andrew at the beginning of the chapter, he was struggling in third grade because his reading skills were weak. If his teachers had been able to recognize his needs and respond to them earlier using an RTI approach, Andrew might have had a better chance of success.

Following is what Andrew's kindergarten classroom would have looked like if the RTI approach had been in place.

Ms. Brown, Andrew's kindergarten teacher, uses a guided reading approach to help all her students get ready to learn to read. This approach focuses on early reading skills, including print awareness, phonemic awareness, vocabulary building, word recognition, reading fluency, and reading comprehension. At the beginning of the year, as part of the schoolwide screening, Ms. Brown assessed all of her students on letter naming, letter sound recognition (phonemic awareness), word recognition, story retelling (retelling the story from memory after it had been read aloud), and story sequencing (placing pictures in order to show the story as it was told). Andrew had a very difficult time with most of these skills, but he was very good at story retelling and picture sequencing. Ms. Brown noted Andrew's initial skill levels in each area and began her instruction with Andrew. She also sent a note home to Andrew's parents asking them to read with and to Andrew as often as possible. She included two books that she thought might interest Andrew, with a list of questions to be used in discussion of the books.

Andrew was placed with a group of his classmates who all needed to strengthen their early reading skills. For six weeks Ms. Brown collected weekly progress monitoring data on letter naming, letter-sound matches, and word recognition. At the end of this period she used this information to review what her students had mastered. At this point, she realized that Andrew was not making appropriate gains in his phonemic awareness and that he was falling further behind his classmates in word recognition. Ms. Brown decided that Andrew's needs required even more intensive instruction, so she brought Andrew's file to the kindergarten team meeting. In addition to the kindergarten teach-

ers, the team meeting included the school's reading specialist and special education teacher. At the team meeting, it was decided that Andrew would benefit from short-term intensive instruction on letter recognition and phonics and that Andrew would receive reading support with Tier II "targeted" services.

▲ Tier II: "Targeted"—Collaborative Interventions

As the intensity of the students' needs increases, the level of support to meet the needs must also increase. In Tier II, general and special education come together to provide the support needed. Interventions at Tier II are characterized by instruction that is more explicit or directive, along with expanded learning opportunities that are embedded in the students' daily learning experience. Learning supports at Tier II are often provided in smaller groups to increase the intensity of the instruction, and the frequency of progress monitoring is also increased. Tier II learning activities act as supplements to Tier I and are designed to correct problems early and to prevent further problems from developing. The general classroom teacher works with specialists to design and implement Tier II interventions. Through this collaborative process the team selects **standard protocol** interventions and works together in a problem-solving mode to determine what else should be done for the child. Progress monitoring in Tier II is used to see whether the intervention has been successful and to help in determining whether the child needs more intense supports (Fuchs & Fuchs, 2006).

In Andrew's case, he joined two other students who worked three times a week with the reading specialist on mastering letter-sound matches (phonemic awareness) and word recognition. An evidence-based curriculum was selected to teach these skills, and this support was provided in addition to all the early reading instruction that Andrew received in his general classroom. Andrew's progress on both skills was monitored three times per week, and records were kept to show his **slope of improvement** (see Figure 4.5).

A meeting was held with Andrew's parents to share Andrew's progress and discuss his needs. Andrew's parents suggested that they could help more with word recognition and wondered whether there might be any computer software that they could use for this. They also asked his teachers to remember his outstanding memory for stories that were read to him, and together they decided to use this strength to help him develop

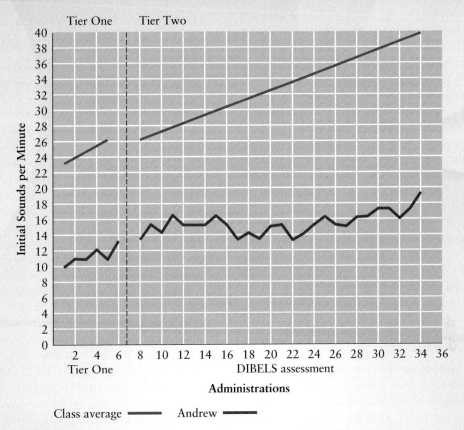

FIGURE 4.5
Andrew's Progress Monitoring Chart for Phonemic Awareness
Source: W.N. Bender & C. Shores. (2007). *Response to Intervention*. (p. 59). CA: Sage.
Reproduced with permission of Sage Publications Inc. Books in the format Textbook via
Copyright Clearance Center.

a word bank of his favorite words from the stories he heard. Andrew created a notebook with pages for each letter and began adding words the next afternoon after story time. In addition to the word, his teacher helped him write a sentence using the word, and Andrew drew a picture in his word bank showing the part of the story in which this word occurred (see Figure 4.6).

Andrew's teaching team met again with his parents to review his progress at the end of nine weeks. It was decided that, although Andrew had made substantial

SNAKE

The snake was
fast and sneaky.

SPIDER

The spider
sat on her web.

FIGURE 4.6
Sample Page from Andrew's Word Bank

progress in both his phonemic awareness and his word recognition, he still needed the intense support to be successful. The team also agreed that more information about Andrew's learning needs should be gathered through a comprehensive evaluation. The planned evaluation included individual assessments of Andrew's listening, thinking, speaking, reading, writing, spelling, and math—the seven domains identified in the legal definition of specific learning disabilities. An occupational therapist was brought onto Andrew's team to assess his handwriting, sensory integration, and motor skills. These assessments, in combination with the progress monitoring data, gave a comprehensive picture of Andrew's strengths and challenges to help the team determine how to meet his needs. The assessment would also be used to decide whether Andrew would need the more intensive services provided through the school's special education program.

▲ Tier III: "Intensive"—Individualized Educational Services

When the results of Andrew's assessments had been compiled, the team met again. This time the team members reviewed all of the assessment information and discussed Andrew's eligibility for special educational services. Andrew's assessment verified the observations that his teachers and parents had made and helped them understand the complexity of his needs. Andrew's strengths and challenges placed him in the gifted range and also showed that he was eligible for learning disabilities services. With both giftedness and learning disabilities present, Andrew is a youngster who is twice exceptional. The psychological report indicated that "Andrew's reading and writing deficits will impact all academic areas. But in spite of these problems, he understands concepts easily, has an advanced vocabulary, and demonstrates very superior verbal abilities. Andrew's listening comprehension is very advanced, and his critical thinking is strong." The areas of difficulty included significant delays in visual-motor integration, early reading skills, and writing, and moderate difficulties with early math achievement. This information, along with the progress monitoring data, indicated that Andrew should be identified for special education services for learning disabilities and that he would also need support for his gifted strengths. The team agreed that an IEP would be needed for Andrew to help him with the transition to first grade.

Strategies That Work to Support Students with Learning Disabilities

Earlier in this chapter we looked at the IPM as a way to think about the impact that a learning disability can have. Tables 4.4 through 4.7 show learning strategies that can help to address difficulties with each component of the IPM system. These strategies are presented for reading, writing, and math, but they can be used in all of the content areas. Each of the strategies chosen for inclusion in these tables has an evidence base for success. Taken together, these strategies form a set of options that can be matched to the students needs. Assistive technology has also been listed when technological supports exist for learning. Some of the ideas given focus on the teacher and the learning environment, whereas others are suggestions the student can use.

Table 4.4 shows strategies that can be used to support students who have difficulties with processing input. Remember that students with learning disabilities have problems with perception, or how the brain interprets the information, not with acuity or the ability of the sensory organ to take in stimuli. Ray, the second child we met in this chapter, has severe auditory processing difficulties. This means that it is very hard for him to take in information when he is reading or listening; but remember that Ray is very good with hands-on projects. The strategies that will support Ray need to focus on using multiple pathways for processing the information. Look at the ideas presented in Table 4.4 and identify strategies that you think would help Ray learn. Which of these would be helpful for his Tier I supports? Which might need collaboration between his classroom and special education teacher? Which of these would be helpful for his Tier II supports? Which strategies should be taught or delivered within his special education services, Tier III?

Some students with learning disabilities have problems with processing information. These problems make it difficult for them to organize their thoughts and ideas and to retrieve information that they have learned. Ray has a very hard time with memory, and he often finds organizing his ideas to be a daunting task. In addition to the strategies you identified to help Ray with his input difficulties, what strategies do you think would help him with his memory and organization of ideas? Review Table 4.5 to see whether there are things you feel could be done to support Ray's learning within each tier of intervention (Tiers I, II, and II).

TABLE 4.4
Support Strategies for Students with Learning Disabilities: Using the Information Processsing Model (Input Problems)

Information-processing component	General strategies	Reading strategies	Math strategies	Writing strategies	Assistive technology
Input problems	1. Content outlines 2. Advanced organizers 3. Syllabus or class overview 4. Reduce distractions 5. Use multiple learning styles (e.g., visual, auditory, kinesthetic) 6. Preferential seating 7. Carrell or screen	1. SQ3R (survey, ask questions, read, recite, review) 2. Think about what you already know 3. Self-check and "fix it fast" if you don't understand something	1. Use manipulatives 2. Learn multiple problem-solving approaches (e.g., guess and check, draw a picture, simplify, etc.)	1. Use writing process that includes: a. prewriting organization b. "note cards" for references c. all your senses to set the stage for writing (e.g., listen, look, feel)	1. Text-to-voice readers 2. Calculators 3. Franklin spellers that "speak" 4. End notes software for references
Visual difficulties	1. Graphic organizers 2. Color code information 3. Black-and-white, clearly printed handouts 4. Highlight direction words 5. Use a cover sheet, reduce distractions	1. Use card to guide eyes across the page 2. Read out loud so you "hear" the words 3. Books on tape	1. Use graph paper with large squares to keep numbers organized 2. Turn lined paper sideways to create columns for your work	1. Reduce or eliminate "far point copying" from board	1. Large-print screens, text 2. Reduce glare on computer screen 3. Color "gels" to overlay on page
Auditory difficulties	1. Use headphones to reduce noise 2. Tape lectures to listen to again 3. Listen to music as you work	1. Scan the written material; focus on understanding charts, graphics, and pictures 2. Use chapter features (e.g., headings, bold print, summaries, etc.) 3. Watch the movie	1. Use pictures and visual prompts to support problem solving 2. Make sure all directions are written down in clear steps (1, 2, 3,...)	1. Reduce or eliminate dictated writing	1. Tape recorders

(Continued)

TABLE 4.4
Support Strategies for Students with Learning Disabilities: Using the Information Processsing Model (Input Problems) (*continued*)

Tactile difficulties	1. Wear comfortable clothing	1. Role-play to act out word problems	1. Trace letters, words on sandpaper or textured surface
	2. Cut tags out of shirts and avoid rough seams		
	3. Avoid foods with unpleasant (for you) textures (seeds, stickiness, etc.)		

ADD/ADHD Problems with output often create difficulties such as those faced by Jason, one of the students we have discussed in this chapter. Jason has a very hard time with handwriting, and his behavior is becoming increasingly more disruptive as his frustration escalates. Reviewing Table 4.6, what kinds of things might be put in place to reduce Jason's frustration with output difficulties while supporting his strengths in thinking, or processing? What levels of assistive technology support (i.e., low, middle, and/or high) would Jason need to be successful? How do you think these supports could be implemented within a tiered, or RTI, approach? What kinds of collaboration will Jason's classroom and special education teacher need to form in order to help Jason become successful?

Some of the most challenging difficulties faced by students with learning disabilities are those that affect the executive function abilities. Angelina, a student discussed in this chapter, has ADHD. She is easily distracted and finds it very hard to stay on task. Because ADHD and problems with executive functioning will affect all areas of information processing, many of the strategies listed in Tables 4.4 through 4.7 will be important for her. Take a look at these and identify key strategies you feel could be used within Tier I, the general classroom; Tier II, the collaborative intervention; and Tier III, special education services.

The emotional context within which individuals learn is also key to understanding the IPM. Thinking about Ray, Jason, and Angelina, how can their teachers create the emotionally supportive environment they will need to thrive in school? Often, when we begin to look at how we can support students with special learning needs, we find that the same strategies would benefit many of our other students. How would all of our students' learning be enhanced if some of the strategies you have identified for Ray, Jason, and Angelina were more broadly implemented in general education classrooms? Visit the Education CourseMate website for tips on helping students with learning disabilities be successful with test taking.

The National Research Center on Learning Disabilities at the University of Kansas has an outstanding website that gives evidence-based strategies for working with students with learning disabilities.

National Research Center on Learning Disabilities
www.nrcld.org

Educational adaptations should be designed to minimize the impact of the disability while maximizing the student's ability to be successful. Adaptations that help the student become more autonomous

TABLE 4.5
Support Strategies for Students with Learning Disabilities: Using the Information Processing Model (Processing Problems)

Information-processing component	General strategies	Reading strategies	Math strategies	Writing strategies
Processing problems	1. Sit near a study buddy 2. Break up longer work periods with short breaks to stretch and move 3. Create or use study guides 4. Allow movement to help anchor learning 5. Use simulations and action games for learning	1. Get the assignments ahead of time and start reading early 2. Highlight key words and ideas 3. Write margin notes in book as you read 4. Summarize key ideas as you read	1. Use real-life examples as the basis for math problems	1. Talk your work over with someone 2. Backward-map your work to see if the flow is logical (i.e., look at the ending and work backward to make sure that all the supporting details have been included)
Memory challenges	1. Learning concepts versus isolated facts 2. Chunking information 3. Mnemonic devices such as My Dear Aunt Sally for the order of operations (multiplication, division, addition, subtraction) 4. Rehearsals or repetition of information, often as a chant 5. Keep lists and use flash cards to study	1. Use headings to outline material and take notes 2. Write short summaries 3. Create a visual to help remember main ideas and sequences (time lines, story lines, etc.) 4. Retell the story/ material 5. Discuss with others	1. Use mnemonics 2. Use strategies to help with memorization of facts and formulas 3. Focus on math problem solving and understanding processes	1. Use note-taking and prewriting strategies 2. Keep a to-do list 3. Insert a "next steps" note to remind yourself where you are going when your writing is interrupted 4. Stop writing with a sentence left half finished so you can start back easily
Thinking challenges	1. Concept webs 2. Learning frames (Edwin Ellis, www.graphicorganizers.com/downloads.htm) 3. Make relationships across ideas explicit 4. Start reviewing for tests early	1. Listen to class discussions and ask questions 2. Ask yourself questions about the material	1. Model the thinking by "thinking out loud" 2. Discuss the relationships and patterns to understand the "why" of math	1. Dictate your thoughts prior to writing so you will remember them 2. Talk to yourself about the ideas you want to share 3. Find editorial support

TABLE 4. 6
Support Strategies for Students with Learning Disabilities: Using the Information Processing Model (Output Problems)

Information-processing component	General strategies	Reading strategies	Math strategies	Writing strategies	Assistive technology
Output problems	1. Separate grades for content and mechanics (e.g., spelling, grammar, punctuation) 2. Reduce assignment length; focus on the essentials 3. Ask for extra credit		1. Remember that less is often more (reduce the number of "practice" problems)	1. Dictate responses 2. Allow short written answers when appropriate 3. Use note-taker support	1. Use *all* available technology for support (e.g., voice activation software, photocopies, etc.)
Speaking difficulties	1. Make notes ahead of time of key points you want to make in a discussion and practice these	1. Practice ahead when you need to read out loud	1. Draw pictures of problems 2. Use charts and graphs to communicate	1. Use notes and emails to communicate versus phone calls	1. Use software to "read" written material
Writing difficulties	1. Use prewriting techniques		1. Use math talks to share what is learned	1. No penalty for poor handwriting 2. Use the drafting process and seek feedback (start early!) 3. Learn essay-writing techniques and use them	1. Computers (spelling and grammar check) 2. Inspiration software as a prewriting tool 3. Voice-activated software

TABLE 4.7
Support Strategies for Students with Learning Disabilities: Using the Information Processing Model (Executive Function Problems)

Information-processing component	General strategies	Reading strategies	Math strategies	Writing strategies	Assistive technology
Executive function problems	1. Use assignment books 2. Create schedules for day and week, and calendar for semester (color code what you must do, what you should do, and what you want to do) 3. Make lists and check things off 4. Create quiet study place with everything you need handy 5. Keep materials organized with a system that works for you (e.g., color-coded notebooks)	1. Focus on topic sentences, conclusions, and summaries 2. Use Cliffs Notes to help you summarize learning 3. Understand that different kinds of written material need different kinds of reading and adjust accordingly	1. Focus on one step or direction at a time 2. Check your work to verify accuracy 3. Work slowly and try to be neat 4. Use reading strategies to help with word problems (e.g., highlight key words, etc.)	1. Think about who your audience is and what it needs to know to understand your message 2. First focus on your key points (what would the bumper sticker say), then expand them 3. Ask for peer editor feedback	1. Day planners and Palm Pilots 2. Electronic calendars and schedulers

and independent are optimal. The responsibility for learning and for self-regulation ultimately rests with the individual, but it is the job of educators to provide the support needed so that the individual can thrive. Fortunately, the child's family can play a critical role in the support system.

▶❚❚ TeachSource **VIDEO CONNECTION**

Learning Disabilities

Please visit the Education CourseMate website to access the TeachSource Video Case for Chapter 4. In this video, you will meet Laura Sestito, mother of three boys (Joseph, Christian, and Nicholas) each of whom has a learning disability. As you watch this video, reflect on the following questions: In addition to their learning disabilities, what other challenges does each of the boys face? How has parental advocacy helped each of the Sestito boys meet with success? How do other families that you know cope with having a child, or children, with disabilities?

Assistive Technology for Students with Learning Disabilities

Assistive technologies play a key role in supporting students with learning disabilities (TAM, 2009; Dell, Newton, & Petroff, 2008). Assistive technology helps to support students by minimizing the impact of their disability (Castellani & Warger, 2009). Tables 4.4 through 4.7 suggested several levels of assistive technology, such as text-to-voice readers, calculators, and spellers. These range from the use of tape recorders to help students with auditory processing problems to voice-activated software for students with output challenges. One thing you might also notice as you review the assistive technology suggestions is that these ideas will often work for many children in a given classroom. This means that when we make assistive technology available to support students with learning disabilities, we can actually enhance learning for other students in the class as well.

- •
Technology and Media Division
of Council for Exceptional
Children
www.tamcec.org

Evidence-Based Practices for Students with Learning Disabilities

While each student is unique, there are some instructional approaches we know help students with learning disabilities master new content. Research supports teaching that is explicit, strategic, scaffolded, and metcognitive (Faggella-Luby, & Deshler, 2008; Maccini, Mulcahy, & Wilson, 2007; Wolegmuth, Cobb, & Alwell, 2008; Ellis, Farmer, & Newman, 2005; Deshler et al., 2001; Graham & Harris, 2009; Coleman, 2005).

- **Explicit teaching** involves using language that is both precise and concise, giving clear examples of what is to be learned (e.g., avoiding vague, disorganized, and cluttered presentations of information), and providing schemas that show the organization of ideas to be learned (Scheuermann, Deshler, & Schumaker, 2009; Maccini, Malcahy, & Wilson, 2007; Fuchs, Fuchs, Prentice Hamlett, Finelli, & Courey, 2004).

- **Strategic teaching** includes mnemonics, organizational strategies (e.g., graphic organizers, advanced organizers, and outlines), and specific approaches that facilitate memory, making connections across information being learned, and the ability to apply information within new contexts (Wolegemuth, Cobb, & Alwell, 2008; Deshler, Robinson, & Mellard, 2009; Gildroy & Deshler, 2008).

- **Scaffolding** of instruction includes moving from concrete to abstract; from simple to complex, and from supported to independent (Ellis, Farmer, & Newman, 2005; Coleman, 2005; Deshler, Robinson, & Mellard, 2009).

- A **metacognitive approach** to teaching means helping students understand how to "think about their thinking" as they work to solve problems, activate or select strategies to use, and anchor learning in their memory. It also helps students with self-regulatory skills that facilitate learning (Wery & Nietfeld, 2010; Faggella-Luby & Deshler, 2008; Maccini, Mulcahy, & Wilson, 2007; Wolegmuth, Cobb, & Alwell, 2008; Ellis, Farmer, & Newman, 2005; Deshler et al., 2001; Graham & Harris, 2009; Coleman, 2005).

You will see that these approaches are reflected in the ideas presented in Tables 4.4 through 4.7. How does teaching that is explicit, strategic, scaffolded, and metacognitive fit with what you know about learning as information processing?

individual spends the majority of his or her time and energy sorting the letters and decoding the words. This leaves little room for understanding meaning, which is essential for moving information into short-term memory (see Figure 4.3).

Moderate problems with input will also hamper processing and thinking, making it difficult to learn. This will inhibit output (the ability to share what has been learned), because the information has not been deeply processed and stored in long-term memory. In contrast, for good readers, the decoding becomes automatic. This automaticity means that while they are reading, they can also process the information; they can think about what they are learning. When all the components work together, this facilitates understanding and keeps the IPM operating smoothly. In addition to the influences of each IPM component on the others, disabilities are further complicated because of the multiplicity of problems. It is not unusual, for example, for a student to have problems with visual perception, short-term memory, sequencing information, organizing thoughts, and handwriting. This same individual might be strong in auditory perception, creative insights, and talking. In fact, this combination reflects Andrew's learning profile, but each individual will have a unique combination of strengths and problems.

Remember that when we use the term *learning disability* we are referring to a wide range of learning problems that coexist with a variety of learning strengths. Therefore, each student with a learning disability will have a unique profile and will need an educational environment that can address these differences.

Families provide support to help their child find success.
(© Ronnie Kaufman/Blend Images/Corbis)

Family and Support Issues

Families are a critical part of the support system for individuals with learning disabilities. Because a learning disability is often not identified until the child reaches school age, the adjustment of the family to the child's needs comes later than it will in some other areas of disability, as discussed in Chapter 3. Families of children with learning disabilities are at risk themselves if they lack social support and are undergoing stress in coping with their child's disability. Because learning disabilities seem to run in families, parents may feel guilty that they have genetically passed this on to their child. Parents may also be struggling with some of the same problems that their child is experiencing, and so they may feel ill equipped to help. However, families are unique, and often they display amazing strengths, as well as needs. Many recognize that their child with learning disabilities needs to be taught strategies (executive functions) for learning, as well as information and facts. Families are also key to convincing their children with learning disabilities that they are not "stupid" or "lazy," and families can play a major role in challenging their children to persist in the face of academic challenges (Shattell et al., 2008).

Teachers working closely with families can develop an IEP or 504 plan for the child. Strong partnerships with parents help both the teacher and the parents understand the child's needs. The parents play two key roles for their child with learning disabilities (Baum & Owen, 2004). The first is as an advocate for the child, working to ensure that the school addresses their child's needs. As teachers, it can sometimes be difficult when parents ask us to change our practices to better meet the needs of their child. But it is critical that we listen. If we have formed a strong partnership with the parents, we can work together, and the parents' knowledge of their child can help us meet the child's needs.

The second key role of parents is to create a support system at home to provide a safe and loving environment with the necessary structures for the child's success. Table 4.8 shows a few things parents can do to support their child with learning disabilities.

Although the suggestions in Table 4.8 may seem like solid ideas for any family, the consistency, organization, and positive tones are even more critical for the healthy development of children with learning disabilities. The major task of every family with children is to prepare them for a meaningful life. This is no different for families who have a child who has learning disabilities.

 # Transitions to Postsecondary Life for Individuals with Learning Disabilities

> It is important that we follow children with learning disabilities into adulthood to confirm the impact of interventions.

The transition from adolescence to young adulthood can be a difficult time for anyone (Levine, 2005). The normal struggles with independence, identity formation, and lifestyle choices are compounded when a disability is added. The challenges of transition to adult life can be even more daunting for Latino youth with learning disabilities who face barriers due to language, citizenship status, and lack of community resources (Povenmire-Kirk, Lindsrom, & Bullis, 2010). Studies of risk-taking behaviors indicate that compared with their non–learning-disabled peers, adolescents with learning disabilities engage more

TABLE 4.8
Ideas for Parental Support for Students with Learning Disabilities

- As much as possible, create a consistent household schedule for daily routines (bedtimes, wake-up times, dressing, leaving for school, meals, room cleaning, TV time, chores, etc.).

- Develop clear guidelines for expected behavior framed from the positive (what you want rather than what you don't want), and place these in a chart or contract if needed for a reminder.

- Consistently reinforce expectations from a positive point of view and, if necessary, develop consequences for inappropriate behavior. Consequences should be naturally linked to behavior. For example, if a child breaks a toy out of anger, the consequences may be to clean up the mess and to give one toy away to a child who does not have many toys. For a teenager who stays out too late and does not call, the consequence may be grounding for a week with no phone privileges.

- Use prompts and checklists for normal chores if needed (prepare a get-ready-for-school checklist to use the night before).

- Organize, organize, organize!

- Set up things you need for the next day the night before (clothes out, lunch made, everything gathered together by the door, etc.).

- Provide a quiet study place and time.

- Check to see that homework has been done and verify that the agreed-on amount of time has been spent working on assignments.

- If needed, seek out the help of a tutor or study coach.

- Help your child regulate blood sugar with healthy snacks and foods.

- Help your child get appropriate exercise to regulate mood and stress.

- If medications are needed, monitor these and their impact.

- Monitor TV time, programs watched, computer time, and Internet access.

- Communicate your love and appreciation of your child often and in very concrete ways.

- If there are other siblings in the family, make sure that their needs are also addressed, and do not set siblings in competition for your approval.

frequently in risk-taking behaviors such as smoking, using marijuana, acts of delinquency, aggression, and gambling (McNamara & Willoughby, 2010). Students with learning disabilities may also use passive coping strategies (e.g., ignoring the problem and hoping it will just go away) (Firth, Greaves, & Frydenberg, 2010). Given the increased likelihood of risk-taking behaviors in combination with limited coping strategies, counseling support may be important for adolescents with learning disabilities when they face difficult life choices.

Transition plans, as discussed in Chapter 2, need to consider the student's current levels of performance, interests and aptitudes, postsecondary goals, and transition activities. These plans must also address who is responsible for implementing the plan and how the plan will be reviewed (Lerner & Johns, 2009). The plan may focus on transition to work or to postsecondary educational opportunities.

For many students with learning disabilities, school has been a place where they have struggled, and so decisions about postsecondary options are filled with mixed emotions. Yet in spite of these challenges, students with learning disabilities are attending college in growing numbers (DaDeppo, 2009; Coleman, 1994; Kosine, 2007; Kravets, 2006). Colleges and universities that receive any federal funds are legally required to provide support for students with disabilities (Block, 2003a). In spite of this requirement, supports and services vary widely from campus to campus and graduation rates for students with learning disabilities continue to lag behind those of their nondisabled peers (DaDeppo, 2009; Kirby, Silvestri, Allingham, Parrila, & LaFave, 2008). A solid support system at the college level is important for students with learning disabilities because, as Block (2003b) points out, college is different from high school. Think of the many things that you, as a college student, are expected to do that were never part of your high school experiences (Kirby et al., 2008). Now imagine the impact these differences would have on you if you also were coping with a learning disability. Not all students with learning disabilities will go to college; many will choose other options. The most important thing is that during their early educational years we have prepared them for the many opportunities that will come their way in life so that they can make sound personal decisions and meaningful contributions to those around them.

moral dilemma
Classroom Modifications

Students with leaning disabilities often need modifications in their assignments in order to minimize the impact of their disabilities and to facilitate their success. Kevin's IEP, for example, includes extended time on exams, no penalty for spelling errors on essays written in class, and ability to use the computer for extensive written work. You are Kevin's high school English teacher, and one of your students has protested that giving these accommodations to Kevin is not fair. The protest is growing, and now several students have voiced their resentment of "Kevin's special treatment."

How will you handle this? What are your personal beliefs about this issue, and how will your beliefs affect your professional decisions? What does "fair" mean in the educational context for individuals with special learning needs?

Go to the Education CourseMate website to share your thoughts on this dilemma.

✱ Summary

▶ The field of learning disabilities has evolved over many years as we come to understand more about child and brain development. Individuals with learning disabilities are a heterogeneous group, and each student has his or her own unique set of strengths and challenges.

▶ Although the origins of learning disabilities are largely unknown, the most commonly accepted cause is a problem related to how individuals process information at the neurological level.

▶ A comprehensive evaluation that includes overall cognitive abilities and academic achievements in combination with progress monitoring data is essential to accurately diagnosing and planning services for students with learning disabilities.

▶ Determining if an English language learning student has a learning disability can be difficult because of the challenges children face when mastering two or more languages. Because of this a bilingual assessment is important.

▶ While the prevalence of students identified with learning disabilities has gone down, this remains the largest group within special education.

▶ Recognizing the early indications of a learning disability allows for support to begin before a child has met with failure.

▶ The response to intervention (RTI) approach promotes the collaboration between general and special educators needed to fully support students with learning disabilities.

▶ Most students with learning disabilities are served in general education classrooms with appropriate modifications (outlined in their IEPs) and/or 504 plans to help them be successful.

▶ The information processing model (IPM) can be used to help understand learning disabilities and to help us plan interventions and supports to help students overcome their challenges.

▶ Evidence-based teaching approaches include the use of explicit, strategic, scaffolded, and metacognitive strategies to support learning.

▶ Instructional and assistive technologies can greatly minimize the impact of a learning disability.

▶ Families of students with learning disabilities are critical both in their advocacy role and in the home support they provide for their child.

▶ Because adolescents with learning disabilities often show poor judgment and engage in risk-taking behavior to a greater extend then their nondisabled peers, counseling support may be needed.

▶ More and more students with learning disabilities are attending college and finding ways to use their strengths in meaningful and productive lives.

Future Challenges

1 *How will the use of RTI affect the identification of and services for students with learning disabilities?*

As RTI becomes more widely used, patterns of identification and services are likely to change, and we do not yet know what the full impact of this will be for students with learning disabilities. The following questions will need to be addressed: How will RTI change which students are identified?

Will RTI reduce the current overrepresentation of students from culturally diverse families? How will collaborative services be delivered in ways that ensure that the needs of students with learning disabilities are met? What will be done for those whose needs are in math or in other nonreading areas? How will parents' rights continue to be addressed as RTI becomes more prevalent?

2 *Increasing numbers of students with learning disabilities and attention-deficit disorders are attending colleges. What should be done to ensure smooth transitions and comprehensive services in the postsecondary setting?*

The wonderful news is that more and more students with disabilities are attending colleges. The difficulty is that institutions of higher education may not be fully prepared to meet the needs of these students. Questions that will need to be answered include: How can we make sure that colleges and universities are equipped to meet the needs of students with disabilities? What changes are needed in institutional policies (for example, admissions, drop-add periods, support services, housing, full-time-student criteria, and so forth) in light of this changing student population?

3 *How can the needs of twice-exceptional students be addressed?*

As more students are recognized as being twice exceptional—that is, gifted and with disabilities—supports and services need to be developed to address their complex needs. We need to ensure that the strengths of twice-exceptional students are nurtured and addressed through challenging learning experiences while, at the same time, appropriate supports are provided for the areas of disability. How can collaborative teams work to include gifted education specialists to address the needs of twice-exceptional students?

Key Terms

anticipatory anxiety
   p. 127

attention-deficit
   hyperactivity
   disorders p. 112

auditory perception
   p. 122

collaborative problem
   solving p. 120

dysgraphia p. 124

dyslexia p. 108

episodic memory p. 123

evidence-based
   interventions p. 112

executive processing
   p. 120

executive function
   p. 120

explicit teaching p. 138

heightened sensitivity
   p. 122

information processing
   model (IPM) p. 120

intervening hierarchy
   p. 129

long-term memory
   p. 123

metacognition p. 120

metacognitive approach
   p. 138

motor memory p. 123

progress monitoring
   p. 112

proprioceptive p. 122

scaffolding p. 138

self-regulatory skills
   p. 125

semantic memory
   p. 123

sensory integration
   p. 122

sensory memory p. 123

short-term memory
   p. 123

slope of improvement
   p. 130

standard protocol p. 130

strategic teaching
   p. 138

tactile defensiveness
   p. 122

twice exceptional p. 108

unexplained
   underachievement
   p. 108

visual perception p. 121

Resources

References of Special Interest

Division for Learning Disabilities. (2007). *Thinking about response to intervention and learning disabilities: A teacher's guide*. Arlington, VA. This publication of the Council for Exceptional Children's Division for Learning Disabilities is a brief, user-friendly guide to how the RTI approach can be used with students who have learning disabilities. It provides an excellent overview for teachers who will be working to implement RTI in their schools and classrooms.

Baum, S., & Owen, S. (2004). *To be gifted and learning disabled*. Mansfield, CT: Creative Learning Press. The paradox of students who are twice exceptional is discussed. Comprehensive guidance is provided for teachers, parents, and students on how to cope with the complexities of gifts in combination with areas of extreme challenge. The use of student case stories brings the book to life and makes the strategies presented readily applicable for use with students who may face similar difficulties.

Lerner, L., & Johns, B. (2009). *Learning disabilities and related mild disabilities*. Boston, MA: Houghton Mifflin. This is the definitive text on learning disabilities written by leading authors in the field. It shares the current strategies and ideas for identifying and serving students with learning disabilities and those with mild disabilities. It is a critical body of work that forms an essential foundation for teachers who work with these students.

Schumaker, J. B., & Deshler, D. D. (2010). Using a tiered intervention model in secondary schools to improve academic outcomes in subject-area courses. In M. R. Shinn & H.M. Walker (Eds.), *Intervention for achievement and behavior problems in a three-tier model including RTI*. Bethesda, MD: National Association of School Psychologists.

Journals

Learning Disabilities Research and Practice. A publication of the Division for Learning Disabilities, Council for Exceptional Children
www.TeachingLD.org

Learning Disability Quarterly. The journal of the Council for Learning Disabilities
www.cldinternational.org.

Journal of Learning Disabilities. A publication of the Hammill Institute on Disabilities, 512-451-3521.

Professional Organizations

National Research Center on Learning Disabilities
www.nrcld.org

Division for Learning Disabilities, Council for Exceptional Children
cec.sped.org
www.TeachLD.org

National Center for Learning Disabilities
www.ncld.org

Learning Disabilities Association (LDA)
www.ldanatl.org

Council for Learning Disabilities
www.cldinternational.org

 Visit the Education CourseMate website for additional TeachSource Video Cases, information about CEC standards, study tools, and much more.

Children with Autism Spectrum Disorders

 Focus Questions

▶ What are autism spectrum disorders?

▶ What are the presumed causes of these conditions?

▶ Why has the prevalence of individuals with autism spectrum disorders increased so dramatically?

▶ How are children with autism spectrum disorders identified?

▶ How does the theory of mind relate to autism spectrum disorders?

▶ What are some of the educational programs designed for children with autism?

▶ What are some special teaching strategies for working with these students?

▶ What specialized knowledge and skills should parents of children with ASD acquire?

▶ What public policy initiatives are available for children with ASD?

Courtesy of Cengage Learning

Mike Dolan's Story

Mike Dolan was a poster boy of a child. With his blond curly hair and clear blue eyes, he was, as neighbors and relatives said, a beautiful 2-year-old. But Mike's parents were worried about him. Something was clearly wrong with their child. He wasn't talking as 2-year-olds do. He made a series of physical motions with his hands that he kept repeating. And, above all, he didn't interact socially with his parents or others the way he should. For example, he didn't look directly at people when they talked to him, and he appeared not to pay attention to many of the things his parents said to him. He seemed preoccupied with his toy trucks and would play with them incessantly. When he wanted something, such as a glass of milk, he would go to the refrigerator, grab a bottle, and hand it to his mother rather than ask.

Finally, Mrs. Dolan decided to take him to the family pediatrician. Dr. Phinney examined Mike and found nothing physically wrong with his development, with the exception of some motor coordination difficulties. However, having seen a child with similar behavior two months before, the doctor suggested that the Dolans take Mike to a university clinic that had a multidisciplinary staff that could review Mike's needs.

Mike was evaluated by physicians, psychologists, and speech pathologists at the university clinic. Then they met with the Dolans and explained that in their judgment, Mike had a condition known as autism.

The lack of communication, his inability to interact socially, his obsession with particular toys, and his strange motor movements all pointed in that direction. It was fortunate that the Dolans had come to them so soon. Early intervention was essential, and it would be important to begin a treatment regimen right away.

The Dolans had many questions. What was this condition? What had caused the autism? Could future children that they might have contract the condition as well? Could it be cured, and if so, what would the treatment be? Mrs. Dolan wanted to know whether the schools could handle a child with this condition or whether Mike would need to go to a special school.

These are all good questions—ones that any parent might ask in a similar situation. Awareness of autism, with its patterns of symptoms, has grown. Now, children such as Mike can be diagnosed by age 2 or even earlier.

Pivotal Issues

- What problems within the classroom could you anticipate with Mike? Name and discuss them.

- Why is early identification so critical for a child like Mike?

Of all the groups in the category of exceptional children, the prevalence and knowledge of groups within autism spectrum disorders (ASD) have shown the greatest changes and modifications over the past two decades. The prevalence of children with ASD has increased by over 500 percent since 1992 (Volkmar et al., 2007)! Brain imaging techniques have uncovered suspected physiological differences in function between children with autism and typical children, and genetic involvement has also been documented. There have also been multiple innovations providing educational interventions, particularly with young children with ASD. We will discuss all these topics within this chapter.

What is important to remember is that autism is treatable! We can't cure the condition, but the language difficulties and social interaction problems faced by children with ASD can be meaningfully improved through education and therapeutic intervention.

Over the past two decades, there have been major controversies about the causes of autism, major legislative initiatives aimed at addressing the challenge of autism (the Combating Autism Act of 2006), and active advocacy groups of parents and professionals (Autism Speaks and Autism Society of America) who have been calling attention to these children and their educational and health needs. Mike, the boy introduced in the "Exceptional Lives, Exceptional Stories" box, exemplifies many of the special characteristics of children with autism. As

Autism Society of America
www.autism-society.org

we attempt to answer some of the Dolans's questions, it is important to keep in mind that there is still a great deal we do not know about autism or about the most effective ways to treat it.

What Are Autism Spectrum Disorders?

Autism spectrum disorders are a variety (or *spectrum*) of related disorders that affect a child's social development and ability to communicate and that include unusual behavioral manifestations such as repetitive motor movements. Included in the category of autism spectrum disorders are Rett syndrome, pervasive developmental disorders–not otherwise specified (PDD–NOS), Asperger's syndrome (observable in high-functioning children with autism-like symptoms), and childhood disintegrative disorders, which cause children to regress in their development (such as in a child who once had speech but is no longer communicating) (Lord, 2001).

Rett syndrome is a condition included within autism spectrum disorders because its symptoms resemble autism. It is a progressive neurological disorder in which individuals reveal a loss of muscle functions, hand flapping, and autistic behavior. Symptoms appear in children 6 to 18 months old, and educational treatment is similar to treatment for autism.

Pervasive developmental disorder–not otherwise specified (PDD–NOS) refers to a group of disorders characterized by delays in the development of socialization and communication skills. Individuals with PDD–NOS usually have some but not all of the full symptoms of autism and, as a result, may not be diagnosed until later on in childhood.

Asperger's syndrome (AS) has gained much public interest over the past few years. Named in 1944 for Viennese physician Hans Asperger, this autism spectrum disorder has received renewed attention in recent years due to increased interest in the general condition of autism and to its increased prevalence. One of the distinguishing characteristics of students with AS is an observable developmental imbalance. On the one hand, they can be of average or superior intelligence; on the other, they are unfailingly years behind in their social development.

In addition, students with AS may have a preoccupation with certain subjects almost to the exclusion of other subjects (for instance, the solar system or computers) and can become experts in a narrow field that includes things but not people. They may also show stereotypical behavior, such as "hand flapping," and various nonfunctional rituals, such as insisting that the objects on a shelf always

Exercises like these are useful in helping students with Asperger's syndrome feel more comfortable with eye contact.

(AP Photo/Minnesota Public Radio, Tim Post)

Play from an Asperger's View

Anything related to the human body seemed to me bad news. In the fourth grade, when my affliction was most intense, I would be herded out to play kickball during our physical-education classes. Teams were chosen, and I was embedded among the strongest kids, to provide some chance of even battle. In memory, it is forever bases loaded with two outs when my turn at the plate comes, and I am as well suited as a giraffe to meet the big red ball that rolls toward me with frightening speed.

Still, for a moment, the same people who generally disdained or bullied me became my friends, cheering me on to hitherto unsuspected athletic glory: "You can do it, Tim!" If I could make the ball lose its gravity, as my best pal, Annie, did so effortlessly with those balletic *whomps* from her long legs, I might redeem myself. Our gym teacher, Miss B.—scowling, beefy, and, after four decades, the only person in the world I just might swerve to hit on a deserted road—had no such illusions and waited for the inevitable, with her festering contempt and ready whistle. Grinning stupidly, shirttail out and flapping, underwear pulled halfway up my back, I would lope toward the ball, which would eventually collide with my ankle or heel and then bounce off into the woods or into the waiting arms of the catcher. My chance was up, and I was a freak once more.

"*So?*" I wanted to scream. "There are things that I know; things that I can do. Can you name the duet from *La Bohème* that Antonio Scotti and Geraldine Farrar recorded in Camden, New Jersey, on October 6, 1909? What was the New York address of D. W. Griffith's first studio? How many books by *David Graham Phillips* have you read? Who was Adelaide *Crapsey*? I learned to play the entire Chopin Prelude in E Minor in a single night!" And then tears, of course, and the taunts redoubled.

In the years since the phrase became a cliché, I have received any number of compliments for my supposed ability to "think outside the box." Actually, it has been a struggle for me to perceive just what these "boxes" were—why they were there, why other people regarded them as important, where their borderlines might be, how to live safely within and without them.

Pivotal Issues

- How can we make the playground a safe place for children like Tim?

- What alternative activities would you suggest for Tim to build social relationships?

be in the same place and order (Attwood, 1998). In addition, awkwardness in motor skills is often a part of Asperger's syndrome.

In American society today, both boys and girls are expected to show some minimum level of athletic skill. Tim, a boy with AS whom we met above, tells how his athletic incompetence and lack of motor skills affects his self-image and his relationships with peers.

Neurological disorders like autism lead to deficits in the child's ability to communicate, understand language, play, develop social skills, and relate to others. The federal government's definition of autism is as follows:

> A developmental disability significantly affecting verbal and non-verbal communication and social interaction, usually evident before age 3, that adversely affects a child's educational performance. Other characteristics often associated with autism are engagement in repetitive activities and stereotyped movement, resistance to environmental change or change in daily routines, and unusual sensory experiences (U.S. Department of Education, http://idea.ed.gov/).

> Autism significantly affects verbal and nonverbal communication and social skills.

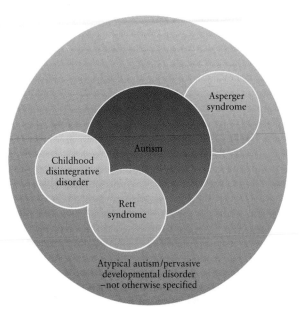

FIGURE 5.1
The Relationship Among ASDs
Overlapping circles show that some symptoms of autism spectrum disorders overlap, although the individual disorders do not. The prototypical disorder, autism, appears in the center; other disorders extend from this prototype in decreasing severity and in decreasing number of domains affected.

Source: From Lord and Risi, "Diagnosis of Autism Spectrum Disorders in Young Children," in A. Wetherby & B. Pizant (Eds.), *Autism Spectrum Disorders*, 2000, p.12. Reprinted by permission of the publisher, Paul H. Brookes Publishing Co., Inc., Baltimore, MD, and the author, Catherine Lord, PhD.

The *Diagnostic and Statistical Manual of Mental Disorders* (DSM-IV) adds unusual sensory experiences as associated behaviors rather than as part of the basic definition. A variety of conditions are included in the category of autism spectrum disorders, as is shown in Figure 5.1. Although the disorders vary in terms of onset, intensity, and cause, they often possess a common set of characteristics, including lack of eye contact, difficulty interacting with peers or adults, language delay, and sometimes random motor movements such as hand flapping (Lord & Risi, 2000).

 # History of Autism

The discovery of the condition of autism has been relatively recent. We have known about children with intellectual and developmental disabilities for more than a century, but autism was first brought to our attention by Leo Kanner (1943), a psychiatrist at Johns Hopkins University. He described a group of children who did not relate to others, had delays in speech development, engaged in repetitive behavior, were upset by changes in routines, and so forth. (See the box "Leo Kanner's Discovery of Autism" for Kanner's description of one of the patients brought to his clinic in the late 1930s.)

Leo Kanner's Discovery of Autism

In October 1938, a 5-year-old boy was brought to my clinic from Forest, Mississippi. I was struck by the uniqueness of the peculiarities which Donald exhibited. He could, since the age of 2½ years, tell the names of all the presidents and vice presidents, recite the letters of the alphabet forwards and backwards, and flawlessly, with good enunciation, rattle off the Twenty-Third Psalm. Yet he was unable to carry on an ordinary conversation. He was out of contact with people, while he could handle objects skillfully. His memory was phenomenal. The few times when he addressed someone—largely to satisfy his wants—he referred to himself as "You" and to the person addressed as "I." He did not respond to any intelligence tests but manipulated intricate form boards adroitly. (Kanner, 1943, p. 93)

Later on in England, Michael Rutter (1996) reported a study that compared children diagnosed as autistic with children who displayed other emotional disorders. He found three characteristics that almost always were present in the children with autism but only occasionally in children with emotional disorders:

1.   Failure to develop social relationships

2.   Language retardation with impaired comprehension

3.   Ritualistic or compulsive behaviors

Causes of Autism

During the 1970s and 1980s, it became popular in the social sciences to emphasize the effects of environment on children and adults. Now, with the growing capabilities of genetic research, it seems clear that many conditions that produce special needs in children are linked to an intertwining of genetics and environment. Conditions such as Fragile X syndrome, intellectual and developmental disabilities, attention-deficit hyperactivity disorder (ADHD), and dyslexia (all learning disabilities), as well as autism, all seem to have genetic components (McGuffin, Riley, & Plomin, 2003).

> Evidence is accumulating for a strong genetic linkage for autism.

Genetics and Autism

Genetics, too, seem to play a role in the causation of autism spectrum disorders. One line of evidence lies in the observation that autism appears to run in families (Newschaffer et al., 2007). A more dramatic finding of the role of genetics is the discovery that monozygotic twins (with the identical genetic makeup) are much more likely to both have autism than dizygotic twins (where the genetic makeup of the twins is different) (see Figure 5.2).

Within these studies, special attention is being paid to chromosome 7, which has been identified as a potential source of the problem in children with autism spectrum disorders. Because the role of genes within the chromosome is to produce proteins that further the growth of the child, any aberration in genetic

---

Neurology and Brain Development
Recent Findings Related to ASDs

The presence of unusual symptoms in children with autism spectrum disorders has suggested that some neurological dysfunction or genetic factors or a combination of both are at play. The rapid development of magnetic resonance imagery (MRI) has allowed us to literally peer into the brain, for the first time, and observe its functioning.

The Center for Cognitive Brain Imaging at Carnegie-Mellon University is one center for examining the brain function of children and adults who have been diagnosed with autism. Marcel Just, director of the Cognitive Brain Imaging Center, has observed that important cognitive, language, and social skills require many parts of the brain to work together.

Just (2007) believes it is the white matter of the brain that contains the cables that connect parts of the brain that hold the key to the functioning of the individual with autism. The research now being done with MRI technology will almost certainly yield more exciting information in the immediate future.

Another line of investigation involves the discovery of mirror neurons. These are neurons that fire not only when a person acts (e.g., bouncing a ball) but also when the person sees someone else act. **Mirror neurons** have been assumed to be the basis for human imitation. Mirror neurons are important because imitation of others seems so difficult for children with autism to perform. The lack of ability to imitate motor or speech production is, in fact, one of the diagnostic signs for the presence of autism (Winerman, 2005).

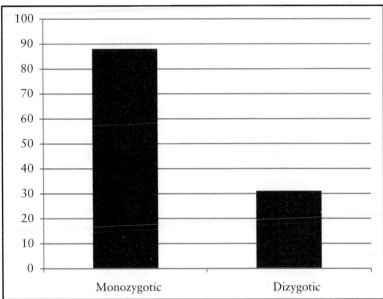

FIGURE 5.2
Genetic Concordance of Twins with Autism

Source: Rosenberg, R., Law, J., Yenskyan, G., McGrady, J., Kaufman, W. & Law, P. (2009) Characteristics and concordance of autism spectrum disorders among 277 twin pairs. *Archives of Pediatric and Adolescent Medicine.* 163, (10) 9-7-914

> The great increase in prevalence of autism spectrum disorders is still not fully understood.

function can result in conditions such as autism. We are only beginning the many investigations that are needed to learn more about the role of genetics in the development of ASD (Dawson, 2008).

Environmental Causes of Autism

With the advance of more sophisticated diagnostic tools, several previously held ideas about the causes of ASD have been abandoned. One of these was that the mother's coldness or lack of emotional feelings for the child had resulted in the child's social distancing. An unfortunate term had been used to describe this situation: "refrigerator mother" (Bettelheim, 1978). Not only was this insulting to the mothers who were already stressed; it was totally incorrect. The term apparently came from observations of the frustrations of the mother being unable to establish social contact with her child.

Another discredited theory is that thimerosal, one of the ingredients in vaccinations, might have some side effect causing the condition of ASD. This idea has been widely circulated in the public press and has resulted in some parents fearing to get vaccinations for their child. Thimerosal as a possible cause of ASD has been studied extensively by scientific panels and found to be without merit (Taylor et al., 2002). Nevertheless, such ideas die hard, and Mike's parents agonized over whether to vaccinate him until they were convinced by their pediatrician that the danger of thimerosal in vaccinations is far less than going without protection from childhood diseases. In addition, vaccines without this ingredient are now available. The pain and confusion caused by these discredited ideas underline the importance of scientific studies to test various propositions to keep the public informed.

Prevalence of Autism

The prevalence of autism spectrum disorders has been steadily rising as the spotlight of attention focuses on them. Fombonne (2003) reviewed the data in ten countries, and he estimated a prevalence of 4.8/10,000, or about 1 in every 2,000 children. Other estimates suggested it may be as high as 1 in every 1,000; the Centers for Disease Control (2009) estimate is 1.0 to 1.8 percent, or 1 in 100. The number of children with autism may now exceed the number of children with Down syndrome and children with Fragile X syndrome. Autism has moved from a low-incidence condition to a high-incidence condition (see Chapter 1)—similar to children with intellectual and developmental disabilities (IDD) or emotional disturbance.

Experts explain that they do not necessarily see a major epidemic of autism striking the country. Instead, the increase seems due to an increased sensitivity to the condition so that children who had previously been labeled "mentally retarded," emotionally disturbed, and so forth, are now correctly diagnosed as children with autism. Also, children with high-functioning autism and/ or Asperger's syndrome have been added to the total. In short, it probably has been professionals' ability to differentially diagnose the ASD condition that has resulted in the increase in the prevalence reported.

Autism is more common among boys, with about four times as many boys as girls identified. Some children with autism may appear to be developing normally until around 2 years of age. Others may be noticeably different from early infancy (Newschaffer et al., 2007).

How Are Children with ASD Identified?

The early identification of these children is made possible through a few tasks provided to pediatricians, who are often the first professionals to come into contact with the family. Children with autism have difficulty with *pretend play* (e.g., pretending to drink from a teacup), *imitating adult behavior* (e.g., rapping on the table), *pointing at objects on request* (e.g., pointing at the dog). In addition, pediatricians may note repetitive motor movements that have no context. The failure to respond well in these instances is often the cue to enter into a more comprehensive examination of child and family.

> Early intervention can greatly improve a child's social development and communication.

The Importance of Early Identification

Early identification of children with autism is one of the key elements of treatment. The development of language and social skills is critical from ages 18 months to 3 years, and these skills, in addition to imitation of motor behaviors and using eye gaze to communicate, must be fostered during this time. If we wait for the child's autism to be discovered in kindergarten, we have lost valuable time that will be very difficult to recover.

Fortunately, a number of studies have shown that diagnosticians have the ability to correctly identify children with autism at age 2 or earlier (Baron-Cohen et al., 1996; Lord, 1995; Stone et al., 1999). This ability affords an early opportunity to begin therapy in language functioning and improvements in peer relationships. It is important for parents and pediatricians to be aware of the existence of such diagnostic services in their communities so that this early identification and treatment can be carried out. Autism spectrum disorders are very troubling to parents, who tend to seek a cure or a miracle to transform their once-developing child back to age-appropriate developmental functioning (Cohen, 1998). As Cohen notes, there is almost a sense of desperation among parents trying an array of approaches that may work for some children, but rarely work for many, and never work for all.

Early identification and intervention allows younger children with ASD to make significant gains. The therapist above is helping this young girl with autism to learn the skill of turn taking.

(iStockphoto.com/ktaylorg)

Typically Developing Child   Child with Autism

FIGURE 5.3
Theory of the Mind: An Illustration

Source: Geoffrey Cowley. Understanding autism. NewsWeek July 25, 2000. Copyright 2000 by NewsWeek Inc. Reprinted by permission.

Special Characteristics of Children with Autism

Many have wondered what might be the fundamental mechanisms at the heart of the problems observable in children with autism like Mike Dolan. What is behind the inability to socialize or to communicate effectively with others?

Theory of Mind

One of the indicators of a fundamental developmental disability in children with autism has been lack of a **theory of mind**, the ability of human beings to understand the thinking and feelings of other people. A theory of mind is necessary for understanding, predicting, and shaping the behavior of others. Typical 4-year-old children have a developing theory of mind (Twachtman-Cullen, 2000).

One example of a test of theory of mind is known as the Sally and Anne Test (see Figure 5.3). In this test, the child watches while a doll named Sally puts a marble in a round box and leaves the scene. While she is away, the other doll, named Anne, moves the marble to the square box sitting beside the round box. On Sally's return, participants are asked to predict where she will look for her ball. To answer correctly, one must be able to understand what Sally's mental state would be—namely, that since she put the ball in the round box, she would expect to find it there.

Most children as young as 4 can correctly guess where Sally will look. But children with autism have a great deal of difficulty with this test, and this suggests that they are not able to get inside Sally's thinking processes. A variety of tasks that depend on understanding the feelings or thinking processes of others have been presented to children with autism, and they often do extremely poorly on them. An analysis of a series of studies on this topic (Yirmiya, Erel, Shaked, & Solomonica-Levi, 1998) revealed that children with autism have a major fundamental deficit in the development of theory of mind compared with typically developing children. They seem even less able to do these tasks than children with intellectual and developmental disabilities who also have deficits in theory of mind ability.

> Autism spectrum disorders affect every domain of the information processing model.

The Information Processing Model

Figure 5.4 provides a portrait of the various elements of information processing that are likely to be affected in children with ASD. The sensory or receptive abilities seem to be affected by the inability to moderate incoming experiences.

Hypersensitivity to Sensory Stimuli (Input)

One of the characteristics shared by many persons with autism is a **hypersensitivity** to noises in the environment. It almost seems as if they have lost the ability to modulate sounds, as these sounds come through with terrifying impact. The following quote from Temple Grandin (1988), as an adult with autism, is typical:

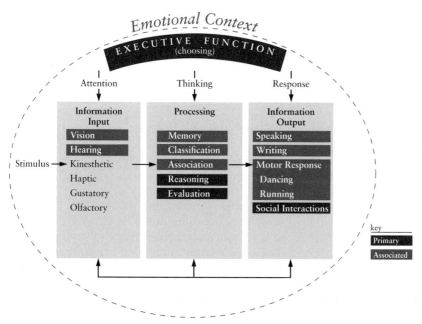

FIGURE 5.4
Information Processing Model for Children with Autism Spectrum Disorders

Loud, sudden noises still startle me. My reaction to them is more intense than other people's. I still hate balloons, because I never know when one will pop and make me jump. Sustained high-pitched motor noises, such as hair dryers and bathroom vent fans, still bother me, lower frequency motor noises do not (Cowley, 2000, p. 23).

This sensitivity is part of a larger condition called "sensory integration dysfunction" (or sensory processing disorder)—a huge problem for many individuals on the autism spectrum. In addition to sound sensitivity, sensitivity to stimuli can extend to the tactile—some children with autism are sensitive to touch and will shy away from relatives hugging them or from being touched by others—and to other sensory systems, such as the visual (seeking out or avoiding visual stimulation), oral (limited food repertoire, excessive chewing or mouthing of objects), and so forth. Such behavior can easily be misinterpreted and compound the social difficulties such children face.

Central Processing

As seen within the information processing model, most individuals with ASD have trouble with important thinking skills like decision making, problem solving, executive function, and the more complex mental processes of reasoning and evaluation. The inability to make choices between activities or toys shows up in this area. However, the memory and classification areas seem less

Children with autism often have sensory sensitivities to sound, touch, taste, and movement, but occupational therapy that targets these sensitivities can help significantly. The occupational therapist in this picture is performing sensory integration therapy that targets sensitivity to movement and touch.
(© Elizabeth Crews)

involved, and a child with high-functioning autism can collect an amazing body of information about specific content areas (e.g., ocean-going fish or various forms of transportation). When asked to use that information in social contexts like the classroom, however, the child shows clear limitations.

Response Mode (Output)

Children on the autism spectrum also have difficulty with a range of motor skills—such as gross motor skills (e.g., running and jumping), fine motor skills, and motor planning (moving one's body in space). Although children with ASD may meet motor milestones on time, the quality of the child's movements can appear stiff or clumsy.

An example of a motor task that is particularly difficult for children with ASD is motor imitation. A careful study (Stone, Ousley, & Littleford, 1997) compared the ability of children between 2 and 3 years of age to imitate actions of adults, from pushing a toy car across a table, to clapping hands, to opening and closing fists, to banging spoons on a table.

In this study, three groups matched for mental age were tested: a group of 18 children with autism spectrum disorders, 18 children with developmental delays, and 18 children with average development. The results clearly indicated that the abilities of the group with autism were sharply inferior in motor imitation to the other two groups. The abilities of the group with developmental delays approached the average group in motor imitation and were clearly superior to the group with autism.

It is important to note that although the group with autism had great difficulty in imitating, they still produced scores greater than zero. Therefore, there is reason to believe that with careful training they could improve their current performance. Such findings seem to be concordant with the mirror neuron observations discussed earlier.

It is in the response or output parts of the model that serious problems arise. The inability to interact socially or even to make eye contact with others is evident—as is the delayed development of expressive language. Some secondary effects also appear often in motor responses, with the child appearing clumsy, and sometimes in repetitive movements or gestures that seem "weird" to their peers.

The combination of social interaction problems along with the inability to think at a complex level results in a serious challenge for education and certainly for the classroom teacher. The degree of involvement (i.e., high- or low-functioning autism) is a key to how much and what kind of intervention may be called for.

As we review the puzzling behavior of Mike Dolan noted earlier in this chapter, we need to consider what is happening in his information processing system. As shown in Figure 5.4, he seems to have major problems in the executive function. He has difficulty focusing attention, is unable to organize his thinking to address problems, and has major communication problems. In addition, his background of socioemotional adaptations appears to be weak.

It is important to also note what is right about his information processing system. Mike has no problem hearing or seeing, and his memory for the things he likes or wants ("Where are the cookies and milk?") is sound. Except for some hand flapping, his motor skills seem acceptable, if somewhat uncoordinated. We can activate the relative strengths in his information processing as a base for instructional planning.

Although there are great individual differences in youngsters with ASD diagnosis, the problems just mentioned are found at the heart of many of their learning problems. Therefore, a major focus of special education procedures must be on improving attention and communication skills in children with ASD.

A child with ASD should have very clear educational objectives, systematically taught with structure and repetition.

EDUCATIONAL RESPONSES
to Children with Autism Spectrum Disorders

One of the themes of this text is that special education is a team game. In other words, no individual teacher should be expected to meet the needs of the children under discussion alone. This is especially true in cases involving children with ASD, where it is necessary for a team of multidisciplinary personnel to diagnose and plan treatment. Also necessary are modifications in the educational infrastructure, such as personnel preparation, technical assistance, research, and evaluation to ensure continuing support. The positive reports about interventions, described in this section, are encouraging.

There are a wide variety of suggestions as to how to improve the educational opportunities for children with ASD. One major question is this: Do we have evidence-based practices to offer? There are two major groups of interventions that can be separated. The first is *focused intervention practices*. These practices are designed to cope with specific behavioral or developmental goals for individual children, can be added to individual education programs (IEPs), and typically last three months or less. They include such strategies as prompting, reinforcement (providing rewards for appropriate responses or behavior), social stories (focusing on illustrating appropriate behavior), and peer-mediated interventions (Volkmar et al., 2009).

The second group of interventions is *comprehensive treatment models*. These consist of systematic practices that address the core symptoms of ASD and are presented over an extended period of time (a year or more) with intensive treatment. Recognized programs include the UCLA Young Autism Program or TEACCH (Odom, Boyd, Hall, & Hume, 2008). These programs are discussed further later in the chapter.

The emphasis on early diagnosis means that educational programming for the child with autism should begin early—sometimes as early as 2 years of age. During the preschool years, the goals are to help the child master basic skills that provide the foundation for future learning. The child must be able to communicate with others, so a major building block is to help him or her attain a *functional communication system*. Second, the child must be able to interact socially with adults and peers, so *basic social skills* (paying attention when others speak, not pushing people out of the way, and so forth) should be learned and practiced.

Strong one-on-one attention seems needed to help many children with autism interact socially.

(© Agefotostock)

Functional behavioral assessment (FBA) may be needed to cope with particular behavioral problems on an individual basis. The FBA describes the event that has taken place (Mike has hit Peter, so they are coming in early from recess), the antecedent conditions (Peter had been bullying Mike on the playground), and the consequences (the teacher separated them). The FBA determines the cause and how to change the antecedent conditions to bring about different consequences. Once these basic communication and social skills have been learned during the preschool period, the child with autism should be ready to participate meaningfully in the educational system, if there is proper staffing and support for the classroom teacher.

> The classroom teacher should have paraprofessionals present to help and should also have easy consultation available if needed.

RTI Model and Treatment of Children with Autism Spectrum Disorders

The range and the intensity of autism spectrum disorders in individual children make it likely that all three tiers of the response to intervention (RTI) model will be brought to bear on these issues. As we have noted before, Tier I is not merely the general education class without any additions. At the least, the general education teacher needs to be sensitized to the special needs of children with autism and have some instructional strategies to cope with problems that might arise in that setting. Having a phone number other than 911 to call for help is desirable as well. It is likely that some degree of consultation with a specialist in autism is necessary if the child with autism is to remain in Tier I.

▲ RTI Model Tier I

George, a nine-year-old fourth grader, has a mild form of ASD and is placed in the regular classroom with some outside professional help. Mrs. Holcomb, his teacher, is bothered by George's verbal outbursts in the class and her inability to form a social contract with George regarding his lessons and behavior.

She needs a specialist in autism to help her with suggestions on behavior control and in adapting lessons. The Universal Design for Learning (UDL) is a good idea (similar curriculum but different delivery methods) but means little without the practical knowledge of how to modify the standard curriculum to take into account George's behavior and academic lagging. Given some qualified help, Mrs. Holcomb can create a good learning environment for George.

▲ RTI Model Tier II

Tier II might be devoted to small-group or individual lessons built around applied behavior analysis (ABA), discussed later in this section, to help the child develop language and learn some social skills. Obviously, having a person specially trained in the use of ABA will be necessary. Special educators who have experience interacting with children with autism should be close by, if not directly involved.

Sally, an eight-year-old, has a moderate form of ASD symptoms, which calls for some Tier II support, even though she may not be qualified for a full-scale diagnosis of ASD. One would expect some out-of-classroom activity such as meeting with a small group of other students with social difficulties. Sally's inability to learn to share with others and difficulty working on cooperative tasks may be addressed by matching her with a small group of children to practice these skills. Someone with special knowledge of the development of social skills may be called upon to conduct these small-group activities focused on social learning. This specialist can also consult with Sally's third grade teacher about Sally's behavior in the classroom and the rules to establish to help her interact positively with her peers. George can be provided with similar Tier II experiences.

▲ RTI Model Tier III

In Tier III, full-scale intensive work with special educators will be called for. The more intense the symptoms are, the longer the time period is needed to help the student by providing some alternative behaviors for these students. Most specialists in this field believe that twenty hours a week or more of special programming over a considerable amount of time will be needed to make a difference—a measure of how difficult these sessions can be before some tangible results can be expected (Lord, 2001).

Bob is in the fourth grade, although his unusual behavior and academic issues have been long recognized. He has a definite diagnosis of ASD and may need more intense programs than either George or Sally. He should receive Tier III services for twenty hours or more, with primary responsibility for his education given to a special educator with a background in autism. This intensive program may have to go back to the fundamentals of language development and give support for attention levels to help Bob establish the basis of learning that he has not yet acquired. He may be a part of a comprehensive program described in the following section. The key to success is commitment over a long period of time and extensive supports designed for Bob's special needs.

> Centers all over the United States are studying autism spectrum disorders.

Educational Programs for Early Childhood

A wide variety of treatment programs have been suggested for young children with autism spectrum disorders, based on the proposition that many of the social and communication skills that typical children learn easily by observation and experience must be learned by children with autism through direct instruction.

Because language and communication are key problems for children with autism, methods for stimulating communication have received a great deal of attention. For children who are essentially without language or who are noncommunicative, we must start with very basic steps, often using applied behavior analysis (ABA) methods to form the basis of communication. This means linking isolated words with objects such as a ball, a car, or a block and rewarding the child for correct identification and speech. This can be the beginning of social and educational interaction for the child.

The inability of children with autism to imitate or learn through observation means that they do not learn as well as other children do through **incidental learning** (i.e., learning that occurs but is not explicitly taught). Typically developing children, through observation and imitation, learn not to run to third base when they hit the ball or not to go to the front of the line in the cafeteria. Such basic life lessons have to become part of the special curriculum for children with autism—some of whom can learn them only through direct teaching.

Later on, many therapists follow a developmental approach (Greenspan & Wieder, 2006). One of the common features of that approach is that it is "child directed." The child's environment is arranged to provide opportunities for communication, the child initiates the interaction or teaching episode ("I want the toy!"), and then the teacher or communicative partner, perhaps a parent, follows the child's lead by being responsive to the child's communicative intentions and by imitating or expanding on the child's behavior.

Greenspan and Wieder (2006) make an important observation about teaching to the strengths of the child. The key point is that the diagnosis has to be based on the top of the range. If the child can walk sometimes, then the child can walk. If the child can relate with others sometimes, then he or she can relate, and we can help him or her relate more often (p. 25). So, when we say the child with autism has difficulties in creating social relationships, it does not mean that the ability to do so is totally absent. It may mean that we have to put more energy and effort into nurturing such skills. The same is true of motor skills or language. A deficit is not an absence of a skill; it represents a delay or shortage!

In some cases in which the child is unable to respond even at this basic level, an approach known as augmentative and alternative communication (AAC) and assistive technology may be used. This approach includes supporting existing speech. Extensive use may be made of pictures displayed on communication boards so that the child, by pointing to the pictures, can communicate his or her wishes. AAC provides ways to communicate needs and can prevent the development of nonadaptive child behavior, such as head banging, biting, throwing objects, and so on, when the child is frustrated with his or her inability to communicate in standard ways.

Major Centers for Children with Autism

The special nature of this condition has led to the development of special centers for research and treatment in which multidisciplinary staff members can be drawn together to work on these issues. There are many variations of treatment, but the few listed here are among the most popular.

▲ UCLA Young Autism Project

This program has used the principles of applied behavior analysis or operant conditioning to directly provide positive rewards when the child behaves correctly. In this way, the child learns to pay attention to adults, to imitate, and to use language for social purposes. This one-on-one interaction, with trained students or parents, is often an intensive and painstaking process, and Lovaas, director of the UCLA Center on Autism, insists that forty hours a week be spent on working directly with the child to ensure that he or she can be ready for first grade with typical children. The approach requires teaching many discrete skills, which are then chained into functional routines (Olley, 1999). The Lovaas program reports significant gains when these methods are closely followed (Lovaas & Buch, 1997).

The applied behavior analysis approach that has been a central part of the Lovaas method has been utilized by many others in the field who have adopted it and established treatment programs of their own. Subsequent results (Butter, Mulick et al., 2006; Sallows & Graupner, 2005) confirm the usefulness of the ABA approach for many young children with autism. Other investigators have suggested that initiated communication, allowing the child to begin the interaction based on his or her needs ("I want some milk."), is more effective.

> UCLA Young Autism Project
> **http://www.semel.ucla.edu/ autism**

▲ TEACCH—University of North Carolina at Chapel Hill

TEACCH is a statewide program in North Carolina with six regional centers. Intensive work is done with parents to help them become teachers of their own child with autism. Pictures and other visual symbols are used extensively to help communicate with the child (e.g., "Time to go to the bathroom"). The communication curriculum is based on behavioral principles but applied in more naturalistic settings (home and child care centers) (Schopler, Mesibov, & Hearsey, 1995).

TEACCH has also developed an extensive curriculum (Eckenrode, Fennell, & Hearsey, 2007) that includes domestic skills, such as cleaning, cooking, and putting things away, and independent living skills, such as using calendars, hygiene, handling money, and so on. TEACCH makes parental counseling available to help parents cope with stress that is caused not only by daily stresses but also by their growing concerns about what their child is going to do in adulthood and how they, the parents, can help them on this path. Individual counseling for children and youth with high-functioning ASD is also available.

> TEACCH University of NC at Chapel Hill
> **www.teacch.com**

▲ LEAP—University of Colorado at Denver

This program, at its base, attempts to improve the social behavior of children with autism. The curriculum emphasizes independent play and social interaction in naturally occurring routines. Social skills are taught as discrete skills such as "play initiation." Applying the program in an integrative setting with typical children allows practice in social skills. LEAP has used peer-mediation skills intervention, training typically developing peers in ways of enhancing social interaction with children with autism. Numerous studies have demonstrated the effective acquisition of social skills by preschool children with autism (Strain, Kohler, & Goldstein, 1996).

> LEAP, University of Colorado at Denver
> **http://depts.washington.edu/ pdacent/sites/ucd.html**

▲ Pivotal Response Model—University of California at Santa Barbara

This program often starts with discrete trial behavior analysis, similar to the UCLA model, but then moves on to a goal of social and educational proficiency in natural settings. The goal is to achieve change in pivotal areas that have broad generalizations. The emphasis is placed on self-management, motivation, self-initiation, and other abilities that can be transferred from one situation to another. Koegel and Koegel (2007) have developed specific curricula with an emphasis on parental involvement to obtain their reported positive results.

> Pivotal Response Model
> **www.education.ucsb.edu/ autism/NIMH.2003.in**

These four comprehensive approaches are only some of the widening professional efforts to cope with ASD. These initiatives are encouraging because of the reports of successful gains in each (Odom, Rogers, McDougle, Hume, & McGee, 2007). These comprehensive programs all tend to stress the differences between their programs and others providing similar services, but we should also consider their similarities. In a preschool program, all children face the daily greeting of teacher and peers, a morning snack, reinforcement of the classroom rules, a lunch break (a fine time for natural lessons of conversation and social skills), nap time, and leaving for the day. These events are roughly similar from one program to another, even with the differences in therapeutic approaches noted by their program leaders. So while we learn the treatment differences, we can remember they are all in a roughly similar educational environment, which may be one reason they all report favorable outcomes with little to distinguish them from one another.

Autism Intervention Effectiveness

Of the two types of interventions, focused intervention practice and comprehensive teaching models, there are growing bodies of evidence as to effectiveness. In the **focused intervention practice,** which is short term with specific goals (e.g., reduce random motor behavior or increase verbal language output) the results are positive regarding the use of ABA (Odom, Boyd, Hall, & Hume, 2008).

In the case of the **comprehensive treatment models**, there are similar positive results reported but with little to choose between the effectiveness of models. Seida et al. (2009) summarizes these results:

> There is evidence of positive outcomes for many of the interventions examined in systematic reviews of ASDs, suggesting that some form of treatment is favourable to no treatment.... There is little evidence of the relative effectiveness of these interventions; therefore, uncertainty remains about "best practices" for the treatment of autism. (p. 103)

There is good reason to tailor the treatment to the individual needs of the child and good reason to believe that systematic intervention will pay off in meaningful developmental outcomes, particularly when the treatment is begun early in the preschool years.

The extensive reviews of literature devoted to evaluating comprehensive programs has allowed for some clear conclusions regarding these programs and the strategies they used. These conclusions are summarized in the National Standards Report (2009) (see Table (5.1). This report was compiled by professionals working together through the National Autism Center and was reviewed by over fifty specialists in autism.

The basic message here is that there is a wide diversity of approaches designed to improve the communications, social relationships, and motor behaviors of children with ASD, and they all have sufficient evidence of success to be included in this major report. These extend from the ABA approaches in the Antecedent and Behavioral Packages to peer training, schedules, and training in self management.

One of the issues that has not yet been solved, or even confronted, is where the funding for these projects will come from. If one takes the clinical advice that children with autism should have 25 to 40 hours of special instruction weekly, and 1 in 100 children have this condition, how do we pay for all of the trained personnel needed (Schwartz & Sandall, 2010)? There are simply not that many specially prepared personnel to meet the demand, and schools and special educators need to adapt their programs to take this into account. Similarly, budgets at local and state levels for general and special education are already seriously stretched. Such a demand for extensive clinical services would be met with skepticism, if not opposition. In addition, the report includes some emerging treatments that look promising but do not yet have the evaluation evidence to justify their inclusion in the established treatments. In a relatively short time, we have demonstrated that the treatments listed here pay off as evidence-based approaches.

In addition, most programs put major emphasis on *family involvement,* although the nature of the involvement may vary from one program to another (Gresham, Beebe-Frankenberger, & MacMillan, 1999; Mesibov, 2006).

Inclusion in Context: School-Age Children with Autism

Children with autism at school age will undoubtedly have an IEP planned for them. A multidisciplinary team will be necessary to provide a comprehensive set

TABLE 5.1
National Standards Project Approved Treatments

Antecedent Package (99 Studies)	The modification of situational events that typically precede a target behavior. Treatments falling into this category reflect research in applied behavior analysis (ABA), behavioral psychology, and positive behavior supports.
Behavioral Package (231 Studies)	Reduce problem behavior and teach functional alternative behaviors or skills through the application of basic principles of behavior change.
Naturalistic Teaching Strategies (32 Studies)	Using primarily child-directed interactions to teach functional skills in the natural environment.
Peer Training Package (33 Studies)	Teaching children without disabilities strategies for facilitating play and social interactions with children on the autism spectrum.
Pivotal Response Treatment (14 Studies)	PRT, Pivotal Response Teaching, and Pivotal Response Training focuses on targeting "pivotal" behavioral areas—such as motivation to engage in social communication, self-initiation, self-management, and responsiveness to multiple cues.
Schedules (12 Studies)	Presentation of a task list that communicates a series of activities or steps required to complete a specific activity.
Self-Management (21 Studies)	Promoting independence by teaching individuals with ASD to regulate their behavior by recording the occurrence/non-occurrence of the target behavior, and securing reinforcement for doing so.
Story-based Intervention Package (21 Studies)	A written description of the situations under which specific behaviors are expected to occur. Social Stories ™ are the most well-known story-based interventions and they seek to answer the "who," "what," "where," and "why" in order to improve perspective-taking.

Source: *National Standards Project. (2009).* Randolph, MA: National Autism Center.

of plans and experiences for the child. Whether the child is successful or not will depend on the makeup of the team. There must surely be someone on the team who knows something about autism and its special issues. We would not think of planning for a child who is deaf without engaging a specialist in the education of children with hearing disabilities, yet too often we engage in a program for children with autism with only minimal expertise present.

It is important for the teacher to know that when things get difficult someone will be available to help. Few things can be more depressing to the teacher than believing herself or himself totally alone in attempting to help the children with autism and feeling that the burden is not shared.

The academic lessons that the child with autism receives can be planned in advance by a team of teachers and aides so that they fit the child's own developmental

▶❚❚ TeachSource VIDEO CONNECTION

Autism in Girls

Please visit the Education CourseMate website to access this ABC News video. This video is a presentation of a girl with autism in early elementary school whose major difficulty is how to interact socially with other students. The video also shows a group of teenage girls describing their problems interacting socially while dealing with high-functioning autism (Asperger's).

Based on your observations, what aspects do you think are most difficult for these students?

If you were their teacher, how would you support these students?

The poem "Ironing Out the Wrinkles" is a good illustration of personal progress.

A Teenager with Asperger's Syndrome Reporting Her Struggles

IRONING OUT THE WRINKLES

Life was once a tangled mess.
Like missing pieces, in a game of chess.
Like only half a pattern for a dress.
Like saying no, but meaning yes.
Like wanting more, and getting less.
But I'm slowly straightening it out.
Life was once a tangled line.
Like saying yours, and meaning mine.
Like feeling sick, but saying fine.
Like ordering milk, and getting wine.

Like seeing a tree, and saying vine.
But I'm slowly straightening it out.
Life is now a lot more clear.
The tangles are unraveling. And hope is near.
Sure there are bumps ahead.
But no more do I look on with dread.
After fourteen years the tangles have straightened.

—Vanessa Regal

Source: "Ironing Out the Wrinkles" by Vanessa Regal from Tony Attwood, *Asperger's Syndrome: A guide for parents and professionals* (London: Athenaeum Press, 1998), p. 153. Reprinted with the permission of the author.

Pivotal Issues

- What are the wrinkles Vanessa is referring to?
- How can we help Vanessa and other teenagers in their struggles?

level. The assignments can be short and not complex, so that the child can see progress and success in these appropriate tasks.

One would expect that each IEP would have some special plans for improving the social skills of the child and would also pay some attention to his or her language development, together with specific plans to cope with disturbing behavior patterns, if they are present. Sam, now in fifth grade, attended a rural school where teachers tried their best but were unfamiliar with ASD or the remedial techniques that might help him. His behavioral problems became worse. His parents moved to a more suburban setting that had more support personnel who formed a team approach to address Sam's difficulties.

Table 5.2 shows some elements of an IEP that might be planned for Sam. Such planning necessitates the presence of specialized assistance, consultation, aides, and others for the general education teacher if it is to work, because few such teachers have the skills or background knowledge or time to carry out the program unaided. Because Sam is behind in fundamental reading and mathematical skills, some specific attention is paid to special *tiered assignments* (assignments adjusted to the developmental level of the child).

Sam's social skills are in substantial need of improvement. Placing him in a small group stressing cooperative learning is one approach to giving him experience working with others toward a common goal. The question as to what Sam's fighting is achieving for him (perhaps security, revenge, attention, or status) can be addressed through a functional behavioral analysis. We may be able to discover Sam's motivation and prepare some substitute or alternative behaviors to replace the fighting while still obtaining the same psychological result for him. One detriment to Sam's social adjustment has been his "hand flapping," which seems to emerge when he is under stress. His classmates view this repetitive motor movement with his hands as "weird," and that doesn't improve his social standing. It seems appropriate to work on all of these problems simultaneously, and that also requires more personnel than just one classroom teacher in this situation.

Adapting Teaching Strategies

▲ Structure and Routine

Because the child with autism often has difficulty confronting unorganized environments and becomes anxious in an unpredictable classroom, one adaptive

TABLE 5.2
IEP Elements for Sam

Area	Goals	Short-Term Objectives
Academic	1. Sam will improve reading skills to third-grade level. 2. Sam will master fundamentals of addition and subtraction.	1. Sam will complete a book relevant to class topics but directed to his limited reading skills. 2. Sam will be given tiered assignments to match his developmental level in arithmetic. He will reach 90 percent correct level in addition and subtraction problems with two numerals.
Social	1. Sam will improve his social skills. 2. Sam will reduce by one-half his episodes of challenging behavior (fighting).	1. Sam will be placed in cooperative learning groups that have been primed to include him in activity. 2. Functional behavior assessment will be carried out by a specialist to determine appropriate replacement behaviors for Sam.
Behavioral	1. Sam will reduce by 50 percent the repetitive movements with his hands (hand flapping).	1. Tasks will be chosen that will require Sam to use his hands in a constructive manner. 2. The teacher will reduce sensory overload and provide calming periods for Sam.

strategy has been an approach called "structured teaching" (Mesibov, 2009). The desire for structure among children with ASD can be met by visual representations for the day ahead. Figure 5.5 shows two types of schedules that can bring structure and security to the student. In Maxwell's case, the sequence is presented in language so that he can check off each event as it occurs and can read the next upcoming event.

In Jordan's case, there is a visual representation of the day. Jordan has a card with a large checkmark on it, and as each event occurs, he moves the checkmark next to the action and can see what is coming next. Such scheduling can bring necessary routines to the child's attention and allow him or her to live in a predictable world. Of course, it is up to the teacher to see to it that these sequences are honored in practice, or the student with ASD will be plunged into a chaotic world again.

Creating a consistent physical environment around the child (everything is in the same place from one day to another) can be another source of security. A daily schedule and a consistent environment are critical for a child with autism to feel secure.

Many children with autism need structure and order so that they can proceed academically. Although children with high-functioning autism or with Asperger's syndrome can have generally good proficiency in language, they tend toward literal interpretation, which causes a lack of understanding of jokes that depend on

plays on words, metaphors, or common idioms such as these (Attwood, 1998, p. 77):

Has the cat got your tongue?

Keep your eye on the ball.

You're pulling my leg.

Pull yourself together.

The literal-mindedness of the child with autism lends an appearance of naiveté that can interfere with socialization.

Improving Social Skills

Because one of the prime areas concerning the education of children with autism is the lack of social sensitivity and social skills that most typical children display, there have been many attempts to counteract that lack. Of course, children with autism are not totally devoid of social skills. McGee and her colleagues (McGee, Feldman, & Morrier, 1997) found that young children with autism engage to some degree in play, social participation, and social interaction, but they do so much less often than typical children of the same age. The special needs of children with autism spectrum disorders often require a change in the teaching approach to each student. Neihart (2000) suggests frequent use of diagrams, visualization,

Jordan

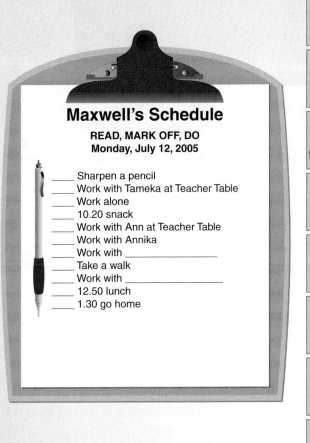

FIGURE 5.5
Visual Schedules for Students with ASD
Source: Mesibov, G. (2009). TEEACH programming. Chapel Hill, NC: University of North Carolina at Chapel Hill. Reprinted by permission.

and pictograms in the lessons provided to children with Asperger's syndrome or to high-functioning children with autism, as they think best in concrete and literal pictures.

> Using visual aids and pictures helps the child with autism to grasp concepts more easily.

Since children with ASD seem to learn visually rather than verbally, lessons focusing on the visual are useful. Figure 5.6 indicates one type of social situation depicting the right way and wrong way to play with peers. Baker (2001) has produced a large collection of such pictures portraying both acceptable and unacceptable approaches to common social situations.

Such pictures can become the basis of role playing, where children play out situations like those shown in Figure 5.6 and then discuss with the teacher the merits of the various approaches taken. In some cases the teacher may play one of the roles or ask peers to play out the social interaction. If the child sees himself or herself in these pictures, then some necessary insight has been achieved.

The teacher can use social stories, which involve the child writing a very short story that describes a specific social situation with which the child struggles. These social stories are designed to teach the cues and behaviors for specific social situations.

FIGURE 5.6
Visual That Illustrates Appropriate Social Skills
Source: Baker, J. (2001) *The Social Skills Picture Book.* Arlington, TX: Future Horizons, Inc.

One attempt to intervene on behalf of children with autism was described in a study in which photographs of various play areas are identified and the children with autism are asked to pick the areas they intend to play in (Morrison, Sainato, Benchaaban, & Endo, 2002). Their choices of photographs of play areas are placed on a bulletin board, and they are encouraged to follow their choices.

Children with autism can follow such a schedule with encouragement, and the result is that children with autism can engage in more effective and interactive play behavior with other children. The lesson here is that the teachers have to be proactive in designing activities that increase the play and social behavior of the child with autism.

A wide variety of approaches has been tried to enhance these children's social abilities, and an attempt to summarize the results of many studies of these various approaches has been completed (McConnell, 2000). McConnell concluded that promoting social interaction development should be a routine component of any comprehensive treatment program for children with autism.

Functional Behavior Assessment

One of the favorite educational strategies designed to cope with some of the behavior manifestations of autism is *functional behavior assessment.* This means that instead of concentrating on the specific behavior of the child, the teacher, therapist, or parent tries to assess the meaning of that behavior to the child. This has been referred to as the ABC approach:

- Antecedents—What preceded the behavior
- Behavior—The nature of the event
- Consequences—What happens as a result of the behavior.

Source: Baker, 2002.

If Mike hits or bites other people, in addition to dealing directly with the behavior, the educational team tries to understand how his behavior benefits Mike. Is he using this as a means for gaining attention, for communicating some need that he is unable to express verbally? We can then try to help him use alternative means for attaining his goals.

This does not mean, of course, that you allow Mike to continue to hit people while you figure out the true meaning of his behavior, but if these attacks have become a constant problem, it means trying to deduce the motivation behind them and substituting some more acceptable way, or *replacement behavior,* for him to use to achieve his goals. For example, if Mike's behavior is aimed at obtaining parental or teacher attention, perhaps a small bell to ring when he wants his parents' attention or a physical sign such as raising his arm in class could be substituted for the hitting and biting. This search for the child's intentions has proven to be more effective in modifying the child's actions than using direct punishment for unacceptable behavior (see Chapter 6).

Assistive Technology for Children with ASD

The importance of communication to the child with autism is universally agreed upon. When the child does not develop speech and receptive language in the usual fashion, a wide variety of devices (called augmentative and alternative communication; AAC) are tried to augment or increase the child's communication skills (Fossett & Mirenda, 2007). This may include the Picture Exchange Communication System (PECS) or, on occasion, teaching the child some elements of American Sign Language. Visit http://www.pecsusa.com to see and learn more about the use of PECS with children on the autism spectrum.

Sometimes a communication board is used so that basic communication is established between child and adult. The child can communicate basic needs and feelings, and the adult can respond in kind. The use of photographs to aid in this type of communication is increasing. Children with autism may learn eye-hand coordination using a computer mouse. A touch screen helps a child understand sending commands to the computer by using a tactile approach.

Now available are also voice output communication aids (VOCA) that store recorded messages that the child can trigger. These can range from a series of twenty messages, each twenty seconds long, to complex messages that can be changed according to the situation so that the student can participate ("Hi, how are you today?").

Also, a computer can be combined with synthetic speech, allowing the child to enter the initial letter of a word to produce an onscreen list of common words that begin with the selected letter. Those who cannot read can use a mouse or arrow key to select words that are recited out loud by the speech synthesizer.

The improvement of communication devices also seems to have a favorable effect on controlling or reducing challenging behavior. Some challenging behavior seems to be caused by the inability to communicate needs and wishes. Augmentative communication aids that set up pictorial or written schedules help the individual to follow predictable sequences (Wood, Lasker, Siegel-Causey, Beukelman, & Ball, 1998), which, in turn, helps reduce these behaviors.

In addition to using assistive technology to support communications skills for children with autism, new programs are being developed to teach social skills (Moore, Chen, McGrath, & Powell, 2005; Lacava, Golan, Baron-Cohen, & Smith, 2007; Dautenhahn & Billard, 2002). In one study, robotic dolls were used to help children learn appropriate social interaction (Dautenhahn & Billard, 2002). Children engaged in structured interactions with a humanoid robot, Robata, to learn about turn taking, imitation of behaviors, and appropriate social exchanges. This work holds promise for helping children with autism generalize interactions from inanimate objects to humans.

Moore and colleagues have set up a similar approach to teaching social skills through software that uses humanoid avatars to model emotions (Moore, Chen, McGrath, & Powell, 2005). With this software, virtual environments (e.g. three dimensional computer simulations) are created that allow children to interact with others through their "avatar" character. Using these simulations, one study showed that children with autism were often able to recognize the emotions of the other avatar representatives (Moore, Chen, McGrath, & Powell, 2005). This type of software may prove useful to support children's development of theories of mind.

Another software package, *Mind Reading: The Interactive Guide to Emotions*™, has been used to help children with Asperger's syndrome recognize emotions and plan appropriate responses to emotions (Lacava, Golan, Baron-Cohen, & Smith, 2007). With *Mind Reading*, students are shown pictures of individuals displaying complex emotions (e.g., insincerity, ambition, intimacy) and are guided through an understanding of what these states mean. The voice accompanying the picture also helps students learn how to "read" various communications when the words do not match the messages (e.g., "you look *wonderful*" said with sarcasm). Initial studies show that this kind of software holds promise for helping children with autism expand their understanding of theory of mind (Lacava, Golan, Baron-Cohen, & Smith, 2007).

Family and Lifespan

To provide an appropriate education for their children, parents of children with autism need specialized skills. Prime among these are the mastery of specific teaching strategies, such as ABA, that enable them to help their child acquire new behaviors. Parents also need an understanding of the nature of autism and how it influences their child's learning patterns and behavior. They need to know special education laws and regulations and how to negotiate on behalf of their child. In addition, some parents need help in coping with the emotional stress that can follow from having a child with a significant developmental disorder. Many parents of children with ASD have become autism experts in their own right and create their own books, websites, and blogs in order to share information and support with other parents. Visit the website of author Susan Senator for an example of a high-quality website and blog authored by a parent of a child with ASD.

www.susansenator.com

The siblings of children with autism can have their lives seriously disrupted, and they should be considered part of a comprehensive treatment program (Konidaris, 1997). Because siblings are often enrolled in the same school, a sensitive teacher can sometimes help a child respond to questions about his or her sibling's autism (Lord, 2001), but professional help for siblings should still be sought out by parents.

One of the promising attempts to modify the behavior of young children with autism focuses on the relationship between the parents and the child. Mahoney and Perales (2003) report a year-long intervention with twenty young children with autism spectrum disorders (80 percent under the age of 3, the rest under 6). The approach is a **relationship-focused intervention (RF)** and encourages parents to use responsible interaction strategies (e.g., "take turns") during routine interaction with their children. Parents of children with autism were seen in one-hour sessions for an average of thirty sessions. The parents were taught a variety of techniques for "responsive interaction" with their child, and they reported using these strategies with that child at home for about two hours a day.

The authors reported significant improvements in social-emotional functioning that included decreases in detachment and underactivity and increases in social competence, including empathy and cooperation. The authors concluded that enhanced maternal responsiveness encourages children to use the behaviors necessary to attain higher levels of social-emotional and developmental functioning.

Gains in social behaviors and communication were reported in those children whose mothers showed substantial improvement in becoming more responsive, and few children gained when the mothers did not improve.

Koegel and Koegel (2007) reported on the importance of the child's mastering pivotal response behaviors such as attachment,

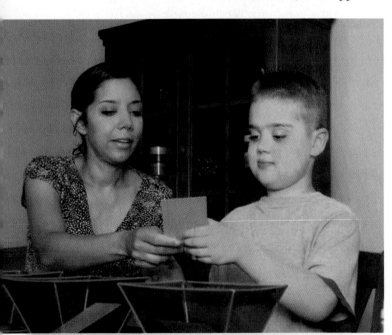

It is important for parents and family members of individuals with ASDs to spend enjoyable leisure time with their affected family member. This child with ASD is playing a card game with his favorite aunt.

(iStockphoto.com/Kim Gunkel)

empathy, cooperation, and self-regulation. These pivotal response behaviors then form the base for more advanced developmental behaviors for the child. It is extremely important that the parents be encouraged, or they may give up attempts to communicate with the child following initial frustrations and failure. A fine example of help for parents is shown in the box "Holiday Tips for Families Living with Autism."

Holiday Tips for Families Living with Autism

The holiday period can be a stressful time for those on the autism spectrum because it is a breach in their daily routine. However, if we anticipate the holidays and what they entail before they arrive, the person with autism can be made more comfortable and at ease—ensuring joy for all throughout the holidays.

"Everyone in the Car!" Starting Off on Successful Outings

- To help day trips run more smoothly, travel in two cars so that one person can return home with your loved one on the autism spectrum if he or she gets distressed.

- Eat before leaving home or bring food with you.

- Bring a quiet toy or books to a restaurant, religious services, or other social activities.

"We Are Going to Grandma's!" Tips for Social Gatherings

- When going to large social gatherings, arrive early to let the person on the autism spectrum get accustomed to the growing number of people.

- If he or she becomes distressed during a social gathering, pick a quiet place to go or take him or her out for a walk.

- When visiting someone's home, ask for breakables to be removed from reach; think carefully about visiting those who refuse to accommodate your request.

- Bring a preferred item, favorite toys, or stuffed animals to a family gathering or other social event.

- Before going to a family event, look at individual pictures of family members and teach your child their names.

- Before going to a social event, use "social stories" and practice simple courtesy phrases and responses to questions, either verbal, with pictures or gestures. ("How are you?" "I am fine." "How is school?" "Good.")

- Let trusted others spend time with your child if they volunteer.

- Ask for help if you need it. Families and friends are often eager to participate.

"Do We Have to Go to the Mall?" Shopping Without Stress

- To help your loved one with autism get used to malls, go early before the stores open. Walk around, get familiar with the building, buy a snack when the stores open, and leave. Extend the amount of time at the mall each time you go.

(continued)

- When shopping, be positive and give small rewards, such as a piece of candy, for staying with you.

- To teach your child not to touch things when shopping, visit a clothing store or another store with unbreakable objects; this gives him or her an opportunity to model behavior and minimize risk.

- When shopping, bring a helper to have an extra set of eyes and hands until you are confident of a safe experience.

- Provide headphones or earplugs to the person with autism spectrum disorder to moderate the noise and activity around him or her.

Source: Adapted from Autism Society of America (2007) http://www.autism-society.org/site/

We can sum up the family issues for the child with autism as follows:

1. Parents can learn how to teach adaptive skills and manage the behavior of their child with autism.

2. For some families, having a child with autism creates measurable stress, and support services should be available for the parents.

3. Parents' use of effective teaching methods for their child with autism can have a measurable impact on the reduction of family stress.

Many parents of children with autism have found to their dismay that although legislation has established their children's right to a free and appropriate public education (FAPE), this does not mean that these laws and regulations will be implemented at the local level. The huge expense (often $20,000 to $60,000 per child) of the intensive treatment programs have led local schools to plan for something less than the intensive treatment that many Lovaas followers and others insist on. Indeed, the National Academy of Sciences' report, *Educating Children with Autism,* recommends no fewer than twenty-five hours of treatment a week for young children with ASD—far fewer than the forty insisted on in the Lovaas program (Lord, 2001).

Although it is a well-accepted practice to involve families in the treatment program through individual family service plans (IFSPs) or IEPs, the evidence for its effectiveness is limited by a lack of research or appropriate measuring instruments testing family effectiveness. Friend, Summers, & Turnbull (2009) have reviewed the existing literature and concluded that "intervention research suggests that parent training programs improved parenting skills and parent satisfaction and reduced parental stress" (p. 468).

Naturally, success in "two-generation" programs (child and parent) depends on the intensity and relevance of the program involved. According to current research, *respite care* (providing child care so that the parents have some time off from their responsibilities) seems to have only short-term benefits (Pollack, Law, King, & Rosenbaum, 2001).

Transition to the Teen Years and Young Adulthood

What happens to children with autism spectrum disorders when they become young adults? The National Academy of Sciences report (Lord, 2001) calls for more longitudinal research, but the truth is that the field has paid much more attention to young children with autism than to what happens to them when they leave school for the adult world. Mesibov, Schopler, & Hearsey (1994) did one follow-up of fifty-nine children with autism and found a decrease in physical movements and repetitive motor behavior but a continuation of the social difficulties so manifest in early autism.

It is easy to see why there has been so much attention to early childhood. There have been positive results from early intervention studies. However, the result of this emphasis on early life and schooling, and the relative newness of this field, means that we have all-too-little information on the long-term adaptation of such children and are forced to fall back on anecdotal reports from adults with autism. An elevated rate of depression in adults with autism is possible, and this depression sometimes necessitates medical and psychiatric attention.

The general recommendation for vocational placements stresses the strengths of the child with autism and downplays the social problems. The requirement in the Individuals with Disabilities Education Act (IDEA) for beginning planning for adult adjustment in the IEPs of teenagers with disabilities seems very appropriate here. We would expect these students with autism to be working with computers or going into engineering or a similar occupation that downplays social interaction and emphasizes focused work. Others with high-functioning autism have successfully made adaptations to the social needs of their jobs.

Currently, information is still being gathered about what happens to the greater number of children with autism when their time in school is finished and they must find a way into the larger world. We do have some individual memoirs by persons with autism (Grandin, 1995), which remind us that even though the basic condition remains, these adults have made effective adaptation and are gainfully employed. One of the next steps, surely, is how we can help youths with autism to make the shift from school to work.

> Many different approaches have shown significant improvement with children and youth with autism spectrum disorder.

Public Policy: The Courts and Legislation

The importance of the courts in the development of programs for children with special needs has been noted in previous chapters. In no other category have the courts played such a significant role than with children with autism. A total of nineteen cases were brought into federal court between 1998 and 2002 as a result of disputes between parents and school districts on the appropriate way of educating autistic children (Nelson & Huefner, 2003).

In many instances, the parents insisted that the school district employ a particular method, such as ABA, whereas the school system wished to provide an alternative training program. The parents' intensity of feeling is not hard to understand because the Lovaas program, which uses ABA, has claimed that children under this program have reached "normality" in many instances. The school districts, however, aware of the high expense and the stringent requirements of the Lovaas approach, have often sought alternatives to this method (or have tried to do it cheaply). This has resulted in parental distress and legal disputes.

In general, the courts have been unwilling to substitute their judgment for that of the school system as to what was appropriate for an individual child, assuming that the districts worked closely with the parents and followed the provisions of IDEA. One case established the legal standard for sound education policy in these disputes (*J. P.* v. *West Clark Community Schools,* 2002):

1. Can the school district articulate its rationale or explain the "specific benefits" of using that approach for the given child?

2. Do the teachers and special educators involved have the necessary experience and expertise to do so successfully?

3. Are there "qualified experts in the educational community who consider the school district's approach to be at least adequate under the circumstances"?

If the answer to these questions is "Yes," the school system will prevail in such disputes.

Although these three requirements would seem to be reasonable propositions, many school systems may have difficulty in meeting them, especially in poor or rural districts. Until there exists a much larger cadre of specially trained teachers or other support personnel capable of meeting the needs of children with autism, it is likely that these disputes will continue.

As noted earlier, there has been a major dispute over whether vaccines (in particular those with the ingredient thimerosal) may cause ASD. In 2007, the U.S. Court of Federal Claims took up the issue (see *Cedillo* v. *Secretary of Health and Human Services,* case #98-916v). The court found no reason to link thimerosal with autism in this as well as two similar cases.

How Legislation Affects the Education of Children with ASD

Over the past few years, a growing number of parents and advocates became concerned that their children with ASD were not receiving proper education and treatment within the public schools. They also wondered whether the Centers for Disease Control and other authoritative voices were giving appropriate weight to the concerns of those who believed that diet or vaccines were possible causative factors of ASD.

The popularity of inclusion as an educational strategy also worried some parents, who wondered who was going to provide the specialized lessons or instruction that their children needed and how that would be accomplished.

In 2006, this alliance of parents and professionals was able to persuade Congress to pass the Combating Autism Act of 2006 (P.L.109–416), and President George W. Bush signed it into law.

This act

- Authorizes establishment of regional centers of excellence for autism spectrum disorders research

- Authorizes activities to increase public awareness of autism, to improve the ability of health care providers to use evidence-based interventions, and to increase early screening for autism

- Calls on the Interagency Autism Coordinating Committee (a state multidisciplinary group) to enhance information sharing

It is still uncertain what level of funding will be appropriated to support this legislation given the wide variety of priorities facing the nation, but the support necessary to pass the legislation was obviously present.

moral dilemma

Jerry's Situation

Jerry Boyd, age 8, has been diagnosed as having high-functioning autism and has the various solitary interests that mark this condition. He loves playing computer and video games but pays little attention to his peers. He has no interest in team games or in attending birthday parties or other social functions of his class and age group.

This is upsetting to Mrs. Boyd, his mother, who thinks that this lack of interest in social matters will hurt his adjustment later on in school and community. She has embarked on campaigns to have friends sleep over. She also enrolled Jerry in dance classes and encourages him to participate in Little League baseball.

So far, Jerry couldn't care less about his mother's campaigns and wants her to stop. Mr. Boyd, his father, is uncertain whether to support Jerry in his wishes or to support his wife, who has Jerry's long-range adjustment in mind.

What should the Boyds do? What is your strategy? If Jerry was your student, how would you advise his parents?

To answer these questions online, visit the Education CourseMate website.

 *Summary*

▶ Autism is a pervasive developmental disorder affecting communication and social development and causing, at times, a variety of unusual behaviors and unusual reactions to sensory stimulation.

▶ There are clear indications of neurological and genetic factors in causes of autism. No environmental factors, such as vaccinations or family patterns, have been implicated.

▶ This condition of autism can be recognized in a child as young as 2 years of age. Beginning intensive treatment for language development and social skills immediately is strongly recommended.

▶ Although the majority of children with autism seem to be developmentally delayed, there is a subgroup, children with Asperger's syndrome, who can be highly intelligent and academically able but who have the same social problems as children with autism.

▶ The prevalence of children with autism spectrum disorders appears to be steadily rising. It now is estimated at 1 in 110, or even more. The reason for the increase is not clear. It may be that we are now identifying as autistic many children who previously would have been labeled differently (developmentally disabled, for example). Or there may be a genuine increase in autism, for reasons not yet known. The gender ratio remains constant: Four times as many boys with autism are found as girls.

▶ The ability to read the feelings and needs of others (Theory of Mind) is diminished in children with ASD.

▶ Applied Behavior Analysis is a treatment of choice for forming the base for social and cognitive learning.

▶ Focus on social skills development includes changes in environment, the teaching of collateral skills, direct social skills training, or peer-mediated intervention.

▶ Improvements in communication are often carried out in natural environments, both home and school, using the child's natural interests in play to develop and expand communication.

▶ Both the courts and legislation have acted to protect the rights of families with children with ASD and provide resources for their education and treatment.

▶ For children without the use of language, augmentative and alternative methods of communication are employed, such as pictures that are organized especially for communication.

▶ Many programs of treatment for ASD exist, and all report clinical successes in terms of improving social and academic skills, but we still need careful research to document these treatments and their long-term effects.

▶ Despite the variety of approaches, all major treatment programs include common elements, such as similar curriculum content, structured teaching environments, predictable routines, functional approaches to problem behavior, and the teaching of transition skills to prepare children for kindergarten.

▶ The major problems with implementation in the schools are the high costs of such treatment and the lack of trained personnel to administer it.

▶ We need more information on the transition to adulthood and adult adjustment of children who were given early help through the schools.

Future Challenges

1 *Will there be enough trained personnel?*

The education of children with autism requires very special preparation. Few teachers, in either general or special education, have mastered the methods of applied behavior analysis or the other instructional strategies designed to enhance the social development and communication skills of children with autism. How will these needs for trained personnel be met?

2 *Will new medical treatments become available?*

To date, medical or pharmaceutical treatments have had uncertain effects on children with autism. With our increasing sophistication and understanding of brain function and the genetic code, can there be some future help for families affected by autism?

3 *Who will pay for expensive educational treatments?*

Some states have established emergency funds to aid the ability of local schools to supplement the education costs for these children. Medicaid has been used in other states to defray the education costs. No easy way out of financial difficulties seems currently available.

4 *Where is the special programming for adolescents with ASD?*

While we are developing impressive adaptations for early childhood and elementary age children with ASD, the literature is almost silent about adaptations in all three of the RTI tiers for adolescents with ASD. This is a major problem, as the environments in secondary education are so different, with the emphasis on content specialists and even movement between classes (including the social milieu that secondary school creates). One big thrust in special education has to be in programming for these adolescents and in planning for their transition into further schooling or the world of work.

Key Terms

applied behavior analysis (ABA) p. 158

Asperger's syndrome p. 148

comprehensive treatment models p. 161

focused intervention practice p. 161

functional behavioral assessment (FBA) p. 158

hypersensitivity p. 154

incidental learning p. 159

mirror neurons p. 151

pervasive developmental disorders–not otherwise specified (PDD–NOS) p. 148

relationship-focused intervention (RF) p. 168

Rett syndrome p. 148

theory of mind p. 154

Resources

References of Special Interest

Boswell, S. (2005). *TEACCH preschool curriculum guide: A curriculum planning and monitoring guide for young children with autism and related communication disorders.* Chapel Hill, NC: TEACCH. A detailed description of activities in the preschool age range that can enhance the language and social development for the child with autism.

Greenspan, S., & Wieder, S. (2006). *Engaging autism.* Boulder, CO: Perseus. A comprehensive review of Stanley Greenspan's floortime approach to helping parents cope with children with autism spectrum disorders. He takes a developmental approach, encouraging parents to interact with their child. Floortime means exactly what it says: The parents need to get down on the floor for twenty to thirty minutes a day and communicate, play, and interact with their child. Many helpful suggestions for parents.

Koegel, R., & Koegel, L. (Eds.). (2007). *Pivotal response treatments for autism.* Baltimore: Brookes. Stresses the importance of teaching and intervention under naturalistic environmental conditions in the home, community, and school. Using multidisciplinary programming with an emphasis on parents, this book stresses the redirection of disruptive behaviors using functional assessment with self-management strategies and the fostering of social interactions with typically developing peers.

Lord, C. (Ed.). (2001). *Educating children with autism.* Washington, DC: National Academy of Sciences. A multidisciplinary committee assembled by the National Academy of Sciences reports on the effectiveness of various attempts to provide educational programming for children with autism. A series of recommendations confront remaining problems and issues and point the way toward better resources and results.

Mesibov, G. B., Shea, V., & Schopler, E. (with Adams, L., Burgess, S., Chapman, S. M., Merkler, E., Mosconi, M., Tanner, C., & Van Bourgondien, M. E.). (2005). *The TEACCH approach to autism spectrum disorders.* New York: Kluwer Academic/Plenum.

Padiyar, K. (2009). *Targeted, taunted, tormented: The bullying of children with autism spectrum disorders.* Boston, MA: Massachusetts Advocates for Children. A report focusing on a special problem faced by children with ASD. These children are especially vulnerable to bullying as they have few psychological and physical defenses. These interviews with parents leave little doubt that their children have suffered serious bullying, and the parents expose the issues with the educators' responses to these events.

Volkmar, F., Paul, R., Klin, A., & Cohen, D. (2005). *Handbook of autism and pervasive developmental disabilities.* New York: Wiley. A comprehensive review of the many aspects of autism spectrum disorders from diagnosis to the variety of treatment programs and options currently available. The multidisciplinary approach is clearly evident.

Volkmar, F., & Wiesner, L. (2009). *A practical guide to autism: What every parent, family member & teacher needs to know about autism.* Hoboken: John Wiley and Co. A much-needed description of the causes and treatments of autism aimed at persons with little technical knowledge of the disorder. The book stresses the importance of educational and behavior treatments that have been shown to produce positive results. Also includes references to other books on the subject.

Winerman, L. (2005). The mind's mirror. *Monitor on Psychology, 36*(9), 1–5. The description of mirror neurons and their impact on the development of the child.

Journals

Journal of Applied Behavior Analysis
http://seab.envmed.rochester.edu/jaba/

Journal of Autism and Developmental Disorders
http://www.springerlink.com/content/104757/

Journal of Child Psychology and Psychiatry
http://www.wiley.com/bw/journal. asp?ref=0021-9630

Topics in Early Childhood Special Education
http://tec.sagepub.com/

Professional Organizations

Autism Network International
www.ani.ac

Autism Research Institute (ARI)
www.autism.com

Autism Society of America
www.iidc.indiana.edu/irca

Online Asperger's Syndrome Information and Support (OASIS)
http://www.aspergersyndrome.org/

National Dissemination Center for Children with Disabilities (NICHCY)
www.nichcy.org

 Visit the Education CourseMate website for additional TeachSource Video Cases, information about CEC standards, study tools, and much more.

Children with Intellectual and Developmental Disabilities

 Focus Questions

▶ Who were the key pioneers in the early evolution of the field of intellectual and developmental disabilities (IDD)?

▶ How do educators define IDD, and what are some of the typical characteristics of students with IDD?

▶ What are challenges in processing information that children with IDD experience?

▶ What are some of the biological and environmental factors that can cause IDD?

▶ How are children with IDD identified?

▶ What are important educational issues related to inclusion of students with IDD?

▶ What are some of the changes in curriculum and teacher strategies useful in teaching students with IDD?

▶ How do we adapt technology for students with IDD?

▶ What are some of the problems students with IDD may have in making the transition to the community?

Heide Benser

The category of *intellectual and developmental disabilities* (IDD), formerly termed *mental retardation*, has evolved though many changes over the last century. Since 1908 there have been ten changes in the definition, and even the current definition has received its share of criticism. There seem to be two reasons for this dynamic state: the proliferation of research, which is a strong change agent, and the changes in the way society views IDD and those who have it (Greenspan & Switzky, 2006).

A Few Pioneers

Organized attempts to educate children who learn slowly began less than two hundred years ago. A French physician, Jean Itard, tried to educate a young boy who had been found living by himself in the woods—the so-called Wild Boy of Aveyron. Although Itard's attempts to tutor the boy met with only modest success, one of his students, Edouard Seguin, later extended Itard's approaches and became an acknowledged leader of the movement to help children and adults with IDD.

Another notable person in the field, Maria Montessori (1912), worked with young children with IDD using what is now called sense training. This approach uses the visual, auditory, tactile, gustatory, and olfactory senses to help preschool-age children learn about the world around them. Today, versions of Montessori's methods are still used at the preschool level for all children, although her original work was with children who had IDD. This is yet another example of how the education of children with disabilities may benefit all children eventually.

> The change in terminology to "IDD" is a response to negative reaction to the term "mental retardation."

What Is in a Name?

Between 2006 and 2007, the key professional organization in this field, the American Association on Mental Retardation, changed its name to the American Association on Intellectual and Developmental Disabilities (AAIDD). It also changed the title of its key journals; now the names refer to the basic condition as *intellectual and developmental disabilities* rather than *mental retardation*. This name change was made, in part, to eliminate the negative connotations that had been attached to the previous term (Prabhala, 2007). Current efforts are being made to change all references in legislation from *mental retardation* to *intellectual and developmental disabilities*.

Not only the professional community and the courts have objected to the term *mental retardation*; those who have been designated "mentally retarded" also take issue with the label:

- A lot of people on the outside world would run and make fun at "retarded people". . . . but when you get in the position of being the person they are making fun of it's different. That's why I won't poke fun at anybody. I have lived with that. I understand that if I had somebody poke at me, I wouldn't like it.

- I think I was sort of an outcast because when I was growing up everyone was calling me retarded. It was hard to deal with.

- I never thought of myself as a retarded individual but who would want to? I never had that ugly feeling down deep (Snell & Voorhees, 2006).

Maria Montessori was a true pioneer in the education of young children.

(© Mary Evans Picture Library/The Image Works)

Defining Intellectual and Developmental Disabilities

Over the past decades, emphasis in the diagnosis of intellectual and developmental disabilities has shifted from strictly a measurement of cognitive abilities (primarily IQ tests) to a mix of *cognitive abilities* and *adaptive behaviors*. This change has been due in part to the realization of the role played by the environment (particularly elements of poverty) in the development of mild IDDs. Educators do not merely try to help a child adjust to his or her disability; they also try to intervene early in a child's life to keep the condition from becoming more serious or from even appearing at all.

> The definition of intellectual and developmental disability (IDD) must include significant delay in intellectual development and adaptive behavior.

Identification of Intellectual and Developmental Disabilities

Table 6.1 highlights the current definition of mental retardation, now IDD. It refers to two separate domains in which limitations must be found before a person can be identified as having IDD. The first area is significantly *below average intellectual functioning*; the second domain reflects limitations in three general indicators of *adaptive skills*. Most special educators and psychologists see the wisdom of using the dual criteria—*intellectual below average/developmental delay* and *adaptive behavior deficits*—in identifying mild IDD.

The Diagnostic Manual (Schalock, 2010) also stresses the importance of having a "system of support" available to cope with the special needs of a child with IDD. The context of the child can determine his or her ability to adapt positively or negatively, and this can have a life-long impact (as discussed in

---

TABLE 6.1
The AAIDD Definition of Intellectual and Developmental Disability

IDD is not something that you *have,* like blue eyes or a heart defect. Nor is it something you *are,* like short or thin. It is neither a medical disorder nor a mental disorder. An **intellectual and developmental disability** *is a particular state of functioning that begins in childhood and is characterized by limitation in both intelligence and adaptive skills.* IDD reflects the "fit" between the capabilities of individuals and the structure and expectations of their environment.

IDD is a disability characterized by significant limitations both in intellectual functioning and in adaptive behavior as expressed in conceptual, social, and practical adaptive skills. The disability originates before age 18.

Five Assumptions Essential to the Application of the Definition:

1. Limitations in present functioning must be considered within the context of community environments typical of the individual's age peers and culture.

2. Valid assessment considers cultural and linguistic diversity as well as differences in communication, sensory, motor, and behavioral factors.

3. Within an individual, limitations often coexist with strengths.

4. An important purpose of describing limitations is to develop a profile of needed supports.

5. With appropriate personalized supports over a sustained period, the life functioning of the person with mental retardation generally will improve.

Source: From American Association on Mental Retardation (now AAIDD) (2002). Reprinted with permission.

Chapter 1). The term **developmental disabilities** includes intellectual and developmental disabilities as well as other mental and physical limitations for which the child is likely to need lifelong support from a variety of health, social, and educational agencies.

Levels of IDD

One traditional way for further classifying children with IDD has been to indicate the level of delay. This has been done by using IQ scores as ranking measures as follows:

- Mild (IQ 50–70)
- Moderate (IQ 35–50)
- Severe (IQ 20–35)
- Profound (IQ below 20)

A more functional approach has been to indicate the intensity of support needed by the individual. The four levels of intensity of support roughly match the four levels noted above (mild, moderate, severe, and profound).

Levels of Support

The definitions of levels of support help us understand how intense the supports need to be for individual students with IDD.

The formal definition given in the previous section reminds us that both intrinsic function and external support should be taken into consideration. The individual's level or intensity of support needed to operate effectively is shown in Table 6.2. The intensities of support are measured as *intermittent, limited, extensive,* and *pervasive* (Greenspan & Switzky, 2006).

Care must be taken that such identification must not limit the planning and opportunities developed for the child with IDD. The question remains how we determine levels of function and need. IQ testing serves the purpose of determining the level of mental functioning that the student shows, but it also can be used to determine the student's cognitive strengths and weaknesses. Students who are identified as having IDD reveal a wide range of performance that can then be used to direct the individualized education program (IEP) by focusing on the strengths revealed by the student (Bergeron & Floyd, 2006).

TABLE 6.2
Intensity of Support for Persons with IDD

The levels of support needed by a person who has an intellectual or developmental disability:

- *Intermittent* refers to support as needed, but that is not necessarily present at all times.
- *Limited* refers to support provided on a regular basis for a short period of time.
- *Extensive* support indicates ongoing and regular involvement.
- The *pervasive* level of support describes constant high-intensity help provided across environments and involving more staff members than the other categories.

Two Students with IDD

Let us meet two students who have IDD. Bob, a student with mild IDD, is a ten-year-old of average physical development; his mental functioning, however, more closely resembles a seven-year-old in understanding. The information processing model (Figure 6.1) shows where the major problems are in Bob's development. His ability to use his memory, associate concepts, and problem solve are limited (his Wechsler IQ, to be defined later, is 67). These primary problems have resulted in secondary problems, including an inability to participate in peer activities and a lack of motivation for academic performance.

His family lives at a borderline poverty level. His father is an unskilled laborer and his mother is a part-time sales clerk in local stores. They both love Bob, but they are having such problems with their own lives that they often can't give him the support that he or his siblings need. If we were to use the scale of "Intensity of Needed Support" (Table 6.1), Bob would probably require both intermittent and limited professional attention.

Carol is also a ten-year-old. She has been diagnosed with Down syndrome. She is at the IDD moderate level, and she has made limited academic gains in primary school. Carol clearly needs support provided on a regular basis, and this support will continue into adulthood. Her fifth grade teacher is working to integrate her within the general classroom setting but finds that Carol requires substantial help from the special education teacher. Both teachers worry about her ability to fit into the middle school environment next year. Her family has more resources than Bob's, but her parents are still quite puzzled as how to help Carol, who has a pleasant and unassuming personality. Her challenges within the information processing model seem similar to Bob's, only more intense. Like many children with Down syndrome, she is delayed in language development but has relative strengths in social relationships. Everyone seems to like Carol.

> To help children learn, teachers need to know how children with IDD process information.

The Information Processing Model and Special Characteristics

In previous chapters, we have explained that a child's ability to learn about his or her world happens through the processing of information. As there is a great diversity within categories of children with special needs, there are variations in the impact of IDD from one child to another—including how well they are able to process information.

The most obvious characteristic of children with mild or moderate IDD is their limited cognitive ability, or the *central processing* of memory, association, classification, reasoning, and evaluation (see Figure 6.1). This limitation inevitably reveals itself in their academic work. These students may lag by two to five grades in language-related subjects (e.g., reading or social studies).

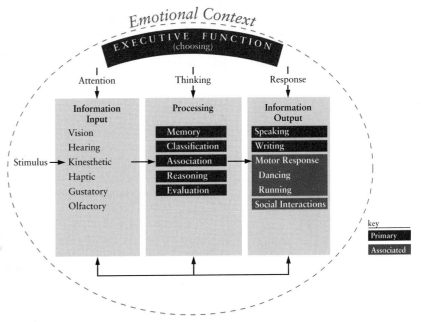

FIGURE 6.1
The Information Processing Model for a Child with Mild IDD

Unless the student has an additional disability (e.g., a learning disability or autism), the input or receptive abilities would not likely be seriously impaired. It is the ability to absorb information, not to sense it, that is affected. Children with IDD often have difficulty with memory, which can stem from differences in understanding. It is hard to remember what you never understood. Most typically developing students use "rehearsal" as a memory aid, saying a string of words or a poem to themselves until they remember it. Children with IDD are less likely to use this method unless they are directly taught how to do so.

Classification, or the organization of information, is also affected for children with IDD. Children in elementary school learn quickly to cluster or group items into useful classifications: chairs, sofas, and tables become furniture; apples, pears, and oranges become fruit. Children with IDD tend to need direct instruction and much practice to learn classification. For example, a teacher may need to explain how a car and train are similar before a child with IDD can classify them both as means of transportation. *Reasoning and evaluation* are contributors of information that may also need extra attention for children with IDD.

The *executive function* is particularly affected in children with IDD. Their ability to make good decisions and make good judgments with the information available is limited. Because of **central processing** differences, children with IDD may have difficulty expressing themselves (*output processing*). Differences in speaking and writing in turn can influence social interactions. All of these information processing functions are listed separately in the model but are actually closely intertwined in practice. For example, the interaction between cognition and language in information processing can lead to many variations of speech. Children with Down syndrome show delay in language that is lower than their general exceptionality (Yoder & Warren, 2004), while children with Williams syndrome seem to have language advanced beyond their developmental delay.

The *emotional context* is also linked closely to IDD (see Figure 6.1). But whether that link is due to negative academic experiences or whether it is a basic part of the neurological and genetic conditions that lead to IDD is not clear. What is apparent is that the learned helplessness (the feeling that one is powerless to cope with a challenge) that some children with IDD display as a result of continual academic difficulties can be addressed with educational programming.

> Adaptive behavior can be divided into conceptual skills, social skills, and practical skills.

Adaptive Skills

The current emphasis on the environment and the context of the child has resulted in an extended attempt to distinguish among various categories of adaptive behavior. Adaptive behavior is an important aspect of the definition of IDD. In the most recent definition, key components of adaptive skills have been reduced to three major categories: conceptual skills, social skills, and practical skills (see Table 6.3 that lists subsets of the skill sets).

A number of concerns still exist. For example, do "conceptual skills" really differ from "intellectual ability"? And how intense must a student's naïveté or gullibility be before it is invoked as a sign of lack of intellectual ability? It is safe to say that the details of adaptive behavior are still being worked out.

It is possible to have a low IQ score and still possess usable adaptive skills, be self-sufficient in the community, be able to interact reasonably with other citizens, and maintain a part-time or full-time job. Under such circumstances,

TABLE 6.3
Major Categories of Adaptive Behavior

Conceptual Skills	Social Skills	Practical Skills
Receptive and expressive language	Interpersonal	Instrumental activities (preparing meals, taking medication, using telephone, managing money, using transportation)
Reading and writing	Responsibility	
Money concepts	Self-esteem	
Self-direction	Gullibility	
	Naïveté	
	Follows rules	
	Obeys laws	
	Avoids victimization	

Adapted from R. Luckason, D. Coulder, E. Polloway, S. Russ, R. Schalock, M. Snell, D. Spitalnick, and I. Stark, Mental Retardation: *Definition, classification, and systems of support* (Washington, DC: American Association of Mental Retardation, 1992), pp. 40–41. Reprinted with permission.

an individual would still be below average intellectually, but would not be considered "intellectually or developmentally disabled." The lowest score on an IQ test that a child with an intact, undamaged nervous system would achieve is not 0 but about 65 or 70. Any score lower than that is generally an indication of some type of damage to the nervous system.

A Special Population?

There are special educators who insist that children with IDD at the mild level of intensity, like Bob, need to be considered as a separate population from other children with IDD like Carol (MacMillan, Siperstein, & Heffert, 2006). Earlier, in definitions by Tredgold and Doll, even mild IDD was considered incurable because genetic causes were assumed to be at the heart of these difficulties (Spitz, 2006). The more that environment has assumed a role in the development of disability, the more professionals believe that cure or improvement should be considered possible.

Children with IDD are children first—with some special characteristics that require educational attention.

(© Lauren Shear/Photo Researchers, Inc.)

Haywood (2006) also discusses the question of subdividing this large category of IDD for the purpose of education and treatment:

> Mental retardation (IDD) is not a single entity and can only be further misunderstood if we insist upon regarding persons who are profoundly

retarded and multiply handicapped under the same broad concepts that govern our conception of persons who are barely discriminable from those who actually escape the "retardation" label altogether (p. xvii).

This chapter focuses on what steps can be taken to help children like Bob and Carol reach an independent or semi-independent adulthood with a high degree of self-sufficiency.

Social Significance of the Definition

The definition of mental retardation (or IDD) took on a greater social significance with the Supreme Court's consideration of whether persons with intellectual and developmental disabilities should be given the death penalty in capital cases. In *Atkins* v. *Virginia* (2002), the Supreme Court ruled, six to three, that executing a citizen with intellectual and developmental disabilities violates the Eighth Amendment's ban on cruel and unusual punishments.

Justice Stevens, in his majority opinion, focused on the adaptive behavior characteristic of *gullibility*, the inability to see through manipulation by a less disabled confederate or by police officers seeking a confession, plus the person's inability to understand the court proceedings well enough to be of assistance to his or her counsel (Greenspan & Switszky, 2006, p. 300).

Measuring Intelligence and Adaptive Behavior

How do we measure intelligence and adaptive behavior? Unless we have adequate measures of these concepts, we still are in a difficult position in diagnosing IDD. The development of intelligence measures actually can be traced back to Alfred Binet in France, who was given the task of finding children who were not capable of responding to the traditional educational program in France in the early twentieth century.

Later individual tests of intelligence were developed by Lewis Terman (the Stanford-Binet Intelligence scales) and David Wechsler (Wechsler Scales of Intelligence). The Stanford-Binet was originally designed to test the "g" factor, or general intelligence and has lately branched out to test multiple abilities. The Wechsler scales generated subtests measuring verbal and performance IQs, which allowed psychologists to develop a profile of strengths and weaknesses for further planning (Salvia & Ysseldyke, 2007).

A third test, the Woodcock-Johnson Tests of Cognitive Ability, has recently received considerable attention. There are also nonverbal intelligence tests that have been developed primarily to help assess students who have verbal difficulties or have English as a their second language. The Peabody Picture Vocabulary Test is an example of such a nonverbal measure where the student is shown four pictures and then asked which picture most closely resembles the verbal clue (e.g., a train).

A more current version of these adaptive rating scales is the Vineland Adaptive Behavior Scales (Sparrow, Cichetti, & Balla, 2006). It is completed by a parent or guardian and covers communication, daily living skills, socialization, motor skills, and maladaptive behavior. The Vineland results seem to match fairly well with other adaptive scales.

The closer one gets to all of these measures, the more cautious one becomes about using the data from them unsupported by other diagnostic information. A fine collection of test and scale reviews may be found in the text by Salvia & Ysseldyke (2007), *Assessment in Special and Inclusive Education*.

Biological Causes of IDD

A large number of possible causes of IDD have been cited, including genetic malfunction, toxic intrusions, neurological insults, and even environmental factors, such as poverty. We review some of the major ones here, but all of them negatively influence the development of cognitive and social abilities needed to adapt to the world without help. Whatever the original cause of the condition, it is the cognitive and social problems that are its end product that call for educational adjustments. Therefore, similar educational strategies may be used with children whose disabilities result from widely differing causes.

Genetic Factors and IDD

The question of how a tiny gene can influence the complex behavior of children and adults has puzzled scientists for many years. The breakthroughs of James Watson and Francis Crick helped to explain the functions of DNA and RNA, and because of them it is now possible to provide a general answer to that question. Watson and Crick discovered that genes influence the proteins that are critical to the functioning of organ systems that determine behavior (Tartaglia, Hansen, & Hagerman, 2007). Thus, genes can influence the development of anatomical systems and their functions—the nervous system, sensory systems, musculature, and so on.

Do certain patterns of genes predetermine certain types of behavior? Are we unwitting automatons driven by mysterious bursts of chemicals? Not really. No particular gene or protein forces a person to drink a glass of whiskey, for example, but some people have a genetic sensitivity to ethanol that may increase their tendency to become active drinkers. Similarly, genetics plays a special role in some types of IDD.

Down Syndrome

One of the most common and easily recognized genetic disorders is **down syndrome.** The child in the photograph on page 188 shows the physical manifestations of Down syndrome, resulting in a somewhat flattened facial profile. It occurs

---

Neurology and Brain Development
What We Know about IDD

What does the brain have to do with developmental disabilities? Everything. Thanks to new methods of investigation, we have been successful in discovering more about this organ and IDD. For example, "It is well established that the brain forms new neurons in response to environmental stimulation. Remarkably, exposure to novel information can rewire the brain" (Doug & Greenough, 2004). The notion that the brain can be rewired through experiences can be good news for educators who are trying to create experiences that can have an impact on children with IDD.

The technique of magnetic resonance imagery (MRI) can show brain activity in action. The electric activity of the brain will change when a child is doing an arithmetic problem, and we can see where in the brain this activity is taking place. Many research endeavors are underway that promise to answer the questions about how brain activity is different in children with IDD. Such discoveries can open doors to our understanding of cortical activity that previous generations had been unaware of. We are on the edge of a major leap in knowledge that promises changes in diagnoses and in education of individuals with IDD (Sandman & Kemp, 2007).

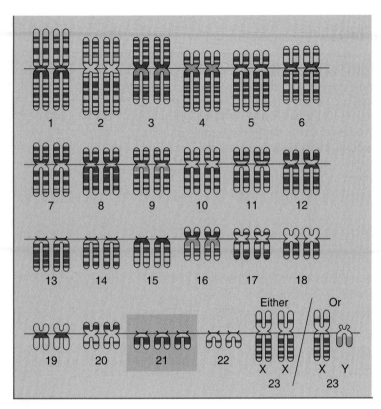

FIGURE 6.2
Down Syndrome
The inheritance of three copies of the twenty-first chromosome results in Down syndrome. Down syndrome usually causes mild retardation and a variety of characteristic physical features.

Source: From Freberg, L. (2006). *Discovering biological psychology* (p.146). Used by permission of Cengage Learning.

once in every 600 to 900 live births, and results form a genotype that features three copies of chromosome 21 (see Figure 6.2). The genotype is often responsible for mild or moderate IDD and often includes a series of other medical complications as well. Even here, environment seems to play a role, as there is a clear link to maternal age and Down syndrome, with older mothers more at risk for having a child with Down syndrome.

Phenylketonuria

Normal growth and development in the embryo and fetus depend on the production of enzymes at the right time and place. When enzymes are not produced or fail to perform their normal functions, a number of unfavorable developmental conditions can result. These conditions are called *inborn errors of metabolism*. One of them is **phenylketonuria (PKU)**, a single-gene defect that can produce severe retardation. In PKU, the absence of a specific enzyme in the liver leads to a buildup of the amino acid *phenylalanine* with serious consequences.

PKU is an unusual genetic disorder in that it can be modified by environmental treatment—a special diet. The diet is very strict, however, and many families have difficulty holding to its requirements. PKU can be detected at birth, and every state has established a screening program to identify children with PKU so that they can be started on an appropriate nutritional regimen early (Simonoff, Bolton, & Rutter, 1998). As a child with PKU grows, he or she can eat only small quantities of high-protein food (such as meat and cheese) but can have fruits and vegetables (low protein). Peer pressure, however, can often pull the child off this restrictive diet. The importance for children of staying on this strict diet can be judged by the following facts: The earlier treatment is begun, the less will be lost in intelligence scores. Children with PKU who abandon the diet at school age suffer social and intellectual setbacks. Mothers with PKU can have a high proportion of children with birth defects unless they maintain this diet.

Fragile X Syndrome

Fragile X syndrome (FXS) is the leading cause of inherited developmental disability, and results from a mutation on the long arm of the X chromosome. It affects about twice as many males as females—overall prevalence is about one in four thousand. Extensive investigation has found that the condition causes a deficiency in protein production necessary for normal brain development. The diagnosis can be determined by DNA testing (see the accompanying box for a further description). The wide range of individual differences in this condition calls for individual planning and treatment based on a child's own profile and patterns of development.

A Child with Fragile X Syndrome: Early Identification

Amy Tyler noticed a problem with her son, Max, within weeks of his birth. He was not easy to comfort and always seemed to keep his hands clasped. When he was 6 weeks old, Amy tried unsuccessfully to get Max to look at her when she clapped her hands. At 15 months, Amy's doctor expressed concern that Max's language development was behind. She took Max to an early intervention service provider, who recommended that he be tested at the local children's hospital. At 20 months, Max was diagnosed with Fragile X syndrome (FXS).

Compared with most families of children with FXS, the Tylers were fortunate. Max was diagnosed with FXS earlier than most children. According to a Frank Porter Graham Child Development Institute study, the average child with FXS is not diagnosed until nearly age 3, and many others not until much later. Had these children been identified earlier, they would have been immediately eligible for early intervention services under the Individuals with Disabilities Education Act (IDEA, 2004).

Source: Frank Porter Graham Child Development Institute, University of North Carolina at Chapel Hill. Screening newborns for Fragile X. *Early Developments*, 8 (2004): 11–13. Reprinted by permission of Frank Porter Graham Child Development Institute.

> Fragile X syndrome is a condition that results in moderate IDD and often behavioral difficulties.

Children with Fragile X syndrome appear to have strengths and weaknesses in information processing that require changes in educational planning and strategy. They have early language delays that call for early speech and language therapy, plus some ADHD (hyperactivity and lack of attention) symptoms that need to be addressed. They also appear to have memory disorders, so a teacher may not be able to count on a child's memorization of facts (Ornstein et al., 2008).

On the other hand, children with Fragile X seem to be relatively good at object recognition and in work with computers that can enhance written language. Of course, these are generalizations, and individual patterns of strengths and weaknesses should be documented. Children with Fragile X (30 percent of whom can also be diagnosed with autism) require substantial multidisciplinary help: medical interventions for mood instability, behavioral support to help with aggression and social adjustment, and speech and language therapy for conversational skills. These supports would be a part of Tier III services in the response to intervention (RTI) model. With appropriate team efforts, meaningful developmental improvements can be shown with Fragile X in students (Tartaglia, Hansen, & Hagerman, 2007).

RTI

Toxic Agents and Causation

The remarkable system whereby a pregnant mother transmits nutrients through the umbilical cord to her fetus is also the highway by which many damaging substances can pass to the developing child. Drugs (including alcohol) and cigarette smoke are prime examples of **teratogens**, which include any agent that causes a structural abnormality following fetal exposure during pregnancy.

Fetal Alcohol Syndrome

For centuries we have been generally aware of the unfavorable effects that alcohol consumption by the mother may have on her unborn child. About

Down syndrome results in mild to moderate intellectual and developmental disabilities and a flattened facial profile.
(© Steve Dunwell/Getty)

7 out of 10,000 births result in **fetal alcohol syndrome (FAS)**, which produces moderate retardation and behavioral problems such as hyperactivity and inattention.

Far too many women are unaware of the potential consequences of drinking while pregnant. The National Organization on Fetal Alcohol Syndrome (2004) presents three key facts:

● When a pregnant woman drinks, so does her baby.

● The baby's growth can be altered and slowed.

● The baby may suffer lifelong damage.

This is not to say that these outcomes are inevitable, but drinking increases the chances that such outcomes will occur.

The Effects of Lead

Ingesting heavy metals, such as lead, cadmium, and mercury, can result in severe consequences, including IDD. Most attention is currently focused on lead, and much of the lead that enters the brain comes from the atmosphere. One of the most effective steps that has been taken on a societal level is the reduction of lead amounts permitted in gasoline. This reduction resulted in a lowering by one-third of the average lead levels in the blood of U.S. men, women, and children. The reduction in lead levels paralleled the declining use of leaded gasoline, showing how public policy can have a positive impact (Beirne-Smith, Ittenbach, & Patton, 1998).

Also, legislation has restricted the use of lead in paint and mandated that lead paint be removed from the walls and ceilings of older homes—a common source of lead poisoning in youngsters. Children, who will place anything in their mouths, are known to ingest peeling paint chips with some regularity. Medications can be prescribed that flush the system of lead once it has been discovered (Pueschel, Scala, Weidenman, & Bernier, 1995).

Infections

The brain begins to develop about three weeks after fertilization. Over the next several weeks, the central nervous system is highly susceptible to disease. If the mother contracts **rubella** (German measles) during this time, her child may be born with IDD and other serious birth defects. A rubella vaccine that is now available has drastically reduced the number of children with defects caused by rubella. Children and adults are also at risk of brain damage from viruses that produce high fevers, which in turn destroy brain cells. **Encephalitis** is one virus of this type. Fortunately, it is rare, as are other viruses like it.

Environmental Factors That Influence IDD

There has long been an enormous gap between what we know about the brain and its function and the set of behavioral symptoms by which we define IDD. With current advances in understanding the central nervous system, we are able to make some reasonable assumptions about the links between the nervous system and behavior. It appears that experience also influences the development and maintenance of certain structures and connections in the brain. The implications are exciting. If the development of the nervous system is not preset by genetic factors, then the nervous system can grow and change as the individual experiences new events (Dong & Greenough, 2004).

This means that environment and human interactions can play a role in neurological and intellectual development. The influence of experience on brain development has been largely confirmed (Jensen, 1998; Sameroff, 1990). We have already seen the results of various early intervention programs in Chapter 3. Some children who are on the borderline of IDD classification can be improved through environmental enrichments, though they may still need support in Tier II of the RTI model.

Psychologists such as Hunt (1961) and Bronfenbrenner (1989) have long championed the idea that the experiences young children have in their families and their surrounding social systems can have a significant impact on their development (See Chapter 1 for information on the ecological model). We can see for ourselves that flowers or vegetables or puppies can, even though they possess specific genetic potential, be stunted or enhanced by their surrounding environment. It remains for educators and special educators to take such knowledge and transform it to the developmental benefit of children—the earlier the better (Dunst, 2007).

We also must not forget that there remains an interactive role for genetics in the mild category of IDD. As we learn more from research such as the Human Genome Project, we become more conscious of the continued interaction between environment and genetics. A study of 3,886 twins (Spinath, Harlaar, Ronald, & Plomin, 2004) focused on pairs who ranked in the lowest 5 percent in verbal and nonverbal abilities. The researchers found twin concordance (when one twin had the condition, the other did as well) for mild mental impairment in 74 percent of the monozygotic (single-egg) twins; this happened in only 45 percent of same-sex dizygotic (two separate eggs) twins (see Figure 6.3). Such a finding suggests that genetics, as well as experience and environment, plays a role in mild IDD.

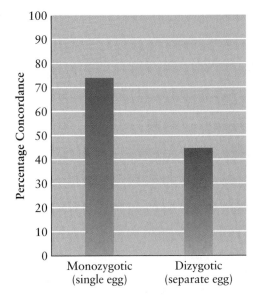

FIGURE 6.3
Twin Concordance Rates of Mild Mental Impairment
Source: F. Spinath, N. Harlaar, A. Ronald & R. Plomin, Substantial genetic influence on mild mental impairment in early childhood, *American Journal of Mental Retardation, 109,* (2004): 34–43. Reproduced with permission of American Association on Intellectual and Developmental Disabilities in the format Textbook via Copyright Clearance Center.

 # Characteristics of Children with Intellectual or Developmental Disabilities

Special programming for children with mild and moderate IDD is shaped in part by the characteristics that distinguish these children from their agemates. There are marked differences in factors linked to levels of intellectual development, such as the ability to process information, the ability to acquire and use language, and the child's emotional development. There are substantial differences also in the relative strengths that individual children bring to their development.

Cognitive Processes

One of the questions posed by researchers in this area is "Do children with IDD follow the same developmental patterns of cognitive growth, only slower, or do they have a unique pattern of development?" Weisz (1999) synthesized the results of many experiments and came to the conclusion that the evidence strongly supports a similar developmental sequence for children with IDD—only developing slower than a typical student. This finding raises another issue, that of *learned helplessness,* the feeling that nothing you can do can make a positive difference. If the child with IDD consistently fails on tasks, does he or she have a tendency to quit trying because of a feeling built up by consistent failure in academic tasks and situations? Think of your own abilities in some sports. If you are not able to kick the ball well in soccer and cannot run fast, isn't there a strong tendency to abandon that game in favor of something that provides some measure of success? Several studies that matched children with IDD with nonidentified children of the same mental level indicated that following failure experiences, the children with IDD showed a significant decline in the use of effective problem-solving strategies (Weisz, 1999). This issue of *learned helplessness* becomes a significant challenge in inclusion, because children with IDD are often faced with the fact that their performance does not match those of typically developing children in the classroom.

> Emotional and behavioral issues associated with IDD may lower social acceptance by peers in the inclusive classroom.

Ability to Acquire and Use Language

The ability to develop language is one of the great achievements of humans, and there always has been curiosity as to how, if at all, language development is

changed or modified in children and adults with IDD. The close link between language and cognition has long been noted along with their reciprocal interactions. Not only is language limited by cognition, but cognition (especially thinking, planning, and reasoning) is also limited by language (Fowler, 1998). In addition, limited input and an impoverished language environment during the language-learning years can add up to an impoverished linguistic system.

Yet there are intriguing variations on this generalization. Children with Down syndrome have deficits in language that are even lower than that of their general mental functioning (Yoder & Warren, 2004), whereas children with *Williams syndrome* seem to have advanced language beyond their general mental abilities. These puzzling patterns guarantee that there will be much more research on these topics in the future (Fowler, 1998).

Ability to Acquire Emotional and Social Skills

For many years, we have had a modest understanding of the link between emotional and social problems and the condition of IDD. But what that link signifies and what should be done about it remain issues of some dispute. We know that emotional and social difficulties can undermine vocational and community adjustment. We are also aware that emotional and behavior problems probably lower the level of social acceptance for children with IDD in comparison with their peers in the classroom.

It is particularly important to find ways to improve the social relationships and emotional functioning of children with IDD.

(Cengage Learning)

As has been the case with language development, studies on social development have focused on the specific problems of children with special causal factors of IDD such as Down syndrome (Kasari & Bauminger, 1998). A range of studies has revealed many problems in peer relationships for children with IDD. With the current emphasis on inclusion, it is particularly important to find ways to improve the social relationships of children with IDD, as the formation of relationships is one of the key purposes of inclusion. Certain skills

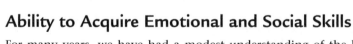

appear to be important for social acceptance. They include sharing, turn taking, smiling, attending, and following directions. A person with social competence uses such skills appropriately in social situations.

Social Adaptation

Because social adaptation, or adjusting to living in accordance with cultural demands, has become critical for the child with IDD, both in the classroom and later in vocational settings, it is important to determine what barriers stand in the way of social adaptation. A study on the interpretation of social cues was most revealing in this regard (Leffert, Siperstein, & Millikan, 2000). One hundred seventeen students in elementary grades, with and without IDD, were shown videotapes depicting various social conflicts (e.g., a child knocking a book off another child's desk accidentally and being rejected when wanting to join a group on the playground). The students watching the videotapes were then asked for their reactions.

>
> **TeachSource VIDEO CONNECTION**
>
> **Serving a Student with Down Syndrome in an Inclusive Classroom**
>
> Visit the Education CourseMate website to access this TeachSource Video Case. This video is a good depiction of how a collaborative team of general educators, special educators, and parents can work to modify general education goals to meet the special needs of Bobby, a first grader with Down syndrome. After watching the Video Case, reflect on the benefits and drawbacks for Bobby in the inclusive classroom. What difficulties does he face? What is he gaining from his environment?

The children with IDD were much more likely to interpret the child who knocked over the book in the first scene as being mean. They were focusing on the negative outcome of the event and ignoring social cues that would indicate that the event was an accident. They also more often referred to an adult authority to solve the social crisis rather than suggesting social strategies for resolving the incident.

These results suggest one reason that children with IDD are sometimes not well received in peer groups and also point the way to some necessary curricular additions for them. Children with IDD clearly need practice in identifying social cues so that they can better interpret social situations; practice through role-playing or discussions about useful strategies for prosocial interaction is essential. One of the helping roles that the special educator, working as a collaborator with the general education classroom teacher, can play is to provide such experiences in small-group situations and help children with IDD to work out their own strategies for appropriate social response.

Two of the common characteristics ascribed to persons with IDD have been *credulity* (inability to see through untruthful assertions) and *gullibility* (the ease with which one can be duped); in other words, the inability to judge the truthfulness of even highly ridiculous statements (Greenspan, 1999). When taken together, these cognitive shortcomings in evaluation and adjustment can result in serious social consequences for children with IDD and should be addressed through educational programming.

Identification of Children with IDD

The first step in adapting the standard educational program to meet the needs of children with IDD is to identify the children who need special help. How do we find a child in need of special education services? Although referrals can come from many different sources, most students with IDD come to the attention of special education services because they have failed in school. The inability of the child to adapt academically or socially to the expected standards of his or her age group sets off alarm bells in the teacher and calls for action.

RTI

As we seek strategies and proper environments for children with IDD to thrive in school, we should remind ourselves that their limitations in information processing are only relative. It means that although a child with IDD's ability to remember or associate ideas may be limited, it is not absent. With proper instruction and teacher support, Bob and Carol can learn and become productive adults. Most of us learn much about the world through incidental learning (observations or imitations). We don't have to receive direct instruction to know to run to first base instead of third, to stay away from Mike on the playground when he is angry, or not to talk when the teacher is explaining something. Children with IDD can learn these things as well, but it often takes direct instruction and practice for them to master the skills necessary to navigate their environments. Their *executive function* skills are likely limited, so they need special help in decision making and choices between options.

> Lack of good judgment is one characteristic of many children with IDD.

Special education adaptations for children with IDD should take into account the characteristics of these youngsters. We cannot assume that they will learn from observation or imitation as other children do. They usually don't have strategies for attacking problem situations, and their judgment is often off base.

Because of these limitations, knowledge and skills must be explicitly taught to children with IDD. It may be necessary to spend some time in specifically modeling and practicing behaviors, such as putting materials away after a lesson. Children with IDD are not being ornery; they literally may not know what behavior is expected of them. Time and patience are required in teaching both the standard curriculum and the social rules and social survival skills to succeed in the classroom.

RTI Model

The RTI model is brought into play at all three levels, or tiers, for children with IDD. At Tier I, the inclusive classroom, attention still needs to be given to ensure that the key lesson elements have been mastered, and additional

Children with IDD can learn many skills through direct instruction and practice.

(© Ellen Senisi)

practice is needed for children with IDD so that they don't fall behind and become confused and discouraged. A special education teacher can be valuable here in proposing adaptations that fulfill the goal of Universal Design for Learning (UDL), learning the same concepts through different methods or approaches.

Tier II may include special lessons for small-group instruction in social skills or in making good choices, conducted by knowledgeable staff. These choices will necessitate removing children for a time for this special instruction, but Bob, and especially Carol, need this special small group experience for reading and math lessons and social skills.

And in Tier III, some of the students may not be able to master the standard curriculum and may have to be given individualized instruction in a special education setting for at least a part of the day or even in a separate setting (Bambara & Knoster, 2005). For instance, Carol could be given social skills practice with her special education tutor.

> All four of the major areas of change—learning environments, curriculum content, skills mastery, and technology—require attention for students with IDD.

Program Differentiation

There are four basic ways to modify the existing program: changing the learning environment, changing the teaching strategy, changing the curriculum content, and changing the special uses of technology. In all of these changes, we assume that a "system of support" is present.

Changing the Learning Environment

▲ Inclusion in Context

How should the educational program be adapted to meet the needs of children with IDD? Proponents of *inclusion* (the practice of including children with disabilities in the regular classroom) want the child with disabilities to be welcomed into a community of equals in the classroom. Implementation of inclusion requires support personnel to assist the classroom teacher, who otherwise would have to bear sole responsibility for inculcating such values.

How does inclusion work in actual practice? We obviously don't expect the special educator to have mastered all of the content fields in the middle school curriculum (e.g., English, social studies, math, and science). Where would he find appropriate content material for special exercises or tasks for children with disabilities? How would he manage the content area instruction?

This is where the *team approach* becomes necessary. Working with the general education teachers, who provide the content for lessons, special education teams can make modifications to meet the needs of the student or suggest ways for the general education teacher to present lessons to include these students. Increased responsiveness of students like Bob and Carol can be important rewards for the staff's collaborative efforts.

The U.S. Congress left little doubt as to its preference of education in the general education classroom for all children with special needs with the following language (from the IDEA amendments of 1997 and repeated in IDEA 2004):

> To the maximum extent appropriate, handicapped children, including children in public or private institutions or other care facilities, are educated with children who are not handicapped, and that separate schooling, or other removal of handicapped children from a regular educational environment occurs only when the nature or severity of the handicap is such that education in regular education classes *with the use of supplementary aids and services* cannot be achieved satisfactorily [20 U.S.C. §1412(5)(B)].

Teachers in inclusive classrooms should be able to call on reading specialists, special education personnel, school psychologists, school counselors, physical and speech therapists, other classroom teachers, math and science teachers, and a variety of other people to participate in the classroom to help the classroom become more flexible and relevant to the needs of all students. The RTI model, with its tiers of support, can be most useful in meeting these needs and utilizing these specialists.

▲ The Socialization Agenda of Inclusion

One of the distinguishing features of inclusion is the emphasis on socialization of the child with disabilities within the inclusive setting. This is a primary objective of the schools, from the standpoint of inclusion advocates; in their view, it is as important as academic achievement.

Research findings suggest that changes in the *learning environment* alone do not make a striking difference. Many studies have tested the effectiveness of inclusive education for children with IDD, but the information derived from such studies is not necessarily educationally significant, as few of the studies discuss the nature of the program the students received. This is surely just as important as, if not more important than, "where" the student has been placed (Guralnick et al., 2006).

Changing Content and Strategies

▲ Special Settings

The greater the degree of disability, the more likely a child like Carol will need a special learning environment in order to learn distinctively different material. In this special setting, a special education teacher can provide a distinctive curriculum for a small group of children, typically no more than fifteen. The curriculum may include exercises in personal grooming, safety, preprimary reading skills, or any other subjects not needed for the typically developing child in the regular classroom. These life skills are highly appropriate for a child like Carol, whose cognitive development is limited and will need these life skills to reach a level of independence.

▲ Individualized Education Programs (IEPs)

One of the first efforts to develop long-range plans for child and family came forth from the IEPs, noted earlier, to increase the collaboration between professionals and parents and to ensure thoughtful consideration about how children would be served within the general and special education program.

One of the major changes in the educational planning for children with disabilities is a shift from focusing on the deficits and disabilities to documenting the developmental and personal strengths of each student in order to plan the most effective educational intervention. Students with limited verbal proficiency may be able to express themselves through dance or through other arts, or they may be relatively proficient in working with their hands, as in carpentry (Bateman & Linden, 2006).

Table 6.4 shows briefly some of the IEP goals and objectives for Ben, a ten-year-old with mild IDD with resistant behavior but with clear strengths as well. Ben's strong communication skills will be brought forth in the **reciprocal teaching** model to improve his academic performance. Here, Ben is the teacher and the teacher is the student. By teaching the lesson himself, Ben should gain some more insight into the content by playing a different role.

His good physical skills are also taken advantage of by encouraging him to play soccer and, through that experience, to improve his respect for rules and his peer interactions while under adult supervision.

> Improving the social relationships of children with IDD is one of the main goals of inclusion.

TABLE 6.4
Ben's IEP Goals and Objectives (CA = 9-8, IQ = 67)

Area	Annual Goals	Short-Term Objectives
Academic	Ben will increase his reading and math scores by one year each on standard tests.	Reciprocal teaching will be used to improve his reading performance and peer-adult interaction by 25 percent.
Social	Ben will reduce his resistant and oppositional behavior episodes by one-half by end of school year.	Positive behavior supports will be used to decrease the basis for oppositional behavior. Resistant episodes charted should be down by 25 percent.
Physical	Ben will be involved in team sports to encourage sharing and cooperative behavior.	Ben will be invited by physical education teacher to play after-school soccer. Number of confrontations and resistant behaviors will be counted and reductions noted.

Differentiating Curriculum

▲ What Are the Goals?

Another way to adjust the program for children with special needs is to modify the curriculum. There has been much discussion about the most desirable curriculum for children with IDD. Should the content be modified from that given to the average child? If so, where in the educational sequence should the branching take place? In secondary school? In middle school? Or should the curriculum be different from the beginning? The important questions to be answered in the development of curricula for students with IDD are, "What are our goals? What are our immediate objectives to reach that goal?"

For students like Carol, who have moderate IDD, reasonable goals are to:

- Learn to read at least the "survival words" *(stop, poison, restroom, school bus, and so on)*. (You may create a list of survival words for your community.)
- Master basic arithmetic and understand the various denominations of money.

- Learn social skills, such as the ability to work cooperatively with others.
- Develop some leisure-time activities and skills.
- Communicate effectively with persons such as storekeepers and community helpers.
- Learn work skills to be partially or fully self-supporting in adulthood.

The more difficult curriculum decisions must be made for children like Bob, with mild IDD, who can be expected with appropriate support to reach a middle school level of skills and knowledge. The curriculum will be the general education curriculum—supplemented by adaptations (e.g., more time to master the material) needed for his success.

At what point does the student with mild IDD branch off into a separate secondary school program that is designed to provide work skills rather than academics that help the student reach the next level of education? Inclusion advocates do not expect students with mild or moderate IDD to take advanced high school physics or calculus. It is in the secondary program that attention is traditionally paid to community adjustment and work skills.

Children with moderate IDD should focus on learning problem solving and motor skills in addition to their academics.

(© Ellen Senisi)

One of the distinctive characteristics of the educational reform movement is its commitment to high standards and accountability. "High standards" generally refers to high conceptual learning in traditional subjects such as language arts and mathematics. If all children are required to meet the same challenging standards, this is surely not good news for students with IDD who do not do well on high-level conceptual material. For some students with IDD, a secondary program focused on learning community living is most appropriate. Yet the No Child Left Behind legislation insists on including most children with disabilities in these districtwide assessments, following these principles:

- All students should have access to challenging standards.

- Policymakers and educators should be held publicly accountable for every student's performance.

Although the federal government, through No Child Left Behind, requires assessment of all students, it is clear that alternative or modified assessments must be made for some students with disabilities. The number of students allowed an alternative assessment option was originally 1 percent of all students. Later a new rule was established that "states could have an alternative assessment for an additional 2 percent of students who evidence persistent academic differences and thus are working toward 'modified achievement standards'" (Salvia, Ysseldyke, & Bolt, 2007, p. 660).

This percentage still amounts to only 3 out of 10 students discussed in this text, so the clear expectation is that the majority of students with exceptionalities will be expected to take the state tests for content competence. For example, Bob would be expected to take the state tests, while Carol might receive alternative or modified assessments because her academic program is significantly different from the standard course of study.

What do alternative assessments look like? Typical examples are:

- *Portfolio assessment:* An assessment of a compilation of selected work of the student over the year that links to the standards.

- *Performance assessment:* An assessment of tasks performed by the students, which are linked to standards.

- *Teacher observations:* Descriptions or formal ratings of the student as connected to standards.

States have the responsibility of showing how the results of modified assessments fit into the required annual yearly progress (AYP) for the school.

Teacher Strategies

The most common adaptation suggested to teachers for children with IDD is *differentiated curriculum,* but what exactly does this term mean? It means that the teacher adjusts the level of difficulty of tasks to fit the level of development of the child with IDD. For example, in math, if the rest of the class is doing complex multiplication or division problems, the child with IDD may be given addition and subtraction problems at his or her level of comprehension. Or in a cooperative learning situation, teams of four or five students might be working on a particular problem related to the early American colonists in our country. The child with mild IDD could be given a task such as finding pictures of colonial life to be used in a report, and other students would be challenged with a complex question, such as why these settlers abandoned their homeland to come to the New World. Sometimes differential lessons are referred to as tiered assignments—that is, assignments of varied difficulty that allow the child with IDD to participate meaningfully in the group activity.

When the teacher is using differentiation, it becomes important to have the special education teacher help design *tiered assignments*. Failure to differentiate lessons for the child with IDD runs the risk of discouraging the child, who faces failure once again in the academic setting (see the earlier discussion on learned helplessness).

▲ Case Study: Ronald

Ronald and his parents have been told that he will be part of a new program at school, called *inclusion,* that will bring Ronald into the regular fifth grade, even with his diagnosis of mild IDD. Previously he was in a school program where he spent an hour or more each day with a special education teacher who worked with him in areas of language and basic arithmetic. He was achieving at the second-grade level.

His parents felt gratified that Ronald would now be with all the other fifth graders, but worried, too. Would he get along with the other children? How could he keep up with the other students, when he was reading at only a second-grade level? The school principal told Ronald's parents that Ronald would be seeing

American Speech-Language-
Hearing Association
www.asha.org

his special educa-
tion teacher for
some lessons—
but within the
general education classroom. The fifth-grade classroom teacher worried about the very same issues as
the parents, knowing that having him in a seat in her
class didn't mean that Ronald would find friends there
or that he would be happy. How will she differentiate
the curriculum to meet his needs? One major task for
this teacher is to make Ronald feel at home, feel like
part of the class. A second is to ensure that he receives
individualized instruction to meet his needs. Making
inclusion work for
Ronald will require
much professional
teamwork.

> The functional use of language is a critical goal for children with moderate IDD.

Two key areas
where students with IDD will need additional support
are language/communication and social skills.

▲ Language and Communication

There is a substantial effort in elementary schools
to help children with mild and moderate IDD use
language as a tool for communication and reading as an essential skill. Teaching students the
most common sounds represented by letters and
a strategy for sounding out words, such as explicit
phonics, has proven effective for children with IDD
(Browder et al., 2007). In math instruction, the use
of money management can be role-played in banks
and grocery stores to teach the use of addition and
subtraction.

Language exercises for children with moderate
intellectual impairment like Carol aim to foster the
development of speech and the understanding and
use of verbal concepts. Communication skills focus
on the ability to listen to stories, discuss pictures, and
tell others about recent experiences. Two important
areas of study are
the home and the
community. Chil-
dren learn about
holidays, transpor-
tation, the months of the year and days of the week,
and how to contribute to home life. Teachers may
make use of dramatization, acting out a story or a
song, playing make-believe, and using gestures with
songs, stories, and rhymes.

> For students with IDD, gaining social acceptance in the inclusive classroom requires special planning by educators.

▲ Social Skills

Social skills are a critical component of the preschool
and primary school curriculum for children who have
IDD, but instruction
at this level should
be informal. Skills
such as taking turns,
sharing, and working cooperatively can be embedded
into their daily activities. The lunch table for young children is an excellent location for teaching social skills.
Here, youngsters learn table manners, as well as how
to pass and share food, help others (pouring juice, for
example), and wait their turn. The lunch table is also a
good place to review the morning's activities and talk
about what is planned for the afternoon or the next
day. Although the teaching is informal, it is both effective and important to the child's social development.

> Role-playing helps children with IDD to identify social cues.

Because, as previous studies have indicated, children with IDD have difficulty establishing social acceptance in the classroom and in their other social environments, we need to prepare them by practicing social
skills. A major effort to do this was a study conducted
with forty-five children with IDD (IQ ranging from 50
to 80, ages 4 to 6) that introduced, over two years,
individualized programming in play groups, increased
parent-child interaction, and coaching on social skills
(Guralnick, Hammond, Conner, & Neville, 2006).

A comparison of effects was done with a control
group that was matched in important developmental
areas to the target (intervention) group. In addition
to ratings of teachers and mothers over time, special observations of each target child were made in a
simulated preschool classroom with three children of
typical ability in 30-minute play sessions, noting the
amount and kind of social interaction that took place.

This comprehensive effort to improve the social
skills of developmentally delayed students, in the
author's words, "produced only modest results with
children with lower cognitive abilities benefitting the
most" (p. 352). There was some reduction in the children's negativity and reduction in unusual play patterns in the children with the lowest measured abilities.

This study shows again that interventions to
change the behavior of children and students must be
intense and administered over a considerable amount
of time for there to be manifest improvement. There
is no simple pill to take to improve social skills and
relationships.

Children with IDD sometimes have difficulty transferring or applying ideas from one setting to another.

Thus, we teach some needed social skills directly (such as greeting of other students).

If we are asked how we meet strangers, break unpleasant news, communicate with someone we haven't seen for a long time, or tell someone that he is intruding on our space and time, it is likely that we will have to think for a while before we can recall the coping strategies that we use without conscious effort. These skills are the lubrication that allows each of us to move smoothly through our daily contacts and tasks. Someone who is markedly lacking or awkward in social skills stands out in a crowd. Many children with IDD need direct instruction in social skills if they are to establish an effective personal and community adjustment.

Bob, for example, usually got too close to the person he was speaking to. Thus, he made the other person uncomfortable but was not aware of this reaction. Through role-playing a number of social situations with Bob and others, the teacher was able to establish that each person has a personal space that is not to be invaded without permission (for example, to kiss an aunt good-bye). Such social rules may seem trivial, but their importance is magnified substantially when they are violated.

It is important that the sense of privacy is established and understood when the child begins to cope with sexual relationships. Parents and other adults worry about the susceptibility of young people with IDD to sexual abuse or unwanted sexual contact merely because they lack the social skills to fend off others in sexual encounters (the gullibility factor). Therefore, some type of counseling and role-playing of relationships or situations with the opposite sex should be a part of the curriculum for students with IDD.

To meet the socialization goal of inclusion, special educators have developed a series of activities that enhance social contact and learning. In *peer-buddy systems,* a classmate may help a classmate with disabilities negotiate the school day; *peer support networks* help students become part of a caring community; and in *circles of friends,* an adult facilitator helps potential peer buddies sensitize peers to the friendship needs of students with disabilities.

Positive Behavior Interventions and Supports

One of the most effective moves made for children with IDD has been the introduction of **positive behavior interventions and supports (PBIS)** in educational programming. Behavior problems and disruption have, unfortunately, been a major part of the lives of too many children with IDD. It may be that these children have been reacting to their inability to live up to adult expectations at home and at school. Unfortunately, the teacher response to disruptive behavior is often punitive, which compounds the problem.

The strategy of PBIS espouses that, when faced with some form of behavior disruption, the teacher should focus on *human motivation,* not just on human behavior. For example, Ben, a student with mild IDD who we met through his IEP discussion on page 199, has shouted "No!" to the teacher's request to pick up his reading book. Why would Ben do such a thing, considering that it will surely bring unpleasant reprimands? What hidden rewards must Ben receive from this situation that would cause him to burst out like that? There must be rewards of some sort, or he wouldn't have done it.

The goals of PBIS are to achieve (1) improved academic performance, (2) enhanced social competence, and (3) safe learning and teaching environments (Eber, Sugai, Smith, & Scott, 2002). The seeking of the "why" of human behavior has traditionally been the role of the psychologist and the psychiatrist—not the teacher, who has immediate circumstances to deal with. Once Ben has been settled down, after either a quiet talk with the teacher or a short visit to a quiet place, it can pay to reflect on the *why* of the situation. The teacher or a child study team can take some time to analyze the event, particularly if it has been only one of many resistant actions taken by Ben. Ben's **functional assessment**, presented in the nearby box, shows how we can come to understand his behaviors.

> ### Ben's Functional Assessment
>
> 1. What were the environmental circumstances surrounding Ben's outburst? (Ben had an altercation with Sylvia at lunchtime, which upset him a lot. He has not been doing well in his reading exercises in past days. He feels the teacher has been too demanding of him, and his father gave him a hard time at breakfast this morning.) Any or all of these might be the cause.

2. Develop some hypotheses about the motivation for Ben's behavior. Is he trying to avoid reading recitation time, at which he has been doing poorly? Is this a general reflection of his fight at lunchtime? Has his relationship with the classroom teacher soured, and he wants to strike back? Is school or the classroom an unpleasant place to be and he wants to get out?

3. Let us test one of the hypotheses by changing the environmental circumstances. Instead of Ben reciting in a group, the teacher's aide, Mrs. Rosseli, who Ben likes very much, will take him aside and work with him one-to-one with his reading lesson so that he will not show his deficiencies to the entire classroom. If we are right, Ben's events of resistance should be reduced, and his reading may even improve.

We will take regular measurements of Ben's behavior and chart these changes coincident with the change in environment that we have made.

If there is no reduction in Ben's resistant behavior, we might move on to another hypothesis and test it (for example, by not including Sylvia in small-group work).

Once we have found an environmental change that works (that is, reduces the undesirable behavior), we can see whether it generalizes to other situations and employ it there.

Although PBIS has generally focused on individual children, there have been attempts to apply it to a total school setting, with positive results—a reduction in discipline referrals (Bohanon et al., 2006).

▲ Scaffolding

In **scaffolding,** the teacher or aide models the expected behavior and then guides the student through the early stages of understanding. As the student's understanding increases, the teacher gradually withdraws aid (hence the name *scaffolding*). The goal is to have the student internalize the knowledge and operate independently.

▲ Reciprocal Teaching

Reciprocal Teaching is an educational strategy where small groups of students and teachers take turns leading a discussion on a particular topic. This exercise features four activities: questioning, clarifying, summarizing, and predicting. In this strategy (as in scaffolding), the teacher models how to carry out the activities successfully. The students then imitate the teaching style while the teacher plays the role of the student. In this way, students become active players in a role they find enjoyable.

▲ Cooperative Learning

Interestingly, emphasis has switched from a focus on one-on-one instruction for the individual student with special needs, as represented in the policies for an IEP, to the importance of student participation in *cooperative learning* or *team-assisted individualization* (Browder et al., 2007).

In **cooperative learning,** the teacher gives a task to a small group of students (typically four to six), who are expected to complete the task by working cooperatively with one another. The teacher may assign different responsibilities to different members of the group or ask each child to play a specific role (such as recorder, reporter, searcher, or praiser). The child with disabilities may have the same overall objective as other students but be operating with a lower level of task expectations, a reduced workload, or tiered assignments. As long as the child feels a part of the enterprise, some good social interactions can occur.

Group instruction may actually be more advantageous than one-on-one instruction because of the economy of teacher effort, students learning how to interact with peers, and students learning from peers. Small-group instruction (RTI Tier II) is the mode for the regular classroom if the students with special needs are to be included (King-Sears & Carpenter, 2005).

▲ Motivation

One of the most important questions facing the teachers of children with IDD is how to motivate them to learn. There are many reasons that they may not be motivated in school. Bob, for example, comes from a home in which there is little interest in school learning. He is 10 years old and has had a few years' experience in school. But those years have not been full of positive experiences. Bob has known a lot of failure, and failure is a distinct turn-off for most children and adults. Building on Bob's strengths becomes important to avoid feelings of learned helplessness.

▲ Self-Determination

One of the long-term goals for students with IDD is **self-determination,** or the ability to set personal goals and to take appropriate actions to achieve them. The capability of making choices and solving problems within the range of their abilities is an often-stated IEP goal (Wehmeyer, 2006)

Practice at decision making can strengthen the executive function in the information processing model. If the teacher makes all the decisions for the student about what to do next or what to read, this undermines this key ability for adult adjustment.

Teaching strategies for self-determination is a priority for children with IDD. A total of 891 elementary and middle school teachers in six districts were asked whether they valued and *provided instruction* in seven self-determination domains: (a) choice attainment (b) decision making, (c) goal setting and attainment, (d) problem solving, (e) self-advocacy and leadership, (f) self-awareness and self-knowledge, and (g) self-management and self-regulations skills (Stang, Carter, Lane, & Pierson, 2009). Both general educators (elementary and middle school) and special educators clearly stated self-determination as a curricular priority, although special educators rate it somewhat more important than general educators. A call has been made to blend these goals into the elementary program and to stress these strategies more in personnel preparation.

While Bob's program will focus on general education, Carol faces a different situation. Many special educators believe that for students with moderate to severe IDD, the fundamental goal should be not the mastery of knowledge or academic skills but the mastery of adaptive behaviors such as social skills, communication skills, and work skills. After all, they ask, who cares very much whether Carol reaches third-grade or fourth-grade mastery of academic skills? If it is most important for Carol to develop adaptive skills that will serve her well in adulthood and in the world of work, she should participate in cooperative learning exercises—not necessarily to learn what the other students learn but to experience positive social interaction and learn how to work constructively with others.

The first step of the problem-solving strategy can be taught that helps the student to achieve more independent behavior. It needs some practice.

1. Find the problem (problem).

2. Discover as many options as possible (option building).

3. Choose the option you think is best (best option).

4. Act on the choice (action).

5. Judge the effectiveness of the choice (success or no success).

For example, Mary is faced with a dilemma: The printer in the classroom is out of paper. No one will be able to finish his or her assignments (problem). Mary can think of the following options: to complain to peers that the printer is not working again; to tell the teacher about it; to go to the supply closet and get another ream of paper; to start doing something else (options).

Mary doesn't know how to put the paper in, so she chooses to tell the teacher about it. This is the option choice (decision). She gets out of her seat and goes to tell the teacher (action). The teacher either gets more paper and refills the printer (success) or says that she is too busy and will get to it later (no success).

This sequence can be followed for most people's daily problems, but for the child with IDD, it may have to be illustrated through role-playing, in which two students play the roles of student and teacher. Or reciprocal teaching can be used, in which the teacher plays the role of the student and verbalizes her thoughts and actions through the process. The teacher can also use modeling by showing the group the steps of getting the paper and filling the printer, and then asking the students to follow the same process (King-Sears & Carpenter, 2005).

We should not assume that, because students have learned the problem-solving process in filling the printer, they will apply the same process to the problem of spilled water under the sink. The sequence of problem solving should be posted on the bulletin board and specifically gone through each time. Generalization from one situation to another is very difficult and must be pursued vigorously by the educational team.

Another skill related to **self-management** is choice making. Josh may be asked, "Would you like to complete your work at your desk or at the table? Would you like to do your math now or after lunch?" Such choice making gives the student a sense of being in control. Of course, once the decision is made, it should be honored (Bambara & Koger, 2005). The outcome of these problem-solving and choice-making activities is students with more self-confidence who are more in control of their environment.

Adapting Technology

The rapid development of technology linked to education provides a variety of opportunities for children with disabilities. As we have discussed earlier in the text, these technological aids can be divided into two areas: assistive and instructional. *Assistive technology* exists to help the child with disabilities gain access to the information needed for learning. *Instructional technology* is used to help the student learn that information. The *universal design for learning (UDL)* is a way of presenting the information to be learned in the style most accommodating to the individual student's needs.

> Technology, when properly used, can help the child with IDD to grasp unfamiliar ideas.

Effectiveness of Intervention

As with other programs in special education, we are interested in knowing how much and in what ways intervention is paying off for children with intellectual or developmental disabilities. Guralnick (1997) has summarized the literature on early intervention and concluded that the basic question, "Can intervention make a difference?" has been answered and that the answer is, "Yes." Our task now is to determine the relative effectiveness of various models of intervention.

Bryant and Maxwell (1999) have reviewed the series of studies that attempted to chart gains from special programming for these children. They found support for an *intensity* or *duration-of-treatment* effect. In other words, the heavier the dose of educational treatment, the greater the children's gains. The same can be said for the length of time that the treatment is applied: the longer, the better. As a matter of fact, when special treatment stops, there is a tendency for the children to lose some of the gains they have made.

We might make an analogy with diabetes in that the patient must *keep receiving treatment* (insulin or other medication and adherence to diet) in order to get the desired results. What we have learned is that special education needs to be intensive and ongoing for the children's initial gains to hold.

The child with IDD needs guided practice with technology.
(Cengage Learning)

Assistive Technology for Students with IDD

One of the support features of an IEP can be assistive technology—equipment or product systems that can meet some of the special needs of individual children with developmental disabilities.

Many students with IDD have difficulty reading. **Hypertext** software programs can provide assistance to learners with words they do not recognize or understand. In such programs the student can select the unknown word. The student can make the computer read and define the word and read the definition. Some programs may also have pictures to support the meaning of the word. For example, a hypertext program could be created for vocabulary found in a general academic science class. A student could independently study the pronunciation and definitions found in the science curriculum through the use of a program that provides words and definitions in an auditory format.

Whereas assistive technology can provide the avenue through which knowledge can be accessed, instructional technology provides the means for presenting content in alternative approaches, and, as such, the computer is a critical tool for the special educator.

For the child with IDD, the computer is actually a window on the world, given capable instruction in its use and the availability of appropriate software. As Foshay and Ludlow (2005) point out, "computers can be the means of curriculum modification, to facilitate the access to content areas such as science and social studies in the academic curriculum and to develop peer relations through interactive games and collaborative learning" (p. 101).

Sometimes children with IDD need additional multimedia stimulation to master concepts. For example, the Doppler effect, often illustrated by a whistle of an approaching and then departing train, may be more richly portrayed through audio and video formats that can be repeated to ensure that the student has mastered the concept.

Technology allows a child to avoid learned helplessness by allowing him access to knowledge and allowing him to complete required tasks. Students with mild IDD can use text to speech software (e.g., ReadPlease, http://www.readplease.com) so that the student can listen to the information as it is read by the computer (Edyburn, 2006). In computational math, a student can use WebMATH, which gives instructional support for solving math problems.

One occasionally hears a complaint that using such technology prevents the IDD student from actually learning to read. Some technologies use scaffolding that can gradually be withdrawn as the student gains skill and confidence; others may remain throughout his or her life (Edyburn, 2006). Consider Braille or spellcheck. Who would want to give them up if they are needed to do important tasks?

WebMATH
www.webmath.com

Do not be deceived, however. Much teacher or teacher aide time must be invested in preparing the student for the proper use of the computer for learning. Still, through the Assistive Technology Act (P.L. 105–394), Congress provided funds for obtaining hardware and also requires, through IDEA (2004), that IEP committees take technology needs into account when developing IEPs for the student in question. It is highly likely that special education programs for teachers in training will be spending larger and larger amounts of time on the uses of technology in the classroom.

Source: J. Foshay & B. Ludlow (2005). Implementing computer-mediated instructional supports. In M. C. Wehmeyer, D. C. Browder, & M. Agran (Eds.). *Teaching students with intellectual disabilities: Empirically-based strategies*. Boston: Pearson Custom Publishing, pp. 101–124.

Until recently, the response to these alarm bells was a diagnostic examination by the school psychologist to determine whether the child was eligible for some form of special education. Now, many school systems use a *prereferral team,* which may include the classroom teacher, the principal, someone from special education, and relevant other special personnel. The team tries to help the classroom teacher devise some adaptation of the general classroom program to cope with the student's problems without more intensive (and more expensive) intervention (Salvia, Ysseldyke, & Bolt, 2007). If the school is using the RTI model, the team may suggest Tier II supports for the child. If the student makes no apparent gain as a result of the recommendations of the prereferral team, the child may then be referred for more detailed diagnostic examination by the psychologist and, if found eligible, placed in more intensive special education services with an IEP, decided on by the multidisciplinary IEP team working with the child's parents.

What is the purpose of a multidisciplinary team? Each team member brings important information to an IEP meeting. Members share their information and work together to write the child's IEP. The team membership always includes the general education teacher, a parent, and the special education representative. Also included, depending on the nature of the child's needs, can be a speech and language pathologist, school psychologist, school principal, occupational therapist, the student, and others as appropriate. Each person's information adds to the team's understanding of the child and what services the child needs.

Transition from School to Work and Community

The ultimate goal of transition is for students with IDD to achieve independence in the community. To reach such a goal, we need to organize our resources along four separate lines (Odom, Horner, Snell, & Blacher, 2007):

- Systematic planning over several years
- Careful attention to the development of essential skills
- Assistance in the transition process, and
- Ongoing support in adulthood.

An acceptable quality of life depends on income, a sense of self-worth, and social connections provided through work, so there are many people responsible for supporting a student with IDD in the adult community.

> Students with IDD can and often do make good adaptations in adulthood.

Ryan's Readjustment

Ryan, a 22-year-old with mild IDD, was referred to an occupational therapist after unsuccessful community-based job placements. Several professionals recommended that he return to a sheltered day program for "work skills training."

While working with a new occupational therapist, Ryan said he'd like more jobs similar to the ones he had previously lost due to excessive absence or poor performance. Ryan was capable of doing the necessary tasks for those jobs but had seemed to lose interest in them very quickly.

He took a look at some new job ideas on video and was excited about the possibility of working as a housekeeper at a motel. It wasn't easy to

(continued)

find an employer who was willing to give him a try. But one motel owner agreed to give Ryan a job on a 30-day trial basis. It took only a short time for Ryan to become one of the most efficient and reliable housekeepers on the motel's staff. His employer was so impressed that she requested other people with disabilities seeking employment.

Ryan had many successes at this job. He was named Employee of the Month and given a cash bonus, and later he was promoted to "second floor supervisor" and given a raise. Ryan eventually moved up to supervising a group of motel employees without disabilities.

Source: Adapted from Becky Blair. (2000). Ryan's story: From job placement challenge to employee of the month. *Teaching Exceptional Children* 32(4), 47. Copyright by the Council for Exceptional Children. Reprinted with permission.

Today, a growing number of studies have indicated how students with IDD are doing in adult life. The news is mixed. A seminal study looking at eight thousand youths with disabilities, the National Longitudinal Transitional Study of Special Education Students (Blackorby & Wagner, 1996), has established a baseline for future results. Researchers used a careful sampling design to ensure that their sample was nationally representative and generalizable to the population as a whole, as well as to students in eleven disability categories. Large samples of youngsters with disabilities from three hundred public school districts and from twenty-five state-operated schools for children who are deaf or blind were surveyed and interviewed. In addition, a subsample of more than eight hundred parents of youths who had been out of secondary school between two and four years was interviewed.

What happened to youths identified as having IDD?

Half of the students with IDD graduated from high school; the rest either dropped out or aged out of school. The reasons for dropping out of school appeared to be related to behavior rather than to academic performance. Twenty-eight percent of the students who dropped out had serious discipline problems.

What about responsibilities at home?

Youths with IDD had roughly the same amount of household responsibilities as youths in other disability categories. Although the number of students with IDD who were performing in an unsatisfactory fashion at home was not encouraging, their adaptation seemed to be at the same level as that of students with other disabilities.

What about living independently?

In the first or second year after secondary school, fewer students with IDD were living independently than were students with other disabilities. For example, 24 percent of adults with IDD were living independently three to five years after high school (Blackorby & Wagner, 1996).

Figure 6.4 indicates the percentage of youths with IDD who were competitively employed within three to five years after they left school. On the graph, the general population

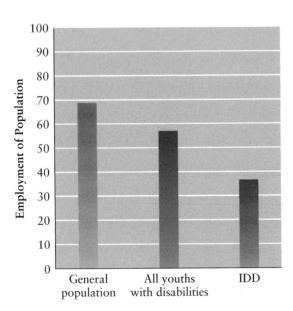

FIGURE 6.4
Youths Competitively Employed 3-5 Years out of School

Source: M. Wagner & J. Blackorby Transition from high school to work or college: How special education students fare in D. Terman, M. Lerner, C. Stevenson & R. Behrman (eds) The Future of Children 6 (1) (1996) 4-24

of students shows a 70 percent rate of employment, and when all the figures for youths with disabilities are included, slightly more than half are competitively employed. In contrast, the number of youths with IDD is between only 30 and 40 percent. Yamaki and Fujiura (2002) took a national profile of U.S. adults with IDD living in community households and found an employment rate of 28 percent, with typical jobs found in service occupations (i.e., cashier) or unskilled labor. These low-income jobs mean that people with IDD will continue to rely on family or public support (Stancliffe & Lakin, 2007). Affordable housing, stable employment, and transportation are keys to independence.

Table 6.5 provides a series of events for secondary students who have IDD. Basically, by getting a part-time job at age 16, enrolling in vocational classes at age 17, and setting vocational goals at age 18, the student is preparing for a transition to work and the community. It does not make much sense to continue to enroll students with IDD in traditional secondary courses, many of them designed for college-preparatory programs where transition to work is a more appropriate goal.

Such results have convinced special educators that assistance for many students with IDD has to be continued beyond the school years if the goals of becoming self-sustaining and independent are to be achieved. Accordingly, there has been more attention paid to the transition years between school and vocational work (and adulthood). Although inclusion appears to be a viable goal for children with IDD through middle school, a strong transition plan must be established earlier in the child's program. (See Table 6.5.)

TABLE 6.5
Planning for Secondary Students with IDD

AT AGE 16

- Find and hold a part-time job in school or in the community.
- Write transition knowledge into the IEP meetings.
- Invite adult service providers to IEP meetings.
- Discuss how long student will attend high school—for four years or until age 21.
- Attend information night meetings that offer information about future planning.

AT AGE 17

- Enroll in vocational education classes.
- Establish a graduation date.
- Write transition goals into IEP.
- Invite adult service providers to IEP meetings.
- Investigate guardianship procedures and determine what is in the best interest of the child.

AT AGE 18

- Apply for SSI and Medicaid card.
- Apply to adult service provider. Take time to visit all providers to find the best match.
- Schedule a vocational evaluation to better assist in determining the child's interest and setting a vocational goal.
- Write transition goal in IEP. Discuss services needed for best transition from high school to adult services.
- Attend a job fair.

Source: From A. M. Goldberg. Transition timeline, retrieved July 15, 2004, from www.ndss.org. Reprinted with permission.

The lesson here is that we cannot release young people with IDD from school and expect them to adjust to a working environment without support and planning. With organized training programs and support services, many of these individuals can adjust well. The support resources fall into four categories:

- *Individuals:* skills, competencies, the ability to make choices, money information

- *Other people:* family, friends, coworkers, cohabitants, mentors

- *Technology:* assistive devices, job or living accommodations, behavioral technology

- *Services:* habilitation services that can be used when natural resources are not available

Parents can become effective partners in planning for children with IDD.

Family Support

One of the common feelings of parents whose children have IDD is loneliness. They feel different from their neighbors and often do not know how best to help their child. An important resource designed to help them cope can be an organized parents' group such as The Arc of the United States (established in 1951 as the National Association for Retarded Citizens), a national organization with many chapters throughout the country. It is able to provide access to resources for parents and to advocate for them and for their children. Often another parent who has been through the same experience can be a valuable friend and confidante, and parents' organizations such as The Arc have well-developed support help. Visit The Arc's website for leads to a wide variety of useful information.

The Arc of the United States
www.thearc.org

One of the strategies that professionals use to help families cope with the extra stress that often accompanies living with children with disabilities is respite care. **Respite care** is the provision of child-care services so the parents are freed for a few days of their constant care responsibilities. Parents who may not have had a "day off" from child-care responsibilities for years greatly appreciate such assistance. Respite care is an effective way of reducing parental depression and stress and enabling parents to be more effective in their role (Botuck & Winsberg, 1991).

Too often in the past, when professionals said they were involved with the family, they really meant only the mother. We now realize the importance of relating to the father as part of the family unit. This is especially true in light of evidence that the typical father tends to play less of a family role when there is a child with disabilities (Blacher & Hatton, 2007). Some direct counseling and support for the father in his role may be important in achieving the sustainable daily routine that seems so necessary to keeping the family on an even keel.

MUMS: National Parent-to-Parent
www.netnet.net/mums

A popular program called MUMS: National Parent-to-Parent Network matches a trained "veteran parent" (someone who has experience as a parent of a child with disabilities) and a "referred parent" (one who is dealing with the issues for the first time). Today, there are 650 Parent-to-Parent programs serving nearly every state. An example of what such a program can mean comes from a referred parent:

> Parent-to-Parent has been my lifeline. When I first heard the diagnosis, I was devastated. Well-meaning doctors and nurses, as well as friends and family, simply did not understand. It was only when I finally connected with another parent through the Parent-to-Parent program that I could begin to hope for a future for us all. My veteran parent was generally there for me whenever I needed her. (Turnbull & Turnbull, 1997, p. 181)

Eunice and Me

I sometimes wonder what was going through Eunice Kennedy Shriver's head when she came up with the idea of Special Olympics and turned her backyard into a day camp for disabled kids. They say it was for Rosemary, her older, learning-disabled sister. That Eunice saw how difficult things were for Rosemary and was inspired by her struggle, and that she also saw that including Rosie with the right support worked out well. It is certainly true that having a disabled person in your life can really alter your perspective. You become very familiar with the dark underside of the world, the realm of "can't do" and "will never be."

My autistic son is 18, and I have been jamming my foot into closing doors all his life: from the renowned doctor who shrugged and pronounced him "retarded" to the synagogue that would not let him have a Saturday bar mitzvah to the local principal who was afraid to have him attend her school.

One day, however, a door swung open wide where we least expected it: sports. Nat tried a gymnastics class run by Special Olympics. The coach was inexperienced with autism but full of energy and patience. She worked him hard and got him to the State Games that summer. We experienced the odd sensation of feeling both proud of our son and being able to trust others with him. Then, at 14, Nat learned how to swim on the local Special Olympics swim team, and it was the first time he ever seemed to look forward to something. "Swim races, swim races," he would say over and over, with a huge grin. Now, at 18, Special Olympics taught him how to be a part of a basketball team.

Our life with Nat is often very hard, but at Nat's sporting events it is not. There, he's just another team member playing his hardest. Nat is just one of the guys, and we are like everyone else. There is no "can't" in Special Olympics. Whether she knew it or not back then, I think that this is what Eunice Shriver had in mind when she set up the day camp. Even though the Special Olympics athlete's pledge is "let me be brave," the secret is, at Special Olympics, we parents don't have to be.

This essay aired on November 16, 2007, on WBUR-FM. Susan Senator is the author of *Making Peace with Autism: One Family's Story of Struggle, Discovery, and Unexpected Gifts*. Shambhala, 2005. Reprinted by permission of WBUR.

Pivotal Issues

Discuss some other ways that students with IDD might find self-satisfaction similar to Special Olympics (such as art or music).

Transition to Community: Special Olympics

A goal of almost everyone, regardless of their educational philosophy, is to increase community contacts and interaction for students with IDD. Whether it is on-the-job vocational training, boarding a community bus to an athletic event, or field trips to various community sites, there is a manifest advantage in these students interacting in the community in which they will live as adults.

One of the most successful of these ventures is a program called Special Olympics, which uses the format of the Olympic Games but in which all the persons participating have developmental disabilities. The program was begun in 1968 by Eunice Kennedy Shriver, a sister of President John F. Kennedy. It has grown to an international event, with several thousand participants and many thousands of spectators. The purpose of the games is to allow children and adults with disabilities to participate in races, swimming meets, field events, and team games and to feel what other athletes feel in competition, in winning and losing—an experience they rarely are able to achieve elsewhere. It has received substantial community support and is touted as one of the largest athletic events now operating, second only to the traditional Olympics.

Interestingly, some negative voices are heard about the Special Olympic games—that they are not designed to integrate the students into the mainstream but are special games only for individuals with disabilities, emphasizing that they are different from the general public. Of course, most of these people could never compete for the basketball or track and field teams of their mainstream schools, so offering alternative participation opportunities is essential. The sheer joy that these competitors and their families get from their Special Olympics experience is obvious to any observer.

moral dilemma
Inclusion and Student Harassment

A teacher in training, Ms. Bascomb, has been concerned about Max, a 9-year-old who has just moved into town with his family. Max joined the fourth-grade class under the school policy of inclusion, although he clearly was not performing at the same level as the other students. The other students have noticed this as well and have begun to comment about it. Today, while on the playground, a group of boys more or less surrounded Max and made some comments that he was a "dummy" and a "retard," asking why he didn't go to a school where he belongs. Max clearly didn't know how to handle the situation and tried to slip away from his tormentors.

What is Ms. Bascomb's responsibility in this situation? What should she say to the boys who were harassing Max? When they have dispersed, what should she say to Max? How should the incident be reported to the classroom teacher, who has been having troubles of her own getting Max oriented? Develop a dialogue between Ms. Bascomb and the boys; Ms. Bascomb and Max; and Ms. Bascomb and the classroom teacher. How should Max's parents be involved?

To answer these questions online, visit the Education CourseMate website.

✳ Summary

- ▶ Pioneers such as Itard and Montessori laid the groundwork for current educational practices.

- ▶ The current definition of children with intellectual and developmental disabilities (IDD) focuses on two major components: intelligence and adaptive behavior. An educational diagnosis of IDD depends on the characteristics of the child and on the demands of the social environment.

- ▶ Many factors contribute to the development of IDD. They include genetic abnormalities, toxic agents, infections, neurological insults, and negative environmental factors.

▶ There are different developmental levels found in children with IDD, and those levels determine the educational placement and strategies that meet the child's needs.

▶ Children with IDD have difficulty processing information. For many, the problem lies in limited memory, perception, reasoning, classification, and the way they organize information and make decisions. Children with IDD often have a general language deficit and specific problems using interpretive language.

▶ Early intervention programs are one means of preventing IDD caused by environmental factors, but they are not a cure-all for the effects of poverty and social disorganization in the home. They are an important first step; the earlier, the better.

▶ The IEPs of children with IDD are encouraged to stress strengths that can lead to positive accomplishments.

▶ The elementary and secondary curricula for students with IDD stress academic skills, communication and language development, socialization, and prevocational and vocational skills. The emphasis, particularly for students with moderate IDD, is on functional language.

▶ By reducing failure, increasing success, and modeling appropriate behaviors, teachers can improve the attitudes and behaviors of children with IDD.

▶ Families with a child with IDD may need support and assistance in their attempts to cope with the challenges they are presented. This could be both from professionals and from other parents in similar situations.

▶ Planning and vocational training are needed to ease the transition of those with IDD from school to work. Many of these students make good adult adjustment, often with community help.

Future Challenges

1 *What aspects of the culture of poverty influence developmental delay?*

We know that a disproportionate number of children growing up in a culture of poverty show early developmental delays. We don't yet know what factors, or interaction of those factors, in that culture are responsible. Our current emphasis on preschool development and intervention promises better answers to this puzzle in the near future.

2 *How can positive employment prospects be increased?*

The future of students with IDD depends as much on the environment or context in which they live as on their education and training. The increasing complexity of modern society casts a shadow over the goal of independence for these students, although many may be able to get jobs in the service sector.

3 *How can more effective instruction be offered to students with IDD who come from a variety of cultures?*

The changing demographics of the American population make it certain that more and more students from different cultures and ethnic backgrounds will be referred for special education services. Some will be mislabeled because of the difficulties of communication; others will find it difficult to adapt to classrooms in which the demands are high and not in line with their own experience or even their family values. Special educators need to develop greater understanding and sensitivity to the cultural diversity of families bringing children to the schools in order to serve the students well.

4 *How can inclusion and the best community options be achieved?*
By including individuals with mild IDD in the general education classroom at the secondary level, we limit them to a standard curriculum. Yet these students need special instruction in prevocational and survival skills. How do we balance the benefits of inclusion with these special vocational needs?

Key Terms

central processing p. 182

cooperative learning p. 199

developmental disabilities p. 180

Down syndrome p. 185

encephalitis p. 188

fetal alcohol syndrome (FAS) p. 188

fragile X syndrome (FXS) p. 186

function assessment p. 198

hypertext p. 202

intellectual and developmental disabilities p. 179

phenylketonuria (PKU) p. 186

positive behavior interventions and supports (PBIS) p. 198

reciprocal teaching p. 194

respite care p. 206

rubella p. 188

scaffolding p. 199

self-determination p. 199

self-management p. 200

teratogen p. 187

Resources

References of Special Interest

Schalock, R., Bothwick-Duffy, S., Brodley, V., Berntinx, W., Coulter, D., Craig, E., Gomez, S., Lachapelle, Y., Luckasson, R., Reeve, A., Shogun, K., Snell, M., Spreat, S., Thesse, M., Thompson, J., Verdugon-Alonso, M., Wehmeyer, M., & Teager, M. (2010). *Intellectual disability: Definitions, clarifications, and systems of support* (11th ed.). Washington, D.C.: American Association for Intellectual and Developmental Disabilities. This impressive volume represents the results of ten years of work to recast the definition of children with intellectual and developmental disabilities. There is a special emphasis on the need for systems of support to provide the special services needed for those children.

Agran, M., & Wehmeyer, M. (2005). *Mental retardation and intellectual disabilities: Teaching students using innovative and research based strategies*. Boston: Merrill/Prentice Hall. A review of the many kinds of special intervention techniques to be used with children with IDD. Special attention is paid to positive behavior supports and the teaching of problem-solving techniques to build the capacities of these students.

Beirne-Smith, M., Ittenbach, R., & Patton, J. (2001). *Mental retardation* (6th ed.). Upper Saddle River, NJ: Merrill. A comprehensive view of children with mental retardation from definition to assessment to characteristics. Much space is devoted to lifespan issues, including infancy and early childhood, educational programming in the school years, and the transitional years preparing for adulthood. Family consideration, individual rights, and legal issues are also addressed.

Blacher, J., & Baker, B. (2002). *Families and mental retardation*. Washington, DC: American Association on Mental Retardation. This book is a compilation of thirty-two articles about families and mental retardation that were originally published in AAMD journals over one hundred years. It reviews how professionals have changed their views concerning families over that period of time. The content covers family responsibilities, the reactions of families to mental retardation (they are not all negative, by any means), and family interventions and support.

Davis, S. (Ed.). (2003). *A family handbook on future planning*. Silver Spring, MD: Arc of the United States. A guide to help families develop a plan for their sons and daughters with cognitive, intellectual, or developmental disabilities. The plan deals with issues of personal finances and how to ensure the safety and well-being of the children after their parents' deaths.

Lakin, K., & Turnbull, A. (Eds.). (2005). *National goals and research for people with intellectual and developmental disabilities*. Washington, D.C.: American Association on Mental Retardation. This volume puts into writing the conference findings from 200 national experts who wished to summarize the progress that has been made over the past few decades in providing multidisciplinary assistance for children with IDD and their families. The National Goals that were agreed upon provide a basis for special programming and policies for such students.

Switzky, H., & Greenspan, S. (Eds.). (2006). *What is mental retardation?* Washington, D.C.: American Association on Mental Retardation. A comprehensive view by many different experts on the problems of defining and implementing the concept of mental retardation. The role of the environment and adaptive behavior are explored, with widely varying views on the appropriate answers.

Turnbull, A., & Turnbull, H. R. (2003). *Families, professionals and exceptionality: Collaborating for empowerment* (5th ed.). Upper Saddle River, NJ: Prentice Hall. A rich text that focuses on the many roles played by the family members of a child with disabilities. It is designed to help professionals understand families, collaborate with families to help family empowerment, and aid family roles in the community and educational system improvement. Many practical quotes from family members bring the issues to life.

Journals

American Journal on Intellectual and Developmental Disabilities
aaidd.allenpress.com/

Education and Training in Intellectual and Developmental Disabilities
www.cec.sped.org

Intellectual and Developmental Disabilities
www.aaidd.allenpress.com

Research in Developmental Disabilities
www.elsevier.com

Professional Organizations

American Association on Intellectual and Developmental Disabilities
www.aaidd.org

Association for Retarded Citizens (The Arc)
www.thearc.org

National Down Syndrome Society
www.ndss.org

United Cerebral Palsy Association
www.ucp.org

 Visit the Education CourseMate website for additional TeachSource Video Cases, information about CEC standards, study tools, and much more.

Children with Emotional and Behavior Disorders

 Focus Questions

▶ How do we define children with emotional and behavior disorders (EBD)?

▶ What are some of the risks for externalizing and internalizing factors for children with EBD?

▶ What are some proposed causes of EBD?

▶ How can we use the Information Processing Model and RTI model to plan for children with EBD?

▶ How do positive behavior supports differ from other types of approaches for coping with problem behaviors?

▶ What techniques can we use to teach children to manage and control their own behavior?

▶ What kinds of teacher strategies and program modifications are needed for students with EBD?

▶ How do we help students with EBD adapt in the community after their schooling is completed?

© Ellen Senisi

Few experiences are as disturbing to teachers as trying to teach children who are chronically unhappy or driven to aggressive, antisocial behavior. The teachers feel distressed, knowing there's a problem but feeling unable to do anything about it. Managing behavior problems in the classroom is rated as one of the most serious problems facing teachers (U.S. Department of Education, 2005).

Children with behavior problems carry a burden that children with other disabilities do not. We do not blame children who have intellectual and developmental disabilities or who have cerebral palsy for their different behaviors. But many people assume that children with behavior disorders *can* control their actions and *could* stop their disturbing behavior if they wanted to. The sense that they are somehow responsible for their disability colors how others respond to children with emotional and behavior disorders (EBD): their peers, their families, their peers, their teachers (Gresham, 2007).

History of Emotional and Behavior Disorders

We have always been painfully aware of children with behavior or emotional problems. Yet for generations there has been amazing variation in what were believed to be the causes of such behavior and, correspondingly, there have been a wide array of treatments. Two centuries ago, children with behavior problems were believed to be possessed by the devil, insane, or mentally retarded. When attention was paid to them at all, they were shut away in large institutions with very little effort directed to their education. The professionals who dealt with them were largely physicians or clergy (if they were "possessed," it was up to the "holy men" to cure them) (Kauffman, Brigham, & Mock, 2004).

In general, our views of the causes and cures of mental disturbance have followed the broader trends of the times. That is, when we as a society became interested in genetics, heredity came to be considered an important cause of behavioral aberrations. When the society became interested in Sigmund Freud's style of psychoanalysis, we became fascinated with the inner life of the child with behavior problems.

In the late 1800s, children who were manifestly different from their age-mates were being put into special ungraded classes, with little attention paid to their individual or special needs. Jean Itard and Edward Seguin, both physicians, became important figures in treating children with behavior problems, as well as children with intellectual and developmental disabilities, as there had been few other attempts to differentiate the two conditions.

After World War II, the responsibility for children with exceptionalities gradually shifted from the medical or mental health professionals to educators. The schools assumed greater responsibility for their treatment, and the treatment became increasingly behavioral and educational. As we became aware of the power of ecological and social factors to influence children's development (Chapter 2), treatment also included changing and improving their social and educational environment. This chapter discusses the current view of causes, as well as the methods and current curricula based on humanistic, ecological, and behavioral principles (Kauffman, Brigham, & Mock, 2004).

The definition of EBD stresses the intensity and long-lasting nature of the observed behavior.

Definition of Emotional and Behavior Disorders

It is not easy to define emotional and behavior disorders in children. There is no clear dividing line, such as an IQ score or the syndromes of autism spectrum disorders. Readers are tempted to skip lightly over technical matters such as definitions in order to get to the more meaty sections that describe students with exceptionalities and how to plan programs for them. We urge that you not do that in this case because the definition of children with EBD is knee deep in many of the problems faced by this special field. Table 7.1 provides the legal definition (IDEA Amendments of 2004), and it is often easy to recognize oneself in this definition. After all, which of us has not been concerned with interpersonal relationships or depression or inappropriate behavior?

What separates children with EBD from their more average peers is not the *kind* of behavior shown but the *intensity* and *long-lasting nature* of that behavior. Everyone can be unhappy from time to time but not every day or in many different circumstances. But here is one of the problems with this definition: How can we separate those students who have a normal amount of unhappiness from those with such intense unhappiness that it threatens to swallow them up and destroy any attempt to do their schoolwork? Where is the dividing point?

Another problem with this definition is in the final statement in Table 7.1, which says that the term "does not apply to children who are socially maladjusted unless it is determined that they have an emotional disturbance." Few professionals are in agreement with this statement; they believe that we should be trying to cope with both emotionally disturbed and socially maladjusted disturbed children (Cullinan, 2004). Gresham (2007) has suggested that lawmakers assumed that students who were acting out were doing so on their own accord and could stop if they wished to do so. Another line of thought has been that lawmakers, having passed legislation dealing with delinquency, thought that having two different kinds of legislation would create a confusing overlap.

The schools have, by and large, handled this problem by assuming that any child showing serious behavior problems can automatically be assumed to be emotionally disturbed and thus eligible for treatment. Whether this is really true or not remains an open question.

This definition of emotional disturbance does have some other serious shortcomings. A number of observers have pointed out that the federal definition places *all* responsibility for the problem on the child and none on the environment in which the child exists, thus making it the responsibility of the special education program to change the *child* but not the *learning environment*, which

Council for Exceptional Children's Division of Children with Behavior Disorders.
www.ccbd.net

TABLE 7.1
Federal Definition of Emotional and Behavior Disorders

... a condition exhibiting one or more of the following characteristics over a long period of time and to a marked degree that adversely affects educational performance:

A.	An inability to learn that cannot be explained by intellectual, sensory, or health factors;
B.	An inability to build or maintain satisfactory interpersonal relationships with peers and teachers;
C.	Inappropriate types of behavior or feelings under normal circumstances;
D.	A general pervasive mood of unhappiness or depression; or
E.	A tendency to develop physical symptoms or fears associated with personal or school problems.
F.	The term does not apply to children who are socially maladjusted unless it is determined that they have an emotional disturbance.

Source: Code of Federal Regulations, Title 34, §300.7(b)(9)

can be considerably flawed (Nelson, Crabtree, Marchand-Martella, & Martella, 1998). This chapter is divided into two main groups of students—those who externalize their difficulties (behavior disorders) and those who internalize them (emotional disorders).

The term *behavior disorder* implies that the child is causing trouble for someone else. A serious emotional disturbance can be merely a manifestation of personal unhappiness. But almost all children reveal age-inappropriate behavior at one time or another. Moreover, a child's behavior is not the only variable that determines classification in this category. The person who perceives the child's behavior as "inappropriate" plays a key role in the decision. Clearly, some kinds of behavior, such as physical attacks, constant weeping or unhappiness, and extreme hyperactivity, are unacceptable in any setting. But the acceptability of a wide range of other behaviors depends on the attitude of the perceiver.

Cultural Perspectives on Defining EBD

In our pluralistic society, behavior that is acceptable in some groups or cultures is unacceptable in others. Can we say that a child's behavior is deviant if that behavior is the norm in the child's cultural group, even though *we* may find the particular behavior socially unacceptable? A definition of acceptable behavior must allow for cultural differences.

We noted that this definition focuses on the child but not on the child's environment. The learning environment may be exactly what is at issue for children who come to school from very different cultures with different lifestyles and values. Let us introduce you to a few students.

Pete is a good example of a child with both academic and behavior problems that interfere with school performance. He has been a constant trial to his middle school teachers. He belongs to a gang known as the Griffins who, on occasion, terrorize other students in the school. They are suspected of stealing from local stores and perhaps dealing drugs in the school. Pete does not appear to be depressed or anxious, but his acting-out behavior causes great stress for his teachers and his parents.

Juan, a child newly arrived from Mexico, has trouble with the different ways he is supposed to react to authority. He is expected to look teachers in the eye when they are talking to him. But if he did that at home, he would be severely reprimanded because such eye contact would be considered defiance of parental authority. Juan's reaction to this very different environment may cause him to exhibit behavior within the range of the current definition of behavior disorder. That behavior would not be due to some underlying pathology but to the clash of cultural values between school and home (Harry & Klingner, 2006).

What treatment is prescribed for such a child? Should Juan be made to change his behavior patterns to fit the new environment, or should we try to reach an accommodation between the two? The issue of an individual child with maladaptive behavior may turn out to be an issue of clashing societies with a very different prescription for social remediation that extends far beyond the reach of special education.

The student caught between two cultures can still manifest behaviors that are certain to cause him or her trouble now and in the future in the school environment and in the community. In short, the problem may start out as a cultural clash, but it is transformed into a personal adjustment problem. Should the child receive some type of intervention? In this situation, it is appropriate to

Because practically all children exhibit inappropriate behavior from time to time, criteria for identifying problem behavior depend largely on the frequency and intensity of specific behaviors.

(© Ellen Senisi)

> Fewer children with EBD are being served than are estimated to be in the general population.

think of the entire family as the focus of attention. Increasingly, the family unit is involved in the attempts at behavior change in the child.

Prevalence of Children with EBD

There is a disturbing gap between the number of children receiving special services in the schools (about 1 percent) and the number of children who are judged to have either **serious emotional disturbance** or behavior disorders (variously estimated between 5 and 15 percent). Many of the judgments are subjective and left to local personnel; this is the reason it is hard to arrive at a definitive prevalence figure.

This is not to say, however, that there is not a core of children who can readily be identified as having emotional or behavior disorders. A child who attacks another child with a weapon such as scissors, a knife, or a hammer leaves little doubt; neither does a child who weeps five or six times a day without apparent cause. As always, confusion about whether a child is eligible for special services exists at the margin of the category

When a first-grade teacher sees a child who harms others and damages property, who breaks the rules, fights, lies, and yells, the teacher first wonders what to do about this child, then worries about what is to become of him or her. Will he or she continue to show these aggressive tendencies? Will they fade away as the child gets older? Will the child, in fact, be in trouble with society as an adult?

►ǁ TeachSource **VIDEO CONNECTION**

Teaching Strategies for Students with Emotional and Behavioral Disorders

Visit the Education CourseMate website to access this TeachSource Video Case. In this video case, you will meet Brittany and Trisha—two girls having emotional difficulties in middle and secondary school. The emphasis within the case is on social interactions, and role-playing is described as one strategy for helping the students cope. As you watch this video, reflect on how teachers can support students who are experiencing difficulties with social adjustment. How should teachers respond to these students?

Diagnostic Fads

The lack of a clear line separating severe from mild emotional and behavior disorders has led to other diagnostic difficulties. Children can be diagnosed with a label that may have major negative consequences, when in reality a temporary condition is being seen.

A current fad in psychiatry is the diagnosis of **bipolar disorder** to describe children experiencing nonepisodic temper outbursts. This, in turn, can lead to medical treatments that have serious side effects (Frances, 2010). There has been a large growth in the diagnosis of bipolar disorder among children, despite the fact that a significant section of the medical community disagrees as to whether bipolar exists in children at all. This overdiagnosing and overtreatment has already been evident with autism spectrum disorders and ADHD, and there can be serious consequences for providing powerful drugs when behavioral treatments may well be sufficient.

> A child's emotional or behavior disorders in school are strong indications of future difficulties in school and society.

Is This Aggression Long-Lasting?

One of the hopes of educators is that behavior problems and academic problems may ease or become less severe over time as the child physically and socially matures. But longitudinal studies tend to lessen that hope. One such study (Montague, Enders, & Castro, 2005) followed kindergarten students identified as at moderate or high risk for behavior and academic problems into later elementary and middle school. These students were primarily from culturally diverse and poor families.

The authors found that those at risk in kindergarten continue to be at risk for poor school outcomes that included truancy, delinquency, and school failure, through middle school. The critical importance of early intervention to support such children with EBD is obvious.

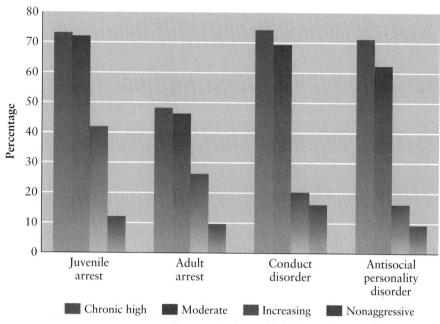

FIGURE 7.1
Predictor of Adult Aggressive Behavior Based Upon Behavior of Young Children

Source: Schaeffer, C., Petras, H., Ialongo, N., Pofuskea, J., & Kellam, S. (2003) Modeling growth in boys aggressive behavior across elementary school; Links to later criminal involvement, conduct disorder and antisocial personality disorder. Developmental Psychology 19, 1020–1035

Another longitudinal study, in which a sample of 297 male children who were first assessed at age 6, then evaluated at each grade level through seventh grade, and finally evaluated through interviews at ages 19 and 20, provides some answers to these questions (Schaeffer, Petras, Ialongo, Poduska, & Kellam, 2003).

The authors were able to sort children into four groups: *chronic high aggressive* (the child was aggressive when starting school), *moderate aggressive, increasing aggressive* (including those who seemed to become aggressive while in school and increased their aggressiveness over the years), and *nonaggressive*. Figure 7.1 shows the comparison of aggressive behavior in school with later adult consequences. The figure shows that almost three-quarters of the children in the chronically high aggression and the moderate groups were arrested as juveniles and that half of them were arrested as adults. Also, almost three-quarters of the children in the chronically high aggressive and the increasing aggressive groups were identified as having conduct disorder or antisocial personality disorder that continued through young adulthood.

Attention Deficit Disorder/Attention Deficit Hyperactive Disorder (ADD/ADHD)

As we have seen in the preceding chapters on children with intellectual and developmental delays and children with learning disabilities, the condition of ADHD blends into these categories and our current focus on emotional and behavior disorders. That is because children with ADHD carry many of the features or

ADD/ADHD

A Teenage Student Comes to Terms with Medication

My name is Amy. I am a 15-year-old girl from Erie, Pennsylvania, and I have attention deficit disorder (ADD). Part of my treatment is working with Jennifer Girts, a counselor at the Achievement Center near my home. One afternoon when I was really frustrated, she gave me an article on ADD and adolescents. Wow! I loved it! It really helped me understand a lot about myself. Now I feel moved to write my own article telling my story about when I was diagnosed, the ways I felt about it then, and how I am coping now. Having dealt with ADD for nine years I know how other kids with ADD feel. I was there at one time too, and I hope my story will help.

Before we found out about ADD, my childhood was good. I have wonderful parents and a younger brother, Brian, who means the world to me. I was good and bad, just like any other child. Then, in first grade we found out I have ADD. My life changed from then on.

Coming to Terms with ADD

When I first heard about ADD, I did not know what it was. I remember asking my parents about it. They explained it to me and I asked, "Will it ever go away?"

The answer: "No." This made me really upset. They assured me that ADD could be treated, but that I needed to want the help.

My parents thought bringing me to a psychiatrist, who could give me medication, would help me. I thought I was going to lose my head trying all the different kinds of medications suggested. I ended up trying eight different kinds. Can you believe it? I took kinds that made me less hungry, some that made me depressed, and others that made me confused. Finally, my doctor found a combination that works. Now I am on Adderall and Clonidine.

Making a Choice

Finally we found the right medication, but then I never wanted to take it. I would hide it in my dog's chew toys or put it up my sleeve. Now I find myself wondering why I would want to do that since the medication really does help me. My mom assures me there was a time when I didn't care if it did or not. Here is the real reason: I wanted to be normal. After all, no other kid I knew took medication. But when I did not take my medication, I always had difficulty paying attention, and my grades dropped. I was a grouch—

characteristics of those other conditions: acting-out behavior, the inability to focus on a task, and the jittery actions that can drive teachers and parents to distraction.

There also seems to be a linkage between aggressive behavior and attention-deficit hyperactivity disorder that suggests a contributing or comorbid (joint) relationship (Kauffman, 2002). The fact that the child with increasing aggression may suffer from concentration problems in school contributes to the portrait of a student having difficulty adjusting to the classroom. Kauffman called for increasing and improved screening and tracking of behavior problems in elementary schools, or even in preschool, so that preventive intervention can take place before the problems ripen.

Matt, an eight year old, has been diagnosed with ADHD and with some aspects of EBD as well. The most frequent description of Matt is that he is "out of control." His constant activity seems almost "driven," according to his mother. Physicians and psychiatrists impressed by this aberrant behavior have increasingly prescribed drugs such as Ritalin as a way for calming Matt so that the teacher has a chance of communicating with him. The story of Amy in the nearby Exceptional Lives box and her encounters with drugs make it clear that there is no easy or simple solution to these problems. A combination of multidisciplinary medical, behavioral, and educational treatment seems called for.

definitely not a nice person—all because I did not take my medication.

Finally, my counselor said to me, "Amy, it is your choice to take your medication or not. A lot of people take medication for all different kinds of reasons. You need to decide if you want to be in control of your moods and impulsivity. What kind of person do you want to be: someone in control or a grouch?" I finally realized that I need the medication to help myself. That's the way my father put it. He would say, "You need to help yourself before you can help others."

Listen, it's up to you. It's your choice; no one can force you to take your medicine. I know which person I would rather be. It was up to me to make the right choice—not my parents or my counselor. Other people can ask me to take medication, but I need to be smart enough to realize that I need it. I found out that it was the best thing for me. So my advice to others is: be smart and take your medication. It will help you—take my word for it.

Now my life is pretty good. I am in the eighth grade. I make good grades and have tons of friends. I still take my medication every morning and at night. And I still see my counselor every once in a while. She helps me sort out my feelings and ask myself the right questions. But, hey, I have ADD. And I am normal.

Don't get me wrong, I still have my ups and downs—everyone does. It's not because of ADD; it's because I am human. My life has changed over the years. I've come to understand what ADD can mean to me. ADD may never go away, but I have the power to control it. I will not let it control me again. I have made my choice. The right choice. You have to decide how you want to live: as Oscar the Grouch, or as a person in control with a wonderful life. What is your choice?

*When this article was written, Amy was an eighth-grader at Walnut Creek School in Erie, Pennsylvania. Her favorite school subject is English and favorite pastimes are hanging out with her friends, going to the mall, school dances, camping with her family, and helping other people. She wants to be a counselor for children with ADD. She enjoys talking with Jennifer Girts, her own counselor, and feels that it would benefit children with ADD to talk to a counselor who has had first-hand experience with the disorder.

Source: From Amy Wojtkielewicz, My choice for my life: Coming to terms with ADD, *Exceptional Parent Magazine* (November 2000): 113. Reprinted with permission.

Pivotal Issues

- What can you do to support students with ADD/ADHD in your classroom?

- What support will you need from other professionals in order to work with complex students like Amy?

- How would you begin to discuss ADD/ADHD with a student's family?

Causation of Emotional and Behavior Disorders

Neurology and Genetic Factors

What causes EBD? Some ideas are harder to accept than others. One hypothesis is that future behavior is determined at birth. Many books and media have adopted the theme of the "evil child" (see the film *The Bad Seed*). The essential unfairness of such a concept repels us and makes genetic research findings harder to accept. Fortunately, we can now say that the final determination of adult behavior is a mix or blend of genetics and environment. Criminal behavior, for instance, is *not* fixed at birth.

What the genetic evidence does tell us, though, is that some children have a predisposition toward behaviors such as hyperactivity, attention problems, or impulsiveness. Those behaviors may call for some special educational or social environments to ensure that such predispositions do not flower into real behavioral problems (Rutter, 1997):

> Some children have a genetic predisposition toward behavior problems. This can be helped through both special education and social environments.

Interaction Between Genetics and Environment

Although it has now been widely accepted that there is an interaction between genetics and environment in the development of aggressive and hostile behavior in children, if we are to develop good remedial practices, we need to know *how* such an interaction works.

As we have learned more about the brain, we have come to realize that how we are wired at birth by genetics and prenatal conditions have much to do with our behavior in such characteristics as impulsiveness. On the other hand, we also know that children such as Matt are not inevitably doomed to a life of aggression and hyperactivity. We also realize that more energy and resources will be needed to prevent such an outcome—more than needed with typical children. An extensive review of the research of such topics (Beauchaine et al., 2008) concludes:

> [A]lmost all forms of psychopathology emerge over the course of development as a result of complex interactions between biological vulnerabilities and environmental risks, neither of which can be ignored in efforts to prevent the debilitation psychiatric conditions (p. 762).

Prescribed medication is often part of the treatment program for children with EBD.

Although there clearly is some genetic influence in conduct disorders, particularly those associated with hyperactivity, inattention, and poor peer relationships, there is no reason to believe that environmental experiences cannot counteract those influences. What does seem clear is that there are two-way interactions between the various forces at work. That is, just as aggression can change psychosocial factors, so can psychosocial factors change levels of aggression.

Neurology and Brain Development
What We Know about Emotional and Behavioral Disorders

When children have extreme emotional and/or behavioral difficulties, the neural chemistry of the child's brain may need to be adjusted and medication may be considered as part of the treatment and support (NIMH, 2010). When medication is considered for a child, the multidisciplinary team will need to include a physician (psychiatrist, neurologist, or pediatrician), and will often include a psychologist, a psychiatric nurse, and/or a behavioral therapist as well. As our understanding of brain development increases, we are better able to recognize and treat early stages of mental illness and emotional disturbances in children.

The use of **psychotropic** (affecting the neurosystem) medication as a part of the intervention support for young children, however, must take into consideration the related risks (NIMH, 2010). Some risks associated with medications include side effects like nausea, decreased appetite, excessive sweating, confusion, and dizziness (Bank, 2010). For children who are trying to manage extreme anxiety disorders, depression, obsessive-compulsive disorders, post-traumatic stress disorders, attention deficits, eating disorders, and schizophrenia, the benefits of medication may outweigh the risks. While the specific medication needed for an individual child will, of course, be identified by the child's physician, medications may include antidepressants, mood stabilizers, antipsychotics, and stimulants to support attention (Bank, 2010).

This medication creates a feeling of well-being and a sense of control (Bank, 2010). Young children respond to medications differently than older children and adults because their brains are developing so rapidly. As a result, they may metabolize medications at a different rate (NIMH, 2010). Because psychotropic medications affect the brain chemicals related to mood and behavior, children taking these medications must be closely monitored.

Child Abuse

One of the environmental factors clearly related to EBD is child abuse. This physical and psychological mistreatment of children, mainly by parents, is so strongly predictive of EBD that unless preventive action is taken, we will see this misfortune repeated generation after generation. The enormous scope of the situation is not well known. As Barth & Haskins (2009) note:

> More than 3 million American children are investigated for child mistreatment each year, and 800,000 children, about 1 in every hundred, are identified by state agencies as having been abused or neglected. More than 1,500 children die as a result of this mistreatment (p. 1).

What is also not well known is that it doesn't have to be that way. We know techniques and treatments that can reduce this problem significantly through parent training and support (Forgatch, Patterson, Degarmo, & Beldavs, 2009). We spend a great deal more time teaching each other how to drive a car than how to parent—how to cope with stress and frustration without taking it out on vulnerable children.

Think about how your own parents learned how to cope with you and your worries and behaviors. If they were fortunate enough to have loving and caring parents themselves, this was a good start. In addition, there are methods, such as positive behavior supports, not well known to even the most caring parents, that can make a clear difference in the family, in the classroom, and in the community. We will discuss some of these methods later in the chapter.

> Children who are victims of abuse and violence often learn to inflict those behaviors on others.

Risk Factors for Externalizing Disorders

There is a tendency to react to aggressive acts as isolated events at face value, especially under the pressure of many other things going on in the classroom. However, there is impressive data that suggest that our behavior is the result of integrated contributions of factors, both internal and external and that these factors work together as a dynamic system (Drews et al., 2007).

Table 7.2 provides some **correlated constraints** that affect aggression, both positively and negatively (Farmer, Farmer, Estell, & Hutchins, 2007). On the positive side, good academic performance, good relationships with peers, the presence of supportive adults, and athletic competence all tend to interrelate to one another and operate as a brake on aggression. On the other hand, there is a series of negative constraints, also interrelated, that can predict aggression. A combination of academic problems, attention difficulties, coercive family relations, and

TABLE 7.2
Aggression and Correlated Constraints

Positive	Negative
Academic success	Academic difficulties
Positive peer relations	Attention problems
Athletic competence	Peer rejection
Supportive adults	Coercive family systems
Sufficient resources	Poor parental monitoring

Source: Farmer, T., Farmer, E., Estell, D., & Hatchens, B. (2007). The developmental dynamics of aggression and the prevention of school violence. *Journal of Emotional and Behavioral Disorders, 15*(4), 197–208, copyright (c) 2007 by Sage Publications. Reprinted by permission of SAGE Publications.

poor parental monitoring all can operate as a dynamic system supporting aggressive behavior (Farmer, Farmer, Estell, & Hutchins, 2007).

When we realize that we are dealing with a correlated dynamic system of factors, we see the limited use of a single effort—such as improving social skills, for example—in the face of this system of correlated constraints. These constraints have likely been in place for a large part of the developmental history of a student.

There also appears to be, based on an extended literature review, a series of correlated constraints (factors related to one another that add to or reduce the challenges occurring) that predict internalizing behaviors such as anxiety, depression, self-hatred, and so forth. Some of these are the presence of a chronically ill sibling, other learning disabilities, poor social status, and parental divorce. Such correlated factors also form a dynamic system that defies easy modification (Crews et al, 2007).

Family Risk Factors

One interesting indicator of a family risk factor is family violence, which includes child abuse. Violence against children is a behavior that the children themselves are likely to display when they are old enough to inflict violence on those weaker than they. The intergenerational aspect of this disorder is distressing. A child with serious behavior disturbance rarely comes from a stable home with warm and loving parents. And the child who is abused is likely to be an abusive parent and to reproduce the entire negative pattern unless the school or community intervenes (Mattison, 2004).

A generation ago, feelings were strong that parents were in large part responsible for their child's behavior problems. Today, many believe that the child's atypical behavior may cause parents to react in ways that are inappropriate and make the condition worse in a downward spiral of unfortunate sequential events.

Children with conduct disorders learn that aggressive behavior is a way of getting what they want, particularly when parental punishment is sporadic and ineffective and provides another model of aggressiveness.

(© Carl Glassman/The Image Works)

School Risk Factors

The risk factor most frequently associated with social and emotional disturbance is below-grade achievement in school. Do these children act out *because* they are academically slow and not able to keep up with their classmates? Is their acting out a reaction to their failure in school? The idea is an interesting one, but the evidence does not seem to support it. For one thing, the aggressive behavior that gets these youngsters into trouble in school is clearly observable *before* they enter school.

Risk Factors for Behavior Problems

Jim, for example, was in trouble in school as early as kindergarten. His school records are peppered with teachers' statements: "He seems bright but doesn't want to apply himself." "He's unmotivated and an angry little boy." "This boy will not take the time necessary to learn the basics." Jim had myriad correlated constraints: a **coercive family system** (the use of physical or psychological force for imposing will), peer rejection, academic difficulties, and attention problems.

Violence in the Schools

We said earlier that the schools are a mirror of our society. Whatever bright spots we see in society, such as a sense of optimism about the future, or whatever problems we see, such as the rise of drug use or extensive violence, are likely to show up in the classroom and schoolyard. We need to remind ourselves that over 55 million students are in school right now, or about one in every five citizens of this country. Since we see a great deal of violence in our communities, we should not be surprised to see it reverberating in our schools. Here are some recent statistics on the kind and rate of violence in our schools:

- In 2007, 62 percent of public schools reported an incident of crime that occurred to the police; 75 percent reported one or more incidents of violent crime.

- In 2007, about 5 percent of students ages 12 to 18 reported that they were afraid of attack or harm at school.

- In 2007, 23 percent of students ages 12 to 18 reported gang activity at their school.

- During the 2007–2008 school year, 25 percent of public schools reported that bullying occurred among students on a daily or weekly basis.

- In 2007, 22 percent of students ages 12 to 18 reported that someone had offered, sold, or given them an illegal drug on school property.

- In 2007, 34 percent of teachers said that student misbehavior interfered with their teaching.

- 18 percent of students in grades 9 to 12 reported that they had carried a weapon, and 6 percent said they had carried a weapon on school property.

- Over the last decade, the use of safety and security measures in schools increased sharply, including controlled access to school and school property (90 percent), faculty wearing badges and picture IDs (58 percent), one or more security cameras installed (55 percent), and telephones placed in every classroom (72 percent).

Source: USDE. (2009). *The condition of education.* (Washington, DC: National Center for Educational Statistics, United States Department of Education.)

All of these statistics can be misread, of course, to make schools appear to be a vast arena of misbehavior and conflict. In almost every case, the statistics on violence reported were much higher in the community at large than in schools, but they do remind us that violence is a part of students', teachers', and administrators' lives in the school setting.

Can we identify children prone to violence? The answer is yes, and they can be identified quite early. Loeber and Farrington (1998) suggested that a small subset of juveniles commits virtually all of the serious offenses and that these students began their violent activities when quite young. Sprague and Walker (2000) suggest that 6 to 9 percent of children account for more than 50 percent of total discipline referrals and virtually all of the serious offenses. Furthermore, early discipline problems predict later adjustment problems quite accurately (Walker, Calvin, & Ramsey, 1995), so it is important to intervene as early as possible.

What can be done? First of all, we should consider what does *not* appear to work with the violent child. The "zero tolerance" approach adopted by many schools, which includes suspensions, expulsions, metal detectors, guards in the hallways, and so forth, seems to reduce violence only temporarily. This "zero tolerance" amounts to counterhostility on the part of the school rather than an attempt to deal with the individuals. Some suggest that such strategies may well be used to impress or reassure parents and other citizens that "action" is being taken on the problem.

Also, there appears to be sufficient evidence now that counseling alone does not seem to have an effect on antisocial or predelinquent youths (Elliott, Hamburg, & Williams, 1998; Gottfriedson, 1997). Of course expulsions may solve the "problem" of the school administration but not that of the community, because violent youths can roam the neighborhoods, free of monitoring or supervision.

School Bullying

One of the problems facing schools in their attempts to establish school rules and regulations (Tier I) is the presence of school **bullying.** This is particularly a problem for children with special needs who are likely to be the victims of such behavior, unless this behavior is counteracted. One definition of bullying is:

> A display of interpersonal violence in which the bully asserts power through some form of aggression and the victim experiences distress and the loss of power, resulting in an unequal relationship (Carran & Kellner, 2009).

It is hard to calculate the damage done when children go to school not to learn, but to worry about how to avoid the bully or bullies who physically threaten, extort money, or write hurtful or threatening emails. The size of this problem can be seen in Figure 7.2, which shows that in the sixth grade more than four out of ten students report incidences of bullying; even in the twelfth grade, one out of five report such behavior.

There is a gender difference, with boys experiencing physical bullying and girls receiving more psychological intimidation. One of the most striking examples of such bullying with girls is seen in the accompanying box, which is shown in the injury column of Figure 7.2. We rarely know the extent of psychological harass-

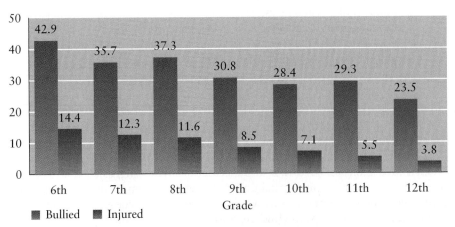

FIGURE 7.2
Percentage of Students Bullied and Injured from Bullying
Source: Data from Table 11.2 in Indicators of School Crime and Safety: 2009; National Center for Education Statistics, U.S. Department of Education (http://nces.ed.gov/).

ment, but it surely can be deadly as the story details. This involves not only individual teachers but the entire school faculty, which has the responsibility to curb such behavior. Teachers should point out to students that bullying is not only wrong but actually breaks the law when it becomes stealing, assault and battery, extortion, sexual harassment, and other criminal acts (National School Safety Center, 2009).

Another approach identifies school staff who are "safe contacts," from whom a student can receive counseling and support and with whom he or she can feel free to share experiences. What might have happened in Phoebe's situation if she had received such support we cannot tell, but it is clear that school staff have the responsibility to act when such behavior is revealed.

The harm is done not only to the bullied but also to the bully himself or herself, who carries such behavior and sense of power into adulthood and will possibly commit more serious offenses. It is not just the bullied who need counseling but the bullies themselves. Chances are the bullies are working out their own psychological needs through their use of power over others (see following box).

When Bullying Goes Unresolved

South Hadley seems like the perfect place for a teenager growing up in Massachusetts: safe, comfortably middle-class, with good schools. But when 15-year-old Phoebe Prince moved there in the fall of 2009, she found herself the target of a group of bullies. The girls, who called themselves the "Mean Girls," called Phoebe names, stalked her at school and home, and spread rumors about her on the Internet. Witnesses later recalled that drawings were scribbled over Phoebe's photo at school, and girls even called her "slut" in front of her teachers, with no reprisal. On January 14, 2010, one girl drove past Phoebe as she walked home from school and threw a drink can at her head, screaming out insults. That afternoon, Phoebe hung herself in her closet, where her 12-year-old sister found her.

The Mean Girls posted mocking eulogies on Facebook and publicly bragged about her death at a dance two days later. This incident exposed an epidemic of bullying at South Hadley High School, mostly by girls who were known as pretty, popular, and athletic. Weeks after Phoebe's suicide, all of the perpetrators were still in school, unpunished, even though what they had done was covered by the local news, and the bullying continued. One girl who reported the bullying to the local television station was beaten up physically by one of the Mean Girls. Finally, local police arrested six of the perpetrators two months later when they felt the school did not handle the situation properly.

What responsibility did the school have to prevent Phoebe from being bullied? What should the school's response have been to her death? What might be the motivation for the Mean Girls' behavior?

Cultural and Ethnic Risk Factors

Many observers have noted the increased prevalence of culturally and linguistically diverse children who are identified as having social or emotional disturbances (Osher et al., 2004). However, even though there might be

Recent violence has led schools to adopt programs to help students deal with their emotions.

(Courtesy of Cengage Learning)

a clear *correlation* between ethnic background and behavior, this does not mean there is *causation*—that is, that their condition was caused by their ethnic or racial membership.

Bronfenbrenner (1989) focused on the family as a child-rearing system, on society's support or lack of support for that system, and on the effects of that support or lack of support on children (Chapter 2). He maintained that the alienation of children reflects a breakdown in the interconnected segments of a child's life—family, peer group, school, neighborhood, and work world. The question is not "What is wrong with children with emotional or behavior disorders?" but may be "What is wrong with the child's social system?"

The conflict between the values of those in authority in society (and in the school) and the values of their culture can create tension. For example, what does a child do who sees a friend cheating? Honesty—a valued societal ethic—demands that the child report the incident. But loyalty—also a valued cultural ethic—demands silence. Even more serious in its impact is the situation in which the peer group devalues education or pressures the individual to use drugs or violence.

Substance Abuse Risk Factors

One of the serious side problems of many children with behavior disorders is *substance abuse*. The public's attention is often directed to the use of exotic drugs, but the use and abuse of alcohol and tobacco are much more common. There is evidence (Davis, Kruczek, & McIntosh, 2006) that children with behavior problems have rates of substance abuse higher than the rates of their peers in special education or in general education. Despite this information, there appears to be little systematic effort to include prevention programs in the school curriculum for these students. Does the presence of behavior or emotional problems predispose an individual to use drugs? If you are anxious, depressed, or angry, are you more likely to take drugs? Common sense would answer "yes," but research is not clear.

Substance abuse is a growing problem in U.S. schools. The prevalence of alcohol abuse and drug use is substantial (18 percent of adolescents used alcohol during the month of the survey) (Department of Health and Human Services [DHHS], 2003), and it has been theorized that exceptional children may be overrepresented among those who use drugs and alcohol. Think about the characteristics of drug users: low self-esteem, depression, inability to handle social experiences, and stress. These same characteristics mark children with behavior disorders. The primary disability is a behavior disturbance; the secondary disability is a chemical dependency. Special educators, then, must know the signs of chemical dependency, what to do when they suspect drug abuse in their students, and how to work with drug treatment programs.

In addition to the general teen culture that can encourage substance abuse in some communities, children or teenagers with behavior and emotional problems often are influenced by a series of additional factors that may predispose them to substance abuse. These factors would include prescribed medication, chronic medical problems, social isolation, depression, and a higher risk of being in a dysfunctional family (McCombs & Moore, 2002).

The link between substance abuse and behavior problems has been well established. One notable study is the longitudinal Pittsburgh Youth Study of inner-city boys. Substance use was classified into five categories: beer and wine, tobacco, hard liquor, marijuana, and other drugs. Tobacco was being used by 23 percent of the 13-year-olds, whereas beer and wine had already been experienced by 32 percent of those boys. By the time the boys in this study reached 13 years of age, 9 percent of them had used marijuana.

These investigators (Loeber & Farrington, 1998) found that the different levels of substance use correlated with the severity of delinquent acts. The factors that seemed to be most linked to substance abuse were low achievement, depressed mood, the presence of attention deficit disorders, and a lack of guilt on the part of the child about such substance use. Substance abuse cannot be said to cause emotional problems or problem behavior, but it is clearly part of the syndrome of behaviors linked to early problems and later delinquency.

Violent Video Games

One of the recent developments in the culture of young people has been the proliferation of violent video games. Along with these games comes the inevitable question: Does the playing of these games have some kind of effect on young people who seem addicted to them? A synthesis of the various studies that have attempted to answer this question has emerged with an answer (Anderson et al. 2010).

The results suggest that the more such games are played, the greater the aggressive feelings and reduction of sensitivity to others. It is true that these results are small; yet think of all of the other forces that might affect the growth of aggressive feelings or behavior. The important point here is that while we may not be able to do anything about poverty, we could surely do something to limit the playing of violent video games, especially since we seem to have evidence that they are having a negative effect on the students who play them.

What Have We Learned About Externalizing Behaviors?

Rutter (2003), in summarizing what has been learned, also presented what we have yet to learn, and these statements represent a challenge for the next generation of researchers and educators:

1. Most of the research falls well short of identifying the crucial mediators of the causal process or the effective elements of prevention or treatment.

2. We have only a very limited understanding of what is required to bring about beneficial change. It is evident that parental abuse and neglect provide significant risks for children, but it is not obvious what would prevent abuse and neglect.

3. Even when we know which interventions are effective, we lack good means of ensuring that those who might benefit from the interventions participate.

4. Most research has focused on individual differences rather than on (a) differences in level, (b) why the crime rate now is much higher than in 1950, (c) why most forms of antisocial behavior are more common in males than in females, or (d) why the homicide rate in the United States is some dozen times the rate in Europe. (p. 376)

Risk Factors for Internalizing Disorders

> Children develop chronic anxiety when they are frequently exposed to stressful situations and are unable to control or remove themselves from those situations.

Children who are anxious or withdrawn are likely to be more of a threat to themselves than to others around them. Because they usually are not disruptive, they generally do not cause classroom management problems. In contrast to children with conduct disorders, children who are anxious and withdrawn have problems with excessive internal control; in most settings they maintain firm control over their impulses, wishes, and desires. Children who are anxious and withdrawn may be rigid and unable to be spontaneous (Gresham & Kern, 2004).

Where do fearful children come from? We know that many of them have parents with similar problems. In addition, most professionals agree that chronic anxiety in children comes from being in a stressful situation, not being able to get out of the situation, and not being able to do anything to improve it. This inability to change the situation adds to feelings of helplessness and reinforces low self-image.

For students, a crucial examination looming on the horizon can create chronic anxiety. For younger children, anxiety can stem from homes in which they feel unwanted or are abused. Children are often too young to understand that their parents may be working out their own problems or that their parents' actions have little to do with them. All they understand is that no matter what they do, they are not getting praise or love from their parents.

Learned Helplessness

> Learned helplessness comes from low self-esteem and depression.

Learned helplessness in children is the belief that nothing they do can stop bad things from happening. Learned helplessness results in severe deterioration in performance after failure, as though the children have said to themselves, "It's all happening again." These children often have such low self-concepts that failure in a school task or a social setting only confirms for them their worthlessness and helplessness in the face of an unfriendly environment. These children's poor performance in the classroom may be much worse than they are capable of, simply because they are so pessimistic about themselves and their abilities. Low self-esteem seems to be at the heart of much of the underachievement of children who are anxious and withdrawn.

The placement of a disproportionate number of culturally and linguistically diverse students in special education programs has raised questions about the process that many school systems use to identify students with behavior problems. Are these systems mistaking cultural differences for aberrant behavior? Are the personal biases of some decision makers playing a role in decision making? Or are some groups especially likely to show the symptoms of behavior problems? These questions can be answered only on an individual basis by a multidisciplinary team of professionals who design individual supports for the child.

The individualized education program (IEP) can be an effective guide for teachers who are trying to cope with children who show emotional or behavior problems. The IEP is shaped not only by the student's specific problem but also by available resources. The presence of professional consultants in the mental health area or of an active remedial program in the school gives both the assessment team and the parents more options to consider.

Suicide

A strong feeling of hopelessness can be the predominant reason for teenagers to think about suicide or even attempt it. For some time, suicide has been one of the major causes of adolescent death. Today it is the third leading cause of teenage deaths in the United States, with 272 deaths recorded and about 8 times more suicides attempted. The ratio of males to females in such attempts is about 4:1 (National Institute of Mental Health, 2001). A number of suicides are also linked to substance abuse.

The following are some currently cited signs of a potential suicide:

- Extreme changes in behavior
- Previous suicide attempts
- Suicide threats and statements
- Signs of deep depression

Special education or general education teachers who note such signs should make referrals to appropriate crisis teams or mental health facilities. Most communities now have such services available. In addition, there is a National Suicide Prevention Lifeline (1-800-SUICIDE; 1-800-784-2433) that is available twenty-four hours a day and seven days a week for emergency counseling (English and Spanish). The teacher remains the first line of defense in these crisis situations and needs to be alert for any signs that students may provide.

Adolescents need to find their way out of learned helplessness through learning alternative coping mechanisms and being offered experiences designed to improve their feelings of self-esteem and self-worth. In these situations, as well as many others we have discussed, multidisciplinary teams of professionals are necessary.

One effort to thwart suicide attempts has been the formation of crisis teams at both the school and the district levels. Team members learn procedures to cope with suicidal individuals, and the team has access to resources that it can bring to bear quickly. A teacher who sees the danger signs has the immediate task of providing relief from the feelings of helplessness or hopelessness that the student may be expressing and of instilling in the student some feeling of being in control. Some positive change, no matter how small, must be made to prove to the student that the situation is not hopeless.

Long-range treatment may demand services from community and mental health agencies, and teachers should be aware of good referral sources. For schools, the best method of prevention is an educational program that enhances

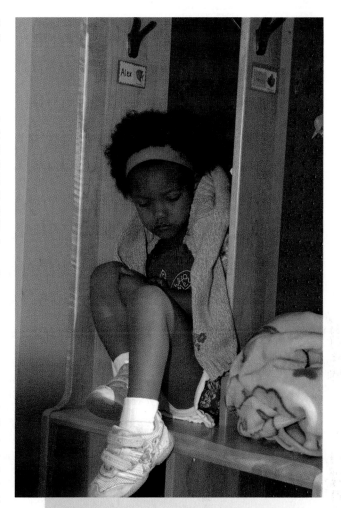

It often is difficult to distinguish between children with behavior disorders and those who just have a series of transient adaptation difficulties.
(Courtesy of Cengage Learning)

> Children with serious EBD are affected in all dimensions of information processing.

feelings of self-worth and self-control. Explicit instruction in positive coping skills can be one way of providing feelings of self-control.

Information Processing Model

As indicated in Figure 7.3, emotional and behavioral disorders have an impact on all aspects of information processing. Although vision, olfactory, and auditory abilities may test as normal, how the child perceives the stimulus may be altered. Pete, very aware of his power status in his group, may misinterpret actions and words of others as a threat to him and his status.

Anxiety and stress can influence all of the central processing mechanisms from memory to evaluation. The child's attempt to communicate through speaking and writing is clouded by either externalizing or internalizing concerns, as well as social relationships. The decision making of the student (executive function) is at the mercy of the emotional forces working on him or her at any given time. In short, a child with emotional and behavioral disorders has serious problems in every major aspect of information processing.

Two students, Jim and Molly, both eight years old, have information processing models that appear similar, but Jim is externalizing aggression while Molly is internalizing aggression. Jim has not been able to control his temper and seems to be in an angry rage most of the time. As a result, he is not able to fully use his good central processing skills—memory, reasoning, evaluation, and so forth—to apply to schoolwork. He comes from a father-absent family, and his mother appears disorganized and depressed. His social relations are poor, and he has been in a number of fights. His decision-making ability (executive function) appears to be overwhelmed by the waves of negative emotions sweeping over him.

A multidisciplinary team, including community mental health services, has been planning to place Jim in special learning sessions where he can get some self-confidence in his abilities, but there is a tough road ahead since Jim did not have the preschool care that might have helped considerably.

Molly also has central processing problems. She is depressed and in tears much of the time, so, like Jim, she is unable to use the abilities she has. She has seen a psychiatrist with minimal success, and her parents wish Molly had the social skills of her older sister, who seems to succeed effortlessly in academic and social settings. Molly is not the personal threat to her teachers that Jim is, because she does not challenge their ability to control the classroom. Nevertheless, her teachers are distressed by their inability to help her sadness and low self-concept. Again, a team of professionals from physician to psychologist to educator, are needed to help turn around Molly's information processing and her increasing levels of academic difficulties.

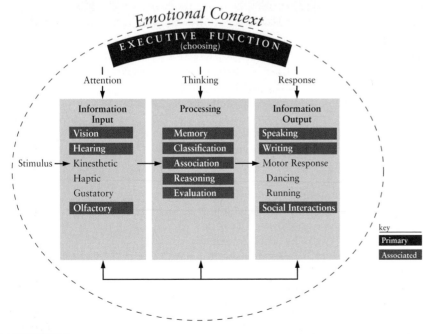

FIGURE 7.3
Information Processing Model for Students with Emotional and Behavior Disorders

EDUCATIONAL RESPONSES
to Students with Emotional and Behavior Disorders

In earlier chapters, we discussed the various ways that educators can modify the standard educational program to meet the special needs of exceptional children. They can change the *learning environment* and the *content* of the lessons, they can teach the child *skills* to process information and to work effectively with peers and adults, and they can use *technology* to aid communication. In addition, teachers must have intervention strategies, as well as training, to accomplish these differential tasks. It is important to think of modifications in all these areas for children with behavior and emotional disorders.

Preschool Children with EBD

It is particularly important to identify children at the preschool age with symptoms of EBD, since we have good evidence that preschool problems do not go away but persist and become more serious in later grades unless action is taken early (Egger & Angold, 2006).

The most common problems found at this age are ADHD, oppositional defiant and conduct disorders, anxiety disorders, and depressive disorders. We are not well equipped to apply diagnostic services and subsequent treatment at the preschool age because preschool services such as child care centers do not have the resources of the public schools, so it is important for child caretakers to be aware of the community mental health resources available.

There is a concern that "normal" aggression may be tagged as a sign of an emotional or behavior problem, so it must be clear that oppositional behaviors be *persistent, pervasive, and severe* to warrant mental health referral. (Still only about one in four children who would be identified as emotionally and behaviorally disturbed are referred for treatment, representing a major gap in services [Egger and Angold, 2006].)

Some attention has been given to the issue of preschool depression, with the predominant symptoms being sad and irritable mood, low energy, eating and sleeping problems, and low self-esteem (Luby et al., 2003). These conditions are often **comorbid,** that is they exist alongside other disorders such as anxiety and fearful feelings. The availability of technical assistance services that can find appropriate treatment facilities for children with EBD would be a great advance for many communities.

In one study, the special education outcomes of 3,608 children who had a preschool history of developmental disability were followed into the fourth grade. Over three-fourths of preschool children who had a designated disability continued to have a disability in fourth grade, but not necessarily with the same label. The most consistent of the labels was that of autism, with 87 percent of the children continuing with the same label. However, for preschool children identified as having an emotional disability, only 69 percent were still considered to have the same label; 18 percent at fourth grade were referred to as "specific learning disabled" and another 6 percent as having autism. The most flexible of the labels were those children described as having an "educable mental handicap" or a "mild intellectual or developmental disability." Five years later, only 20 percent retained the same label, while 36 percent are now described as being learning disabled, 11 percent emotionally disturbed, 7 percent autistic, and 13 percent speech impaired (Delgado, 2009).

For our purposes as educators, however, it is important to note that these children were still in academic trouble, whatever the labels. These findings indicate that the best plan may be to move ahead with IEPs that specify the student's difficulty and outline specific supports and services to meet the child's needs.

The RTI Model

How does the response to intervention (RTI) model fit into these various attempts to create a plan for behavior adjustment? Figure 7.4 reveals the RTI model for children with emotional and behavior disorders. The bottom of the RTI triangle (Tier I) is concerned with the universal interventions—the *schoolwide behavior system*. It should not be assumed that this band is represented by the usual classroom program. Instead, there may need to be a determined effort to ensure that the regular classroom *is* a place for healthy social interaction and the presentation of good mental health programming, as well as adequate content knowledge.

Three levels of behavioral support seem to be necessary for good school operation (Sugai & Horner, 2006). The first of these is *universal group behavior support* for most students. This involves establishing schoolwide management strategies, setting rules and standards for expected student behavior in such venues as the cafeteria, the hallways, and the bus. Such an approach has been documented as sharply reducing office referrals for misbehavior.

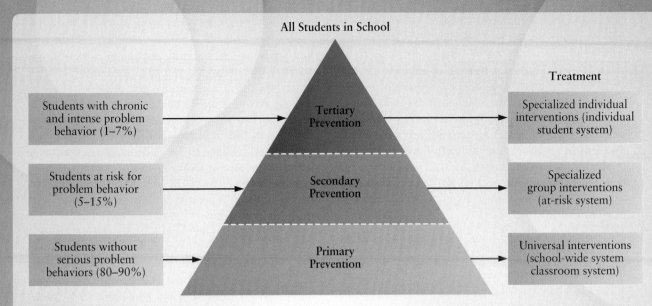

FIGURE 7.4
Response to Intervention, EBD
Based on Sugai, G., & Horner, R. (2006). A promising approach for expanding and sustaining the implementation of school-wide positive behavior support. *School Psychology Review, 35,* 245–259.

The Tier II activities (for about 5 to 15 percent of students) would apply the positive behavior supports through small-group work or individual tutoring. Such intervention should start as early as possible to prevent the flowering of even more difficult behavior problems.

The Tier III activities involve a small number of students (1 to 7 percent), those with the most serious emotional and behavioral problems. They are dealt with on an individual basis with carefully designed IEPs and professional support to lessen the negative impact that the environment and bad personal interactions have had on these impaired children.

▲ Tier I—Schoolwide Adjustments

When we realize that poor academic performance is one of the key elements for children with EBD, our attention needs to be focused on all of the tiers of the RTI model. Included in Tier I must be a strong core reading program that is adaptable for students currently doing poorly (Simonsen et al., 2008). A consensus on school rules and classroom performance expectations is also part of the Tier I model. Such rules should be enforced schoolwide and applied in every classroom to give students a sense of stability and few surprises.

There has been a sharp increase in the number of research studies testing positive behavior approaches. For example, in a carefully controlled study, a three-

year application of schoolwide behavior supports in elementary schools in Hawaii and Illinois resulted in the improvement of the perceived safety of the school and the proportion of third graders meeting or exceeding the state reading assessment standards. A reduction in office discipline referrals was also noted (Horner et al., 2009).

▲ Tier II—Small Group Interventions

Positive Behavior Supports
If we are to urge teachers to abandon punishment and punitive responses to behavior problems (primarily because they don't work in the long run), then what will we replace them with? This is particularly relevant because the influential No Child Left Behind Act stresses the importance of evidence-based practices and research-supported procedures.

A review of such innovative practices includes positive behavior supports, functional behavior assessments, social skills instruction, and self-management practices (Lewis, Hudson, Richter, & Johnson, 2004). These reviewers point out that it is essential not only that teachers understand these techniques but also that they have ample opportunity to practice them! It is one thing to read a piece of music and quite another to play that piece with grace and style. Such performance requires quality monitoring of the necessary practice.

Case Example: Mrs. Cabot

Mrs. Cabot, a sixth-grade teacher, does not necessarily believe in punishment as a way of restoring order in the classroom, but she sometimes is driven to it as a last alternative to chaos. What she may not realize is that Jim and Pete, her most troublesome students, would really prefer a calm and reasonable learning environment, too, if their needs were appropriately met. The question is how to keep Mrs. Cabot from reaching that level of desperation and how to have available to her alternative strategies for classroom control. She needs, and should have, professional supports to aid her.

The history of **positive behavior supports** is quite short, but its influence is growing rapidly across the country. The basic concept is that misbehavior should not necessarily be followed by punishment of one sort or another but with attempts to understand the causes or antecedents of the misbehavior (Dunlap & Carr, 2007). Then the teacher should introduce measures to create a positive environment that would make the misbehavior unnecessary. If we can create an educational climate in which personal needs and interests are being met, we will generate less of the anger and cruelty that so often accompanies social transgressions. None of these procedures is easy to learn or implement. The Teacher and Inclusion box gives a brief description of what may face an elementary school teacher without such training.

Functional Behavior Assessment

Functional behavior assessment (FBA) is a key part of positive behavior supports. It can be described as a collection of methods for gathering information about a child's behavior that tries to answer the question "Why did he or she do that?" rather than, "What did he or she do now?" To answer this key question, a child study team may wish to seek the *antecedent behaviors* to the event or to comprehend the child's understanding of the consequences of his or her actions.

Gresham (2007) describes five major ways in which unwanted behavior can accomplish certain goals for the individual child or adult:

1. Gain social attention (positive social reinforcement)
2. Gain access to tangibles or preferred activities (material or activity reinforcement)
3. Escape, delay, reduce, or avoid aversive tasks or activities (negative reinforcement)
4. Escape or avoid other individuals (negative social reinforcement)
5. Gain internal satisfaction (automatic or sensory reinforcement)

When Bobby suddenly hits another boy for being in his way or Sally tears up a drawing done by someone else, there probably is a cause that fits into one of these five categories, but which one? Careful observation may be required to discover which one and to plan alternative activities that will reduce the need for the unacceptable behavior (Fox & Gable, 2004). Bobby may be avoiding working with numbers, which he hates, whereas Sally may be trying to avoid Midge, whom she has just been told to work with. If we feel confident in our conclusions, then we can plan environmental changes or social activities that make such behavior unnecessary. You might recall some unusual behavior that you have seen over the past week. See if you can categorize it into one or more of the motives in the preceding list.

▲ Tier III—Intensive Interventions

Applied Behavior Analysis

One of the most frequently used methods of modifying student behavior is applied behavior analysis (ABA), procedures that follow the work of B. F. Skinner on operant conditioning. In addition to the attention paid to the problem behavior, the procedure focuses on the *antecedents* to the behavior and the *consequences* following it; this is sometimes referred to as the A-B-C approach (antecedents–behavior–consequences). By modifying the antecedent behavior and the consequences that follow, we can often modify the behavior itself (Lewis, Lewis-Palmer, Newcomer, & Stichter, 2004).

For example, Matt has developed the disturbing habit of physically escaping from frustrating situations, and this means that teachers and administrators must be alert lest Matt leave school and take off into the surrounding neighborhood, leading his mentors on a long and exasperating chase. The answer that ABA gives is to focus on antecedent behavior. What was happening immediately before Matt headed for the outdoors? If it is discovered that it was direct conflict with one of the other boys in the class, then steps can be taken to reduce the likelihood of such conflicts, or they can be stopped before a crisis develops.

Also, if the consequence of Matt's sojourns is that the other students pepper him with attention when he returns to the room, the teacher can instruct the other students to ignore Matt when he runs away or to praise him for being a member of the group. Matt can even earn points in a token system for resisting the temptation to flee. Such points can later be turned in for such rewards as time to listen to music or read special books.

It is not easy to always determine the antecedents and consequences of problem behavior. Once we are looking for them, however, we are often able to make a reasonable conclusion as to what is happening. There will be many students with diverse needs and capabilities in the same physical space; this fact makes even more necessary the establishment of a solid basis for **schoolwide behavior supports** at the Tier I level in the RTI model.

Residential Care

Despite the strong tendency to try to place children with emotional and behavior disorders in inclusive settings, other alternatives are being investigated. A small residential unit in North Carolina enrolls twenty-four children with severe behavior problems (ages 6 to 12) for periods up to six months and provides them with an organized program using the reeducation model (Fields, Farmer, Apperson, Mustillo, & Simmers, 2006).

Teams of teacher/counselors, licensed special education teachers, and qualified mental health professionals work with a group of eight children who attend school and complete therapeutic and daily living activities five days a week, returning for the weekend to family or foster care homes. The reeducation program stresses positive wellness as well as academic competencies (Fields et al., 2006). This approach would be an extreme example of a Tier III operation in the RTI model for children who need maximum support.

Substantial gains in appropriate behavior were noted using both the Child Behavior Checklist and the Behavioral and Emotional Rating Scale, with the majority of students appearing in the normal range following this program. Readings taken six months after treatment reported that most children maintained a large part of the gains they had made in the program.

Obviously, the intensity of treatment provided and the high staff-to-student ratio makes such an approach very expensive and not likely to be adopted by public school programs, but it could be one part of a state comprehensive program for children with emotional and behavior disorders (Fields et al., 2006).

▲ Will the American Public Pay Now to Benefit Later?

Foster & Jones (2006) pose this question in their review of a ten-year project to prevent crime by highly aggressive children. This project worked with schools in North Carolina, Tennessee, Washington State, and Pennsylvania; children in fifty-four schools were screened in kindergarten, and those that scored high on aggressiveness and reported by parents to be problem children were asked to participate. A total of 445 children were randomly selected as the treatment group, with 446 children as the control.

Small group meetings were led for twenty-two biweekly sessions with the parents and children as they reached the first grade. Group leaders practiced a combination of social and interactive skills with their groups. The sessions continued, on a lessening basis, over a ten-year period. In addition, the curriculum of the classrooms with the targeted children used a Universal Design for Learning (UDL) approach, focusing on social and emotional development. Individualized intervention plans were developed and implemented with each youth in the seventh grade.

The results were favorable for the students who revealed the most aggressive behaviors. A self-report at the tenth-grade level on the Index of Criminal Offenses (including items such as "I sold heroin or LSD" or "I attacked someone with the intention of causing harm") was collected.

This project was enormously expensive, totaling over $58,000 per child. Yet the money saved in projected prison incarceration costs and property damage is larger. To keep a long-term prisoner in jail costs over 1 million dollars. However, the payment for these programs must come before the benefits are seen. The cost is incurred by the public education system, but the benefits accrue to the criminal justice system and the community. Who should be responsible? Will the public support these costs? These questions must be answered.

Special Teacher and Program Strategies for Children with EBD

▲ Social Skills Training

One of the clear goals in remediation of emotional and behavior disorders is to improve the social skills of the student to produce socially acceptable learned behaviors such as cooperation, assertion, responsibility, empathy, and self-control. There has even been some suggestion that improvement in academic skills instruction, as much as social skills instruction, might improve the behavior of many students. One of the biggest problems has been the failure of *generalization*; that is, the student might learn a skill in one setting (for example, proper greeting in a classroom) but be unable to generalize it to other settings, such as the playground. Gresham (1998, p. 22) has proposed a contextual approach to teaching social skills that would take advantage of events that occur naturally in the school environment; most social skills instruction in home, school, and community settings can be characterized as informal. Thousands of behavioral incidents occur in these settings, creating numerous opportunities for successful learning experiences every day.

A comprehensive review of social skills training and its effect on children with behavior and emotional disorders (Kavale, Mathur, & Mostert, 2004) found limited positive results and concluded that social skills training is still an "experimental intervention and needs to be rebuilt as part of a comprehensive treatment for students with EBD" (p. 459). This serves to remind us that it took years for many of these students to develop their dysfunctional behavior patterns, which cannot be eliminated without substantial effort and professional attention.

Although the various attempts at meta-analyses (syntheses of past studies) of the effectiveness of social skills training have reported modest and sometimes discouraging results (see Kavale & Forness, 1999), a more recent study (Gresham, Van, & Cook, 2006) provides more encouragement. These authors suggest that the reason for the small results in previous studies was due to (1) lack of intensity of treatment and (2) failure to target the specific behaviors in need of modification.

The finding that "treatment intensity" is important has many applications in other special education attempts to modify behavior. Because of the chronic lack of resources for treatment, we are tempted to try to use as few resources as possible to get the changes we want. We lose faith in some methods because they were not provided in specific intensity or for a specific length of time with follow-up. The hard lesson is that it takes time and considerable effort to modify well-ingrained behavior patterns.

Students with behavior problems need joint planning with the support teacher.
(Courtesy of Cengage Learning)

▲ Developing Social Skills

Many children with behavior disorders not only engage in nonadaptive behaviors that cause them trouble with their peers and teachers but also lack positive social skills. Some students may have little opportunity in their neighborhoods or in their families to see positive social skills in use. One specific goal of a special education program, therefore, is to enhance the use and practice of socially acceptable behaviors.

> Students using self-management assume greater responsibility for changing undesired behaviors.

Self-Monitoring, Self-Instruction

There is a family of strategies currently known as the *cognitive strategy approach*. Whether called *self-monitoring*, *self-instruction*, or *self-control*, these methods rely on the cooperation of the child and encourage the development of effective conscious coping skills. One attraction of **self-management** techniques is that students who successfully apply them assume greater responsibility for their behavior instead of being externally controlled or "forced" to change by various kinds of conditioning (Polsgrove & Smith, 2004).

Suppose Pete has trouble staying in his seat. The first step is to teach him to recognize the behavior and then to record its frequency. Next, Pete negotiates a reward that is satisfying to him (perhaps some time to work on the computer) for staying in his seat for a specified period. Once he has shown the ability to control the behavior, he can be given the opportunity to control his own schedule and make decisions about the content or skills he would like to work on in the time slot.

There are several self-management techniques:

- *Self-monitoring* requires students to determine whether a target behavior has occurred and then record its occurrence. For example, if Pete feels an aggressive attack coming on, he can note it in a journal. This helps him become increasingly aware of the clues that identify a potential outburst.

- *Self-instruction training* (SIT) is a strategy for teaching any sequential thinking skills such as problem solving, handling frustration, managing anger, or resisting peer pressure (Polsgrove & Smith, 2004).

- *Self-evaluation* asks the student to compare his or her behavior with some criteria and make a judgment about the quality of the behavior being exhibited; for example, "On a scale of 1 to 5, how much attention am I paying to the teacher?"

- *Self-reinforcement* means that the student rewards himself or herself with a token or a tally after meeting some performance standard, such as avoiding aggressive outbursts for a set period of time. For example, a timer set for ten minutes that goes off without an aggressive outburst earns for the student a token that he or she can cash in later for game-playing time or a specially designed activity.

These techniques are designed to increase students' awareness, competence, and commitment to eliminating negative behaviors and to encourage the acquisition of constructive ones. For Pete, this means that the teacher works with him to improve self-awareness skills that will enable him to increase his own control over his hyperactivity or distractibility. One practical way of increasing the student's personal responsibility is to let the student participate in developing his or her own IEP.

The greatest advantage of this approach is that the child gains self-confidence by exerting control of his or her previously out-of-control behavior. There is an important additional advantage. Many children with behavior disorders spend much of their time in the general education classroom as a result of inclusion. Many general education classroom teachers do not wish to, or feel they cannot, engage in the complex monitoring and recording of individual student behaviors that some of the other behavior-shaping techniques require. Once the students learn what they are to do in a self-management program, they can proceed with only modest teacher supervision.

How do all the approaches work with individual children such as Pete, who is having special problems with a fellow student, Jason? Part of Pete's volatility around Jason is a reaction to feeling left out. Pete is angry at being abandoned by Jason, who had been his friend when they were younger, and his behavior with Jason is a misplaced attempt at getting something: Jason's attention and friendship. At this point we can work with Pete to help him see how his aggressive behavior drives more people away from him. Part of the positive behavioral supports for Pete will include working with the school counselor on (1) recognizing the consequences of negative behavior and (2) developing specific **replacement behaviors** that will help him make and keep friends.

When we look at Pete's functional behavior assessment, we see that there are a few things we can do to modify the classroom environment and provide positive supports for his better behavior. We might, for example, establish a work carrel for Pete in which distractions are minimized and he has all supplies (such as pencils, Franklin speller, paper, etc.) in one place. This might help with his initial "out of the seat" behavior, but we need to go further if we want to address his task avoidance. We already know that Pete avoids tasks with reading and writing because they are very difficult for him, so we look for ways to support his academic progress with tasks that are at his level of development and thereby foster competence and success.

In addition to working on his IEP goals, we might establish a *behavior contract* with him that focuses on his interactions with classmates, especially with Jason. The contract might look like the "Behavior Contract for Pete" in the nearby box.

Behavior Contract for Pete

Behavior and impact: I, Pete Walker, understand that when I start fights with Jason, I disrupt the class, I don't do my own work, I make my teacher mad at me, and Jason and I sometimes get hurt.

Target for change: This week I will work on leaving Jason alone.

Reward for change: If I do not get into a fight with Jason this week, I can pick three classmates to play my favorite computer math game with me on Friday during independent work time.

Consequence for no change: If I do fight with Jason this week, I will use my independent work time to do a classroom chore. That way, I can give something back to my classmates.

Date: 9/15/2010

Student Signature: _____

Teacher Signature: _____

What is most important about behavior contracts is that they are directed by the student: The student identifies specific objectionable behavior, articulates the impact of this behavior, identifies its consequences, and describes rewards for not indulging in it. This ownership, for students, is critical to helping them take responsibility for their behavior and for the impact it has on those around them. It is also essential to remember that the more specific a contract is regarding the targeted behavior, the more likely it is that the student will be able to succeed in changing it. So in Pete's case, the wording "leaving Jason alone" is much better than a vague phrase like "trying to get along with Jason." The reward, too, is critical: It should appear desirable to the student, but it should also foster positive growth. For Pete, the ability to invite other students to play a math game fosters growth in both academic and social skills. Finally, the consequence for *not* fulfilling the contract must be logical and must be seen by the student as undesirable. In this instance, Pete's behavior disrupts the class and takes away class time, so it is logical that his consequence should give something back to the class.

Teacher Preparation

Policy makers differ as to whether the field of emotional and behavior disorders merits a specialist training program or whether it can be folded into the usual special education program.

▲ The Teacher and the Pressures of Inclusion

Anne, a devoted elementary school teacher in a local rural school district for fifteen years, tells me that her job has become emotionally and physically overwhelming. After her school district moved to "full inclusion" several years ago, her fifth-grade classroom of twenty-five now includes two children diagnosed with autism, three with EBD, eight with learning disabilities (LD), and about five others with mild cognitive disabilities. Anne is not certified in special education, but she gets some support from a special education teacher who works with the children with autism and a child with LD about thirty minutes each day. Although the reading levels of the children range from preprimer to grade level, she is required by the state to use standard textbooks for the fifth-grade level. She is finding it an increasingly difficult struggle to meet the needs of such a widely diverse class of students and is seriously considering resigning her position at the end of the year.

Source: From L. Polsgrove, Reflections on the past and future, *Behavioral Disorders 28* (2003): 221–226. Reprinted with permission.

What is needed in the above situation is not a "super teacher" but a *team* of professionals working together to meet the students' needs.

▲ Personnel Preparation

Personnel preparation studies of teachers in the EBD field yield good news in terms of the increasing confidence that such prospective teachers have in controlling classroom behavior (Henderson et al., 2005). Students respond positively to statements such as "I am skillful in managing behavior" and "in collaborating with non-special education teachers, including prereferral interventions."

The bad news is that not enough of these teachers are available. The teacher shortages in the EBD field are severe, as is attrition, causing many school systems to hire persons under emergency certificates to handle these responsibilities. SPeNSE (Study of Personnel Needs in Special Education supported by the U.S. Department of Education) has conducted surveys that reveal the continued need for qualified personnel (SPeNSE, 2002). Among other things, these results probably mean that some inservice training of general and other special education teachers in local districts should be provided by certified EBD teachers in such problematic areas as classroom management and behavior challenges.

> The support teacher concept fits well into the inclusive classroom.

▲ The Support Teacher (EBD Specialist)

One innovative suggestion for supporting classroom teachers is to use a **support teacher**, a person with special education training in many of the approaches noted earlier. She or he comes into the general classroom to support the teacher in working with children with special needs and sometimes takes responsibility for small groups of students. Obviously, a classroom teacher with twenty-five or thirty children cannot cope with all aspects of the classroom environment without help. Who can provide that help? The strategy rests on five assumptions and principles:

- Even a child who has serious behavior problems is not disturbed all the time. There are only certain periods during which the pupil cannot function in the larger group setting. These periods may come at certain regular times or in the press of a crisis. But most of the time, the child can benefit from and fit into the class.

- Teachers need direct assistance. Consultation is one thing, but real help is something else. Psychologists and similar professionals might offer advice, but they do not know what it is like to try to administer a classroom that includes children who have behavior disorders.

- The direct-service support teacher should work full time in the school to which he or she is assigned, should not be itinerant, and should be trained as a special teacher. The support teacher should be able to respond to the child who is in crisis but also be able to help all children with academic and emotional problems. Many of these youngsters need direct counseling help with issues such as self-concept, but just as many can achieve growth through therapeutic tutoring.

- Sometimes the support teacher can assist best by taking over the classroom while the regular teacher works through a phase of a problem with a child.

- Help should be based on the reality of how the child is able to cope with the classroom and not on categories, labels, or diagnostic criteria.

The support teacher generally uses techniques that are an extension of regular education procedures, emphasizing positive behavior supports. In addition, the support teacher is able to provide important liaison services that are not within the capabilities of the heavily burdened classroom teacher. Children with behavior problems often need the help of a multidisciplinary team of pediatricians, psychologists, and paraprofessionals, and the support teacher can be the case manager and coordinate these sources of assistance.

▲ The Wraparound Approach

The **wraparound approach** makes extensive use of agencies outside the school program, though they are expected to include school personnel in the planning. The family is also a critical part of this planning if it is to work, and strong efforts are made to involve them (Eber, Sugai, Smith, & Scott, 2002). Because behavior problems seem to include many different dimensions of self, family, culture, and community, it makes good sense to try a multidisciplinary approach using professionals from education, psychology, psychiatry, social work, and perhaps other related fields, combined into a treatment team that produces a system of care (Eber & Keenan, 2004).

With regard to Jim, such wraparound planning might include counseling for his mother, who has become depressed about her inability to handle his behavior; some psychological counseling for Jim to help him understand the reasons for his hostile outbursts; and plans for the teacher to find some examples of success for Jim in his schoolwork so that he will get some satisfaction from being in school.

The plan focuses on the strengths of the student, as well as on attempts to mute any deficits in performance that the student may have. Although it is often used as a vehicle for maintaining the student in the general education classroom by bringing additional resources into that classroom, services might be delivered in a resource room or a self-contained special class if that is what represents the least restrictive environment for that student (Kerr & Nelson, 2002).

Teachers can use various strategies with students who have behavior disorders, but each strategy imposes costs or demands on the teachers, whether they are trying to communicate with students, support desirable behavior, or control problem behavior. For example, reminding a student about the rules of the classroom (RTI, Tier I) costs the teacher less in energy or effort than does conducting a group meeting on a problem behavior (Tier II). High-cost teacher behavior, however, may be needed to bring some benefits to the situation. Teachers often find themselves having to decide whether to use these high-cost strategies, and all sorts of factors—professional and personal—can affect the final decision.

▲ Peer Tutoring

One of the instructional strategies in use with students with mild disabilities such as EBD is *peer tutoring*. Obviously, if peers can be helpful in improving the performance of children with disabilities, it could be a substantial boon for the teacher.

One of the most active and well-researched programs is the peer-assisted learning strategies (PALS) used primarily in elementary schools (see Fuchs et al., 1997). This approach consists of pairing students, one of whom is the player (student with a disability) and the other the coach (a student who has been prepared to help). In twenty-five-minute segments, the pairs meet to take turns in reading to one another, identifying words, and so forth.

Over a fifteen- to twenty-five-week period, meeting four times a week,

Peer Assisted Strategies
www.peerassistedlearning strategies.net

this approach has shown growth in reading that is sustainable over time for many, but not all, students. Much appears to depend on the nature of the students and the kind of preparation given to the tutors before beginning. One of the great potential advantages of such an approach is that expert outside help is not needed for its operation. Once the classroom teacher has set up the pairs and the learning periods, she or he has only to monitor the progress periodically. This approach would be especially valuable in rural schools, where little outside help can be expected for the classroom teacher.

Senhoff and Lignugaris-Kraft (2007) reviewed twenty articles on peer tutoring at the secondary level and reported good results. These favorable results occur when the teacher spends some time in providing the tutors with a clear understanding on how to conduct lessons, how to provide feedback for correct responses, procedures for correcting errors, and so forth. Role-playing the tutor-tutee procedures seems particularly useful.

As with inclusion, it is not enough to ask one student to help another with his or her lessons. This peer tutoring approach requires considerable planning and preparation to be successful. One of the interesting

Peer tutoring can be of great assistance to the teacher.
(Courtesy of Cengage Learning)

Students with ADHD may benefit from working on a computer.

side benefits is that the tutors themselves showed academic gains, reduced school absences, and increased positive social interactions. It seems that giving students increased responsibility in the academic setting pays off for both tutor and tutee!

Technical Assistance

One of the marks of the success of the positive behavioral intervention movement has been the establishment of the OSEP Technical Assistance Center on Positive Behavioral Interventions and Supports, a collaboration between the U.S. Department of Education and eleven technical assistance units across the United States. The Center is based on the demonstrated success of PBIS in improving social behavior and academic performance as a practical classroom implementation. Its goal is to encourage the widespread implementation of PBIS through demonstration, dissemination, and evaluation.

A number of technological aids can provide some supportive help for those working with children with behavior or emotional difficulties. Some take the form of board games that enhance social skills development with topics such as social greetings, handling anger at school and work, appropriate and inappropriate touching, good sportsmanship, and so on. In another classroom behavior game, students move around the board and are exposed to ten strategies that are positive solutions for managing anger. They include taking responsibility for one's own actions, encouraging self-control, and dealing with the acting-out behavior of others.

PCI Education
www.pcicatalog.com

Time-Out

One of the techniques used most frequently to control the behavior of children with behavior disorders is the time-out—sending students who have violated classroom rules to a secluded place in the room or in a space nearby with instructions to come back when they feel they have regained control of themselves. Time-out takes the student away from possibly negative interactions with other students and gives him or her a chance to cool off.

One version of the time-out approach is the Think-Time strategy (Nelson, Crabtree, Marchand-Martella, & Martella, 1998). This approach requires the cooperation

⇨ Assistive Technology for Students with Emotional and Behavior Disorders

A computer can be an especially useful learning tool for a student with a behavior disorder because it provides an objective, neutral response to the child's sometimes provoking or challenging behavior. Children with long histories of social interaction problems may respond poorly to teacher feedback, particularly when criticism or correction is involved. The child who is adept at manipulating others can quickly change the focus of a discussion from his or her inadequate academic performance to the teacher's behavior. "Why are you always picking on me?" is a common theme. With a computer, however, the student must find a different approach.

Obviously, a computer is not able to interact emotionally with the child. If the student has difficulty solving a problem, he or she must find out why and determine the right answer in order to proceed with the computer program. The student cannot resort to emotional manipulation or accuse the computer of being unfair.

Computer assisted learning can support the child's academic performance by helping with spelling, word definitions, text-to-speech options for reading, and organizational support for writing his or her thoughts and ideas. When technology is used to enhance the student's performance and success, the child learns more and feels better about herself or himself and school (Edyburn, 2006). Assistive technology support can help by increasing success and reducing stress for children with emotional difficulties (Edyburn, 2006).

Children who are hyperactive or who have ADHD often have difficulty concentrating and can be helped by a computer. When working with a computer, they must pay some degree of attention to get results. The orderliness and sequence of the software programs can provide a systematic structure for students who have very little cognitive structure or self-discipline.

of another teacher who can provide the think-time area. The student engaging in disruptive behavior is sent to an area in another classroom previously designated in cooperation with another teacher. This enables the teacher to cut off a negative social exchange or a power struggle and provides the student with time to think about future performance. Once the student has calmed down, the cooperating teacher can get the student to review the inappropriate behavior, what the student was trying to do, and what he or she needs to do on returning to the classroom. Such an intervention cuts short what could be a serious situation.

There is a version of time-out, however, that has received negative reviews from the professional community. *Seclusionary time-out* (placing an individual in an area that he or she cannot leave until others decide that he or she can) is a highly intrusive behavior and should be used only as a last resort. As with any other technique, time-out should be used as a positive behavior-enhancement tool, not as punishment.

The Role of the Family

The importance of the family, in both positive and negative ways, has long been recognized for children with EBD. This is one of the reasons parents play a significant role in the IDEA legislation. Table 7.3 summarizes the various interactions the family will have with the school.

> The goal is for the parents to become partners with the school in coping with their child.

As you can see in Table 7.3, parents must be fully informed about activities related to their child. Sopko and Reder (2007) provide detailed statements from the law itself that leave little doubt as to the intentions of the lawmakers.

A relatively new way of viewing the professional and parent relationship is by seeing it as a *partnership of experts.* The parents are experts on their own children and on those children's feelings and behaviors. They are case managers, policy makers, and legislative advocates. The professionals are experts in such general fields as special education and mental health. Under these assumptions we can establish a relationship between the two parties with the best interests of the child in mind (Turnbull, Turbiville, & Turnbull, 2000).

A possible problem in establishing such collaboration or partnership emerges when there are cultural differences between families and professionals. Sometimes the parents of children from culturally and linguistically diverse families are seen by the professionals as "needing training" rather than as being full-fledged partners in the support efforts. A sense of "learned helplessness" felt

TABLE 7.3
Parental Involvement in IDEA

- Understand what consent is and provide informed consent for services under IDEA.
- Notified in advance about any proposed changes to a child's evaluation, IEP/IFSP, or educational placement to ensure the opportunity to participate in meetings regarding the education of their child.
- Informed about the process used to assess the child's response to scientific, research-based intervention, appropriate strategies for improved achievement, and the right to request an evaluation.
- Informed about disciplinary processes and disciplinary actions regarding their child.
- Given a copy of the procedural safeguards, the evaluation report, the documentation of determination of eligibility, and a copy of the child's IEP at no cost to the parent.
- Informed about the state procedures for filing a complaint and the right to records of hearings, findings of fact, and decisions.
- Allowed to inspect and review all education records related to their child, and request that information be amended.

Source: Sopko & Reder (2007). *Public and Parent Reporting Requirements: NCLB and IDEA Regulations.* Alexandria, VA: Project Forum National Association of State Directors of Special Education.

by many parents has to be combated by the professionals, so that the parents can maintain self-respect and their desire to partner with professionals (Harry, 1997).

 # Transition

One of the unsolved challenges involving the education of students with emotional and behavior disorders is their poor record of school completion, together with limited success in the vocational arena following school. The Office of Special Education Programs (2003) reported that only about 40 percent of students with EBD completed their secondary schooling. These findings suggest (1) the difficulty of entering a labor market with low and uncertain wages, (2) the possibility of trouble with the law, and (3) the unlikelihood of their seeking additional training on their own.

The findings are consistent with those of earlier studies (Rylance, 1997; Valdez, Williamson, & Wagner, 1990). Kortering, Braziel, and Tomkins (2002) individually interviewed thirty-three students who were receiving services for behavior disorders to find out their perceptions of the problems with completing school. Students' responses are listed in Table 7.4 and indicate that additional support is needed during the difficult transition period.

TABLE 7.4
Responses from Students with EBD on Staying in School

Are There Any Advantages or Disadvantages to Staying in School?	
Advantages	Better education and jobs. Getting a better job and better pay. Diploma means a better job. Good education and a job. So I can get in the army and get a job. You will get a better job. Good job.
Disadvantages	Getting into trouble with peers. A lot of homework and not much free time. Can't get a job. Can't work. Working in class is too hard. Don't get a lot of time with friends.
What Changes Would Help an Individual Student Finish School, and How?	
More Support	Help me pass. Help me with my homework. Help me get good grades. Give me more help. Help me control my anger.
What Changes Would Help More Students Stay in School?	
Curriculum	More detail in classes. Up-to-date books. Newer texts. Social studies books should be easier for kids in special education classes. Some of the books are too difficult. More fun things in class. Put tutors in [classes].

Source: From L. J. Kortering, P. M. Braziel, & J. R. Tomkins. (2002). The challenge of school completion among youths with behavioral disorders: Another side of the story, *Behavioral Disorders*, 27: 142–154. Reprinted with permission.

One of the goals for children with EBD is to help them complete their secondary programs and adapt meaningfully to their community or gain further education towards adult competence. It is clear that we must pay increased attention and commit resources to strengthen the bridges from school to community for children with EBD.

moral dilemma
Emotional and Behavior Disorders

Mrs. Stern, a special education teacher working with children with behavioral disorders, has been on increasingly good terms with Ralph since she has listened quietly to Ralph's complaints and protests about the unfairness of life from his standpoint. Ralph has had numerous escapades in and out of school

One day Ralph, a twelve-year-old, asked Mrs. Stern to sit down and talk with him about a problem he was having. He asked Mrs. Stern to swear to keep secret what he was about to tell her, and she said she would. He then told her about his belonging to a gang that was systematically stealing from local Wal-Marts and drugstores. This activity was fairly limited in scope, and Ralph did not seem too concerned. Recently, however, drugs had entered the situation, with members of the gang urging Ralph to deliver drugs from their supplier to various other sites. Part of the reward for his being a delivery boy would be that he would get a small amount of drugs for his own use. Despite the pressure put on him by other members of the gang, he had resisted so far, but now he was being threatened with expulsion from the gang or worse.

He wanted advice and perhaps moral support for his action.

What should Mrs. Stern do? She has already promised him confidentiality. What should she say to Ralph? What is her responsibility to the larger school and neighborhood community concerning the presence of drugs in and out of school? Write some dialogue that might follow in this situation.

 To answer these questions online, visit the Education CourseMate website.

✳ Summary

▶ The definition of *emotional and behavior disorder* takes into account the intensity and duration of age-inappropriate behavior, the situation in which the behavior is exhibited, and the individual who considers the behavior a problem.

▶ Unlike children with other disabilities, children with emotional and behavior disorders are often blamed for their condition. This affects their interactions with the people around them.

▶ Although less than 1 percent of schoolchildren are receiving special education services for emotional and behavior disorders, the number of children who actually need those services is at least 5 percent and may range as high as 15 percent.

▶ In many instances, the causes of EBD appear to be a blend of neurology, genetics, and environmental factors.

▶ Children who externalize problems require different planning and intervention from those who internalize problems.

▶ Intervention for the child who is anxious and withdrawn should have as its primary objective instilling a sense of self-worth and self-control. Positive experiences play an important role in preventing suicide—a serious problem among students who are deeply depressed and withdrawn.

▶ Violence in the schools has been a continuing problem. Serious physical violence is caused by a small percentage of students, many of whom can be identified at an early age.

▶ There is an increased prevalence of children from culturally and linguistically diverse families referred for special services for social and emotional disturbance. Favorable changes in the school environment for these children have positive results.

▶ The RTI model's three-tier approach provides the opportunity for students to move between intense treatment and less intense professional involvement as the situation requires.

▶ Social skills training has been a modest success and should focus on the need for generalization from specific training to general classroom behavior.

▶ Functional behavior assessment and positive behavior supports do seem to have favorable results.

▶ Self-management and self-control training has shown promising results. The wraparound approach, which features a multidisciplinary system of care, also has potential for positive results.

▶ Much remains to be done to assume good community adjustment following school for children with emotional and behavior disorders.

Future Challenges

(1) What are the conditions for emotional health for culturally diverse students?

Despite findings of increased prevalence of social and emotional problems in culturally and linguistically diverse groups, the vast majority of such children are not so affected. A study of emotionally healthy children from these backgrounds and their families could help us understand and assist in the emergence of emotional health in these groups.

(2) Can increasing uses of multidisciplinary teams provide the necessary increase in services?

One serious condition limiting the delivery of quality educational services to children with behavior problems is the need for highly trained personnel.

Unless a way can be found to use paraprofessional personnel, as has been done in applied behavior analysis programs, it will not be possible to provide the help needed by many students identified as having behavior problems.

3 *How early should we begin?*

The more research that is done, the stronger is the felt need to begin education and therapy as early in the child's life as possible—and that includes family counseling. For children with emotional and behavior disorders, this would mean starting well before the school years. Ideally, some therapeutic treatment for children with EBD and their families should begin by ages 2 or 3. This often means arranging for relationships with pediatricians and other professionals, who frequently are the first contact that the family has about these problems.

4 *How can violence be prevented?*

Longitudinal studies of children who are socially maladjusted and act out their aggressive feelings suggest strongly that they do not outgrow these tendencies. Unless something significant is done with these children or with the environment surrounding them (positive behavior supports), we can predict that aggressive children who hurt peers will become aggressive adults who hurt people. The need for large-scale intervention within the school, family, and neighborhood is clear.

Key Terms

bipolar disorder p. 216

bullying p. 224

coercive family system p. 223

comorbid p. 231

correlated constraints p. 221

functional behavior assessment (FBA) p. 233

learned helplessness p. 228

positive behavior supports p. 233

psychotropic p. 220

replacement behaviors p. 236

schoolwide behavior supports p. 234

self-management p. 236

serious emotional disturbance p. 216

support teacher p. 238

wraparound approach p. 238

Resources

References of Special Interest

Committee for Children. (2002). *Second step: A violence prevention curriculum.* Seattle, WA: Committee for Children. This curriculum is a classroom-based social skills program for children ages 4 through 14. Designed to teach socioemotional skills, its goals are to reduce impulsive and aggressive behavior in children and to increase their levels of social competence. The program teaches, models, practices, and reinforces skills in empathy, impulse control, problem solving, and anger management and is packaged in a teacher-friendly format for use in the classroom. Over twelve evaluations of the second-step curricu-

lum have been conducted; all have found overall decreases in aggression (both verbal and physical), along with a decrease in discipline referrals.

Fields, E., Farmer, E., Apperson, J., Mustillo, S., & Simmers, D. (2006). Treatment and posttreatment effects of residential treatment using a reeducation model. *Behavior Disorders, 31*(3), pp. 312–322. A description of residential treatment that can supplement a total program for EBD students.

Forum. (2003). *Behavioral Disorders, 28,* 197–228. A special issue of this journal containing the retrospective thoughts of key figures in the field. Steven Forness, James Kauffman, C. Michael Nelson, and

Lewis Polsgrove sum up what they have learned and what they believe to be the key issues of the present and the immediate future. Younger leaders in the field comment on these summaries with ideas of their own.

Kerr, M., & Nelson, C. (2002). *Strategies for managing behavior problems in the classroom* (4th ed.). Upper Saddle River, NJ: Merrill. This book is rich in the wide varieties of strategies and techniques for dealing with children with behavior problems. It includes principles for selecting interventions and for dealing with specific behavior problems, aggressive behaviors, and psychiatric problems. It also presents survival skills for the teacher.

Lane, K., Gresham, F., & O'Shaughnessy, T. (Eds.). (2002). *Interventions for children with or at risk for emotional and behavioral disorders*. Boston: Allyn & Bacon. A multiauthored text whose sections include coverage of prevention and identification, academic instruction, management of challenging behaviors, and the integration of services to children with EBD. One section deals with internalizing disorders such as phobias, anxiety, depression, and so forth. Much of the book focuses on the specific problems teachers have in coping with these children, and there is a call for continued research on the linkage between academic difficulties and behavior problems.

OSEP. (2010). *Ideas that work*. Washington, DC: Office of Special Education Programs, U.S. Department of Education. A series of short publications dealing with issues of instructional practice, assessment, behavior, and accommodations. These publications are aimed at parents and teachers, containing the best of evidence-based practices currently available. Such topics as functional behavior assessment and oppositional defiant behavior and childhood depression are covered.

Reading and Writing Interventions for Students with, and at Risk for Emotional and Behavioral Disorders (Special Issue). *Behavioral Disorders* (2010), *35*(2) 81–184. There is a growing interest in the link between academic performance and emotional disturbance. This special journal issue explores a variety of studies and research syntheses dealing with academic performance of children labeled emotionally and behaviorally impaired. The results indicate a strong link between the two that require educational adaptations.

Rutherford, R., Jr., Quinn, M., & Mathur, S. (Eds). (2004). *Handbook of research in emotional and behavorial disorders*. New York: Guilford Press. The editors have gathered together many of the most outstanding researchers and scholars in this field to present the most recent knowledge, research, and practices for educating students with emotional and behavior disorders. The content allows easy access to historical and conceptual foundations, assessment and evaluation, student characteristics and intervention, and treatment. It is an admirable source book for anyone interested in this field.

Journals

Behavioral Disorders
www.ccbd.net

Beyond Behavior
http://www.ccbd.net/beyondbehavior/

Exceptional Children
www.cec.sped.org

Journal of Applied Behavior Analysis
http://seab.envmed.rochester.edu/jaba/

Teaching Exceptional Children
http://www.cec.sped.org/content/navigation menu/publications2/teachingexceptional children/

Journal of Emotional and Behavior Disorders
http://www.hammill-institute.org/journals/ JEBD.html

Professional Organizations

American Psychological Association
www.apa.org

Council for Children with Behavioral Disorders
www.ccbd.net

National Alliance for the Mentally Ill
www.nami.org

National Mental Health Association
www.nmha.org

Society for Research in Child Development
www.srcd.org

 Visit the Education CourseMate website for additional TeachSource Video Cases, information about CEC standards, study tools, and much more.

Children with Communication, Language, and Speech Disorders

 Focus Questions

▶ How did the field of speech and language disorders evolve?

▶ What are some characteristics of children with communication, language, and speech disorders?

▶ How are communication, language, and speech defined and related to each other?

▶ What are the critical components of language, and how does typical language develop?

▶ What kinds of problems and/or disorders can affect communication, language, and speech?

▶ What are the prevalences for children with communication, language, and/or speech disorders, and why are these difficult to determine accurately?

▶ How do other disability areas interact with and impact communication, language, and speech disorders?

▶ Why must a child's culture and linguistic background be factored in when assessments and services are determined?

▶ What kinds of supports and services can be provided to children and their families?

© Ellen Senisi

247

The desire to communicate seems as basic a human need as food. Communication begins early as the infant works to make his or her needs known to the parent. Initially, the infant uses cries, grunts, gestures, and facial expressions to get the message across. At 3 or 4 months of age, the baby begins cooing and babbling—using sounds that approximate speech and imitate the language the baby has been listening to from birth. Finally, at around 1 year, the first "words" appear. These first words are usually repetitions of sounds, such as *ma-ma, da-da,* or *pa-pa.* So is it any wonder that in many languages these words mean "mother" and/or "father"? Nothing is more exciting to parents than their infant's amazing ability to acquire speech and language in the first year of life.

When a child shows delays in language development or has difficulty producing speech sounds, early intervention is essential to improve his or her ability to communicate. In this chapter, we look at communication, language, and speech, examining the ways that children develop and the difficulties they encounter when they have problems in these areas. We look briefly at the history of the speech-language field; reflect on how we define communication, language, and speech; examine typical human development of language; review the disorders and disabilities that can affect these areas; and present strategies that can be used to support children and youths who have disorders in communication, language, and/or speech. Throughout this chapter, we refer you to other chapters for information on the impact that specific disabilities may have on a child's development, because difficulties with communication, language, and speech often coexist with other disabilities.

History of Communication, Language, and Speech Disorders

The formation of the American Speech and Hearing Association (ASHA) in 1925 marked a significant point in the emerging field of speech-language pathology, but attempts to correct speech patterns and to enhance communication date back at least as far as the early Greeks in the fifth century BC (Coufal, 2007). In the United States during the 1800s, the focus was on elocution, or the ability to speak with elegance and propriety (Moore, 1802, as cited in Duchan, 2008). With the emergence of public schools, curricula for teaching elocution were developed, and some attention was given to helping students who had speech impediments. Alexander Graham Bell founded the School of Vocal Physiology in 1872 to help improve the speech of children who were deaf or who suffered from stuttering and/or articulation problems (Duchan, 2008).

American Speech and Hearing Association **www.asha.org**

By the twentieth century, the science of speech and communication began to influence practice. Early studies showing areas of the brain that were associated with speech and language began to emerge with the work of Paul Broca and Carl Wernicke. As Figure 8.1 shows, parts of the brain were named after Broca and Wernicke as a result of their pioneering work in this area. By the middle of the twentieth century the conception of speech-language disorders began to move beyond the production of sounds to include the "inner language," or thoughts that underlie communication. Key contributors to the importance of symbol formation were Karl Goldstein, Helmur Myklebust, and Charles Osgood. Goldstein worked with aphasics, individuals who had lost or failed to develop language, whereas Myklebust concentrated on individuals with auditory processing difficulties. Osgood added the idea of a mental component to communication. Their combined work began

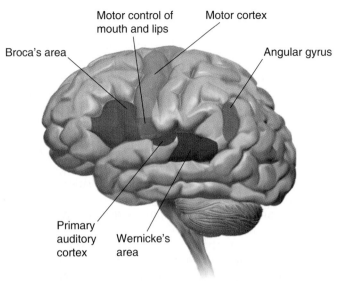

FIGURE 8.1
The Major Brain Structures Participating in Language
Source: Freberg, L. (2006). *Discovering Biological Psychology,* 392. Used by permission of Houghton Mifflin Harcourt Publishing Company.

Neurology and Brain Development
Studying Brain Injury to Understand Language

Neurologists often try to determine the specific function for areas of the brain by examining the impact of brain injury or damage. The generalized notion that language is largely associated with the brain's left hemisphere (see Broca and Wernicke's areas in Figure 8.1) is supported by the language disruption that occurs when there is a lesion or injury to the left hemisphere (Lansing et al., 2004). This pattern of hemispheric specialization, however, seems to be better defined for adults than for children (Bates et al., 2001). For young children, when the brain is still developing, there seems to be far more plasticity (i.e., the ability of the brain to compensate for and reorganize functions to draw on the nondamaged areas) than there is for adults (Bates et al., 2001). In their comparison of the effects of left hemispheric brain lesions on language for children and adults, Bates and her colleagues (2001) found that while adults showed the classic signs of aphasia (i.e., language loss) after their injuries, children did not seem to be impacted in the same way. In their study, they saw no differences in the language development of children, ages 5 to 8, who had either left- or-right hemisphere lesions. The language of children and adults with unilateral brain injury was severely impaired. These findings support the hypothesis that language outcomes, as a result of brain injury, differ for children and adults and depend on the extent of damage to both hemispheres.

to show that communication was complex, involving interactions among speech production, language development, and thought (Duchan, 2008).

During the 1960s and 1970s, the field emphasized linguistics. Noam Chomsky led the way by examining the rules and sequences governing the acquisition of language (Chomsky, 1965). Over the last 30 years, the area of **language pragmatics**—ways that language is used to communicate in a variety of contexts—has emerged as a critical area of study (Duchan, 2008; Hyter, 2007). The social aspects of communication in everyday life also play a central role in our current thinking about speech and language disorders (Duchan, 2008; Olswang, Coggins, & Svensson, 2007; Salvia, Ysseldyke, & Bolt, 2007). Current research also focuses on the role of cognition in language development and the importance of learning as part of language acquisition (Hoff, 2009, 2005). Language acquisition, from the cognitive perspective, depends to a large extent on the child's exposure to language (Slobin, 2006). The more language a child hears, and the greater the complexity of this language, the more likely the child will learn the structural properties of language (Hoff, 2004). From this perspective, providing language-rich environments is critical for young children. The impact of learning two languages for children growing up in bilingual or multilingual families or communities is also an emerging area of study. We will explore this issue in greater detail later in this chapter (Maguire et al., 2010). Because communication is so vital to being a member of society, life can be difficult for children who have speech and/or language disorders.

Characteristics of Children with Communication, Language, and Speech Disorders

Communication is central to our ability to fit into society successfully, and when difficulties with language and/or speech interfere with communication, children often experience problems (Brinton & Fujiki, 2006). These problems can affect the formation of a child's friendships, school success, and self-esteem (Girolametto & Weitzman, 2007).

Meet Johnny and Michelle, Two Students with Speech Disorders

Johnny: Johnny is a 10-year-old boy who has a moderate articulation and phonology disorder (he mispronounces specific sounds). A speech disorder may signal an underlying language problem, and a comprehensive assessment indicated that Johnny also has a language-related learning disability. Academically, he is performing below grade level on skills that require language mediation. Johnny also demonstrates a range of intraindividual differences. At this point, his sound substitutions and omissions are not so severe, and he can usually be understood, but his oral productions still call attention to his speech and sometimes set him apart from his peers.

Johnny's speech is characterized by consistent sound substitutions (w/r, as in *wabbit* for *rabbit;* t/k, as in *tome* for *come;* and l/y, as in *lello* for *yellow*). He also sometimes omits sounds at the ends of words, including the sounds that represent verb tense and noun number (for example, the final /s/ in *looks* and *cats*). When he was younger, his expressive language was delayed, and he spoke very few words until he was 2 years old. When he did begin to talk, his speech was almost unintelligible, and non-family members had difficulty understanding him. Johnny's receptive language, however, was excellent, and his understanding of language spoken to him allowed him to be an active member of a busy family with three older siblings. Careful listening to his conversational language reveals that he still omits articles and that his sentence structure is not as elaborate as that of most 10-year-olds.

Johnny is in a general classroom, RTI Tier I, but he seems reluctant to participate in class. It has not been determined whether this reluctance stems from his sensitivity to others' reactions, an inability to formulate speech and complex language to express his ideas, or both. When we look at Johnny's strengths, we note that he is bright and has strong athletic abilities and that he gets along well with other children. A sensitive teacher can do much to help Johnny feel comfortable in spite of his speech disorder and can help him develop a positive self-concept.

Michelle: Michelle also has difficulty with speech. Her problems, however, are not with articulation—that is, the pronunciation of words. Michelle has difficulty with speech fluency, and she often stutters when she is talking. Michelle's speech is characterized by sound repetitions (for example, "W-W-W-What do you need?"), sound prolongations (for example, "ShShShShould I go too?"), and a series of interjections that insert pause words into the sentence (for example, "I can-um-um-you know-do this"). Sometimes when Michelle opens her mouth to speak nothing comes out. Michelle is a shy child by nature, and her difficulties with speaking have made her very hesitant to interact with others. When Michelle was in the second grade, she had a teacher who made the situation even worse. Michelle remembers Mrs. Cooke forcing her to stand before the class and give her book report. Mrs. Cooke said loudly in front of the class, "Now, Michelle, just take a deep breath and talk slowly and you will be fine." When Michelle did begin to stutter, Mrs. Cooke interrupted her and said, "Just start from the beginning and you can get it right." Michelle was mortified by her continued difficulties in front of the whole class, and the more nervous she became, the worse her stuttering became. Finally, she was allowed to slink back to her seat and try to make herself invisible; she has tried hard to maintain her invisibility ever since.

One of Michelle's strengths is written language, and she has won several awards for her poetry. Michelle is comfortable talking at home, and her stuttering does not seem to be a problem when she is with her family. In school and other settings Michelle finds it very difficult to participate in conversations in which there are more than a few people.

Both Johnny and Michelle have speech disorders, and both receive support from a speech-language pathologist. Later in the chapter we discuss the supports and services these children need to be successful, and we return to Johnny and Michelle to check their progress.

Definitions of Communication, Language, and Speech

Although we sometimes use the terms *communication, language,* and *speech* interchangeably, each means something different. The following definitions clarify how these terms are being used in this chapter and give us a shared platform for looking at the kinds of problems that can emerge with each of these areas.

> Communication, language, and speech are related concepts, yet each has its own meaning.

Communication

The ability to communicate is essential to our participation in society. It is what links us to others and helps us form a shared sense of belonging. **Communication** is the exchange of thoughts, information, feelings, and ideas, and it requires three

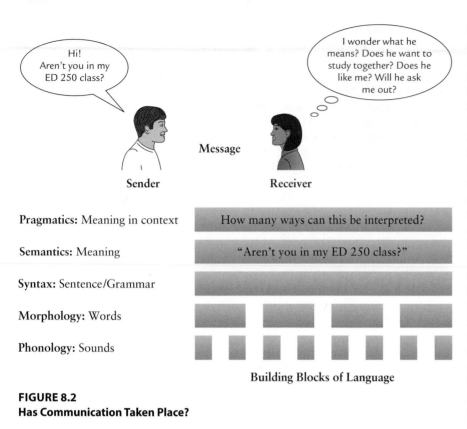

Pragmatics: Meaning in context

Semantics: Meaning

Syntax: Sentence/Grammar

Morphology: Words

Phonology: Sounds

Building Blocks of Language

FIGURE 8.2
Has Communication Taken Place?

Communication involves all aspects of the information processing model (IPM). Difficulties in any part of the IPM will lead to problems with communication.

things: a *sender*, a *message*, and a *receiver* (see Figure 8.2). This statement may seem like common sense, but it is important to note that communication has not taken place unless all three elements are in place *and* are working. The sender initiates the communication and determines the message, and the receiver gets the message and must interpret it to understand what it means, thus completing the communication loop. If you think about the information processing model (IPM) we have discussed in earlier chapters, you can see how communication involves input (hearing or seeing), central processing (thinking about and understanding), and output (speaking, signing, writing, etc.). Communication also involves the use of the executive function (decision making) and all of this takes place within an emotional context that must be factored in to correctly understand the message. Communication problems can emerge when there are difficulties with any one of these elements.

There are many ways to communicate. Messages can be transmitted through writing, telegraphy, and pictures. As humans we also use the arts to communicate through drama, dance, music, and all of the fine arts. Communication can be nonverbal, through gestures and facial expressions. Think of all the things you can express with just a look. Sign language uses an ordered form of gestures to convey meaning. The primary vehicle that humans use for communication, however, is language.

Language

Lahey's classic definition of **language** as "a code whereby ideas about the world are represented through a conventional system of arbitrary signals for communication" is still viable today (Lahey & Bloom, 1988, p. 3). Through this definition we see that language, as a *code*, represents *ideas*, or mental constructs, and that these are *separate from the actual objects and events*. These mental constructs are inherent to the person and not to the word, object, or event. Further, Lahey's definition reminds us that language is symbolic; that it relies on signals, sounds, and signs to represent objects and events; and thus that it is an abstraction of these. And finally through this definition we see that the primary function of language is to communicate.

Two kinds of language are involved in communication: **receptive language** and **expressive language**. *Receptive language* involves the ability to take in the message and understand it (that is, listening with understanding to oral language and reading written language with comprehension; input and central processing). *Expressive language* is the ability to produce a message to send; this typically involves speaking and writing (output). So, as part of communication, language is an organized system of symbols that humans use to express and receive meaning (Jusczyk, 1997; Salvia et al., 2007). Language systems evolved over time and largely replaced the innate communication system of gestures and facial expressions, which convey a more limited range of meaning. The key elements that help to define a language can be thought of as belonging to three categories: form, content, and function.

> There are two aspects of language development that are critical: receptive language, or hearing with understanding, and expressive language, or talking.

Language Form

The form that a language takes can be seen in the sounds, the words, and the grammar that underlie the language (Sylvia, Ysseldyke, & Bolt, 2007). Each language has its own individual form, or structure, but languages that share a common origin may be similar to each other in form (Gleason, 2005). **Language form** includes:

1. **Phonology** the sound system and patterns for the combinations of these sounds into speech

2. **Morphology** the rules that address how words are formed and the structure of words

3. **Syntax** the rules that guide how words are combined to form sentences and the relationships of components within the sentence

A language's grammar is the combination of its morphology and syntax. The structure of a language helps to convey the content. For example, in English we often use the sentence form article/noun/verb: "The cat pounced." When we see a sentence like this but with a word we do not know (in case a made-up word): "The cat zupped" we understand that "zupped" is an action.

Language Content

The content of a language is the information being communicated. This is an essential element of language because the meaning of the symbols used is the heart of the message. **Language content**, or *semantics,* is the meaning of words and sentences. You may have heard someone say, when arguing a point, that something is "just semantics," dismissing a point of difference by implying that the ideas are the same regardless of the words used. This argument is incorrect, however. *Meaning is semantics*, and this may be the most essential aspect of language. Meaning, however, must be interpreted within the context of the communication.

> Language includes form, content, and function and each component is essential for communication.

Language Function

Language function, or use, addresses language as appropriate communication within a given society and a specific context. The two concepts that are critical to how language is used are language **pragmatics** and **supralinguistics** (Salvia et al., 2007). *Language pragmatics* address the social context in which the communication occurs. The social context is important because it helps to clarify the meaning of the communication. Thus, the sentence "Can you feed the dog?" may mean one of the following: Please feed the dog. Are you physically able to feed the dog? or Do you have the resources needed to feed the dog? depending on the circumstances and person to whom the question is addressed. Pragmatics also addresses the different expectations for communication in different settings. Children are asked to use very different rules when they communicate in the classroom versus on the playground, and sometimes expectations for communication are different for the home and the school. To be successful we must learn to adapt our communications to the specific expectations in a variety of settings.

Supralinguistics is the sophisticated analysis of meaning when the literal meaning of the word or phrase is *not* the intended meaning (Salvia et al., 2007). Being good at supralinguistics means that one can understand sarcasm, indirect requests, subtle inferences, and figures of speech. This skill is also important for understanding puns, wordplay, and verbal humor. Because people often communicate with indirect language, individuals who have difficulty with this may be at a loss to interpret meaning and understand needs. For example, a teacher may say, while rolling her eyes, "Well, of course I *expect you* to talk out in class," when she means the opposite. A youngster who has difficulty understanding social cues and interpreting nonliteral language (such as sarcasm) will be very confused by this statement. This is one of the challenges faced by children with Asperger's syndrome, discussed in Chapter 5 (Hughes-Lynch, 2010).

Next, we discuss speech. When a given community selects a series of sounds to convey meaning, it creates speech. Spoken language can be used to convey abstract meanings and to address the past and future, as well as the present.

Speech

Speech is the systematic oral production of the words of a given language. Sounds become speech only when they produce words that have meaning. Speech has a rhythmic flow, with stress and intonation, and it uses words with stressed and unstressed syllables. We think of normal speech as combining **articulation**, **fluency**, and **voice**. *Articulation* is the clear pronunciation of words, *fluency* refers to the appropriate flow of the words, and *voice* is the intonation and quality of the production (pitch, loudness, and resonance). Figure 8.3 presents a simplified overview of the production of speech. A thought occurs in the brain; it is translated into symbols and sent to the larynx area for phonation and resonation, which takes place in the vocal tract; then air is sent to be modified by movements of the tongue and passage over the teeth and lips, which combine to form the sounds, words, and sentences of a particular language (articulation).

The thought transformed into words is received by a listener through hearing, in a process called **audition.**

The following four processes are involved in the production of speech:

- **Respiration** (breathing) generates the energy that produces sound.

- **Phonation** is the production of sound by the vibration of the vocal cords.

- **Resonation** gives the voice a unique characteristic that identifies the speaker (it is the product of sound traveling through the speaker's head and neck).

- **Articulation** is the movement of the mouth and tongue that shapes sound into phonemes (the smallest unit of sound), which combine to make speech.

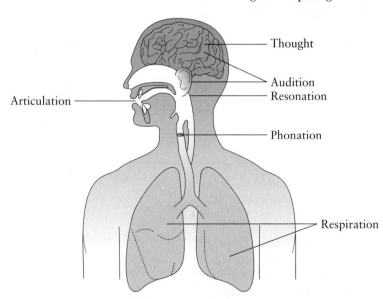

FIGURE 8.3
Processes Involved in the Production of Speech

Early Childhood Typical Language Development

An infant is innately programmed to communicate through smiles, eye contact, sounds, and gestures (the prelinguistic system). Infants are very social beings and are motivated to relate to persons in their environment (Bloom, 2000). The language system uses these talents, and parents teach the child that people and objects have names and particular sounds to identify them. Although the specific language that each child learns will depend on the language spoken in the home, the pattern of language development seems to be similar across languages. The aforementioned two aspects of language, receptive language and expressive language, are critical to a child's development. Understanding typical language development is essential to understanding when and how problems with language can manifest themselves. Table 8.1 shows the typical emergence of language for children from birth to age five.

There are many reasons that a child's individual language progression may differ somewhat from the typical sequence given in Table 8.1. A bilingual child, for example, who is learning two languages at the same time may have fewer words in each language and so may appear to be delayed in vocabulary or language acquisition when only one language is assessed (Hoff, 2004; Hart, 2009; Brice & Brice, 2009). When words in both of the child's languages are considered, however, we get a more accurate understanding of the child's true vocabulary (Holt, 2005, Brice & Brice, 2009). Children who are bilingual may also be somewhat delayed in their phonemic awareness (the relationship between letters and sounds) and they may need additional time and support in early reading (Brice & Brice, 2009; Brice, Carson, & O'Brien, 2009).

> The range of typical development can be quite large. However, if a child's speech or language is significantly delayed, this is cause for concern.

Infants begin to communicate the moment they utter their first cry.
(© ICHIRO/Getty)

(milestones)

TABLE 8.1
Typical Language Development for Children from Birth through Age Five

Chronological age in months and years	Expectations for typical receptive language development (hearing and understanding)	Expectations for typical expressive language development (talking)
Birth–3 months	• Startles to loud sounds • Quiets or smiles when spoken to • Seems to recognize your voice and quiets if crying • Increases or decreases sucking behavior in response to sounds	• Makes pleasure sounds cooing, gooing • Cries differently for different needs • Smiles when sees you
4–6 months	• Moves eyes in direction of sounds • Responds to changes in tone of your voice • Notices toys that make sounds • Pays attention to music	• Babbling sounds more speech-like with many different sounds including *p*, *b*, and *n* • Vocalizes excitement and displeasure • Makes gurgling sounds when left alone and when playing with you
7 months–1 year	• Enjoys games such as peek-a-boo and pat-a-cake • Turns and looks in direction of sounds • Listens when spoken to • Recognizes words for common items, such as *cup, shoe,* or *juice* • Begins to respond to requests (e.g., "come here" or "want more?")	• Babbling has both long and short groups of sounds, such as *tata upup bibibibi* • Uses speech or noncrying sounds to get and keep attention • Imitates different speech sounds • Has one or two words (e.g., *bye-bye, dada, mama*), although they may not be clear
1 year–2 years	• Points to a few body parts when asked • Follows simple commands and understands simple questions (e.g., "What's that?" "Roll the ball," "Kiss baby," "Where is your shoe?") • Listens to simple stories, songs, and rhymes • Points to picture in book when named	• Says more words every month • Uses some one- or two-word questions (e.g., "Where kitty?" "Go bye-bye?" "What's that?") • Puts two words together (e.g., "More cookie," "No juice," "Mommy book") • Uses many different consonant sounds at the beginning of words
2 years–3 years	• Understands differences in meaning ("go/ stop," "in/on," "big/little") • Follows two-step requests ("Get the book and put it on the table")	• Has a word for almost everything • Uses two- or three-word "sentences" to talk about and ask for things • Speech is understood by familiar listeners most of the time • Often asks for or directs attention to objects by naming them
3 years–4 years	• Hears you when you call from another room • Hears television or radio at the same loudness level as other family members • Understands simple *wh-* (*who, what, where, why*) questions	• Talks about activities at school or at friends' homes • Speaks clearly enough that people outside the family can usually understand his or her speech • Uses a lot of sentences that have four or more words • Usually talks easily without repeating syllables or words

4 years–5 years	• Pays attention to a short story and answers simple questions about it • Hears and understands most of what is said at home and in school	• Makes voice sounds clearly like other children's • Uses sentences that give lots of details (e.g., "I like to read my books.") • Tells stories that stick to a topic • Communicates easily with other children and adults • Says most sounds correctly (except perhaps certain ones such as *l, s, r, v, z, ch, sh, th*) • Uses the same grammar as the rest of the family

Source: Reprinted with permission from "How does your child hear and talk?" Available from American Speech-Language-Hearing Association website, www.asha.org/public/speech/development/chart.htm, accessed 5/24/2010.

The ability to communicate in more than one language is a strength that will ultimately be an asset to the individual. Because, however, bilingualism may impact the early development of language, children can be misidentified as having language delays when they are actually on target given the demands of learning two languages. During assessments, we must make sure that the child's language and cultural context are understood as we look at the child's needs (Hart, 2009; Hoff & Elledge, 2005).

Genetics and Communication Disorders

There appears to be a genetic component that manifests itself in 50 percent of the children in families with a history of communication disorders (Dionne, Dale, Boivin, & Plomin, 2003). Children whose families have a history of communication disorders tend to have significantly lower language scores in comparison with their age-matched peers. The interaction between genetics and environment, discussed in Chapter 1[CE22], plays a major role in language development influencing the child's language acquisition rates (Flax et al., 2003). Because of these interactions, the child and family may need additional support with the development of language. When a child's language development differs substantially from the typical pattern, however, it may be due to a disorder with communication, language, and/or speech.

Disorders in Communication, Language, and Speech

It is important to distinguish between disorders in communication, language, and speech because they have different origins and they require different interventions. Table 8.2 gives the American Speech-Language-Hearing Association's (ASHA) definitions of these disorders. **Communication disorders** are often related to other areas of disability. Those related to hearing are discussed in Chapter 10. Communication difficulties also impact children with autism (Chapter 5), learning disabilities (Chapter 4), visual impairments (Chapter 11), and physical disabilities (Chapter 12). We will explore these relationships in greater detail later in this chapter.

TABLE 8. 2
American Speech-Language-Hearing Association's Definitions of Communication Disorders Including Language and Speech

I. Communication Disorders	A *communication disorder* is an impairment in the ability to receive, send, process, and comprehend concepts of verbal, nonverbal, and graphic symbol systems. A communication disorder may be evident in the processes of hearing, language, and/or speech. A communication disorder may range in severity from mild to profound. It may be developmental or acquired. Individuals may demonstrate one or any combination of communication disorders. A communication disorder may result in a primary disability, or it may be secondary to other disabilities.

A. A *speech disorder* is an impairment of the articulation of speech sounds, fluency, and/or voice.

1. An *articulation disorder* is the atypical production of speech sounds characterized by substitutions, omissions, additions, or distortions that may interfere with intelligibility.
2. A *fluency disorder* is an interruption in the flow of speaking characterized by atypical rate, rhythm, and repetitions in sounds, syllables, words, and phrases. This may be accompanied by excessive tension, struggle behavior, and secondary mannerisms.
3. A *voice disorder* is characterized by the abnormal production and/or absences of vocal quality, pitch, loudness, resonance, and/or duration, which is inappropriate for an individual's age and/or sex.

B. A *language disorder* is impaired comprehension and/or use of spoken, written, and/or other symbol systems. The disorder may involve (1) the form of language (phonology, morphology, syntax), (2) the content of language (semantics), and/or (3) the function of language in communication (pragmatics) in any combination.

1. Form of Language
   a. *Phonology* is the sound system of a language and the rules that govern the sound combinations.
   b. *Morphology* is the system that governs the structure of words and the construction of word forms.
   c. *Syntax* is the system governing the order and combination of words to form sentences, and the relationships among the elements within a sentence.
2. Content of Language

   Semantics is the system that governs the meanings of words and sentences.
3. Function of Language

   Pragmatics is the system that combines the above language components in functional and socially appropriate communication.

Source: Reprinted with permission from "How does your child hear and talk?" Available from American Speech-Language-Hearing Association website, www.asha.org/public/speech/development/chart.htm, accessed 5/24/2010. All rights reserved.

Communication Disorders

Communication is often used as a general term to include pragmatics, speech, and language. Communication disorders disrupt the individual's ability to send, receive, and process information. If you think about the information processing model, you can see how problems with input could undermine an individual's ability to take in messages. Difficulties with processing can make understanding or interpreting the message hard, and output problems can make it hard to send a

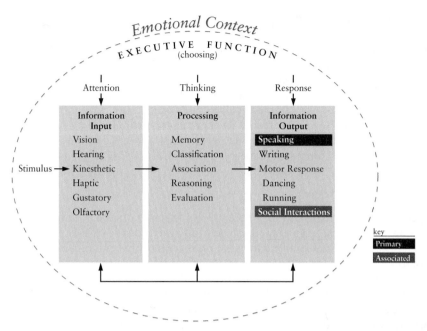

FIGURE 8.4
Michelle's Information Processing Model

message. In some cases, the processing difficulties affect a child's ability to under-stand nonliteral meanings of words, and so the child misses the nuances of the communication. The brain's executive function system also oversees and moni-tors communication; so if there are problems with attending, communication will be difficult. The emotional context of communication can also contribute to an individual's inability to send, receive, and/or understand the message. Strong emotions, such as anger and high levels of anxiety, can make communication difficult. Remember Michelle, the girl we met at the beginning of the chapter, and how painful speaking in front of the class was for her because of her speech disorder? Speaking in front of the class became even more difficult as her anxiety increased when her teacher put pressure on her. Michelle's early experience with public speaking was connected with strong negative emotions that stayed with her and inhibited her desire to communicate for years to come. Figure 8.4 shows the information processing model for Michelle and indicates the areas that cause her the most difficulties. A failure to appropriately interpret the context or setting can also lead to problems with communication and the pragmatics of language use. Communication disorders often involve language and speech disorders.

Language Disorders

As we explained earlier, culturally determined rules govern the form, content, and function of language. Table 8.2 shows that each element of language—phonology, morphology, syntax, semantics, and pragmatics—is a potential source of **language disorders.** For example, some children are able to express age-appropriate ideas in correct sentence structures but are not able to use accepted rules of morphology; they might have difficulty with pluralization (*foot-feet*), with verb tenses (*run-ran, walk-walked*), or with the use of prefixes (*pre-, anti-*).

Language involves both *reception* (taking in information) and *expression* (giving out verbal information and producing written language). In some man-ner, language is processed internally during both reception and expression, but language production and language comprehension do not always proceed at the same pace. Some children will speak but do not seem to understand the meaning of the sentence (Slobin, 2006). And remember from our discussion of the information processing model that processing errors interfere with all types of learning, including language learning.

The stages and sequences of normal language acquisition give clues to language disorders. But it is often difficult to determine a specific cause for a child's language disorder. Speech problems, developmental disorders, or other disabilities may all influence the child's ability to use language. Speech disorders are a specific form of language disorders that affect a child's ability to produce oral language.

Speech Disorders

Speech disorders may include problems with articulation and phonological processing, voice, and/or fluency. One cause of speech disorders is a **cleft palate**, which is a congenital abnormality that occurs when the roof of the mouth has not joined completely during prenatal development (Lee, Law, & Gibbon, 2009). The incidence of cleft palate range from 1:500 to 1:2000 depending on racial and gender differences (Lee, Law, & Gibbon, 2009). The cleft may be only on one side (unilateral) or on both sides (bilateral) and is usually closed by surgery during the first 18 months of the child's life (Henningson, Kuehn, Sell, Sweeney, Trost-Cardamone, Whitehill Speech Parameters Group 2008; Priester & Goorhuis-Brouwer, 2008). While early surgery can repair the cleft, an estimated 50 to 75 percent of children born with a cleft palate will require speech intervention at some point in their life (Lee, Law, & Gibbon, 2009).

www.smiletrain.org

Studies looking at the development of speech for children born with a cleft palate indicate differences in pronunciation, word usage, and vocabulary for children at age 2.5 to 3 years (Scherer, Williams, & Proctor-Williams, 2008; Scherer, D'Antonio, McGahey, 2008). Scherer, Williams, and Proctor-Williams (2008) compared the early language development of children born with and without cleft palates and found persistent difficulties in vocalization and vocabulary for children even after their cleft palate had been repaired surgically. While the two groups of children (those born with and without a cleft palate) were similar in their frequency of early babbling, the complexity of the child's early babbling was significantly lower for children with cleft palates. The authors conclude, in part, that the children with cleft palates use fewer and less complex sounds and receive more limited motoric feedback from their babbling practice and that this limits their spoken word acquisition at three years.

Early intervention with a multidisciplinary team (e.g., surgery, dentistry, audiology, speech language pathologies, and parents) can help to support speech acquisition (Henningson et al., 2008). Parents can also be taught to provide early intervention support to help their child's speech development (Scherer, D'Antonio, & McGahey, 2008; Priester & Goorhuis-Brouwer, 2008). The areas of speech therapy that are often needed for children born with cleft palates include disorders of articulation and phonological processing and voice.

Articulation and Phonological Processing Disorders

The number and kinds of misproductions and their effect on intelligibility are among the criteria for judging an articulation disorder on a continuum ranging from mild to severe. **Articulation disorders** may range from a mild frontal lisp or a fleeting hesitation in words to mispronunciations of speech sounds that are so severe that the speaker is unintelligible to listeners in his or her own community. Imprecise phoneme (sound) production or articulation errors include substitutions, distortions, omissions, and, infrequently, the addition of extra sounds.

When the intended phoneme is replaced by another phoneme, the error is one of *substitution*. Common examples are *w* for *r* (*wight* for *right*), *t* for *k* (*toat* for *coat*), and *w* for *l* (*wove* for *love*). The influence of multiple substitutions on intelligibility becomes apparent when *like* becomes *wite*. In other instances, a misproduction makes a phoneme sound different but not different enough to change the production into a phoneme with a different meaning. These productions are known as *distortions* (for example, *bru* for *blue*). When a disorder involves *omissions,* certain sounds are omitted entirely (*pay* for *play, ka* for *cat* or *cap*). Misarticulations are not always consistent. In some phoneme sequences, sounds are articulated correctly; in others, they are not. Often the position of a sound (at the beginning, middle, or end of a word) or the position of a word influences the production. Johnny,

Speech therapists encourage production of speech with articulation that can be understood.

(© Ellen Senisi)

the boy discussed earlier in the chapter, had difficulties primarily with articulation. Even with intense early speech therapy, his speech was almost unintelligible until he was 8 years old.

Disorders of Voice

Voice is the production of sound in the larynx and the selective transmission and modification of that sound through resonance and loudness (you may want to look back at Figure 8.3 to remind yourself how speech is produced). When we talk about voice, we usually think of three characteristics: quality, pitch, and loudness (ASHA, 2008). We evaluate these characteristics in terms of the speaker's age, sex, and culture (Moores, 1996). A **voice disorder** is an inappropriate variation in one of these. Disorders of voice quality, generally called **dysphonia**, can be related to phonation, resonation, or both. Breathiness, hoarseness, and harshness are disorders of phonation. Problems with resonation include hypernasality (excessively nasal-sounding speech) and hyponasality (speech that sounds as if the speaker has a bad cold). For children born with a cleft palate, voice disorders often include hypernasality, hyponasality, audible nasal air emissions, and/or turbulence and difficulties with controlling voice quality (Henningson et al., 2008). Often phonation and resonation disorders are present in the same person, but they can be separate disorders. Pitch indicates whether the speaker is male or female, young or old. Pitch breaks, a common problem, occur in adolescents and affect boys particularly when their voices are maturing.

With the growing numbers of children from culturally and linguistically diverse families in today's schools, we must be extremely careful that we take the child's language background into consideration as we look at possible areas of concern (Guiberson et al., 2006; Salvia et al., 2007; Brice, Carson, & O'Brien, 2009).

> Speech disorders may include problems with articulation, fluency, or voice.

Disorders of Speech Fluency

Fluency is the flow of speech. The most common fluency disorder is stuttering, which is characterized by repetitions and prolongations of sound, syllables, or words; tension; and extraneous movement (ASHA, 2010). **Stuttering** is a complex speech disorder with a variety of assumed causes. Speech patterns often include:

- repetitions of words or word parts ("W-W-W- Where are we eating?)

- prolongations of speech sounds ("SSSSave me a chair.")

- interjections of sounds ("We can meet at um, um, you know, like, six o'clock.")

- stopped or blocked speech where the sounds will not come out (ASHA, 2010).

Stuttering is diagnosed when these disfluencies stand out and disrupt the person's ability to communicate. A skilled speech-language pathologist is needed to assess the speech patterns and develop and implement a support program to help the individual cope with his or her speech challenges. Treatment programs for people who stutter often focus on teaching behaviors to help them monitor and control speech rate, control breathing, and reduce tension during speaking (ASHA, 2010). Some researchers believe that there may be a genetic component to stuttering as more boys than girls have disfluencies in their speech (Dworzynski, Remington, Rijsdijk, Howell, & Plomin, 2007). Many children who stutter show spontaneous recovery by school age (Ward, 2008). But others, like Michelle, continue to have difficulties. As with most disabilities, early intervention (begun by the age of 3) can be very effective in reducing stuttering (Ward, 2008).

 # Bilingual Language Differences and Dialects

Children learn to speak the language that is spoken in their homes and neighborhoods. They tend to use language to express their needs and thoughts in the same way that their parents or caregivers do.

Bilingual Learners

For children who are bilingual, the increased language demands may cause delays in vocabulary acquisition in each of the languages used. As noted earlier in the chapter, these "delays" are a normal by-product of learning more than one language. To accurately assess vocabulary development for bilingual children, we must include word counts for both languages used by the child (Brice & Brice, 2009).

Brice, Carson, and O'Brien (2009) studied articulation and phonology for preschool bilingual (Spanish/English speaking) children and noted differences in pronunciations for some phonemes. In these cases the use of two languages may cause interference patterns to emerge when one language structure is imposed on to the other language. These differences may lead to the misdiagnoses of some children as having speech disorders. The articulation differences were further complicated by the various Spanish dialects used by the child (see discussion

It is essential to remember that language differences and dialects are not disorders.

of dialect in a later section). The study highlights the need for speech-language pathologists with bilingual and bicultural experience to appropriately assess children who are dual language learners.

Language Differences

In some homes, parents use language in ways that are different from the language some teachers expect students to use. For example, teachers may demand explicitness in language (Justice, Mashburn, Hamre, & Pianta, 2008). Whereas the two sentences "He took it" and "Arthur took my truck" convey the same meaning, the listener has to be in the immediate environment to understand the former, less explicit communication. Children who have not been exposed to explicit communication in the home may have difficulty when they encounter a teacher who expects it. Teachers must be aware that differences in language usage such as this are not treated as disorders. These

Children from communities that speak a language other than American English need assessments by speech-language pathologists who are skilled in the child's primary language.
(© Ellen Senisi)

differences can be addressed by teaching rather than by therapy. Comparing the child's communication skills with the skills of peers from the same cultural background helps us to avoid labeling the child as language impaired rather than language different (McCabe & Champion, 2010; Hart, 2009).

Dialects

The picture can be further complicated by differences in a child's language due to family, community, or regional accents and dialects. Variations in word usage, pronunciation (phonology), word order (syntax), and meaning (semantics) influence the child's use of language (pragmatics). A **dialect** is a variation of language that differs in pronunciation, vocabulary, or syntax from the literary form of the language. It is used and understood by a group within a larger community. Dialects reflect regional, social, occupational, and other differences: "He done sold his car"; "We be there tomorrow"; "She be sick to her stomach." The use of a dialect is *not* a sign of a speech disorder but is part of the linguistic diversity of society (Hwa-Froelich, Kasambira, & Moleski, 2007). Saying "warsh" for "wash" is not a sign of a speech defect but a regional dialect. The following ASHA definition for communication differences and dialects reminds us that these are *not* considered to be speech or language disorders:

Communication difference/dialect is a variation of a symbol system used by a group of individuals that reflects and is determined by shared regional, social, or cultural/ethnic factors. A regional, social, or cultural/ethnic variation of a symbol system should not be considered a disorder of speech or language. (American Speech-Language-Hearing Association website, www.asha.org/public/speech/development/chart.htm, accessed 5/24/2010).

A dialect is very much a part of a child's self-concept, and teachers must react to it carefully. Teachers should model standard literary usage when speaking, and encourage children to use it when reading aloud and writing, but they should allow children to use dialect in their informal speech if communication is clear.

A major problem for teachers is that the existence of a dialect may mask a delay or disorder that will become increasingly difficult to diagnose the longer it remains undetected (Guiberson, Barrett, Jancosek, & Itano, 2006). A major failing of language assessment tools is that they are based on the average child's use of language, which is not necessarily the way language is used, taught, and encouraged in all families and communities (McCabe & Champion, 2010). Speech-language pathologists and teachers need to learn what a specific community considers accurate pronunciation and usage, and then they can teach children the expectations for communication in different settings (Brice & Brice, 2009).

Prevalence of Communication, Language, and Speech Disorders

Because of the complexity of communication problems, it is difficult to get an accurate picture of how many communication disorders are speech disorders and how many are language disorders. Speech and language disorders affected over 1 million children in 2004, composing 18.8 percent of the total number of children with disabilities (U.S. Department of Education, 2008). Not all children with speech-language disorders are in special education classes. In fact, 88 percent of children with speech and language disorders are served primarily in general education classes; only 4.7 percent spend more than half their day outside of the general classroom and 0.5 percent in separate classes (U.S. Department of Education, 2008). Children with speech and language disorders are more likely than children with other disabilities to be served in the general classroom.

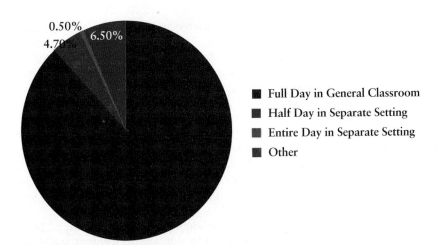

FIGURE 8.5
Placement of Children with Communication Disorders
Source: U.S. Department of Education. (2008). *Twenty-Eighth Annual Report to Congress.* Washington, D.C.: Office of Special Education Programs

Determining prevalence figures can be difficult because younger children, in kindergarten through second grade, may be overidentified due to mild speech disorders. Prevalence figures also tend to be distorted because intellectual and developmental delays, cerebral palsy, hearing loss, and many other disabilities affect communication. Although a communication disorder may be secondary to another disability, it still requires treatment and therapy as part of a total special education program.

> It can be difficult to establish the prevalence of communication, language, and speech disorders because these often overlap with other disability areas.

 # Disability Areas and Problems with Communication, Language, and Speech

Throughout this text we look at the ways that a disability can affect a person's life. The impact that a disability can have on an individual's ability to communicate with others is perhaps one of the most poignant of these effects. Table 8.3 shows the possible problems with communication, language, and speech that can coexist with other areas of disability.

Because problems with communication, language, and/or speech are often present along with other disabilities, the law requires that speech-language

TABLE 8.3
Possible Problems with Communication, Language, and Speech That May Accompany Disability Areas

Disability Area	Possible Communication, Language, and Speech Problems
Intellectual and Developmental Delays	Delayed language is a universal characteristic; disorders may be present in all aspects of speech production and with both expressive and receptive language.
Cerebral Palsy	Poor muscle control and difficulty breathing may result in communication difficulties ranging from speech disorders of articulation and voice to the inability to speak; may need augmented communication support. For many individuals language delays will also be present.
Learning Disabilities	Language difficulties can cause major problems in learning to read, write, spell, and do arithmetic. Problems with communication include understanding social cues, contextual needs, and interpreting nonliteral language.
Severe and Profound Multiple Disabilities	Difficulties with speech production. May experience delays in language development; may need an augmented communication support.
Autism	Communication difficulties can stem from an inability to "read" and interpret social cues, facial expressions, and gestures; a lack of interest in communication, difficulties with interpreting nonliteral language and language delays may be present.
Deaf/Hearing Loss	Generalized language delays, alternative communication needs (e.g., sign language, cued speech, lip reading, etc.); may have articulation difficulties, voice problems, and limited use of speech.
Visual Impairments	Difficulties with language reception in reading; can require use of Braille or audio augmentation. Communication difficulties may be present if individual is unable to see social cues, facial expressions, and gestures. Abstract ideas (e.g., colors) may be hard to communicate if child has no vision.
Emotional and Behavioral Problems	Communication difficulties can arise from the inability to appropriately "read" social cues and from impulsivity related to difficulties with self-regulation. Language delays lead to further frustration and can exacerbate existing problems.

Sara's Story

Have you ever wondered what it would be like not to be able to communicate? It's very frustrating. It's very lonely. It hurts.

Think about it. You feel, you think, you know and understand the words, yet you cannot speak them. You hear everyone around you in an interesting conversation, but you cannot join in.

You cannot express any of the feelings or emotions that are just as deep inside of you as anyone else. You are furiously angry and you have to hold it in; or you are extremely happy and you can't show it. Your heart is so full of love you could just burst, but you can't share it. I know what it is like because for years I could not communicate or express myself. I am a 19-year-old girl. I have cerebral palsy and cannot talk. I do not have coordination in my hands to write or use sign language. Even a typewriter was out of the question when I was younger. I know what it is like to be fed potatoes all my life. After all, potatoes are a good basic food for every day, easy to fix in many different ways. I hate potatoes! But then, who knew that but me?

I know what it is like to be dressed in reds and blues when my favorite colors are mint greens, lemon yellows, and pinks. I mean, really, can you imagine?

Mama found me one night curled up in a ball in my bed crying, doubled over in pain. I couldn't explain to her where or how I hurt. So, after checking me over the best she could, she thought I had a bad stomachache due to constipation. Naturally, a quick cure for that was an enema. It didn't help my earache at all!

Finally, help came! I was introduced to Blissymbols.

My life changed! Blissymbols were originally developed for a universal language, but they have been a miracle for me and others like me. Blissymbols are a combination of the written word and a symbolized picture that anyone can learn, which are displayed in a way that can be easily used. There was a tray strapped to my wheelchair. It was covered with a sheet of paper, which was divided into little blocks of words to form sentences. At last, I could communicate!

Naturally, one board could not hold all the words needed. I had to learn to make up my own, combining two or more words to mean another. As in "story sleep" for dream or "bad night horse" for nightmare.

My teachers started me on ten words a day to see if I could learn them. I learned as fast as they could give me new words. I was ready to communicate! I could even stutter! That's what my uncle calls it when it takes three or four tries to point to one word.

Once I mastered Blissymbols, I left the symbols behind and changed to words and sentences. I got my first computer. It was an Autocom™. I programmed my Bliss board into it and much more. It also had a printer. Finally, I could write!

I didn't stop there. I went on to a more advanced system. I had fun learning about computers by using my Express III™. I was doing the programming all by myself and even did some of the "funny" spelling.

The first thing I learned about computers was to think of them as "hotel." My "Hotel Express III™" had 99 floors or levels. Each floor had 128 rooms or spaces for programming. In each room I could put one person as in a letter or a number, or a whole family as in a sentence; or I could just throw a wild party with several paragraphs. So you see my "Hotel Express III™" had almost unlimited accommodations.

Did I stop there? Surprise, I got a new device. It is called a Touch Talker™ with Mindspeak software. This one has the same basic features as my Express III™, but I can connect it to an Apple computer to either store the memory on a disk or just use the screen to make my paragraphs all in one instead of having to say bits and pieces at a time. Everything in it is coded like my Express III™, but it is much easier to get the words or sentences out because everything is coded by pictures instead of numbers, and it is a lot easier to remember pictures. The Express III™ had number levels, and it was harder to remember where I put everything, so as you can see, the Touch Talker™ makes it a lot easier for me to communicate with you or anyone else.

Communicating for me has opened a lot of doors. It even let me act in a play. I have been a guest speaker at a Kiwanis Club meeting. It has done a lot more, too. There's help out there, just don't give up.

Source: "Sara's Story" from *Keyhole Communique,* 3(3), May 1989. Reprinted by permission of the author.

Pivotal Issues

- How did the ability to communicate change Sara's life?

- Assistive technology and augmentative communication are improving at a rapid pace. What additional kinds of support are available today for Sara?

- You may have noticed that Sara has excellent writing skills as she tells her story in this article; how would you identify the strengths of students in your classroom if they have communication disorders?

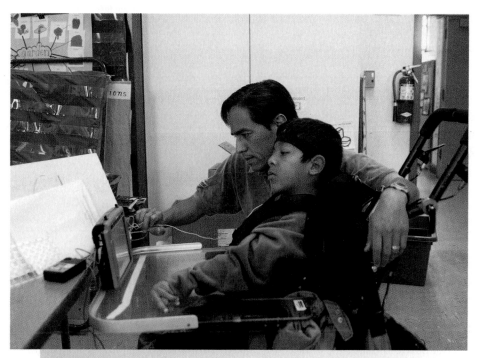

Difficulties with speech, language, and communication may affect many children with disabilities.

(© Elizabeth Crews)

therapy be available as a related service for children with disabilities if they need it (CEC, 2010). **Related services** are defined as support services that are required to assist the child in benefiting from special education (CEC, 2010). In most cases, a speech-language pathologist will be part of the multidisciplinary team that helps in assessing the child's needs, in planning to address these needs, and in carrying out the services required to support the child. The early detection of problems related to communication, language, and speech is essential because early intervention can make a significant difference in the outcomes for children with problems in these areas.

 ## Assessment and Identification of Problems with Communication, Language, and Speech

A comprehensive evaluation of a child's ability to communicate will include an assessment of both receptive and expressive language strengths and needs. Because the demands of communication are complex, it is essential to assess each element of language to establish areas in which difficulties are encountered. Table 8.4 shows the language element that should be assessed and what it will look like for both receptive and expressive language.

A comprehensive evaluation will likely include both formal and informal assessments, combining standardized tests with systematic observations and recordings of spontaneous uses of language (Hyter, 2007; Olswang et al.,

A speech-language pathologist is a key member of the multidisciplinary team that is needed to identify and support children with speech and language disorders.

TABLE 8.4
Language Elements for a Comprehensive Assessment of Communication Difficulties

Language Elements	Receptive Language	Expressive Language
Phonology	Hearing and discriminating speech sounds	Articulating speech sounds
Morphology and Syntax	Understanding the grammatical structure of language	Using the grammatical structure of language
Semantics	Understanding vocabulary, meaning, and concepts	Using vocabulary, meaning, and concepts
Pragmatics and Supralinguistics	Understanding a speaker's or writer's intentions	Using awareness of social aspects of language
Ultimate Language Skills	Understanding spoken or written language	Speaking or writing

Source: Reprinted with permission from American Speech-Language-Hearing Association in the Schools, Definitions of communication disorders and variations, *ASHA, 35* (Suppl. 10) (1993): 40–41. Available from http://www.asha.org/docs/html/RP1993-00208.html.

2007; Salvia et al., 2007). Formal assessments rely on diagnostic test and clinical evaluations done by a speech-language pathologist. As part of the informal assessment, teachers can make a key contribution to understanding the child's needs through their systematic observations of the child. The observations that a teacher makes of the child's language behavior during the course of typical classroom activities helps the team gain a comprehensive portrait of the child's typical verbal and nonverbal communication patterns (Olswang et al., 2007). The teacher can further use her or his observations to shape the kinds of supports that will help to strengthen the child's communications skills.

The speech-language pathologist is primarily responsible for the identification, diagnosis, and design of the treatment plan or curriculum, and the implementation of this plan for children with language and speech disorders. In doing this, the speech-language pathologist works as part of a multidisciplinary team. The team must consider several things as they evaluate the communication strengths and needs of the child. The child's age, general cognitive abilities, sensory acumen, experiences, and the family's primary language will all have an impact on the child's communication. When English is not the primary language of the child and/or the child's family, the assessment for possible problems with language is more complex.

Assessment of Children from Culturally or Linguistically Diverse Backgrounds

Children from homes in which English is not the primary language are likely to encounter difficulty in using English in school. Language differences can and should be identified early, and language pragmatics, that is, how to relate to others and to speak in a school setting, can be taught to minimize problems for the child due to cultural differences in expectations (Brice, Miller, & Brice, 2006). When a language or speech disorder is suspected, children from cultures and communities that speak a language other than English need to be assessed by speech-language pathologists who are skilled in the child's primary language (Brice, Carson, & O'Brien, 2009; Guiberson et al., 2006; Salend & Salinas, 2003).

Ines is a 3-year-old child whose bilingual family lives in New Mexico. English is her primary language, but her range of English vocabulary and language proficiency is lower than would be expected for her age norms. In part, these lower scores reflect the impact of her dialect, called Spanglish, which varies from classic Spanish and includes some English. The school personnel will need to be knowledgeable about this dialect when they assess Ines's functioning (Brice, Miller, & Brice, 2006). Ines is fortunate in some respects, as many children her age in New Mexico have not learned English and will not do so until they attend school. Ines's school success will depend on the skills of her teacher and the speech-language pathologist and on the cooperation and support provided by her family (Saenz & Felix, 2006).

Children who are bilingual vary in their English competence and our assessments of these children should involve a specialist who is bilingual and bicultural. A speech-language pathologist who speaks the language of the child's home and who understands the child's cultural background can answer three basic questions (Metz, 1991): Who speaks what language? When is that language spoken? For what purpose is that language spoken? Answers to these questions will inform the speech pathologist's interpretation of the child's assessment results and should help to prevent misdiagnosis of communication, language, and speech disorders.

> Speech-language pathologists who are bilingual and bicultural can help to accurately identify bilingual children who may have speech or language disorders.

Great care must be taken that children from different cultures who speak a different language receive an accurate assessment by a person well versed in the children's language and cultural mores. For example, Spanish-speaking children who speak a Puerto Rican dialect make a number of phonological "errors" that are consistent with their dialect. If the dialect of these children is not taken into account, lower scores will be obtained (Goldstein & Iglesias, 2001; Brice & Brice, 2009).

When a native speaker of the child's language is not available to conduct the assessment, a mediator who speaks the child's language can be hired as a neutral person to assist the evaluator and help communicate with the family. During the evaluation, the mediator can relieve the family's stress by keeping the family informed about what is taking place (Saenz & Felix, 2006).

Six research-based guiding principles for working with preschool bilingual children have been identified by the Southern California Comprehensive Assistance Center. These six principles include:

- Using the child's home language as a foundation for cognitive development, learning about the world, and emerging literacy

- Creating a learning environment that facilitates social and emotional growth and affirms the child's cultural identify

- Supporting opportunities to allow one language to enhance the other language

- Building strong and effective home-school partnerships

- Providing high-quality professional development for adults on meeting the needs of English-language learners

- Using culturally, developmentally, and linguistically appropriate assessment. Southern California Comprehensive Assistance Center.

▶❚❚ TeachSource VIDEO CONNECTION

Bilingual Education: An Elementary Two-Way Immersion Program

Visit the Education CourseMate website to access this TeachSource Video Case. As you watch the Video Case, reflect on how the teachers worked together to promote vocabulary development for their students. In addition, think about the ways they used the bilingual approach to reinforce concept development and enhance understanding.

Adapting the Learning Environment

RTI

The three levels of intervention that typically constitute the response to intervention (RTI) approach are an excellent match for students with communication, language, and speech disorders. All three levels can play an important role in helping the child meet with success.

▲ Tier I: The General Education Classroom

The general classroom is where most children whose primary area of identification is speech-language are served. Inclusion is the typical option for the child with communication disorders because most children with primary speech disorders respond well to the general education program if they receive additional help for their special communication needs. The general education classroom and inclusion with typically developing peers provides a rich language environment that can enhance the communication of all children.

You may recall that both Johnny and Michelle, the children presented early in this chapter, were students in a general classroom. You may also remember that Michelle's second-grade teacher's insensitivity led to a painful situation in which Michelle's stuttering caused her significant embarrassment. Michelle's current teacher in fifth grade, Ms. Boone, is much more aware of the difficulty that Michelle faces and has worked hard to make the classroom comfortable, engaging, and nonthreatening. Ms. Boone has modeled active listening for her students, and she praises them when they listen respectfully and patiently to each other without interrupting. This is particularly helpful to Michelle, because it has allowed her to feel more at ease talking. In addition, the children in the class have learned about the difficulties that Michelle faces, and they have been asked to show courtesy to Michelle when she is speaking by following these guidelines:

- Disregard short pauses or slow speech
- Show acceptance of what has been expressed rather than how it was said
- Treat Michelle like any other member of the class
- Acknowledge Michelle's speech difficulties without labeling her
- Help Michelle feel in control of her speech

Not surprisingly, because of the open, honest, and compassionate way that Michelle's needs have been addressed, the class is very supportive, and Michelle is making leaps and bounds with her class participation.

Ms. Boone also uses a variety of cooperative learning strategies to promote student-to-student communication (Timler, Vogler-Elias, & McGill, 2007). The classroom environment is set up with engaging materials and small-group arrangements that promote conversations about what is being learned. Ms. Boone believes that learning is facilitated by social interaction, and so she has structured her classroom environment and routine to facilitate communication (Timler et al., 2007). Even with this language-rich environment in which the children's communication is intentionally enhanced, Ms. Boone knows that some of her students will need more support. She works closely with the school's speech-language pathologist, Mrs. Henley, to help her students with more intense needs.

▲ Tier II: Collaborative Interventions

In addition to Michelle, Ms. Boone's fifth-grade class has three students with language-related learning disabilities, two students who are English-language learners, Pedro and Gyanna, and one student with Asperger's syndrome, Drew (see Chapter 5). Many of these children seemed reluctant to participate in the literature seminars that the class held every other week. To help with this, Mrs. Henley worked with a small group of children, giving them explicit instruction on the "language routines" used by Ms. Boone during literacy seminars (Ritzman, Sanger, & Coufal, 2006). She explicitly taught them the rules of participation, and the students practiced their new participation skills until they could use them comfortably (Timler et al., 2007). During the seminars Mrs. Henley prompted the students to remember their "participation rules" when they wanted to contribute. Eventually students were able to participate without explicit prompting. Pedro and Gyanna also worked with the English-language learners (ELL) teacher prior to each seminar to review key vocabulary that would be used and to explore answers to the questions that would be discussed. These preliminary activities helped both children feel more confident in participating during the seminars.

To help Michelle become more comfortable participating in the classroom, Mrs. Henley and Ms. Boone used a similar approach called "planned participation" that gave Michelle time to prepare and practice what she wanted to say. They also focused on Michelle's strength in poetry writing by creating a "Friday Poets Corner," in which students could share their poems. Classroom teachers can be particularly helpful to the child who stutters by working with the speech-language pathologist to create planned opportunities for the child to participate in speaking activities that are appropriate for practicing newly acquired fluency skills at increasing levels of complexity.

Speech-language pathologists increasingly are working directly with children in the general education classroom, supporting the academic program. They may alert students to pay attention to verbal or written instructions, encourage them to ask pertinent questions and to participate in discussions, and assist them in responding in a culture- and classroom-appropriate fashion. The speech-language pathologist helps teachers facilitate communication with the child in natural settings, including the classroom (Salend & Salinas, 2003).

Speech-language pathologists also use many techniques to promote the carryover of newly acquired communication skills into the classroom and everyday conversation. These techniques include children's notebooks prepared by therapists that are kept in the classroom for the teacher's regular review, weekly conferences with teachers regarding specific objectives, the use of devices and props as reminders, and carefully planned in-class "talking" activities. A major task of the communication specialist is to help the classroom teacher use these tools effectively, because the teacher's help is vital to success. The speech-language pathologist helps by suggesting strategies that encourage talk, expand talk, and model correct forms and usage. She may help the teacher set up effective peer-mediated social supports (Goldstein, Schneider, & Thiemann, 2007) and may help teach students self-advocacy skills so that they can communicate their needs (Ritzman, Sanger, & Coufal, 2006).

The teacher's creativity in adapting classroom opportunities to foster ways of talking will help the student to generalize these new skills. The classroom is often the most appropriate setting for incidental and interactive functional teaching (Fey, Windsor, & Warren, 1995). For some children, however, more individualized support is needed, and for these children Tier III services must be provided to help them be successful.

▲ Tier III: Individualized Educational Services

At Tier III, the services are specifically designed to meet the individual needs of the student. The child's individualized education program (IEP) will specify the services needed and will determine the related services that are essential to his or her success. Because the needs of each child are unique, a speech-language pathologist must be prepared to deal with a broad range of disorders. The speech-language pathologist provides support for students who may have primary articulation, fluency, voice, and/or language disorders. She or he must also be able to address the problems found among children with cleft palate, intellectual and developmental delays, cerebral palsy, learning disabilities, and emotional disturbances; children who are learning impaired; and students who are deaf (Hanks & Velaski, 2003). To address the wide variety of needs, the speech-language pathologist must be able to manage multiple roles (Ritzman et al., 2006).

▲ Roles of the Speech-Language Pathologist

Speech-language pathologists support children who have communication needs by:

- providing individual therapy
- consulting with the child's teacher about effective ways to assist the child in the classroom
- Working with the entire class on skills, strategies, and/or creating a climate of support
- Working in close partnership with the family
- Working with vocational teachers and counselors to establish goals for work
- Providing direct support for individual children in the classroom, cuing them as to when to ask questions and encouraging them to participate in discussion and to interact verbally

Classroom teachers work closely with speech language pathologists, so understanding the specialized terminology that they use is important. Table 8.5 gives the definitions of terms that are commonly used in speech-language pathology.

TABLE 8.5
Terms That Speech-Language Pathologists Use to Describe Communication Disorders

Term	Disorder
Apraxia	Impairment in the ability to plan the movement for speech
Aphasia	Impairment in the ability to communicate due to brain damage
Dysarthria	Articulation or voice disorder due to impaired motor control problems of throat, tongue, or lips
Anarthria	Loss of the ability to speak
Dysphonia	A disorder of voice quality
Stuttering	A disorder of fluency: repetitions, prolongations, and hesitations of sounds and syllables

▲ Specific Strategies to Support English-Language Learners

Understanding the linguistic competencies of children whose primary language is not English can be tricky. Earlier in the chapter we looked at a variety of things that make it more challenging to recognize language delays and disorders in children who are English-language learners, and so it should come as no surprise that meeting the needs of bilingual children can also be challenging. The strategies given here are meant to be a starting place for teachers and can provide a foundation for interventions at Tiers I and II.

These strategies address the two areas of language competency that English-language learners need: (1) basic interpersonal communication skills and (2) cognitive/academic language proficiency (Bunce, 2003). In other words, children must be able to communicate with others socially, *and* they need the more specialized language skills required for success in school. Brice, Miller, and Brice (2006) offer the following ideas for teachers to help English-language learners strengthen their communication:

1. Build lessons around the child's background knowledge and bridge this to the new learnings.

2. Provide written copies of directions and key instructions and use pictures to show what is expected.

3. Ask prediction questions that are open-ended to allow children to contribute a variety of knowledge (for example, "What do you think…?").

4. Teach self-study skills (for example, note-taking, organization, and test-taking strategies).

5. Encourage students to ask questions and participate in discussions.

6. Model correct language forms and employ appropriate wait times (e.g., be patient and give 3 to 5 seconds or more to let students think) to allow students to respond.

7. Teach language routines to help the child in typical situations (e.g., asking questions, getting what he or she needs, and providing information).

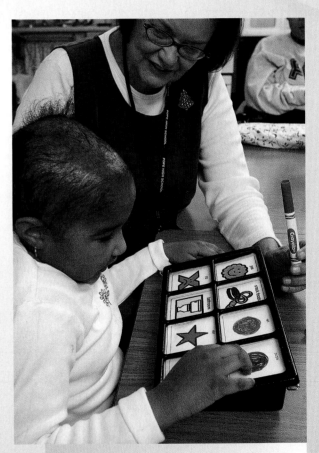

Supporting communication is critical to the child's development.
(© Robin Nelson/Photo Edit)

8. Use grammar drills and direct instruction to support skill development.

9. Practice formalized or structured speaking and allow students to "rehearse."

10. Allow for code switching and code mixing (the use of the primary language interspersed with English is natural as the second language emerges).

11. When students have reached a higher level of proficiency with English, use more complex sentences.

12. Explicitly teach vocabulary that is needed in the learning context.

Perhaps most important, in working to meet the needs of children who are English-language learners and who have communication disorders, we must establish a collaborative team that includes the classroom teacher, the bilingual education specialist, the special education teacher, the speech-language pathologist, and the child's parents.

 TeachSource VIDEO CONNECTION

Tyler: Augmentative Communication Techniques for a Kindergarten Student with Autism and Language Issues

Visit the Education CourseMate website to access this TeachSource Video Case. In this video, you will meet Tyler, his teacher Whitney Mead, and his speech-language pathologist, Becky Paden. Tyler uses the Picture Exchange Communication System (PECS), an augmentative communication approach, to help him express his thoughts, needs, and wants. As you watch this video, reflect on the strategies his teachers use to support Tyler's communication abilities. What strategies did Ms. Paden suggest that might be used with all children to enhance communication? How did Ms. Meade help her students develop their pragmatic language skills?

 ## Assistive Technology for Augmentative and Alternative Communication

When speech disorders are severe enough to make oral communication difficult, students will need additional assistive technology supports to help them communicate. Assistive technology includes approaches and devices that support communication, and help the child to express his or her thoughts, needs, wants, and ideas. The primary forms of assistive technology for children with communication, language, and speech disorders are **augmentative and alternative communication** devices or approaches (ASHA, 2010). Augmentative communication strategies are often used to prompt or promote the development of speech by helping the child use words to communicate. Individuals with severe speech difficulties, however, can use augmentative or alternative communication to supplement or replace talking. Some communication systems do *not* provide voice output, and so the person who is receiving the message must be physically present to understand what is being communicated. In other words, the communication must be seen—such as gestures, body language, sign language, and communication boards. Because of this, these communication approaches are not useful with telephones or for communication from room to room. **American Sign Language (ASL)**, an alternative communication system of gestures that contain meaning, is an example of a non-speech communication system and is discussed in more detail in Chapter 10. Other augmentative communication devices simulate or enhance speech. Assistive technology for communication varies in its level of sophistication. One device for supporting communication is the communication board. Communication boards vary in complexity from a set of simple pictures (for example, pictures of a glass of milk and a glass of juice) to sophisticated groups of letters, words, pictures, and special symbols (DiCarlo, Banajee, & Buras-Stricklin, 2000). More sophisticated communication boards produce speech when they are used.

(continued)

Blissymbolics is a computerized communication system that uses graphic symbols or "blisswords" to help the child communicate. Figure 8.6 shows some sample blisswords that might be used for communication. Using Blissymbolics, the child points to or touches the word he or she wants, and forms sentences to express thoughts. This allows a child with severely limited speech to "talk." This is the system that Sara, who you met in the Exceptional Lives, Exceptional Stories section of this chapter uses to communicate. You may want to revisit her story to think about how assistive technology can change someone's life. The pic-ture exchange communication system is another way to augment communication, helping students increase their vocabulary and expand their communication. Tyler, a kindergartener with Autism, uses this approach in the TeachSource video that you can watch as part of this chapter.

The most important thing to remember about the use of augmentative and alternative communication supports is that the more a child communicates, the stronger his or her ability to communicate becomes! This means that we should support communication through a variety of means to enhance the child's development.

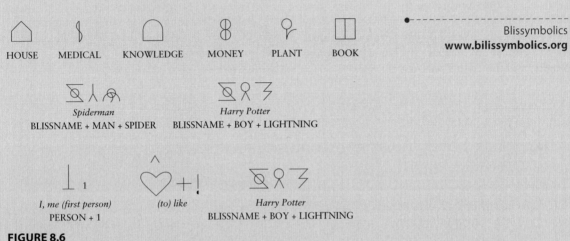

FIGURE 8.6
Sample Blisswords
Blissymbolics is a computerized communication system that uses graphic symbols or "blisswords" to help the child communicate. Almost any word in the English language can be described using a combination of blisswords.

Family and Lifespan Issues

Parents are the child's first teachers, and in no area is this more true than in the language a child develops. If you look back at Table 8.1, you will see the amazing progress that children make in their language during the first few years of life. The parent or primary caregiver can do a lot to support early language development. In the first few years of life, talking with the child is essential. Talking about colors, counting, identifying the names of objects, playing word repetition games, and sharing nursery rhymes are all part of the early language stimulation of young children. The parent can also help the child become more aware of sounds by reinforcing the familiar sounds of the environment (for example, "The clock goes tick-tick-tick"; "The car goes vroom!"; "What does the cat say?"). Reading with young children further extends their understanding of language and can be the perfect time for discussions of pictures, ideas, and actions in the story. As the child grows, it is important that early attempts to communicate are taken seriously. Children thrive when adults listen to them and seem interested in what they have to say. Often grandparents play a special role in the child's life because they take the time to listen to the child and are genuinely interested in what the child has to say.

Technology and Media Division of the Council for Exceptional Children
www.tamcec.org

How Parents Can Support Their Child's Communication

If the child says "Wa doo," the parent may say, "I don't understand; tell me again." The child repeats "Wa doo," looking at the refrigerator. The parent then says, "Oh, you want some juice," and gives it to the child. The parent can also be taught to use *recasting,* or modeling the correct pronunciation without correcting the child's speech. For example, in response to the question "What do we call that big cat?" the child says "a wion," and the parent says, "yes, that big cat is a lion." At no time does the parent interrupt the child and tell him or her, "Say *lion*." Responses by the adult that build on what the child is communicating are also referred to as *following directives,* and they have been shown to facilitate the child's language development (McCathren, Yoder, & Warren, 1995). When adults follow the child's lead, talking about what the child is interested in, the child is likely to be more engaged in the conversation and will use and learn more words (Southern California Comprehensive Assistance Center, 2005; Justice, Mashburn, Hamre, & Pianta, 2008).

When we focus on the social use of language (pragmatics) and stress functional communication, we can support language development in natural environments. Using an interactive approach, the interventionist—a parent, special education teacher, or speech-language pathologist—capitalizes on the natural inclination of the child to talk about what he or she is doing, plans to do, or wants to do. To encourage correct word and language use, the adult provides support while the child is eating, playing, or visiting community settings such as a

Technology can enhance communication in many ways.
(© Able Images/Getty)

Parents are children's first language teachers, and the early language environment of children plays a significant role in their language development.

grocery store (Hyter, 2007). Working in settings in which talking and listening occur naturally helps to increase the child's amount of talk (Bloom, 1991), and the more the child talks, the more he or she will gradually gain accuracy and increase his or her vocabulary.

Transitions for Students with Communication Disorders

What lies ahead for the child who has a communication disorder? The answer to this question depends on the nature and severity of the disorder. Children who have primary articulation disorders (that is, a speech or language disorder not associated with other disabilities) seem to have few related problems as adults. In contrast, follow-up studies of children with severe disorders show that some children with language deficits continue to have problems in academics, interpersonal relationships, and work. What is clear, however, is that early support can help to minimize secondary problems and in some cases it can help a child overcome the speech disorders.

Important changes have come about in helping students with communication disorders make transitions from high school to college and the workplace. Many colleges and universities have support services and special programs for students with disabilities. Special clinics and help sessions are staffed by speech-language pathologists, learning disabilities specialists, and psychologists. Supports offered may include individualized techniques for note taking, class participation, and writing. Job coaches can help individuals with the pragmatics of work-related communication to allow individuals to be successful in employment settings (Montgomery, 2006). Augmentative and alternative communication systems can be developed to meet work-related needs, and assistive technologies can be used to support communication. Because communication is so critical to an individual's successes, every effort must be made to support effective and appropriate communication. Appropriate supports and interventions that are provided early and continued for as long as necessary can help the individual develop his or her communication skills.

moral dilemma

Children with Communication Disorders

Collaboration among classroom teachers, special education teachers, and speech-language pathologists is essential to providing the full support that a child with communication disorders needs across all three tiers of intervention. A good example of collaboration was presented in the Educational Responses section of this chapter (see pages 270–274). But collaboration is not always easy to accomplish. What can you do if one of the professionals who is key to the child's success will not work as part of a team? What are some of the personal and professional obstacles to collaboration, and how can you help a colleague overcome these? What should you do if you feel a child is being harmed by a colleague's resistance to collaboration?

To answer these questions online, visit the Education CourseMate website.

✸ Summary

▶ The formation of the American Speech and Hearing Association in 1925 was critical to the formation of the field of speech and language disorders was.

▶ Children with communication, language, and speech disorders have a wide range of strengths and needs that impact their learning.

▶ Communication is an essential part of being human, and it requires a sender, a message, and a receiver.

▶ Language is a code in which signs, sounds, and symbols represent feelings, ideas, and information.

▶ Language is both receptive and expressive and can be described as having form, content, and function.

▶ Language form includes phonology, morphology, and syntax; semantics refers to content; and function includes pragmatics and supralinguistics.

▶ Speech is the systematic oral production of the words of a given language.

▶ Processes needed to produce speech are respiration, phonation, resonation, articulation, audition, and symbolization/organization.

▶ Typically language development follows a pattern of emerging complexity moving from sounds to words and sentences that convey meaning.

▶ A language disorder is impaired comprehension and/or use of spoken, written, and/or other symbol systems.

▶ Speech disorders include problems with articulation, fluency, and voice.

▶ Understanding normal patterns of language acquisition is an important part of identifying children with language disorders.

▶ A comprehensive assessment is essential to identifying communication, language, and speech disorders.

▶ Because communication, language, and speech disorders often co-exist with other areas of disability it is difficult to determine the prevalence of these for children.

▶ Understanding a child's cultural and linguistic background is necessary to correctly identify and support children with language disorders.

▶ Individuals with disabilities may also have communication disorders.

▶ Recognizing communication disorders in children whose primary language is not English can be challenging and may require a specialist who is both bilingual and bicultural.

▶ The role of the speech-language pathologist has expanded in the schools to include coteaching of children within the general education classroom.

▶ Assistive technologies including augmentative or alternative communication devices and approaches may be needed for individuals with limited speech.

▶ Parents and families can provide essential support for a child's development of language.

Future Challenges

1 *How can schools provide the time and resources needed to allow teachers to collaborate as they work to meet the needs of their students?*

Collaboration between general education teachers and specialists is essential to supporting children with communication, language, and speech disorders, yet often teachers find that this is difficult to accomplish. Barriers to collaboration include a lack of time, limited shared resources, and difficulties with caseloads or class size. If we truly believe that collaboration is necessary, how can we find ways to support teachers and related service providers so that they can work together meaningfully?

2 *How can early intervention materials be made more available to parents and physicians?*

Most speech disorders are not identifiable until a child reaches 2 years of age, when verbal language ability usually appears. Unfortunately, parents frequently do not recognize early signs of potential speech disorders in the prelinguistic stage. How can we make information on prelingual indicators of potential difficulty more available to both pediatricians and parents?

3 *How can we provide appropriate services for children with communication, language, and speech problems who are also English-language learners?*

Our schools are serving increasing numbers of children whose primary language is not English. When communication, language, and speech problems exist in children who are bilingual, it can be more difficult for school personnel to recognize, identify, and meet the child's needs. How can we address the communication, language, and speech needs of bilingual children and their families?

Key Terms

American Sign Language (ASL) p. 273

articulation p. 254

articulation disorders p. 260

audition p. 254

augmentative and alternative communication p. 273

cleft palate p. 260

communication p. 251

communication disorders p. 257

dialect p. 263

dysphonia p. 261

expressive language p. 252

fluency p. 254

language p. 252

language content p. 253

language disorders p. 259

language form p. 253

language function p. 253

language pragmatics p. 250

morphology p. 253

phonation p. 254

phonology p. 253

pragmatics p. 253

receptive language p. 252

related services p. 267

resonation p. 254

respiration p. 254

speech p. 254

speech disorders p. 260

stuttering p. 262

supralinguistics p. 253

syntax p. 253

voice p. 254

voice disorder p. 261

Resources

References of Special Interest

Justice, L. (2010). *Communication sciences and disorders: A contemporary perspective* (2nd ed.). Canada: Pearson. This is a literacy-focused look at the development of speaking, listening, reading, and writing and the ecological impact of communication disorders at home, school, work, and within the community.

Bloom, L., & Tinker, E. (2001). The intentionality model and language acquisition. *Monographs of the Society for Research in Child Development, 66*(4), 1–91.

An excellent presentation of language acquisition, as well as a critique of current theories and the presentation of an integrated theory.

McCormick, L., Loeb, D. F., & Schiefelbusch, R. L. (2003). *Supporting children with communication difficulties in inclusive settings: School-based language intervention* (2nd ed.). Needham Heights, MA: Allyn & Bacon.

Paul, R. (2006). *Language disorders from infancy through adolescence: Assessment and intervention.* St. Louis, MO: Mosby. A comprehensive presentation of assessment strategies for a wide array of speech-language disorders, as well as suggestions for intervention.

Journals

American Journal of Speech-Language Pathology
http://ajslp.asha.org/

Communication Disorders Quarterly
www.proedinc.com; www.cec.sped.org

Journal of Special Education Technology
http://www.tamcec.org/jset/; www.cec.sped.org

Journal of Speech-Language, Pathology, and Audiology
www.caslpa.ca/english/resources/jslpa.asp

Journal of Speech, Language, and Hearing Research
http://jslhr.asha.org/

Topics in Language Disorders
http://www.topicsinlanguagedisorders.com

Professional Organizations

American Speech-Language-Hearing Association (ASHA) **www.asha.org/**

Division for Communicative Disabilities and Deafness **http://www.dcdd.us/**

Division for Communicative Disabilities and Deafness of the Council for Exceptional Children **www.cec.org**

Technology and Media Division of the Council for Exceptional Children **www.tamcec.org**

Visit the Education CourseMate website for additional TeachSource Video Cases, information about CEC standards, study tools, and much more.

Children Who Have Special Gifts and Talents

Focus Questions

- What evidence exists that children with special gifts and talents will play a significant role in society in adulthood?
- What are the current components of definitions for children with special gifts and talents (SGT)?
- What are some of the key dimensions of encouraging creativity in students with SGT?
- What are typical characteristics of students with SGT?
- How does the information processing model explain special gifts and talents?
- How can we find children with "hidden SGT" in communities with poor environmental conditions?
- How are students with SGT identified?
- What are the major elements of a differentiated program for children with SGT?
- What changes in curriculum and teaching strategies are needed for children with SGT?
- What other exceptionalities can students with SGT have?
- How have technological advances aided in educational programming for children with SGT?

© Bob Daemmrich/Photo Edit

We can all picture the two or three most intelligent persons that we have ever met. We have been impressed by the breadth of their knowledge and skills and sometimes are envious of how effortlessly they learn or play an instrument. We may have even wondered where such talent came from. Was it merely a lucky roll of the genetic dice, or did their parents and teachers have something to do with the flowering of this talent? Were they always so superior in development? Are there others in our society who have great talent that, for a variety of reasons, have not been discovered or enhanced?

One thing is certain: As educators we need to do more than stand in awe of their abilities. We need to find ways to help them develop and extend these creative abilities because creations in new art, new scientific inventions, and business innovations will likely come from their gifts and talents.

No matter how intelligent they are, these students won't discover algebra on their own, nor learn how to write a sonnet, or play a saxophone or violin. Their special abilities are raw materials that need to be nurtured. This chapter describes these gifted and talented individuals and shares what we have learned about the best ways to educate them.

 ## Why Should We Care?

Aside from the commitment to help all students do the best they can, why should we spend special time and resources on children with special gifts and talents (SGT)? We have learned that students with SGT can have an important impact on the future of our society.

The National Academy of Sciences assembled a distinguished panel composed of Nobel prizewinners, university presidents, and CEOs of major corporations to produce a report on the status of students with SGT in American society, with particular reference to math and science. This panel concluded with some serious concerns in a report, *Rising Above the Gathering Storm* (2006).

Following are some of the indicators the panel members noticed:

- U.S. 12th graders recently performed below average for 21 countries on a test of general knowledge in mathematics and science.

- In 2004, China graduated about 500,000 engineers and India graduated 200,000, as compared with 70,000 in America.

- In 2001, U.S. industry spent more on tort litigation than on research and development.

Following are a few of the many recommendations made by the panel:

- Create 10,000 four-year scholarships in math and science to capture the best minds in our society.

- Increase teacher training to stress innovation and creativity.

- Increase funds for research for a number of federal agencies, such as the National Science Foundation and NASA.

These recommendations were turned into legislation through the America Competes Act (P.L. 110–69), but it is still not clear what level of resources will be devoted to this purpose. Indeed, it has not yet been determined whether major investments in math and science will help American society more than investments in the social sciences or communications. This is the latest of many efforts to alert the American public to the importance of educating students with SGT. Previous efforts include:

- The Marland Report (Marland, 1972)
- *A Nation at Risk* (D. Gardner, 1981)
- National Excellence (Ross, 1994)
- Rising Above the Gathering Storm (Augustine, 2007)

Definitions of Special Gifts and Talents (Gifted)

> Early rapid development is a key indicator of special gifts and talents.

The term *gifted* traditionally has been used to refer to people with intellectual gifts, and we use it here in the same way. Each culture defines *giftedness* in its own image, in terms of the abilities that that culture values. Ancient Greeks honored the philosopher and the orator, and Romans valued the engineer and the soldier. From a society's definition of giftedness, we learn something about the values and lifestyles of that culture. We also learn that the exceptional person often is defined by both individual ability and societal needs.

Federal Definition of Students Who Are Gifted

Children and youth with outstanding talent perform, or show the potential for performing, at remarkably high levels of accomplishment when compared with others of their age, experience, or environment.

These children and youth exhibit high-performance capability in intellectual, creative, and/or artistic areas; possess an unusual leadership capacity; or excel in specific academic fields. They require services or activities not ordinarily provided by the schools.

Outstanding talents are present in children and youth from all cultural groups, across all economic strata, and in all areas of human endeavor.

Source: P. Ross (Ed.). (1993). *National Excellence.* Washington, D.C.: U.S. Department of Education.

In the United States, early definitions of giftedness were tied to performance on the Stanford-Binet Intelligence Test, which Lewis Terman developed during and after World War I. Children who scored an intelligent quotient (IQ) score above an agreed-on point—such as 130 or 140—were called gifted. They represented from 1 to 3 percent of their age-group population (Terman & Oden, 1947).

Essentially, a high score on the Stanford-Binet or the Wechsler Intelligence Scale for Children (WISC) or on other intelligence tests meant that children were developing intellectually more rapidly than their agemates. What was unique was not so much *what* they were doing as *when*, developmentally, they were doing it. A child playing chess is not a phenomenon, but a child playing chess seriously at age 5 is. Many children write poetry, but not at age 6, when most are just learning to read. Early rapid development is one of the clear indicators of high intellectual ability, and that is what intelligence tests measure.

It was long thought that intelligence was distributed in society in conformity with the normal curve, with many students likely to have about average IQ scores of 100 and much fewer expected to score extremely high. This "normal curve" distribution of scores was one of the reasons for assuming that intelligence was a biological property, similar to characteristics such as height and weight, which showed normal curve distributions.

But now we have evidence that intelligence scores do *not* form a normal distribution, certainly not at the extreme ends (Robinson, Zigler, & Gallagher, 2000; Silverman, 1997). Few children's IQ scores fall below 70 without some pathological cause, and there seem to be many more youngsters at the top end of the distribution (scoring over 140) than would be expected on the basis of a normal curve distribution (Silverman, 1997). (The authors' view of this estimate is shown in Figure 9.1.)

When we combine this discovery with investigations that suggest that entire populations of countries are performing better on tests of ability than they had a generation before (Flynn, 1999), we must confront the notion that IQ scores are *not* fixed for an individual or a society but can be improved with education and experience. We are *not* limited in the number of highly intelligent students we can produce but have as a prospect a gradually increasing number of highly intelligent people—if we are wise enough to create the conditions for their development.

Over the past few decades, periodic efforts have been made to broaden the definition of giftedness to include more than abilities directly related to schoolwork. See "Federal Definitions of Students Who Are Gifted" for a federal definition of children who have SGT. There are many phrases within this definition that reveal our current thinking about these students with SGT. The

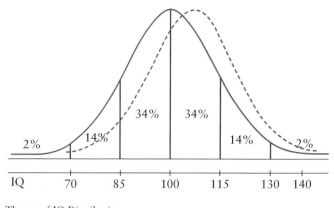

Theory of IQ Distribution _____

Reality of IQ Distribution - - - - - - - - - - - - - ·

FIGURE 9.1
IQ Distribution Over the Population

Chess is one game that can reveal special gifts and talents in young children.

(© Bob Daemmrich/ The Image Works)

> Children from all cultural groups, economic levels, and areas of human endeavor show outstanding gifts and talents.

phrase "show the potential for performing" means that we accept the idea that children can have special gifts without showing excellent performance. "Compared with others of their age, experience, or environment" means that we accept the important role of environment and context in developing students with gifts. The phrase "require services...not ordinarily provided" means that we expect that school systems will and should modify their services and programs to take into account the different levels of development of these students. "Outstanding talents are present in children...from all cultural groups, across all economic strata" means that we expect to find gifted abilities in all racial and ethnic groups.

As far back as one can go in recorded history, concern about the nurturing of children with gifts has been evidenced. Plato, for example, was convinced that Athenian democracy could sustain its greatness only by providing the best educational opportunities for selected young people, who would then become the society's leaders. Other leaders expressed these ideas in similar fashion (Tannenbaum, 2000).

One Gift or Many?

Should giftedness be regarded as one overriding general mental ability or as a series of special abilities? Howard Gardner is one of the latest of a group of psychologists to view giftedness as a series of special abilities (Ramos & Gardner, 2003). He has proposed a list of nine distinct and separate abilities called **multiple intelligences** that need specific educational attention: *linguistic, logical-mathematical, musical, spatial, bodily-kinesthetic, interpersonal, intrapersonal,* and *naturalist.* (*Existential* is another ability which is often included, but it is unconfirmed.) (See Chapter 2 for more detailed descriptions of Gardner's multiple intelligences theory.)

Everyone knows persons who are particularly good at one or two of the abilities listed by Gardner but who are not superior in them all. Think of a student who is a math whiz but is not an expert in linguistic or interpersonal intelligence. Some students seem to be particularly gifted in spatial intelligence but have only above-average ability in other areas. Although all these abilities seem to be positively correlated with one another, and although students who have outstanding talents in one area are often good in the other areas as well, we can find concrete examples of specialists in outstanding performance. Students who score highly on tests of spatial skills tend to do better in mathematics and science courses. Consequently, the educational issue becomes not only how to plan one *overall* program for students who have talents in many of these areas but also

Extraordinary ability has been found in all racial and ethnic groups and genders.

(© Corbis)

what should be done with students who have specialized talents in a single area such as mathematics, visual perception, or interpersonal relationships.

High ability is not the sole predictor of student productivity but only the base on which the student must build. *Extended practice, dedication,* and *high motivation to succeed* are the characteristics necessary to complete the portrait of a productive person. These are easily recognized components of the successful athlete or musician, and so this should be of no surprise to educators. The school and educators can play a significant role by exciting the student about learning, and providing resources and access to advanced knowledge that keep a student's high motivation alive. One strategy to enhance students' motivation was developed by Dweck (2007).

Dweck provided school-age students with an explanation of how the brain develops, an explanation that, in turn, increased their motivation and drive to learn. She explained that the brain is like a muscle—the more they exercise it, the stronger it becomes. They learned that every time they try hard and learn something new, their brain forms new connections that, over time, make them smarter. They learned that intellectual development is not the natural unfolding of intelligence but rather the formation of new connections in the brain brought about through effort and learning (Dweck, 2007, p. 38). This is important information for all educators to have.

> Extended practice, dedication, and high motivation to succeed are the characteristics needed for productive individuals.

Children of Extraordinary Ability

It is generally accepted today that superior intellectual ability often predicts high academic performance and favorable personal adjustment. But doubts linger about the youngster of extraordinary ability—the 1 in 100,000 at the level of an Einstein. What happens to the student who is seven or eight years ahead of his or her age group in intellectual development?

One of the standard assumptions has been that once the threshold of an IQ of 120 or 130 is reached, intellectual or artistic production depends on other factors such as motivation and persistence. These characteristics are certainly important, but the notion that there is a ceiling on the importance of IQ level is incorrect.

Lubinski (2009) reported on over 2,000 students that represented the top 1 percent of ability drawn from the School Mathematics Precocious Youth Project (SMPY). When these students were divided into quartiles, the top quartile was enormously more productive than the bottom, even within the top 1 percent. The top quartile received many more doctoral degrees, wrote more scientific articles, were named on more patents, had higher income, and had more literary publications than did the lowest quartile. As Lubinski commented, "Overall, there does *not* seem to be an ability threshold within the top 1%" (p. 353). So higher IQs can make a difference in performance.

The great developmental distance between youngsters with SGT and their peers necessitates individual programs for them, not unlike the individualized education programs (IEPs) proposed for children with disabilities. These special programs and services should consider **acceleration**, moving the student through the system more rapidly, and some form of tutoring or mentoring by adults with special knowledge in the student's area of special interest (Silverman, 1998).

Extraordinarily precocious students represent one of our greatest and rarest natural resources. We must learn more about them to understand the origin of their giftedness and ways to help them adapt to an often difficult social environment.

> In the federal definition of "Students Who Are Gifted," "shows the potential for performing" means a student can have SGT without performing well academically.

Terry and Lenny

Thanks to Dr. Julian Stanley, who began the Study of Mathematically Precocious Youth (SMPY) in 1971, we have gathered a picture of children of outstanding ability over time. Two of the most outstanding are Terry and Lenny, whose mathematical abilities flourished early. The schools they attended and their parents were flexible enough to adapt to the special abilities of these boys (Muratori et al., 2006).

Terry: Terry, who grew up in Australia, taught himself to read by watching *Sesame Street* at age 2. By age 3 he had learned to read, type, and solve mathematical puzzles designed for 8-year-olds. At age 5 he was placed in a split first- and second-grade class but took math with fifth graders. In three years he had mastered the elementary curriculum and was placed in eleventh-grade mathematics. He finished undergraduate work at age 15 and received a PhD in mathematics from Princeton University at age 21.

His parents and mentors took care that he had social interaction with his peers and was not distracted by the notoriety that accompanied his obviously unusual development. Terry's father commented on his friendly personality. When he was little he was liked by his classmates and teachers, and now he is equally liked by his colleagues, peers, and students. He is now a parent himself and a professor of mathematics at UCLA. When asked what advice he would give to other talented students, he said:

> Well, don't be afraid to explore and be prepared to learn new things continually. . . . I remember in high school thinking I understand what mathematics and physics were all about only to discover so many wonderful things about these subjects in college that I had no idea existed in high school (p. 313).

Lenny: Lenny grew up in a university town in North Carolina. Lenny came to the attention of many people when, as a 10-year-old, he earned a perfect score on the SAT mathematics test. During his participation in SMPY, he was referred to as "the smartest kid in the United States," yet he was a friendly and gregarious boy interested in music and sports, interests he has carried into adulthood.

He excelled on various tests, obtaining a perfect score on the College Board Test of Standard English at age 11 and also on all three parts of the Graduate Record Examination. He led the United States team in the International Mathematical Olympiad and helped the team win two gold medals and one silver medal, the first time the United States was able to do so. He also won distinction in the National Spelling Bee and the Westinghouse Science Competition.

Unlike Terry, Lenny was not moved through the school program so rapidly, skipping only the third grade. His parents discouraged rapid acceleration in favor of good social and emotional development, although he took many university classes while in high school and eventually went to Harvard University at age 16. He now has his PhD from the Massachusetts Institute of Technology and is a professor at Duke University. Despite growing up on different continents, Terry and Lenny both had intelligent and well-educated parents who wished for their boys good achievement but also happy social and emotional development. They will likely make major contributions to mathematics and to our country's scientific advancement. (Students who wish to learn more about Terry and Lenny through their own accounts of their childhood and schooling may visit our website to read detailed interviews with the two men.)

Not all stories of outstanding talent have such happy endings. One counterexample is provided by the early life of Norbert Wiener, another famous mathematics **prodigy** who coined the word *cybernetics*. His unhappy childhood is detailed in his autobiography, *Ex-Prodigy: My Childhood and Youth* (Wiener, 1953).

What is clear is that such unusual talent has to be guided in an intelligent way, with the education system remaining flexible and adaptive to these students' needs. If this occurs, there is no reason not to expect other happy stories such as those of Terry and Lenny.

Pivotal Issues

- How many years should a child like Terry and Lenny be advanced in school?

- What kinds of special mentoring would be helpful for a child like Terry or Lenny?

Do Special Gifts and Talents Persist into Adulthood?

One of the most often-asked questions about students with SGT is What actually happens to them as adults? Do they continue to do well, or do they slump and become average or even underachievers? One way to answer that question is to use longitudinal studies that follow children into adulthood, which we now have.

After his revision and the publication of the Binet-Simon Tests of Intelligence in 1916, Lewis Terman, a professor of psychology at Stanford University, turned his attention to children with SGT. In 1920, he began a study of 1,528 such children, which was to continue for more than sixty years.

Terman used teacher nominations and group intelligence tests to screen California students. He based the final selection of children on their performance on the Stanford-Binet Intelligence Scale. The characteristics of this group of high-IQ students were, on average, favorable in practically every developmental and socioemotional dimension. The group did well not only in school and career but also in areas such as mental health, marriage, and character.

The final volume in the Terman series captures this population in their 60s and 70s (Holahan & Sears, 1995). The group continued to be superior in health, psychological well-being, and survival rates; when compared to the general population, the overall portrait was one of a privileged group of children who contributed substantially to their society as adults.

However, we have come to realize that Terman did not balance his sample of individuals with gifts. Through his identification process of young children using IQ tests as the tool for selecting students for his sample, he eliminated many potentially bright youngsters of low economic or immigrant status from the sample. For example, he failed to find two future Nobel Prize winners who were in school at the time of his study. As a consequence, what we are looking at in these lifespan results is largely what happens to gifted students from already well-established professional or managerial families. We don't know what happens to low-income or culturally different children who are gifted.

The Speyer School, a special elementary school in New York, was established through the work of Leta Hollingworth (1942), a pioneer in the education of children with special gifts. White and Renzulli (1987) conducted a forty-year follow-up of graduates of the school. Like the subjects in the Terman study, the majority of the men had entered professions, whereas the women tended to combine career and family. Their memories of the school were vivid. And "they all believed that their experience at Speyer School was instrumental in providing them with peer interaction for the first time, exposing them to competition, causing them to learn and like school for the first time, giving them a strong desire to excel" (1987, p. 90).

Although no one in the group had made an earth-shaking discovery or contribution, most seemed to be contributing substantially to the quality of society in what they were doing. Remember that individuals can be extraordinarily successful and make major contributions in their own field, such as business, science, the arts, or religion and still be virtually unknown to the general public. (Can you name three of the country's outstanding biochemists? Can you name one?)

One of the recurring questions regarding longitudinal studies such as the one that Terman and his associates did is, Are the results due to the students or to the culture and times (the context) in which the study took place? A more recent study provides some information on this issue (Subotnik, Kassan, Summers, & Wasser, 1993). In the 1940s, a special elementary school was established at Hunter College in New York City. The school was highly selective in the students it

> On average, children who are identified as having gifts grow up to become well-adjusted adults, successful in their chosen careers.

enrolled. In educational attainment, the results were similar to those reported by the Terman group. Over 80 percent held master's degrees, and 68 percent of the men and 40 percent of the women held doctorates in medicine, law, or some other area. They were in good health, mentally and physically, and were earning incomes as impressive as their educational attainments would suggest.

One major difference between the Terman and the Hunter Elementary samples was in the careers of the women. The vast majority of the women in the Hunter Elementary sample were employed and were satisfied with their careers. Fewer than 10 percent were homemakers exclusively. The interviews made it clear that the women's movement (context again!) had a decided effect on their becoming more oriented to work outside the home.

Subotnik and the other authors of the study (1993) were somewhat disappointed by the lack of drive for success or for extraordinary achievement that they found in the Hunter Elementary group. Most members of the group seemed content to do their professional jobs and enjoy their social lives and the opportunities their vocational success provided. The well-rounded students had become well-rounded, complacent adults. One of them remarked,

> This is a terrible thing to say, but I think I'm where I want to be—terrible because I've always thought that there should have been more challenges. I'm very admired and respected where I work.... I don't want to be a senior vice president.... I want to have time to spend with my family, to garden, to play tennis, and see my friends. I'm very happy with my life (p. 78).

There is little difference in emotional adjustment when comparing groups of students with gifts with students of average ability. On the other hand, the vast majority of these students became productive and useful citizens, and we might well ask whether we should expect more of them than that.

Another major study followed over 2,000 participants in the SMPY over 20 years to see what happened to these students who fell in the top 1 percent of measured ability on the SAT at age 13 (Lubinski & Benbow, 2006). The results were comparable to the earlier study in terms of large numbers attaining advanced degrees, even in their early thirties attaining more than five times the number of patents achieved in the general population and being prolific in writing scientific papers and literature. The authors believed that such results solidify the notion that mental ability is central to societal achievement and contribution.

Creativity

Creativity is a process that has fascinated educators and philosophers for centuries. How does one create something novel that was not there before? How did da Vinci, Picasso, the Brontë sisters, Einstein, Curie, Mozart, and many thousands of others accomplish their outstanding works? Can we as educators discover and enhance these talents that seem to be at the apex of human endeavor?

One researcher defined creativity as the ability to generate ideas, products, or solutions that are considered novel and useful for a given problem, situation, or context (Beghetto, 2008). (Note the emphasis on usefulness; many people produce "novel" thoughts, but with little utility.)

From the early work of Paul Torrance (1969) and Gretzels and Jackson (1962), we have tried to unravel the concepts of intelligence and creativity in order to

> Creativity can be seen as an interaction among persons, products, and environment.

TABLE 9.1
The Dimensions of Creativity

Dimensions	Behaviors Needed
Generating ideas	Producing multiple ideas to meet a task Cognitive characteristics like fluency, flexibility and originality, elaboration
Digging deeper into ideas	Desire to understand complexity Analyzing, synthesizing, resolving ambiguities, bringing order from disorder
Courage to explore ideas	Curiosity, playfulness, risk taking, sense of humor, tolerance of ambiguity, openness to experience, self-confidence
Listening to one's inner voice	Understanding of who you are, where you want to go, commitment to do whatever it takes to get there Persistence, self-direction, concentration, work ethic

Source: D. Treffinger, G. Young, E. Selby, & C. Sheperdson, *Assessing creativity: A guide for educators* (Storrs, CT: National Research Center on the Gifted and Talented, 2002). Reprinted with permission.

study and stimulate each. The recognition is growing that creativity is not so much a personal characteristic as it is a process that blends both thinking and personality. Treffinger, Young, Selby, and Shepardson (2002) present four different dimensions of the creative process, shown in Table 9.1

Generating ideas requires cognitive flexibility, whereas digging deeper into ideas requires more synthesis and reasoning power. Personality becomes more central to the courage to explore ideas, requiring risk taking and openness to experience. The final stage, listening to one's inner voice, deals with clearly envisioning what you wish to accomplish and determining to overcome obstacles—again, personality characteristics.

One reason that such disagreement exists among observers as to the essence of creativity is that different persons focus on different properties. Some stress generation of ideas; others possess the courage to explore ideas. What is clear, though, is that educators can help individuals develop these characteristics and reward them when the characteristics are acquired. It is also clear that no one is creative all the time or has all four of these components perpetually in play.

There seems to be substantial evidence from literature on many cultures that people are most creative when they are motivated primarily by the interest, enjoyment, satisfaction, and challenge of the work itself (i.e., "intrinsic motivation"). When we come to those forces that inhibit such motivation, we come to the current emphasis on **high-stakes testing**. By forcing students to learn a cluster of facts to prepare for these tests, we deprive them of the search for new ideas and intellectual adventures leading to creativity.

Hennessey & Annabele (2010) in an extensive review of creativity literature commented:

> One possibility is that with America's newfound emphasis on "high stakes testing" and other manifestations of the accountability movement has come a general de-emphasis on creative behavior in favor of the more easily quantified and assessed mastery of reading, writing, and arithmetic. (p. 587)

A similar finding was made in schools in China—specifically, that societal values and school pedagogic approaches impaired the creativity of students of that nation (Niu & Sternberg, 2003). So what are the positive environments that can enhance creativity?

It is increasingly clear that many general education classrooms, with their standard curricula, worksheets, and routine management, are destined to impede the development of independent thinking without meaning to do so.

Renzulli (2002) has been well known for his three intersecting rings of productivity: superior ability, creativity, and task commitment. He went further with Operation Houndstooth, which asks the question, "What causes some people to mobilize their interpersonal, political, ethical, and moral realms of being in such ways that they place human concerns and the common good above materialism, ego enhancement, and self-indulgence?" (Renzulli & Reed, 2008).

This document proposes that the following combination leads to intellectual productivity: optimism (positive feelings from hard work), courage (moral conviction), romance with a topic (passion), sensitivity to human concerns (empathy), physical/mental energy (curiosity), and sense of destiny (power to change). There is little doubt that such a combination should stir productivity. What remains is how educators can develop instruction that can enhance this collection of assets. How can we nurture the creativity shown in Katrina's poem?

A Poem Written by Katrina, a Gifted 7-Year-Old

INDECISION
She wears a colourful summery skirt
A thick dark purple coat.
Her house has a very dark blue roof
And a light yellow base
Her shutters are half closed half open

She likes to play with Crazy and Adventurous
But every time she goes to see them
She walks out the front door,
Then thinks she should have
Gone through the back door.

She really would like to eat hot food
But she prefers cold food.
She loves to cook
But normally eats out.

She would do things on the weekend
Except it takes till Monday to decide what.

(Katrina, age 7)

Source: D. Fraser, From the playful to the profound: What metaphors tell us about gifted children, *Roeper Review* 25 (4) (2003): 180–184. Reprinted with permission.

 # Characteristics of Children with Special Gifts and Talents

Are children born with SGT? Do outstanding abilities emerge no matter what opportunities or education a person has? What role does heredity play in giftedness? How important is the context for the child with special gifts?

Neurology and Brain Development
What We Know About SGT

Most of the research on brain function has been devoted to what happens when the brain doesn't function well (Newman, 2008). But another significant question is: What happens when the brain is operating efficiently, as it does with children with SGT?

One of the original ideas from neurology was that the frontal lobes were linked to intellectual ability and executive function. Such functions as control processing, strategy formulation, and monitoring the contents of working memory fit into this category.

But more recent evidence from a variety of MRI studies now suggests that the neural basis of giftedness is distributed throughout the brain, and it is the "interconnectiveness" of the brain (those fibers that link one part to another) that determines high efficiency (Just & Varma, 2007). While there are areas within the brain that have specialized functions, it is the ability of these areas to work together in synergy that contributes to giftedness. We are in just the beginning phases of the research on brain function with our new tools, such as magnetic resonance imagery (MRI), and more exciting discoveries await us.

Genetic Factors and SGT

More than one hundred years ago, Francis Galton, in a study of outstanding Englishmen, concluded that extraordinary ability ran in families and was genetic in origin. (Galton overlooked the environmental advantage of being born into an upper-class family.) Ever since, there has been a strong belief in the powerful role that heredity plays in producing mental ability. Certainly, studies of twins and the close relationship of the abilities of adoptive children to the abilities of their natural parents demand that we recognize a hereditary element (Plomin, Defries, Craig & McGuffin, 2003).

One of the strongest arguments for hereditary influences on giftedness lies in the small—but still impressive—number of prodigies, children who develop extraordinarily quickly.

Family

Although researchers make a strong case for the importance of heredity in giftedness, environment, or the context of the child, is important, as well. Extraordinary talent may be shaped by heredity, but it is nurtured and developed by the environment. We have discussed the role that society plays in defining SGT and rewarding individuals with SGT. A more powerful influence, because it is closer, is the family. We stress that intellectual production takes more than talent; it also takes persistence, hard work, and desire. It is clear that the family plays a major role in the development of these traits (Webb et al., 2007).

Creative endeavors support development of special gifts and talents.
(Courtesy of Cengage Learning)

Gender

The observation of gender differences in various aptitudes in students with gifts has been often noted, although such differences have sometimes been linked to differential encouragement and opportunity. Strand, Drury, and Smith (2006) analyzed a representative sample of 320,000 11- and 12-year-olds in the United Kingdom and found striking gender differences in favor of boys at the upper reaches of ability in quantitative reasoning. In general, males seemed more diverse, having both more high scores and more low scores than the girls.

The impact of gender on how students decide to manage their giftedness has been an area of interest to many scholars (Coleman & Cross, 2001; Kerr & Cohn, 2001; Reis, 2003; Roeper, 2003). Sociocultural standards regarding appropriate roles for boys and girls are very clear and may conflict with the emergence of giftedness in some instances. Let's look at how this might work for girls who have SGT.

For girls with gifts, the message to be "feminine," meaning to be passive, modest, dependent, nurturing, and unselfish, can conflict with their expectations of such factors as independence, risk taking, full development of their potential, assertiveness, and a certain degree of competitiveness. These conflicting messages can mean that some girls with gifts elect to camouflage their abilities in order to fit in better with society's expectations (Reis, 2003). Although societal messages have changed somewhat since the women's movement of the 1960s (Roeper, 2003), these dilemmas remain critical for many girls with SGT.

Social and Emotional Development

Despite their demonstrated ability to make friends and generally to adapt well, people who have SGT may shoulder some challenges that stem from their exceptionality.

A volume produced by members of the National Association for Gifted Children presented a summary of what was known about the social and emotional status of students with gifts (Neihart, Reis, Robinson, & Moon, 2002). There have been substantial differences of opinion with regard to the linkage of giftedness to such issues as depression, delinquency, perfectionism, suicide, and response to stress.

Giftedness does not provide an inoculation against emotional problems. The question is whether it provides a buffer against them because of these students' cognitive abilities to solve problems and to examine their own feelings. Silverman (2002) discusses the special problem of *asynchronization of development* of students with gifts: namely that, for example, some may be 14 years old cognitively but only 8 years old physically and socially. This asynchronization causes problems both for these students and for adults around them who are not aware of the effects of this atypical development.

Perfectionism

Another characteristic that seems to be a part of the emotional and social lives of some students with SGT is *perfectionism*. Perfectionism is the combination of thoughts and behaviors associated with high standards or high expectations for one's own performance. Superior performance depends on setting high standards for oneself, and such standards would seem an essential part of the high productivity expected of such students. But sometimes perfectionism shades over into neurotic performance. From their earliest years, children with SGT tend to be successful in almost everything they try—because they are being underchallenged. If perfectionism becomes a neurosis, students can become "failure avoidant." Perfectionist students can have a depressive reaction if they receive a 95 on a paper instead of the usual 100. In such instances it is important for teachers and others to point out to the student that great accomplishments usually are accompanied by failure in some part of the process.

These children can be distraught at the thought of not getting a perfect score on tests and seem to expect much more of themselves than their parents would ever wish (Webb et al., 2007). Jack, who was used to doing well in everything, once struck out three times in a Little League game. He wept uncontrollably. "I'm a failure, a failure," he cried. He could not match his behavior to his expectations. Parents can sometimes help by recounting similar events in their own lives, letting the child know that everyone eventually faces these experiences.

Suicide

Cross (2008) pointed out that an increasing incidence of suicide among adolescents in general would seem to mean that the incidence would likely be increasing in the gifted populations as well. There is some indication that youngsters who are extremely creative artistically are more vulnerable to mental illness than are their classmates with other academic gifts. Periodically the question arises about the relationship between emotional disorder and giftedness and between suicide and giftedness. It is clear that many well-known personalities, scientists, and artists, such as Vincent Van Gogh, have committed suicide, and periodically news stories appear about highly gifted students who have committed suicide. The question lingers.

> There is no greater prevalence of suicide among students with SGT than among typically performing students.

Suicide is the third most prevalent cause of death among teenagers (American Association of Suicidology, 2004), so what about teenagers who have SGT? We do know that depression, which is often closely linked to suicide, is neither higher nor lower in adolescents with SGT (Baker, 1995).

Cross, Cassady, and Miller (2006) explored suicide ideation in 153 teenagers applying to a residential school for advanced mathematics and science and found no higher rates of suicide in this group than in the normal population. Because this was a select group of students of high achievement applying to such a school, however, it still leaves unanswered the question about underachievers with gifts and their emotional status.

The Information Processing Model

The information processing model for students with SGT differs considerably from that of the typical student. In this instance, the differences are assets rather than difficulties. In Chapter 6, on intellectual and developmental disabilities, we discussed *correlated constraints*—features that combined to cause a negative outcome. In the case of students with SGT, **correlated assets** exist, linking high IQ scores to favorable physical, personality, and social factors. These students are generally more popular, have fewer physical problems, and have intact families.

As shown in Figure 9.2, the major assets of students with SGT are the central processing areas of *memory, association, classification, reasoning,* and *evaluation.* Because of these mental strengths, the output area of the model reveals an ability to speak well and write effectively. The ability to think more clearly should allow students with SGT to make better decisions in the *executive function* and to succeed in *emotional and social contexts,* although there are many exceptions to this generalization.

These correlated assets may pose a challenge to the teacher, as students with SGT may be bored with being taught facts and simple processes, making them markedly inefficient and overconfident from being told how smart they are. They

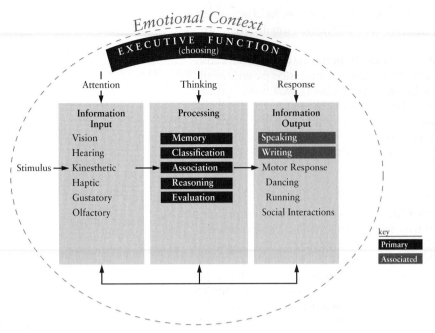

FIGURE 9.2
The Information Processing Model for Gifted Students

bring home good grades, pleasing their parents who are unaware of how their children are being short-changed by the lack of challenge to their abilities.

Characteristics of Three Students with SGT

We would like you to meet three children: Cranshaw, Zelda, and Pablo. They are 10 years old and in the fifth grade. Cranshaw probably meets the criteria for intellectual, creative, and leadership giftedness; Zelda has intellectual gifts; and Pablo's gifts are hidden.

Cranshaw: Cranshaw is a big, athletic, happy-go-lucky youngster who impresses the casual observer as the "all-American boy." He seems to be a natural leader and to be enthusiastic over a wide range of interests. These interests have not yet solidified. One week he can be fascinated with astronomy, the next week with football formations, and the following week with the study of Africa.

His history in school has suggested that teachers have two very distinct reactions to Cranshaw. One is that he is a joy to have in the classroom. He is a cooperative and responsible boy who not only performs his own tasks well but is also a good influence in helping the other youngsters to perform effectively. On the other hand, Cranshaw's mere presence in the class also stimulates in teachers some hints of personal inferiority and frustration, as he always seems to be exceeding the bounds of the teachers' knowledge and abilities. The teachers secretly wonder how much they are really teaching Cranshaw and how much he is learning on his own.

Cranshaw's family is a well-knit, reasonably happy one. His father is a businessman, his mother is an elementary school teacher, and the family is moderately active in the community. Their attitude toward Cranshaw is that he is a fine boy, and they hope that he does well. They anticipate his going on to higher education but, in effect, say that it is pretty much up to him what he is going to do when the time comes. They do not seem to be future-oriented and are perfectly happy to have him as the enthusiastic and well-adjusted youngster that he appears to be today.

Zelda: Zelda shares similar high scores on intelligence tests to those manifested by Cranshaw. Her information processing model is reflected in Figure 9.2. Zelda is a chubby girl who wears rather thick glasses that give her a "bookish" appearance. Her clothes, although reasonably neat and clean, are not stylish and give the impression that neither her parents nor Zelda have given a great deal of thought to how they look on her. Socially, she has one or two reasonably close girlfriends, but she is not a member of the wider social circle of girls in her classroom and, indeed, seems to reject it.

Teachers respond to Zelda with two generally different feelings. They are pleased with the enthusiasm with which Zelda attacks her schoolwork and the good grades that she gets. At the same time, they are vaguely annoyed or irritated with Zelda's undisguised feeling of superiority toward youngsters who are not as bright as she is; they tend to turn away from Zelda when she tries to act like an assistant teacher or to gain the special status that is reserved for the teachers.

Zelda and her family seem to get along very well with each other. The main source of conflict is the fact that the family has values that Zelda has accepted wholeheartedly but that are getting her into difficulty with her classmates. Her parents are college professors—her father in history and her mother in English literature. They seem to value achievement and intellectual performance almost to the exclusion of all other things.

Their social evenings are made up of intellectual discussions of politics, religion, or the current burning issue on the campus. These discussions are definitely adult-oriented, and Zelda is intelligent enough to be able to enter occasionally into such conversations. This type of behavior is rewarded much more by her parents than is the behavior that would seem more appropriate to her age level (Gallagher & Gallagher, 1994).

Cranshaw's adjustment is as good as his academic achievement, but Zelda has social difficulties. She is not accepted by her agemates and doesn't understand why. The pattern of development is different for each of these students because of differing environmental contexts.

Pablo: Pablo, a short compact boy with enormous energy, is very different from Cranshaw and Zelda. As a matter of fact, in years past, he would not have been considered for SGT services at all. His gifts and talents would have likely gone unnoticed.

Pablo came to this country with his parents five years ago from Central America, and so he speaks two languages, English and Spanish. His father works long hours on construction projects, and his mother stays at home with the four children. They were somewhat surprised when the school system told them Pablo was eligible for the program for students with gifts, but now they are very proud and want to help Pablo succeed in his new role.

Pablo is very athletic and physically active. He does best in school with tasks that require him to think, but his performance in English and related subjects, spelling and reading, lags somewhat behind his other abilities. The psychologist says that his mental ability score represents a minimal estimate. Pablo gave evidence on the test of a higher level of ability than his scores show.

Pablo qualifies as having "hidden" gifts. The standard achievement measures would not show his abilities, but classroom observation and new teaching techniques, such as *problem-based learning*, allowed him to show his bright and inquiring mind and encouraged his teacher to refer him for further evaluation. If energy and effort means anything, and it does, Pablo will be a success. He puts as much effort into his lessons as he does on the soccer field.

Pablo's teacher, however, will still have to be careful with his assignments, supporting his verbal skills while stressing his artistic contributions, which are considerable. It is not enough just to place Pablo in a group of students with SGT; the teacher must also be sensitive to his cultural background and linguistic differences and provide appropriate support if he is to thrive.

When we look at Cranshaw, Zelda, and Pablo, we are reminded that individuals within any category of exceptional children are first and foremost *individuals*. Each has his or her own pattern of strengths and areas of need. Indeed, within any category of exceptional children, the intraindividual differences of a single child can seem more important than the interindividual differences across the group. Nevertheless, we need to remember that what students with SGT all have in common is an advanced cognitive ability that will require teachers to provide a more challenging curriculum in these students' areas of strengths.

Identification of Students with Gifts and Talents

Before we can provide children who have SGT with special services to match their special needs, we have to find these children. Identification is not always an easy task. In every generation, many such children pass through school unidentified, their talents uncultivated (Johnsen, 2004).

Identifying these students requires an understanding of the requirements of the program for which they are chosen. If we want to choose a group of students for an advanced mathematics class, we would use a different approach than we would if we were looking for students with high aptitude for a creative writing program. Specific program needs and requirements shape the identification process.

Any program for identifying children who have SGT in a school system should include both subjective and objective methods of evaluation. Classroom behavior, for example, can point out children's ability to organize and use materials and can reveal their potential for processing information, sometimes better than can a test. Products, such as superior essays and term projects, can be kept in a student portfolio and serve as an indication of special gifts.

Project U-STARS~PLUS (Using Science Talents and Abilities to Recognize Students Promoting Learning for Under-represented Students) capitalizes on the teachers' knowledge of their students to help identify young children with outstanding potential (Coleman & Shah-Coltrane, 2010a). The U-STARS approach relies on three key elements:

1. Teachers who know what to look for (how to recognize potential)

2. Teachers who know how to structure their classrooms so that children will be engaged

3. Teachers who know how to provide a psychologically safe environment in which students can show their best abilities (Coleman & Shah-Coltrane, 2010b)

The structured observation approach used by U-STARS includes an observational note-taking system that gives teachers specific behaviors to look for. In this case, children to be observed would include those who learn easily, show advanced skills, display curiosity and creativity, have strong interests, show advanced reasoning and problem solving, display spatial abilities, are motivated, show social perceptiveness, and have leadership strengths. The basic belief underlying this approach and similar ones is that we must go beyond the use of IQ scores and standardized measures of achievement if we hope to identify "hidden giftedness." Other programs that focus on using observational data to help teachers recognize students with outstanding potential have used problem-based learning experiences as the observational platform.

In the visual and performing arts, talent usually is determined by the consensus of expert judges, often in an audition setting. Experts in the arts are not enthusiastic about tests of artistic ability or musical aptitude. They trust their own judgment more, although their judgment is susceptible to bias. Sometimes it is possible to judge the quality of a series of products or a portfolio of drawings or compositions that students produce over a period of time (Clark & Zimmerman, 1998).

Students with SGT Who Are Underachievers

One of the many myths surrounding children with gifts is the "cannonball" theory. The idea, simply put, is that such children can no more be stopped from achieving their potential than a cannonball, once fired, can be diverted from its path. Like most simplistic ideas about human beings, this one, too, is wrong. There is a subgroup of children referred to as **underachievers with SGT**, students whose academic performance consistently falls far short of expectations despite high cognitive abilities (for example, a consistent C average or dropping out).

A substantial proportion of students never achieve the level of performance that their scores on intelligence and aptitude tests predict for them. In the Terman longitudinal study, researchers identified a group of 150 men who had not achieved to the level of their apparent ability and compared them with 150 men who had done well (Terman & Oden, 1947). In their self-ratings and in ratings by their wives and parents, four major characteristics separated the underachieving men from the achieving men: *greater feelings of inferiority, less self-confidence, less perseverance,* and *less of a sense of life goals.* More striking was an examination of teacher ratings that had been made on the men twenty years earlier, while they were in school. Even at that time, their teachers believed that the underachievers lacked self-confidence, foresight, and the desire to excel.

A recent study looked at the predictors of underachievement for gifted students (McCoach & Siegle, 2003). Five factors were examined: academic self-perception, attitudes toward school, attitudes toward teachers, motivation/self-regulation, and goal valuation. Shortcomings in the last two factors, lack of motivation and academic goals, were the best predictors of underachievement. Interestingly, the academic self-perceptions of underachieving students with gifts were high; they knew that they *could* do the work, and their attitudes toward school and teachers were mixed. The authors recommended that "teachers and counselors who work with underachievers with SGT should assess whether these students value the goals of school and whether they are motivated to attain those goals" (McCoach & Siegle, 2003). The authors further pointed out that if these students value neither the specific task they are given (such as solving problems in algebra) nor the outcome of completing the task (an A in math), their motivation is likely to be low.

It is difficult to change the maladaptive behavior patterns of students who for eight to ten years have been developing precisely the wrong approach to academic stress or challenge. This goal of change requires great intensity of effort on the part of both the student and those trying to help that student change. The best-known educational intervention strategies have established either part-time or full-time special classrooms for underachievers with SGT (either Tier II or Tier III in the response to intervention [RTI] model). In these classrooms, as reported by Reis and McCoach (2000), "educators strive to create a favorable environment for student achievement by altering the traditional classroom organization. A smaller student-teacher ratio exists, teachers create less conventional types of teaching and learning activities, teachers give students some choice and freedom in exercising control over their atmosphere, and students are encouraged to utilize different learning strategies" (p. 164).

> Underachievers have greater feelings of inferiority and less self-confidence than achievers.

Classroom behavior can point out a child's ability to organize and use materials and reveal their potential for processing information.

(© Will & Deni McIntyre/CORBIS)

RTI

Culturally Diverse Students with SGT

A consensus is growing about what is needed to support students from different cultural environments to succeed in school. For many students and their families, such support would include a range of health and social services and teachers with broad training in special education methods and understanding of the child's cultural milieu (Callahan, 2007; Ford, 2002).

Just about every research project cites as positive forces in such families a home environment characterized by warmth and stability of mother-child interactions, opportunities for learning (reading books and being read to), and a neighborhood with play resources and security for children and youths (Ford, 2007). A strong partnership between school and families can encourage these favorable conditions for educational success (Coleman & Shah-Coltrane, 2010a).

Kitano (2007) specifically urges "universal access to high-quality early childhood programs for those who face extreme poverty in the first four years of life." Such programs would include a multicultural curriculum, early literacy development, and support for creative thinking, as well as health and social services.

Van Tassel-Baska (2004) has summarized the need for special curriculum units for low-income students with SGT who may have a greater interest in social acceptance and a lesser interest in reading, abstract ideas, and long-term academic performance.

Van Tassel-Baska proposed curricula that place emphasis on openness to experience and that allow creativity and fluency in thinking, opportunity to express ideas through the arts rather than verbally, preference for hands-on applications, and preference for oral expression. The **problem-based learning (PBL)** approach contains many of these characteristics and has been shown to be effective with low-income populations with SGT.

> Structured teacher observations have proved useful in recognizing gifted students from culturally and linguistically diverse families.

Children With Disabilities Who Have SGT (Twice Exceptional)

A student's inability to see, hear, or walk does not mean that he or she does not have special gifts and talents (Hua & Coleman, 2002). It only means that the child stands a good chance of having special talents overlooked. Coleman (2002) studied the coping strategies used by students who had both gifts and learning disabilities. She found that the students who had SGT and learning disabilities had constructive coping strategies, whereas the students with average ability and learning disabilities often displayed learned helplessness, escape/avoidance, and distancing.

Another condition in which giftedness and another exceptionality may be mixed is autism. Although the majority of children identified as autistic have average or below-average ability, a subset of children, sometimes those diagnosed with Asperger's syndrome, can be highly intelligent (Attwood, 1998; see also Chapter 5 in this volume). This high intelligence takes on a special flavor with such children, who can be encyclopedic in their knowledge but very poor in their social relationships. Their *theory of mind* function (the ability to perceive the intentions and thoughts of others) remains a serious problem for them. They need special help in social adaptation, regardless of their academic proficiency. (Chapter 5 includes more information on children with Asperger's syndrome.) There are similar examples of students with SGT who also have vision impairment (Helen Keller), hearing loss (Beethoven), and orthopedic disabilities (Stephen Hawking) that need to be identified for a special education program.

As noted earlier, we have to consider three major questions when we propose to adapt the current program to take into account the special needs of exceptional children: *Where* will the adaptation take place? *What* content changes will be necessary? How will the instruction be modified? *How* can technology enhance their abilities? Much of the early attention given to the education of students with SGT focused on the location of educational adaptations. The probable reason is that moving students around in various groupings creates administrative challenges; thus parents, principals, and superintendents become involved and concerned. Actually, location is less important than what takes place once students arrive at the new location. The change was made in order to provide services and curriculum that would not have been possible in the normal setting.

The RTI Model and Children with SGT

RTI

The RTI model is also appropriate in thinking about the special educational needs of students with SGT. As with other children with special needs, the general education curriculum should be extended to meet the needs of students who often are two or three grades advanced in their knowledge over their classmates.

Although Tier I represents the general education classroom, there are special additions needed to meet the educational needs of these students. The No Child Left Behind Act places emphasis on basic proficiency and has often led the class to focus on exercises that have long been mastered by these advanced students.

In some instances the problem-based learning approach will first present a problem to all students (tier I) and then provide some students additional assignments or projects based on their performance on the original problems (tier II). A gifted education consultant can work with students doing advanced projects while the general education teacher is busy with other lessons.

Tier II also clusters high-performing students for special activities. Advanced Placement courses at the secondary level are an example of curricular changes to accommodate students at this level. Special summer programs that present brief but intense experiences in mathematics, science, or creative writing are also a popular way to satisfy the curiosity and desire for learning among children with special SGT. Gifted

underachievers can also receive special counseling designed to remediate their performance as part of their Tier II activities.

Tier III represents a difference from the regular program as recognition of the huge knowledge and aptitude differences between some students with SGT and students in the average program. Acceleration is often a key component of tier III services. Programs like AP and IB with advanced learning opportunities can be part of them as well. Residential programs such as the North Carolina School of Science and Math may go beyond typical tier III options, as are special classes for students with extraordinary talent that provide a quite different program for learning. Tutoring programs for especially talented students in arts and music also fit into Tier III activities.

Consider the following three general educational objectives for programs or services for students who have SGT:

- Mastering important conceptual systems that are at the level of their abilities in various content fields

- Developing skills and strategies that enable them to become more independent and creative

- Developing pleasure in and excitement about learning that will carry them through the routine that is an inevitable part of the learning process

What holds us back in reaching such objectives?

Values and Schools

Two major values, *equity* and *excellence*, have driven American education for many years. We even accept

TABLE 9.2
U.S. Performance Relative to the International Average at a Glance

Content Area	Fourth Grade	Eighth Grade	Final Year of Secondary School	Advanced Math & Science Students
Mathematics Overall	Above	Below	Below	—
Science Overall	Above	Above	Below	—
Advanced Mathematics	—	—	—	Below
Physics	—	—	—	Below

Sources: National Center for Education Statistics. (1998). *Pursuing Excellence: A Study of U.S. Twelfth-Grade Mathematics and Science Achievement in International Context.* Figure 1, Figure 5, Figure 9, Figure 16. Washington, D.C.: NCES.

the concept of *vertical equity*, the unequal treatment of unequals in order to make them more equal. Programs such as Head Start and legislation such as No Child Left Behind reflect that value of equity.

But, we also want to make sure that all students, including those with extraordinary talent in the arts, sciences, business, and other fields, have full opportunity to develop their gifts (*excellence*). We do this, in part, because we recognize that their excelling in these fields means that our society as a whole will flourish.

Because scarce resources must be divided among our needs and goals, these two values, equity and excellence, sometimes bump into one another. In the first part of the twenty-first century, the scales seem to tip strongly in the direction of equity. So at the present time there are far fewer public resources available for children with SGT than for children who need special help to survive academically and socially in this culture.

A wake-up call to American educators came with the publication of the results of the Third International Mathematics and Science Study (TIMSS, 1998). This study, which involved about 15,000 schools around the world in tests of their students' mastery of mathematics and science at fourth-, eighth-, and twelfth-grade levels, revealed disturbing results for American students.

At fourth grade, American students appeared to be performing above average among the fourteen countries that participated in the TIMSS study. That result changed, however, at the middle school level, with American students falling below average in both subjects. The twelfth-grade results were even

more devastating, with the American students at or near the bottom among more than twenty countries with which they were compared. American middle school students are below average in math and science compared with students in other countries. See Table 9.2 for important results from the TIMSS study.

One myth about students who have SGT is that they "have it easy." They do their school assignments effortlessly, they often do their homework in school while waiting for the other students, and they generally can float through school with few demands. Actually, the story is very different for those students who wish to fully develop their SGT. An extended period of time spent developing their talents is necessary. Nobel Laureate Herbert Simon has commented that it takes ten or more years of extensive practice before one can expect to become an expert in a particular field.

Students with gifts in math and science report working fifty-five to sixty hours a week and expect to do so for the rest of their lives (Lubinski & Benbow, 2006). No matter what your basic talents, long hours of practice and learning are necessary if they are to be translated into high performance. That is why persistence is often mentioned as a key characteristic of gifted performers. Far from having an easy life, these performers with SGT will be working much longer hours than the average citizen for as long as they live. A popular book by Malcolm Gladwell (Outliers, 2008) also states that students with SGT will still need to spend 10,000 hours on their area of specialty if they hope to become eminent.

Adapting the Learning Environment (Where to Teach)

Teachers can change the learning environment in many ways, but most of those ways are designed to bring children who have SGT together for instruction for a period of time. The aim is threefold:

- To provide students who have gifts with an opportunity to interact with one another and to learn with and be stimulated by their intellectual peers

- To reduce the range of abilities and performance within the classroom (past achievement, for example) to make it easier for the teacher to provide appropriate instruction matched to the student's needs

- To place students who have gifts with an instructor who has expertise in working with such students or in a relevant content field

Because changes in the learning environment affect the entire school system, they have received more attention at the school district level than have changes in skills and content, which remain primarily classroom issues. Still, the three elements are closely related: Changes in the learning environment for students who have gifts are often necessary to meet the instructional goals of special skills and differential content mastery.

A number of strategies are being used to modify the placement of gifted students to meet their special needs. The strategies are of two main types: grouping and student acceleration.

▲ Grouping

This strategy brings students with gifts together for learning so that they can go at an advanced pace and be stimulated by others of like ability. This can be done through a special class, a part-time special class, or *cluster grouping*, which brings six to ten gifted students together (Tier II activities) to form a subgroup within the larger classroom (Schroth, 2008).

The **magnet school** is a recent addition to the options available to bright students and is a type of *performance grouping*. Magnet schools often specialize in subject matter such as mathematics or in an activity such as art, and they encourage interested and qualified students to attend. Students who have gifts often are interested in magnet schools that allow them to study at advanced levels and with other highly motivated students. Students are encouraged to volunteer for magnet school participation (Tier III activity).

Among other recent developments are the designs for *charter schools*, which are freed from some of the standard rules for public schools so that they can try innovative approaches to education. Students with SGT can often find a more comfortable setting in these schools, with their emphasis on individual performance and accomplishments. Another type of educational setting for students with SGT is *residential schools*. Established in ten states, these schools bring together highly talented students for their last two or three years of secondary school. Instead of floating through their last two years of high school, as many students with SGT do, students in these residential schools are given a rigorous introduction to higher-level thinking and study (Kolloff, 2003).

▲ Student Acceleration (Flexible Pacing)

We can adapt the educational program by abandoning the traditional practice of moving from grade to grade and by varying the length of the educational program. Because more and more knowledge and skills must be acquired at the highest levels of the professions, students who have talents and gifts, and who are seeking advanced degrees or professional training in fields such as medicine, can find themselves still in school at age 30 and beyond. While skilled workers are earning a living and starting families, students with gifts are often dependent on others for a good part of their young adult lives. The process of **student acceleration**—passing students through the educational system as quickly as possible—is a clear educational objective for some children. Gallagher and Gallagher (1994) described six ways of accelerating students:

- *Early school admission*. The intellectually and socially mature child is allowed to enter kindergarten at a younger-than-normal age.

- *Skipping grades*. The child can be accelerated by completely eliminating one semester or grade in school. The primary drawback here is the potential for temporary adjustment problems for the student.

- *Telescoping grades*. The child covers the standard material but in less time. For example, a three-year middle school program is taught over two years to an advanced group.

Students who have gifts and talents can be challenged by participating in Outward Bound activities, such as this boy working on a nature project.

(© Ellen Senisi)

- *Advanced placement*. The student takes courses for college credit while still in high school, shortening the college program.

- *Dual enrollment in high school and college*. The student is enrolled in college while finishing high school.

- *Early college admission*. An extraordinarily advanced student may enter college as young as 13 years of age.

There is no doubt that special programs such as those for students with SGT increase the level of challenge for these students. Rigorous academic demands throw many students off balance because many never had to study before and few really know how to do it. Coleman (2005) reports on the reaction of one student with SGT who enrolled in a special school: "At home I did my homework all in class and I got straight A's. Here I do homework and I study and I get mostly B's" (p. 36).

Schroth (2008) raises a series of remaining questions about special grouping problems. They relate to justifying increased costs, the need for special personnel preparation, and finding the evidence-based practices and content that are needed to complement these special placements.

From early admission to school to early admission to college, research studies invariably report that children who have been accelerated, as a group, have adjusted as well as or better than children of similar ability who have not been accelerated (Colangelo, Assouline, & Gross, 2004).

Despite these findings, some parents and teachers continue to have strong negative feelings about acceleration, and some educational administrators do not want to deal with these special cases. The major objection to the strategy is the fear that acceleration can displace individual children who have gifts from their social and emotional peers, affecting their subsequent social adjustment. The result of these misgivings is that many students who have gifts spend the greater part of their first three decades of life in the educational system, often locked in relatively unproductive roles, to the detriment of themselves and society.

As more longitudinal studies are completed, it becomes possible to learn what actually happened to students who were accelerated, instead of what people hoped or feared would happen. Lubinski, Webb, Morelock, & Benbow (2001) conducted a ten-year follow-up of 320 students with profound gifts who scored high enough on the SAT to qualify as the top student among 10,000. Of these 320 students, 95 percent had taken advantage of various forms of acceleration (grade skipping, taking college courses while in high school, taking exams for college credit, entering college early, and so forth).

The perceptions of these students regarding their acceleration were highly favorable. They saw the procedures as an advantage in their academic progress and in maintaining their interest in learning. They found little or no effect of such acceleration on their social lives or peer relationships. By their early 20s, 23 had already attained PhDs, 9 had law degrees, and 7 were doctors of medicine. Another 150 or so of this sample continued to work toward advanced degrees.

These results are even more positive than those of similar studies and clearly suggest that the fears of educators and parents that such acceleration would harm the students socially are largely unfounded.

Ideas on Why Schools Hold Back America's Bright Students

- Schools' lack of familiarity with the research on acceleration
- A belief that children must be kept with their age peers
- A belief that acceleration "hurries" children out of childhood
- A concern that acceleration could hurt students socially
- Political concerns about "equality" for all
- The concern that other students will be offended

Research finds these concerns not to be based on facts. Instead, the report *A Nation Deceived* (Colangelo et al., 2004) finds highly favorable results for these acceleration approaches.

There is also little evidence to show that highly gifted students who are radically accelerated (more than two to three years) suffer unfavorable social or emotional effects (Gross & Van Vliet, 2003). These students do not burn out; they do not lose interest in their area of talent; and they do not suffer from large gaps in their academic or social knowledge. Rather, radical acceleration appears to offer extraordinary benefits for these children in both their intellectual development and their social and emotional health. One comprehensive tool that can guide decision-making is the Iowa Scales.

Adapting Curriculum (What to Teach)

▲ Effective Education Programs

An important question to raise in the education of gifted students—and in all education—is: Are the practices we are using beneficial, or do they just represent established practice, which through repetition becomes the established way of doing things?

Although a number of practices, such as problem solving, problem finding, and use of computers, can be used effectively with all students, their use can be especially relevant in the accelerated, high-level curriculum for students with gifts (Robinson, Shore, & Enersen, 2007).

Considerable information is now available on what happens to children with SGT in the regular classroom and in special instruction programs designed to meet their needs. Reis & Renzulli (2009), in a review of this literature, found that teachers in regular classrooms rarely differentiated their curriculum or activities to meet the needs of SGT students. On the other hand, when SGT students were grouped for special instruction in a wide variety of content fields, there were high positive outcomes, as reported by a number of studies. Reis & Renzulli found this evidence compelling and pleaded for more special attention to the instructional needs and opportunities for these students.

They conclude by posing the question, "Why isn't more being done to challenge our most able students?" This is an excellent question, and until we can find a convincing answer, we will face the downgrading of much of our top intellectual potential in the U.S. If we produce underachieving children with SGT in this generation, we are asking for underachieving adults in the next one.

How does one differentiate the curriculum for students with SGT? Do we expect teachers to compose their own curricula? It is enough that they employ the special curriculum with grace and style, as a concert pianist would play music that he or she has not composed. We should not expect individual teachers to design differentiated curricula, but they are capable of implementing quality curricula that are given to them.

Perhaps the educator who has come closest to providing us with a useful approach to differentiating curriculum is Joyce Van Tassel-Baska (2003). Her integrated curriculum model is composed of three interrelated dimensions that are responsive to the learner with gifts:

1. Emphasizing advanced content knowledge that frames disciplines of study
2. Providing higher order thinking and processing
3. Focusing learning experiences on major issues, themes, and ideas that define both real-world applications and theoretical modeling within and across areas of study (Van Tassel-Baska, 2003)

▲ Curriculum Compacting

One strategy to help gifted students avoid the chronic boredom of having to "learn" things they already know is curriculum compacting. The basic principle of compacting is that if students already know something and have the basic skills to apply the knowledge, they should be allowed to move on to other areas of learning (Reis, 2008). The critical point of compacting is that students are allowed to show their knowledge when *they* are ready; they do not have to wait until the whole class is prepared for the assessment (Renzulli, and Reis, 1997).

The most appropriate curriculum areas for compacting are those that focus on mastery of basic knowledge and skills. These might include vocabulary, basic application skills (such as grammar, arithmetic, and spelling), factual knowledge in a given subject, and basic comprehension in reading. These areas can be readily assessed to document student mastery. Once students have shown mastery of the basics, they can be released from further direct instruction, guided practice (class work), and independent practice (homework) on this set of knowledge and skills. Essentially, **curriculum compacting** allows students to "buy time" for other, more appropriate learning experiences. How can this time be used?

▲ Content Sophistication

Content sophistication challenges students who have gifts to use higher levels of thinking to understand ideas that average students of the same age would find difficult or impossible to comprehend. The objective is to encourage children who have gifts to understand important abstractions, scientific laws, or general principles that can be applied in many circumstances.

▲ Advanced Placement and International Baccalaureate

Two approaches to systematic curriculum adaptations for students with SGT have been Advanced Placement (AP) courses and the International Baccalaureate (IB) program (Herzberg-Davis & Callahan, 2008). The AP program consists of more than thirty courses and exams offered by the College Board to provide the opportunity for high school students to take college-level courses while they are preparing to graduate. If the students score high enough on the exam for the course, they may earn credit with the college they choose to attend. Chances are that you took an AP course in high school, as over 1.2 million students took one in 2005 alone. An effort is now being made to ensure that as many students as possible have access to AP classes; in previous years AP classes have been much more available in suburban and middle class communities.

The International Baccalaureate program was designed to provide a rigorous preuniversity course of study focusing on active learning, citizenship, internationalism, and respect for other cultures. IB begins as early as elementary school in some areas. A special Theory of Knowledge course is provided for all IB candidates, and each candidate must write an extended essay on an independent study topic, as well as report on a service activity he or she has performed.

> Two secondary-level programs for students with SGT are Advanced Placement and International Baccalaureate.

Adapting Teaching Strategies (What Skills to Teach)

One of our goals in educating students with gifts—and all students—is to capitalize on skills they already have—that is, the ability to generate new information from existing information. If I tell you that "Mary is taller than Joyce and Joyce is taller than Betty," you most likely will generate the conclusion that "Mary is taller than Betty." You have generated new information from old knowledge.

The ability to generate new information from old is extremely valuable. The cognitive processes for doing so can be simple exercises such as the preceding example of girls, or they can lead to a new solution for global warming, the discovery of genes linked to cancer, or an improved transportation system. All students need to increase their ability to generate new information from old, but this is particularly true for students with gifts, who have the capability to deal with problems of greater complexity than do their age-mates (Linn & Shore, 2008).

Few students, no matter how bright, will be likely to discover on their own topics such as calculus, the scientific method, or the creation of depth perspective in art. These must be taught, and we expect students to produce findings and results that will demonstrate that they have learned the skills required for the generation of new knowledge or information.

▲ Problem-Based Learning

There are specific strategies to help students learn search techniques so that they themselves can gather information that will allow them to solve problems. The essence of *problem-based learning (PBL)* is as follows:

1. *The students are presented with a problem in which the solution is not stated.* For example, a student has suddenly become ill with a number of odd symptoms. The cause of this condition is not evident.

2. *The students are made stakeholders in the problem.* They are to play the role of medical detectives tracking down the diagnosis for the condition and must use a variety of search techniques, such as surfing the Internet, to arrive at an answer.

3. *The instructor plays the role of metacognitive coach,* not information giver. The teacher may point out possible sources of information or ways of accessing various sources, perhaps even suggesting that students interview community medical personnel, but will not provide the answer.

Using a combination of small-group and individual work, the students try to arrive at the answer. (In the preceding problem, the students finally decided that the cause was the West Nile virus. They recommended controlling mosquitoes but not closing the school, as the disorder is not contagious.)

> Students need to be taught how to cultivate higher-level thinking skills such as creativity, problem solving, and problem finding.

Teachers receive special training for the role of coach in the PBL model. These PBL methods have been used to teach economics, social studies, language arts, science, and even medical school subjects. The observations from diverse PBL programs are remarkably similar: The students are energized by the nature of the problems presented, play an active and enthusiastic role in seeking new knowledge to solve each problem, and report excitement and increased interest as a byproduct of the PBL approach (Barrows, 1988; Doig & Werner, 2000; Gallagher & Stepien, 1996; Maxwell, Bellisimo, & Mergendoller, 2001).

Students use brainstorming to extend their intellectual fluency and by discussing a particular problem and suggesting as many answers as possible for the problem.

(© Ellen Senisi)

One example of the use of the response to intervention (RTI) Tier I approach in education for gifted students is a problem-based-learning unit on the Black Death (Gallagher & Bray, 2002). The process begins with the entire class of low-income sixth-grade students taking the roles of council members in a medieval Italian town who have heard that a terrible plague is coming.

The students' task is to determine how to protect their fellow citizens and what actions they need to take as a council. The students study in small groups, explore the Internet, and have discussions and sometimes debates about what should be done. From this Tier I whole-class exercise, a number of high-performing students were identified and placed in a special group that met three times a week (Tier II). They were given special lessons in self-assessment, discussed career goals, and were encouraged to believe in themselves and their special abilities (Gallagher, Cook, & Shoffner, 2003).

Some of these students were then given individual tests and interviews to determine whether they qualified for the school program for students with SGT (Tier III). Using a version of the RTI model, the instructional staff was able to provide exciting adventures for all of the students (Tier I), to offer specialized work for a smaller group of high-performing students (Tier II), and finally to include some of those students in the regular program for students with SGT (Tier III).

In educating children with disabilities, we find many students who need help but do not qualify for special education services. They fall into Tier II of the RTI model, in which some curriculum differentiation seems called for based on the needs of individual children. Similarly, we have students who do not qualify as having gifts but who still need special instruction because of their enhanced talents and abilities. This is particularly true of students who come from culturally different backgrounds and who in some instances need extra stimulation to develop their talents. So students with SGT as well as those with other exceptionalities may receive services under Tier II.

RTI

▲ Adapting to Cultural Differences

Once students with SGT from a variety of cultures are identified, by any of a variety of methods, we must develop an educational plan to meet their special needs and circumstances. One objective is to encourage a child's understanding of and respect for his or her own cultural background (Briggs, Reis, & Sullivan, 2008; Barbarin, 2002). Biographies and the works of noted writers or leaders from the particular cultural group are often the basis of special programs. Because there are so many groups with such diverse backgrounds, these programs are usually unique (Villegas & Lucas, 2002; Baldwin, 1987; Bernal, 1979).

Ford and Harris (1999) are concerned about retaining black children in programs for students with gifts. Placing a child in a program does not guarantee that he or she will be happy to be there or will want to stay (Ford, Moore, & Milner, 2005). This fact underscores a general rule about exceptional children: Merely placing the exceptional child in a different setting is not sufficient for his or her success; special steps need to be taken to ensure that the child's adaptation is appropriate.

Ford (2002; Ford & Grantham, 2003) mentions irrelevant curriculum; social, racial, and cultural backgrounds that are incompatible with those of the majority of the students; and even a lack of support from those parents who find themselves torn between the culture of the school and the culture of the home as reasons for dropping out of a special program.

One of the major attempts to provide special intervention for minority students identified as gifted has been Project Excite (Olszewski-Kubilius, 2010). This was an attempt to provide a stimulating enrichment program to cohorts of twenty-five students, each identified by above-average achievement in math, science, and reading at the third-grade level.

For the next six years, these children received a variety of special programming—from summer enrichment programs in math and science, to one-on-one tutoring, mentoring by college students, field trips, and family counseling—from the Center for Talent Development at Northwestern University.

One of the reasons that this model was easy to implement was that the regular school program was not changed, so there was not a struggle with the school administration over changing curriculum. Also, minority peers were not aware of the special experiences, thus avoiding a negative reaction.

After six years with a cohort of twenty-five students each year, the tentative findings through comparisons with other minority groups and interviews with students and families were very promising. Table 9-3 shows some of the results of Project Excite, which focuses on achievement plus the important element of self-perception. That perception was shared with families and had other positive results.

TABLE 9.3
Tentative Results for Project Excite

Influence on Minority Students

- Viewed themselves as special, different, and gifted
- Had higher expectations for achievement
- Increased commitment to study
- Prioritized study over play
- Selected more rigorous coursework

Academic Influence

- Increased in content knowledge and skills
- Better preparation for next level of schooling

Affective Influence

- Increased confidence to succeed in challenging work and compete with nonminority peers

Adapted from: Olszewski-Kubilius. (2010). Two perspectives on statistics in gifted education. In B. Thompson & R. Subortnik. *Methodologies for conducting research in giftedness.* Washington, D.C.: American Psychological Association.

If outside resources can be assembled to conduct such an out-of-school program, this approach could have promising potential for many other school systems.

▲ Time

The failure of school reformers to recognize *time* as the enemy of teachers and teaching is at the heart of many teachers' concerns. The question is often posed, "Cannot the average student learn what is being taught to students who have gifts?" The answer is "yes," if you disregard the time factor. For example, middle school students with SGT can be taught about the solar system and the various theories about its origin in an enrichment lesson because they have already mastered the required curriculum in less than the time allotted. Could average students also master these theories? Of course, *if* they are given enough time. But they have not yet mastered the required lessons of the regular curriculum, and they also have greater difficulty with the concepts of distance, of orbits, and of centrifugal force—difficulty that will extend further the time they need to master the theories.

Time is a fixed constant. Between 180 and 200 days are available in a school year, so the period in which students can master needed knowledge and skills is not unlimited. Youngsters who learn faster than others will be able to master more knowledge and practice more of the necessary skills than will other students in the same amount of time. Such differences are a fact of life that we, as educators, must adjust to, instead of pretending that they do not exist.

▲ Emotional Context

A team from the American Psychological Association produced a third-grade curriculum called "The Other Three R's: Reasoning, Resilience, and Responsibility." *Reasoning* includes cognitive problem solving, *resilience* means competently surmounting challenges, and *responsibility* implies being accountable for one's actions and inactions and their consequences. The team belief was that if schools teach children to work well with others, regulate their emotions, and constructively solve problems, students will be better equipped to deal with life's challenges, including academic ones (DeAngelis, 2010).

▲ Distance Learning

Distance-learning classes are increasingly becoming available at many sites and should be a great benefit for students with gifts who have exhausted the available coursework in their local schools. Another form of distance learning—interactive television—can bring complex ideas to remote areas. The faculty at the North Carolina School of Science and Mathematics, a special statewide school for highly talented students, constructed a precalculus course and now shares it with all areas of the state (Wilson, Little, Coleman, & Gallagher, 1997).

The role of the local teacher will be changed by technology from one of *direct instruction* to that of *instructional coach* of individual students. Teachers also need to help students evaluate information they obtain from such sources as the Internet. The largely unscreened communications on the Internet allow many outrageously incorrect statements to be widely broadcast. A new challenge is teaching students the difference between legitimate information and spurious information.

➡ Assistive Technology for Students with SGT

The rapid development of educational technology has made mountains of knowledge easily accessible to every student who has access to a computer. This development is a boon for students with SGT. An entire encyclopedia is available on a single small disk—it's like having a library inside the home. The challenge for the teacher is to ensure that students learn the best ways to use the computer as a learning tool.

If teachers know how to access major references or sources of information, they can open the door to more knowledge for their students, who can then explore for themselves. (Students with gifts can—and often do—surpass their teachers in understanding selective fields.) Of course, teachers have access to these new sources of information as well and, by using the same technology, can become continuous learners themselves. (See the teacher website for an expanded list of assistive technology equipment.)

One of the great advantages of the Internet, with its information-storage capacities and search engines, is that it affords students the opportunity to conduct their own research and independent serious investigations. An example of such an opportunity is within the Renzulli Learning Systems (Renzulli & Reis, 2007), which extends the well-known Schoolwide Enrichment Model into a system that matches enrichment resources with student strengths through a three-step process:

1. Create a computer-generated profile of each student's academic strengths and interests, learning styles, and preferred mode of expression.

2. Match, through a search engine, Internet resources to the student's profile from fourteen carefully screened databases that are categorized by subject area, grade level, state curricular standards, and degree of complexity.

3. Use the Wizard Project Maker to guide students through assignments, independent research, and creative projects that they would like to pursue.

Currently, 450 schools systems involving 40,000 teachers and 300,000 students are using the Renzulli Learning Systems (Field, 2009).

Family and Lifespan Issues

Homeschooling

One of the educational phenomena of recent years has been a growing interest in **homeschooling**, involving more than one million children who have been receiving their educations at home (Kunzman, 2008). Although homeschooling originated with parents anxious to maintain a religious element in their children's education, it has also become a vehicle for many parents of students with SGT. Many of these parents have despaired of the public schools' ability to meet the needs of their exceptional children.

Such education has now become more feasible through the Internet. No longer is the school the gatekeeper or exclusive dispenser of knowledge. The access that the Internet provides opens wide the door to knowledge of all sorts. The student can focus on a particular project without having to stop at intervals to change classes, and children being homeschooled do not have to limit themselves to grade-level books or curricula. The concern that such homeschooled children will necessarily be deprived of social opportunities has been proven largely untrue, because many parents make plans for their children to join clubs, recreational sports, and other activities (Kearney, 1999).

There have been few serious efforts to evaluate the overall impact of homeschooling on students, but there have been favorable reports from parents seeking an educational alternative for a child with gifts. It has also caught the attention of educational administrators, who are aware of losing some of their better students to this alternative and who therefore seek ways to entice these children back into public school programs.

Prolonged Schooling and Financial Considerations

The economic and vocational prospects for most individuals with SGT are bright. The vocational opportunities awaiting them are diverse, including the fields of medicine, law, business, politics, and science. Only in the arts, in which a limited number of opportunities exist to earn a comfortable income, do people who are gifted encounter major social and economic barriers to their ambitions.

It is virtually certain that when most students who are gifted finish secondary school, they will go on to more schooling. They often face from eight to ten *more* years of training before they can expect to begin earning a living. This is especially true if they choose careers in medicine, law, or the sciences. The delay in becoming an independent wage earner creates personal and social problems that researchers are just beginning to study. Prolonged schooling means that individuals who have talents and gifts must receive continued financial support. The most common forms of financial support are assistance from family and subsidies from private or public sources. If financial aid takes the form of bank or government loans, then a man or woman who has special gifts may begin his or her career with a substantial debt. This period of extended schooling also tends to cause individuals with gifts to postpone marriage and raising a family.

The psychological problems that result from remaining dependent on others for financial support until the age of 30 or beyond remain unexplored. We need to consider these issues before we burden students who have gifts with more schooling requirements intended to meet the demands of this rapidly changing world.

Transition: Unsolved Questions

For most children with exceptionalities, the discussion of transition from school to community depends on whether they will be able to find useful employment and independent living. Children with SGT face a different set of issues.

It is likely that most students with SGT will seek advanced education and preparation for professional careers. Two obstacles appear in this question: the expense of advanced education and the time that such an education takes. Pablo's parents, who wish for him to go to medical school, face expenses of up to a quarter of a million dollars over a five-year period when considering the combination of school, internships, and residency. Can Mr. and Mrs. Gomez, who have a modest family income, afford to encourage Pablo on this path? Even with scholarships and grants, Pablo is likely to leave school in debt.

In addition, the Gomez family has two other bright children in the public education system. Can they afford to encourage advanced education for them? This is not merely an issue for the Gomez family, but society at large. We continue to need highly-trained scientists, economists, lawyers, engineers, and professors to operate a modern society. We don't want training for these professionals to be left solely to the wealthy who can afford it.

The time involved is also a factor. If Pablo follows the typical school trajectory, he will be 22 when he graduates from college, 26 when he finishes medical school, and nearly 30 when he is a licensed doctor. He will be deeply in debt and just beginning his career when others have already had years of experience. Zelda, discussed earlier, wants to be a professor—she will also be 30 when she finishes her Ph.D., with similar expenses to Pablo's. How can we as a society help Pablo and Zelda? Perhaps they can use acceleration, as noted in this chapter, to finish college and graduate school sooner. But what about the expense? These are real questions we need to address.

moral dilemma
Who Shall Decide?

Earlier in this chapter, we noted the economic threats posed by India and China, as well as the enormous number of engineers, scientists, and other highly-educated persons that their education systems are turning out compared with the United States. We wonder why more of our bright students are getting off the education train before reaching the final station. The answer is right in front of us: time and money.

Whether we wish to excel in agriculture, economics, biology, or education, we must delay the start of careers until age 25 or older and pay more money than we have conveniently available. Who, if anyone, is responsible for doing something about this problem (if we agree that it is, indeed, a problem)? Is it up to each individual, or is it in society's best interest to provide resources to encourage these students with SGT to pursue the highest education goals possible? Should the rest of us be taxed so that a minority of students with SGT succeed and strengthen our society? The largest social experiment of this type was the GI Bill, which financed advanced education for soldiers returning from World War II. This policy was created to compensate soldiers for the sacrifices they made during the war, but it resulted in a major stimulus to society. Should we attempt something like this again? What would be the justification?

 Go to the Education CourseMate website to share your thoughts on this dilemma and email your responses to your instructor.

✳ *Summary*

▶ We care about children with special gifts and talents because we know they will become the leaders of tomorrow in science, arts, and business.

▶ Children who have special gifts and talents may show outstanding abilities in a variety of areas, including intellect, academic aptitude, creative thinking, leadership, and the visual and performing arts.

▶ Intellectual giftedness appears to be created by a strong combination of heredity and environment, with a close and continuing interaction between these two forces.

▶ Creativity depends on the individual's capacity for divergent thinking, a willingness to be different, strong motivation, and a favorable context.

▶ Longitudinal studies indicate that most children who are identified as having SGT are healthy and well adjusted and achieve well into adulthood. There are some exceptions, called *underachievers*. Some students with SGT may be underachievers due to personal characteristics (such as feelings of inferiority, low self-confidence, expectations of failure), whereas others may underachieve because of their resistance to traditional educational programs and practices.

▶ Ability grouping, combined with a differentiated program, has been demonstrated to be an effective strategy that results in improved performance by students who have SGT.

▶ Cognitive strategies—problem finding, problem solving, and creativity—are the focus of many special programs for students who with SGT.

▶ Acceleration, the more rapid movement of students with SGT through their long educational span, has shown positive results.

▶ Society's traditional gender roles may provide special obstacles for girls with SGT, limiting their willingness to explore the full range of their talents.

▶ Many students possess SGT that is "hidden" by differing cultural perspectives, linguistic backgrounds, and life experiences. A variety of tests, observations, and performance indicators are necessary to discover these students.

▶ Children with physical and sensory disabilities may have intellectual gifts (twice exceptional), but often their abilities are undiscovered because less has been expected of them.

▶ The abilities of all students with SGT can be enhanced by comprehensive and rigorous programming to meet their special needs.

Future Challenges

1 Will students with SGT receive an appropriate education in our schools?

The conflicting education priorities between equity and excellence seem to be tilted in favor of equity. It will take deliberate planning and commitment to national excellence to provide our gifted students with a challenging education.

2 Are there programs for young children who are gifted?

The early years are increasingly seen as fundamental to a developing intellect. Prekindergarten programs are blossoming across the country and will need to provide for prekindergarten students with SGT who already can read and do basic arithmetic. This is an early challenge for educators to develop a differentiated curriculum.

3 How can we ensure that gifted and talented students from culturally and linguistically diverse and/or economically disadvantaged families are recognized and served appropriately?

We continue to face the challenge of underrepresentation of some groups of children in our programs for students with SGT. Given the rapidly changing demographics across the country, this disproportionate representation will likely increase unless we take proactive steps to address it. We need to look to models that help teachers recognize and nurture potential, using structured observations of students engaged in meaningful and dynamic lessons.

4 What are best practices for identifying students with SGT?

What can we do to (1) ensure that students who need services provided through education programs for students with gifts are not overlooked and

(2) make sure that we do not identify as having gifts students who do not need those services? We need to use multiple types of information and multiple sources of input in the identification process; we need to match the information directly with the kinds of services that will be provided.

Key Terms

acceleration p. 285

content sophistication p. 304

correlated assets p. 293

creativity p. 288

curriculum compacting p. 304

high-stakes testing p. 289

homeschooling p. 309

magnet school p. 301

multiple intelligences p. 284

problem-based learning (PBL) p. 298

prodigy p. 287

student acceleration p. 301

underachievers with SGT p. 297

Resources

References of Special Interest

Colangelo, N., Assouline, S., & Gross, M. (Eds.). (2004). *A nation deceived: How schools hold back America's brightest students. The Templeton national report on acceleration.* Iowa City, IA: Bolen & Blank International Center for Gifted Education. This report is a comprehensive compilation of the effects of educational acceleration on gifted students. Eleven specialists have written chapters reviewing research and practice.

Dixon, F., & Moon, S. (Eds.) (2006). *The Handbook of Secondary Gifted Education.* Waco, TX: Prufrock Press, Inc. A much-needed addition to the field of gifted education, this book is a series of 25 chapters presented on a largely neglected part of gifted education—secondary school. It covers such topics as Secondary English for High-Ability Students; Guiding Gifted Students Toward Science Expertise; Gender, Adolescence, and Giftedness; and Development of Visual Arts Talents in Adolescence.

Gifted Child Quarterly. (2009). Special issue: Demythologizing gifted education, *53*(4). An entire issue of this journal is devoted to considering the various myths that abound about the education of gifted children. The various specialists have considered myths that were present a quarter of a century ago and consider where they stand now. Myths such as the idea that giftedness is due entirely to genetics, that IQ should be the determining factor for acceptance into gifted programs, and that creativity is too difficult to measure are covered. Sadly enough, not much progress has been made in dispelling these myths either in the teaching profession or in public awareness.

Karnes, F., & Bean, S. (2005). *Methods and materials for teaching the gifted* (2nd ed.). Waco, TX: Prufrock Press. This volume is devoted to updated strategies and resources for differentiating the instruction of learners who have SGT. The 22 chapters are organized into four sections: characteristics and needs of learners with gifts, instructional planning and evaluation, strategies for best practices, and supporting and enhancing gifted programs. The emphasis is on teaching strategies rather than the changes in content fields themselves.

Keyes, D. (1966). *Flowers for Algernon.* New York: Harcourt Brace. This is a science fiction story that is still in print about a man with IDD who is given a special drug and becomes the most intelligent person in the world, yet is unable to relate socially to others. When the drug wears off, Algernon must cope with returning to his original state. An interesting commentary on both intellectual disability and high ability, the book has sold over six million copies and was made into an award-winning movie, *Charly*.

Plucker, J., & Callahan, C. (Eds.) (2008). *Critical issues and practices in gifted education: What the research says.* Waco, TX: Prufrock Press, Inc. This is a comprehensive research review of fifty subjects in gifted education that covers topics such as underachievers, gifted girls, suicide, and differentiated instruction. The chapters were prepared by some of the most noted authorities in this special field and form a baseline for discussions on these various topics.

Robinson, A., Shore, B., & Enerson, D. (2007). *Best practices in gifted education*. Waco, TX: Prufrock Press. This is an effort to bring together the evidence to support the various educational and personal attempts to improve the development of children who have SGT. A relatively small number of educational changes 29 have been identified by the authors as significant, and these have been subdivided into suggestions for the home (developing specific talents), the classroom (inquiry-based learning and teaching), and school (acceleration). The reason for the limited set of practices is no doubt the lack of available funds for the research that would be necessary to meet the evidence-based criteria.

Van Tassel-Baska, J., & Stamburgh, T. (2007). *Overlooked gems: A national perspective on low-income promising learners*. Washington, D.C.: National Association for Gifted Children. A collection of 16 essays by the ranking authorities on students with gifts from low-income environments, addressing issues from how to discover them to how to enrich their educations.

Journals

Educational Leadership
www.ascd.org

Gifted Child Quarterly
www.nagc.org

Journal for the Education of the Gifted
www.prufrock.com

Journal for Secondary Gifted Education (now *Journal of Advanced Academics*)
http://www.jaa.uconn.edu/

Parenting for High Potential
www.nagc.org

Roeper Review
http://www.roeper.org/RoeperInstitute/index.aspx

Professional Organizations

National Association for Gifted Children
www.nagc.org

The Association for the Gifted (TAG)
http://www.cectag.org/

Visit the Education CourseMate website for additional TeachSource Video Cases, information about CEC standards, study tools, and much more.

Low-Incidence Exceptionalities

© Thomas Balsamo

THE THREE CHAPTERS in Part 3 describe the educational needs of exceptional children who constitute less than 0.5 percent of the students in our schools. Special planning and individualized programming are important to support children who are deaf or hard of hearing, children with visual impairments, and children with physical or multiple and severe disabilities. In Chapters 10 through 12, we highlight how these exceptionalities affect students and discuss the supports and services needed to help students with these exceptionalities meet with school success.

Children Who Are Deaf or Hard of Hearing

✳ Focus Questions

▶ How did the field of deaf education evolve, and what is the history of the debate between oral and manual communication?

▶ How are the terms *deaf* and *hard of hearing* defined, and why must we consider the degree, type, and age of onset of the hearing loss?

▶ What is the prevalence of individuals who are deaf or hard of hearing?

▶ What are some genetic and environmental causes of hearing loss?

▶ How are hearing losses detected, and why is early intervention so critical?

▶ How do hearing losses affect a child's cognitive, academic, social, and language development, and what can be done to maximize a child's communication potential?

▶ What is the Deaf culture, and how can being a member help a student who is deaf or hard of hearing?

▶ What kinds of educational supports and services (including technological and medical) are needed for children with hearing loss?

▶ What are bilingual and bicultural approaches to understanding the needs of individuals who are deaf and hard of hearing?

▶ Why is family involvement so important for the child's communication?

© Ellen Senisi

Connecting with the world around us through our senses is important. We learn through what we see, touch, smell, taste, and hear, and when one of our senses is limited, our access to information can be reduced. According to the information processing model (IPM) (see Kiesha's IPM on page 321), *taking information in* is the first component of learning, and we take information in through our senses. Building and maintaining strong connections with the world can be challenging when sensory input is reduced, and living without sensory input can feel isolating. Think of all the information you take in with your ears and all that you would miss if you could not hear.

Listen for a moment to all of the sounds in your environment and think about all that you learn from them. The cars going by outside, the siren, the music from your neighbor's room, and the rain falling on the window all provide information that helps you understand and connect with your world. Hearing individuals are surrounded by a sea of sounds and often take the information gathered through listening to these sounds for granted. For individuals who are deaf or hard of hearing, the world of sound is limited, and information that most people acquire through sound must be gained in other ways. Now think about how the loss of sound would affect your ability to form relationships with others. How would not being able to hear impact you socially?

Chapter 8 discussed the importance of communication to our sense of belonging. Being able to exchange thoughts, feelings, and desires is key to establishing a bond with others. Belonging to a cultural group in which you are accepted and understood is critical, and for many individuals who are deaf or hard of hearing, this acceptance is received within the Deaf community (the capitalized term *Deaf* is discussed later in the chapter). In this chapter we continue to explore the role of communication, including the importance of language, in learning and in social relationships, and we look at a variety of ways that communication can be enhanced for individuals with hearing losses—both within the Deaf community and within hearing society. We discuss the history of education for individuals who are deaf or hard of hearing, review definitions of what it means to have a hearing loss, and consider the supports and services that individuals and families need to help them thrive.

History of Education for Individuals Who Are Deaf or Hard of Hearing

Over the past three decades, we have seen a growing acceptance within the hearing society of individuals who are deaf or hard of hearing. This growing acceptance has come about in part because several individuals who are deaf or hard of hearing have come into prominence in their fields. Phyllis Frelich, an actor who is deaf, won a Tony award for her performance in the Broadway play *Children of a Lesser God*. Marlee Matlin, also deaf, received an Oscar for her performance in the motion picture based on the same play, and she starred in the television dramatic series *Reasonable Doubts* as a deaf lawyer. Miss America of 1995, Heather Whitestone McCallum, is deaf. Following in the athletic footsteps of Luther Taylor, who played baseball from 1900 to 1908, Kenny Walker played professional football in the 1990s and now coaches for the Iowa School for the Deaf. During the 2000 Olympics, Terrence Parkin, a swimmer who is deaf, won a silver medal. Today there are doctors, lawyers, directors of government agencies, and professionals in every walk of life who are deaf. The president of Gallaudet University, Dr. T. Alan Hurwitz, is deaf. There are many students who are deaf or hard of hearing in regular schools and more and more adults who are deaf or hard of hearing in the workplace. But there

Marlee Matlin, a famous actress who is deaf, has lead the way in advocating for individuals who are deaf and hard of hearing.

(Hubert Boesl/Newscom)

While there is growing societal acceptance, challenges still remain for full and meaningful inclusion of individuals who are deaf or hard of hearing in a world that is so speech-language oriented.

has not always been general acceptance by the hearing society of individuals who are deaf or hard of hearing.

The acceptance of individuals who are deaf or hard of hearing has been greatly assisted by government mandates, regulations, and continued advocacy for the rights of all people. Commissions established by Congress in 1986 and 1988 led to the establishment of the National Information Center on Deafness and the Helen Keller National Center for Technical Assistance. Rules and regulations in 1990 that required statewide telephone relaying systems helped ensure phone access for individuals with hearing impairments, and stipulations in 1993 that all television sets with screens 13 inches or larger sold in the United States must be equipped to receive captioned broadcasts have expanded media access. The Individuals with Disabilities Education Act (IDEA; PL 101–476), the Americans with Disabilities Act (PL 101–336), the Rehabilitation Act (PL 102–569), and other laws and regulations have increased public awareness of the talents and educational needs of persons who are deaf and hard of hearing. Some states, such as Colorado, have passed a Deaf Child's Bill of Rights to help ensure that children get the education they need. The key points of this important law are included in the accompanying box.

You may wish to review Chapter 2 as you think about how our laws work to protect individuals with special needs. Through legislation, court actions, and growing societal awareness, the world is becoming more accessible to individuals who are deaf or hard of hearing.

In spite of these gains, there are still challenges. Our speech-language–oriented society has not yet accepted **American Sign Language (ASL)** as a true language, and a lack of understanding can still cause barriers in the

---

Synopsis of the Colorado Deaf Child's Bill of Rights (1996)

● Recognizes the unique needs of children with low-incidence disabilities. Identifies the specific educational needs of children who are deaf or hard of hearing.

● Requires the committee that prepares an individual educational program for a child who is deaf or hard of hearing to consider the child's specific communication needs, including the child's mode of communication; the availability of peers, adult models, and staff with whom the child can communicate; and the availability of appropriate educational services.

● Specifies reasons for which a child may not be denied education in a particular communication mode or language.

● Allows a child to receive education in multiple communication modes or languages.

● Requires that a child receive education in the communication mode or language that is deemed beneficial for the child.

● Clarifies that the committee does not have to ensure the availability of a specific number of peers, that the provisions of the act do not abrogate a parent's statutory rights to educational choice, and that no school district is required to expend additional resources or hire additional personnel to implement these requirements.

acceptance of individuals with differences. Because we are a speech-dominated society, some educators strongly advocate the use of oral-speech language for individuals who are deaf or hard of hearing. Others, however, advocate the use of sign language or some combination of these (see the box below)

Sounds for Sammy

Sammy was born deaf and because of infant hearing screening, this was detected shortly after his birth. Because Sammy has some residual hearing he was fitted with hearing aids by 3 months and he began to respond to the sounds around him. Sammy will need intense language interventions, focusing on interaction with his environment and the development of words and concepts. The family is working with an interdisciplinary team comprised of an audiologist, a speech language therapist, and a special education teacher who is an early interventionist for children with hearing losses. The team has decided that a total communication approach using both oral and manual communication will be the best approach for Sammy. They are also aware that if his residual hearing does not seem to be sufficient for language development, a cochlear implant may be an option. The team has decided to reevaluate these decisions when Sammy is 9 mos. The journey for Sammy and his parents has just begun and it will be a lifelong process of finding the right combination of supports and services to help Sammy develop to his fullest.

National Deaf Education Center: **http://clerccenter. gallaudet.edu/**

Two early leaders in deaf education within the United States, Thomas Gallaudet and Alexander Graham Bell, both had mothers with severe hearing losses.

The dispute over how to teach communication skills to a child with a hearing loss is not new; it began in Europe, with Samuel Heinicke in Germany stressing oralism (speech) and Abbe de l'Epee in France stressing manualism (gestures). An early conference held in Milan in 1880 stressed oralism and claimed that sign language impeded language development (Paul & Quigley, 1994). The debate was intense, with firm believers on both sides.

In the United States, the sign language approach was spearheaded by Thomas Hopkins Gallaudet, who, with Laurent Clerc, founded the first school for the deaf in Hartford, Connecticut, in 1817. Gallaudet College was founded in Washington, D.C., in 1884, and its patron, Abraham Lincoln, signed the school's charter. During the next one hundred years, from 1817 to 1917, schools for the deaf were founded in most of the states. The oral approach to instruction was advocated by Alexander Graham Bell, inventor of the telephone and audiometer, and (as you may remember from Chapter 8) the founder of the School of Vocal Physiology in 1872. Interestingly, both Gallaudet and Bell had mothers with severe hearing losses, and each man was firmly convinced of the correctness of his approach.

Not until the 1970s did Bob Holcomb (Gannon, 1981), a college graduate with a severe hearing loss, advocate the use of both systems and coin the term **total communication method** to describe this approach. In total communication, some type of manual communication is used simultaneously with speech. Because our hearing culture seems to prefer that people learn to speak, educators of students who have hearing losses may stress oral language within the total communication approach (Lynas, 2000). The most important thing, however, is to teach the child a communication system that the child can master, regardless of whether it is manual, oral, or a combination of both. The combination of manual and oral systems in a total communication approach is now being more widely recommended for

While best known as the inventor of the telephone, Alexander Graham Bell was also an advocate of the oral approach.

(© Bettmann/CORBIS)

> Using both oral and manual approaches can support the child's ability to communicate.

those with hearing losses, regardless of whether the loss is moderate or severe (Moores, 2000).

As use of the total communication method increases, the recognition of American Sign Language as a true language will become very important. Through this recognition, individuals whose primary language is ASL would receive protection and support services covered under the Bilingual Education Act as English-as-a-second-language users (Johnson & McIntosh, 2009; Simms & Thumann, 2007).

Recent technological and medical advances with hearing aids and cochlear implants have greatly increased the ability to capitalize on an individual's residual hearing and, through this, to expand his or her ability to communicate. We will learn more about these technological and medical advances later in the chapter. The impact of a hearing loss can vary widely depending on the degree of loss, the type of loss, and the age of onset at which the loss occurs.

Meet Three Children Who Are Deaf or Hard of Hearing

The individual patterns of children with a hearing loss can vary widely as we can see in the cases of three children, Kiesha, Carlos, and Raymond, each of whom has a hearing loss that will affect his or her learning and possibly also his or her social skills. Kiesha is hard of hearing. Carlos has a postlingual hearing loss, and his situation is complicated by the fact that his first language is Spanish. Raymond has prelingual deafness and moderate intellectual delays. The intra-individual differences among these children show the heterogeneous nature of children who have hearing losses.

Kiesha: Kiesha, who is 10 years old, has a moderate hearing loss of 50 decibels. This means that without her hearing aids she will miss most normal conversations. (See Table 10.1 on page 321 for a reference on levels of hearing loss.) Kiesha is of average height, slightly below average weight. Her motor coordination, cognitive abilities, and social maturity are on target for her age. Kiesha's language development, as might be expected, is slightly delayed. She has some difficulty with articulation, so she receives speech therapy. The language delays have affected Kiesha's reading and spelling skills, but her achievement in math is at her grade level (fifth). Kiesha was first fitted with hearing aids when she was in preschool; as she has grown, she has received new hearing aids each year. Kiesha goes to the audiologist every year for a full evaluation, and the special education teacher and the speech-language pathologist work with her to make sure that her hearing aids are functioning well in the school environment. As a fifth grader, Kiesha receives support from the speech-language pathologist once a week, and she works with the special education teacher periodically when she needs some extra help with school tasks.

Even though Kiesha's development and educational achievement are close to those of her peers, she does need some special support from the classroom teacher. Her hearing aids and slight speech differences sometimes make her feel different from her friends, and this may become more of a problem as she moves into middle school. Kiesha's hearing also fluctuates somewhat when the weather changes or when she has a cold. Teachers who are not aware of this fluctuation may not realize that in some circumstances Kiesha may miss key information if she is not encouraged and supported to participate fully in the learning activity. Kiesha's information processing model, showing the areas that are impacted by her hearing loss, is shown in Figure 10.1.

TABLE 10.1
Levels of Hearing Loss

Level of Hearing Loss (Measured in Decibels)	Description	Possible Causes	Sounds Heard
15–20 dB	Slight hearing loss	Otitis media, or fluid buildup in the middle ear due to ear infections; damage to the ear through injury, illness, or noise exposure	Hears vowel sounds clearly; may miss unvoiced consonant sounds (f, s, sh)
20–40 dB	Mild hearing loss	Otitis media; prenatal exposure to infections (e.g., rubella, cytomegalovirus/CMV, herpes simplex virus); damage to the ear through illness, injury, or noise exposure	Hears only some louder-voiced speech sounds
40–60 dB	Moderate hearing loss	Chronic otitis media; middle ear anomalies; sensorineural damage; prenatal exposure to infections; genetic factors; and damage to the ear through illness, injury, or noise exposure	Misses most speech sounds at normal conversational level
60–80 dB	Severe hearing loss	Middle ear anomalies; sensorineural damage; prenatal exposure to infections; genetic factors; and damage to the ear through illness, injury, or noise exposure	Hears no speech sounds at normal conversational level
More than 80 dB	Profound hearing loss	Same as severe hearing loss	Hears no speech or other sounds

Source: Adapted from the American Speech-Language-Hearing Association (ASHA) website, www.asha.org. Retrieved June 15, 2010.

Carlos: Carlos, who is now 11 years old, was born with normal hearing but suffered a severe hearing loss in both ears at age 4 due to a high fever. His family moved from Mexico to the United States when he was 5, and his first hearing aids were fitted when he began kindergarten. Because he was already speaking when he lost his hearing, he is classified as having postlingual hearing loss. Carlos's needs are complicated by the fact that his first language is Spanish, and so, although his hearing loss is postlingual, he still has difficulties with English. Carlos's height and weight are typical for his age, and his motor coordination is above average. He is an intelligent young man, but because of his hearing challenges and his language differences his academic development has lagged behind. Because of his social maturity and

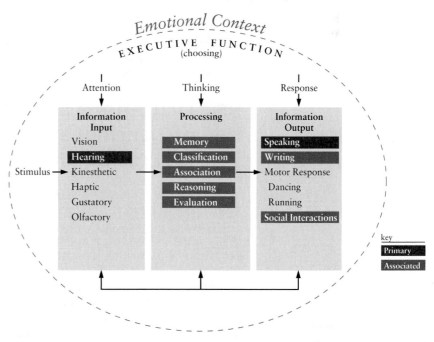

FIGURE 10.1
Keisha's Information Processing Model

excellent physical abilities, he is a leader on the playground, where the game of choice is soccer. The one area of academics in which he performs at grade level is mathematical computation. On audiometric testing, Carlos showed a hearing loss of 75 decibels with the amplification provided by his hearing aids; this is a severe hearing loss. Because Carlos learned to talk before his loss of hearing, he is able to draw on his early language foundation for learning, and with hearing aids, speech therapy, and other special education services, he is moving ahead. For the first three years of schooling, Carlos attended a bilingual special education class for two hours each day. In this class he received academic support in both Spanish and English. He is now receiving weekly speech language support and special education services in reading. Carlos relies a good deal on his lip-reading skills, and he sits at the front of the classroom, facing the teacher. He still needs extra help in developing his academic skills. The audiologist and speech-language pathologist have suggested that Carlos would be an ideal candidate for a cochlear implant. They are working to set up a meeting with his parents to share information on this option for Carlos (we will learn more about this later in the chapter).

Raymond: Raymond's hearing loss is profound, testing at more than 95 decibels. Raymond was born deaf and has never heard a spoken word. Although Raymond is 10 years old, due to his intellectual delays his mental age is estimated at around 4 years, and he has mild problems with physical coordination. Because of the severity of Raymond's hearing loss and the difficulties with learning that he encounters due to his cognitive delays, he is in a self-contained special class. Raymond's limited speech is difficult to understand, and he uses alternative communication picture boards to express his needs. In reading and other academic subjects, Raymond is several grades behind his agemates.

Raymond's communication with his family and peers is limited; so are his sources of information and his social experiences. He often reacts to social situations in ways that are characteristic of a much younger child. Raymond will need intense support throughout his schooling and will need careful transition planning as he moves into adulthood.

These three students show the wide range of needs that are common for individuals with hearing losses. Each individual child will show a unique pattern of strengths and needs, and this pattern will change over time. Later in the chapter we look at the supports and services needed to help students with hearing losses achieve success in school and life.

Definitions of Deafness, Hard of Hearing, and Central Auditory Processing Disorders

A hearing loss is defined by the degree of loss, the type of loss, and the age at which the loss occurred. The Individuals with Disabilities Education Act (IDEA, 2004) defines deafness as a hearing impairment that is severe enough that the child cannot process linguistic information through hearing, even when using amplification or hearing aids. This hearing loss adversely affects the child's educational performance (Council for Exceptional Children, 2010). Being "hard of hearing" is defined as an impairment in hearing that may be permanent or fluctuating and that adversely affects a child's educational performance but that is *not* included under the definition of deafness (CEC, 2010). What we see in both definitions is that the hearing loss can adversely affect the child's education and that we must make special educational adaptations to support children with hearing losses.

> Hearing losses must be viewed in terms of degree of loss, type of loss, and age of onset of loss.

In this chapter we use the term *deaf* to refer to a profound or complete inability to hear and the term *hard of hearing* to refer to all other categories of hearing loss. We also use a capital *D* when referring to the Deaf culture or community (discussed later in the chapter). On occasion, we also use the term *hearing losses* to describe these challenges. Because hearing losses can differ in degree, type, and age of onset, their impact on children can vary widely.

Degree of Hearing Loss

The severity of hearing losses is determined by the individual's reception of sound as measured in **decibels (dB)**. A loss of between 15 and 20 dB is considered slight; increasing degrees of loss range from *mild* (20–40 dBs) to *moderate* (40–60 dBs) to *severe* (60–80 dBs) to *profound* (more than 80 dBs) hearing loss or, to use a more common term, deafness (American Speech-Language-Hearing Association [ASHA], 2010). Table 10.1 presents the range of degrees of hearing impairments, their descriptive classification, and their possible causes. Individuals classified as hard of hearing may be able to hear and understand speech, or they can be helped to do so with hearing aids. Only a small percentage (less than 1 percent) of persons who are deaf are unable to hear speech under any conditions.

The identification during infancy and in early childhood of children who are deaf or hard of hearing means that these children have the opportunity for early access to instruction and assistive technology. This increases their potential for communication development and academic success.

(© Ellen Senisi)

Types of Hearing Loss

The ear is a complicated structure (Figure 10.2), and it functions in a complex way. The outer ear is composed of the **pinna**, the **temporal bone**, and the auditory canal, or **external auditory meatus**. The middle ear is composed of the tympanic membrane, or **eardrum**, and the three ear bones: the **malleus**, the **incus**, and the **stapes**. The stapes lies next to the oval window, called the gateway to the inner ear. The inner ear contains the **cochlea**, the **vestibular apparatus**, and the **cochlear nerve**, or **auditory nerve**. Problems with hearing can be due to either the structure or the function of the ear. Hearing losses can be classified into four categories: **conductive losses**, **sensorineural losses**, **mixed hearing losses**, and **central auditory processing losses**. The first three types of hearing loss are considered to be due to problems with **auditory acuity**, or the ability to take in sounds and get these to the brain successfully. The fourth type of hearing loss is an **auditory processing** difficulty, which means that the individual can "hear" the sounds but has problems understanding them. Within the information processing model, the first three types of hearing loss are related to problems with input—getting the information to the brain—whereas the fourth type is due to difficulties in processing the input once it is received.

A *conductive hearing loss* occurs when something blocks the sound passing through the outer or middle ear (ASHA, 2010). The blockage can be caused by wax, ear infections (otitis media), or any type of malformation of the ear canal. Conductive hearing losses make hearing faint sounds more difficult. This type of loss is usually temporary and can often be corrected by surgery or medication, but the child will also need educational supports to help him

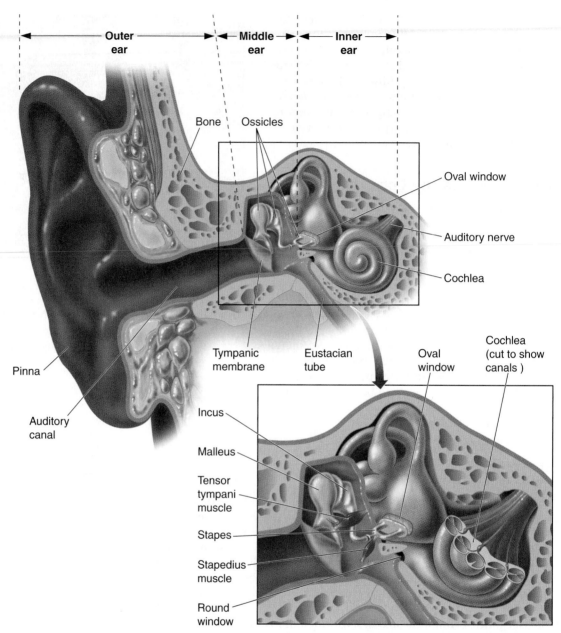

FIGURE 10.2
Anatomy and Structure of the Ear
Source: Freberg, L. (2006). *Discovering biological psychology*. 192. Used by permission of Houghton Mifflin Harcourt Publishing Company.

or her with language development and may need speech-language support to help overcome articulation problems (ASHA, 2010; Herter, Knightly, & Steinberg, 2002).

Sensorineural hearing losses are caused by damage to the inner ear (cochlea) or to the auditory nerve, particularly in the delicate sensory hairs of the inner ear or in the nerves that supply them. Sensorineural hearing losses affect both the ability to hear faint sounds *and* the ability to hear clearly, and this can make understanding speech sounds difficult. These hearing losses may be caused by genetic syndromes, diseases, injuries, or exposure to loud noise (Salvia, Ysseldyke, & Bolt, 2007). Hearing aids will likely be useful for the majority of individuals with sensorineural hearing loss, and cochlear implants can be considered for individuals with profound hearing loss in both ears who cannot benefit from hearing aids (ASHA, 2010). Educational support and related speech-language services will be needed to help the child be able to achieve successfully.

Mixed hearing losses result from problems in the outer ear as well as in the middle or inner ear, combining both conductive and sensorineural difficulties (ASHA, 2010). Persons with this type of loss may hear distorted sounds and have difficulty with sound levels. Depending on the specific site of the difficulty, a combination of medical treatment and amplification with hearing aids can be used to increase hearing. As with sensorineural hearing losses, some individuals may benefit from **cochlear implants** (a surgically implanted device that directly stimulates the auditory nerve), and all will need educational and related service supports.

In addition to the loss of hearing due to auditory acuity problems, an individual may have difficulties processing auditory information. *Central auditory processing* difficulties are considered a type of hearing loss because they limit the individual's ability to use auditory information (ASHA, 2005; Salvia et al., 2007). An individual with a **central auditory processing disorder (CAPD)** may have difficulties with sound localization, auditory discrimination, understanding speech sounds against a noisy background, auditory sequencing, memory, pattern recognition, sounding out words, and reading comprehension (ASHA, 2005; Salvia et al., 2007). Like individuals with other hearing losses, individuals with CAPDs will need the support of a multidisciplinary team to provide appropriate supports and services. We continue to discuss these supports and services later in this chapter.

Age of Onset of Hearing Loss

A hearing loss can be either **congenital**, meaning present at birth, or **acquired**, meaning that it has occurred in either childhood or adulthood. A hearing loss that occurs before the child's language has developed is a **prelinguistic hearing loss**, and one that occurs after the child has acquired some speech and language is called a **postlinguistic hearing loss**. The timing of an acquired hearing loss will have a critical impact on the child's language and speech. The timing of the hearing loss is critical because it shapes the child's early communication, language, and speech development. If the hearing loss occurs congenitally, the child will often have limited experience with the sounds of speech and will likely encounter greater difficulties understanding and producing speech. If the loss occurs before the child has acquired speech, the language delay is likely to be greater than it would be if the child had already developed a solid language and speech foundation. The stronger the child's speech and language foundation is prior to the loss of hearing, the more the child can draw on it to support his or her communication. The specific impact of any hearing loss will depend in part on how early the loss is detected, on whether the child is provided amplification or a cochlear implant, and on the supports and services the child and family receive.

TeachSource VIDEO CONNECTION

Mysteries of the Brain: Unlocking the Secrets of ADHD

Please visit the Education CourseMate website to access this ABC News video. Danny has both ADHD and a central auditory processing disorder that make learning difficult. As you watch this video, reflect on how new technologies can help us understand the brain and on how this information can be used to plan appropriate educational interventions for children.

While the specific impacts of different kinds of hearing losses vary, children with prelingual hearing loss often encounter greater difficulties using and understanding speech.

Prevalence of Hearing Loss

In 2004, an estimated 31.5 million persons in the United States, or 10 percent of the general population, were reported to have some degree of hearing loss (Better Hearing Institute, 2010). Of these, less than 1 percent are likely to be deaf. Hearing losses span the generations, affecting the following estimated numbers:

- 3 in 10 people over age 60

- 1 in 6 people ages 41 to 59

- 1 in 14 people ages 29 to 40

- Approximately 1.4 million children and youths under the age of 18 (Better Hearing Institute, 2008)

An estimated 3 in 1,000 infants are born with serious to profound hearing losses, and, as infant screening increases, this number could be proven to be a low estimate (Better Hearing Institute, 2010). During the 2003–2004 school year, 73,421 students were listed as deaf or hard of hearing (U.S. Department of Education, 2009). Although students with hearing loss reportedly account for 1.3 percent of students with disabilities, this figure is likely to be a low estimate, because many students with hearing losses have other disabilities as well (Jones, Jones, & Ewing, 2006). Students who are deaf or hard of hearing can be served in different educational settings. In 2004, 47.1 percent were served primarily in regular classes (spending over 80 percent of their time in general education classrooms), 18.7 percent received services in both the resource room and general classroom, 20.9 percent received services primarily in special education classes (over 60 percent of the time), and 13.4 percent attended separate environments or residential schools (U.S. Department of Education, 2009). Figure 10.3 shows the placements of children who are deaf and hard of hearing for their primary educational services.

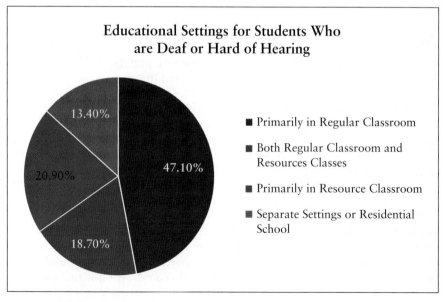

FIGURE 10.3
Educational Placements for Children Who are Deaf or Hard of Hearing
Source: U.S. Department of Education, 2008.

Causes of Hearing Loss in Children

Many factors may produce hearing loss in children. The causes are genetic, environmental or acquired, and or of unknown origin (Herter et al., 2002).

 ## Genetic Causes of Hearing Loss

Genetic factors are likely to be involved in more than half of all the incidents of congenital hearing losses (losses present at birth). The Joint Committee on Infant Hearing (JCIH), (2007) position paper states that there are nearly 600 syndromes and 125 genes associated with hearing that have been currently identified, and genetic research on deafness continues (Kurima et al., 2002). Genetically caused hearing losses are inherited from one or both of the parents and can be inherited from either a hearing parent or a nonhearing parent (ASHA, 2010). Because many forms of deafness are at least partially related to genetic factors, it is now possible to test individuals for various genes associated with deafness (Sparrow, 2010). The use of genetic testing to help determine the probability of conceiving a child who is deaf has become quite controversial as members of the Deaf community are concerned that this information may perpetuate the deficit, or medical, view of deafness (Sparrow, 2010). We discuss this controversy more fully later in the chapter. Approximately 30 to 40 percent of children with hearing losses have associated disabilities that must be considered as part of their treatment (JCIH, 2007). Chapter 12 looks at the needs of children with multiple areas of disability, including children who are both deaf and blind.

Children with other genetically related disabilities may also have associated hearing problems. For example, children with Down syndrome (a genetic

 ## Neurology and Brain Development
Related to Children Who Are Deaf or Hard of Hearing

The **primary auditory cortex**, where sound is initially processed in the brain, is organized in columns that respond to single frequencies while the **secondary auditory cortex** appears to be activated by more complex stimulus like clicks or bursts of noise (Freberg, 2006). Some evidence from research with monkeys indicates that the brain may have specialized neurons for processing speech. You may recall that by around 10 to 12 months of age, a toddler has begun to distinguish between general sounds and speech sounds that are found in his or her native language. Some studies show that by around this time, the brain begins to ignore the sounds that do not fit with the language patterns the child is hearing each day (Sousa, 2001). While processing language is a key function of the auditory cortex, brain scans of children who are deaf show that the secondary auditory cortex also responds to vibration as well as to sound (Freberg, 2006). After losing his hearing, Beethoven is said to have taken the legs off his piano and placed it on the floor so that he could "feel" the music!

One reason that early intervention when a hearing loss is detected is so critical is that the younger the child is when treatment begins, the easier it is for the brain to learn how to interpret the sounds (Jensen, 2000). This is, in part, why cochlear implants have now been approved for infants (NIDCD, 2010).

disorder associated with intellectual and developmental delays—see Chapter 6) often have narrow ear canals and are prone to middle-ear infections, which may cause hearing losses. Individuals with cleft palates (an opening in the lip and aboral ridge—see Chapter 8) also may have repeated middle-ear infections, which can result in conductive hearing losses (Herter et al., 2002).

Not all genetic hearing losses appear at birth. Babies born with perfectly normal hearing may lose their hearing in the early months or years as a result of hereditary factors (Herter et al., 2002). Teachers should be aware that a hearing loss can occur in a child who previously exhibited a normal range of hearing, so continued monitoring of students for signs of hearing loss is important.

Neurology and Brain Development
Related to Children Who Are Deaf or Hard of Hearing

The brain is a complex organ that plays an essential role in all of our functions. Here is a simplified version of normal hearing: Sound comes in through the ear canal, vibrations move from the cochlea along the auditory nerve, and these vibrations are processed in the auditory cortex (within the left hemisphere) (Sakai, 2005). For young children, the sounds of most importance are related to language. So what happens when a child is deaf and the brain receives no input from sound? Early work by Helen Neville and her colleagues (1997) using brain-imaging technology showed that for children born congenitally deaf, their "visual language," American Sign Language, is processed in the auditory cortex (Sakai, 2005) had similar findings in a study of children whose first language was Japanese Sign Language. Other studies, however, found bilateral cortical activity (both hemispheres working) for processing both ASL and British Sign Language (BSL) (Sakai, 2005). The brain's plasticity, or ability to reorganize itself when needed, seems to be at work here (Pennington, 2009).

The result of studies done with children who have received cochlear implants show that the younger the children are when they receive the implants, the more benefit there is for speech and vocabulary outcomes (Fagan & Pisoni, 2010; Hayes, Geers, Treiman, & Moog, 2009; Geers, Tobey, Moog, & Brenner, 2008; Connor, Craig, Raudenbush, Heavner, & Zwolan, 2006). The critical age for the maximum benefit seems to be prior to 2.5 years. While no causal information regarding the brain was attributed to these outcomes, Sakai (2005) notes that language acquisition and dramatic brain growth take place in the early years of the child's life. More research looking at the role of the brain in processing language (both oral and visual/manual) will help us understand these relationships better (Pennington, 2009).

Environmental Causes of Hearing Loss

Environmental causes include exposure to bacteria, viruses, toxins, and trauma, as well as infection during the course of pregnancy or in the birth process (Herter et al., 2002). The environmental effects that begin before birth are associated with illness or infections the mother may have had during pregnancy. For example, uncontrolled diabetes in the mother may cause a hearing loss in her child. A group of infections that affect the mother and that can also cause severe hearing losses in the fetus has been labeled **TORCHS** (de Jong et al., 2010) (see Table 10.2).

TABLE 10.2	
Maternal Infections That May Cause Hearing Loss to the Fetus: TORCHS	
TO	Toxoplasmosis
R	Rubella (German measles)
C	Cytomegalovirus (CMV)
HS	Herpes simplex virus

The *TO* stands for toxoplasmosis, a parasitic disease common in Europe that may be contracted by handling contaminated cat feces or eating infected lamb that has not been cooked sufficiently (Batshaw & Perret, 1992). The *R* stands for rubella (German measles), which, if contracted by the mother, can cause not only serious hearing loss in the child but also blindness and cognitive delays. With the advent of the rubella vaccine, very few cases of the measles are occurring (Steinberg & Knightly, 1997), but this vaccination must be renewed periodically.

Rubella Cases

Between 1964 and 1965, a rubella epidemic broke out with approximately 12.5 million cases. This epidemic caused 12,000 babies to be born deaf in the United States. Today, rubella is largely controlled with vaccination, and in 2004, only nine cases were reported in the entire country (Tharpe, 2010).

The *C* stands for cytomegalovirus (CMV), an infection in the mother's uterus, which is a major environmental cause of deafness in the United States. CMV can go undiagnosed, or it can be misdiagnosed (sometimes as the flu). It is a particularly harmful virus that can pass through the placenta and affect the fetus. It can also be passed through the mother's milk in nursing (Strauss, 1999). CMV is so strongly associated with low-birth-weight and premature infants that it has been considered as a possible cause of prematurity, as well as of hearing loss. Whereas fewer than 25 cases of rubella were reported in 2004, that of CMV has increased from 1 percent to up to 4 percent in women with no antibodies to the illness (CDC, 2005). The *HS* stands for herpes simplex virus, which, if untreated, can lead to death in 60 percent of infected infants. It is also a cause of serious neurological problems and potential hearing loss.

Asphyxia (lack of oxygen) during the birth process may bring about a hearing loss (March of Dimes, 2010). Premature and low-birth-weight infants, particularly those born weighing less than four pounds, are at greater risk of hearing loss. Because of increasingly successful lifesaving techniques now being used in neonate nurseries, we are seeing an increase in the number of infants with hearing losses (March of Dimes, 2010; Raus-Bahrami, Short, & Batshaw, 2002). Infections after birth, such as *meningitis* (an inflammation of the membranes covering the brain and spinal cord), can damage the auditory nerve. Because the antibiotics given to treat the infection may also cause damage to the auditory nerve, the dosage for the infant must be measured carefully (JCIH, 2007; Batshaw & Perret, 1992). Noise pollution, particularly loud and persistent noises, and damage to any part of the ear due to injury can also result in hearing loss.

The most common cause of hearing loss for young children in their preschool years is **otitis media**. A middle-ear infection, very common in children of preschool age, otitis media can lead to hearing loss and language difficulties. Figure 10.2 (shown earlier), shows an area called the middle ear, where the malleus, the incus, and the stapes are located. When a child has otitis media, this area fills with a fluid that decreases the child's ability to hear. Depending on the frequency and severity of infections, the hearing loss may be mild or even moderate (ASHA, 2010). Children are susceptible to ear infections because their Eustachian tubes are small and often more horizontal than those of adults, so fluids do not drain as effectively (ASHA, 2010). Later in the chapter we look at specific strategies teachers can use to support children who may have hearing losses due to otitis media ear infections. The most important thing is to detect the hearing loss as early as possible.

Assessing Hearing Loss in Children

Hearing losses can be detected at birth, and 41 states require a hearing screening for newborns. The Center for Disease Control report, based on data from 46 states, indicated that 85.4% of infants under the age of one month had been screened for hearing losses in 2007 (CDC, 2005). Because 20 to 30 percent of hearing losses occur during early childhood, further screenings should be conducted at regular intervals. If a hearing loss is identified at birth, a comprehensive auditory evaluation can be conducted by 3 months of age, and the infant may be fitted with a hearing aid or may receive a cochlear implant (more information on cochlear implants is found on page 325). Early diagnosis can also alert the parents if the child is deaf and may need to learn sign language or an alternate communication system in order facilitate optimum development and to mitigate any developmental delays (Herter et al., 2002). Testing for a hearing loss will take somewhat different forms depending on the age of the child.

Measuring a Hearing Loss

To assess hearing in an infant, we must first determine whether the ear is functioning appropriately and whether the brain is receiving the sound signal. Three methods for assessing hearing in infants are: **otoacoustic auditory emissions (OAE)**, **auditory brainstem response (ABR)**, and **auditory steady state response (ASSR)** (JCIH, 2007). While both OAE and ABR techniques measure the underlying physical activity for hearing, there are some differences between these approaches. ABR measurements are taken from surface electrodes that record the brains activity in response to sounds delivered via an earphone. OAE is assessed by placing a small microphone in the child's ear. In the ear of a hearing child, when a click sound is played an echo is generated. This echo happens because as sounds move through the ear canal to the middle ear they stimulate thousands of hair cells, causing them to vibrate. The microphone placed in the child's ear makes it possible to receive and record this echo (Mauk & White, 1995). If no echo is received, further evaluation is indicated. The ASSR approach uses continuous stimuli to elicit a response and can provide frequency-specific auditory information that can be important if the child is being considered for a cochlear implant.

National Center for Hearing Assessment Management: **www.infanthearing.org**

A **bone-conductor test** can assess hearing in infants and preschool children younger than 3 years of age by measuring the movement of sound through the bone and the hearing system to the brain, bypassing the ear. The reception of this sound in the brain (auditory brainstem recognition) is recorded on a graph that charts the brain's response in vibrations (Salvia et al., 2007). By comparing the child's responses to the responses of a population of hearing persons, the audiologist can ascertain hearing abilities or losses. A bone-conductor test should *not* be done in a school setting because a special environment is needed.

Play audiometry can be used with very young children to assess their ability to hear. Tests are conducted in a pleasant environment with toys that move and make sounds. The toys are used to elicit responses, such as eye blinks and changes in respiration or heartbeat (slower heartbeats indicate attention).

The child is brought into a room with his or her caregiver. An examiner distracts the child with an attractive toy. Sounds are piped into the room. A change in sound indicates that a curtain will be raised to reveal a more attractive toy. The child is not told that this will happen. After a few experiences of this, children without hearing losses hear the change of sound and turn to look at the hidden toy before the curtain is lifted to reveal it. If the child does not turn when the sound is changed, hearing losses are suspected (Herter et al., 2002).

Play behavioral assessments are based on principles of conditioning children to respond to sound by rewarding them when they indicate that they hear it. The reward is usually allowing them to play with a toy. Play audiometry has long been accepted as both a reliable and feasible technique for assessing hearing in young children (Paul & Quigley, 1994); however, it is not suitable for infants (ASHA, 2008).

The most frequently used hearing assessment is pure-tone audiometry. **Pure-tone audiometry** can be used with children about 3 years of age

FIGURE 10.4
Sample Audiogram
Source: http://www.audiologyawareness.com/hearinfo_agshl.asp

and older. The audiometer—an instrument for testing hearing acuity—presents pure tones (not speech) to the individual, who receives the tones in a headset (Salvia et al., 2007). The audiometer presents a range of sounds and measures the frequency (vibrations) and intensity (pitch) at which the individual is able to hear these sounds. The individual being tested responds to the sounds by raising his or her hand (or speaking into a microphone) if he or she can hear the tone. These responses are recorded on a graph called an audiogram. From an examination of the results, an audiologist can determine the degree and range of hearing loss. Figure 10.4 shows a sample audiogram for a child with hearing losses.

The Importance of Early Intervention for Children with Hearing Losses

Early intervention is critical for children with hearing losses. The Joint Committee on Infant Hearing (2007) stated:

> Before newborn hearing screening was instituted universally, children with severe to profound hearing loss, on average, completed the twelfth grade with a third- to fourth-grade reading level and language levels of a 9- to 10-year-old.

The report further states that infants and children with mild to profound hearing loss who are identified in the first 6 months of life and are provided with immediate and appropriate intervention have significantly better outcomes in vocabulary development, receptive and expressive language, understanding of syntax, speech production, and social and emotional adjustment.

Lauren's Surgery

My only thought when my baby was first handed to me was: "Please tell me my child can hear." I've been profoundly deaf from birth and even though I can speak clearly, I rely on lip-reading to understand. I'm the only deaf person in my family and before Lauren was born, I had tests done with a top geneticist who told me I wasn't a carrier of any known deafness gene. So when Lauren failed the newborn hearing test at just 24 hours old, I was devastated.

At ten weeks old I had her fitted with a hearing aid, and we started making the 2.5-hour round trip every two weeks to the city so she could have auditory verbal therapy. This taught her to give meaning to the sounds she could pick up using her hearing aid. She'd be "shown" a sound, like the splash of water, and helped to memorize it so when she looked away she could still recognize it and attribute it to water. I practiced this with her for two hours a day at home, something I still do now. With the help of the therapy, she grew into a bright, tenacious, communicative little girl. By 7 months, she was using baby signals when she wanted her diaper changed or felt hungry. She could also understand words like "teddy," "dog," and "butterfly" by using her hearing aid and watching my lips, which is incredibly advanced even for a hearing child. I was so proud of her.

But I was faced with a heart-wrenching decision. Doctors said Lauren was a potential candidate for a cochlear implant—a surgically implanted electronic device that directly stimulates the auditory nerves (the hair cells on the inner ear usually do this but in many deaf people they are damaged). I knew the younger she had it done, the more naturally she would learn to hear and the better her speech would progress. Waiting until she was old enough to make her own decision would put her entire development at risk. But I also knew that the implants would involve invasive surgery and carry many risks.

I kept asking myself, "Is it worth exposing Lauren to such major surgery when she's learning to communicate so well on her own?"

Even if the operation was successful, I was terrified Lauren would one day turn to me and say, "Why did you do this to me? Why didn't you let me be?"

The decision was made even harder by the attitudes of some people in the deaf community who believe that if a child is born deaf, the parents should accept it or in fact, embrace it. On the other hand, I knew that if the operation were successful Lauren would fit into the mainstream world in a way I never have. She'd be able to hear leaves rustle and sounds I've never known. It was a long decision process and often my husband David and I veered in different directions, but in the end we were both sure it was the right choice.

Lauren finally had the operation at 1 year and 11 months. Those four hours of waiting were the most harrowing of my life. And I wasn't prepared for what I saw when she was done. The whole side of her face was swollen, and she was badly bruised. I felt horrified, but when she opened her eyes, spoke the words, "Mommy, have I got a new ear?" and asked for chocolate, I knew she was going to be fine.

It took two months before she was ready for the audiologist to switch on the electrodes in her implant. It allowed Lauren to access sound, but she needed our help and hours of therapy to learn how to hook into that sound and make sense of it. I'll never forget that sunny afternoon when David and I were sitting in the garden and Lauren said, "I can hear a birdie!"

David asked her where it was (I, of course, couldn't hear it) and she pointed into the tree, where a bird was tweeting. At that moment I knew Lauren was going to experience the world in the way we'd wished for, in the way I never have, and I couldn't hold back my tears.

The implants aren't a miracle cure—she'll always need therapy because her hearing won't ever be perfect—so she struggles at school when there's a lot of background noise and she can't hear the teacher or her name being called. But three years on, the one thing I'm sure of is that Lauren has had the best start in life we could have hoped for, with the confidence to help her get on in the world.

Source: Adapted by Jennifer Job, from: Jacqui Press as told to Naomi Greenaway, Dec 1, 2009. The parents who faced a heartbreaking dilemma—should their daughter have surgery for deafness despite the risks? *Daily Mail.*

Pivotal Issues

- How can professionals help parents as they struggle with key decisions like this one?

- What kinds of support will the family continue to need as they work to help Lauren?

- How do you think her mother's deafness will impact Lauren as she moves through a dual world with both hearing and deaf experiences?

The impact and importance of early intervention for children with a hearing loss cannot be overstated. Early and intense intervention using a communication system that the child can master (NAD, 2010) is essential. Once a child's hearing loss has been detected, parents are faced with several decisions. Based on the type and severity of the hearing loss, parents must evaluate the use of amplification (hearing aids to maximize the child's residual hearing); communication systems (oral and/or manual); and the possibility of a cochlear implant (NIDCD, 2010; Joint Commission on Infant Hearing, 2007; Duncan, 2009). These decisions are not easy because there are pros and cons associated with each option. Because each child's situation is unique, professionals and parents must carefully review these pros and cons as they work to plan interventions that will be most successful for the child (NAD, 2010). During this decision-making process, parents may feel torn between the urgency of making a decision and starting the intervention and the need to think through the options so that they make the right decision (Duncan, 2009; Archbold, Lutman, Gregory, O'Neill, & Nikolopoulos, 2002). The following guidelines can help professionals provide appropriate support for parents during the decision-making process:

- Remember that parents of young children with hearing loss need time to deal with their feelings.

- Engage parents in discussing and determining their ambitions, aspirations, and desires for their child.

- Display clear, open, and harmonious beliefs, expectations, and assumptions.

- Provide parents with impartial, comprehensive, written, and spoken information presented free of jargon and in a judicious manner.

- Recognize common emotions, beliefs, and knowledge needed to make the decision-making process work (Duncan, 2009).

Early and intense communication with children, particularly in infancy and the preschool years, when the child's central nervous system is ready to learn language, is critical (Moeller, 2000; Spencer, Ertling, & Marschark, 2000). The language of the child, whether it is expressed in manual or oral form, must be provided with strong parental involvement if the child is to learn to communicate.

> Early intervention for children with hearing losses is critical to facilitate their development and their ability to communicate.

Cognitive, Academic, Communication, and Social Development of Children with Hearing Loss

The overall development of each child will depend on the child's strengths and needs in combination with the supports of the family, the medical community, and the school. While we cannot predict any specific outcomes for individuals based on their hearing loss, we can look at overall patterns of development for cognitive abilities, academic achievement, language, and social adjustment.

Cognitive Development of Children with Hearing Losses

Children who are deaf or hard of hearing have the capacity for normal intelligence, and some may be intellectually gifted. However, because the child cannot hear as well as children with normal hearing, he or she may experience developmental delays. Intelligence depends on the interaction between a person's innate capacity and their environmental experiences. A child who is deaf from birth will not have access to sounds, in particular to early language, and this will likely cause delays in their cognitive development. As children with hearing losses mature, they will have different background experiences, communication histories, and access to information, and so they will need specialized instruction to reach the same cognitive and developmental milestones as children who can hear (Marschark, Lang, & Albertini, 2002). A hearing loss may, however, be accompanied by disabilities that impact the child's cognitive abilities (Gallaudet, 2008; Jones, Jones, & Ewing, 2006). An estimated 33 percent of students with hearing loss also have an additional area of disability (Jones, Jones, & Ewing, 2006). One area of special concern is children who are both deaf and blind. This is discussed in depth in Chapter 12.

It can be difficult to determine the intellectual level of children with hearing losses in part because intelligence tests used to measure cognitive abilities are not designed for children with hearing losses. Orally (speech) administered intelligence tests that are heavily based on language often greatly underestimate the abilities of a child whose primary language is manual (Salvia et al., 2007). To assess children who are deaf or hard of hearing in written English is also problematic if the child's primary language is American Sign Language, because the vocabulary, syntax, and grammar of ASL are significantly different from those of English. A child whose first language is ASL should receive the same assessment accommodations that any child whose primary language is not English receives. This means that the assessment should be conducted in the child's primary language (ASL) and that the assessor should be bilingual and if possible bicultural (Johnson & McIntosh, 2009; Simms & Thumann, 2007; Mayer & Askamatsu, 1999). Furthermore, appropriate assessments must address both the child's access to the stimulus (spoken or printed words) and his or her ability to respond to the test prompts by either by speaking or writing (Salvia et al., 2007; Cawthon & Wurtz, 2008). When nonverbal tests are used with a sign language or manual communication system familiar to children, they often perform well within the normal range (Bellugi & Studdert-Kennedy, 1984). The Universal Nonverbal Intelligence Test (UNIT) (Bracken & McCallum, 1998) is a highly recommended nonverbal assessment for students who are deaf (Maller, 2003) (see Figure 10.5 for a sample item on the UNIT).

As part of the validation process of the UNIT, 106 students with hearing losses were assessed (Bracken & MaCallum, 1998). All of the students tested attended a special school for the deaf. When the outcomes for the students with hearing losses were compared with a demographically matched sample of hearing students, the mean differences in scores showed approximately one-third of a standard deviation (Bracken & McCallum, 1998). These differences were considerably smaller than would be expected for a cognitive assessment if it depended heavily on the child's language. The smaller differences indicate that the UNIT is likely to be a better predictor of cognitive abilities for children with hearing losses (Maller, 2003).

FIGURE 10.5
Sample of UNIT Assessment
In the UNIT assessment of analogic reasoning, children are asked to pick which of the pictures best fits in the empty box above.
Source: Reprinted with permissions from Bracken, B. and McCullam, R. S. (1998). *Universal Nonverbal Intelligence Test;* Riverside Publishers, 1998.

Academic Development in Reading for Children with Hearing Losses

Reading levels of children who are deaf or hard of hearing tend to be substantially lower than those of their hearing peers, but we may be closing this gap (Antia, Jones, Reed, & Kreimeyer, 2009; Luckner & Handley, 2008; Reed, Antia, & Kreimeyer, 2008; Schirmer & Schaffer, 2010; Antia, 2007; McGough & Schirmer, 2005; Trezek & Wang, 2006). A child who has not heard the sounds of the language will struggle to decode print if he or she is taught in the usual method of matching speech sounds (e.g., phonemes) to print. Because phonemic awareness, or the ability to use speech sounds, may be limited for children who are deaf or hard of hearing, alternative methods must be used to teach reading (Schirmer & Schaffer, 2010; McGough & Schirmer, 2005; Trezek & Wang, 2006; Luckner & Handley, 2008). If reading is taught visually or by a manual method (e.g., American Sign Language or finger spelling), children who are deaf or hard of hearing are able to learn how to read, write, and use appropriate language forms, such as past tense, questions, and logical propositions, such as *if-then* or *either-or* (Trezek, Wang, Woods, Gampp, & Paul, 2007; Trezek & Wang, 2006; Yoshinaga-Itano et al., 1998).

A study compared teaching methods for teaching reading to children who are deaf or hard of hearing with similar methods used to teach children who can hear (Luckner, Sebald, Cooney, Young, & Muir, 2005/2006). The findings of this review were compared with the National Reading Panel's recommendations for reading instruction (National Institute of Child Health and Human Development, 2000), and key areas of overlap were identified. The promising elements of reading instruction identified in this study for children who are deaf or hard of hearing are given in the accompanying box (Luckner et al., 2005/2006).

Promising Elements of Reading Instruction for Children Who Are Deaf or Hard of Hearing

- Rehearsal of information
- Direct teaching of sight words and morphological rules (how sounds are combined to make words)
- Explicit vocabulary instruction and practice with short passages
- Use of high-interest reading materials
- Instruction in the grammatical principles of ASL and how these translate to written English
- Teacher-modeled discussions of stories and explicit instruction in reading comprehension strategies
- Interaction with text and peers in learning
- Reading to young children
- Use of captions
- Intensified instruction
- Use of word processing
- Use of simple stories and word recognition practice with young readers
- Use of general curriculum for reading reinforcement

Source: Information was drawn from Luckner et al. (2005/2006). An examination of the evidence-based literacy research in deaf education. *American Annals of the Deaf, 150* (5), 443–456.

In addition, there is a movement to teach reading by the whole-word method. First, students learn to read words that stand for persons or things with which they are familiar; for example, *ball*. Then, after students have acquired a basic reading vocabulary, the teacher introduces phonics as a part of a continuing emphasis on teaching whole words (Hammil, 2004). For children who are deaf or hard of hearing, a picture of the object or person may accompany the presentation of the word, and a visual cue can be used for the word sounds (phonons). The child who can hear may have already made the association between the word and the object or person, but one cannot assume that the child who is deaf or hard of hearing has done so.

In summary, through improved teaching strategies, earlier intervention, new technology, and medical treatments (cochlear implants), children who are deaf or hard of hearing are making solid gains in learning to read. In spite of all we do know, however, there is still a critical need for additional research on instructional methods that work with children who are deaf (Luckner et al., 2005/2006; McGough & Schirmer, 2005).

Impact of a Hearing Loss on Language, Speech, and Communication

A hearing loss is a silent disability. It is not accompanied by pain, fear, or physical problems, and it is apparent only when verbal demands are made on the child (Lillo-Martin, 1997). During the first year of life, which is called the *prelinguistic* period (meaning without speech), infants with hearing losses will exhibit the same behaviors as hearing infants. As you may recall from Chapter 8, these early language behaviors include crying, making comfort sounds, and babbling to parents. In babbling, the child produces his or her first sounds that resemble words (*baba, dada*), and the parents reinforce these sounds and transform them into words. What many parents do not realize is that these language behaviors are innately programmed and will appear whether the infant can hear or not (Knight, 2003).

Infants who can hear typically produce their first word around 12 months of age. For the infant who is deaf, babbling does not develop into words. However, in a seminal study, Petitto and Marentette (1991) found that children with severe hearing losses gesture at about the same developmental age at which hearing children babble. They concluded that infants are innately predisposed to learn language and that they do so by stimulating the environment with babbling; if they cannot hear, they use babbling-like hand movements that are sign equivalents of speech sounds. These signs are not words, but they are similar to the babbling sounds. Parents who are deaf recognize these signs and begin teaching a manual form of communication; often this is American Sign Language. Each language, spoken or manual, proceeds in similar

Supporting enriched social interactions between students is an important step in developing social competence.

(© Image Source/Corbis)

fashion. If the parents do not help the child form signs into a language, the child may develop his or her own sign system, called *home sign*.

The innate language mechanism is so strong that children who hear will develop a spoken language and children who are deaf will develop a manual one. Each will develop the language of his or her home. For the child who can hear, it will be whatever language is spoken in the home. For the child who is deaf, it will be the sign language (American Sign Language) taught in the home or sign system (e.g., Signing Exact English or one developed by the child) (Goldin-Meadow, 1998). One difficulty is that 90 percent of children who are deaf or hard of hearing are born into homes with hearing parents who do not recognize the child's early attempts at a manual communication system, and so these attempts are not reinforced and the child's language development is delayed.

The pattern of language development for children who are deaf or hard of hearing and for children who can hear is essentially the same. Most children produce their first word by 12 months of age. By 18 to 22 months of age, they master the logical forms of the language used in their home, and they begin on their own to figure out the rules of language from the spoken examples provided by their environment (see Chapter 8 to review typical language development). This ability to independently generate the rules of grammar (particularly syntax or word order) tends to disappear after 6 years of age. If the child masters these rules of grammar by age 6, he or she can build on them through instruction. If the child has not acquired these rules, it is extremely difficult to teach them to the child.

> Infants who are born deaf will use babbling-like hand gestures in place of sounds, and these can be reinforced to enhance manual communication.

Social and Personal Adjustment of Children with Hearing Loss

Many youngsters who are deaf or hard of hearing will make friends with both their hearing and nonhearing peers. Luckner and Muir (2001) conducted interviews with twenty successful students who are deaf and who were receiving most of their education in general educational settings. They found that many of the students attributed their success to working hard, studying, paying attention, advocating for themselves, getting involved in sports, and *making friends*. Most students acknowledged the importance of their families and the help and support they received from teachers, interpreters, and note takers, but every student spoke about the importance of his or her friends (Luckner & Muir, 2001). The students in this study had all done well and were recognized by their teachers as being successful, and forming friendships was part of this success. But friendships may be difficult for some children who are deaf or hard of hearing. A hearing loss often brings with it communication problems, and communication problems can contribute to social, emotional, and behavioral difficulties (NAD Position Statement on Mental Health, 2010).

Lack of verbal language makes it difficult for children who are deaf to make friends with children who speak and do not sign. Several factors should improve the social adjustment of children who are deaf or hard of hearing (Luckner & Muir, 2001):

- Early identification and intervention that markedly improve the child's overall functioning and increase feelings of self-esteem
- Family support and acceptance of the child
- Sophisticated technological aids such as the Internet that provide access to information and social contacts
- Participation in extracurricular activities (sports, Scouts, service clubs)
- Skilled and caring professionals who work with the child and family

Promoting Alternative Thinking Strategies (PATHS) is a curriculum designed to improve social competence and to reduce behavioral problems for children who are deaf. It teaches self-esteem and interpersonal competencies (Kam, Greenberg, & Kusche, 2004) and aims to assist students in achieving self-control, emotional understanding, and problem-solving skills (Greenberg & Kusche, 1998). The curriculum focuses on problem-solving techniques to resolve social problems and overcome frustrations. PATHS is useful from late preschool through sixth grade (Calderon & Greenberg, 2000).

Being able to communicate is an interactive process that enables a person with hearing loss to participate fully in his or her environment. Hearing is not the issue; communication is (Antia, Sabers, & Stinson, 2006; Bodner-Johnson & Sass-Lehrer, 2003). Recall that approximately 90 percent of the parents of children who are deaf or hard of hearing are not able to communicate fully with their children through speech. Therefore, parents will have to master a communication system that is appropriate for their child.

When expressing frustration over inadequate communication in their homes, five young adult deaf students mentioned family members with limited signing skills, attending gatherings with numerous untrained relatives, and watching television with family members who would summarize the program but not give the details (Bodner-Johnson & Sass-Lehrer, 2003). These students' main complaint was that communication issues prevented them from participating fully in family life. It is rare for all the hearing members of a family to learn a sign language. Communication difficulties may cause individuals with hearing losses to prefer being with others who share their language and communication needs. It is not surprising that some children with severe hearing losses prefer to be with children like themselves, with whom they can feel socially accepted and comfortable (Guralnick, 2001). This desire extends into adulthood and has led to the formation of the Deaf culture or community.

The Deaf Culture or Community

The **Deaf community** exists as a separate cultural group within our society and has exhibited considerable cohesiveness for more than a century (MSM Productions, 2008; Moores, 2000). The community is a very diverse group whose membership is composed of people of many different religious, social, and ethnic backgrounds. The shared bonds, however, are similar values and traditions, a common language (ASL), and specific behavioral protocols that are known to and practiced by group members. Membership in the Deaf community is a part of individuals' identity, and allegiance to the group is often strong. Parents who are deaf often teach ASL to their children who are deaf, and many adults who are deaf learned ASL from their peers in residential schools, where they established close, long-lasting friendships (Stinson & Foster, 2000).

The Deaf community has state and local networks, holds world games for the deaf, hosts a Deaf Miss America Pageant (Moores, 1996), and publishes a newspaper, as well as other material. The community is strongly bonded, and many adults who are deaf in the United States move toward membership and involvement in it. The Deaf community has the status of a minority group within the mainstream culture. Its members are bilingual, using ASL for communication with others and American English for reading and writing. They provide one another with a sense of belonging and pride, and they help one another overcome possible isolation from mainstream society.

> The Deaf community offers strong bonds of acceptance for individuals with hearing losses.

RTI

Students who are deaf or hard of hearing, like most other populations of students with special needs, are a very heterogeneous population (Wachs, 2000). Because of this, each child will need an individualized educational program (IEP), and most will require services provided within all three tiers of the response to intervention (RTI) model. For students with intense and complex needs like hearing losses, the RTI process should include all of the legal requirements of IDEA (see Chapter 1) and special education. Timely and comprehensive evaluations are critical so that appropriate supports and services are not delayed. For children with hearing losses, assessment will need to be completed at least annually and may be needed more often. Annual evaluations are essential for several reasons including:

- The increasing educational and social demands placed on the child as he or she grows up

- The changing physical structure of the ear and the need to make sure that amplification devices and other assistive technologies still fit and still work

- The rapid advancement of technology with new options emerging at a quick rate

- The evolving needs of the child across the grade span

In addition to the need for formal assessments, the RTI approach hinges on data showing how each child is learning and monitoring the progress the child is making so that supports can be adjusted. All of this data is used by the multidisciplinary team to plan for the child's strengths and needs.

The multidisciplinary team is critical in planning for children with hearing losses. This team usually includes an audiologist, a speech-language pathologist, and sign language interpreters, in addition to the child's teachers and parents and other professionals as needed. The audiologist is a critical member of the team because he or she can assess the degree, type, and extent of the hearing loss and can help to monitor the child's

> Annual reviews and frequent monitoring are needed to ensure that the child's supports and services are up to date and appropriate.

use of hearing aids and cochlear implant supports. The speech-language pathologist provides support for speech development and communication skills, and interpreters meet the child's communication needs within the classroom. The classroom teacher is responsible for the general education content, and the special education teacher works with the child on special needs (for example, reading support using finger spelling and visual cues, use of picture boards for augmenting communication, intensive reinforcement of academic skills, and teaching strategies to help the child with academic and social tasks). The parents are critical team members, as they can both help the teachers understand the child's needs and work at home to support the child's development.

Tier I Supports for Children Who Are Deaf or Hard of Hearing

Like most children with a hearing loss, Kiesha, the child we met at the beginning of the chapter, is in a general education classroom for most of her day. Her 5th grade classroom teacher, Ms. Langley, works to make sure that she is included in daily activities. Ms. Langley is also careful to check in with Kiesha periodically to make sure that she understands key information. The classroom library also has reading materials that are of high interest to all the students, and Ms. Langley is always on the lookout for readings on horses, fashion, and women's soccer because these are Kiesha's favorites. The instructional strategies that she uses with Kiesha include more explicit instruction in vocabulary, additional hands-on materials for math and science, and word processing support for writing. Many of Ms. Langley's other students also benefit from these supports. One of the major differences for Kiesha is the periodic presence of the speech-language pathologist, Mr. Jackson. It is sometimes hard for Kiesha to participate in class discussions with all of the external noise and children talking over each other. To help with this problem, Mr. Jackson suggested a new procedure to the class, called "stop and think time," for some of the class discussions. Using this procedure, the class members must count to five before they raise their hands to answer a question, and during this time they must "stop and think." This has slowed down the discussions and allowed Kiesha to keep up and participate more. Interestingly enough, Ms. Langley has noticed that it has also increased the quality and length of the students' responses and has created time for a more reflective dialogue. Although the support of the speech-language pathologist is key to giving Kiesha strategies to help her understand what is happening in the classroom, he is not able to help in many informal situations, such as the playground or cafeteria when Kiesha is with her friends, so building Kiesha's own communication skills is also critical for her success (Stinson & Foster, 2000).

Kiesha is strong in math, and she often helps other students and leads the math talks for the class. This has built her confidence in speaking and has helped her with social relationships. Kiesha's parents know that reading is critical, and they work with her on special reading comprehension materials that Ms. Langley sends home. In addition to the Tier I supports, Kiesha also receives more intensive services at Tier II.

Tier II Supports for Children Who Are Deaf or Hard of Hearing

The supports that a child receives at Tier II provide more intensive instruction in the academic areas and can also address special learning strategies or study skills. For Kiesha, Tier II activities include small group reviews with Ms. Langley to preview topics and skills that she plans to teach the following week or to review key things that have just been taught. Sometimes the special education teacher, Mrs. Cooke, works with small groups of children on study skills and organization strategies; Kiesha usually participates in these sessions. The guidance counselor also provides some Tier II supports in helping students become better self-advocates, and Kiesha has participated in several small-group sessions to learn and practice ways to help others understand and meet her needs.

Planning for the Tier II activities is usually collaborative, and Ms. Langley often works with other members of the multidisciplinary team to determine the kinds of supports Kiesha needs. This collaboration is like a rhythmic dance, with different professionals taking the lead and others following, depending on the child's needs, but with everyone in tune and staying mindful of the importance of appropriate services to help the child be successful (Luckner & Muir, 2001). Even with extensive supports at Tier II, Kiesha, like most children who are deaf or hard of hearing, needs the individualized support of Tier III.

Tier III Supports for Children Who Are Deaf or Hard of Hearing

The supports that a child with a hearing loss will receive at Tier III vary depending on his or her specific needs. Often support includes specific instruction on the use of hearing aids or cochlear implants. Instruction in speech reading and speech production are also important for many children. Specific instruction on communication skills and language development is often needed, though the specific form this takes will be determined by the child's needs. There are examples of several manual communication approaches, including American Sign Language, Pidgin Sign English, Signing Exact English, Cued Speech, and finger spelling on the website given in the margin notes.

Of these manual communication approaches, ASL is the only actual language with its own grammar and syntax. The others are manual coding approaches that use the structure of English, preserving its grammar and syntax. With greater emphasis on total communication, Tier III instruction is likely to focus on approaches that combine manual communication with oral methods.

Sign Languages:
http://www.nidcd.nih.gov/ health/hearing/asl.asp

Kiesha's Tier III services include continued lessons in speech reading and communication strategies. Kiesha is given direct reading instruction using visual prompts and reading comprehension strategies (Schirmer & Schaffer, 2010). She also receives special instruction to help her in developing abstract language. This instruction includes a focus on multiple word meanings (*mole* as an animal and as a spy collecting classified information), similes (*he has a head like a rock*), metaphors (*he is a moose*), onomatopoeia (the *whir* of the engine), idioms (*he pulled himself up by his bootstraps*), and inferences (*the inference taken from the cold wind blew snow around the house* is that it is winter). Explicit instruction that reinforces abstract language is often necessary for children with hearing losses to ensure that they do not miss critical nuances in communications by making literal interpretations of the message. The combined services in Tiers I, II, and III all help to ensure that students have the supports they need to be successful. In addition to meeting the educational needs of children, the general classroom teacher is also key in recognizing warning signs that a child might have a hearing problem.

The General Education Teacher's Role in Recognizing Hearing Problems

How does the classroom teacher identify a child with a possible hearing loss so the child can be referred for comprehensive examination? Indicators of a hearing loss can show up in several ways that allow teachers to recognize the potential problem. A general education teacher can help identify a child with a possible hearing loss by observing his or her articulation, need for a higher volume of sounds, requests that information be repeated, and inattentiveness or unresponsiveness.

The accompanying box gives specific student behaviors (Stephens, Blackhurst, & Magliocca, 1982) that can help teachers recognize potential problems with hearing.

Warning Signs That Should Alert the Teacher to Potential Hearing Problems in Children

- *Does the child appear to have physical problems associated with the ears?* The student may complain of earaches, discomfort in the ear, or strange ringing or buzzing noises. Teachers should note these complaints and also be alert for signs of discharge from the ears or excessively heavy waxy buildup in the ear canal. Frequent colds and sore throats are occasional indicators of infections that could impair hearing.

- *Does the child articulate sounds poorly and particularly omit consonant sounds?* Students who articulate poorly may have a hearing problem that is preventing them from getting feedback about their vocal productions. Omission of consonant sounds from speech is often indicative of a high-frequency hearing loss.

- *When listening to radio, television, or sound recordings, does the student turn the volume up so high that others complain?* Because many young people may turn up the amplification of music, this determination will sometimes be difficult to make. Teachers can get clues, however, by observing students listening to audio media that are not producing music, such as instructional materials and movies.

- *Does the student cock his or her head or turn toward the speaker in an apparent effort to hear better?* Sometimes such movements are obvious and may even be accompanied by a "cupping" of the ear with the hand in an effort to direct the sound into the ear. In other cases, actions are much more subtle. Teachers often overlook such signs, interpreting them as symbols of increased inquisitiveness and interest.

- *Does the student frequently request that what has just been said be repeated?* Although some students pick up the habit of saying "Huh?" as a form of defense mechanism when they are unable to produce what they perceive as an acceptable response, such verbalizations may also indicate a hearing loss. When a particular student frequently requests repeated instructions, teachers should further investigate the possibility of hearing loss.

- *Is the student unresponsive or inattentive when spoken to in a normal voice?* Some students who do not follow directions or do not pay attention in class are frequently labeled as "troublemakers," which results in negative or punitive treatment. Often, however, these inappropriate school behaviors are actually caused by the student's inability to hear. They can also be caused if the sounds that are heard appear to be "garbled."

- *Is the student reluctant to participate in oral activities?* Although reluctance to participate orally may be indicative of other things, such as shyness, insecurity with respect to knowledge of subject matter, or fear of failure, it also may be due to hearing loss. The child might not be able to hear the verbal interactions that occur in such activities.

Source: From T. Stephens, A. Blackhurst, & L. Magliocca (1982). *Teaching mainstreamed students* (New York: Wiley), pp. 43–44.

Instructional Strategies to Enhance Participation for Children with Hearing Losses

With most children who have hearing difficulties served in the general classroom for most of their day, it is essential that teachers incorporate strategies to help students be successful (Antia, 2007; Luckner & Muir, 2001; Luckner, 2006). The educational adaptations listed in Table 10.3 were developed to help children who have hearing loss succeed in the general classroom setting.

In addition to support for academic success, children with hearing losses often need support for social and behavioral adjustments. Table 10.4 shares ideas for social support.

Evaluation and grading are two additional areas where modifications may be needed. Table 10.5 offers some suggested adaptations.

TABLE 10.3
Educational Adaptations for Children Who Are Deaf or Hard of Hearing

Environmental
- Seat student in best place to permit attending and participation.
- Use a swivel chair on casters.
- Set up a semicircular seating arrangement.
- Reduce noise and reverberation by: carpeting, draperies, acoustic ceiling tile, and acoustical wall treatments.

Input
- Use a frequency modulated (FM) system, an induction loop system, an infrared system or a sound-field system.
- Stand where the student can read lips and face the student when talking.
- Use an overhead projector and captioned movies and television programs.
- Cue student visually to indicate that someone is talking during class discussions or during intercom messages and repeat information when needed.
- Team teach with an educational interpreter or teacher of students who are deaf or hard of hearing.
- Preteach important vocabulary and concepts using concise statements or simplified vocabulary, highlight key words, and provide a list of new vocabulary.
- Provide graphic organizers, study guides of the key concepts, outlines, questions, course requirements, short summaries of lessons/chapters, and teacher notes Supplement lesson with visual materials (i.e., real objects, pictures, photographs, charts, videos).
- Provide manipulatives for multi-sensory, hands-on instruction or activities.
- Use peer tutoring, notetakers, cooperative learning and a "Buddy System" to provide support.
- Develop learning centers and use games for drill and practice.
- Use a peer tutor, paraprofessional, or volunteer to review work with student.
- Use commercial software to provide practice and review material.
- Use task analysis to divide and organize lengthy directions into multiple steps and break long-range projects into short-term assignments (post due dates and remind frequently).
- Demonstrate directions to clarify what needs to be undertaken.
- Increase the number of practice examples of a rule, concept, or strategy prior to assigning seatwork or homework and shorten assignments when appropriate.
- Teach organizational skills, reading comprehension strategies (i.e., PARS, RAP) and assist student to generalize these skills, ask students to summarize at the end of the lesson.
- Provide duplicate sets of materials for family use and review.
- Use thematic instruction to unify curriculum.

Output
- Allow more time to complete assignments.
- Allow students to make models, role-play, develop skits, and create art projects to demonstrate their understanding of the information.
- Allow written or drawn responses to serve as an alternative to oral presentations.
- Allow student to use computer/word processor.
- Use cooperative learning experiences to develop cooperative small group projects.
- Provide some self-pacing activities (i.e., matching cards for math facts).
- Use peer tutor, paraprofessional, or volunteer to work with student on task.

Source: Reprinted with permission from: Luckner, J. L. (2006). Providing itinerant services. In D. F. Moores and D. S. Martin (Eds.). *Deaf learners: Developments in curriculum and instruction.* (pp. 93–11). Washington, D.C.: Gallaudet University Press.

TABLE 10.4
Social and Behavioral Supports for Children with Hearing Loss

Social
- Teach hearing students to sign.
- Make books about hearing loss and deafness available.
- Invite Deaf adults to come to school and share stories.
- Implement a circle of friends program.
- Structure activities and experiences for deaf and hearing students to work together.
- Teach a unit on specific topics (i.e., friendship, avoiding fights, emotions, stealing, dating, dealing with divorce).
- Provide direct instruction on specific social skills (i.e., starting conversations, giving compliments, responding to criticism).

Behavioral
- Provide consistent expectations and consequences with regard to classroom routines and rules.
- Use interest inventories to identify positive and negative reinforcers for each individual.
- Use assignment books and/or folders to increase organizational and memory skills.
- Provide regular feedback and check progress often.
- Home-school contracts—develop a contract with student's family whereby when specific behaviors are demonstrated in school, the student receives a specified reinforcer at home.
- Send a daily report card home.
- Use corrective feedback. ("I would like you to take out a book and read when you finish your work, rather than bothering the person sitting next to you.")
- Increase frequency of descriptive praise ("You really paid attention and stayed in your seat for the past 15 minutes.")
- Use behavioral contract (written agreement between teacher and student including regarding student behavior and agreed-upon consequences).
- Use response cost procedures (taking away a privilege, points, or reward)
- Use time out.
- Limit the number of distractions by establishing isolated work/study area.

Source: Reprinted with permission from: Luckner, J. L. (2006). Providing itinerant services. In D. F. Moores and D. S. Martin (Eds.). *Deaf learners: Developments in curriculum and instruction.* (pp. 93–11). Washington, D.C.: Gallaudet University Press.

TABLE 10.5
Evaluation and Grading Modifications for Students with Hearing Losses

Evaluation

- Use peer tutor, paraprofessional, or volunteer to work with student to review for test.
- Allow test items to be signed to the student and the student to respond in sign.
- Allow tests to be taken with teacher of students who are deaf or paraprofessional.
- Provide extra time to complete tests, quizzes.
- Allow test items to be read to the student.
- Provide additional explanation of test questions and instructions.
- Provide a study guide with important vocabulary or facts needed for tests and quizzes.
- Allow student to use notes/study guide/textbook on tests.
- Evaluate daily work/participation in addition to tests.
- Use projects or portfolios in lieu of tests.
- Provide graphic cues (i.e., arrows, stop signs) on answer forms.
- Modify tests to match student abilities (i.e., matching, multiple choice questions, true/false questions, short answer questions, as compared to essay questions).
- Modify vocabulary used in test items to match student abilities.
- Modify the number of test items.
- Provide short tests on a more frequent basis.
- Chart progress or lack of progress.
- Teach test-taking skills.

Grading

- Use IEP as the criteria for grade.
- Develop contract as basis for grade.
- Use a pass/fail system.
- Write descriptive comments and give examples regarding student performance.
- Use a checklist of competencies associated with the course and evaluate according to mastery of the competencies.

Source: Reprinted with permission from: Luckner, J. L. (2006). Providing itinerant services. In D. F. Moores and D. S. Martin (Eds.). *Deaf learners: Developments in curriculum and instruction.* (pp. 93–11). Washington, D.C.: Gallaudet University Press.

Diversity: The Bilingual-Bicultural Approach

The **bilingual-bicultural approach** asserts that persons who are deaf are bicultural in that they belong to the Deaf culture as well as to the broader culture of the society in which they live (NAD, 2010). Many are also bilingual because they use a sign language system (usually ASL) to communicate and use the spoken or written language of their culture. In the United States, the primary language is English, and Deaf individuals that speak a different first language would be considered trilingual if they mastered two oral and written languages in addition to ASL (Baker & Baker, 1997; Easterbrooks, 1999; Moores, 2000).

Some specialists believe that children should be taught a sign language first and be introduced to oral language as a second language. Children with hearing losses who were taught in this manner would be considered bilingual, using ASL as their first language and the written or oral form of English as their second language. Latino children who are deaf make up one of the fastest growing minorities in the U.S. school-age population (Gallaudet, 2008). Think back to Carlos, one of the children we met at the beginning of the chapter. Carlos would be a trilingual child, with Spanish, ASL, and English. Clearly he needs support in all three languages to achieve success. Carlos is also a candidate for a cochlear implant and his parents have decided to pursue this option in hopes that he will be

Assistive and Instructional Technology for Students Who Are Deaf or Hard of Hearing

Assistive technology is the term for any equipment or product that assists the learner with special needs. Federal law requires that assistive technology be considered for every student with an identified disability (CEC, 2006).

Alerting devices and **alarm systems** have been developed for the deaf and hard of hearing that show flashing lights or use vibration. There are numerous devices of this kind, including alarm clocks, fire alerts, doorbell signals, phone signals, and baby-cry alarms.

Hearing aids provide essential amplification for many individuals who are deaf or hard of hearing. The technology of hearing aids has advanced rapidly, and today's aids are small, are powerful, and have special features to help differentiate speech sounds from background noise. In addition to hearing aids, there are several devices that facilitate hearing. These include assistive listening devices (ALDs), which increase the volume of the voice received and reduce other sounds in the environment; an induction loop device, which is an audio loop system that surrounds a seating area connected to a microphone and amplifies the sound received by the hearing aid; frequency modulated (FM) systems, in which the teacher wears a microphone that sends a direct signal into the child's hearing aid; infrared devices, which transmit sound via invisible light waves; and vibrotactile aids, which transmit sound through vibrators worn on the skin. More information on all of these technologies can be found through the Better Hearing Institute and the American Speech-Language-Hearing Association (ASHA):

> **Better Hearing Institute: www. betterhearing.org**
> **American Speech-Language-Hearing Association: www.asha.org**
> **Abledata Assistive Technology database: www.abledata.com**

Cochlear implants involve a surgical procedure in which electrodes are inserted into the cochlea. A microphone worn behind the ear receives environmental sounds and sends them through the auditory system (NIDCD, 2010; Edwards & Tyskiewicz, 1999; Steinberg & Knightly, 1997). Cochlear implants bypass the damaged part of the ear and stimulate the hearing nerve. They do not restore hearing, but they do provide a sound system that can assist the user in understanding incoming auditory stimuli (Marschark, Lang, & Albertini, 2002). They appear to be effective over a longer period of use if used consistently. Recent research indicates that children who receive implants, particularly during the preschool years, develop vocabulary, speech, and reading at nearly normal rates and in sequences similar to those of children who are not deaf or hard of hearing (Fagan & Pisoni, 2010; Hayes, Geers, Treiman, Moog, 2009; Marschark, Rhoten, & Fabich, 2007; Deafness Research Foundation, 2000; Martindale, 2007; Serry & Blaney, 1999).

> Cochlear Implant Association
> **www.cici.org**

Whereas hearing aids simply amplify sounds, cochlear implants with twenty-two to twenty-four wires send sounds of different frequencies to the brain, thereby providing a direct connection between speech and sounds in the environment. Currently more than 41,000 people in the United States have received cochlear implants (over 25,000 are children), and the demand for implants is increasing by 20 percent each year (NIDCD, 2010). However, these implants cost over $40,000, with a follow-up expense of approximately $20,000 per year (ASHA, 2010). Health insurance may cover these expenses depending on the person's health care plan and costs can be covered by Medicare and Medicade for families that qualify (NIDCD, 2010). Once the cochlear implant is in place, this is just the beginning. Extensive therapy so the brain can learn how to interpret sounds is still needed (NIDCD, 2010). The Deaf community has not fully accepted cochlear implants, as many feel that they convey a negative impression of deafness (Sparrow, 2010).

Visual Voice Tools provide a variety of visual displays, such as a balloon getting larger in proportion to the loudness of the speaker's voice. The program is designed to improve voicing, pitch, timing, and sustained production. Several online dictionaries of line drawings of sign language also exist.

> Visual Voice Tools:
> **web.riverdeep.net**

Assistive technology such as hearing aids and cochlear implants allow students to participate in the inclusive classroom.

(© Susie Fitzhugh)

Speech-to-print systems reproduce the classroom dialogue on a computer screen. In some cases a captioner who is in the room types the dialogue as it occurs, but more frequently the computer is equipped with voice-activated software. These approaches have a dual advantage in that the student can read the discussion as it is taking place and can review it later in either a printout or electronic form (Stinson & Foster, 2000).

Telecommunications and **media access** have increased dramatically over the past few decades. Captioned telephone relay services are available in forty-seven states, with a federal mandate being considered by the FCC; phones with text messaging and access to the Internet allow real-time communication; pagers are available; and the media industry is increasingly using captions for movies and productions. *The National Directory and Resource Guide for Telecommunications and Media Accessibility for People Who Are Deaf, Late-Deafened, Hard-of-Hearing, or Deaf-Blind* (2010), known colloquially as *The Blue Book,*

Telecommunications for the Deaf and Hard of Hearing, Inc.: **www.tdi-online.org**

provides up-to-date information on how to use these resources.

Instructional software programs are being developed at a rapid rate. High-speed computers make it possible to combine print, videos, sounds, and signs to help the student who is deaf or hard of hearing understand instruction. Multimedia programs are also available that contain video dictionaries of sign language (usually ASL). When the user encounters an unfamiliar word, he or she moves the mouse and clicks the appropriate key and a video appears with a person signing the word. Applied computer technology has advanced to such an extent that special word processing systems can be used to translate written English into graphic finger spelling signed on the computer screen. The computer enables the student with severe hearing losses to practice both signed and written English. Speech recognition software moves speech to print and print to speech, allowing communication in a variety of settings. (Because advances in technology are so rapid, you may wish to locate more information by visiting the websites listed throughout the chapter.)

better able to fit in with other children in his school and neighborhood community.

Residential Schools for the Deaf

The population in residential schools is approximately 10,000, with only 2,500 full-time students (Marschark, Lang, & Albertini, 2002). Many factors have led to the shrinking attendance in residential schools. These include the increase in newborn screening programs and early intervention, decreasing incidence of severe to profound deafness, increasing numbers of children with cochlear implants, federal legislation directed at providing access to general education curriculum and setting, and the closing of state schools for the deaf (Luckner & Muir, 2001). Students who do attend residential schools tend to have more severe hearing losses, to come from lower income and lower socioeconomic status families, and to have poorer spoken-language skills. Also, a greater number of students have parents who are deaf or hard of hearing (Marschark et al., 2002). Although the trend is clearly toward fewer students attending residential schools, these schools still provide an essential service for students who are deaf.

> Although the numbers of students attending residential schools for children who are deaf and hard of hearing are decreasing, it is important to keep these schools available as an educational option for children who need them.

✳ Family and Lifespan Issues

The family provides essential support for the child who is deaf or hard of hearing (Luckner & Muir, 2001). As members of the multidisciplinary team, the family helps to shape the educational program for the child and reinforces the intervention in the home. Family-oriented approaches lead to better communication skills for children who are deaf or hard of hearing.

Focusing on the family system requires recognition of the family's strengths and respect for their values, beliefs, choices, and aspirations. It helps the family to recognize the critical role that communication plays in the development of children who are deaf or severely hard of hearing. The child's development is facilitated when family members adopt interactive strategies to facilitate communication, encouraging the child to make requests, to respond, and to take the initiative. All these interactive patterns are important factors in effective learning, and they also stimulate the child to strengthen communication skills.

> Identifying families' strengths and needs is critical to helping them support their child's development.

When the parents of a child who is deaf are also deaf, they are likely to prefer having the child learn a sign or manual language, usually ASL, first. Children in this situation can learn a language early and may develop more quickly than children who are deaf and born to hearing parents, who may not recognize their child's needs for some time.

Most parents who can hear have little or no experience with deafness and may not know how to proceed with a child who is deaf. In many instances, they initially misperceive the condition, believing it to be an inability to speak rather than an inability to hear. The earlier the hearing problem is identified, the sooner appropriate support can be provided to the child and the family.

Early intervention for children who are deaf or hard of hearing begins in the home as soon as the child is identified and is continued in early intervention centers (Moeller, 2000). The family, however, continues to play a key role as the child grows. Parents in a study completed by Luckner and Muir (2001) shared stories of moving to a specific location to access better services, driving long distances to get needed supports, learning sign language so they could communicate, securing technology and medical support for their child, and working to provide additional social opportunities for their child. Parents also help to ensure that their child's educational experiences are appropriate and meet his or her needs.

Transitions for Students Who Are Deaf or Hard of Hearing

Transition planning for students who are deaf and hard of hearing must begin in high school and should address the student's interests, strengths, and support needs. Identifying the postsecondary options for each student early in high school is helpful as the student and family begin preparing for young adulthood. Students who are deaf or hard of hearing face the same question as hearing students: What do I want to do when I grow up? The role of the high school guidance counselor is to help the students explore their options and to help the families plan for these options. This exploration may include vocational school, job training, and college. For each option a

Identifying students' interests and strengths is critical to supporting their transitions to post-secondary options.

(© Ellen Senisi)

close look at the student's interests and strengths is essential to see whether it is
a good match. If college is the choice, and currently there are over 30,000 deaf
college students in the U.S. (Smith, 2010), the next step is to identify the school
that best fits the student's needs. Although most colleges have support services
for students with special needs, some are more comprehensive. Key questions
that should be asked to help make the choice of a college are given in Table 10.6.
Many of these questions would be helpful for any student with special needs,

TABLE 10.6
Questions to Ask Colleges About Supports and Services for Students Who Are Deaf or Hard of Hearing

Key Question	Related Questions
Who is eligible for support services?	What are the identification criteria?
	Are further diagnostic assessments required or available?
	What costs are associated with services?
	Are qualified personnel available who have experience working with students who are deaf or hard of hearing?
What academic supports are available for students who are deaf or hard of hearing?	Are qualified interpreters available who use the student's communication methods?
	Can the students have note takers, modified tests, learning strategies support, tutoring, writing labs, math labs, study sessions, computer support?
	Is financial assistance available to help cover costs of assistive technology that may be needed by the student?
What kinds of counseling supports are available?	Personal and social adjustment support?
	Self-advocacy?
	Career guidance?
What are the college's policies regarding . . .	Number of credit hours that count as full time
	Extended drop-and-add periods
	Taping classes and lectures
	Transferring credits from community colleges
	Auditing classes prior to enrollment for credit
	Substitution for foreign language (does ASL count?)
	Grade-point requirements for graduations
	Priority scheduling for students with special needs
	Selection of academic advisors
	Academic probation
	Office hours for faculty
	Teaching loads for faculty

(Continued)

TABLE 10.6
Questions to Ask Colleges About Supports and Services for Students Who Are Deaf or Hard of Hearing
(*continued*)

What lifestyle modification can be made?	Can students have access to study carrels equipped with their technology needs?
	Are health services appropriate?
	Is an audiologist available?
What extra curricular activities and social supports are available?	Is there a Deaf community network on campus?
	What religious affiliations are available and accessible?
	Are clubs, sports, and other campus activities accessible?

Source: Adapted from M. R. Coleman, (1994). Postsecondary educational decisions for gifted/learning disabled students, *Journal of Secondary Gifted Education, 5*(3), 53–59. (Prufrock Press). Adapted with permission.

and you may want to adapt these as you think about the transition needs of students with disabilities discussed in the other chapters.

Students who are deaf and hard of hearing also have another key decision to make about college: whether to attend a college designed specifically for their needs, such as Gallaudet University, or to attend a mainstream college with additional supports. The exciting thing is that more and more students with hearing loss are attending many different colleges across the country.

moral dilemma
Students Who Are Deaf or Hard of Hearing

Family-centered intervention is critical to providing appropriate support for the child, and parents are key members of the multidisciplinary team. The involvement of the family is essential for children who are deaf or hard of hearing because families support and reinforce early communication skills with the child. You are working with the parents of Tony, a preschool child who is deaf. Tony has been fitted with hearing aids, but even with amplification his residual hearing is very limited. The professionals on the team feel that he should receive a cochlear implant. Tony's mother is very worried about the risks of surgery and the fact that this would destroy any residual hearing Tony has, thus making later use of hearing aids impossible. She also feels strongly that they should accept Tony the way he is. You think that Tony's father is more open to the idea of the implant for Tony because he is worried about how his son will fit in to the hearing world.

How can you bridge the gap between the professionals and the parents? How can you support the mother and the father as they wrestle with this decision? What stress does the difference in beliefs place on the family? And how do you as a professional know when to push for what you feel the child needs, in spite of the stress this might cause, and when to back off?

 Go to the Education CourseMate website to share your thoughts on this dilemma and email your responses to your instructor.

✹ Summary

- Since the early 1800s the field of deaf education has been evolving through both legislation and the formation of schools and educational associations focused on teaching children who are deaf.

- Thomas Gallaudet and Alexander Graham Bell were early leaders of deaf education within the United States.

- A hearing loss is defined by the degree of loss, the type of loss, and the age at which the loss occurred.

- The Individuals with Disabilities Education Act (IDEA, 2004) defines deafness as a hearing impairment that is severe enough that the child cannot process linguistic information through hearing, even when using amplification or hearing aids.

▶ Individuals who are deaf or hard of hearing are a heterogeneous group with different strengths, interests, and needs; what they share is difficulty hearing.

▶ The impact of a hearing loss will depend on the degree of loss, type of loss, and age of onset when the loss occurred.

▶ The ear is a complex organ, and problems with any part of the ear or the auditory nerve can result in hearing loss.

▶ Central auditory processing disorders (CAPD) are considered to be a hearing loss because they prevent the individual from making full use of the sounds in his or her environment.

▶ A prelingual hearing loss will likely have a greater impact on language development than a postlingual hearing loss.

▶ Hearing losses span all age groups, affecting approximately 1.4 million children and youths under the age of 18.

▶ There are both genetic and environmental causes of hearing loss. Otitis media is the most common cause of hearing loss in children.

▶ Early identification and intervention is essential to help the child develop the communication skills that will be the foundation for his or her later success.

▶ A hearing loss does not affect a child's overall cognitive level; some children also have special gifts and talents, while others have developmental delays.

▶ Many students who are deaf and hard of hearing will need additional support for language development and academic success.

▶ Many individuals with hearing loss also have other exceptionalities.

▶ Students who are deaf or hard of hearing may need additional support for social adjustment.

▶ The Deaf culture or community provides its members a shared social identity with strong bonds.

▶ A multidisciplinary team is critical to the educational support of children who are deaf or hard of hearing, and an audiologist is a key member of this team.

▶ Total communication combines oral and manual methods to enhance the child's ability to communicate.

▶ Education services will likely be needed across all three tiers of intervention in the RTI model, and an IEP will need to be in place for many children.

▶ Technological advances have had a tremendous impact on the ability of individuals who are deaf or hard of hearing, allowing greater communication and access to information.

▶ Medical advances, especially cochlear implants, have dramatically changed the ability to hear speech sounds for many individuals who are deaf or hard of hearing.

▶ Family support is critical for the child's development.

▶ More and more students who are deaf or hard of hearing are attending college.

Future Challenges

1 *As hearing screening for infants increases, will we be able to provide adequate early intervention support for the children and their families?*

Early intervention is key to the success of individuals who are deaf or hard of hearing. As infant screening programs increase, we are likely to see growing numbers of children and families who need early intervention. How can we ensure that the infrastructure of professionals and resources needed to provide early intervention supports and services is in place?

2 *How can we make sure that the needs of students who are deaf or hard of hearing and who are served in general education classrooms are met?*

With the majority of students who are deaf or hard of hearing being placed in general education classrooms for part or most of the day, making sure that their needs are met is essential. How can we ensure that the multidisciplinary team includes an audiologist, that the interpreter has had experience working with children, and that the teacher receives the support she or he needs to be most effective with the child?

3 *How will the expanding use of cochlear implants affect individuals who are deaf or hard of hearing?*

The demand for cochlear implants is growing each year, and implants are being used with more infants. Cochlear implants seem to have dramatically opened access to speech sounds for individuals who are deaf or hard of hearing. Preliminary research suggests that when cochlear implants are in place and are used, the language and academic trajectory for the child is significantly improved. Yet because this is still a relatively new technology, there are still questions. What impact will these changes have on the Deaf community? How will we ensure equitable access to this technology for children whose parents cannot afford the expensive procedures?

Key Terms

acquired hearing loss p. 325

alerting devices p. 345

alarm systems p. 345

American Sign Language p. 319

auditory acuity p. 323

auditory brainstem response (ABR) p. 330

auditory nerve p. 323

auditory processing p. 323

auditory steady state response (ASSR) p. 330

bilingual-bicultural approach p. 344

bone-conductor test p. 330

central auditory processing disorder (CAPD) p. 325

central auditory processing loss p. 323

cochlea p. 323

cochlear implant p. 325

cochlear nerve p. 323

conductive loss p. 323

congenital hearing loss p. 325

Deaf community (culture) p. 338

decibel (dB) p. 323

eardrum p. 323

external auditory meatus p. 323

hearing aids p. 345

incus p. 323

malleus p. 323

media access p. 346

mixed hearing loss p. 323

otitis media p. 329

otoacoustic auditory emissions (OAE) p. 330

pinna p. 323

play audiometry p. 330

postlinguistic hearing loss p. 325

prelinguistic hearing loss p. 325

primary auditory cortex p. 327

pure-tone audiometry p. 331

secondary auditory cortex p. 327

sensorineural loss p. 323

speech-to-print systems p. 346

stapes p. 323

telecommunications p. 346

temporal bone p. 323

TORCHS p. 328

total communication method p. 319

vestibular apparatus p. 323

Visual Voice Tools p. 345

Resources

References of Special Interest

Bodner-Johnson, B., & Sass-Lehrer, M. (2003). *The young deaf or hard of hearing child.* Baltimore: Brookes. A rich resource for a family approach to early education when a child is deaf or hard of hearing.

Luckner, J., & Handley, M. C. (2008). A summary of reading comprehension research undertaken with students who are deaf or hard of hearing. *American Annals of the Deaf, 153*(1), 6–36. The purpose of this study is to identify, review, and summarize peer-reviewed research published in journals related to reading comprehension and school-age students who are deaf or hard of hearing. The study covers research spanning over 40 years.

Marshark, M., & Spencer, P. E. (Eds.) (2003). *Oxford handbook of deaf studies, language, and education.* Oxford, UK: Oxford University Press. This comprehensive handbook gives a thorough overview of the history of deaf education, impact of schooling, and language acquisition for children with hearing loss. Included are specific examples and instructional ideas, as well as case studies and vignettes.

Moores, D. F., & Martin, D. S. (Eds.) (2006). *Deaf learners: Developments in curriculum and instruction.* Washington, D.C.: Gallaudet University Press. This book reviews the culture of deaf learners and how they should be included in mainstream classrooms. The authors incorporate standards from national associations, including NCTE and NCTM.

Moores, D. (2000). *Educating the deaf: Psychology, principles, and practices* (5th ed.). Boston: Houghton Mifflin.This comprehensive textbook on children with severe hearing losses provides a rich historical background and up-to-date reports on current research, educational trends, and preschool and postsecondary programs.

Journals

American Annals of the Deaf
Gallaudet University

Communication Disorders Quarterly
http://www.ingentaconnect.com/content/ proedcw/cdq

Journal of Deaf Studies and Deaf Education
http://jdsde.oxfordjournals.org

Journal of Speech, Language and Hearing Research (American Speech-Language-Hearing Association)
www.asha.org

The Volta Review
http://www.agbell.org/DesktopDefault.aspx? p=The_Volta_Review

Professional Organizations

Alexander Graham Bell Association for the Deaf
www.agbell.org

Division for Communicative Disabilities and Deafness (DCDD) of the Council for Exceptional Children
http://education.gsu.edu/dcdd/

Gallaudet University
www.gallaudet.edu

National Association of the Deaf
www.nad.org

National Association of the Deaf Captioned Film/ Video Program
http://www.dcmp.org/

National Technical Institute for the Deaf
http://www.ntid.rit.edu/

National Deaf Education Center (formerly known as the National Information Center on Deafness, NICD)
http://clerccenter.gallaudet.edu/ /

National Institute on Deafness and Other Communication Disorders
www.nidcd.nih.gov

PEPnet
http://www.pepnet.org/

Sorenson Communication
www.sorenson.com

 Visit the Education CourseMate website for additional TeachSource Video Cases, information about CEC standards, study tools, and much more.

Children with Visual Impairments

Focus Questions

▶ What is the definition of visual impairment (low vision and blindness)?

▶ What are typical causes of visual impairments?

▶ What special characteristics do children with visual impairment reveal?

▶ What are the goals for a national agenda for children with visual impairments?

▶ How can the Information Processing Model and the RTI model be employed for children with visual impairments?

▶ What is the existing core and expanded core curriculum for children with visual impairments?

▶ What changes in learning environment and teacher strategies are necessary for children with visual impairments?

▶ What is the special role of orientation and mobility in the education of children with visual impairments?

▶ What effect has technology had on communication and mobility of children and youth with visual impairments?

▶ What challenges in transition to the adult world are faced by youths with visual impairments?

© James Shaffer/Photo Edit

Many children have correctable visual problems, but for 3 or 4 in 10,000, the visual impairments are so severe that they cannot be corrected with glasses or contact lenses. In this chapter, we discuss the special needs of children who are visually impaired and the educational adaptations needed to help them meet with success.

 # Definitions of Visual Impairments

Formal efforts in the United States to educate children with visual impairments began in Boston in 1829 with the establishment of the residential school now called the Perkins School for the Blind. In 1834, Louis Braille perfected his literary raised dots code of reading, but it was not until 1900 that the first public school class for children who were blind organized in Chicago. Some thirteen years later, other classes for children with severe visual impairments were established in Boston and Cleveland.

Prior to the twentieth century, no distinctions were made between children with low vision and children who were functionally blind. During the past few decades, a rapid growth in public school services for children with visual impairment has been stimulated by the Education for All Handicapped Children Act (PL 94–142) (IDEA, 2004). Currently, there are teacher preparation programs and orientation and mobility (O&M) programs based in universities that prepare professionals to work with children with visual impairment (Goodrich & Sowell, 1996).

Before the implementation of the Individuals with Disabilities Education Act (IDEA), children with multiple handicaps that included visual disabilities were often refused education in schools for the blind and were placed in settings that focused on their other disabilities while often ignoring the visual problems. As Hatlen (1998) pointed out, it is no longer possible for educators of students with visual impairments to ignore students with multiple impairments.

Today, these previously underserved students constitute the majority of students who have visual impairments. Reported increases in the percentage of students who have visual impairments with other disabilities are dramatic. Since the mid-1980s, estimates regarding the prevalence of these children have risen from 50 percent to as high as 75 percent of the total number of children with visual impairment.

The legal definition of **blindness** sets a physical standard of sight less than 20/2000, meaning that one cannot see after correction at 20 feet what the typical person sees at 200 feet. A person with low vision would have, after correction, 20/70 to 20/200 vision. However, this definition is not as helpful for educational planning. As educators, we think of how a child can use sight for learning. Children who are **blind** cannot use vision for learning but still can be responsive to light and darkness and may have some visual imagery.

Children with **low vision** have difficulty accomplishing visual tasks, but they can learn through the visual sense by the use of various special technologies and teaching techniques. The major educational distinction is that children who are blind use their tactile or auditory senses as their primary learning channels, whereas children with low vision can, with aid, still use the visual sense as their major avenue of learning.

Association for Education and Rehabilitation of the Blind and Visually Impaired
www.aerbvi.org

Prevalence of Visual Impairments

Children with visual impairments qualify as having a low-incidence disability and make up a very small percentage of the school population. There are only about 4 of these children for every 10,000 students (U.S. Department of Education, 2003), so it would be very difficult to cluster them for instructional purposes unless they were in a very large community or enrolled in a state school for the blind. Today there is a strong effort to provide them with an education within local schools. Another complication, described by a teacher of the visually impaired, is that more than half of children with visual impairments also have other exceptionalities, such as cerebral palsy, intellectual and developmental disabilities, autism, and so on, that challenge the education planning for such students.

The fact that visual impairment is a low-incidence disability has a number of challenging consequences. If a school district has 20,000 children, then only 8 of them would on average have visual impairments. Grouping of students for instruction is not likely to be feasible. In addition, a specialist in visual impairment (TVI) would be very expensive due to his or her limited case load. Research programs are difficult to carry out because of the insufficient sample of students present. Indeed, the research reported in this chapter combines a number of school systems across states in order to reach the required number to pursue *evidence-based practice*. And, finally, there is a limited amount of funding available for children with visual impairments, making the possibility of meeting the requirements of legislation such as IDEA difficult. We address these consequences throughout the chapter.

The Human Eye

Vision, or visual interpretation, is a function of the brain, experience, and adequacy of the sense organ that receives stimuli from the outside world: the eye. Faulty visual interpretation can result from a defect in the brain, inadequate experience, or a defective eye (sense organics). The process of visual interpretation is as follows: Light enters the eye, focuses on the retina, and is transmitted along the optic nerve to the brain, where visual information is interpreted. Two people with well-functioning sense organs can interpret a visual experience differently, depending on their training and experience.

> Vision is a function of the sensation and perception of light.

Educators of children with visual impairments are concerned primarily with adapting instruction to the impairment. To accomplish this, they need to understand how healthy eyes operate and what some of the conditions are that can cause problems.

The human eye is a complex system of interrelated parts (see Figure 11.1). Any part can be defective or become nonfunctional as a result of hereditary anomaly, disease, accident, or other causes. The eye has been called a camera for the brain. Just as a camera lens expands and contracts to let in the correct amount of light, the eye uses the **iris**. The iris is the colored muscular partition that expands and contracts to regulate the amount of light admitted through the central opening, or **pupil**. Behind the iris is the lens, an elastic biconvex body that focuses onto the retina the light reflected from objects in the line of vision. The **retina** is the light-sensitive innermost layer of tissue at the back of the eyeball. It contains neural receptors that translate the physical energy of light into the neural energy that results in the experience of seeing.

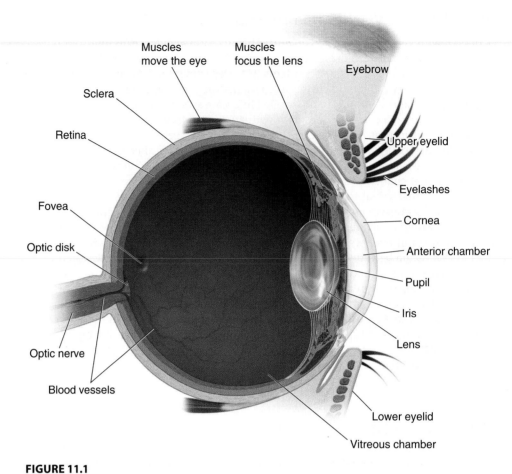

FIGURE 11.1
The Human Eye
Source: Freberg, L. (2006) *Discovering biological psychology.* Reprinted by permission
of Houghton Mifflin Harcourt Publishing Company.

As Figure 11.1 shows, other protective and structural elements in the eye can affect vision. The **cornea** is the transparent anterior (front) portion of the tough outer coat of the eyeball which refracts light to help focus the retina. The **ciliary muscles** change the shape of the lens so the eye can focus on objects at varying distances. In the normal mature eye, no muscular effort is necessary to see clearly objects 20 feet or more away. When the eye looks at an object closer than 20 feet, the ciliary muscles increase the convex curvature of the lens so that the closer object is still focused on the retina. This change in the shape of the lens is called accommodation.

Extrinsic muscles control the movement of the eyeball in the socket. The change made by these muscles is known as **convergence** and refers to the movement of two eyes toward each other when focusing on an object at near range.

For the visual system to function typically, a number of structures and processes needs to be present and operative:

● The eyes and associated structures must be normal in structure and function.

- The neurological pathways from the retina and optic nerve to the visual cortex must be intact.

- The brain must be capable of interpreting the information received (Schwartz, 2010, p. 138).

If any part of the system is damaged and not correctable, the child will have a visual impairment.

Causes of Visual Impairments

A wide variety of conditions can cause serious visual impairments in children from birth to age 5. The potential causes include hereditary conditions, infectious diseases, cancer, injuries, premature birth, and various environmental conditions. The actual cause of the disorder is not of primary interest to the teacher, who must deal with the functional consequences of the disorders; those functional consequences would seem to be similar from one condition to another. So whether the cause was an infection or a hereditary condition, the teacher faces a similar problem of instructing a child with limited vision. In order of prevalence, the most common causes of **visual impairment** for children in the United States are as follows:

- Cortical visual impairment

- Retinopathy of prematurity

- Optic nerve hypoplasia

- Albinism

- Optic atrophy

- Congenital infection (Schwartz, 2010, p. 139)

The widely scattered prevalence of these conditions makes it difficult to assign percentages to particular causes, but some of them are reasonably well known. One of the most common infectious diseases was rubella (German measles), contracted by the mother during pregnancy. Rubella can cause serious birth defects, intellectual and developmental disabilities, and hearing loss, in addition to visual problems, but improved control measures and education have combined to reduce the percentage of children blinded by this and other infectious diseases. (See Chapter 10 for more information on rubella.)

> Low birth weight is an indication of possible visual impairment and requires diagnostic attention.

Another major cause of visual impairment is **retinopathy of prematurity** (formerly called *retrolental fibroplasia*). This genetic disorder was widely believed to be caused by the overadministration of oxygen to premature infants in an attempt to save the life of a child who was threatened by other conditions. However, the condition appears to be more complicated. For example, it seems to be associated with low birth weight as well. A cohort of 137 children (ages 11–13) with very low birth weight were compared with a typical sample and found to have a high incidence of visual impairment (Powls et al., 1997), about one third of the sample. They also showed neurodevelopmental impairment in motor and cognitive areas, presumably due to early neurological damage. For additional information on blindness and multiple disabilities, see Chapter 12.

Genetic Factors and Visual Impairment

Genetic causes of blindness are relatively rare. Vision impairments are often associated with **albinism**, the absence or lack of pigmentation resulting from and inheritance of recessive genes, in approximately 1 in 20,000 individuals (Wikipedia, 2010). The visual problems associated with albinism include **nystagmus**, rapid irregular movements of the eye; **myopia**, **hyperopia**, and **astigmatisms**, refraction errors that create blurred vision; **amblyopia**, a decrease in acuity due to poor transmission of information to the brain; and **optic nerve hypoplasia**, the underdevelopment of the optic nerve. Treatment may include surgurey to reduce eye movements, glasses to reduce the impact of glare and improve vision, and the use of large-print materials.

Leber's congenital amauroisis (LCA), a second inherited eye disease, affects around one in 80,000 infants at or shortly after birth (Wikipedia, 2010). LCA is associated with multiple genes and so the specific form it takes can vary, however, a typical characteristic is a sluggish or non-response of the pupils to light and severe vision loss or blindness. Gene replacement therapies are currently in a trial phase at the Children's Hospital of Philadelphia and emerging results show positive improvements for some subjects (Kaiser & Voss, 2009). As research on genetics continues we will learn more about both genetic causes of, and possible cures for, visual impairments.

Twenty-five years ago, Adam Ockelford was giving a piano lesson to a young girl at Linden Lodge School for the blind in London when a couple and their five-year-old son opened the door to his room. Suddenly, the little blond boy ran over to the piano, pushed Ockelford's student roughly off her stool, and began to bang on the piano keys. Ockelford soon recognized that he was playing, "Don't Cry for Me Argentina." He asked the parents if he could teach the child.

This was in 1985. The child, Derek Paravicini, 30, is a musical savant. He was born 25 weeks premature, and although oxygen therapy saved his life, he incurred brain damage and now suffers from severe learning difficulties and autism. He is blind, is unable to read Braille, and can barely count, let alone read music, but he has an amazing gift: He can play anything after hearing it only once. Ockelford has been his teacher and even wrote his biography, *In the Key of Genius*. It took many months before Ockelford could get close enough to the piano to work with Derek. He met every day with him for an hour and painstakingly taught him how to play correctly.

Derek realized that he could communicate through music. He could copy what others played and memorize any song he liked. And now, he plays in concerts with full orchestras. As for his abilities, Ockelford says, "He has no fear. Most musicians will be very aware if they play a wrong note, but that critical side of it isn't really in Derek's make up. If he does play something wrong, he can cover it up within half a second. But having said that, I don't think he really perceives it as making a mistake."

Persons such as Derek teach us that the brain has remarkable capabilities. We cannot say his story is impossible when he is sitting in front of us playing a concert!

Source: Norman, M. (2009). The human iPod: Meet the musical savant. *The Independent*. May 28.

Because projections predict that children will increasingly have multiple disabilities, it is likely that more children will have visual problems. These children will have visual difficulties which may be complicated by a variety of other problems, which make a team approach necessary for diagnosis and treatment.

Neurology and Brain Development
The Promise of the Bionic Eye

The visual cortex, located at the back of the brain, is highly specialized to process static and moving visual objects and to recognize patterns. The left visual cortex processes information from the right eye, and the right visual cortex responds to stimulus from the left eye. There are an estimated 140 million neurons in the visual cortex of each hemisphere. These neurons can discriminate between small changes in visual orientation, spatial frequency, and color (wikipedia.org, July 2010). Damage to any part of the primary visual cortex can lead to vision problems. If the visual cortex is intact and the difficulty with vision is caused by problems with the eye itself or damage to the optical nerve. then a promising new development called the "bionic eye" may someday be able to restore vision.

The bionic eye involves a small implant behind the retina that captures the visual stimulus and sends the information directly to the visual cortex to be processed (The Future of Things, July 2010; ScienceDaily, July 2010). The bionic eye will only be useful for individuals who had vision that was lost. In addition, the optic nerve must be at least partially functional for the technology to work. Individuals who are born blind do not have the neurological capability to process and interpret the visual stimulation. The bionic eye may eventually help restore some vision for patients with age-related macular degeneration and retinitis pigmentosa (a genetic condition). While research continues on the use of bionic eyes, it is not science fiction. The device is currently being tested with animals and the expectation is that human trials will begin in the next few years (ScienceDaily, July, 2010).

Characteristics of Children with Visual Impairments

Children with visual impairments tend to develop at a slower pace than children without disabilities. There is a wide variation in the patterns of development of children with visual impairments, and with a rich physical environment and encouragement to take reasonable risks, parents can increase the adaptive skills of their children.

A Visit to the Beach for a Child Who Is Blind

Imagine that a girl who is blind goes to the beach for the first time with someone who takes pleasure in introducing her to the joys of summer. Her companion, who may be sighted or blind, has described where they are going so that she has some preparation for what awaits her as she first sets foot on the beach. She anticipates eating a picnic lunch on the beach, and she has helped to buy the food and pack it in the ice chest. The two beachgoers have loaded the chest into the car and carried it from the car to the beach. Together, they have paused to pick up some sand and feel it sift through their fingers before they venture to the shore. Her friend has pointed out how the sand becomes damper the closer they get to the water. She may have picked up some more sand on her own to examine the change in texture. She has helped spread the blanket on the sand, noticing how the wind makes it difficult to spread it flat. When she has listened to an explanation of why it is important to protect her skin from the sun, she is prepared to rub the parts she can reach with sunscreen and to ask for help with the parts she cannot reach. Her attention to the sounds, smells, and tactile sensations at the beach is appreciated and forms an important part of the friends' conversation. With assistance, she has stashed her shoes in a bag on a particular corner of the blanket; her friend hopes she will remember where to retrieve them when it is time to put them on and go home.

The day has been rich in information and less scary than it might have been. Her friend has answered questions and shown her, in small, understandable, and pleasant steps, what is enjoyable and interesting at the beach. She may not comprehend how huge the ocean looks or how beautiful the sky is that day, but she has had a better chance of relaxing in the sun, enjoying a swim, and feeling like one of the magicians who produced the lovely picnic at the beach.

Source: F. Liefert, Introduction to visual impairment, in S. Goodman & S. Wittenstein (Eds.), *Collaborative assessment: Working with students who are blind or visually impaired, including those with additional disabilities,* (pp. 1–22) (New York: American Foundation for the Blind, 2003). Reprinted with the permission of the American Foundation for the Blind.

The Office of Special Education Programs in the U.S. Department of Education funded a large longitudinal study of the development of young children with visual impairment (birth to 5 years) in seven sites around the country. This enabled the investigators to assemble data on a population of 202 youngsters receiving services from these sites and to draw some conclusions about their visual acuity, behavior, temperament, and environment in an effort to discover any differences between these children and typical children of similar age. This longitudinal study was named Project PRISM, and it has administered 2,446 standardized tests to the 202 children during the course of the project (Ferrell, Shaw, & Dietz, 1998).

Some of the major findings from this effort were as follows.

- Sixty percent of these children had additional disabilities, and two-thirds of these disabilities were considered severe.

- The leading diagnoses for these children were cortical visual impairment (21 percent), retinopathy of prematurity (19 percent), and optic nerve hypoplasia (17 percent).

- The majority of developmental milestones for these children were delayed, in comparison with those of typical children. Children with additional impairments achieved these milestones later than children without such impairments.

- Measures of social maturity and cognitive development showed delay.

- Measures of parental stress found more high scores among the parents of these children with visual impairments compared to typical children.

These findings tended to underscore the importance of providing services to the child and family as early as possible and emphasize the importance of special attention to those children with more than one disability.

 # The Information Processing Model

Figure 11.2 shows the impact of lack of vision on the information processing model (IPM). What is clear is that the lack of vision impacts many other aspects of the system. In particular, the *cognitive* and *expressive* aspects are significantly affected. Unlike children who are deaf who may have a serious and obvious communication problem, children with moderate visual impairments are able

to communicate through language but still have limitations in understanding the three-dimensional world in which we live.

Like the girl at the beach, children with visual impairments have little grasp of the vastness of the ocean or space, as it is vision that allows us to understand such concepts. Also, children with visual impairments have limitations in navigating their living space or traveling from one place to another. Much of the special instruction provided for these students has to do with helping them gain some facility in travel and grasping the concepts of space and language.

The *emotional context* of these children with visual impairments is that they can fall into a state of **learned helplessness** and be unable to read the emotional context of others, which they need to be able do to interact with others effectively. This interaction impacts their ability to make decisions and choices and use the *executive function* to its fullest.

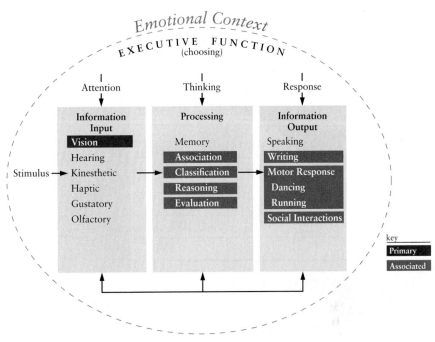

FIGURE 11.2
The Information Processing Model for Children with Visual Impairments

Cognitive Development of Children with Visual Impairments

In the 1940s and 1950s, educators believed that the intelligence of children with visual impairments was not seriously affected by their condition, except for their ability to use certain visual concepts (colors and three-dimensional space, for example). The thinking then was that intelligence unfolds on a genetically determined schedule and is affected by only the most severe environmental trauma.

Today, we hold a different view of cognitive development of children with visual impairments. We recognize that what we measure as intelligence in school-age children has been notably affected by their cumulative experiences in the early years of development. Lack of vision, then, is both a primary impairment and a condition that can hamper cognitive development because it limits the integrating experiences of *association* and *classification* and the understanding of those experiences (*reasoning* and *evaluation*), which the visual sense brings naturally to sighted children. These limitations are especially notable if the children do not receive early intervention in the preschool years. At present, the verbal section of the Wechsler Intelligence Scale for Children (WISC) would seem to provide the best measurement of intelligence for children with visual impairment.

> Visual impairment can sometimes hamper cognitive development.

Language Development for Children with Visual Impairments

Sighted children acquire language by listening, reading, and watching movements and facial expressions. They express themselves first through babbling and later by imitating their parents and siblings. Children with visual impairments acquire

> Visual impairment calls for major efforts in vocabulary development.

World Class surfer Kip Jerger, lying down in water, leads by the hand July 17, 2000 as he teaches blind children surfing techniques in Manhattan Beach, Ca.

Dan Callister/Newsmakers/Getty Images

language in much the same way, but their language concepts are not helped by visual input. A sighted child develops the concept of a ball by seeing different balls; a child with blindness develops the same concept through tactile manipulation of different balls. Both are able to understand the word *ball,* and both are able to identify a ball.

A series of investigations into the language development of school-aged children with visual impairments yielded the following conclusions. Visual impairment does not interfere with everyday language usage or communication abilities. The language of children with visual impairments is similar to that of their sighted peers. However, the children with visual impairments had less understanding of words as vehicles of, or as standing for, concrete experiences. They may talk about a baseball or mountain climbing without a full understanding of the concept.

Sensory Compensation and Perception

Vision provides a continuous source of information. We depend on vision to orient ourselves, to identify people and objects, and to regulate our motor and social behavior. People without sight have to rely on other senses for information and for all the other tasks that vision performs. How this is accomplished has been the focus of much speculation and research. The false doctrine of **sensory compensation** holds that if one sense, such as vision, is deficient, other senses are automatically strengthened, in part because of their greater use. Although this may be true in certain cases, research does not show that the hearing or touch sensitivity of children with visual impairments is superior to that of sighted children (Huebner, 2000).

Personal and Social Adjustment and Nonverbal Communication (Emotional Context)

No personal or social problems *inevitably* follow from being visually impaired. However, the restricted mobility and consequent limited experiences of children who are visually impaired appear to cause, in some children, a state of passivity and dependency.

The increasing interest in the social adjustment of students with visual impairments resulted in a study of the lifestyles of adolescents with blindness, low vision, and sight (Sacks, Wolffe, & Tierney, 1998). Using a device called a **time diary**, in which the students identified their primary and secondary activities in one-hour blocks of time over a 24-hour period, the investigators found that students with visual impairments spent more time on the telephone, engaged in more sedentary activities, spent more time alone, and were bound to their homes by their inability to travel independently. One could anticipate that children with multiple impairments would fare even worse in the social domain than did these students.

What this study seems to indicate is a need for continued implementation of programs designed to prepare students with visual impairments for adult life. That would mean curricula that focus on career development and social skill competencies. Of course, the study also underscores the importance of mobility training as a key component to social contact for these students.

The TVI must deal with many realistic issues; for example, spatial perception and communication. It is understandable that the teacher might overlook an issue that turns out to be one of the most important—how the child feels about his or her situation. Recently, there has been an attempt to focus on the child's feelings and to make them a significant part of the instructional program. The child who is deeply depressed and feels helpless is not a good candidate for Braille, print reading, or any other kind of instruction (Tuttle & Tuttle, 2004). For example, a child who is trying to deny the reality of visual impairment may resist special learning devices such as viewers or magnifying glasses because these symbolize the disability that he or she is denying.

> It is important to let children take control of a task once they demonstrate an ability to do so.

Successful Coping

Several principles have formed the basis of a strategy to help the child go beyond these feelings of despair and create a climate of self-expression and self-esteem.

Successful coping includes the following:

- What a person *can do* is emphasized.

- The areas of life in which the person can participate are seen as worthwhile.

- The person plays an active role in molding his or her life constructively.

- Accomplishments are appreciated in terms of their benefits to the person and others and not depreciated because they fall short of some irrelevant standard.

- Pain that is suffered or difficulties that exist are felt to be manageable.

- The person is overcoming difficulties or lessening them through the application of medical procedures, the use of prostheses and other aids, the learning of new skills, and environmental accommodations (social, legal, economic, and so on).

- The person is living on satisfactory terms with his or her limitations (Tuttle & Tuttle, 1996, p. 169).

Many people who have not had experience with individuals with disabilities react to them by lowering their expectations. But many students with exceptionalities do not want this kind of favor. "Don't treat me like I'm helpless. Let me do it on my own," is their response to well-meaning people who attempt to "help" them.

Great interest has been shown in the self-esteem of students with visual impairment. However, self-esteem appears to be the by-product of good performance on tasks deemed socially valuable (for example, effective mobility around class and school). Good academic and social behavior will result in good self-esteem, rather than the other way around.

When adapting instruction to the educational needs of children who are visually impaired, teachers should emphasize concreteness and tactile experiences.
(Courtesy of Cengage Learning)

One Person's Reflections on the Consequences of Using a Unique Standard

I don't know when it began, this pervasive expectation that others would naturally give me a break because I am blind—probably as a very young child. I do remember in the first grade the teacher asked for volunteers to help me during recesses "so [I] wouldn't get hurt." I didn't need the help, but I have to admit I enjoyed the extra attention.

In fourth and fifth grades, the teachers let me complete only even-numbered problems in arithmetic homework while my classmates had to do them all. They told me that they were making this exception because I was blind and it took me longer to do my work. I had a teacher in seventh grade who required six book reports during the year for an A, but then turned to me and announced that four would be good enough for an A. Who was I to argue with such good fortune? Through high school, I guess I began to work the system to my advantage. I learned that if I looked uncomfortable, I wouldn't be called on in class; if I turned in partial work, I would often get full credit; if I happened to be late turning in assignments, it was OK because I was blind. Before long, I expected everyone to give me a break because of my blindness.

My first summer job after my junior year in high school really jolted me to reality. I was hired by a used car dealer to wash, wax, and vacuum six cars a day. At the end of the first week I questioned my paycheck—I thought they shortchanged me. My boss didn't pull any punches. "You serviced four cars a day this week, so I paid you for four cars a day. If and when you get up to speed and you finish six cars, I'll pay you what we agreed upon." I didn't argue—I knew he was right. I got myself organized, hustled a bit more, and put in some extra time that next week. I was proud to get my first paycheck on Friday; I knew I had earned it fair and square.

Source: Reprinted from D. Tuttle & N. Tuttle, Psychosocial needs of children and youths, in M. C. Holbrook & A. J. Koenig (Eds.), *Foundations of education* (2nd ed.), Vol. 1, *History and theory of teaching children and youths with visual impairments* (p. 167) (New York: AFB Press, 2000) American Foundation for the Blind.

Pivotal Issues

- What was the cumulative effect on the student of all the "help" provided because of his blindness?

- Have you ever had your offers of help indignantly rejected? What do you believe was the psychological basis for that rejection?

What happens to children with visual impairments over time? Does their lack of experience with the world around them cause developmental problems in motor and social domains? These questions have been difficult to answer because the relative infrequency of such children made it hard to bring together a sufficient number of children to conduct a convincing study.

The findings of a national study of children with visual impairments were combined with agency data from a southern state to create a sample of 186 children (ages 1–7) who had developmental curves that could answer these questions (Hatton, Bailey, Burchinal, & Ferrell, 1997). The majority of these children had visual impairments that stemmed from retinopathy of prematurity, optic nerve hypoplasia, cortical visual impairment, and albinism. Forty percent of the sample also had co-occurring conditions of intellectual and developmental disabilities. Personal and social development improved as the impact of the visual disability lessened. (See Chapter 12 for more on multiple disabilities.) The following story gives a good example of a student seeking independence.

Early Intervention

A child's experiences during the period from birth to age 5 are critical to subsequent development and provide opportunities for engagement. It is especially important that the systematic education of children with visual impairment

Children with visual impairments can be very active when they are under supervision.

(© Mitch Wojnarowicz/The Image Works)

begin as early as possible. Sighted children absorb a tremendous amount of information and experience from their environment in the ordinary course of events. Parents and teachers must design parallel experiences for children who are visually impaired (see Chapter 3 for more information).

The characteristics we observe in a 10-year-old who has visual impairment are often a blend of the primary problem (loss of vision) and a number of secondary problems that have developed because the child has missed certain sequential experiences. For example, many youngsters with a visual impairment are passive. Passivity is not a natural or inevitable by-product of low vision; it is present because the child does not have a well-established motivation to move.

> Placement in a typical preschool requires careful planning and support personnel.

For the sighted child, the environment is filled with visual stimulation: toys, enticing foods, bottles, people, color, and shapes. The child has a natural impulse to move toward these elements. The child with a severe visual disability is not aware of these elements unless someone points them out. For an infant who is blind, the feeding bottle appears magically. The child is not motivated to go after it; in fact, the child does not even realize that he or she can do something—be active—to get the bottle.

An easily understood concept for the sighted child is **object permanence**. By the age of 6 or 7 months, sighted children realize that even when objects disappear from their visual field (mother left the room; the ball rolled under the couch), they still exist. This knowledge makes the world more orderly and predictable. And it makes sense to go after objects even if they are not in the line of sight. Object constancy is a more difficult concept for children with visual disabilities to understand. They need deliberate instruction and an organized environment before they can understand the concept and begin to act on it.

The importance of starting education early for children with visual impairments was pointed to in a study of 13 children with visual impairments who were 40 months of age (Hughes, Dote-Kwan, & Dolendo, 1998). The study looked at the play behavior of these children in a special play setting. The results are consistent with earlier studies in that the children with visual impairments were significantly delayed in their play skills, particularly symbolic play. Because the children were functioning at expected developmental levels in other domains, such as receptive language, the study underlined the importance of helping these children to develop and facilitate their play behavior. This is particularly important considering the heavy emphasis on play in most inclusive preschool settings.

IDEA, which mandates services for infants and toddlers with disabilities (see Chapter 2), provides for earlier identification and earlier professional services for children with vision impairment. Such early intervention programs should reduce the number of secondary problems shown by children who did not have the advantages of earlier services. The work cited in Chapter 3 on early intervention provides additional evidence on the usefulness of early attention.

The Role of the Family

Family members are the first teachers of a child with visual impairments. Parents and siblings are key to the development of the child's skills, and that is one reason why legislation requires the family help design and take part in the Individual Family Service Plan (IFSP) (Corn & Lusk, 2010).

Family members may need to be reassured about the child's natural tendency toward exploring or taking risks. Parents are often overprotective of a child with visual impairments because of difficulties with mobility, but they can be reminded that children with typical vision fall, twist ankles, and bruise often as part of the experience of growing up.

While we can create a safe environment for a child with visual impairments to help him adapt to his surroundings, an important goal is to allow him to experience the world and feel successful in his abilities to cope with his environment independently. Children with visual impairments gain confidence through exploring and gaining familiarity with their home and community. A parent's encouragement can coax an infant to turn toward a favorite toy or crawl into a new area (Fazzi & Naimy, 2010). Passageways can be formed with furniture and soft barriers to help a child navigate her home environment. Providing young children with low vision with a rich variety of early life experiences, such as those found in the activities listed here, helps them to comprehend the world they encounter both in life and in books, providing a foundation for literacy. The following box suggests some home and community experiences that a parent may provide to help her child become more self-confident.

Basic Early Experiences for Development

Home Experiences

- Helping prepare a snack or bake cookies
- Picking up the morning newspaper
- Helping stack dishes in the dishwasher
- Helping rake leaves or plant flowers
- Picking up clothes or toys
- Getting the mail from the mail carrier
- Playing with siblings or friends in the backyard
- Calling grandmother and grandfather on the telephone

Community Experiences

- Playing at the city park with siblings and friends

- Splashing in the wading pool at a public swimming pool

- Exploring the grocery store and stores at a mall

- Visiting a farm with animals and machinery

- Eating at a fast-food and at a formal restaurant

- Visiting a petting zoo

- Visiting public places like the post office, fire station, and library (Koenig and Holbrook, 2010, p. 503)

Identification and Assessment

Most children with severe and profound visual impairment are identified by parents and physicians long before they enter school.

Most states require preschool vision screening, which identifies children with moderate vision problems. Throughout this textbook, we discuss the importance of early experiences in cognitive development. Obviously, early identification allows us to broaden those experiences for the child with a visual disability through maximum correction and preschool programs.

The term *assessment* describes a process that must occur before a student with a suspected disability receives special educational services. Four specific steps are taken in assessments: screening, eligibility, instructional planning, and progress evaluation (Lewis & Russo, 1998).

Routine vision screenings are administered to many students before they enter school. Whereas severe visual impairments are readily apparent without formal screening, some milder problems might escape notice. Screening merely identifies students with possible developmental problems. A medical diagnosis of blindness is often sufficient to demonstrate the need for special educational services, but sometimes a functional visual evaluation may be necessary to determine the degree of usable vision. These results can do much to shape the approach taken by special education teachers.

The standard school screening instrument is the Snellen chart, which has rows of letters in gradually smaller sizes that children read at a distance of 20 feet. A variation that is useful for screening young children and people who do not know letter names consists of capital *E*s pointing in different directions. The individual is asked to indicate the direction in which the arms of the *E* are pointing. Scores are based on how accurately the person identifies the letters (or directions of the *E*s) using one eye at a time.

The National Society to Prevent Blindness is the oldest voluntary health agency involved in preventing blindness. For preschoolers and school-age children, it has developed a number of screening tests that use the Snellen chart or modifications of it.

The National Society to Prevent Blindness
www.preventblindness.org

Notice the accompanying examples of some near-acuity cards provided by Lighthouse International. These lists would seem to have considerable advantage over the typical Snellen chart for children with low vision. It becomes important to know what the students can read at near point, and the gradations of size here can give some understanding of the student's limits in responding to print.

More extensive tests use elaborate equipment (such as the Keystone Telebinocular and the Bausch & Lomb Orthorater) to measure vision at far and near points and to test muscle balance, fusion, usable vision, and other characteristics. The Titmus Vision Tester (manufactured by Titmus, P.O. Box 191,

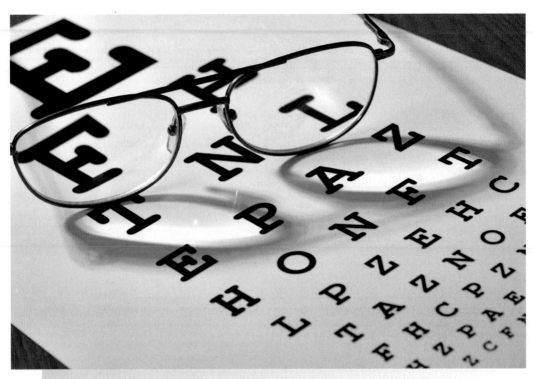

Near-Acuity Cards
(Image copyright ajt 2010. Used under license from Shutterstock.com)

Petersburg, VA 23804) is the most widely used test of visual acuity and is used to screen vision in preschool children, school-age children, and adults. Most people who have taken a driver's license test have been screened for vision problems by the Titmus.

 # A National Agenda

Table 11.1 provides a roster of national agenda items for children with visual impairments. The items include students' and parents' rights, appropriate and timely service, and appropriate caseloads and personnel preparation programs. This list presents the professional expectations of what should be happening if good educational practice for children with visual impairments is to be observed. For those programs that are not meeting these needs, it is a wake-up call that they are falling short of appropriate norms for good practice. The list itself can be a checklist for parents and others who want to make sure good practice is being adhered to. The National Agenda in Table 11.1 represents the work of many professionals and parents to provide goals for effective educational services for children with visual impairments.

In particular, the importance of proper access to instructional materials and the expanded core curriculum, to say nothing of transition services, cannot be overestimated.

TABLE 11.1
National Agenda Goal Statement for Children with Visual Impairments

1. **Early Referral.** Students and their families will be referred to an appropriate education program within 30 days of identification of a suspected visual impairment.

2. **Parent Participation.** Policies and procedures will be implemented to ensure the right of all parents to full participation and equal partnership in the education process.

3. **Professional Personnel.** Universities, with a minimum of one full-time faculty member in the area of visual impairment, will prepare a sufficient number of educators of students with visual impairments to meet personnel needs throughout the country.

4. **Case Loads.** Service providers will determine caseloads based on the needs of students and will require ongoing professional development for all teachers and orientation and mobility instructors.

5. **Array of Services.** Local education programs will ensure that all students have access to a full array of placement options.

6. **Assessment.** Assessment of students will be conducted, in collaboration with parents, by personnel having expertise in the education of students with visual impairments.

7. **Access to Instructional Materials.** Access to developmental and educational services will include an assurance that instructional materials are available to students in the appropriate media and at the same time as their sighted peers.

8. **Expanded Core Curriculum.** Educational and developmental goals, including instruction, will reflect the assessed needs of each student in all areas of academic and disability-specific core curricula.

9. **Transition.** Transition services will address developmental and educational needs (birth through high school) to assist students and their families in setting goals and implementing strategies throughout the life continuum commensurate with the student's aptitudes, interests, and abilities.

10. **Professional Development.** To improve student learning, service providers will engage in ongoing local, state, and national professional development.

Source: A. L. Corn & K. M. Huebner (Eds.), *A Report to the Nation: The National Agenda for the Education of Children and Youth with Visual Impairments* (New York: American Foundation for the Blind, 2001).

Multicultural Issues and Underserved Populations

As in the case of children with other exceptionalities, the presence of children from different ethnic or racial backgrounds adds an element of complexity to the planning and programming for children with visual impairments. This is particularly an issue whenever English is not the primary language of the child or family (Milian, 2000). Again, a collaborative team of professionals seems called for, although in this case it might include a translator familiar with the first language of the student. Consultations between the English Language Learners (ELL) teachers and the teachers of students with visual impairments can yield positive results. An ELL teacher can learn how to modify the curriculum to take visual problems into account, while the TVI can learn about the sequence of acquiring a second language.

A substantial percentage of children with visual impairments come from African American families (perhaps 10–15 percent). The variety of possible cultural backgrounds make it important that cultural factors such as family views on education, on child-rearing practices, and on the origins of disability be factored into the plans for the student. Adding to the challenge of planning is a shortage of minority teachers in special education, but a determined effort to recruit more teachers from these ethnic or racial backgrounds is under way (Milian & Ferrell, 1998).

Additional support may be needed if the visually impaired child's first language is not English.

The impact of visual impairment on a child is widespread, as noted in the information processing model. All of the elements, from central processing to output to emotional context, require attention. The learning environment, curriculum, teaching strategies, and technology must be adapted for use. The adaptations differ considerably depending on whether the child has low vision or blindness.

To design an instructional plan, one must first find out what the student's current level of achievement is, what his or her potential is, and other information about learning style and responsiveness to various forms of instruction. A comprehensive assessment would contain information about the child's skills and assistive technology needs:

- Concept development and academic skills
- Communication skills
- Social and emotional skills
- Sensory motor skills
- Daily living skills
- Orientation and mobility skills
- Career and vocational skills

In addition to a variety of formal tests designed to capture the preceding skill areas, assessment is made from observations and criterion reference tests. For example, if you want to know whether the student can borrow in subtraction, you give him or her some additional problems and watch what the student does (Lewis & Russo, 1998; Silberman & Brown, 1998).

All this information is drawn together, with input from the parents, in an individualized education program (IEP) meeting in which the basic goals and objectives of the program for the student are determined, together with the strategies that will be used to reach those goals.

Finally, there is the question of whether the student is progressing toward these goals in a satisfactory manner. If a student is not progressing satisfactorily, readjustments in the IEP and the instructional program are called for.

Learning Environments

Because of the special nature of the adaptations that have to be made (e.g., teaching of Braille or use of technology), there are questions as to what is the least restrictive environment for children with visual impairment. Is it the regular classroom with special help or a special separate setting? It is here that the team approach is not only desirable but also essential. The team includes the general education teacher, the TVI, and an orientation and mobility specialist (O&M), in addition to others as appropriate.

▲ Adapting the Learning Environment

The goal of moving students with visual impairments into the general education classroom or as close as possible (least-restrictive environment) is getting closer, as Figure 11.3 indicates. Fifty-seven percent of children with visual impairments are found in the general education classroom 16 or more hours a week, another 16 percent are out of the classroom 21 to 60 percent of the time, and 15 percent are away more than 15 hours a week. A little more than 12 percent of these children can now be found in residential schools or in other settings. Many of these students, but by no means all, probably have a variety of disabilities requiring very specialized education and care.

As is true of children with other kinds of exceptionalities, the various learning environments provided for children with visual impairments represent a continuum of services. The goal of full inclusion is modified by the particular needs of the individual child and, sometimes, by the availability of services.

The successful inclusion of the exceptional child requires a well-thought-out plan and capable people; otherwise, there is a good possibility for social isolation of the child. An additional complicating factor is cultural differences between the child with visual difficulties and the school. For example, a child who is blind and from a Hispanic background has numerous challenges to overcome as well as, possibly, a language barrier and a set of family values that may differ from the values taught at school.

The following vignette shows how classroom adjustments and technology operate to create a positive learning environment.

Jeanie and Wes

Jeanie, a second grader, entered the classroom and hung her pink baseball cap on the hook by the door. Her teacher of students with visual impairments, Ms. Carlyle, and her second-grade general education teacher, Ms. Burkette, had put up the hook so Jeanie

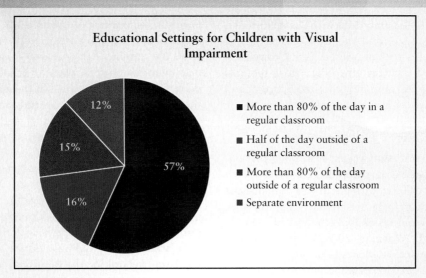

FIGURE 11.3
Time Spent in School Services by Students with Visual Impairment
Source: U.S. Department of Education. (2009). *Twenty-Eighth Annual Report to Congress*. Washington, D.C.: Office of Special Education Programs.

would have a place to keep her cap and not have to hunt for it each time she went out. In preschool, Jeanie had usually crouched in the shade at recess before it was discovered that she had ocular albinism and photophobia. Jeanie's visual acuity was 20/200. She wore tinted eyeglasses, and maybe when she was older she would wear contact lenses. With the tinted eyeglasses, indoor light almost never bothered her; but when outdoors, Jeanie really needed a cap with a visor as well. In the classroom, Jeanie sat at a desk in the front row, away from the windows. She read regular second-grade books, sometimes propping them up on a reading stand, and occasionally used a handheld magnifier to view small print or the details of a picture. She was able to write using the same sort of pencil and paper as her classmates—and she could read what she had written, too.

Ms. Carlyle and Wes were practicing copying from the chalkboard with his handheld monocular. Wes had no trouble reading from the board with the device, but he habitually held the monocular in his right hand. The trouble was that Wes also *wrote* with his right hand, so he had to lay down the monocular and pick up his pencil each time he was ready to write. It was an ineffective process, and Wes was having trouble keeping up when Mr. Taylor, the mathematics teacher, wrote a series of problems on the board. Ms. Carlyle had written several typical problems on the board, and Wes was

experimenting with holding the monocular in his left hand while he copied part of a problem down with his right hand and then looking back at the board. This way, he did not have to put down either the monocular or the pencil. It was definitely a faster method, but Wes felt clumsy holding the monocular in his left hand. Ms. Carlyle told him that with practice, he might feel more comfortable and become more skilled in doing so.

Source: Holbrook, M. Cay., & Koenig, A. J. (2000). *Foundations of education*. New York: AFB Press, p. 464–465.

Wherever the child with visual impairments is placed, ideally one professional—the classroom teacher or the TVI should take the role of **case coordinator**. This individual brings together all the information that relates to the child (the comprehensive assessment, for example) and leads a team of professionals who, with the parents, develop an IEP for the student. A working team made up of persons of different backgrounds and skills is of paramount importance in producing an IEP.

▲ Removing Barriers

In most cases, we increase the mobility of individuals who are visually impaired by teaching them ways to get around or to use available tools. But there is another way to ease the restrictions on those who are blind. Society has a responsibility to remove obstacles wherever possible. That responsibility became law in 1991 with the passage of the Americans with Disabilities Act, which directs businesses and public officials to remove barriers for persons with disabilities (see Chapter 2). Removing barriers includes attaching Braille symbols to elevators, widening aisles for wheelchair access, and providing open spaces in the classroom.

▲ Special Schools

Before the emphasis on the least restrictive environment and the inclusive classroom began in the 1980s, the education of children with visual impairments was often conducted in large residential state schools. There are still fifty-one residential schools in the United States and Canada (Hoetling, 2004). With the rapidly growing trend for such students to be educated in the local schools, the question of what happens to the residential school and its often-elaborate facilities arises.

The children attending residential schools may have additional disabilities, and the schools may have been redesigned to provide an effective environment for such children. Also, these schools can provide outreach services, offering information, assessment, and technical assistance to students who are visually impaired and to their teachers in the public schools. There is also an opportunity to introduce major shifts in program and curriculum not possible in public schools. This can be done by creating the following:

- *Life skills centers for students with severe disabilities.* These centers would specialize in assisting students with severe and multiple disabilities, with an emphasis on those with visual impairments.

- *Magnet schools for students with visual impairments.* These schools would provide direct instruction for the academic learner with a visual impairment. Short-term placements that would be arranged by contract with individual school districts and that would address functional needs would be common.

In short, residential schools could address children with diverse needs while playing a role in the future education of children with visual impairments.

Another reason for placing a child with visual impairment in a special school is to receive a curriculum that cannot be provided in the general education classroom. The Texas School for the Blind and Visually Impaired, for example, is implementing a career education model that

begins in the elementary school and continues through secondary school and beyond. At the elementary school level, the emphasis is on career awareness. Students may interview persons about their jobs and what they do to function in those jobs. At the middle school level, the emphasis is on career investigation. Students take a course in Introduction to Work and assess their own abilities, aptitudes, and interests. At the secondary school level, students focus on career preparation and career specialization, and the academic subjects are tailored to those objectives.

Obviously, such a curriculum would not be appropriate for students without disabilities in the public school. For children with visual disabilities who attend public schools during the school year, the Texas School for the Blind and Visually Impaired also provides summer programs with an emphasis on career education.

RTI Model

The special needs of children with visual impairments necessitates a heavy investment in Tier II and Tier III activities since they often need special personnel and communication activities to carry out the program for the student. Nevertheless, Tier I of the RTI model, the enhanced regular classroom, reportedly serves 62 percent of children with visual impairments (U.S. Department of Education, 2006). Children with visual impairments will need additional help to prosper in Tier I activities if they are to keep up with their sighted peers. A specialist trained in visual impairment instruction needs to supervise, if not directly be a part of, the intervention. The following additions are important:

- Technology to aid students' visual acuity in reading and using computer programs

- The regular use of the extended core curriculum for those students who need it

- A teacher of the visually impaired who can give help to the regular classroom

Bishop (2004) provides a variety of ways in which to improve the regular classroom learning environment for children with visual impairments, outlined on the next page.

Dim light may be more comfortable for students with low vision.

General Suggestions for Classroom Teachers During the Upper Elementary and Middle School Years

1. Allow preferential seating or "roaming privileges" for best use of available vision.

2. Allow enough time for the student's best work—and *expect it.* Don't "give" grades; expect the student to earn them.

3. Monitor lighting conditions; especially watch for glare. (Do not stand with your back to windows when lecturing, as this forces the visually impaired student to look into the light source.)

4. Encourage the visually impaired student to take responsibility for his or her own time management and assignment completion; encourage neatness and organization.

5. Provide clear, dark copies of notes if a visually impaired student is a visual learner.

6. Verbalize whatever you write on the board.

7. Remind blind students in particular to face the speaker (orienting both face and body in that direction). Some students with low vision may need to be similarly reminded. Reminders should be as unobtrusive as possible, so as not to embarrass the student in front of his or her peers.

Source: Bishop, V. (2004). *Teaching Visually Impaired Children.* Springfield, IL: Charles C. Thomas.

Adaptations in both materials and equipment are needed to fully utilize the visually handicapped person's senses of hearing, touch, smell, vision, and even taste. Lowenfeld (1973), a pioneer in educating children with visual impairments, proposed three general principles that are still important for adapting instruction to the educational needs of children who have visual impairments:

1. *Concrete experiences.* Children with severe and profound visual disabilities learn primarily through hearing and touch. To understand the surrounding world, these children must work with concrete objects they can feel and manipulate. Through tactile observation of real objects in natural settings (or models, in the case of dangerous objects), students with visual handicaps come to understand shape, size, weight, hardness, texture, pliability, and temperature.

2. *Unifying experiences.* Visual experience tends to unify knowledge. A child who goes into a grocery store sees not only shelves and objects but also the relationships of shelves and objects in space. Children with visual impairments cannot understand these relationships unless teachers allow them the *experience* of the grocery store. The teacher must bring the "whole" into perspective, not only by giving students concrete experiences—in a post office or on a farm—but also by explaining relationships.

   Left on their own, children with severe and profound visual impairments live a relatively restricted life. To expand their horizons, to enable them to develop imagery, and to orient them to a wider environment, it is necessary to develop experiences by systematic stimulation: Lead children through space to help them understand large areas, and expose them to different sizes, shapes, textures, and relationships to help them generalize the common qualities of different objects and understand the differences. Their verbalization of similarities and differences stimulates mental development.

3. *Learning by doing.* To learn about the environment, these children have to be motivated to explore that environment. A blind infant does not reach out for an object unless that object attracts the child through other senses (touch, smell, hearing). Stimulate the child to reach and to make contact by introducing motivating toys or games (rattles, objects with interesting textures).

Tier II activities would concentrate on individual or small-group instruction in independent living skills such as eating, household chores, money, and time management. Orientation and mobility training for safe and independent travel will also require close supervision until the skills have been mastered. Much of these activities will be under the supervision of the TVI or the O&M specialist who would be consulting with the general education teacher, school psychologist, and other relevant personnel.

Tier III activities, which require a separate curriculum and the learning of Braille and other means of communication, can often be done in a separate setting such as individual tutoring, magnet schools, or state schools for the blind. The extended core curriculum becomes especially important for students with serious visual impairment so that the senses of hearing and touch become the primary channels for learning. The learning of the Braille system may be a central part of these Tier III activities. Nineteen percent of children with visual impairment fit into this group (U.S. Department of Education, 2006).

Adapting Curriculum

Two major challenges related to the curriculum for children with visual impairments face special educators. Table 11.2 lists the existing core curriculum and the expanded core curriculum. In the existing core curriculum, major adaptations have to be made to the standard lessons in English, social studies, science, and so forth to allow children with visual impairments to absorb the concepts.

> The TVI helps to ensure that instructional materials can be easily used by children with visual impairments.

In addition, there is need for an expanded core curriculum exclusively for children with visual impairments that deals with the use of assistive technology, orientation and mobility, independent living skills, and career education. Specially trained teachers who have learned how to present the expanded core curriculum to these students will be needed.

▲ Existing Core Curriculum

How are we to educate children who have visual impairments when so much of the standard education is based on the ability to see? Table 11.2 shows the components of both a core curriculum and an expanded core curriculum for children with visual impairments. The core curriculum makes clear that there are expectations that these children will and should master the standard curriculum of such subjects as language arts, mathematics, social studies, and science.

An important thing to realize in the increasing trend toward including children with visual impairments in the general education classroom is that they require special adaptations of the environment and the instruction, as well as specially trained personnel.

TABLE 11.2
Curricula for Children with Visual Impairments

Existing Core Curriculum		Expanded Core Curriculum	
English/language arts	Other languages to the extent possible	Compensatory academic skills, including communication modes	Orientation and mobility
Mathematics	Science	Social interaction skills	Independent living skills
Health	Physical education	Recreation and leisure skills	Career education
Social studies	History	Use of assistive technology	Visual efficiency skills
Economics	Business education		
Fine arts	Vocational education		

Source: From P. Hatlen. (2000). The core curriculum for blind and visually impaired students, including those with additional disabilities, in A. J. Koenig & M. Cay Holbrook (Eds.), *Foundations of education* (2nd ed.), Vol. 2, *Instructional strategies for teaching children and youths with visual impairments* edited by A. J. Koenig and M. Cay Holbrook, (p. 781) (New York: AFB Press, American Foundation for the Blind, 2000).

▲ Facilitating the Three Components of Emergent Literacy with Children Who Are Visually Impaired

Promote oral language in young children with visual impairments through the following strategies:

- Encourage children to initiate communicative exchanges and follow the children's lead.

- Expand the children's language by adding meaningful descriptive information.

- Encourage children to tell stories to learn more about narrative structure.

Promote metalinguistic awareness (phonological and syntactical awareness) through the following strategies:

- Play rhyming games that encourage attention to the end sounds of words.

- Encourage awareness of letters and sounds in words that are used throughout the day.

- Use chants, rhymes, and songs related to the daily routine to encourage awareness of the sounds of words.

Promote print and Braille literacy knowledge:

- Encourage pretend reading and writing during pretend play (at an office, restaurant, and school).

- Provide adaptive materials and opportunities for print and Braille scribbling and writing.

- Encourage parents to teach their children how to write and spell during developmentally appropriate activities at home.

Source: K. A. Erickson and D. Hatton, Expanding understanding of emergent literacy: Empirical support for a new framework. *Journal of Visual Impairment and Blindness* 101(5), (2007): 261–277. Copyright 2007 by American Foundation for the Blind (AFB). Reproduced with permission of American Foundation for the Blind (AFB) in the format Textbook via Copyright Clearance Center.

Koenig and Rex (1996) suggest targeted practice in reading fluency so that a student with visual impairment becomes comfortable with the use of optical tools and becomes comfortable reading in front of others. Other devices, such as *echo reading* (teacher and student reading together) and *choral reading* (small groups of readers

> Choral reading brings confidence to the child with visual impairments.

read aloud at the same time), can bring more confidence to the child with visual problems.

The writing skills of students with visual impairments can be helped by the use of bold-lined paper, felt-tipped pens, and mounted magnifiers. Manuscript and cursive writing are always desirable and need to be practiced, but keyboarding skills are equally important. Computers can be equipped with screen enlargement programs and **synthetic speech** output to allow students to use all aspects of the writing process: prewriting, drafting, revising, editing, and publishing.

▲ Mathematics

With children who are visually impaired, direct teaching of mathematical concepts is essential and should not be left to incidental learning. Because mathematics involves the manipulation of symbols, as well as of words, the teacher has to have a well-organized set of lessons so that the fundamental understandings of arithmetic and the most abstract algebra and geometry can be grasped.

Special attention must be paid to the use of measurement tools and to the concepts underlying the addition, subtraction, multiplication, and division of fractions, difficult for many students with visual impairments. Creating examples of these operations can test the ingenuity of the teacher but is essential if the student is to master these abstract ideas (Kapperman, Heinze, & Sticken, 2000).

Children who are blind can master fractions by working with three-dimensional circles of wood and placing them in a form board nest that can include fractional parts to make up a full circle. Once they have placed a whole circle, the children can learn to assemble blocks representing a third of a circle and put them together in the nest to form the whole. This kind of tactile experience helps children who are blind not only master the idea of fractional parts but also discriminate among the relative sizes of various fractional parts (for example, halves versus quarters), along with their sighted peers.

In the middle grades (fourth through eighth or ninth grade), students who are visually impaired work with supplementary materials to help themselves absorb the information that sighted children learn.

A standard tool for learning mathematics is the abacus, used in many Asian countries to instruct all children. The Cranmer Abacus, a special version of the device, is a substantial help to persons who are visually impaired. The beads in the Cranmer Abacus do not move as rapidly as the beads in the usual abacus and thus can be read more easily by touch.

> A student with visual impairment should have an extended core curriculum that includes independent learning skills, visual efficiencies, and recreational leisure skills.

Expanded Core Curriculum

In addition to adjustments to the core curriculum, Hatlen (2000) points out that there needs to be an *expanded core curriculum* that includes those skills needed especially by the child with visual impairments. One of these is *orientation and mobility,* which enables a child to master spatial concepts and physical environments. Trained specialists (certified orientation and mobility specialists, or COMS) help children who are blind learn to orient themselves in space and to travel safely around their homes or their communities. The goal is to make children with visual impairments as independent as possible.

Independent living skills also need to be specifically taught. These would include dining, bathing, toileting, and so on (Koenig & Holbrook, 2000). These need to be taught in natural environments at home and in school, and they are needed to combat learned helplessness, the child's feeling that he or she cannot do anything worthwhile or useful.

Recreation and Leisure Skills

Recreation and leisure skills are important, as they offer opportunities for relaxation and social interaction. The teacher might wish to assess the student's ability to manage leisure time; to play independently or with friends; and to acquire skills related to physical games and sports, arts and crafts, and music and dance (McGregor & Farrenkopf, 2000).

Many people find amazing the range of sports and leisure activities that students with visual impairments can participate in, given special instruction and aids. Such activities include bowling, bicycling, skiing, swimming, ice skating, and wrestling. In addition, card games and board games such as Scrabble and various arts and crafts are well within their capabilities when the materials are modified to accommodate children with a visual impairment. It must be stressed, though, that special instruction is needed before the student with a visual impairment will feel comfortable and seek out such activities.

One way to think about this issue is to think of a recreation or leisure activity that you enjoy. Analyze the activity on the following basis.

Social interaction within the classroom is an important part of the education program.

(© Mitch Wojnarowicz / The Image Works)

- What modification would need to be made for a blind person or someone with low vision to participate in the activity?

- Would someone with a visual impairment need to take more time in order to participate in the activity?

- Are there other benefits of this activity (social interactions, physical fitness)? (McGregor & Farrenkopf, 2000)

Sex Education for Children with Visual Impairment

One important element in the curriculum for children with visual impairment is how to cope with sexual encounters. The fact remains that much of the information students accumulate about sexuality has a visual base, and visually impaired students are at a disadvantage in learning about male–female bodies and body changes, roles, and relationships. It is extremely important for visually impaired students to have a specific, carefully planned and structured sex education course in school. Such a course should be sequenced and concrete, utilizing anatomically accurate models (even at the earliest levels). Care must be taken to balance the physiological aspects of sexuality with the interpersonal (moral and sociological) implications so that visually impaired students have sufficient and correct information upon which to develop their own standards of conduct. In a world where the consequences of sexual ignorance can literally be fatal, it is of extreme importance that visually impaired students be able to make informed decisions for their own lives.

Source: Bishop, V. (2004). *Teaching Visually Impaired Children*. Springfield, IL: Charles C. Thomas.

Universal Design for Learning

The **Universal Design for Learning (UDL)** framework helps us to see that inflexible curricular materials and methods are barriers to diverse learners, just as inflexible buildings with stairs as the only entry option are barriers to people with physical disabilities. Universally designed curricula include a range of options for accessing, using, and engaging with learning materials—recognizing that no single option will work for all students (Hitchcock, Meyer, Rose, & Jackson, 2002).

The increasing emphasis on inclusion as a policy for all of special education has led policymakers to try to ensure that children with visual impairments receive the special services they need. The IDEA Amendments of 2004 (PL 105–17) require that IEP teams make provision for instruction in Braille and the use of Braille for children who are blind or visually impaired, unless the IEP team determines that instruction in Braille or the use of Braille is not appropriate.

A similar addition to the "related services" part of the law adds "orientation and mobility services" to the list of supportive services identified, so there is no doubt that such services should be made available to students in need of them.

Social Interaction Skills

Fulfilling social needs should be one of the most significant dimensions of educational programs for children with visual impairment. Such needs can be shortchanged in inclusive settings if the general education teacher knows little about the special needs of visually impaired children. Organized efforts to improve social skills are required because visually impaired children are rejected by classmates more often than other children. Students needs special role-playing and increased sensitivity in auditory cues that help in social relationships.

Adapting Teaching Strategies

▲ Communicating with Print and Braille

Some students can be instructed in both print and Braille. They can learn readiness skills and word identification strategies in this style of parallel instruction, and the decision about which channel to emphasize can be postponed until the teacher and the school gain experience with the child's learning style.

> Listening skills may need to be developed through practice and planned experiences.

The language experience approach to reading offers many advantages. It uses students' actual experiences as the basis for reading instruction and is a highly motivating approach for a student. But adaptations have to be made for children with visual impairments. For example, the class visits a local fire station. Afterward, the student with a visual impairment dictates a story about the experience, and the teacher writes down exactly what the

Recordings for the Blind
and Dyslexic
www.rfbd.org
and National Library Service
(NLS) for the Blind and the
Physically Handicapped
www.loc.gov/nls

student says, using a Braille writer or a special slate and stylus. The student and the teacher then read the story together. They can continue to discuss and elaborate on the story, and the teacher can develop reading strategy lessons using the story as a base—for example, thinking about the firefighters' various activities at the firehouse and when fighting a fire.

▲ Listening Skills

In order to learn through the auditory sense the most important skill a child with visual impairment can learn is listening. This directed listening begins at birth when the child turns his or her attention to speakers and listens to language that describes the child's environment. Directed listening continues in preschool, when young children listen to their classmates telling about experiences and describing favorite objects brought from home. The most direct teaching of listening skills occurs during orientation and mobility instruction, in which auditory cues are used for orientation to the environment and for safe travel (Koenig & Holbrook, 2000).

"What Is It?"

The teacher plays a tape recording or record of isolated sounds. The child must correctly identify the sound or its cause. The sounds can progress from easily recognizable sounds to sounds that normally require visual clues for recognition. Easily recognizable sounds can include a telephone ringing, a clock ticking, a police officer's whistle, a car horn, a doorbell's chimes, a jet plane overhead, and water pouring from a faucet. Sounds that normally require visual clues, but that should be auditorily recognizable, can include dialing of a telephone, striking a match, fire burning, chewing crunchy vegetables, a person walking or running, and pages of a book being turned rapidly.

Source: Bishop, V. E., (2004). *Teaching visually impaired children*. Springfield, IL: Charles C. Thomas Publishing, p. 270.

As the child with visual impairments grows older, he or she tends to gather information from audiotaped materials and books. Talking books can become a favorite source of information and pleasure, and a number of organizations provide specially prepared tapes for visually impaired students. Many users find that listening to information while simultaneously reading along in print or Braille allows them to cover the information faster and maintain better comprehension. Pairing the auditory with Braille or print is key because listening alone does not help students develop or reinforce certain literacy skills. It is strongly recommended that a student not rely on auditory as the only method of accessing information

Auditory Tools

- human readers
- tape and digital recorders and players
- digital talking book players
- e-text or e-book readers, including MP3 players
- talking calculators
- talking dictionaries and other reference materials
- accessible personal digital assistants (PDA)
- scanning systems with speech
- talking computers
- talking GPS devices (Presley, 2010, p. 597)

The use of *live readers* to read aloud mail, memos, bills, textbooks, and so forth is another way to develop listening skills. As with other devices or tools, working with the live reader requires practice and effective interaction between the reader and the student. The student can ask the person who is the live reader to skip around or to read the table of contents or summaries of materials. This gives the listener more flexibility than with audiotapes.

▲ Teaching Braille or Print

People with profound visual disabilities must develop a series of special communication skills. For children who are blind, using Braille is a key skill for communicating with the sighted world.

Braille is a system of touch reading developed in 1829 by Louis Braille, a Frenchman who was blind. The system uses embossed characters in different combinations of six dots arranged in a cell two dots wide and three dots high (see the "Braille Alphabet and

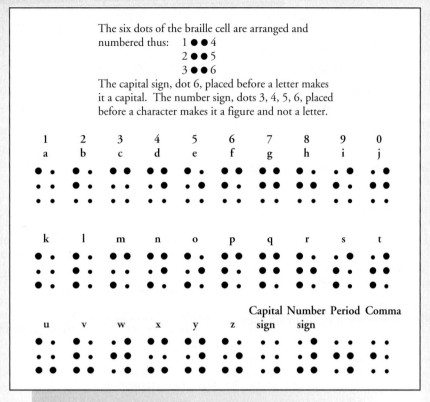

The six dots of the braille cell are arranged and
numbered thus: 1 ●●4
                  2 ●●5
                  3 ●●6
The capital sign, dot 6, placed before a letter makes
it a capital. The number sign, dots 3, 4, 5, 6, placed
before a character makes it a figure and not a letter.

Braille Alphabet and Numerals
Division for the Blind and Physically Handicapped, Library of Congress

Numerals" box above). The symbols are embossed on heavy paper from left to right, and users usually read with both hands—one leading, the other following. Advanced readers may use the second hand to orient themselves to the next line while reading the line above, and they may read as much as one-third of the lower line with the second hand. Punctuation, music, and mathematical and scientific notations are based on the same system. Standard English Braille was accepted in 1932 as the system for general use, although many other communication systems have been tried.

One of the problems faced by teachers and administrators is whether the child is capable of being a print reader or should be taught how to read Braille. Such a decision has long-term implications for the student. Table 11.3 lists characteristics of candidates for print reading and for Braille reading and can help educators decide which path is appropriate for a given youngster.

In many communities, itinerant teachers manage a growing caseload of children. These teachers have less and less time to teach Braille and to transcribe print to Braille for their students. Teachers in some communities have only three hours a week on average to provide direct services to children with visual impairments, and many teachers have even less time. Under such circumstances it is understandable that these children are not able to read rapidly or efficiently (Ferrell & Suvak, 1995). When highly specialized instruction is needed to help a youngster learn other material—whether the child has auditory problems and is trying to learn total communication or has visual problems and is trying to learn Braille—it becomes very important for the school to provide sufficient time and practice so the children can master these crucial skills at a functional level.

Braille, by its very nature, will be read more slowly than print. A reasonably good Braille reader will read at a rate of around 100 words per minute. A reasonably good print reader will read at a rate of 250 to 300 words per minute. Thus the sighted high school reader will cover three times as much material in the same

TABLE 11.3
Characteristics of Candidates for Print Reading and Braille Reading Programs

Characteristics of a Likely Print Reader	Characteristics of a Likely Braille Reader
• Shows interest in pictures and demonstrates the ability to identify pictures or elements of pictures	• Shows a preference for exploring the environment tactilely
• Uses vision efficiently to complete tasks at near distances	• Uses the tactile sense efficiently to identify small objects
• Identifies his or her name in print or understands that print has meaning	• Identifies his or her name in braille
• Uses print to perform other prerequisite reading skills	• Braille or understand that Braille has meaning
• Has stable eye condition	• Has an unstable eye condition or a poor prognosis for retaining the current level of vision in the near future
• Shows steady progress in learning to use his or her vision as necessary to ensure efficient print reading	• Has a reduced or nonfunctional central field to the extent that print reading is expected to be inefficient
• Is free of additional disabilities that would interfere with progress in a developmental reading program in print	• Shows steady progress in developing the tactile skills necessary for efficient Braille reading
	• Is free of additional disabilities that would interfere with progress in a developmental reading program in Braille

Source: Adapted from A.J. Koening & M. C. Holbrook, *Learning media assessment of students with visual impairments: A resource guide for teachers* (Austin, Texas: Texas School for the Blind and Visually Impaired, 1995). Reprinted with permission.

period of time as a Braille reader. (This is not a condemnation of Braille; it simply reflects the differences between visual reading and tactile reading.) Therefore, most blind high school students use recorded books or live readers as a supplement to Braille to cover the amount of reading material they are assigned in a regular school (Hatlen, 2003).

It is ironic that in these days of including greater numbers of visually impaired students in the general classroom and curriculum, instructional materials are becoming more elaborate and ever-more difficult to use. On a single print textbook page, there are likely to be sidebars, boxes, graphs, pictures, boldfaced words, colored words, words of all different sizes, italicized words, and charts. What was once a simple format consisting of words printed in uninterrupted lines has now become an exciting multimedia production for the sighted student.

Orientation and Mobility

One of the greatest problems imposed by blindness is becoming oriented to one's environment and to one's need for mobility in that environment. The situations that force dependence and can cause the greatest personal and social problems for individuals who have visual impairments usually involve mobility. To improve mobility, adults use tools such as long canes, guide dogs, and sighted guides. But children also must learn to move about their environment independently and safely, so *orientation* and *mobility* have become part of the curriculum in all programs for children with visual impairments.

> The goal of an O&M program is to develop a child's mobility skills to the safest, most independent level possible.

Simply defined, **orientation and mobility (O&M) training** involves developing an understanding of one's location in a given environment (orientation) coupled with the ability to physically move through that environment safely and independently (mobility) (Fazzi & Naimy, 2010). The goal of any mobility program is to bring the individual to his or her highest desired level of safe, independent travel.

A key element of special education for such children has been O&M services. Much of the O&M training involves teaching visual skills that can be used. Table 11.4 shows the necessary skills for negotiating the school environment.

Exceptional Lives, Exceptional Stories

Blindness Is Not a Barrier

Sure but sightless, Timothy Cordes arrived on the campus of the University of Notre Dame four years ago, an 18-year-old freshman from Eldridge, Iowa, who wanted to enroll in the biochemistry program.

Faculty members tried, politely, to dissuade him. Just how, they wondered aloud, could a blind student keep up with the rigorous courses and demanding laboratory work of biochemistry?

Mr. Cordes graduated Sunday from Notre Dame with a degree in biochemistry and a 3.991 grade-point average on a four-point scale. His German shepherd, Electra, led him to the lectern to deliver the valedictory speech as his classmates rose, applauded, and yelled his name affectionately.

Mr. Cordes starts medical school in two months, the second blind person ever admitted to a U.S. medical school. He does not plan to practice medicine, preferring research. "I've just always loved science," he said. . . .

Armed with Electra, a high-powered personal computer, and a quick wit, Mr. Cordes received the top grade—A, in all his classes except for an A-minus in a Spanish class. Two weeks ago, he earned a black belt in the martial arts tae kwon do and jujitsu.

"He is really a remarkable young man," said Paul Helquist, a Notre Dame biochemistry professor. Mr. Helquist had doubts at first but ultimately recommended Mr. Cordes for medical school. "He is by far the most brilliant student I've ever come across in my 24 years of teaching." . . .

"I don't see myself as some sort of 'Profiles in Courage' story," [Mr. Cordes] said. "If people are inspired by what I've done, that's great, but the truth is that I did it all for me. It was just hard work. It's like getting the black belt. It's not like I just took one long lesson. It was showing up every day and sweating and learning and practicing."

His sophomore-year roommate, Patrick Murowsky, said: "The thing about Tim is that he's fearless and he just seems to have this faith. Once we were late for a football game and we had to run to the stadium. He had no qualms about running at top speed while I yelled 'jump,' or I would yell 'duck' and he would duck. And we made it. He is simply amazing to be around sometimes."

Mr. Cordes has Leber's disease, a genetic condition that gradually diminished his vision until he was blind at age 14.

When doctors at the University of Iowa first diagnosed the disease when he was age 2, "it was the saddest moment of my life," his mother, Therese, said. She said the doctors told her, "He won't be able to do this, and don't expect him to be able to do this."

"So I went home," she said, "and just ignored everything they said." . . .

The study of biochemistry relies heavily on graphics and diagrams to illustrate complicated molecular structures. Mr. Cordes compensated for his inability to see by asking other students to describe the visual aids or by using his computer to recreate the images in three-dimensional forms on a special screen he could touch. . . .

"Tim has always exceeded people's expectations of him," said Therese Cordes, who, with her husband, Tom, watched him graduate. "He really does inspire me."

Pivotal Issues

- What are some of the ways you can encourage students with visual impairment in your classroom?

- How can you instill in them the confidence that people with visual impairments can achieve their dreams of attending college?

TABLE 11.4
School Orientation and Mobility Checklist
Classrooms
• Is the student oriented to all classrooms and easily able to manage personal effects and negotiate crowded areas?
Campus Routes
• Classroom to cafeteria
• Classroom to playground
• Classroom to bus or car pickup line
Cafeteria
• Can the student negotiate the line to purchase food and handle his or her tray and other personal effects?
Auditorium
• Is the student fully oriented to the auditorium?
School Office
• Is the student fully oriented to the main office?
Playground
• Is the student fully oriented to the playground?
• Can the student negotiate the play equipment with and without other children present?
Restrooms
• Does the student know the routes to the closest restroom from each classroom or other location throughout the day?
• Can he or she comfortably locate individual stalls, toilet tissue, sink, soap, and towels as needed?

Source: Adapted from Fazzi, D., & Naimy, B. (2010). Orientation and mobility services for children and youth with low vision. In A. Corn & J. Erin (eds.) *Foundations of low vision* (2nd ed). New York: American Foundation for the Blind.

> O&M practitioners believe the cane has many advantages.

Despite a variety of experiments with more sophisticated devices to aid in travel, the long white cane, so long recognized as a symbol of the individual with visual impairments, continues to be the instrument of choice, even with preschoolers (Pogrund, Fazzi, & Lampert, 2002). There seems to be a consensus among active O&M practitioners that the cane has numerous advantages over alternatives, even though there is little firm research evidence to support this position (Leong, 1996). It certainly extends the mobility of young children during a period in which exploration and orientation to objects in the environment are very important.

Children with Other Exceptionalities

As we noted earlier in the chapter, many children with visual impairments may have other disabilities, such as learning disabilities, neurological disabilities, behavioral disorders, or deaf-blindness (Silberman, 2000). It has been estimated that the prevalence of children with visual impairments who have dual

Assistive Technology for Students with Visual Impairments

It is likely that of all the groups of students with special needs, students with visual impairments have profited the most from developments in technology. As reported by the American Foundation for the Blind (2007), students with visual impairments can complete homework, do research, take tests, and read books along with their sighted classmates thanks to advances in technology. Advances in computer technology have been responsible for students with visual impairments being able to receive information and also to deliver information to others.

IDEA mandates that assistive technology be "considered" when developing a student's IEP. The term "considered" has not been defined in detail. However, best practice indicates that consideration includes an evaluation of the student's assistive technology needs, the writing of goals and objectives related to assistive technology, and the acknowledgement of assistive technology as part of the expanded core curriculum for students with visual impairments (Presley, 2010, p. 607). The following questions need to be addressed in each student's assistive technology assessment, based on the categorization of devices discussed in the first part of this chapter:

- How will the student access print information up close and information on chalkboards, whiteboards, or elsewhere at a distance?

- How will the student access electronic information?

- How will the student produce written communication?

- What tools will be needed for the student and his or her service provider to produce materials in alternate formats? (Presley, 2010, p. 609).

Handheld monocular telescopes are used for short-term distance viewing tasks, such as reading street signs, chalkboards, or dry erase boards at school. For people with low vision, handheld monoculars are often the preferred distance viewing devices because of the following qualities:

- They are small and lightweight and can be carried in a pocket or handbag or worn on a cord around the neck.

- They are less expensive than spectacle-mounted devices of comparable power.

- They generally can focus on objects whose distance is from 10 inches to very far away.

- The user can choose the preferred eye or dominant hand to use and can position and adjust the focusing mechanism with either hand.

- A full range of magnification is available (from 2.5X to 10X) (Zimmerman, Zebehazy, & Moon, 2010, p. 221).

Often, the biggest stumbling block to using assistive technology is the child's reluctance. Many youngsters are self-conscious about devices that make them look "strange" or "weird." To overcome

Many items, like the cell phone above, can be adapted for the visually impaired

(© AFP/Getty Images)

this self-consciousness, it is important to introduce these tools in a positive way (by playing games, for example) when the children are young.

Technology has given us the capability to transcribe printed language into spoken language and Braille. It also allows us to move easily from one form of communication to another, such as transferring Braille to print and back again. Obviously, this technology has enormous potential for students with visual impairments and for their teachers.

There is a wide range of assistive technology devices to help children with visual impairments exchange information with sighted persons. Table 11.5 provides a brief summary of the more common of these devices (Hatlen, 2003).

> Computers with an enlargement screen or synthetic speech allow students with visual impairments to work on writing skills.

TABLE 11.5
Assistive Technology Devices

Assistive technology device: any item, piece of equipment, or product system, whether acquired commercially off the shelf, modified, or customized, that is used to increase, maintain, or improve functional capabilities of individuals with disabilities (P.L. 100–407, P.L. 101–476). May include low-vision aids, bold line paper, Braille writers, screen readers, Braille printers, communication devices, etc.

Adaptive keyboard	This offers a variety of ways to provide input into a computer through various options in size, layout (i.e., alphabetical order), and complexity.
Augmentative communication device	A device that provides speech for people unable to communicate verbally. The device may talk; the user indicates communication through the use of tactile symbols, auditory scanning, large-print symbols, and so on.
Braille embosser	A Braille printer that embosses computer-generated text as Braille on paper.
Braille translation software	Translates text and formatting into appropriate Braille characters and formatting.
Braille writing equipment	Manual or electronic devices used for creation of paper Braille materials.
Closed-circuit television	As an assistive device, it magnifies a printed page through the use of a special television camera with a zoom lens and displays the image on a monitor.
Portable note takers	Small portable units that employ either a Braille or standard keyboard to allow the user to enter information. Text is stored in files that can be read and edited using the built-in speech synthesizer or Braille display. The file may be sent to a printer or Braille embosser or transferred to a computer.
Refreshable Braille displays	These provide tactile output of information presented on the computer screen. Unlike conventional Braille, which is permanently embossed onto paper, refreshable Braille displays are mechanical in nature and lift small, rounded plastic pins as needed to form Braille characters. The displays contain twenty, forty, or eighty Braille cells. After the line is read, the user can "refresh" the display to read the next line.
Scanner	A device that converts an image from a printed page to a computer file. Optical-character-recognition (OCR) software makes the resulting computer file capable of being edited.
Screen magnification	Software that focuses on a single portion (1/4, 1/9, 1/16, etc.) of the screen and enlarges it to fill the screen.
Screen reader	Software program that works in conjunction with a speech synthesizer to provide verbalization of everything on the screen, including menus, text, and punctuation.

or multiple disabilities may be over 50 percent (Hatlen, 1998). More involved cases of such multiple disabilities, including children with deaf-blindness, are covered in detail in Chapter 12.

Silberman (2000) considers the *transdisciplinary* model for educating such students the most desirable method. In this model, therapists and other specialists provide direct services to students in classrooms or other natural environments as part of the daily routine, instead of in some isolated therapy room. The IEP needs to reflect the goals of all of the professionals working with the child.

Individualized Education Programs

IEPs for children with visual impairment should include a variety of goals—some focusing on the effective use of the learning environment, some on instructional content, and some on skills that the student will need to perform effectively in the inclusive classroom. It will likely take a team of professionals to implement the goals.

As Sacks (1998) point out, one of the consequences of the diversity of children with visual and other disabilities is that the teacher becomes a team member rather than teaching in isolation.

They are working as members of a team that includes professionals in specializations such as visual impairment, severe disabilities, deaf-blindness, early childhood, learning disabilities, general education and occupational and physical therapies and also includes to come in revises the families of these children and youth (p. 33).

Some sample IEP goals for such children are shown in Table 11.6. Note that Jerry has both academic and social goals in his IEP, reflecting the comprehensive goals of the program. The general education classroom teacher may need some help from an itinerant teacher to carry out these objectives successfully.

Erin proposed a future in which such schools could play three distinct roles:

- *Resource centers for students with visual impairments.* These facilities would function as state or regional sites to distribute materials and provide technical assistance and outreach services to neighborhood schools. They would also participate in professional preparation activities.

TABLE 11.6
Sample IEP Goals and Objectives for a Student Who Is Visually Impaired

Long-Term Goals	Short-Term Objectives
Jerry will use special devices and materials in order to perform at grade level in reading and mathematics.	1. Jerry will demonstrate effective use of various tools of magnification. 2. Jerry will demonstrate effective keyboarding skills that allow him to do word processing. 3. Jerry will score within one grade level of the class norm in academic achievement tests.
Jerry will establish effective social relationships with some of the nondisabled members of the class.	1. Jerry will join and participate in one of the clubs or organizations in the school that stresses social interactions. 2. Jerry will receive a number of votes by other students to work on class projects with them. 3. In class parties, Jerry will join in the activities and interact with other class members.

Source: Reprinted from A. Corn, P. Hatlen, K. M. Huebner, F. Ryan, and M. Siller, *National Agenda for the Education of Children and Youths with Visual Disabilities, Including Those with Multiple Disabilities, Revised.* Kathleen M. Huebner, Brunhilde Merk-Adam, Donna Stryker, and Karen Wolffe, pp. 5–6, New York: AFB Press, American Foundation for the Blind, 2004.

Transition to Independent Living Skills

Independence at Home and in the Community

Mastering the environment is especially important for the physical and social independence of children with visual impairments. The ease with which they move about, find objects and places, and orient themselves to new physical and social situations is crucial in determining their role in peer relationships, the types of vocations and avocations open to them as adults, and their own estimation of themselves.

How do we help children who are blind master the environment? We have to teach them, from a very early age, not to be afraid of new experiences or injury.

Life Skills Training for Children with Visual Impairments

How do people with visual impairments pay for things when they can't see their money?

Coins are easy to recognize by feeling them. Dimes are small and slim with ridges around the edges; pennies are small with smooth edges; nickels are bigger and thick; quarters have ridges and are bigger but thinner than nickels.

Many people who are visually impaired use this trick to recognize dollar bills: In their wallet, one-dollar bills are left unfolded; five-dollar bills are folded in half the short way; and ten-dollar bills are folded in half the long way.

How do children who are visually impaired find their toys and clothes?

Children with visual impairments have to be very neat. They have to put their things in the same place every day in order to find them.

To pick out what to wear in the morning, children who are visually impaired can feel the texture of their clothes. They know jeans feel different from wool pants. Or they may remember in what order their clothes are hung in the closet.

To decide what top matches what bottom, aluminum clothing tags can be sewn in each piece of clothing. On the tags, Braille markings indicate the color. Children with visual impairments must learn what colors go together.

How do children with visual impairments find the food on their plate?

To find the food on their plate, imagine the plate as a clock. They are told at what clock time the food is placed.

For example, the hamburger is placed at 12 o'clock, the salad is at 3 o'clock, and the French fries are at 8 o'clock.

How do children with visual impairments gain confidence in their physical abilities?

Sighted children skin their knees, bump their shins, fall from trees, and step in holes. Children who are blind must have the same chance if they are going to learn to control their environment.

Transition: From School to Work

The transition from school to work is an extremely important aspect of the total educational program for children with visual impairments. Although there have been attempts to use sheltered workshops, in which students produce goods in a protected setting that is publicly subsidized, the more recent emphasis is on placement in real job settings whenever possible. The secondary school program then becomes a part-time academic and part-time workplace program to give the student a chance to experience employment while still in a supervised setting. The academic program focuses on functional reading and other skills that can enhance the student's chance of success in the workplace.

John, a teenager with a visual disability, was exposed to several jobs and learned a series of generic work skills (such as greeting and conversation skills). This type of experience should serve John well in whatever occupation he decides to enter.

In the preceding chapters, we have been concerned with what happens to exceptional children after they leave school and try to make their way in the world. After all, educational programs are supposed to prepare students for life in the community. We have the same concerns for children with visual impairments.

As for what happens to children with disabilities after secondary school and what kind of life adjustment they make as young adults, there is increasing evidence that social adjustment, rather than specific vocational training, is what is central to successful adult adaptation.

In recent years a careful study was made of groups of children who were blind, children who had low vision, and children who were sighted. Sixteen students ages 15 to 21 were in each group. Extensive questionnaires about their daily activities and interests were given to the students and their parents, along with time diaries asking the participants to identify their activities in one-hour blocks over a 24-hour period (Sacks, Wolffe, & Tierney, 1998).

This investigation yielded a variety of interesting facts. The majority of students with sight had worked for pay, whereas only 31 percent of students with low vision and 19 percent of students with blindness did likewise. The majority of the students with blindness and low vision reported that they spent their after-school time alone. Many of the students who were visually impaired, particularly those with low vision, required extensive support to succeed academically in inclusive school environments. Adaptive computers and other devices specially designed for such students were not widely used. The authors of the study concluded that the secondary curriculum for adolescents with visual impairments should include a stronger focus on career development and social skill competencies and that travel training also seemed advisable.

> The lack of support for infrastructure is hindering progress in the field of transitioning students with visual impairments from school to work.

A Final Word

The low prevalence rate of children with visual impairments has caused the professional field to depend upon a small but strong cadre of professionals who have devoted their careers to these students. If this field is to flourish, there will have to be meaningful changes in the way programs are financed and research and personnel preparation are supported.

Kay Ferrell (2007) has described the "crumbling research base," which has had to depend upon single case studies, anecdotal reports, and small, heterogeneous samples. Her status report notes, "We are often left with best practices that are more philosophical than proven, more descriptive than empirical, and more antiquated than modern" (p. 2).

Perhaps we can find a foundation willing to commit itself to this cause. We have advocated for the team approach to plan for children with visual impairment, but we need to have the members of the team present to play their special roles, which is not always happening today. We in special education have learned a great deal from the work of these leaders in this field and hope to profit more in the future from their work with students who are increasingly faced with multiple problems in learning and social adaptation.

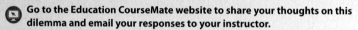

moral dilemma

To Braille or Not to Braille

Ruth, age 8, is a severely visually impaired girl who has been having trouble adjusting to the regular school program and has been referred for evaluation. After a comprehensive examination, the IEP committee has decided that Ruth needs to receive Braille training to aid her ability to master her lessons. Ruth, however, is seriously resisting such a move and is close to outright rebellion over the idea. The source of Ruth's concerns is clear. She is afraid that if other children see her using Braille, they will brand her as a blind girl, and Ruth desperately wants to be like other children. After all, a number of the girls in her class wear glasses. Ruth would much prefer to continue to struggle with trying to decipher her lessons visually, even if unsuccessfully.

What should be the approach of the teacher in such a situation? What would you say to Ruth or to her classmates? Should her academic progress be bought at the price of social isolation?

Go to the Education CourseMate website to share your thoughts on this dilemma and email your responses to your instructor.

Summary

▶ Children with visual impairments are classified in several ways. Educational classifications rest on the special adaptations necessary to help these children learn.

▶ A visual impairment can hamper the individual's understanding of the world, but such understanding can be enhanced through extending the experiential world of the child with visual impairments.

▶ Hereditary factors are one major cause of visual impairments in young children. Other causes are infectious diseases, injuries, and poisonings.

▶ Today most educators agree that the cumulative experiences of children as they develop affect intelligence. Youngsters with visual impairments lack the integrating experiences that come naturally to sighted children. The challenge for educators is to compensate for this lack of integration through special instructional programs.

▶ One of the important areas of curriculum adaptation is how to modify the standard core curriculum (e.g., math, language arts, social studies, science) to take into account the special needs of children with visual impairments.

▶ Another major need is to implement the expanded core curriculum. That includes such items as orientation and mobility, independent living skills, uses of assistive technology, and so forth. Very specially trained personnel are needed for this expanded program.

- One of the by-products of restricted mobility and limited experience can be a passive orientation to life. Teachers play a critical role in helping students with visual impairments be active and independent.

- It is important for parents and teachers to help children with visual impairments develop their skills. It is equally important to let these children do things for themselves and to experience as much as possible the things that sighted children experience.

- Braille reading is slower than regular reading, a fact that can affect the academic performance of students with profound visual impairments.

- Orientation and mobility training are critically important parts of the curriculum for children with visual disabilities. Such services should be available in the public schools.

- Technology is improving the means of communication for those with visual impairments. It has also broadened their occupational choices. Keyboarding and word processing are particularly useful skills, along with access to necessary technology.

Future Challenges

1 *Will technology become more accessible for students with vision impairment?*

Technology is wonderful—when it is usable. The widespread distribution of technological developments for those with visual disabilities has been impeded by the cost and size of equipment. In the same way, we have to increase accessibility to the computers and word processors that are transforming the academic and work worlds of those with visual disabilities.

2 *Where will the specially trained teachers come from?*

There has always been a thin supply of teachers with expertise in dealing with children with visual impairments. This situation has grown worse because of the many complications and multiple disabilities that are becoming the responsibility of the special education teacher. We are sure to face a major teacher shortage despite the financial help given by the Office of Special Education Programs in the U.S. Department of Education.

Key Terms

albinism p. 360
amblyopia p. 360
astigmatisms p. 360
blind p. 356
blindness p. 356
Braille p. 380
case coordinator p. 373
ciliary muscles p. 358
convergence p. 358
cornea p. 358
hyperopia p. 360
iris p. 357
learned helplessness p. 363
Leber's Congenital Amaurosis, p. 360
low vision p. 356
myopia p. 360
nystagmus p. 360
object permanence p. 367
optic nerve hypoplasia p. 360
orientation and mobility (O&M) training p. 382
pupil p. 357
retina p. 357
retinopathy of prematurity p. 359
sensory compensation p. 364
synthetic speech p. 377
time diary p. 364
Universal Design for Learning (UDL) p. 379
visual impairment p. 359

Resources

References of Special Interest

Corn, A., & Erin, J. (Eds.). (2010). *Foundations of low vision: Clinical and functional perspectives* (2nd ed.) New York: American Foundation for the Blind. A valuable text covering the various challenges faced by children with low vision and their families. Special attention is directed to the various elements of assistive technology that can be of help. Educational adaptations to the core curriculum and the extended core curriculum are touched on, as well as the special additions necessary for children with multiple impairments.

Goodman, S., & Wittenstein, S. (Eds.). (2002). *Collaborative assessment.* New York: American Foundation for the Blind. The theme of this book is an appropriate assessment of children with visual impairments through a multidisciplinary team, each member bringing his or her own specialty to an overall collaborative assessment. Separate chapters are written by speech-language pathologists, psychologists, orientation and mobility specialists, and others. This professional collaboration is stressed not only in the initial planning for the child but also as continuing through the core curriculum.

Holbrook, M., & Koenig, A. (Eds.). (2000). *Foundations of education*: Vol. I. *History and theory of teaching children and youths with visual impairments* (2nd ed.). New York: American Foundation for the Blind. This volume, along with the companion Volume II, provides a solid basis for anyone interested in the education of children with visual impairments. The book focuses on the special developmental issues and problems that children with visual impairments face—challenges that require adaptations of the general education curriculum. Each chapter is prepared by a specialist on the topic being discussed.

Pogrund, R., & Fazzi, D. (2002). *Early focus* (2nd ed). New York: American Foundation for the Blind. This volume focuses its attention on young children, ages birth to 5, who are in need of early intervention and early education services. Educational vision specialists have been increasingly called upon to provide identification and services at an early age because of the developmental importance of this age span. The eleven chapters are written by experts in the various developmental processes (e.g., cognition and language) and explain how the family can be helpful in a team approach.

Silberman, R., Bruce, S., & Nelson, C. (2004). *Children with sensory impairments*. Baltimore: Brookes. A thorough review of the challenge presented by children with visual impairments. Topics range from definitions to causation to the special techniques and technologies that can present a level playing field for these children in the public schools.

Spungin, S. (Ed.). *When you have a visually impaired child in your classroom: A guide for teachers*. New York: American Foundation for the Blind. A book filled with important ideas and techniques for teachers who have children with visual impairments in their classrooms. Covers the environmental changes that should be made, the curriculum adjustments to be introduced, and the technical tools that have to be included to meet the special needs of these students. Written by important veterans in this field.

Tuttle, D., & Tuttle, N. (2004). *Self-esteem and adjusting with blindness: The process of responding to life's demands* (3rd ed.). Springfield, IL: Charles C. Thomas. A book that focuses on the personal and social adjustment of children with visual impairment. A good review of what is known up until the present time.

Journals

Journal of Special Education Technology
   http://www.tamcec.org/jset/

Journal of Visual Impairment and Blindness
   www.afb.org/jvib.asp

Professional Organizations

American Foundation for the Blind
   www.afb.org/afb

Association for Education and Rehabilitation of the Blind and Visually Impaired
   www.aerbvi.org

Division on Visual Impairment
   c/o Council for Exceptional Children
   www.cec.sped.org

National Association for Parents of the Visually Impaired, Inc.
   www.napvi.org

National Association for Visually Handicapped
   www.navh.org

 Visit the Education CourseMate website for additional TeachSource Video Cases, information about CEC standards, study tools, and much more.

Children with Physical Disabilities, Health Impairments, and Multiple Disabilities

 Focus Questions

▶ What are some of the historical events that contributed to disability awareness and legislation?

▶ What are some characteristics of children with physical disabilities, health impairments, and multiple disabilities?

▶ How have advances in medical interventions changed outcomes for individuals with disabilities and health impairments?

▶ How are physical disabilities, health impairments, and multiple disabilities defined?

▶ What are the prevalences of physical disabilities and health impairments in children?

▶ What challenges are associated with the assessment of children with physical disabilities?

▶ What services and supports can be provided for students with physical, health, and multiple impairments at each intervention tier?

▶ How can technology enhance the lives and increase the autonomy of individuals with physical disabilities?

▶ What special issues face the families of children with physical disabilities, health impairments, and multiple disabilities?

▶ What challenges and supports are part of the individual's transition into adulthood?

© Ellen Senisi

393

Philosophers and theologians have debated for millennia about what makes us who we are—what makes us human. We have bodies, minds, and hearts, and many religions believe that we have souls, or spirits. None of these things alone is "us," but they combine to make us both amazingly unique and simultaneously just like everyone else. Often we are distracted by external things. We are judgmental about appearances, and we are fearful, dismissive, or just uncomfortable when the appearance of another is different from our own. We may experience this uneasiness with others of different races or cultures, and we may experience it with others who have physical disabilities. These outer differences, however, are like the waves on the ocean: They can sometimes look blue, sometimes green; they distract us with their constant motion; but they are not the ocean itself. The ocean consists of deep currents that flow with a steady power that can be felt but not easily seen. Just like the waves, the surface differences we see in the appearances of others may mask the deeper humanity that we all share. In this final chapter, we reflect on how the deep currents of humanity can allow us to connect with others in spite of our surface differences.

> While each of us is a unique individual, we are all connected by our shared humanity.

We explore the impact that physical disabilities, chronic health problems, and multiple disabilities can have on a child's life and look at how we can address the educational needs of these children and their families. The physical, health, and psychosocial needs will be uniquely individual for each child. Meeting these needs, however, requires that a comprehensive infrastructure be in place to support the child and family. Nowhere is the need for a multidisciplinary team more evident than in the identification of and planning for children with the complex needs discussed in this chapter. Working together, the multidisciplinary team provides that support network to help the child meet with success. Throughout this text we have looked at the social forces (Chapter 1) and the policies and institutions (Chapter 2) that affect the lives of children with disabilities. We have focused on issues related to early intervention (Chapter 3), on the communication needs (Chapter 7) of children, and on specific areas of disabilities (Chapters 4, 5, 6, 8, 10, and 11) and of gifts and talents (Chapter 9). In this final chapter you will need to draw on all that you have learned thus far as you think about how the unique and complex needs of children with physical disabilities, health impairments, and multiple disabilities can be met.

History of Special Education for Children with Physical Disabilities, Health Impairments, and Multiple Disabilities

The first major legislative response to individuals with physical disabilities was passed in 1917 to help meet the vocational needs of World War I veterans with disabilities (Best, Heller, & Bigge, 2005). President Franklin Delano Roosevelt is credited with advancing the cause of individuals with disabilities through his New Deal; the 1935 Social Security Act provided funds for vocational rehabilitation, retirement support, and insurance benefits (Best et al., 2005). World War II veterans with disabilities added another powerful voice for physical access to jobs for individuals with disabilities. The civil rights movement served as a model for the disabilities rights movement, and the 1968 Architectural Barriers Act laid the groundwork for later accessibility legislation. In Chapter 1 we discussed the evolution of society's relationship with individuals with disabilities, and in Chapter 2 we reviewed the policies and laws that have helped shape the ways we integrate and support individuals with disabilities. The laws, however, are a means and not an end. They provide a platform that guides practice and allows us to advocate for needed supports and services. Laws in and of themselves do not, however, prevent prejudice, ignorance, or malice—they only mediate it. People with physical disabilities may still face intentional and unintentional discrimination from other people and from the "system." Fear, ignorance, lack of experience, and inflexibility are the most common causes of discrimination, but with mandatory accessibility and expectations for inclusion, we are moving toward full participation for individuals with disabilities within all aspects of life.

Three key areas in which we have made substantial progress in supporting full participation for individuals with physical disabilities are in *universally designed access, medicine,* and *technology.* Universal designs and modifications like curb cuts, accessible bathrooms, wheelchair ramps, and elevators all help individuals gain mobility and offer accessibility for wheel-chair-mobile individuals.

Advances in medicine have led to lifesaving interventions for children with physical disabilities and health impairments. As medical interventions have improved, the life expectancy for preterm infants has increased, and the overall life expectancy for children with severe disabilities has been extended. Improved medical interventions are also increasing the survival rate for soldiers who have been wounded in battle and who, like the returning veterans from previous wars, have disabilities. Medical supports also can enhance the quality of life and prevent secondary complications. Newly developed prostheses can help individuals who have lost limbs regain functioning, new blood sugar monitors can maintain a continuous check to help regulate diabetes, improvements in surgical procedures for infants allow doctors to repair heart defects, and new treatments for cancer have led to 75 percent survival rates for children (Porter, 2008).

> Advances in medicine and technology have improved support for individuals with physical and health needs.

The third area in which we have seen dramatic advances that affect the lives of individuals with disabilities is technology. Through technology we can now greatly increase mobility, communication, and independent functioning for individuals with disabilities. Later in this chapter, we look at the role of assistive technologies in supporting autonomous living for individuals with disabilities.

Characteristics of Children with Physical Disabilities, Health Impairments, or Multiple Disabilities

The unique needs of children who have physical disabilities, health impairments, or **multiple disabilities** require that each child must be considered individually. The following profiles describe two fifth-grade children, Pam and Henry. Both children have special needs, but each is unique in her and his developmental profile. Pam and Henry both have *cerebral palsy,* but, as you will see, Henry has multiple disabilities that are more severe.

Pam: Pam is a happy young girl who is slightly built and small for her age. She has spastic cerebral palsy (CP). Her CP is hemiplegic; it affects her ability to control the right side of her body. She uses a wheelchair with special supports to help her sit and move. Although Pam's motor control on her right side is severely affected by the CP, her cognitive and academic abilities are not affected; in fact, Pam is intellectually gifted, and her academic achievements are above grade level. She is an especially good speller and is always chosen first for class spelling bees. She has won the districtwide spelling bee twice.

Pam seems to make friends easily, and other students enjoy helping her get around. She is usually at the center of things in the lunchroom but sometimes

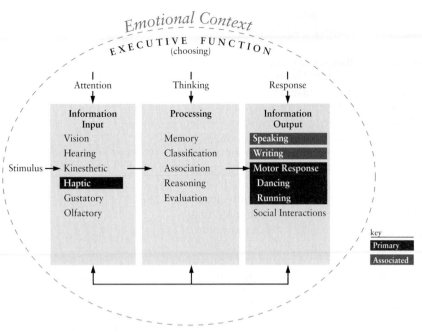

FIGURE 12.1
Pam's Information Processing Model

feels left out when it comes to recess and physical education. Pam spends most of her day in the general education fifth-grade class, but because of her unique needs she also receives supplemental services. Twice a week she receives services for students with gifts and talents, and twice a week she receives services for students with disabilities with a multidisciplinary team. In her gifted education services, she participates in seminar discussions of advanced books and works on an independent project studying robotics. She is very interested in how robotics can be used to help people accomplish things that they cannot physically do. In her special education services she works on mobility, has occupational and physical therapies, and gets specific support for such things as self-advocacy and the use of assistive technology. Even with her special services, which take her out of the general education class for as much as four hours a week, Pam is doing well academically, but her teachers must be attentive to her fatigue level and responsive to her physical and emotional needs. The information processing model in Figure 12.1 shows the impact for Pam.

Henry: Henry, like Pam, has spastic cerebral palsy, but he has quadriplegia, meaning that all four limbs and his torso are affected, making his motor control very limited. Henry also has speech difficulties and severe intellectual delays. Because his needs are intense and complex, Henry attends a special self-contained class all day. His related services are integrated into his day, and he receives occupational therapy, speech-language therapy, and physical therapy weekly. The goals for Henry are more functional than academic, and his teachers are working to help him with basic communication skills. Henry uses a touch Dynavox (for digital speech) that is configured for each portion of his day to help him make choices and express his wants. The Dynavox shows pictures and icons and produces digitalized speech when the picture is touched. Because he has the most control over his neck muscles, Henry uses a head stick to point to the picture of his choice. When he arrives at school he chooses whether he wants to start his day with a story or with music; Henry must point to a picture of either a book or a CD player. His teachers have added a second level of choice that requires him to select the specific music or story he would like to hear. At lunch Henry can choose from pictures that show his menu options, and throughout the day he can select some of his learning activities. Because of his cognitive level, Henry is still learning to communicate simple, direct needs and wants. Making choices is key to developing Henry's ability to communicate and to supporting his development of self-determination. At home his parents use a similar system to reinforce and extend his communication.

Henry's teachers work to help him initiate activities and ask for things that he wants. Recently they have begun using a self-activating system that allows Henry to start his morning activities on his own by selecting and turning on the recordings. His teachers prompt him to start but wait for him to actually select the program. Some days this works smoothly, but on other days Henry stubbornly waits for his teachers to help him. Building autonomy in daily routines can be a slow process, and it is sometimes very hard for Henry's parents and teachers to allow him to do things for himself that they could do more quickly and easily. The reward for their patience, however, is seeing the pleasure in Henry's eyes when he does something for himself.

 # Definitions of Physical Disabilities, Health Impairments, and Multiple Disabilities

As we look at definitions of the disability areas addressed in this chapter, we first turn to IDEA 2004, but because the law includes only some of the areas we are addressing, we augment these definitions. IDEA 2004 specifically includes children with **orthopedic impairments**, **traumatic brain injury (TBI)**, **deafblindness**, multiple disabilities, and **other health impairments** within its definitions (Council for Exceptional Children, 2006). Table 12.1 gives the legal definitions for each of these areas.

Physical Disabilities

Understanding the physical disabilities that can affect a child can be difficult because of the wide variety of problems that can exist. Children with physical disabilities will require direct special education support, and thus it is important that teachers have a basic understanding of the conditions. Here we address

TABLE 12.1	
Federal Definitions for Areas That Include Physical Disabilities, Multiple Disabilities, and Other Health Impairments	
Disability Area	**Definition from IDEA 2004**
Orthopedic impairments	A severe orthopedic impairment that adversely affects a child's educational performance (e.g., cerebral palsy, amputations, and fractures or burns that cause contractures)
Traumatic brain injury	An acquired injury caused by an external physical force, resulting in total or partial functional disability and/or psychosocial impairment that requires special educational services
Deafblindness	Concomitant hearing and visual impairments, the combination of which causes severe communication, developmental, and other educational needs that require special services
Multiple disabilities	Concomitant impairments (such as intellectual and developmental disabilities–blindness or intellectual and developmental disabilities–orthopedic impairment) that result in severe educational needs that require special services
Other health impairments	Limited strength, vitality, or alertness, including heightened alertness to environmental stimuli, that are due to chronic or acute health problems such as asthma, attention deficit disorders, diabetes, epilepsy, cystic fibrosis, heart conditions, hemophilia, lead poisoning, leukemia, nephritis, ulcerative colitis and Crohn's disease, rheumatic fever, sickle cell anemia, and Tourette syndrome and that require special educational services

Source: Material was drawn from the Council for Exceptional Children (2006). *Council for exceptional children policy and advocacy services: Understanding IDEA 2004 regulations.* Arlington, VA: Council for Exceptional Children.

> **TABLE 12.2**
> **List of Physical Disabilities**
>
> *Neuromotor impairments*
> - Cerebral palsy (CP)
> - Neural tube defects
> - Seizure disorders
> - Traumatic brain injury (TBI)
>
> *Degenerative diseases*
> - Muscular dystrophy
> - Spinal muscular atrophy
>
> *Orthopedic and musculoskeletal disorders*
> - Juvenile arthritis
> - Spinal curvatures
> - Limb deficiencies
> - Hip conditions
> - Other musculoskeletal conditions/Osteogenesis Imperfecta

Source: From K. W. Heller, P. A. Alberto, P. E. Forney, & M. N. Schwartzman (Eds.). *Understanding physical, sensory, and health impairments: Characteristics and educational implications.* Copyright © 1996. Adapted with permission of the authors.

some of the physical disabilities that are most likely to affect children. Resources provided at the end of this chapter offer a more comprehensive study of this topic. Table 12.2 gives a detailed list of some of the areas of physical disability.

Cerebral Palsy

Cerebral palsy (CP) refers to a disorder of movement and posture caused by damage to the motor control centers of the brain (Liptak, 2002; Pellegrino, 2002). *Cerebral* refers to the brain and *palsy* to disorders of movement (March of Dimes, 2010). The damage that results in cerebral palsy can occur before birth, during the birth process, or after birth from an accident or injury (for example, a blow to the head, lack of oxygen). The condition affects muscle tone (the degree of tension in the muscles), interferes with voluntary movement and full control of the muscles, and delays gross and fine motor development.

There are four major classifications of CP: spastic, dyskinetic, ataxic, and mixed. Children can have one or a combination of types of cerebral palsy. The form and degree of physical involvement vary from child to child, as do the affected areas of the body (Best et al., 2005). Figure 12.2 shows the brain areas involved and the regions of the body that will be affected for each type of CP.

In **spastic cerebral palsy**, muscle tone is abnormally high (**hypertonia**) and increases during activity. Muscles and joints are tight or stiff, and movements are limited in the affected areas of the body. Some children are *hemiplegic*; just one side of the body (either left arm and left leg or right arm and right leg) is affected. Others are *diplegic*; the whole body is involved, but the legs are more severely involved than the arms. Still others are *quadriplegic*; involvement is equally distributed throughout the body.

United Cerebral Palsy Association
www.ucp.org

The specific physical impact of cerebral palsy depends on the areas of the brain that are involved.

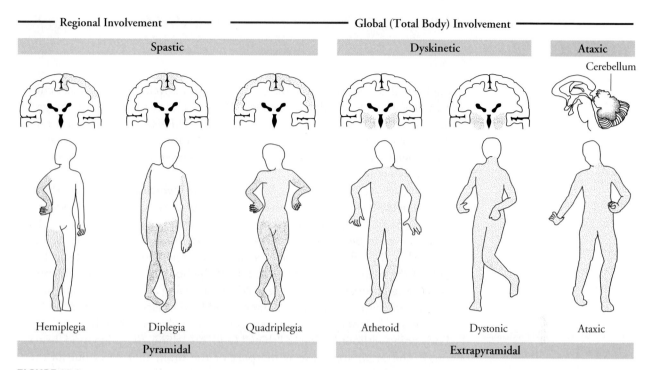

FIGURE 12.2
Regions of the Brain and Body Affected by Various Forms of Cerebral Palsy
Source: J. P. Dorman & L. Pellegrino, *Caring for children with cerebral palsy: A team approach* (p. 12) (Baltimore: Paul H. Brookes, 1998).

In **dyskinetic cerebral palsy**, tonal abnormalities involve the whole body. The individual's muscle tone is changing constantly, often rigid while he or she is awake and decreased when asleep (Best et al., 2005).

Ataxic cerebral palsy is a condition in which voluntary movement involving balance is abnormal. Individuals with ataxic CP have difficulty controlling their hands and arms, and their gait is unsteady.

A child with **mixed cerebral palsy** will have a combination of spastic, dyskinetic, and ataxic CP. This combination and its impact will be different for each child, but all will likely have severe problems with balance and coordination that affect ambulation as well as bodily and hand control.

Additional problems that can be associated with cerebral palsy include learning disabilities, intellectual and developmental disabilities, seizures, speech impairments, eating problems, sensory impairments, and joint and bone malformations such as spinal curvatures and contractures (permanently fixed, tight muscles and joints). Although CP can bring with it concomitant problems with vision, hearing, speech, and cognition, it is essential to remember that many individuals with CP have normal intelligence and that some, like Pam, are gifted and talented (Best et al., 2005). An individual's cognitive abilities can *never* be assumed by looking at the severity of the physically disabling condition; and as we discuss later in the chapter, cognitive abilities can be hard to assess in the presence of physical disabilities (Best et al., 2005).

> A child's cognitive abilities should never be assumed by looking at the severity of his or her physical limitations.

Neural Tube Defects

A **neural tube defect (NTD)** occurs when the neural tube (surrounding the spine) does not close properly and the developing brain or spine is left exposed to the amniotic fluid during gestation (March of Dimes, 2010). An estimated one in every one thousand children born in the United States will have NTDs (Duke Center for Human Genetics, 2010). The most common type of NTD we see in children is **spina bifida**.

Neurology and Brain Development
What We Know About Cerebral Palsy

Throughout this text we have looked at how brain development impacts children as they grow, learn, think, and feel. When a part of the brain is damaged in some way, the impact can be significant. Cerebral Palsy literally means brain weakness or problems with bodily positioning and movement. CP can result from damage to any part of the brain and can be either mild or severe depending on the extent of the damage.

The largest part of the brain is the cerebrum, which accounts for about 85 percent of the brain's weight. The cerebrum helps us reason, and there is some evidence (Jensen, 1998; Sousa, 2001) of hemispheric specialization (e.g., the right side seems to be more involved with abstract things like music and spatial abilities, while the left side may be more analytical and language oriented). The left side of the brain controls the right side of the body, so damage to different parts of the cerebrum will impact the child's functioning and body lateralization.

The cerebellum controls coordination and how muscles work together for movement and balance. The brain stem controls involuntary muscles that keep the body going without having to "think" (e.g., breathing, digesting food, heart beating). The brain stem also is the part of the brain that sorts out all the messages sent between the brain and nervous system. The pituitary gland controls growth, and the hypothalamus controls the body's temperature regulation. Emotional regulation seems to be located in the amygdala cells (almond shaped cluster of cells) on either side of the brain.

Think back to Pam and Henry—the two children you met early in the chapter. Each has CP, but the degree and type of impact are very different. See if you can determine, by looking at the type and extent of abilities and functions, which areas of the brain are damaged for both Pam and Henry.

Source: Information was adapted from KidsHealth website kidshealth.org; July 10, 2010.

Spina bifida can vary in severity and long-term impact depending on the location of the lesion and shunt (i.e. a medical device implanted to help drain fluid away from an impacted area) (Johnson, Dudgeon, Kuehn, & Walker, 2007). Surgery can often close the spinal opening, and some children with spina bifida must undergo multiple surgeries, but the damage to the nerves will cause lasting difficulties.

Researchers believe that 50 to 75 percent of NTDs could be prevented by adding folic acid (a type of vitamin B) to the diet prior to and early on in pregnancy (Duke Center for Human Genetics, 2010). The U.S. Public Health Service recommends that all women of childbearing age take 0.4 milligrams of folic acid a day as a preventive measure, because spina bifida occurs in the first twenty-six to twenty-eight days of pregnancy, usually before a woman is aware that she is pregnant (March of Dimes, 2010). Medical interventions have advanced to include prenatal surgery, which can now be done to reduce the effects of some NTDs.

Spina Bifida
www.spinalcord.org

Seizure Disorders

A seizure is caused by abnormal electrical discharge within the brain that disrupts the brain's normal functioning. Seizures can be general, in which the individual often loses consciousness, or partial, in which the individual maintains awareness of the environment (Porter, 2008). The intensity of the seizure varies from mild to severe and may include muscle contractions, purposeless movement, vocalizations, urinary and fecal incontinence, and frothing at the mouth. Most seizures will end spontaneously within a few minutes, but they will leave the individual disoriented and sleepy, with a headache and sore muscles. Absence seizures (formally called *petit mal*) may last only 10 to 30 seconds, during which time the child's eyelids may flutter and the child appears to be "spaced out." If not treated, these seizures can occur several times a day and cause the child to miss much of what is happening in the classroom.

A **seizure disorder** is considered to be symptomatic of an underlying problem and requires a full medical evaluation, including EEG and a possible MRI and CAT scan of the brain. Seizures occur in up to 1.4 percent of full-term infants and in 20 percent of preterm infants (Porter, 2008). With school-age children, the major cause of seizures is likely to be **juvenile myoclonic epilepsy.** There are an estimated two million children and adolescents with seizure disorders in the United States (Porter, 2008). Most seizure disorders respond well to medical treatment (either medication or surgery). All teachers should be aware of how to respond to the immediate needs of a child during a seizure. The *Merck Manual for Neurological Disorders* (Porter, 2008) recommends the following:

> During a seizure, injury should be prevented by loosening clothing around the neck and placing a pillow under the head. Attempting to protect the tongue is futile and likely to damage the patient's teeth or the rescuer's fingers. The patient should be rolled onto his or her side to prevent aspiration (www.merck.com, 2008).

Once the child awakes from the seizure, teachers must provide immediate comfort and security to ensure that the child has time to rest and recover both physically and emotionally. The child may feel embarrassed and will need reassurance that things are back to normal. For children with known seizure disorders, teachers should plan ahead with the parents to have clean clothes available at school and contact information for immediate notification if the child has had a seizure. If the seizure is prolonged, lasting more than 5 minutes, or if seizures are occurring repeatedly, medical help should be sought. Parents and the child should also help decide what information should be shared ahead of time with classmates who may witness a seizure. Students who have witnessed the seizure must also be comforted and must be given appropriate information regarding the seizure. It is not unusual for children to worry that they might "catch" the disorder and to react by either withdrawing from or teasing the child. Negative reactions can usually be prevented if the teacher has prepared the students and takes time to help them process their feelings, but teachers must in all cases intervene when children are behaving in a hurtful manner to each other.

With appropriate support, children with cerebral palsy can participate fully in life.
(Courtesy of Cengage Learning)

Epilepsy Foundation of America
www.epilepsyfoundation.org

Traumatic Brain Injury

Severe head injury is the most common acquired disorder in the category of traumatic brain injury (TBI) (Michaud, Semel-Concepcíon, Duhaime, & Lazar, 2002). With more than two million brain injuries occurring annually within the United States, it is also the most common cause of accidental death and disabilities (Porter, 2008). Injuries may be either closed (i.e., covered by flesh) or open, and the trauma caused to the brain can be mild or severe. Severe injuries may result in learning disabilities, attention-deficit disorders, personality changes, cerebral palsy, or

Brain Injury Association of America
www.biusa.org

other physical disabilities, but traumatic brain injury is considered a separate category of disability. TBI can result in cognitive, social, and language deficits as well (Pershelli, 2007). In the evaluation of students with TBIs, a multidisciplinary team approach is necessary to ensure that the most appropriate education placement and intervention are provided (Keyser-Marcus et al., 2002). Individual cases of TBI may vary in terms of the severity of injury, manifestations of disability, and potential for recovery (Carter & Spencer, 2007; Keyser-Marcus et al., 2002).

> TBI can have a major impact on a child's ability to learn.

Muscular Dystrophies

Muscular dystrophies and **spinal muscular atrophy (SMA)** are inherited, progressive disorders of the muscles that affect movement and function (Porter, 2008). The most common form, Duchenne muscular dystrophy, occurs primarily but not exclusively in boys (Leet, Dormans, & Tosi, 2002). The disease appears at about 2 to 5 years, and by age 12 the child may not be able to walk. The disease gradually weakens the respiratory system, eventually leading to death (Batshaw, 2002; Bigge, Best, & Heller, 2001; Porter, 2008). Approximately one-third of children with Duchenne muscular dystrophy will have mild, nonprogressive intellectual impairments that will affect their verbal abilities (Porter, 2008). There are currently no cures; however, there are treatment protocols. Treatment often consists of:

1. Low resistance training to reduce muscle damage

2. Proper nutrition

3. Medications as required

4. CPT for respiration

5. Avoiding a tracheotomy by the use of cough suppressants and noninvasive interventions

Muscular Dystrophy Association
www.mdausa.org

Planning for the educational needs of a student with muscular dystrophy must be done by a multidisciplinary team and must be seen as a dynamic process, allowing the team to respond to the changing needs of the student as the disease progresses.

Juvenile Arthritis

Juvenile rheumatoid arthritis begins at or before age 16 and causes swelling, stiffness, effusion, pain, and tenderness in the joints (Leet, Dormans, & Tosi, 2002; Porter, 2008). Initial diagnosis is often accompanied by persistent fever of unknown origin and rash. Complete remission is possible for 50 to 75 percent of children, and others can be treated with disease-modifying drugs. Prolonged inflammation, however, can lead to joint deformities, which eventually can affect mobility and the child's use of her or his hands and fingers. Students may require frequent medication or may miss school if surgery is needed or a flare-up of the disease occurs. A multidisciplinary team is required to evaluate, identify, and recommend appropriate therapies, medications, exercises, counseling, and educational adaptations (Bigge et al., 2001).

Arthritis
arthritis.org

Spinal Curvatures

The spinal column consists of a stack of thirty-three vertebrae, with a disk between each, held in place by long ligaments enclosing the spinal cord (Ford, 2008). Problems with the spine function or curvature can lead to spinal disorders. **Scoliosis**, most common in adolescent females, is a form of **spinal curvature** in which the spine forms a "c" or an "s" when it is viewed from behind. Scoliosis may begin in infancy, early childhood, or adolescence, and although there are many potential causes of spinal curvatures, including congenital genetic neuromuscular difficulties, in many cases they cannot be determined (Ford, 2008). Treatments include wearing a brace, doing special exercises, and, in more severe cases, surgery to halt the progression of the curvature. The outcome is dependent on the cause, location, and severity of the curve. Educational supports and related services should include physical therapy and emotional support if needed to help with self-image and personal adjustment.

National Scoliosis Foundation
www.scoliosis.org

Osteogenesis Imperfecta (OI)

Osteogenesis imperfecta (OI) is an inherited congenital fragility of the bones caused by a dominant genetic mutation that occurs in approximately 1:20,000 births. There are seven types of OI; other syndromes resembling OI exist with a recessive genetic inheritance. Bone fragility leads to fractures on different bone sites, causing extremely short statures, scoliosis, long-bone bowing, and skull fractures. Additional problems may include hearing loss, lax ligaments, and teeth abnormalities. Some children with OI become wheelchair mobile. While there is no cure for OI, orthopedic management for fractures and corrective devices for scoliosis, as well as addressing the hearing loss (in some cases with choclear implants, see Chapter 10), are used to manage difficulties and improve outcomes for the child. In some cases the use of bisphosphonates to increase bone density is helpful (Zeitlin et al., 1994). Teachers must meet the child's physical needs in modified education programs and be alert to problems in hearing and vision. Children with OI are usually of normal intelligence, but they can experience fatigue and low self-esteem, so counseling support may be needed.

Osteogenesis Imperfecta Foundation
www.oif.org

Major Health Impairments

When children are dealing with serious health problems, their life and education will be impacted. The support needed for each child will depend on the range and severity of the problem. In this section we discuss some of the major health issues that children face, (see Table 12.3). Medical experts take the lead on diagnosis and planning medical interventions, while the general education teacher takes responsibility for needed daily supports and for knowing the appropriate protocols for initial response in an emergency. Children with health concerns may also need some support from the special education teacher as well, and this support may be consultative in nature. In the following text we briefly discuss each health concern and general guidelines for teachers.

Juvenile Diabetes

Juvenile diabetes is a disorder in which the blood sugar of the individual is abnormally high because the body does not produce enough insulin (Type 1 diabetes) or because the body is insensitive to the insulin that is produced (Type 2 diabetes) (Porter, 2008). Type 1 diabetes can develop at any time (including in infancy) but usually begins between ages 6 and 13. Type 2 diabetes was considered a disease of adolescents or adults, but it is becoming more common in children who are overweight or obese, and 10 to 50 percent of the newly diagnosed childhood cases of diabetes are Type 2 (Porter, 2008). Symptoms of Type 1 diabetes may develop rapidly over the course of a few weeks and include an excessive need to urinate (**polyuria**); increased thirst (**polydpsia**); dehydration leading to weakness, lethargy, increase in appetite (**polyphagia**) and rapid pulse; and possibly blurred vision (Porter, 2008). Dietary changes, exercise, and weight loss can prevent or delay the onset of Type 2 diabetes, but nothing can prevent Type 1 diabetes. The treatment of diabetes involves regulating the blood sugar with additional insulin and nutritional management. Controlling blood sugar levels in children can be

Juvenile Diabetes Research Foundation
www.jdrf.org

> **TABLE 12.3**
> **List of Health Impairments**
>
> *Major health impairments*
> - Juvenile diabetes
> - Asthma
> - Cardiac conditions
> - Blood disorders & hemophilia
> - Cancer
> - Cystic fibrosis
> - Other conditions (ulcerative colitis, Crohn's disease, sickle cell anemia)
>
> *Congenital diseases*
> - HIV/AIDS
> - TORCHS infections (congenital diseases that include toxoplasmosis, rubella, cytomegalovirus infections, and herpes simplex infections)
>
> *Acquired diseases*
> - Hepatitis B
> - Meningitis
> - Encephalitis
> - Other conditions

Source: From K. W. Heller, P. A. Alberto, P. E. Forney, & M. N. Schwartzman (Eds.). *Understanding physical, sensory, and health impairments: Characteristics and educational implications.* Copyright © 1996. Adapted with permission of the authors.

difficult because of problems following a consistent diet, normal growth, hormonal changes during puberty, and problems in recognizing warning signs of high or low sugar levels.

Asthma

Asthma, an immune system-allergy disease, is a condition affecting an individual's breathing due to bronchial swelling. It usually has three features: the lungs are swollen, breathing is difficult, and the airways react negatively to a variety of environmental triggers (such as dust, smoke, cold air, mold, and exercise). Asthma may also cause acute constriction of the bronchial tubes (Batshaw & Perret, 1992). Asthma affects about 23 million Americans (7 million under 18 years of age) and account for between 3,000 and 4,000 deaths each year (CDC, 2009). Asthma is the leading cause of hospitalization for children and the number one cause of elementary school absenteeism (Porter, 2008). In children, the condition varies from mild to severe.

Childhood Asthma Foundation
www.childasthma.com

Cardiac Conditions

Each year in the United States an estimated 40,000 (1 in 125) are born with **heart defects** that range from ones that are so slight that problems might not appear for years to ones that are so severe that they are immediately life threatening

(March of Dimes, 2010). Medical advances have led to dramatic increases in survival rates for children with serious heart defects (March of Dimes, 2010). Whereas some infants with heart defects do not show any symptoms at all, others can be recognized by the following indicators: heart murmurs; rapid heartbeat and breathing difficulties (especially during exercise or eating); swelling of the legs, abdomen, or areas around the eyes; and, in some cases, a change in skin coloring to a pale grayish or bluish cast (March of Dimes, 2010). A full medical review should be completed if the infant or child shows any of these indications of heart complications. Some children will need medications for their cardiac conditions to control heart rate, hypertension, and blood flow.

American Heart Association
www.americanheart.org

Hemophilia

Hemophilia is a hereditary bleeding disorder caused by a clotting factor deficiency (e.g., factor VIII: hemophilia A; factor IX: hemophilia B; factor XI [rare]: hemophilia C). The percentages of clotting factors determine the severity of the disease. The symptoms of hemophilia include deep internal bleeding, swelling of a limb, bleeding in an organ (such as liver or gall bladder), cerebral bleeding (characterized by headache and vision problems), joint immobility, stiffness in throat, skin bruising, and prolonged bleeding from minor cuts.

National Hemophilia Foundation
www.hemophilia.org

Cancer

Cancer is rare in children, occurring in only 1 in 5,000 children in the United States each year (Porter, 2008). The most common forms of cancer in children are leukemia, lymphoma, and brain tumors. In contrast to cancers in adults, cancers in children are much more curable. About 75 percent of children with cancer will survive at least five years, and many researchers now consider childhood cancer to be a chronic illness. However, in spite of optimal treatments, approximately 2,000 children with cancer will die each year (Porter, 2008). Medical treatments for children with cancer include a combination of chemotherapy, radiation, surgery, and medications. Because children are still growing, the side effects of these treatments may differ from those in adults; for example, an arm that receives radiation therapy may not reach its full growth (Porter, 2008). Long-term impacts of the treatments may also include such things as infertility, poor overall growth, damage to the heart, and secondary cancers (Porter, 2008). Treatments for children with cancer must be overseen by specialists with expertise in childhood cancers.

With modern medical treatments, more children are surviving cancer and will need the support of their teachers to ensure that their progress in school is maintained.

The impact of cancer on the family and child can be overwhelming. In addition to anguish and worry for the child's well-being, the family is often faced with an intense medical regimen that requires full-time management, leaving little time for siblings, work, or "normal" activities. Meeting the needs of the child and family can be more stressful if the treatment center is located far from the family's home. The family and child will need as much support as possible to cope with these difficulties. Children who are attending school will need academic support, emotional support, and health support to help them cope successfully (Key, Brown, Marsh, Spratt, & Recknor, 2001; Mukherjee, Lightfoot, & Sloper, 2000; Shiu, 2001).

American Cancer Society
www.cancer.org

Cystic Fibrosis

Cystic fibrosis is an inherited disease that affects a child's breathing and digestion. An estimated 30,000 children and adults in the United States have cystic fibrosis; advances in medical treatments have increased the survival rate for adults into their thirties and forties (March of Dimes, 2010). Cystic fibrosis affects the movement of salt in and out of the cells that line the lungs and pancreas, and this causes secretions of mucus and other thick fluids that clog the lungs and the ducts connecting the pancreas with the small intestines (March of Dimes, 2010). Lung infections, difficulties gaining weight, and problems with nutritional intake are common complications for individuals with cystic fibrosis, and medical supervision is important throughout the person's life. Medical treatments include providing breathing assistance (for example, respiratory therapy and vibrating vests that help loosen and clear mucus) and drugs that thin mucus, clear airways, prevent and treat infections, and reduce inflammations (March of Dimes, 2010). Most children with cystic fibrosis can attend school. Doctors may recommend exercise to help strengthen the child's heart and lungs and to help loosen mucus.

Cystic fibrosis
www.cff.org

Ulcerative Colitis and Crohn's Disease (IBD)

Both **ulcerative colitis** and **Crohn's disease** involve inflammation of the intestine. Ulcerative colitis affects the colon, while Crohn's may affect any part of the intestinal system—causing thickness of the bowel wall. Causes of both ulcerative colitis and Crohn's disease include heredity, weakened immune and inflammatory response, and intestinal bacteria.

Symptoms include abdominal pain, fever, diarrhea with blood in the stool, and joint pain. Treatment includes the use of anti-inflammatory drugs, steroids, immune system medicines, antibiotics, pain relievers, vitamin and iron supplements, intestinal corrective surgery, exercises to reduce stress, biofeedback, and probiotics. Children and teenagers with these conditions may have significant self-image issues and need support from teachers, family, friends, and health care providers to help maintain their social, mental, and physical growth (CCFA, 2010).

Crohn's and Colitis
Foundation of America
www.ccfa.org

Sickle Cell Anemia

Sickle cell anemia is a form of anemia caused by a mutation in the gene that tells the body to make hemoglobin A (the red iron rich compound), which allows red blood cells to carry oxygen to all parts of your body. Sickle cell is most common among African Americans and individuals of Middle Eastern and Indian ancestry. The symptoms of sickle cell anemia include stroke, speech difficulties, seizures, painful joints and extremities, vision problems, fatigue, fever, and infection.

Treatment for sickle cell anemia includes pain relievers, antibiotics, blood transfusions, and, in some cases, therapeutic oxygen. Most children with sickle cell anemia can continue to function well in school, but teachers must help them avoid trauma, extreme temperatures, and dehydration.

Sickle Cell Disease Association
of America
www.sicklecell.org

HIV/AIDS

Acquired immune deficiency syndrome (AIDS) is a breakdown of the body's immune system caused by the **human immunodeficiency virus (HIV).** When HIV enters the bloodstream, the body reacts with antibodies to fight the infection; it is the presence of these antibodies in the blood that leads to the diagnosis of "HIV positive." A person can carry HIV and can infect others for ten or more years without developing AIDS. People with AIDS are more susceptible to certain diseases and cancers because their immune systems are compromised. Ninety percent of AIDS cases in children are the result of the virus being transmitted from the infected mother during pregnancy, the birth process, or breastfeeding (Rutstein, Conlon, & Batshaw, 1997). Because many women do not know that they are infected with HIV, the Centers for Disease Control and Prevention (CDC) recommends HIV screening for all pregnant women. HIV is now being treated before birth with some success, and the number of babies born with HIV in the United States has dropped from a high of about 1,650 in 1991 to an estimated 100 to 200 in 2005 (March of Dimes, 2010).

HIV-infected infants should be treated with antiretroviral agents approved by the Food and Drug Administration (FDA) (Spiegel & Bonwit, 2002). A child may also become infected through a transfusion of contaminated blood. Adolescents who are exposed through sexual contact or contaminated needles through drug use are at risk of contracting the disease.

With early diagnosis and medical treatment, 75 percent of infants born with HIV in the United States are still living at age 5, with the average survival rate for children born with HIV being 9.4 years (Franks, Miller, Wolff, & Landry, 2004). This means that increasing numbers of HIV-infected children are attending preschool and elementary school (Grier & Hodges, 1998). AIDS is a serious concern in our society, and communities are still formulating policies on how to work with infants and children who have the infection. The likelihood of a child with HIV infecting others during normal classroom activities is low, but all teachers should still learn and use **universal precautions** (Edens, Murdick, & Gartin, 2003; Franks et al., 2004). Universal precautions at a minimum include the following (Edens et al., 2003):

> Many children who are HIV-positive are attending schools, and their health needs must be addressed.

1. Use of gloves when dealing with any body fluids (for example, blood, urine, fecal material, vomit) produced by a child. This protects the teacher from contamination and also reduces the risk of spreading an infection to the child if the teacher is in direct contact with an open wound. Teachers should practice "gloving," which is the safe way to don and remove gloves.

2. Proper hand washing when accidents occur that involve bodily fluids. Any areas of contact with the biohazard (the contaminated bodily fluids) should be washed immediately because some pathogens can enter the body even through skin that is chapped but not broken. If no direct contact occurs with the biohazard, hand washing should occur after taking care of the child or cleaning the site of contamination. Hand washing should be completed even when gloves have been worn. All surface areas should be scrubbed with soap for between 10 and 30 seconds and rinsed in warm water. Drying hands with paper towels or air driers is recommended.

3. Cleanup procedures for biohazards should follow a protocol using appropriate disinfectants and placing all clean-up materials in a biohazard waste disposal container. Gloves should be worn during cleanup, and hands must be thoroughly washed after cleanup.

> CDC National Prevention Information Network (HIV and AIDS)
> **www.cdcnpin.org**

Because there is no way of knowing for sure which children may be HIV-positive, *universal precautions should be used with all children in all classrooms.*

Acquired Diseases

Children who become seriously ill may require regular medication or other medical treatment. Some serious or chronic illnesses, such as chronic Lyme disease, encephalitis, and meningitis, will require a prolonged hospital stay for the child. If this is the case, everything should be done to continue the child's educational support in the hospital (Shiu, 2001). Many large children's hospitals have educational programs. Ideally the educational support received in the hospital should be coordinated with the child's school so that reentry can be facilitated for the child when he or she is able to attend school again. Teachers working with these children should be knowledgeable about medical procedures needed at school, limitations on activities, and emergency procedures that may be necessary if problems arise (Best et al., 2005).

Teacher's and School's Roles in Supporting Children with Serious Health Needs

While the specific needs will be different for each child, there are some general guidelines that will help teachers be prepared to support a child with serious health problems. When a teacher has a student who has serious health problems he or she should:

1. Learn about the child's health diagnosis and the impact that this may have on learning, social development, emotional well-being, and physical needs for support.

2. Learn about the medical treatments the child is receiving and what impact these may have on learning, social development, emotional well-being, and physical needs for support.

3. Plan for any specific medication or medical needs that may need attention during the school day (e.g., use of an inhaler for breathing or an EpiPen for allergies).

4. Develop a plan, with the child and the child's family, to share information about the health issues with others (including peers).

5. Learn about the other support systems the child has and how you can coordinate with them when needed (i.e., family, counselors, nurses, etc.).

6. Be prepared for extensive absences while the child receives needed medical treatments, and have a plan in place for helping the child make up work by targeting only critical work for completion.

7. Learn about specific limitations and needs so that you can modify the environment and/or activities for the child (e.g., remove sharp items that may cause bleeding, limit contact sports, keep the child hydrated, remove food allergens).

8. Be prepared to recognize signs of an emerging health-related difficulty (i.e., fatigue, faintness, stress, flushing, etc.) and know how to support the child.

9. Be prepared for medical emergencies and have a response plan in place.

10. Learn about the child's interest and strengths so that these are nurtured and supported as well,

Teachers must be alert to signs of fatigue or pain and to the vitality needs of their students (Mukherjee et al., 2000; Shiu, 2001). Parents and teachers must also watch for indications of depression and should plan ahead for emotional and social support (Key et al., 2001). It is important for all members of the child's environment (medical personnel, therapists, parents, teachers) to prepare a detailed plan once the child is ready to enter or reenter the school environment following an illness or chronic condition (Prevatt, Heffer, & Lowe, 2000). This plan should provide a detailed description of all aspects of the child's day, including what exercise is recommended, periods of rest and quiet times, and ways of encouraging a positive self-concept (Mukherjee et al., 2000; Prevatt, Heffer, & Lowe, 2000). Because wellness-illness is a continuum and health needs can fluctuate, these plans must be individualized and reviewed when circumstances change.

In addition to the plans for individual children, a comprehensive district plan should also be developed that includes policies at the school and district levels that address provision of services, provision of emergency care, steps for supporting the child in school, and guidelines for related service personnel (Hill & Davis, 1999).

Genetic Factors and Disabilities

Many disabilities are caused by genetic differences that include mutations, damage, and general anomalies. Genetics-related disabilities can be inherited (i.e., they are passed from one generation to the next) or they can be specific to the individual who is impacted. In this chapter we look at several disability and health areas that have their origins in genetic differences including muscular dystrophies, sickle cell anemia, hemophilia and blood-related diseases, cystic fibrosis, and juvenile diabetes. One area of emerging research to address some genetic defects is **gene replacement therapy** (Smith, Bainbridge, & Ali, 2009), where the defective genetic material is replaced and corrected. There are two approaches being developed. The first is **germ line therapy,** in which sperm or egg cells are modified by introducing functional genes ("gene therapy", 2010). The genetic change is then integrated into the genome and is passed to future generations. The second type of therapy is **somatic gene therapy,** in which the therapeutic genes are transferred into the somatic cells and only impact the patient ("gene therapy", 2010). Current studies are underway to use gene replacement therapies for spinal muscular atrophies (University of Sheffield, 2010), muscular dystrophies metabolic liver disease (Hoglund, 2010), sickle cell disease and other blood disorders (Townes, 2010), and retinal degeneration (Smith, Bainbridge, & Ali, 2009). While the results for genetic replacement therapies are promising, the techniques are not without controversy. The ethical implications of genetic replacement include concerns about bioengineering, the use of genetics to alter the natural course of human development and the use of genetic replacement technology to create "smart" biological weapons that could target groups based on their genetic makeup. These ethical issues will need to be explored as research on gene replacement continues.

Severe and Multiple Disabilities

In addition to the definitions of physical disabilities and health impairments presented earlier, TASH (formerly known as The Association for Persons with Severe Handicaps) has defined what it means to have a severe disability. The TASH definition, by and large, addresses children who have multiple disabilities, but it also includes those whose primary area of disability creates extreme limitations. The TASH defines severely disabled individuals as those

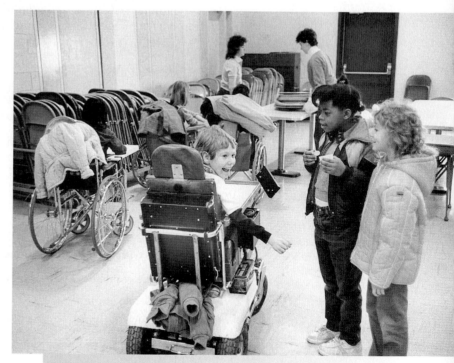

Children form friendships as they work and learn together.
(© Alan Carey/The Image Works)

who require extensive ongoing support in more than one life activity in order to participate in integrated community settings and to enjoy a quality of life that is available to citizens with fewer or no disabilities. Support may be required for life activities such as mobility, communication, self-care, and learning as necessary for independent living, employment, and self-sufficiency. (Bureau for the Education of the Handicapped, April 1985; revised and adopted by TASH, December 1985, and revised November 1986; see Meyer, Peck, & Brown, 1991, p. 19)

Any definition of individuals with multiple or severe disabilities must be broad, because it includes a very heterogeneous population: for example, persons with psychiatric disorders, deafblindness, and combinations of health, motor, or cognitive impairments (Best et al., 2005).

Deafblindness

Although the term "deafblind" seems to imply a complete loss of vision and hearing, it actually includes children with a range of vision and hearing losses, as shown in Table 12.4 (Malloy, 2009).

Because of the range of sensory abilities for children who are deafblind (sometimes written "deaf-blind"), it is essential that the multidisciplinary planning team carefully assess the child's vision and hearing to determine how to support the maximum use of the child's sensory input for learning (Riggio, 2009). Many children who are deafblind have other disabilities, including 66 percent with cognitive disabilities; 57 percent with physical disabilities; 38 percent with complex health needs; 9 percent with behavior challenges; and 30 percent with other complications (Malloy, 2009). Deafblindness is not always associated with other disabilities; more than half of the deafblind population have Usher syndrome, which is an inherited condition. Individuals with **Usher syndrome** have progressive sensorimotor deafness, retinitis pigmentosa (vision

TABLE 12.4
Vision and Hearing Loss in Children Identified as Deafblind
Vision Loss Within the Deafblind Population
17% totally blind or light perception only
24% legally blind
21% low vision
17% cortical vision impairment
21% other
Hearing Loss Within the Deafblind Population
39% severe or profound hearing loss
13% moderate hearing loss
14% mild hearing loss
6% central auditory processing disorders
28% other

Source: Adapted from Malloy, P. (2009). Who are children who are deaf-blind? *Division on Visual Impairments Quarterly, 54*(3), 5–7.

loss), and central nervous system problems (Batshaw, 2002). A person with Usher syndrome has a hearing impairment and a vision disability that worsens over time. In its extreme form, referred to as Usher syndrome type I, the individual is deaf from birth and has severe balance problems. In the second type, children are born with moderate to severe hearing impairments and can perform well in the general education classroom. In the third type, the person has normal hearing that worsens over time, followed by blindness beginning in adolescence.

There is no cure for Usher syndrome, but children with this condition can profit from early identification and appropriate technological and educational assistance (National Institute on Deafness and Other Communication Disorders [NIDCD], 1999). Cochlear implants (see Chapter 10) may be appropriate for children who are deafblind if they cannot use hearing aids to increase their hearing (Stremel, 2009).

Helen Keller National Center
www.helenkeller.org/national

The National Consortium on Deaf-Blindness estimated that there were 10,766 individuals with deafblindness in 2008 (NCDB, 2009). Because of the intensity of their needs, most children who are deafblind are served in separate settings. Figure 12.3 shows the educational placements for children who are deafblind.

Helen Keller, the most famous deafblind individual, is reported to have said that being blind isolates you from things, while being deaf isolates you from people. This double isolation can make it challenging for individuals to learn (Riggio, 2009; Anthony, 2009). It takes a great deal of time, patience, empathy, and repetition to establish the first word (usually a sign) with the child who is deafblind. The goal is to connect a movement made by the child to a sign. The learning process often begins with the names of parents (*mama, papa*) or a toy or activity the child likes (*swing,* for example).

If the child is blind, the sign is taught by placing both hands on the child and encouraging the child to respond. Bear in mind that children who can see and hear do not speak until they have heard thousands of words. Children with deafblindness need similar multiple experiences with the activity and the corresponding sign (McKenzie, 2009; Miles & Riggio, 1999).

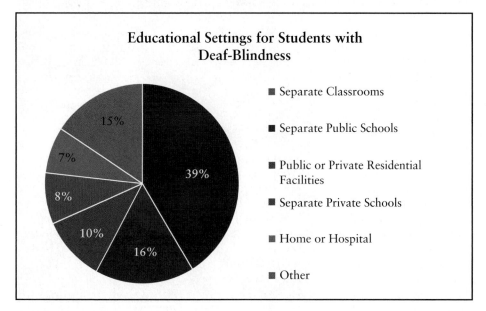

FIGURE 12.3
Educational Settings for Students with Deaf-Blindness
Source: U.S. Department of Education. (2009). *Twenty-Eighth Annual Report to Congress.* Washington, D.C.: Office of Special Education Programs.

My Amazing Maisy

My 7-year-old daughter Maisy was born with a chromosomal disorder. We were so frightened for her from the minute we looked into her eyes for the first time. She was born with two holes in her heart that required open-heart surgery as a toddler, and she also needed reconstructive surgery on her knee. By the time she was 9 months old, I realized that she wasn't meeting developmental milestones. She didn't walk until she was 18 months old, and I became concerned about her communication. Her pediatrician tried to reassure me that I was being overly sensitive because of my background in special education, but by the time she was a year old, she wasn't talking at all.

That was when she was diagnosed with a developmental delay. Undiscouraged, we encouraged her to try to speak as much as possible. When she turned three, she qualified for a state program that provided occupational and physical therapy. This seemed to help her development, but we got so many conflicting messages! We had begun to teach Maisy sign language to help her communicate, but her new school told us sign language might slow down her emerging speech. Then, when Maisy began kindergarten, we tried to get her IEP team to agree to five days a week of speech therapy. One of the team members told us not to jump the gun—that if we didn't pressure Maisy to speak, one day she would just start talking on her own. I couldn't believe an expert was handing out such false hopes! We kept pushing until Maisy got her five days a week of therapy. Perhaps the most frustrating aspect of Maisy's speech delay is that none of her doctors ever suggested testing her hearing. Everyone assumed her communication difficulties were due to her developmental delay, so she didn't get her first hearing test until she was almost seven! It breaks my heart to think she may have had an easier time learning how to speak if we had known whether her hearing was ok.

Now, at 7, Maisy communicates with us in her own way. There is almost always a smile on her face. She speaks in repetitive, short sentences that we encourage her to use all of the time, like when she wants something. She is learning inflection and has a great sense of humor, so she'll use certain noises or words just to make us laugh. When she is surprised or pleased by something, she'll drawl, "Oh my gosh!" just like a Jersey girl. She says, "W-ow!" when she is happy, and opens her eyes wide and says, "Noooo!" when she doesn't like what is happening around her.

It warms my heart to see her talking with her best friend, Wilson. Wilson has Down syndrome and a speech delay similar to Maisy's. But when they are together, they talk up a storm! They get along really well and always seem to know what the other is thinking. When Maisy is in school, she constantly asks her teacher to go to the "green hall," where Wilson has his classes. I really admire the way my daughter finds so much joy in her life. And when she comes up and kisses me, I know exactly what she's saying.

Source: Written by Jennifer Job for Melissa Schaffer Miller, Maisy's mother and a professor of education at UNC-Chapel Hill.

Pivotal Issues

- What should parents do when advice from professionals goes against what they feel is best for their child?

- How can we help children develop friendships, and why are friendships so important for children with disabilities?

Maisy and Wilson enjoy time together in the park.
(Courtesy of M.S. Miller)

Mobility instruction is also critical for independent functioning and the use of the cane is still considered to be an optimal mobility strategy (Tellefson, 2009). Children can begin "caning" as soon as they learn to walk, and can even use the cane with a baby stroller (Tellefson, 2009). The use of assistive technologies will is discussed later in this chapter; there are many support devices to enhance independence and learning (Westmaas, 2009).

Early Intervention with Children Who Have Severe and Multiple Disabilities

Children with multiple and severe disabilities need early intervention so that the parents can provide appropriate and consistent care. Parents and therapists need to help children with severe disabilities recognize that they are persons in an environment and that they can influence their environment. The adults need to teach the children to turn outward—from their internal world to the external world of the environment and other people for stimulation. If they do not, children with multiple and severe disabilities tend to respond to internal rather than external stimuli and to use their genetic capacity for curiosity to explore by manipulating their internal world through body movements. As with many areas of disabilities, early intervention can both mediate the impact of the disability and prevent secondary problems from emerging.

> While we may see broad patterns for individuals with multiple and severe disabilities, we must remember that each child is unique and will have his or her own strengths and needs.

All of the definitions presented earlier help us understand the broad categories that are addressed by physical disabilities, health impairments, and multiple or severe disabilities, but we must remember that the specific needs of children within each category will be unique.

Prevalence of Physical Disabilities, Health Impairments, and Multiple Disabilities in Children

The U.S. Department of Education (2009) reports that in the fall of 2004 the number of individuals ages 6 through 21 receiving special education services was 6,118,437. Table 12.5 shows the distributions within this category for orthopedic impairments, deafblindness, traumatic brain injuries, multiple disabilities, and other health impairments.

TABLE 12.5
Disability Distribution for Children Ages 6–21 Who Receive Special Education and Related Services, Fall 2004*

Area of Disability	Percentage of Special Education	Numbers of Children*
Orthopedic impairments	1.1%	73,421
Deafblind	0.03%	1,835
Traumatic brain injury	0.4%	24,473
Multiple disabilities	2.2%	134,605
Other health impairments	8.4%	513,985

Numbers are based on the total population of children, 5,959,282, ages 6–21 reported as receiving special education and related services in the fall of 2002.
Source: U.S. Department of Education (2009). *Twenty-eighth annual report to Congress: Implementation of the Individuals with Disabilities Act.* Washington, D.C.: Office of Special Education Programs.

Counting on Me

I've always believed life to be a continual learning process. January 23, 1998, my greatest lesson began with the birth of my daughter, Isabel Soledad. Isabel was born in Germany two weeks postterm via emergency caesarean, weighing only five pounds. She had to be revived. No one knew and no one was prepared, least of all me. It was later determined that Isabel has a chromosomal disorder, a unique genetic rearrangement, never before documented (a partial trisomy 22 and a partial trisomy 7)—and so it began.

Motherhood can be an overwhelming experience itself, but when a grave disappointment for the dreams you so carefully envisioned is suddenly replaced with a lifelong responsibility to a difficult unknown, it's like being hit over the head with a hammer. Once your head stops spinning and the realization sets in, you focus on what you can control and move on. There is no time for mourning.

The first year was the most frightening. In my case, there was no information, no research, no data, nor studies. Even still, I sought second and third opinions. I conducted my own research online and in libraries and medical universities around the world. I have refused to accept anything less than the best I can provide for my daughter; and because of this, I have excused many professionals from my child's care over the years whenever I have felt that her best interests were not on their forefront.

Isabel's condition is responsible for a wide range of developmental delays. She has received physical, occupational, and speech therapies from a very early age. Although I was warned that my child would never walk, most frequently I am continually given the frustrating prognosis of "wait and see." I view this as a mixed blessing. There are no other children like Isabel to compare missed milestones with, and, therefore, no predetermined shortcomings.

By the time Isabel was 18 months old, her amazing little spirit had emerged in full. Many of my fears had subsided and much of my faith was restored; however, a new challenge arose to the occasion when I returned to the U.S. as a single parent.

Isabel and Crystal have learned to count on each other.
(Courtesy of the Author)

Encountering the System

Becoming established into the system was relatively easy through Wake County's Early Intervention Services, which, in turn, led me to Community Partnerships, Inc., and Smart Start. These exceptional organizations helped provide funding for child care, special equipment, as well as additional therapies which insurance would not cover. Eventually we also received a CAP-C slot, which provides respite care and Medicaid. Once my daughter turned 3, however, the bulk of support and assistance (which had been such a godsend) ended abruptly. In its place a different system arose, with lots of paperwork, policies, red tape, and many, many closed doors.

Frustration and disappointment landed me on the doorstep of The Arc of Wake County, where I met one of the most remarkable and passionate human beings I have ever known, Ms. Lynn Schwartz, family resource coordinator and guardianship specialist. For years now, she has been at my side through hours of individual education program (IEP) meetings with the school board, as our advocate and our dear friend. Sometimes, that makes all the difference.

Through the unending trials and transitions, I quickly learned to lean on those I could count on and cut the losses from those I could not. I called upon friends when I needed support and reassurance. I called upon family when I needed a break. I called upon caseworkers when I ran out of ideas, and in the midst of desperation, I have even enlisted the aid of politicians and local news media. I have built my own vast invaluable support network.

No doubt, over the years, my heroes have had many faces—countless doctors, nurses, caseworkers, therapists, advocates, teachers, counselors, mothers, friends, and family. I could not have survived with less; however, my greatest debt of gratitude I owe to my daughter; she is my strength, my angel, and the most extraordinary teacher I have ever known.

Currently, Isabel is 5 years old, but developmentally she functions mentally and physically at a 2-year-old level (and yes, we are now in the terrible 2's!). She does not walk independently nor does she speak; we communicate primarily through ASL (American Sign Language), as this is far more efficient than mind

reading. She has made incredible progress and every day is a celebration.

Changing Horizons

Isabel is beginning public school this fall (a terrifying experience for me). When we went to meet her new teacher, Isabel quickly extinguished my fears of my precious little one being trampled by some mean old fifth grader when she proudly tore off down the halls with her walker, running over toes and taking no prisoners! She has no idea that she is any different than anyone else. ... I think this is going to be a good year!

Because of Isabel, I am more patient, more persistent, and more understanding than I ever imagined possible. I am more educated and knowledgeable in matters of health, humanity, and humility. I have learned more about government systems, care, and resources (or lack of) than I ever cared to. I have learned how to ask for help when I cannot do it alone, and I have learned how to ask again. I have found that there are small groups of wonderful people out there who do care and want to help. I've learned about Medicaid and IEPs (having once been accused of being a lobbyist!). I have mastered the art of effective letter writing for my causes. I know how to smile proudly at the weak-minded apologies of those who see my life as misfortune. Because of Isabel, I am a passionate advocate, a loving mother, and a better human being because I have learned the hard way how to laugh, how to cry, and how to keep going—all because there is a strong, beautiful, and determined little person who believes in me and who calls me "mama." For Isabel, I have learned to count on me.

Source: Crystal de la Cruz, Counting on me, *All Together Now!* 9(3), 2003. Reprinted by permission of Partnerships for Inclusion.

Pivotal Issues

- How does the life of the family change when a child is born with disabilities? What are the good things that can emerge?

- What does the family face as the child grows up? What kinds of support do they need to help them?

- Why are parent-advocates so critical?

Assessment of Children with Physical Disabilities, Health Impairments, and Multiple Disabilities

The initial assessment of children with physical disabilities and health impairments is primarily the responsibility of pediatricians; neurologists, who specialize in conditions and diseases of the brain, spinal cord, and nervous system; orthopedists and orthopedic surgeons, who are concerned with muscle function and conditions of the joints and bones; and doctors who specialize in childhood diseases. Other specialists involved in identification include physical therapists, speech-language pathologists, and occupational therapists.

The identification process involves a comprehensive medical evaluation, which includes a medical and developmental history (illnesses, medical history of family members, problems during pregnancy and labor, and developmental progress), a physical examination, and laboratory tests or other special procedures needed for accurate diagnosis. When the child enters preschool or kindergarten, a comprehensive educational assessment must be completed.

Educational Assessments for Children with Physical or Multiple Disabilities

You may want to refer back to Chapter 2 to remind yourself of the legal requirements of assessments, remembering that IDEA requires that assessments be timely, comprehensive, and multidisciplinary (CEC, 2006). The greater the impact of the disability, the more challenging it can be to assess the child's abilities. Federal regulations about assessing or evaluating the skills of individuals with multiple and severe disabilities are, however, quite clear: The evaluation must be appropriate to the needs of the individual and the family, and it must take into account the child's culture and primary language. There is currently a movement for the development of "universally designed assessments" (Salvia, Ysseldyke, & Bolt, 2007). Universal design, you may recall from Chapter 2, is a concept that emerged in our attempt to create architectural designs that give everyone access (for example, curb cuts that work for wheelchairs also help with baby carriages). As more test designers work toward incorporating universal design features in their assessments, it will likely become easier to assess children with disabilities. Until then, however, educational assessment of children who have physical disabilities remains a complex and challenging task. These challenges involve both the administration of the assessment and the interpretation of the assessment results.

Administration of Educational Assessments

Depending on the specific impact of the disability, the assessment will need to be modified to allow the child to participate. These modifications are made to accommodate the student's disability and to ensure that we get an accurate picture of his or her abilities and needs. Accommodations can include changes in the testing materials or procedures that allow students to participate so that their abilities rather than their disabilities are assessed

(Salvia et al., 2007). Salvia et al. (2007) have identified the following four areas in which assessment accommodations can be made for students with disabilities:

1. Presentation (repeated directions; readers, translators, interpreters; large print; Braille)

2. Response (marking the answer in a book; using computers; using push buttons, pointers, or other assistive technologies; dictating answers)

3. Setting (access for a wheelchair or accommodations for other physical needs; special lighting; separate rooms or study carrels)

4. Timing/schedule (allowing extended time and frequent breaks to avoid fatigue)

The specific accommodations needed for each student should be listed in the student's IEP and should be available for all assessments that the student takes. In addition to administering assessments so that children with disabilities can take them, we also must be careful how we interpret the results of these assessments.

Interpreting Assessment Results

Interpreting the results of assessments of children who have physical and/or multiple and severe disabilities presents very specific challenges. The primary difficulty is with **norm-referenced tests.** These are tests that are "standardized" on groups of children in order to allow us to compare an individual child's score with the typical score for other children in his or her age group. With this comparison we are primarily interested in where the specific child is in relation to what can typically be expected for a child within a given age range. State assessments that look at a student's progress are generally norm-referenced, as are standardized achievement and IQ tests. The difficulty with the use of norm-referenced tests for children with disabilities is that the group of children we are using as the comparison base (the norm group) rarely includes other children who have disabilities, and so drawing conclusions about the child with disabilities in comparison with this group can lead to faulty assumptions.

Imagine for a moment that you were to be assessed on your ability to navigate the Amazon River *and* that your performance would be rated against the performance of individuals who lived on the river and traveled it daily. You would likely, and justifiably, feel that you were at a distinct disadvantage in this comparison because of the norm group—people with lots of Amazon River experience. Similarly, the experiences of individuals with disabilities may differ dramatically from those of the norm group.

If, for example, we wish to assess the cognitive abilities of a child with cerebral palsy, we will likely use an intelligence test that has been normed with children who do not have the motor difficulties that are part of the experience of the child with CP. If the test requires the physical manipulation of materials, a timed physical response, or even an abstract response based on a working knowledge of physical properties (for example, pictures that show typical objects and ask the child to estimate which one weighs more), the child with CP will be at a distinct disadvantage when compared with the norm group. Because of this disadvantage, the test results for this child will not necessarily be valid and will likely underpredict the child's cognitive abilities.

Students with physical disabilities, health impairments, and multiple or severe disabilities will need supports and services at all three tiers of the response to intervention (RTI) model.

Many students with physical disabilities and most students with health impairments will receive the majority of their services in the general education classroom (the benefits of inclusion are discussed later in this chapter). These students will, however, also need specific supports at Tier II to address academic, functional and life skills, assistive technology, and counseling needs. Tier III supports are also critical to address individualized supports and services. The development of an IEP is critical to guiding the instructional modification and to ensuring that the transition needs of the student have been addressed. The role of the special education teacher may include collaboration with the general education teacher in the provision of supports at Tier II and direct services for students within Tier III. The special education teacher may also serve as the case manager for the multidisciplinary team working to address the students needs.

Pam, the 5th grade student we met at the beginning of the chapter, spent most of her day in the general classroom receiving solid instructional support, but she also received services that required collaboration among her teachers (Tier II). For Pam, these Tier II supports focused on self-advocacy and general career planning and were taught by the guidance counselor. Pam also received intervention support at the Tier III level, with special education and physical and occupational therapy, and she will soon begin transition planning. What we can see from Pam's example is that RTI is not a linear set of services by which a student begins in Tier I, moves to Tier II, and finally is served in Tier III. All three levels of services are often needed by the same child for different aspects of their support. The conception of the three tiers is to help teachers and service providers determine the level of the child's needs and to organize their responses to meet these needs. Again, remember that the greater the need of the child, the more intensive the service must be to meet the need.

Henry, the second child discussed in the chapter, has multiple and complex needs, and he requires more intense services to meet these needs. Henry spends most of his day in the special education class, where intensive supports can be provided to him on an individualized basis. His related services and therapies are integrated into his day. Henry, and most children with physical disabilities, will require support at the Tier III with motor skills and mobility.

Motor Skills and Mobility

Motor skills and mobility constitute a critical area of skill development for children with physical disabilities. These skills are necessary to maintain upright postures (sitting, standing), to perform functional movements (reaching, grasping), and to move around in the environment. The programming priorities for motor skill development should include developing functional movements and postures that are needed to perform classroom and school activities. Appropriate positioning techniques include developing the following:

- Sufficient head and trunk control to maintain an upright sitting posture in order to perform needed activities throughout the school day (attending and listening, writing, using a computer or communication device, eating)

- Arm movements and fine motor skills for performance of needed activities throughout the school day (holding a pencil and paper to write, holding a book and turning pages, using keyboards or switches to access a computer or communication device)

- Standing and balance for assisted ambulation (using braces and crutches)

- Skills needed to maneuver a wheelchair in the classroom and throughout the school environment (using arms to propel, learning to use an electric wheelchair with a joystick or other control, turning corners and entering doorways, negotiating ramps and curbs, and crossing streets)

Physical and occupational therapists assume the primary responsibility for setting goals in motor development and mobility. They must work closely with teachers, other professionals, and parents, however, for the child to meet these goals. Teachers should become familiar with the basic working components of mobility

> The multidisciplinary team for children with physical disabilities will likely include both a physical and occupational therapist.

equipment (wheelchairs, braces, crutches, walkers) and report needed repairs or adjustments to the child's therapist. Therapists should provide teachers and others with information related to the child's physical condition, limitations, and abilities.

Classroom teachers and others may be required to learn special techniques to help children perform motor tasks during the school day. Positioning, handling, lifting, and transfer techniques are physical management procedures that teachers and others use to help the student maintain good body alignment in a variety of positions (postures) and perform functional movements and skills in the context of daily activities.

A child with spastic cerebral palsy who constantly leans sideways in the wheelchair will have tremendous difficulty reaching the keyboard on the computer and striking the correct keys or using the mouse. With help from a physical therapist or occupational therapist, the teacher can learn to position the student in the wheelchair, use a slant board to move the keyboard closer to the child, and relax the child's arms and bring them forward to rest on the keyboard.

American Physical Therapy Association
www.apta.org

Increasingly, children with cerebral palsy are involved in motor skill activities under the guidance of a physical therapist. These activities include swimming, dance, martial arts, horseback riding, and other real-life experiences. The activities prevent atrophy of damaged muscles. The vast majority of children with disabilities will spend part or most of their days in the general education classroom. The inclusion of children with disabilities in general educational settings is encouraged, and the use of an RTI approach can help to ensure that the collaboration needed for successful inclusion can be accomplished.

Inclusion in General Education for Students with Physical, Health-Related, and Multiple Disabilities

A substantial body of research conducted over many years has established the following benefits of inclusion of students with physical, multiple, and health-related disabilities in public schools and community settings:

- Children with disabilities have shown greater academic gains (Wehmeyer & Schwartz, 1998; Zang, Katsiyannis, & Kortering, 2007).

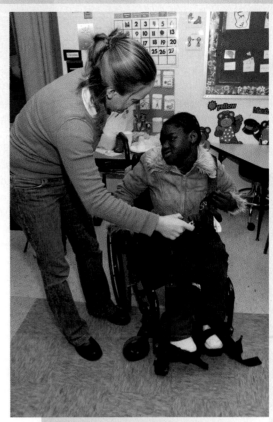

Physical therapists are key members of the multidisciplinary team.
(© Ellen Senisi)

- Positive changes have been reported in the attitudes of nondisabled individuals toward their peers with severe disabilities at various age levels (Grenot-Scheyer, 1994; Ryndak & Alper, 2003; Voeltz, 1980).

- Inclusion has led to improvements in the social and communication skills of children with severe disabilities (Jackson, Ryndak, & Billingsley, 2000; Jenkins, Speltz, & Odom, 1985; Newton, Horner, Ard, LeBaron, & Sapperton, 1994).

- Inclusion has improved interaction between students with severe disabilities and their nondisabled agemates (Downing & Eichinger, 2003; Roberts, Burchinal, & Bailey, 1994).

- Inclusion facilitates adjustment to community settings as students transition into adulthood (Hasazi, Gordon, & Roe, 1985; Helmstetter, Peck, & Giangreco, 1994).

One of the foundational findings about including persons with multiple and severe disabilities in general education classrooms is that inclusion increased the students' social and interpersonal skills. Students displayed increased responsiveness to others, increased reciprocal interactions, and increased displays of affection toward others (Buyssee, Goldman, & Skinner, 2002; Grenot-Scheyer, 1994). In addition, the inclusion of students with physical disabilities in general education classrooms was found to have a positive impact on their peers who do not have disabilities. Nondisabled peers showed increased tolerance for others, increased tolerance for diversity, and growth in their own personal development (Helmstetter, Peck, & Giangreco, 1994).

Full and meaningful inclusion, however, does not happen simply by placing children with disabilities in the same room with their nondisabled peers (Schwartz, 2000). Teachers must specifically and intentionally plan for full inclusion and must be prepared to help develop a sense of belonging for each student (Solish, Perry, Minnes, 2010). Three aspects of full and meaningful inclusion are membership, relationships, and skills (Schwartz, 2000). When these three are working together effectively the child experiences a sense of belonging to and being valued by the group (Schwartz,

2000). Establishing a sense of belonging can lead to the formation of friendships, which in turn increases the child's emotional well-being and language development. Yet creating the environment for full inclusion and belonging can be challenging for children with multiple and/or severe disabilities (Solish, Perry, & Minnes, 2010). Guralnick and colleagues (2009) found that while mothers believed that social networks were important for their child with intellectual and developmental disabilities, actually establishing these networks was difficult. Schwartz (2000) identified some difficulties that impact helping children with disabilities become true members of the group; these include the time the child is out of the group to receive needed supports, expanded curriculum, and therapies; physical or cognitive challenges that limit participation in some group activities; participation in fewer activities; and more limited access to others in the group. To overcome these difficulties, teachers must take an ecological approach to facilitating belonging and the formation of relationships that can develop into friendships (Schwartz, 2000; Solish, Perry, & Minnes, 2010).

Still, however, inclusion must go beyond the social benefits to be of most value. The student must learn both functional and academic skills. For children with

Meaningful inclusion must allow for participation in social and academic activities in the classroom.

(© Ellen Senisi)

physical disabilities, an expanded core curriculum must include functional skills for daily living (Best et al., 2005).

▲ Functional Skills for Individuals with Physical and Multiple Disabilities

Whatever the age of the students or the severity of their disabilities, we must provide them with an **expanded core curriculum** that is functional and as **age appropriate** as possible.

Functional skills can be used immediately by the student, are necessary in everyday settings, and increase to some extent the student's independence. Folding a sheet of paper in half is not a functional skill; folding clothes is (Campbell, 2000; Kaiser, 2000). Teaching functional skills that students will use in daily living is an important part of the curriculum because this helps to build autonomy for the student.

For individuals with intellectual delays, we need to teach age-appropriate skills that match the student's chronological age, not his or her mental age. A 16-year-old boy who has severe disabilities is taught

how to engage in activities similar to those that his nondisabled agemates participate in. Skills appropriate for a 16-year-old, for example, may include eating in a restaurant, using a neighborhood health club, or operating a television set or personal stereo. If the skills are not age appropriate, they are not as likely to be functional. Moreover, age-appropriate skills give students with severe disabilities a measure of social acceptance. Table 12.6 shows age-appropriate life skills for students across the grade levels.

Systematic activity-based instruction teaches skills in the context in which they will be used. Basic academic skills will often be embedded in the skill training. For example, Colin, a young man with cerebral palsy, is being taught how to buy food in the cafeteria. He learns how to maneuver his wheelchair into the line, survey the food, make a selection and take it to the cashier, pay for it, and count his change. Reading the name of the food and its price, knowing whether he has enough money to pay for it, and determining whether the change is correct all involve basic academic skills (Hunt, Soto, Maier, & Doering, 2003).

TABLE 12.6
Life Skills Across the Grades

Student	Domestic	Community	Leisure	Vocational
Tim (elementary age)	• Picking up toys • Washing dishes • Making bed • Dressing • Grooming • Practicing eating skills • Practicing toileting skills • Sorting clothes • Vacuuming	• Eating meals in a restaurant • Using restroom in a local restaurant • Putting trash into container • Choosing correct change to ride city bus • Giving the clerk money for an item he wants to purchase • Recognizing and reading pedestrian safety signs • Participating in local scout troop • Going to a neighbor's house for lunch	• Climbing on swing set • Playing board games • Playing tag with neighbors • Tumbling activities • Running • Playing kickball • Playing croquet • Riding bicycles • Playing with age-appropriate toys	• Picking up plate, silverware, and glass after a meal • Returning toys to appropriate storage spaces • Cleaning the room at the end of the day • Working on a task for a designated period (15–30 minutes) • Wiping tables after meals • Following two- to four-step instructions • Answering the telephone • Emptying trash • Taking messages to people

(Continued)

TABLE 12.6
Life Skills Across the Grades (*continued*)

Student	Domestic	Community	Leisure	Vocational
Mary (junior high age)	● Washing clothes ● Preparing simple meals (e.g., soup, salad, sandwich) ● Keeping bedroom clean ● Making snacks ● Mowing lawn ● Raking leaves ● Making grocery lists ● Purchasing items from a list ● Vacuuming and dusting living room	● Crossing streets safely ● Purchasing an item from a department store ● Purchasing a meal at a restaurant ● Using local transportation system to get to and from recreational facilities ● Participating in local scout troop ● Going to a neighbor's house for lunch on Saturday	● Playing volleyball ● Taking aerobics classes ● Playing checkers with a friend ● Playing miniature golf ● Cycling ● Attending high school or local basketball games ● Playing softball ● Swimming ● Attending craft class at city recreation center	● Waxing floors ● Cleaning windows ● Filling lawn mower with gas ● Hanging and bagging clothes ● Busing tables ● Working for 1–2 hours ● Operating machinery (e.g., dishwasher, buffer) ● Cleaning sinks, bathtubs, and fixtures ● Following a job sequence
Sandy (high school age)	● Cleaning all rooms in place of residence ● Developing a weekly budget ● Cooking meals ● Operating thermostat to regulate heat and air conditioning ● Doing yard maintenance ● Maintaining personal needs ● Caring for and maintaining clothing	● Utilizing bus system to move about the community ● Depositing checks into bank account ● Using community department stores ● Using community restaurants ● Using community grocery stores ● Using community health facilities (e.g., physician, pharmacist)	● Jogging ● Archery ● Boating ● Watching college basketball games ● Playing video games ● Playing card games (e.g., Uno) ● Attending athletic club swimming class ● Gardening ● Going on a vacation trip	● Performing required janitorial duties at J.C. Penney ● Performing housekeeping duties at Days Inn ● Performing grounds keeping duties at college campus ● Performing food service at K Street cafeteria ● Performing laundry duties at Moon's Laundromat ● Performing photocopying at Virginia National Bank headquarters ● Performing food-stocking duties at Farm Fresh ● Performing clerical duties at electrical company ● Performing job duties to company standards

Source: From S. Best, K. Heller, & J. Bigge, *Teaching individuals with physical or multiple disabilities* (5th ed.). (Upper Saddle River, NJ: Merrill-Prentice, 2005). Reprinted with permission of Pearson Education, Inc., Upper Saddle River, New Jersey.

▲ Teacher's Support Needed for Inclusive Classrooms

RTI

Teachers who work within an RTI framework should have the support they need to recognize and respond to the needs of children with disabilities. Coordination of these services through the child's individual family service plan (IFSP) or IEP helps to ensure that the child will not get lost in the myriad of service providers. The multidisciplinary team provides the individual expertise needed to meet the child's needs. For children with physical and health-related needs, the medical members of the team (such as the child's physician or nurse) are critical. In addition to the medical expertise, the team must include someone with expertise in the use of technology to support the child. Inclusion will not work for the child or the teacher without the provision of a supportive infrastructure that provides time for the team members to collaborate in meaningful ways.

➡ Assistive Technology for Students with Physical Disabilities, Health Impairments, and Multiple Disabilities

The child with multiple impairments may have diverse technology needs—such as for instructional technology (see Chapter 4), **assistive technology (AT)**, and technology related to augmentative communication.

The first step in providing AT is determining what kinds of supports are needed. Table 12.7 is a checklist that can be used to help assess the child's needs for AT.

TABLE 12.7
Matching Assistive Technology to a Disability

Type of Disability	Objectives/Tasks	Devices	Applications
Cognitive learning	Reading	Electronic reading machine	WYNN
	Reading		L&H
	Reading	Portable reading pens	Kurzweil 3000
	Reading	Portable hand-held dictionaries	Quicktionary Reading Pen Scan-a-Word
	Language arts	Instructional software	Speaking Language Master
	Writing	Instructional software	The American Heritage Dictionary
	Writing	Word cueing and prediction programs	My Reading Coach
	Writing	Speech synthesis software	Simon Sounds It Out Co:Writer
	Writing	Speech recognition software	Write:Outloud IntelliTalk II DragonDictate
	Note taking	Spelling, grammar, and style checkers	ViaVoice
	Mathematics	Portable keyboards	Write This Way Alphasmart 2000
	Mathematics	Instructional software	Math for Everyday Living
	Auditory memory	Talking calculators	Math Sequence
	Reading	Portable prompting devices	Radio Shack Talking Calculator Mobile Digital Recorder
	Reading	Video magnifiers	Aladdin Pro+ Magnicam
	Reading	Scanner/OCR systems	Reading Edge
		Braille translation software	Duxbury Braille Translator MegaDots

Source: Sze, S. (2009). The effects of assistive technology on students with disabilities. *Journal of Educational Technology Systems, 37*(4), 419–429, Table 1.

(Continued)

Once a full review of the child's needs has been completed, appropriate AT devices can be selected or designed for the child (Sze, 2009). Several kinds of AT devices can be used to meet students' needs, ranging from low- or no-teach to high-teach supports and devices.

Selecting the appropriate technology is just the first step. Once this has been done, the child will need direct instruction with the technology and time to practice with it (Watson, Ito, Smith, & Anderson, 2010). He or she may need emotional support while learning how to manage this new aspect of life. The most important factor in the successful use of the AT device is not which device is selected but how the teacher adapts it for the students (Sze, 2009). The sustained use of any AT device depends on how well it matches the students capabilities and limitations; how easy it is to use; and how appropriate it is for the individual based on gender, age, and personal preferences (Sze, 2009). AT is designed to help the individual gain autonomy, and this is especially true for technologies that help the individual communicate. (See the nearby TeachSource Video Connection box about Jamie.)

Augmentative Communication

Students with physical disabilities who cannot acquire understandable speech or legible writing skills must be provided with **augmentative communication** (Okolo, 2006; Light, Beukelman, & Reichle, 2003). Some children with cerebral palsy, for example, have severe impairment of the oral muscles used in speech and limited fine motor abilities that hamper their writing skills. Muscular dystrophy or arthritis can leave children so weak that they tire easily when writing. Teachers and parents should work closely with speech therapists in selecting, designing, and implementing augmented and alternative communication devices for children with physical disabilities.

▲ Speech: Boards and Electronic Devices

The most common augmented and alternative methods for speech are communication boards and electronic devices with synthesized speech output. Henry, you may recall, used a Dynavox to select his daily activities. Some key points pertaining to the use of speech technologies are:

- Most children use the board or electronic device by pointing with a finger or fist to a word or symbol.

- Children who are not able to point accurately can use a hand-held pointer, a head-mounted wand, a mouthstick, or a laser pointer.

- Youngsters with limited use of their hands may use their eyes instead, visually focusing on the intended word or letter.

A single switch may be necessary for students who have limited or no use of their hands. The type of switch depends on the child's movement abilities. Numerous commercial switches are available, and many can be made at home. A switch is used with devices that light each possible selection on the board by rows, then by columns. When the correct row is lit and the child presses the switch a second time, the correct sentence, phrase, word, or letter is "spoken." Although this method is slower than accessing the device by pointing or using a keyboard, it can accommodate students with severe physical impairments. Many electronic communication devices can be connected to a computer for word processing or computer-assisted instruction (Ashton, 2006).

Supplemental boards or overlays for electronic devices may be needed for academic content areas. For example, a mathematics board contains numbers, mathematics symbols, and words related to current classroom instruction. Other subject boards reflect the content and vocabulary of the specific academic subject (science, social studies, history). These boards should be revised or replaced as classroom content changes throughout the school year. Without augmented communication support, many students might be denied placement in a less-restrictive environment (resource room or general education classroom) because of their lack of spoken language.

▲ Writing Aids and Systems

A variety of **writing aids** and augmented and alternative systems are available for written communication. Students with physical disabilities that cause muscle weakness, involuntary movements, and poor coordination of the fingers and hands may require a writing aid or an alternative system to complete written assignments in school and at home in a neat and timely manner. Some specific aids to help a child with writing include:

- Hand splints to aid in grasping a crayon or pencil

- Special pencil holders

- Slant board to support forearms

- Clipboard, heavy weight, or masking tape to secure paper while writing

- Wide-lined paper (Bigge & Best, 2000)

Computers provide another alternative means of written communication. Word-processing software can be used to complete written assignments. Keyguards are available for most types of computer keyboards. For students who cannot use a standard keyboard because they lack fine motor skills, expanded keyboards with large keys are easier to use. A student with muscular dystrophy might use a miniature keyboard if he or she lacks the range of motion in the arms required to use a standard keyboard yet has good finger movement within a limited range. Alternative keyboards are placed directly on the student's lap, desk, or lap tray for easy access.

▶ⅠⅠ TeachSource VIDEO CONNECTION

Assistive Technology in the Inclusive Classroom: Best Practices

Visit the Education CourseMate website to access this TeachSource Video Case. In this video, you will meet Jamie—a kindergarten child with cerebral palsy. Jamie is an active member of Mr. Byers's classroom, and she participates with her classmates in all of the learning activities. As you watch this video, reflect on how assistive technologies help Jamie communicate and on the ways her teacher (Mr. Byers) and the inclusion specialist (Ms. Woodruff) work together to make sure that Jamie is learning.

Enhancing Self-Determination and Autonomy

Although there are some things that will need to be done for an individual with physical and health needs, the goal of all supports and services is to enhance the autonomy of the individual whenever possible. The first step toward autonomy is self-awareness and self-determination (Field & Hoffman, 2007). Henry, the fifth-grade student we met at the beginning of the chapter is sometimes resistant to doing things without help. Henry's teachers and parents, you recall, are working hard to teach him how to choose what he wants and to eventually self-initiate his morning routine. This may seem like a small thing, but it leads to life skills and habits that will be essential as he grows to adulthood.

Being able to take care of themselves is of critical importance for children with physical disabilities. Self-care skills include eating, toileting, dressing, bathing, and grooming. Students with severe physical involvement may require physical assistance in eating or may have to be fed. Some children need assistive devices or physical help to perform many of these tasks; for example, utensils with built-up or larger handles, special plates and cups, or nonskid mats to stabilize the child's plate.

Social and Emotional Adjustment

Children with physical disabilities sometimes feel powerless. Christie, for example, knows that she has leukemia and that she will probably live only a few more months. She is frequently absent from school. She misses her friends when she is away from school, but when she returns, she no longer feels a part of the group. Besides being sick, she is lonely and is keeping to herself more and more. Josh faces an entirely different problem. He is recovering from a traumatic brain injury that has left him using a wheelchair. He is no longer able to do many things for himself, and he has discovered that temper tantrums are an effective way to get people to respond to his needs immediately. It sometimes seems that the more people try to help Josh, the more aggressive he becomes.

Although withdrawal and aggression are normal when we encounter life-changing circumstances, support to cope with changes may be needed. In addition to coping with changes and feelings of being out of control, individuals with disabilities are also often coping with pain, loss of independence, fears about life, feelings of isolation, rejection from peers, and a host of other issues related to personal acceptance of difficult circumstances. Early research showed that people are more likely to accept their physical disabilities when the environment is supportive (Heinemann & Shontz, 1984), when they achieve some sense of control over their disabilities, and when they begin to demonstrate new competencies. Teachers can enhance the social and emotional adjustment of children with physical disabilities by increasing the understanding of the disabling condition, emphasizing quality of life, and increasing a sense of control. Because of the challenges that individuals with disabilities face, direct instruction on self-advocacy is often needed. Showing students how to assert their rights helps to ensure that they can secure the needed supports and services. Assertiveness training should focus on the individual's ability to express his or her rights clearly, concisely, appropriately, and firmly. Although Josh and Christie cannot control the circumstances leading to their physical disabilities, they can control many other aspects of their lives. It is revealing to have children with physical disabilities list the aspects of their lives that they believe they cannot control. Josh knew he could no longer move independently, and he thought he was powerless. School personnel worked with Josh and his family to show him that his temper tantrums were in fact one way to control people and events. They also helped Josh understand how he could achieve the same results in a more constructive way. Josh learned that his family and classmates were happy to help him when necessary and were in fact still interested in being with him. He found that people understood his frustration and could help him find ways to express that frustration without damaging his relationships with others. Although he still has a severe physical disability, Josh now sees that he can control many aspects of his life.

Family and Lifespan Issues

Parents are the child's first teachers, first advocates, and first caregivers. They provide the support needed to help the multidisciplinary team understand their child and often spend hours securing appropriate supports to meet their child's needs. As the child grows, these needs will change, and parents need to be prepared for lifelong issues that they and their child may face. Table 12.8 offers an overview of some of these issues.

Parenting any child is challenging, but parenting children with disabilities and health impairments can be even more daunting. Parents are constantly walking the fine line between protecting their child and allowing the child to develop independence. Finding the balance between protection and fostering independence can be hard when the parent or the child is fearful or worried. This balance creates unique dilemmas for the child and the parent. The balance between protection and independence often changes as the intensity or severity of the child's situation progresses. There are many excellent websites and blogs written by parents who grapple with these dilemmas, such as the website of writer Ellen Seidman, who chronicles the joys and challenges of raising her young son Max, who has CP.

Love that Max
**http://lovethatmax
.blogspot.com**

TABLE 12.8
Possible Issues Encountered by Parents at Each Stage of Their Child's Life

Early Childhood, Ages 0–5	• Obtaining an accurate diagnosis • Informing siblings and relatives • Locating services • Seeking to find meaning in the exceptionality • Clarifying a personal ideology to guide decisions • Addressing issues of stigma • Identifying positive contributions of exceptionality • Setting great expectations
Elementary School, Ages 6–12	• Establishing routines to carry out family functions • Adjusting emotionally to educational implications • Clarifying issues of mainstreaming vs. special class placement • Participating in IEP conferences • Locating community resources • Arranging for extracurricular activities
Adolescence, Ages 12–21	• Adjusting emotionally to possible chronicity of exceptionality • Identifying issues of emerging sexuality • Addressing possible peer isolation and rejection • Planning for career/vocational development • Arranging for leisure time activities • Dealing with physical and emotional change of puberty • Planning for postsecondary education
Adulthood, Ages 21 On	• Planning for possible need for guardianship • Addressing the need for appropriate adult residence • Adjusting emotionally to any adult implications of dependency • Addressing the need for socialization opportunities outside the family • Initiating career choice or vocational program

Source: From A. P. Turnbull, H. R. Turnbull, E. Erwin, L. Soodak, & Shogren, K. *Families, professionals, and exceptionality: Positive outcomes through partnership and trust* (6th ed.). (Upper Saddle River, NJ: Prentice Hall, 2010). Reprinted by permission of Prentice Hall., Upper Saddle River, New Jersey.

Family support is critical to the well-being of the child with disabilities.
(© Ellen Senisi)

Culturally Responsive Practices

The areas of race, culture, language, and disabilities all combine when we look at special education practices and equitable support for children with exceptionalities (Klingener, Blanchett, & Harry, 2009). Culturally responsive communication and support are critical to building the partnerships with families that help children be successful (Nehring, 2007). Cultural sensitivity includes a focus on the family's strengths and a valuing of the family's input into goal setting for their child (Nehring, 2007). Klingener and her colleagues (2009) offer ten suggestions for working with students of color with disabilities and their families:

1. Recognize the effect of race, culture, language, and social class issues on families' access to relevant special education services.

2. Acknowledge that special education and related services provisions are based on White, middle-class, English-speaking cultural norms and values and may not reflect the child and family's culture.

3. Communicate with students and families in their native language.

4. Communicate using lay and cultural terminology and avoid overreliance on professional jargon.

5. When meeting families, ask about their hopes and dreams for their child and recognize that these may be different from those of the typical of mainstream culture (but are just as valid).

6. Make sure print material is prepared in the native language.

7. Be familiar with and acknowledge within-group difference.

8. Whenever possible, provide services to ethnically, culturally, and linguistically diverse families within the context of relevant community or cultural centers.

9. Involve individuals of color in the development of appropriate IEPs and IFSPs.

Transition for Students with Multiple and/or Severe Disabilities

Table 12.9 lists ten things that can help prepare adolescents with disabilities for their transition to adulthood (Cobb, 2004).

For all individuals with disabilities, the transition from school to work and independent living presents a range of challenges, such as obtaining a driver to take them to and from work, remodeling an apartment so that all appliances

TABLE 12.9	
Top Ten Things to Think About in the Transition to Adulthood	
1. Know your disability.	How does it affect you, your learning, and your activities, and how have you learned to manage it?
2. Know your needs.	What will be required of you in the new setting(s) and what will you need to be successful?
3. Weigh your options.	Gather information and seek advice from others, but most important, look at what you want out of life and set your goals accordingly.
4. Plan for "gatekeepers" (for example, college entrance exams, job-related exams).	Plan early for any known gatekeepers that you will need to negotiate in order to reach your goals.
5. Document your disability and your abilities.	Create a portfolio that documents your disability and your accomplishments.
6. Advocate for yourself.	Your ability to advocate for yourself is critical to your success. Know the laws and requirements and how to ask for what you need and deserve.
7. Use all services available to you.	Find and use *all* possible supports (such as vocational rehabilitation, student support services, special financial aid support, and community-based services).
8. Plan for independence in your living space.	Review your needs and plan ahead for appropriate supports, modifications, and accessibility to your new home, work, and/or learning environments.
9. Learn to manage your time.	Know what you must do, what you should do, and what you want to do, and plan twice as much time as you think you need!
10. Remember that making mistakes is *not* the end of the world.	Everyone struggles with change. Learning as you go is natural and will help you in the future.

Source: Adapted from J. Cobb (2004). *Top ten things to think about as you prepare for your transition into adulthood.* Washington, DC: GW HEATH Resource Center.

can be reached from a wheelchair, or having a live-in aide with special knowledge of how to deal with various kinds of equipment. The focus of this transition should move beyond the individual's limitations to include a recognition of the individual's skills and strengths so that independence and self-fulfillment are enhanced. Growing up means becoming as autonomous as possible in all environments, self-regulation, self-evaluation, self-confidence, and finding ways to reach desired goals (Cobb, 2004).

In Chapter 10 we focused on the transition into college or postsecondary educational settings. Many students with physical disabilities will indeed go on to colleges and universities. A review of the transition planning for selecting a college may be useful in thinking about what this transition may require for individuals with physical disabilities. In this chapter, we focus on the transition to independent living and work.

To be able to accomplish the transition, the individual needs to be taught to move from high school vocational skills development to the community setting in which the work is to take place. This requires a **transition coordinator**, who plans for and assists in the transition (Bellamy, Rhodes, Mank, & Albin, 1988; Falvey, Coot, Bishop, & Grenot-Scheyer, 1989; Kochhar-Bryant, 2007; O'Neill, Gothelf, Cohen, Lehman, & Woolf, 1991).

An individual transition plan (ITP) is required for each student with disabilities. The ITP requires a great deal of information from the school, the individual, the parents, and the community. Questions to be answered by the ITP include the following:

- What will the student need to learn before leaving school?
- Where will the person live as an adult?
- What activities will replace school for recreation?
- How will this individual support himself or herself?
- What will he or she do in leisure time?
- How will this person travel using community transportation?
- How will he or she gain access to medical care?
- What will be the relationship with his or her family? (adapted from O'Neill et al., 1991)

Naturally, every person with multiple and severe disabilities is unique and will need individualized planning. Advice, support, and guidance can be found through a state's center for independent living and center for vocational research. The coordinator must have the skill to develop a plan for each person. The teacher or coordinator collects information on the individual to find the most suitable community site, to conduct a task analysis of what will be required at that work site, and then to initiate a prescriptive program to meet these demands. The coordinator will try to match the individual to activities on the basis of the person's preferences. Key to the successful transition are services provided by vocational rehabilitation services (see Table 12.10).

The National Information Center for Children and Youth with Disabilities (NICHCY, 2000) has prepared a Transition Summary for parents, teachers, and individuals to assist individuals with disabilities in moving into work and

Workworld
www.workworld.org

ILRU Directory of State Centers for Independent Living
http://www.ilru.org/html/publications/directory/index.html

TABLE 12.10
Vocational Rehabilitation Services

Service	Description of Service
Evaluation	To determine a person's interests, capabilities, aptitudes, and limitations and the range of services needed to prepare the individual for employment
Counseling and guidance	To help the person aim for a job in keeping with his or her interests, capabilities, aptitudes, and limitations
Medical and hospital care	To attend, if needed, to mental or physical problems that are obstacles to job preparation
Job training	To provide training that fits the person's needs and that leads to a definite work goal; can include personal adjustment training, prevocational training, vocational training, on-the-job training, and training in a sheltered workshop
Maintenance payments	To cover increases in a person's basic living expenses because of participation in vocational rehabilitation
Transportation	To support and maximize the benefits of other services being received
Services to family members	To help the person achieve the maximum benefit from other services being provided
Interpreter services	To assist the person with visual impairments
Reader services	To assist the person with visual impairments, including note-taking services and orientation and mobility services
Aids and devices	To provide the person with needed aids and devices, such as telecommunication devices, sensory aids, artificial limbs, braces, and wheelchairs
Tools and equipment	To provide the person with tools and equipment needed to perform the job
Recruitment and training services	To provide new work opportunities in public service employment
Job placement	To help the person find a job, taking into consideration the person's abilities and training; includes placement into supported employment
Occupational licenses or permits	To provide the person with the occupational licenses or permits that the law requires a person to have before entering an occupation
Other	To provide other services that an individual may need to become employable

Source: L. Kupper (Ed.). (1991). Options after high school for youth with disabilities, *NICHCY Transition Summary,* no. 7, p. 8. Available from the National Information Center for Children and Youth with Disabilities, P.O. Box 1492. Washington, DC 20013.

independent living. The center indicates that research has demonstrated an enormous qualitative difference in the lives of people with disabilities because of recent legislation leading to changes to assist these individuals throughout the transition process. Postsecondary programs, on-the-job education, internships and apprenticeships, adult education, trade school, and technical schools, as well as college and career education, are all available with some support (NICHCY, 2000).

The National Information Center for Children and Youth with Disabilities
www.nichcy.org

moral dilemma
Meeting the Needs of Every Child

Anew family has just moved into your small rural school district. One of their children has cerebral palsy. The child, Hanna, has spastic CP of the quadriplegic type. She also has problems with speech. This is the first child with these kinds of complex needs that you have served in your district. You are the special education director and must make the decisions regarding Hanna's placement and services.

What steps will you take to get a comprehensive and accurate assessment of Hanna's abilities and needs? Who will you ask to be part of the multidisciplinary team? How will you prepare the school and the teachers who will be responsible for Hanna's education? And how will you provide the needed assistive technologies to support Hanna?

Go to the Education CourseMate website to share your thoughts on this dilemma and email your responses to your instructor.

Summary

▶ History of services for children with physical disabilities, health impairments, and multiple disabilities shows an evolution from isolation toward meaningful inclusion with the support of a multidisciplinary team.

▶ Children with physical disabilities, health impairments, and multiple disabilities are a heterogeneous group, and each child will have unique physical, health, educational, and psychosocial needs.

▶ Legislation supports and protects the rights of individuals with disabilities and requires accessibility to allow participation in social, educational, recreational, and vocational activities.

▶ Advances in medical technologies continue to extend the life expectancy and enhance the quality of life for individuals with physical disabilities and health impairments.

▶ Federal definitions for each area of exceptionality have been given in IDEA, but each child's specific combination of strengths and areas of need must be taken into consideration in educational planning.

▶ The 2009 data from the U.S Department of Education indicates that just under 4 percent of students receiving special education have been identified with orthopedic impairments, Deafblindness, traumatic brain injuries, multiple disabilities, and that another 8.4 percent have been identified as other health impaired.

- Assistive technologies, including augmentative communication devices, help individuals gain independence.

- Universally designed assessment may someday help us get fair and accurate information regarding children's abilities and needs, but until then assessments are likely to underpredict children's capabilities.

- Children with physical disabilities will likely need an expanded core curriculum that includes functional and life skills, and they will likely need services at all three tiers of intervention (RTI).

- Families of children with physical disabilities, health impairments, and multiple disabilities face special challenges and may need intensive and ongoing support.

- Planning for transitions to adulthood must begin early and will require careful consideration of the student's strengths and needs.

Future Challenges

1 *How will we ensure that supports are available for the increasing numbers of adults with complex needs?*

As medical advances help to extend the lives of individuals with severe disabilities and complex health needs, more individuals are living longer with more debilitating conditions. Currently, vocational rehabilitation services can work with only a fraction of the individuals who need support, and long-term care options for individuals with severe disabilities are often not available. How will we provide appropriate supports to ensure quality of life for these individuals?

2 *As assistive technologies are developed, how can we make sure that all children who need them have access to them and that they are supported by experts who can fix them when they malfunction?*

The benefits of assistive technology are so great that they can mean the difference between dependence and independence for individuals with physical disabilities, but assistive technologies can be expensive. How can we make sure that cost is not a barrier to access for children who need the new technologies? How can we also ensure that support services include a person who can fix the technology when it breaks?

3 *How can we enhance meaningful collaboration that is transdisciplinary in nature?*

The numbers of people needed on the multidisciplinary team to meet the needs of individuals with physical disabilities, health impairments, and multiple disabilities are substantial. These teams require individuals with expertise in health, education, social services, and technology. How can we enhance collaboration that moves from being cross-disciplinary to transdisciplinary in nature, in which professionals engage in meaningful collaboration?

Key Terms

acquired immune deficiency syndrome (AIDS) p. 406

age appropriate p. 421

assistive technology (AT) p. 423

asthma p. 404

ataxic cerebral palsy p. 399

augmentative communication p. 424

cancer p. 405

cerebral palsy p. 398

Crohn's disease p. 406

cystic fibrosis p. 405

deafblindness p. 397

dyskinetic cerebral palsy p. 399

expanded core curriculum p. 421

functional skills p. 421

gene replacement therapy p. 409

germ line therapy p. 409

heart defects p. 404

hemophilia p. 405

human immunodeficiency virus (HIV) p. 406

hypertonia p. 398

juvenile diabetes p. 403

juvenile myoclonic epilepsy p. 401

juvenile rheumatoid arthritis p. 402

mixed cerebral palsy p. 399

motor skills and mobility p. 418

multiple disabilities p. 395

muscular dystrophies p. 402

neural tube defect (NTD) p. 399

norm-referenced tests p. 417

orthopedic impairments p. 397

osteogenesis imperfect p. 403

other health impairments p. 397

polydpsia p. 403

polyphagia p. 403

polyuria p. 403

scoliosis p. 402

seizure disorder p. 401

sickle cell anemia p. 406

somatic gene therapy p. 409

spastic cerebral palsy p. 398

spina bifida p. 399

spinal curvature p. 402

spinal muscular atrophy (SMA) p. 402

transition coordinator p. 430

traumatic brain injury (TBI) p. 397

ulcerative colitis p. 406

universal precautions p. 407

Usher syndrome p. 410

writing aids p. 425

Resources

References of Special Interest

Batshaw, M., & Perret, Y. (2002). *Children with handicaps: A medical primer* (5th ed.). Baltimore: Brookes. The fifth edition of this exemplary text explains how genetic abnormalities, problems during pregnancy and early infancy, and nutritional deficiencies can cause disabilities. It also describes how these problems affect the nervous and musculoskeletal systems and, in turn, child development. A few physically disabling conditions also are discussed.

Best, S., Heller, K., & Bigge, J. (2005). *Teaching individuals with physical or multiple disabilities* (5th ed.). Upper Saddle River, NJ: Merrill-Prentice Hall. A recent edition of a comprehensive work that discusses educational and treatment issues. Practical suggestions and the names of vendors specializing in assistive technology are provided.

Bradley, V., Ashbaugh, J., & Blaney, B. (1994). *Creating individual supports for people with disabilities*. Baltimore: Brookes. This guide helps individuals change community- and state-based agencies to organizations that become community supports for individuals with disabilities.

Browder, D. (Ed.). (2001). *Curriculum and assessment for students with moderate and severe disabilities*. New York: Guilford Press. A basic orientation to the range of issues confronting the teaching and assessment of disabled students. Includes family-centered planning, communication and leisure skills, academic skills, inclusion, and transition.

Dormans, J. P., & Pellegrino, L. (1998). *Caring for children with cerebral palsy*. Baltimore: Brookes. A comprehensive text emphasizing an interdisciplinary team approach to assessment, management, treatment, and total functioning of persons with cerebral palsy and their families.

Elias, S. (2005). *Special needs trusts*. Berkeley, CA: Nolo Press. Provides instructions and forms for establishing a trust fund to pay for the needs of individuals with disabilities. A CD-ROM is also available.

Hill, J. L., & Davis, A. C. (1999). *Meeting the needs of students with special physical and health needs*. Upper Saddle River, NJ: Prentice-Hall. Richly documented, with multiple checklists, diagrams, anatomical drawings of all major body systems, and helpful suggestions for teaching, this highly recommended volume contains a complete description in understandable language of a wide range of physical and health disorders.

Krajicek, M., Steinke, T., Hertzden, D., Anastasiow, N., & Skandel, S. (2003). *Handbook for the care of infants and toddlers with disabilities and chronic conditions.* Austin, TX: PRO-ED. This manual is designed to assist day-care and home-care workers in integrating children with physical disabilities and health problems into general education classes.

Snell, M., & Brown, F. (2005). *Instruction of students with severe disabilities* (6th ed.). Baltimore: Brookes. Twenty leaders in the field discuss in twelve chapters issues of teaching, policy, integration, research, and suggestions for practice. This book presents current thinking on persons with multiple and severe disabilities.

Wehmeyer, M. L., Agran, M., & Hughes, C. (1998). *Teaching self-determination skills to students with disabilities.* Baltimore: Brookes. A broad compendium of ideas and techniques for teaching independence skills to students. The acquisition of these skills will contribute greatly to students' transition.

Journals

Journal of Applied Behavior Analysis
  http://seab.envmed.rochester.edu/jaba/

Journal of the American Physical Therapy Association
  www.ptjournal.org

Physical and Occupational Therapy in Pediatrics
  www.informacare.com/pop

Research and Practice for Persons with Severe Disabilities (formerly *Journal of the Association for Persons with Severe Handicaps [JASH]*)
  http://www.tash.org/publications/rpsd/rpsd.html

Professional Organizations

The Association for Persons with Severe Disabilities (TASH)
  www.tash.org

Brain Injury Association, Inc. (formerly National Head Injury Foundation)
  www.biausa.org

Division for Physical and Health Disabilities (DPHD)/ Council for Exceptional Children (CEC)
  http://web.utk.edu/~dphmd/

Epilepsy Foundation of America (EFA)
  www.epilepsyfoundation.org

March of Dimes Birth Defects Foundation
  www.modimes.org

National Consortium on Deafblindness
  http://nationaldb.org/

National Information Center for Children and Youth with Disabilities (NICHCY)
  www.nichcy.org

National Rehabilitation Information Center
  www.naric.com

United Cerebral Palsy Association, Inc.
  www.ucp.org

 Visit the Education CourseMate website for additional TeachSource Video Cases, information about CEC standards, study tools, and much more.

Appendix

 **Council for Exceptional Children**

The voice and vision of special education

COUNCIL FOR EXCEPTIONAL CHILDREN

Special Education Professional Ethical Principles

Professional special educators are guided by the CEC professional ethical principles and practice standards in ways that respect the diverse characteristics and needs of individuals with exceptionalities and their families. They are committed to upholding and advancing the following principles:

A.   Maintaining challenging expectations for individuals with exceptionalities to develop the highest possible learning outcomes and quality of life potential in ways that respect their dignity, culture, language, and background.

B.   Maintaining a high level of professional competence and integrity and exercising professional judgment to benefit individuals with exceptionalities and their families.

C.   Promoting meaningful and inclusive participation of individuals with exceptionalities in their schools and communities.

D.   Practicing collegially with others who are providing services to individuals with exceptionalities.

E.   Developing relationships with families based on mutual respect and actively involving families and individuals with exceptionalities in educational decision making.

F.   Using evidence, instructional data, research and professional knowledge to inform practice.

G.   Protecting and supporting the physical and psychological safety of individuals with exceptionalities.

H.   Neither engaging in nor tolerating any practice that harms individuals with exceptionalities.

I.   Practicing within the professional ethics, standards, and policies of CEC; upholding laws, regulations, and policies that influence professional practice; and advocating improvements in laws, regulations, and policies.

J.   Advocating for professional conditions and resources that will improve learning outcomes of individuals with exceptionalities.

K.   Engaging in the improvement of the profession through active participation in professional organizations.

L.   Participating in the growth and dissemination of professional knowledge and skills.

Approved by the CEC Board of Directors, Jan. 22, 2010

Glossary

academic aptitude A combination of general cognitive abilities that measure a student's potential for learning (such as an intelligence test or an IQ score) and achievement within specific content domains. Knowing a student's academic aptitude helps us predict the optimal level of curriculum that will allow him or her to be successful.

acceleration An intervention for students with special gifts and talents by which the school moves the student through the system more rapidly.

acquired hearing loss A hearing loss that has occurred in either childhood or adulthood.

acquired immune deficiency syndrome (AIDS) A breakdown of the body's immune system, allowing the body to become vulnerable to a host of fatal infections that it normally is able to ward off.

age appropriate Skills that match the student's chronological age, as opposed to his or her mental age.

alerting device/alarm system Devices and systems for the deaf and hard of hearing that use flashing lights or vibration to provide notification of events that hearing people detect through sound, such as a baby crying, fire alarm, or alarm clock.

American Sign Language (ASL) A manual language used by many people with hearing impairments that meets the universal linguistic standards of spoken English.

amniocentesis A procedure for analyzing the amniotic fluid (a watery liquid in which the embryo is suspended) to discover genetic defects in the unborn child.

anticipatory anxiety A fear and undermining of self-confidence caused by past experiences of failure and frustration that can sabotage success with new experiences.

Apgar test A screening test administered to an infant at one minute and five minutes after birth.

applied behavioral analysis (ABA) A learning approach that is based on individual analyses of a student's functioning and relies on the learning of behaviors to remediate learning problems.

articulation disorder Difficulty forming and stringing sounds together, usually characterized by substituting one sound for another (*wabbit* for *rabbit*), omitting a sound (*han* for *hand*), or distorting a sound (*ship* for *sip*).

articulation The movement of the mouth and tongue that shapes sound into speech.

Asperger's syndrome A form of autism that features the usual social and behavior problems, but where the cognitive abilities may be average or above.

assessment A process for identifying a child's strengths and weaknesses; it involves five steps: screening, diagnosis, classification, placement, and monitoring or discharge.

assistive technology Tools that enhance the functioning of persons with disabilities.

asthma A respiratory condition that results in difficulty breathing or coughing.

ataxic cerebral palsy A condition in which voluntary movement involving balance is abnormal.

attention deficit hyperactivity disorder (ADHD) A disorder that causes children to have difficulty settling down to do a particular task, especially desk work.

audition Thought transformed into words and received by a listener through hearing.

auditory acuity The ability to take in sounds and get them to the brain successfully.

auditory brainstem response (otoacoustic emissions) A neurological hearing test for infants which is used to determine whether the ear is functioning appropriately and the brain is receiving the sound signal.

auditory nerve The bundle of nerve fibers that carries hearing information from the cochlea to the brain (also known as the *cochlear nerve*).

auditory perception One's ability to process information from different sources, including hearing speech against background noise, sound discriminations, and sound recognition.

auditory processing The brain's ability to recognize and interpret sounds.

auditory steady state response (ASSR) A hearing evaluation that uses continuous stimuli to elicit a response and can provide frequency-specific auditory information.

augmentative communication alternatives Non-traditional methods of communication, including the use of assistive technology devices, for children with physical and other disabilities who cannot acquire understandable speech or legible writing skills.

augmented and alternative communication A variety of assistive technologies that help an individual communicate. These range from sophisticated voice synthesizers to relatively simple story boards with pictures that indicate words and actions.

authentic assessment Measuring a child's ability by means of an in-class assignment.

behavioral support plan A plan of services devised by teachers and parents to give support to children trying to overcome challenging behavior. This plan focuses on antecedents to the difficult behavior, what the actual behavior is, and the consequence of the behaviors in order to provide the child with support.

bilingual-bicultural approach Cultural viewpoint that persons who are deaf are bicultural because they belong to both the Deaf culture, and the society in which they live. Many who are deaf are also bilingual because they use both a sign language system (usually ASL) and the spoken or written language of their culture, such as English.

bipolar disorder A condition involving the experience of nonepisodic temper outbursts. There has been a large growth of the diagnosis of bipolar disorder among children, despite the fact that a significant section of the medical community disagrees as to whether bipolar exists in children at all.

blended practices Practices that bridge the gap between special and general education by creating one comprehensive approach for teaching young children with and without disabilities.

blind Sight ability less than 20/200. Children who are blind cannot use vision for learning, but may still be responsive to light and darkness and may have some visual imagery.

blindness A visual impairment so severe that the student must learn through other senses than the usual (tactual and auditory).

bone-conductor test A test used to assess hearing in children under age 3 by bypassing the ear and measuring the movement of sound through the bone and the hearing system to the brain.

braille A system using embossed characters in different combinations of six dots arranged in a cell that allows people with profound visual impairments to read by touch as well as to write by using special aids.

bullying A display of interpersonal violence in which the bully asserts power through some form of aggression and the victim experiences distress and the loss of power, resulting in an unequal relationship.

cancer A malignant abnormal growth or tumor. This is rare in children and the most common forms are leukemia, lymphoma, or a brain tumor.

case coordinator An educator who takes the lead on the child's multidisciplinary team. The coordinator is generally responsible for setting up the meetings, ensuring that all paperwork is completed, and sharing information about students' needs and progress with other team members.

central auditory processing disorder (CAPD) Disorder characterized by difficulties with sound localization, auditory discrimination, understanding speech sounds against a noisy background, auditory sequencing, memory, and pattern recognition, sounding out words, and reading comprehension.

central auditory processing loss Hearing difficulty which limits the individual's ability to process and use auditory information.

central processing Classification of a stimulus through the use of memory, reasoning, and evaluation; the second step in the information-processing model.

cerebral palsy A condition caused by damage to the motor control centers of the brain before birth, during the birth process, or after birth.

Child Find Public awareness activities, screening, and evaluation designed to locate, identify, and refer as early as possible all young children with disabilities and their families who are in need of Early Intervention Program (Part C) or Preschool Special Education (Part B/619) services of the Individuals with Disabilities Education Act (IDEA).

child with exceptionalities A child who differs from the norm in mental characteristics, sensory abilities, communication abilities, social behavior, or physical characteristics to the extent that special education services are required for the child to develop to maximum capacity.

ciliary muscles Muscles that control changes in the shape of the lens so the eye can focus on objects at varying distances.

cleft palate A congenital abnormality that occurs when the roof of the mouth has not joined completely during prenatal development.

cochlea Part of the inner ear that contains part of the hearing organs.

cochlear implant A small electronic device that can be surgically implanted into the ear of a person who is profoundly deaf or severely hard-of-hearing to provide a sense of sound. It consists of a microphone, a speech processor, a transmitter and receiver/ stimulator, and an electrode array.

cochlear nerve Bundle of nerve fibers that carries hearing information from the cochlea to the brain (also known as the *auditory nerve*).

coercive cycle Describes a situation where the child misbehaves, the adult responds punitively, and the child in anger is driven to misbehave some more creating a downward cycle in relationship.

coercive family system The use of physical or psychological force for imposing will within the family.

collaborative problem solving Working with a multi-disciplinary team of individuals and parents to design services that address the student's needs.

communication disorder Impairments in articulation, fluency, voice, or language.

communication The exchange of thoughts, information, feelings, or ideas.

comorbid Existing alongside one another. Used to refer to conditions such as anxiety and fearful feelings.

comprehensive treatment models A group of interventions that address the core symptoms of autism spectrum disorders and are presented over a period of time (a year or more) with intensive treatment. Examples include the UCLA Young Autism Program and TEACCH.

conductive loss Hearing loss caused by something (wax, ear infections [otitis media], or any type of malformation of the ear canal) blocking the sound that passes through the outer or middle ear, which makes hearing faint sounds more difficult.

congenital hearing loss Losses present at birth.

congenital Present at birth.

content sophistication Curriculum modification that challenges students who are gifted to use higher levels of thinking to understand ideas that average students of the same age find difficult or impossible to understand.

context of the child The combination of forces in the child's environment that impact his or her development. This context includes the child's family, neighborhood, school, community, and even state and country.

continuum of services A range of personnel to provide needed specialized services such as speech, physical, or occupational therapy.

convergence Change in the extrinsic muscles of the eye.

cooperative learning A set of instructional strategies that emphasize the use of groups for teaching students techniques of problem solving and working constructively with others.

cornea The transparent anterior portion of the tough outer coat of the eyeball.

correlated assets Conditions linked favorably with one another, such as high IQ scores with personality.

correlated constraints Conditions that tend to appear with one another and perform on another condition. For example, good academic performance and the presence of supportive adults tend to operate as a brake on aggression.

creativity Mental process by which an individual creates new ideas and products or recombines existing ideas and products in a fashion that is novel to him or her.

criterion-referenced tests Tests designed to measure a child's development in terms of absolute levels of mastery, as opposed to the child's status relative to other children.

Crohn's disease A disease resulting from heredity, weakened immune and inflammatory response, and intestinal bacteria that affects the intestinal system and causes thickness of the bowel wall. Children with Crohn's experience pain, fever, and diarrhea.

culture The attitudes, values, customs, and language that form an identifiable pattern or heritage.

curriculum compacting Content modification that allows students who are gifted to move ahead. It consists of three steps: finding out what the students know, arranging to teach the remaining concepts or skills, and providing a different set of experiences to enrich or advance the students.

cystic fibrosis A genetic disease that affects a child's breathing and digestion.

deafblindness The condition of little or no useful sight and little or no useful hearing, the combination of which causes severe communication, developmental, and other educational needs that require special services.

decibel (dB) Unit used to measure the intensity of a sound.

developmental delays see **developmental disabilities**.

developmental disabilities Mental retardation and related conditions (e.g., cerebral palsy) that create a substantial delay in the child's development and require intervention from many professional disciplines.

developmental profile A chart presenting the intraindividual differences in development for a particular student.

developmentally appropriate practice (DAP) Curriculum practices that match the level of development of the child and are presented in ways that children learn (e.g., play).

diagnostic achievement tests Tests help educators understand how a student solves a problem by examining the strategies that he or she uses when learning. Diagnostic assessments help us determine why a child is struggling so that we can offer appropriate support or remediation.

dialect A variant in pronunciation and syntax of a spoken language.

differentiated instruction Refers to the changes in teacher strategies and curriculum made necessary by the characteristics of the exceptional child.

Down syndrome A chromosomal abnormality that leads to mild or moderate mental retardation and, at times, a variety of hearing, skeletal, and heart problems.

dysgraphia Brain dysfunction or disease that causes an inability to write, or write legibly.

dyskinetic cerebral palsy A condition characterized by tonal abnormalities that involves the whole body and muscle tone that changes constantly.

dyslexia A severe reading disability involving difficulties in understanding the relationship between sounds and letters.

dysphonia A disorder in voice quality.

eardrum A thin layer of skin at the end of the external ear canal.

early intervention Systematic efforts designed to prevent deficits or to improve an existing disability in children between birth and age 5.

ecological model A view of exceptionality that examines the individual in complex interaction with environmental forces and believes that exceptionalities should be remediated by modifying elements in the environment to allow more constructive interactions between the individual and the environment.

ecology of the child Those forces surrounding and impacting on the child from family, culture, peers, physical setting, etc.

embedded instruction The use of a child's daily activities to teach and reinforce key skills. This allows teachers to use typical classroom routines to strengthen and reinforce learning.

encephalitis An inflammation of the brain, usually refers to brain inflammation caused by a virus. It's a rare disease that only occurs in approximately 0.5 per 100,000 individuals-most commonly in children, the elderly, and people with weakened immune systems (i.e., those with HIV/AIDS or cancer).

episodic memory One's ability to recall whole scenes or episodes from one's past, often brought on by smells.

evidence-based interventions Intervention strategies which research has demonstrated to be effective.

executive function The hypothesized decision-making element that controls reception, central processing, and expression.

executive processor According to the information processing model, the mechanism for decision-making in information processing and learning.

expanded core curriculum A plan of study which includes functional and life skills as well as academic skills.

explicit teaching Instruction that involves using language that is both precise and concise, giving clear examples of what is to be learned, and providing schema that show the organization of ideas to be learned.

expressive language The ability to produce a message to send; typically involves speaking and writing.

external auditory meatus The channel through which sounds are led from the outside ear to the middle ear. Also known as the *external auditory canal*.

family centered early intervention An attempt to involve the family in the treatment programs in the early years of a child with a disability. The family will play a role in the treatment process and in monitoring the progress of the child.

family empowerment The family plays a major decision role in the planning and execution of the program for their child with disabilities through the IEP process and subsequent planning and treatment.

family-centered model A model of family dynamics that empowers families to take the lead in determining what is best for their child. This is done through support that focuses on the strengths of the child and family.

family-focused approach Helping parents become more autonomous and less dependent on professionals.

fetal alcohol syndrome spectral disorder Defects in a child as a result of the mother's heavy use of alcohol during her pregnancy.

fluency The flow of speech.

focused intervention practice An intervention which is short term with specific goals (e.g., reduce an undesirable behavior).

Fragile X syndrome A restriction at the end of the X chromosome that may result in mental retardation or learning disabilities.

free and appropriate education The courts have affirmed that children with exceptionalities are guaranteed the right to an education provided by the state that is suitable to their needs.

functional behavioral assessment (FBA) Valuations of behavior that define a behavior, explain why this behavior occurs, describe where and when the behavior is present, and demonstrate how the behavior impacts the child and his or her surroundings. The premise behind FBA is that there is a rational purpose for every behavior and that it is necessary to understand why and how negative or destructive behaviors are triggered in order to reduce them.

functional skills Skills that can be used immediately by the student, are necessary in everyday settings, and increase to some extent the student's independence (e.g., folding clothes).

gene replacement therapy A method by which defective or damaged genetic material is replaced and corrected.

gene-environment interaction A description of how certain conditions are caused by both genetics and environment. Neuroscience has shown us that almost all behavioral traits emerge from complex interactions between multiple genes and environments; thus, we cannot say that genes cause depression or ADHD, but rather that the complex mix of environments and multiple genes can result in some unfavorable outcomes.

genetic counseling A source of information for parents about the likelihood of their having a child with genetically based disabilities.

germ line therapy A method by which sperm or egg cells are modified by introducing functional genes.

hearing aids Small electronic devices that provide sound amplification for individuals who are deaf and hard of hearing.

heart defect A congenital cardiac condition that can range from slight to severe and be characterized by heart murmurs; rapid heartbeat and breathing difficulties (especially during exercise or eating); swelling of the legs, abdomen, or areas around the eyes; or change in skin coloring to a pale grayish or bluish cast. It is also possible that no symptoms may be present.

heightened sensitivity Oversensitivity to sensory input, including lights, sounds, smells, and tastes.

hemophilia A hereditary bleeding disorder caused by a clotting factor deficiency. The symptoms include deep internal bleeding, swelling of a limb, bleeding in an organ, cerebral bleeding, joint immobility, stiffness in the throat, skin bruising, and prolonged bleeding from minor cuts.

high-incidence disabilities The categories of disability that are most prevalent in the U.S., composing at least one percent of the school population.

high-stakes testing Any examination whose results can substantially change the future of a student, such as course failure or admittance to college.

home schooling Educating at home. The home-schooling movement involves over a million parents who have chosen to educate their children at home rather than send them to schools. This movement began as a response to parental concerns about appropriate religious instruction, but today many parents home school because they feel their child's needs cannot be met within the traditional school setting.

human immunodeficiency virus (HIV) A virus that breaks down the body's immune system, causing AIDS.

hypersensitivity A shared characteristic of persons with autism spectrum disorders in which they cannot modulate sounds or other stimuli.

hypertext A link on a Web site or document that will lead you to other relevant references or material.

hypertonia Having abnormally high muscle tone.

IDEA The law originally passed in 1975 as PL 94-142 and reauthorized in 2004 addressing the school's responsibility to children with exceptionalities in the classroom.

incidental learning Learning that occurs but is not explicitly taught.

inclusion The process of bringing children with exceptionalities into the regular classroom.

incus One of the three small bones in the middle ear; also known as the *anvil*.

individualized educational program (IEP) A program written for every student receiving special education; it describes the child's current performance and goals for the school year, the particular special education services to be delivered, and the procedures by which outcomes are to be evaluated.

individualized family service plan (IFSP) An intervention program for young children and their families that identifies their needs and sets forth a program to meet those needs.

information processing model (IPM) A model that describes learning as a series of components that involve sensory stimulation/input, processing/thinking, and output, or the sharing of what has been learned.

instructional technology A growing field of study which uses technology as a means to solve educational challenges, both in the classroom and in distance learning environments.

intellectual and developmental disabilities Significant delay in intellectual development and adaptive behavior, formally known as *mental retardation*.

interindividual difference A substantial difference among people along key dimensions of development.

intervening hierarchy A model for organizing intervention strategies from least to most intensive; with three or more tiers in which Tier I is a high-quality general learning environment and the additional tiers provide more help for students whose needs require more intensive supports.

intraindividual difference A major variation in the abilities or development of a single child.

iris The colored muscular partition in the eye that expands and contracts to regulate the amount of light admitted through the pupil.

juvenile diabetes A disorder in which the blood sugar of the individual is abnormally high because the body does not produce enough insulin (Type 1 diabetes) or because the body is insensitive to the insulin that is produced (Type 2).

juvenile myoclonic epilepsy A disease that causes seizures in school-age children.

juvenile rheumatoid arthritis A condition that begins at or before age 16 and causes swelling, stiffness, effusion, pain, and tenderness in the joints.

language A code whereby ideas about the world are represented through a conventional system of arbitrary signals for communication.

language content The meaning of words and sentences. Also called *semantics*.

language disorder The impairment or deviant development of comprehension or use (or both) of a spoken, written, or other symbol system.

language form The sounds, words, and grammar that underlie a language to create its individual form, or structure; includes phonology, morphology, and syntax.

language function The use of language within a given society and a specific context.

learned helplessness The belief that nothing one does can prevent negative things from happening.

least restrictive environment The educational setting in which a child with special needs can learn that is as close as possible to the general education classroom.

long–term memory A way of storing information in the brain for future retrieval.

low vision Visual acuity of 20/70 to 20/200. Students with low vision can still benefit from visual learning through the use of various technologies to enhance their sight.

low-incidence disabilities The categories of disability that comprise less than one percent of the school population in the U.S.

magnet school Public school that exists outside of zoned school boundaries and typically have something special to offer over a regular school, such as alternative modes of instruction.

malleus One of the three small bones in the middle ear known as the *hammer*.

media access Availability of information that can be accessed and utilized by individuals with disabilities, including captioned television.

medical model A view of exceptionality that implies a physical condition or disease within the patient.

metacognition The ability to think about one's own thinking and monitor its effectiveness.

metacognitive approach Helping students understand how to "think about their thinking" as they work to solve problems, activate or select strategies to use, and anchor learning in their memory.

mirror neurons Cells in the nervous system which allow the individual to imitate others' speech and actions. Apparently, not fully functional in children with autism.

mixed cerebral palsy A condition with a combination of spastic, dyskinetic, and ataxic cerebral palsy that impacts each child differently, but affects balance and coordination for almost all children.

mixed hearing loss Hearing loss resulting from problems in the outer ear, as well as in the middle or inner ear.

morphology The rules that address how words are formed and their structure.

motor memory The ability to program one's body movements to learn patterns and retain them for future use.

motor skills and mobility Skills that are necessary to maintain upright postures (sitting, standing), to perform functional movements (reaching, grasping), and to move around in the environment.

multidisciplinary team A group of professionals who work together to help plan and carry out intervention or treatment for children with disabilities to help them achieve their full potential.

multiple disabilities A combination of impairments, such as mental retardation-blindness or mental retardation-orthopedic impairment, that results in severe educational needs that require special services.

multiple intelligences A theory associated with Howard Gardner that proposes nine separate intelligences instead of one general intelligence.

muscular dystrophy A genetic, progressive deterioration of the muscles that affects movement and function.

natural environment Setting that is typical for children who do not have disabilities.

neural tube defect (NTD) A condition that occurs during fetal development when the neural tube surrounding the spine does not close properly and the developing brain or spine is left exposed to the amniotic fluid.

norm-referenced test Standardized assessment used to compare an individual child's score with the typical score for other children in his or her age group.

object permanence The understanding that objects that are not in the visual field still exist.

orientation and mobility (O&M) training Teaching a person with visual loss or with blindness how to move through space.

orthopedic impairment A severe injury or disorder of the skeletal system and surrounding muscles, joints, and ligaments that adversely affects a child's educational performance (such as cerebral palsy, amputations, and fractures or burns that cause a distortion of the scar tissue or joints).

osteogenesis imperfecta An inherited congenital fragility of the bones caused by a dominant genetic mutation that occurs in approximately 1:20,000 births. The condition leads to fractures on different bone sites, causing extremely short statures, scoliosis, long bone bowing, and skull fractures. Some children with OI need to use wheelchairs or hearing aids.

other health impairments Limited strength, vitality, or alertness, including heightened alertness to environmental stimuli, that are due to chronic or acute health problems such as asthma, attention deficit disorders, diabetes, epilepsy, a heart condition, hemophilia, lead poisoning, leukemia, nephritis, rheumatic fever, sickle cell anemia, and Tourettes syndrome and that require special educational services.

otitis media Middle-ear infection that can lead to hearing loss.

otoacoustic auditory emissions (OAE) A technique for measuring hearing ability by placing a small microphone in the child's ear and testing for a child's ability to hear the echo produced by the stimulation of hair cells in the ear.

performance assessment A measure of the application of knowledge.

pervasive developmental disorders not otherwise specified (PDDNOS) These are autistic-like conditions that do not fulfill all of the diagnostic characteristics for autism, but show strong resemblance in terms of social and communication problems. Increasingly referred to as Autistic Spectrum Disorders reflecting the variations found in these conditions.

phenylketonuria (PKU) A single-gene defect that can produce severe retardation because of the body's inability to break down phenylalanine, which when accumulated at high levels in the brain results in severe damage; can be controlled by a diet restricting phenylalanine.

phonation The production of sound by the vibration of the vocal cords.

phonology The science of speech sounds and the rules that govern how these sounds combine to form words and to convey meaning.

pinna The outer part of the ear.

pivotal response model A play based intervention model made popular by Koegel & Koegel for children with autism. It focuses on pivotal behaviors which are central to a wide area of functioning and so transferable to many situations.

PL 107-110 Otherwise known as No Child Left Behind, this law, enacted in 2001, requires that schools must show that not only are students as a group meeting state standards, but that individual categories (e.g., children with exceptionalities) are as well.

PL 94-142 The original law, passed in 1975, that became IDEA (originally known as Education for All Handicapped Children Act).

play audiometry Hearing tests for young children conducted in a pleasant environment using toys that move and make sounds to elicit responses, such as eye blinks and changes in respiration or heartbeat (slower heartbeats indicate attention).

polydpsia A symptom of Type 1 diabetes involving increased thirst.

polyphagia A symptom of Type 1 diabetes involving dehydration leading to weakness, lethargy, and increase in appetite.

polyuria A symptom of Type 1 diabetes involving an excessive need to urinate.

positive behavior interventions and support (PBIS) An approach to intervention based on behavior science principles and meant to replace punitive measures for behavior control. It includes functional assessments, positive interventions, and evaluative measures to assess progress.

postlinguistic hearing loss The loss of hearing after spontaneous speech and language have developed.

pragmatics Language rules that address the social context in which the communication occurs.

prelinguistic hearing loss The loss of hearing before speech and language have developed; referred to as *deafness.*

primary auditory cortex The center of the brain where sound is initially processed.

problem-based learning (PBL) A problem that encourages the student to define the issue, organize the components, and then solve the problem.

prodigy A child who has shown extraordinary development in his or her early years of development so that they are capable of adult behavior while still very young, such as chess playing, musical composition, or poetry writing.

progress monitoring Using data (such as test results or performance on screening measures) on student's achievement, performance, and other needs to monitor progress, guide decision making, and plan for future needs.

proprioceptive An awareness of where one's body is in relation to the space around it.

psychotropic Affecting the neurosystem.

pupil The central opening of the eye through which light enters.

pure-tone audiometry The most frequently used method for assessing hearing in which an audiometer presents pure tones of varying frequency and intensity to an individual wearing a headset.

receptive language The ability to take in a message and understand it (that is, listening with understanding to oral language or reading written language with comprehension).

reciprocal teaching A technique in which small groups of students and teachers take turns leading a discussion.

related services Support services that are required to assist the child in benefiting from special education.

relationship-focused intervention Intervention that help parents develop responsive interactions with their children that build on the social nurturing between the parents and the child. This approach was first developed to support parents of children who have autism.

replacement behavior Positive behavior for children with behavior disorders, such as asking for permission to talk, that are designed to replace unacceptable behavior. This practice is based on the principle that the child often has no acceptable behaviors in his repertoire and is in trouble as a consequence.

resonation The process that gives the voice its special characteristics.

respiration Breathing; the process that generates the energy that produces sound.

Response to Intervention (RTI) A multilevel approach to helping children face difficulties in school. Proposes a range of interventions from general classroom to special education.

retina The light-sensitive innermost layer of tissue at the back of the eyeball.

retinopathy of prematurity A disease of the retina in which a mass of scar tissue forms in back of the lens of the eye. Both eyes are usually affected, and it occurs chiefly in infants born prematurely who receive excessive oxygen.

Rett syndrome A condition included within autism spectrum disorders because its symptoms resemble autism. It is a progressive neurological disorder in which individuals reveal a loss of muscle functions, hand flapping, and autistic behavior. Symptoms appear in children 6 to 18 months, and educational treatment is similar to treatment for autism.

rubella German measles, which in the first three months of pregnancy can cause visual impairment, hearing impairment, mental retardation, and birth defects in the fetus.

scaffolding A strategy in which a teacher models the expected behavior and guides the learning of the student.

schoolwide behavior support An attempt to use behavior principles to create an emotionally healthy school environment. This would include rules for behavior and guidelines for punishment. The goal is to bring to the entire school population the positive behavior supports usually given to specific students.

scoliosis A form of spinal curvature that begins in infancy, early childhood, or adolescence in which the spine forms a "c" or an "s" shape when it is viewed from behind.

secondary auditory cortex The center of the brain activated by complex stimuli, such as bursts of noise.

seizure disorder A condition characterized by multiple seizures (i.e., abnormal electrical discharge within the brain that disrupts the brain's normal functioning). This is considered to be symptomatic of an underlying problem that requires a full medical evaluation.

self-determination The ability to set personal goals and to take appropriate actions to achieve them.

self-management Having children with disabilities make decisions and to be responsible for their lives.

Many intervention programs are designed to help students attain this responsibility gradually.

self-regulatory skill An individual's ability to continuously adapt thoughts, speech, and actions to accomplish goals and adapt to the environment.

semantic memory Stores concepts, words, symbols, and generalizations; most often used in school.

sensorineural loss Hearing loss caused by damage to the inner ear (cochlea) or to the auditory nerve, particularly in the delicate sensory hairs of the inner ear or in the nerves that supply them. These losses affect both the ability to hear faint sounds and the ability to hear clearly, making understanding speech sounds difficult.

sensory compensation The theory that if one sense avenue is deficient, other senses are automatically strengthened.

sensory integration The ability to use two or more senses simultaneously and smoothly.

sensory memory The ability to accommodate a large amount of information for a short period of time (2-3 seconds) and allows us to take in information and interpret what we are seeing, hearing, tasting, smelling, etc.

serious emotional disturbance (SED) An emotional disturbance that creates unhappiness for the individual and often leads to behaviors that are socially disruptive or self-destructive. To be considered serious, these problems must be persistent and must interfere with life functioning and/or learning.

short-term memory Temporarily storing information while simultaneously completing tasks; involves strategies for consciously storing information, such as rehearsal.

sickle cell anemia A form of anemia caused by a mutation in the gene that tells the body to make hemoglobin A (the red iron rich compound) which allows red blood cells to carry oxygen to all parts of your body. The symptoms include stroke, speech difficulties, seizures, painful joins and extremities, vision problems, fatigue, fever, and infection.

slope of improvement A visual graph depicting the change in a student's rate and level of growth on skills.

somatic gene therapy A method by which therapeutic genes are transferred into somatic cells and therefore only impact the patient, not future generations.

spastic cerebral palsy A form of cerebral palsy marked by tight muscles and stiff movements.

speech disorder Disorder of articulation (how words are pronounced), voice (how words are vocalized), or fluency (the flow of speech).

speech The systematic oral production of words of a given language.

Speech Viewer III A computer program designed to improve voicing, pitch, timing, and sustained production that provides a variety of visual displays that represent sound, such as a balloon getting larger in proportion to the loudness of the speaker's voice.

speech-to-print system Computer program that reproduces the classroom dialogue on a computer screen, either through typing captions or voice-activated software.

spina bifida The most common neural tube defect where part of the spinal cord protrudes from the spinal column.

spinal muscular atrophy (SMA) An inherited, progressive disorder of the muscles that affects movement and function.

standard (norm-referenced) achievement test Test that measures the student's level of achievement compared with the achievement of students of similar age or grade. Also called *norm-referenced test*.

standard protocol A prescribed manner of conducting interventions. It may include a specified lesson or series of steps.

stapes One of the three small bones in the middle ear known as the *stirrup*.

strategic teaching Using mnemonics, organizational strategies, and specific approaches that facilitate memory; making connections across information being learned; and the ability to apply information within new contexts in order to instruct students.

student acceleration Passing students through the educational system as quickly as possible.

stuttering A disorder of fluency.

support teacher A teacher who provides direct assistance to the student with disabilities and to their teacher within the regular classroom setting. This support may include assistance with behavior management, focused work with learning activities, therapeutic tutorials, and general assistance with classroom needs to allow the regular classroom teacher time to work with the student with disabilities.

supralinguistics The sophisticated analysis of meaning when the literal meaning of the word or phrase is *not* the intended meaning.

syntax The rules that guide how words are combined to form sentences and the relationships of components within the sentence.

synthetic speech The production of sound—of phonemes into words—by means of a computer.

tactile defensiveness Oversensitivity to touch that causes discomfort.

telecommunication The transmission of signals over distance for the purpose of communication, such as television and radio.

temporal bone A bone situated at the sides and base of the skull that supports the part of the face known as the temple.

teratogen A substance ingested by the mother that can damage the growth and development of the fetus.

theory of mind A condition where children are unable to put themselves in the place of others in order to understand what they are feeling or thinking. This inability leads to predictable social problems.

tiered assignment Assignment of greater or lesser difficulty to students to match their level of possible attainment. In this way, all students can be involved in the same problem but at levels that match their capabilities.

time diary A method of data collection in which the user records their activity in set blocks of time (e.g., investigators used time diaries to collect information about how children with visual impairments spent their time during the day).

TORCHS A group of infections that affect the mother and that can also cause severe hearing losses in the fetus; toxoplasmosis (*TO*), rubella (*R*; German measles), cytomegalovirus (*C*; CMV), and herpes simplex virus (*HS*).

total communication method A method of teaching deaf students that combines finger spelling, signs, speech reading, speech, and auditory amplification. Also called *combined method* and *simultaneous method*.

transition coordinator The individual who plans for and assists the individual in the transition from school to work.

transition services Programs that help exceptional students move from school to the world of work and community.

traumatic brain injury (TBI) An injury of the brain caused by an external physical force, resulting in total or partial functional disability and/or psycho-social impairment that requires special educational services

twice exceptional Presence of both giftedness and a learning disability.

ulcerative colitis A disease resulting from heredity, weakened immune and inflammatory response, and intestinal bacteria that affects specifically the colon and causes thickness of the bowel wall. Children with ulcerative colitis experience pain, fever, and diarrhea.

underachievers with SGT Students whose academic performance consistently falls far short of expectations despite high cognitive abilities.

unexplained underachievement A learning disability that does not have a neurological base but which is characterized by performance below expected levels.

universal design for learning (UDL) A variety of strategies that give all students access to the curriculum. These strategies include the use of technology to reduce the impact of sensory and learning disabilities, the incorporation of flexible entry points to allow students to begin work at a level that is appropriate to their needs, and the use of multiple instructional approaches to respond to the different learning needs and styles of the students.

universal precautions Methods for reducing the spread of germs and infections (such as AIDS), including proper handwashing routines, use of gloves to clean up bodily fluids, and following biohazard cleanup protocols.

Usher syndrome A progressive degeneration of vision and hearing occurring some years after birth.

vestibular apparatus The vestibule and three semicircular canals of the inner ear. These structures work with the brain to sense, maintain, and regain balance and to perceive one's body orientation relative to the earth.

visual impairment Any form of visual loss. These visual difficulties can include very moderate (such as the need for glasses) or a complete loss of vision.

visual perception One's ability to process information from figure-ground input (seeing an object against the background), closure (completion of a figure: a\/u) and spatial relationships.

Visual Voice Tools A computer designed to improve voicing, pitch, timing, and sustained production of users with hearing loss.

voice disorder A variation from accepted norms in voice quality, pitch, or loudness.

voice The intonation and quality of the production of words, such as pitch, loudness, and resonance.

wraparound approach An approach to interventions for children with disabilities and their families that offers full support from multiple perspectives across the community. The support is tailored to the family and their needs but may include things like counseling, educational assistance, medical services, and assistance from social services. The purpose is to provide a full-support network to help the child and family move toward success.

writing aids and systems Augmented and alternative systems that are available for written communication.

References

Agran, M., & Wehmeyer, M. (2005). *Teaching problem solving to students with mental retardation.* Boston: Pearson/Merrill/Prentice.

Albinism. (2010, July). In *Wikipedia, The Free Encyclopedia.* Retrieved July, 2010, from http://en.wikipedia.org/w/index.php?title=Albinism&oldid=388946528.

Allgood, M. H., Heller, K. W., Easterbrooks, S. R., & Fredrick, L. D. (2009). Use of picture dictionaries to promote functional communication in students with deafness and intellectual disabilities. *Communication Disorders Quarterly, 31*(1), 53–64.

Allison, C., Baron-Cohen, S., Wheelwright, S., Charman, T., Richler, J., Pasco, G., et al. (2008). The Q-CHAT (quantitative checklist for autism in toddlers): A normally distributed quantitative measure of autistic traits at 18–24 months of age: Preliminary report. *Journal of Autism & Developmental Disorders, 38,* 1414–1425.

America competes act. (2007). (PL) 110-69. Washington, DC: U.S. House of Representatives.

American Association of Suicidology: Kochanek, K. D., Murphy, S. L., Anderson, R. N., & Scott, C. (2004). Deaths: Final data for 2002. *National Vital Statistics Reports, 53*(5). Hyattsville, MD: National Center for Health Statistics. DHHS Publication No. (PHS) 2005–1120. (p. 92, Table 29).

American Psychiatric Association. (2000). *Diagnostic and statistical manual of mental disorders.* (4th ed., p. 92). Washington, DC: Author.

American Speech-Language-Hearing Association. (1991). *ASHA, Supplement H, 33*(3).

American Speech-Language-Hearing Association. (1998). *Provision of instruction in English as a second language by speech-language pathologists in school settings* (Position statement). Retrieved from www.asha.org/policy

American Speech-Language-Hearing Association. (2005). *(Central) auditory processing disorders: The role of the audiologist* (Position statement). Retrieved from www.asha.org/policy

American Speech-Language-Hearing Association. (2008). *The prevalence and incidence of hearing loss in children.* Retrieved from www.asha.org/public/hearing/disorders/children.htm.

American Speech-Language-Hearing-Association. (2010). *Stuttering.* Retrieved from www.asha.org/public/speech/disorders/stuttering.htm

Anastasiow, N., & Nucci, C. (1994). Social, historical, and theoretical foundations of early childhood special education and early intervention. In P. Safford (Ed.), *Early childhood special education: Vol. 5. Yearbook in early childhood education,* (pp. 7–25). New York, NY: Teachers College Press.

Anastasiow, N. J. (1982). *The adolescent parent.* Baltimore, MD: Brookes.

Anastasiow, N. J. (1996). Psycho-biological theory of affect and self-development. In S. Harel & J. Shonkoff (Eds.), *Early childhood intervention* (pp. 111–112). Jerusalem, Israel: JDC-Brookdale Institute.

Anastasiow, N. J., Frankenberg, W., & Fandall, A. (1982). *Identifying the developmentally delayed child.* Baltimore, MD: University Park Press.

Anderson, C., Shibuya, A., Ihori, N., Swing, E., Bushman, B., Sakamoto, A., Rothstein, H., & Saleem, M. (2010). Violent video game effects on aggression, empathy, and prosocial behavior in Eastern and Western countries: A meta-analytic review. *Psychological Bulletin, 136*(2), 151–173.

Anthony, T. (2009). Deafblindness: One TVI's story. *DVI Quarterly, 54*(3), 16–17.

Antia, S. D., Jones, P. B., Reed, S., & Kreimeyer, K. H. (2009). Academic status and progress of deaf and hard-of-hearing students in general education classrooms. *Journal of Deaf Studies and Deaf Education, 14*(3), 293–313.

Antia, S. D., Sabers, D. L., & Stinson, M. S. (2007). Validity and reliability of the classroom participation questionnaire with deaf and hard of hearing students in public schools. *Journal of Deaf Studies and Deaf Education, 12*(2), 158–171.

Antia, S. (2007, February 19). *Teachers College Record.* Retrieved from http://www.tcrecord.org.

Archbold, S. M., Lutman, M. E., Gregory, S., O'Neill, C., and Nikolopoulos, T. P. (2002). Parents and their deaf child: Their perceptions three years after cochlear implant. *Deafness and Education International, 4*(1), 12–40.

Ashton, T. M. (2006). Assistive technology centers: Getting technology into the hands of users. *Journal of Special Education Technology, 21*(4), 55–57.

Atkins v. Virgina, 536 U.S. 304, (2002).

Atrophy. In *The Medical News.* Retrieved from www.news-medical.net/news/20100610/Novel-gene-replacement

Attwood, T. (1998). *Asperger's syndrome: A guide for parents and professionals.* Philadelphia: Kingsley.

Bahr, D., & Rosenfeld-Johnson, S. (2010). Treatment of children with speech oral placement disorders (OPDs): A paradigm emerges. *Communication Disorders Quarterly, 31*(3), 131–138.

Baker, J. (1995). Depression and suicidal ideation among academically gifted adolescents. *Gifted Child Quarterly, 39*(4), 218–223.

Baker, J. (2001). *The social skills picture book: Teaching play, emotion, and communication to children with Autism.* Arlington, TX: Future Horizons, Inc.

Baker, S., & Baker, K. (1997). Educating children who are deaf or hard of hearing: Bilingual-bicultural education. Council for Exceptional Children. Retrieved from www.cec.sped.org

Baker, S., & Baker, K. (1997). Educating children who are deaf or hard of hearing: Bilingual-bicultural education. *ERIC Digest, 533.*

Baldwin, A. (1987). Undiscovered diamonds. *Journal for the Education of the Gifted, 10*(4), 271–286.

Bambara, L., & Knoster, T. (2005). Designing positive behavior support plans. In M. Wehmeyer & M. Agran (Eds.), *Mental retardation and intellectual disabilities: Teaching students using innovative and research-based strategies.* Boston: Merrill/Prentice Hall.

Bambara, L. M., & Koger, F. (2005). Opportunities for daily choice-making. In M. Wehmeyer & M. Agran (Eds.), *Mental retardation and intellectual disabilities: Teaching students using innovative and research-based strategies* (pp. 213–233). Boston: Pearson.

Bank, P. (2010). Brief overview of common psychotropic medications: A practical guide from a clinical viewpoint. University of Michigan. Retrieved from www.ssw.umich.edu/.../Brief_Overview_of_Common_Psychotropic_Medications.pdf

Banks, R., Milagros, R., & Roof, V. (2003). Discovering family ancestry, priorities and resources: Sensitive family information gathering. *Young Exceptional Children, 6*(3), 11–19.

Barbarin, O. (2002). Set for success: Building a strong foundation for school readiness based on the social-emotional development of young children. *The Kauffman Early Education Exchange, (1)*1.

Barbarin, O. A. (2002). Culture and ethnicity in social, emotional and academic development. *The Kauffman Early Education Exchange, 1*(1), 45–61.

Barnett, D. W., Elliott, N., Wolsing, L., Bunger, C. E., Haski, H., McKissick, C., & Vander Meer, C. D. (2008). Response to intervention for children with extremely challenging behaviors: What it might look like. *School Psychology Review, 35*(4), 568–582.

Baron-Cohen, S., Cox, A., Baird, G., Sweettenham, J., Nightingale, N., Morgan, K., Drew, A., & Charman, T. (1996). Psychological markers in the detection of autism in infancy in a large population. *British Journal of Psychiatry, 168,* 1–6.

Barrere, I. (2000). Honoring difference. *Young Exceptional Children, 3*(4), 17–26.

Barrows, H. (1988). *The tutorial process.* Carbondale: Southern Illinois School of Medicine.

Barth, R., & Haskins, R. (2009). Will parent training reduce abuse, enhance development, and save money? Let's find out. (Policy brief: *The Future of Children*) Princeton, NJ.

Basu, S., Salisbury, C. L., & Thorkildsen, T. A. (2010). Measuring collaborative consultation practices in natural environments. *Journal of Early Intervention, 32*(2), 127–150.

Bateman, B. D., & Linden, M. A. (2006). *Better IEPs: How to develop legally correct and educationally useful programs* (4th ed.). Champaign, IL: Research Press.

Bates, E., Reilly, J., Wulfeck, B., Dronkers, N., Opie, M., Fenson, J., Kriz, S., Jeffries, R., Miller, L., and Herbst, K. (2001). Differential effects of unilateral lesions on language production in children and adults. *Brain and Language, 79,* 223–265.

Batshaw, M. (Ed.). (2002). *Children with disabilities* (5th ed.). Baltimore, MD: Brookes.

Batshaw, M., & Perret, Y. (1992). *Children with handicaps: A medical primer* (5th ed.). Baltimore, MD: Brookes.

Baum, S. M., & Owen, S. V. (2004). *To be gifted and learning disabled.* Mansfield Center, CT: Creative Learning Press.

Baum, S., Renzulli, J., & Hebért, T. (1995). Reversing underachievement: Creative productivity as a systematic intervention. *Gifted Child Quarterly, 39*(4), 224–235.

Baumeister, A., & Woodley-Zanthos, P. (1996). Prevention: Biological factors. In J. Jacobson & J. Mulick (Eds.), *Manual of diagnostic and professional practice in mental retardation* (pp. 229–242). Washington, DC: American Psychological Association.

Bausch, M. E., Ault, M. J., & Hasselbring, T. S. (2006). *Assistive technology planner: From IEP consideration to classroom implementation.* Lexington, KY: National Assistive Technology Research Institute.

Beauchaine, T., Neuhaus, E., Brenner, S., & Gatzke-Kopp, L. (2008). Ten good reasons to consider biological processes in prevention and intervention research. *Development and Psychopathology, 20,* 745–774.

Beghetto, R. (2008). Creativity enhancement. In J. Plucker & C. Callahan (Eds.), *Critical issues and practices in gifted education* (pp. 139–154). Waco, TX: Prufrock Press.

Beirne-Smith, M., Ittenbach, J., & Patton, J. (2001). *Mental retardation* (6th ed.). Upper Saddle River, NJ: Merrill.

Beirne-Smith, M., Ittenbach, J., & Patton, J. R. (1998). *Mental retardation* (5th ed.). Upper Saddle River, NJ: Merrill.

Bellamy, G., Rhodes, L., Mank, D., & Albin, J. (1988). *Supportive employment.* Baltimore, MD: Brookes.

Bellugi, U., & Studdert-Kennedy, A. (Eds.). (1984). *Signed and spoken language.* Deerfield Beach, FL: Verlag Chemie.

Bender, W. N. (2001). *Learning disabilities: Characteristics, identification, and teaching strategies* (4th ed.). Needham Heights, MA: Allyn & Bacon.

Bergeron, R., & Floyd, R. (2006). Broad cognitive abilities of children with mental retardation: An analysis of group and individual profiles. *American Journal on Mental Retardation, 111*(6), 417–432.

Bernal, E. (1979). The education of the culturally different gifted. In A. Passow (Ed.), *The gifted and the talented: Their education and development* (78th Yearbook of the National Society for the Study of Education, Part 1). Chicago, IL: University of Chicago Press.

Berninger, V. W., & Amtmann, D. (2003). Preventing written expression disabilities through early and continuing assessment and intervention for handwriting and/or spelling problems: Research into practice. In H. L. Swanson, K. R. Harris, & S. Graham (Eds.), *Handbook of learning disabilities* (pp. 345–363). New York, NY: Guilford Press.

Best, S. J., Heller, K. W., & Bigge, J. L. (2005). *Teaching individuals with physical, health, and multiple disabilities* (5th ed.). Upper Saddle River, NJ: Merrill-Prentice Hall.

Bettelheim, B. (1978). *A home for the heart.* New York, NY: Alfred A. Knopf.

Better Hearing Institute (2010). *Better Hearing Institute: Advocates for America's Ears.* Retrieved from: http://www.betterhearing.org/.

Bigge, J., Best, S., & Heller, K. (2001). *Teaching individuals with physical, health, or multiple disabilities* (4th ed.). Upper Saddle River, NJ: Merrill-Prentice Hall.

Bigge, J. L., & Best, L. (2000). *Teaching individuals with physical and multiple disabilities.* Upper Saddle River, NJ: Merrill.

Bishop, V. E. (2004). *Teaching visually impaired children.* Springfield, IL: C.C. Thomas.

Blacher, J., & Hatton, C. (2007). Families in context: Influences on coping and adaptation. In S. Odom, R. Horner, M. Snell, & J. Blacher (Eds.), *Handbook of Developmental Disabilities.* New York, NY: The Guilford Press.

Blackorby, J., & Wagner, M. (1996). Longitudinal outcomes of youth with disabilities. *Exceptional Children, 62*(5), 399–413.

Blair, R. J. R. (2004). The roles of orbital frontal cortex in the modulation of antisocial behavior. *Brain and Cognition, 55,* 198–208.

Block, L. (2003a). Legal considerations for learning disability programs. In *Colleges for students with learning disabilities or ADD* (7th ed.) (pp. 5–7). Lawrenceville, NJ: Thomson-Peterson's.

Block, L. (2003b). Distinctions between K–12 and higher education requirements. In *Peterson's colleges for students with learning disabilities or ADD* (7th ed.) (pp. 1–2). Lawrenceville, NJ: Thomson-Peterson's.

Bloom, L. (1991). *Language development from two to three.* New York, NY: Cambridge University Press.

Bloom, L. (2000). Commentary. In G. Hullich, K. Hirsch-Pasek, & R. Golinkoff (Eds.), Breaking the language barrier: An emergent coalition model of word learning. *Monographs of the Society for Research in Child Development, 65*(Serial No. 262), 121–135.

Bloom, L., & Tinker, E. (2001). The intentionality model and language acquisition. *Monographs of the Society for Research in Child Development, 66*(4), 1–91.

Bodner-Johnson, B., & Sass-Lehrer, M. (2003). *The young deaf or hard of hearing child: A family-centered approach to early education.* Baltimore, MA: Brookes.

Bohanon, H., Fenning, P., Carney, K., Minnis-Kim, M., Anderson-Harriss, S., Moroz, K., et al. (2006). Schoolwide application of positive behavior support in an urban high school. *Journal of Positive Behavior Interventions, 8*(3), 131–145.

Bondy, A. S., & Frost, L. A. (1994). The picture exchange communication system. *Focus on Autistic Behavior, 9*(3), 1.

Boswell, S. (2005). *TEACCH preschool curriculum guide: A curriculum planning and monitoring guide for young children with autism and related communication disorders.* Chapel Hill, NC: TEACCH.

Botuck, S., & Winsberg, B. (1991). Effects of respite on mothers of school-age and adult children with severe disabilities. *Mental Retardation, 29*(1), 43–47.

Boyd, B. A., Odom, S. L., Humphreys, B. P., & Sam, A. (2010). Infants and toddlers with autism spectrum disorders: Early diagnosis and early intervention. *Journal of Early Intervention, 32*(2), 75–98.

Bracken, B., & McCallum, R. (1998). *UNIT: Universal nonverbal intelligence test (examiner's manual).* Itasca, IL: Riverside Publishing Co.

Bradley, R., Danielson, L., & Doolittle, J. (2007). Responsiveness to intervention: 1997 to 2007. *Teaching Exceptional Children, 39*(5), 8–12.

Bradley, V., Ashbaugh, J., & Blaney, B. (1994). *Creating individual supports for people with disabilities.* Baltimore, MD: Brookes.

Bredekamp, S., & Cupple, C. (Eds.). (1997). *Developmentally appropriate practice in early childhood programs* (Rev. ed.). Washington, DC: National Association for the Education of Young Children.

Brice, A. E., Carson, C. K., & O'Brien, J. D. (2009). Spanish-English articulation and phonology of 4- and 5-year-old preschool children. *Communication Disorders Quarterly, 31*(1), 3–14.

Brice, A. E., Miller, K. J., & Brice, R. G. (2006). Language in the English as a second language and general education classrooms: A tutorial. *Communication Disorders Quarterly, 27*(4), 240–247.

Brice, R. G., & Brice, A. E. (2009). Investigation of phonemic awareness and phonic skills in Spanish-English bilingual and English-speaking kindergarten students. *Communication Disorders Quarterly, 30*(4), 208–225.

Bricker, D., & Cripes, J. (1992). *An activity based approach to early intervention.* Baltimore, MD: Brookes.

Briggs, C. J., Reis, S. M., & Sullivan, E. E. (2008). A national view of promising programs and practices for culturally, linguistically, and ethnically diverse gifted and talented students. *Gifted Child Quarterly, 52*(2), 131–145.

Brinton, B., & Fujiki, M. (2006). Social intervention for children with language impairment: Factors affecting efficacy. *Communication Disorders Quarterly, 28*(1), 39–41.

Bronfenbrenner, U. (1989). Ecological systems theory. In R. Vasta (Ed.), *Annals of Child Development, 6,* (pp. 187–249). London: Jessica Kingsley.

Browder, D. (Ed.). (2001). *Curriculum and assessment for students with moderate and severe disabilities.* New York, NY: Guilford Press.

Browder, D., Trela, K., Gibbs, S.L., Wakeman, S., & Harris, A.A. (2007). Academic skills: Reading and mathematics. In S.L. Odom, R.H. Horner, M. Snell, & J. Blacher. *Handbook in developmental disabilities.* NY: Guilford Press, p. 292–309.

Brown, C. W., Olson, H. C., & Croninger, R. G. (2010). Maternal alcohol consumption during pregnancy and infant social, mental, and motor development. *Journal of Early Intervention, 32*(2), 110–126.

Brown, W. H., Odom, S. L., & Conroy, M. A. (2001). An intervention hierarchy for promoting preschool children's peer interactions in natural environments. *Topics in Early Childhood Special Education, 21,* 162–175.

Bruder, M., & Dunst, C. (2000). Expanding learning opportunities for infants and toddlers in natural environments. *Zero to Three, 20*(3), 34–36.

Bryant, D., & Maxwell, D. (1999). The environment and mental retardation. *International Review of Psychology, 11,* 56–67.

Buchanan, M., & Cooney, M. (2000). Play at home, play in the classroom, parent/professional partnerships in supporting child play. *Young Exceptional Children, 3*(4), 9–26.

Buck, G., Polloway, E., Smith-Thomas, A., & Cook, K. (2003). Prereferral intervention process: A survey of state practices. *Exceptional Children, 69*(3), 349–360.

Bunce, D. (2003). Children with culturally diverse backgrounds. In L. McCormick, D. F. Loeb, & R. L. Schiefelbusch (Eds.), *Supporting children with communication difficulties in inclusive settings* (pp. 367–407). Boston, MA: Allyn & Bacon.

Burchinal, M., Peisner-Feinberg, E., Pianta, R., & Howes, C. (2002). Development of academic skills from preschool through second grade: Family and classroom predictors of developmental trajectories. *Journal of School Psychology, 40*(5), 415–436.

Burchinal, M., Roberts, J., Riggins, R., Zeisel, S., Neebar, E., & Bryant, D. (2000). Relating quality of center-based child care to early cognitive and language development. *Child Development, 71*(2), 339–357.

Bush, T. W., & Reschly, A. L. (2007). Progress monitoring in reading. *Assessment for Effective Intervention, 32*(4), 223–230.

Butter, E. M., Mulick, J. A., et al. (2006). Eight case reports of learning recovery in children with pervasive developmental disorders after early intervention. *Behavioral Interventions, 21*(4), 227–243.

Buysse, V., Goldman, B. D., & Skinner, M. L. (2002). Setting effects on friendship formation among young children with and without disabilities. *Exceptional Children, 68*(4), 503–517.

Buysse, V., Skinner, D., & Grant, S. (2001). Toward a definition of quality inclusive child care: Perspectives of parents and practitioners. *Journal of Early Intervention, 24*(2), 146–161.

Buysse, V., & Wesley, P. W. (Eds.). (2006). *Evidence-based practice in the early childhood field.* Washington, DC: Zero to Three.

Cairns, R. B. (1983). The emergence of developmental psychology. In W. Kessen (Ed.), *Handbook of child psychology: Vol. 1* (4th ed., pp. 41–102). New York, NY: Wiley.

Calderon, R., & Greenberg, M. (2000). Challenge to parents and professionals in promoting socio-emotional development. In P. Spencer, C. Ertling, & M. Marschark (Eds.), *The deaf child in the family and at school* (pp. 275–291). Mahwah, NJ: Erlbaum.

Campbell, F. A., & Ramey, C. T. (1995). Cognitive and school outcomes for high-risk African-American students at middle adolescence: Positive effects of early intervention. *American Educational Research Journal, 32*(4), 743–772.

Campbell, F. A., Ramey, C. T., Pungello, E. P., Sparling, J. J., & Miller-Johnson, S. (2002). Early childhood education: Young adult outcomes from the Abecedarian Project. *Applied Developmental Science, 6*(1), 42–57.

Campbell, P. (2000). Promoting participation in natural environments by accommodating motor disabilities. In M. Snell & F. Brown (Eds.), *Instruction of students with severe disabilities* (5th ed., pp. 291–330). Upper Saddle River, NJ: Merrill.

Campbell, P., Milbourne, S., Dugan, L., & Wilcox, M. (2006). A review of evidence on practices for teaching young children to use assistive technology devices. *Topics in Early Childhood Special Education, 26*(1), 3–17.

Campbell, P. H., & Sawyer, B. (2007). Supporting learning opportunities in natural settings through participation-based services. *Journal of Early Intervention, 29*(4), 287–305.

Campbell, P. H., Sawyer, B., & Muhlenhaupt, M. (2009). The meaning of natural environments for parents and professionals. *Infants & Young Children, 22*(4), 264–278.

Campos, J. J., Frankel, C.B. & Camaras, L (2004). On the nature of emotion regulation. *Child Development, 75*(2), 377–394.

Carran, D. T., & Kellner, M. H. (2009). Characteristics of bullies and victims among students with emotional disturbance attending approved private special education schools. *Behavior Disorders,* (34), 3.

Carta, J. J., & Kong, N. Y. (2007). Trends and issues in interventions for preschoolers with developmental disabilities. In S. L. Odom, R. H. Horner, M. E. Snell, & J. Blacher (Eds.), *Handbook of developmental disabilities* (pp. 181–198). New York, NY: Guilford Press.

Carter, B. B., & Spencer, V. G. (2007). Another beautiful mind: A case study of the recovery of an adolescent male from a TBI. *Physical Disabilities: Education and Related Services, 25*(2), 33–58.

Casey, A. M., & McWilliam, R. (2008). Graphical feedback to increase teachers' use of incidental teaching. *Journal of Early Intervention, 30*(3), 251–268.

Casey, A. M., & McWilliam, R. A. (2007). The STARE: The Scale for Teachers' Assessment of Routines Engagement. *Young Exceptional Children, 11*(1), 1–15.

Castellani, J., & Warger, C. (Eds.). (2009). *Accommodating students with disabilities: Instructional and assistive technology tools that work!* Reston, VA: Exceptional Innovations, INC.

Castellanos, F, Lee, P., Sharp, W., Jeffries, N., Greenstein, D., Clasen, L., Blumenthal, J., James, R., Ebens, C., Walter, J., Zijdenbos, A., Evens, A., Giedd, J., Rapaport, J. (2002). Developmental trajectories of brain volume abnormalities in children and adolescents with attention-deficit/hyperactivity disorder. *JAMA, 288*(14), 1740–1748.

Catlett, C. (2009). What do we mean by "early childhood inclusion?" Finding a shared definition." *Impact, 22*(1).

Cawley, J., Hayden, S., Cade, E., & Baker-Kroczynski, S. (2002). Including students with disabilities into the general education science classroom. *Exceptional Children, 68,* 423–436.

Cawthon, S. W., & Wurtz, K. A. (2008). Alternate assessment use with students who are deaf or hard of hearing: An exploratory mixed-methods analysis of portfolio, checklists, and out-of-level test formats. *Journal of Deaf Studies and Deaf Education,* Advance Access 7/23/2008.

Cedillo v. Secretary of Health and Human Services, 98-916v (2010)

Centers for Disease Control and Prevention. (2005). Achievements in public health: Elimination of rubella and congenital rubella syndrome—United States, 1969–2004. *Morbidity and Mortality Weekly Report, 54*(11), 279–282.

Centers for Disease Control and Prevention. (2009). FastStats: Asthma. Retrieved from http://www.cdc.gov/nchs/fastats/asthma.htm

Center on the Social and Emotional Foundations for Early Learning (a). *Research synthesis: Infant mental health and early care and education providers* [Web report]. Vanderbilt University. Retrieved from http://csefel.vanderbilt.edu

Center on the Social and Emotional Foundations for Early Learning (b). *Research synthesis: Early childhood mental health consultation* [Web report].Vanderbilt University. Retrieved from http://csefel.vanderbilt.edu

Chandrasekaran, B., Hornickel, J., Skoe, E., Nicol, T., & Kraus, N. (2009). Context-dependent encoding in the human auditory brainstem relates to hearing speech in noise: Implications for developmental dyslexia. *Neuron, 64,* 311–319.

Chomsky, N. (1965). *Aspects of the theory of syntax.* Cambridge, MA: MIT Press.

Clark, G., & Zimmerman, E. (1998). Nurturing the arts in programs for gifted and talented students. *Phi Delta Kappan, 79,* 746–751.

Clarke, S., & Campbell, F. (1998). Can intervention early prevent crime later? The Abecedarian project compared with other programs. *Early Childhood Research Quarterly, 13*(2), 319–343.

Cobb, J. (2004). *Top ten things to think about as you prepare for your transition to adulthood.* Washington, DC: G. W. Heath Resource Center.

Cohen, S. (1998). *Targeting autism.* Berkeley, CA: University of California Press.

Colangelo, N., Assouline, S., & Gross, M. (2004). *A nation deceived: How schools hold back America's brightest students. The Templeton national report on acceleration.* Iowa City, IA: Bolen and Blank International Center for Gifted Education.

Coleman, L. (2002). A shock to study. *Journal of Secondary Gifted Education, 14,* 39–52.

Coleman, L., & Cross, T. (2001). *Being gifted in school: An introduction to development, guidance, and teaching.* Waco, TX: Prufrock Press.

Coleman, L. (2005). Nurturing talent in high school: Life in the fast lane.New York, NY: Teachers College Press.

Coleman, M. R. (1994). Postsecondary educational decisions for gifted/learning disabled students. *Journal of Secondary Gifted Education, 5*(3), 53–59.

Coleman, M. R. (2000). *Conditions of special education teaching: CEC commission technical report.* Washington DC: Council for Exceptional Children.

Coleman, M. R. (2005). Academic strategies that work for gifted students with learning disabilities. *Teaching Exceptional Children, 38*(1), 28–32.

Coleman, M. R., Buysse, V., & Neitzel, J. (2006a). *Recognition and response: An early intervening system for young children at risk for learning disabilities.* Chapel Hill, NC: University of North Carolina at Chapel Hill, FPG Child Development Institute.

Coleman, M. R., Buysse, V., & Neitzel, J. (2006b). Establishing the evidence base for an emerging early childhood practice: Recognition and response. In V. Buysse & P. W. Wesley (Eds.), *Evidence-based practice in the early childhood field* (pp. 195–225). Washington, DC: Zero to Three Press.

Coleman, M. R., & Hughes, C. (2009). Meeting the needs of gifted students within an RTI framework. *Gifted Child Today, 32*(3), 15–17.

Coleman, M. R., Roth, F., & West, T. (2009). *Roadmap to pre-K RTI: Applying response to intervention in preschool settings.* New York, NY: National Center for Learning Disabilities.

Coleman, M. R., Shah-Coltrane, S., & Harrison, A. (2010). *Teacher's observation of potential in students: Teacher Guidebook.* Arlington, VA: Council for Exceptional Children.

Coleman, M. R., & Shah-Coltrane, S.(2010). *U-STARS ~PLUS Science & Literature Connections.* Arlington, VA: Council for Exceptional Children.

Coleman, M. R., West, T., & Gillis, M. (2010). *Early learning observation and rating scales (ELORS): Teacher-individual child form.* New York: National Center for Learning Disabilities.

Compton, D. L., Fuchs, D., Fuchs, L. S., & Bryant, J. D. (2006). Selecting at-risk readers in first grade for early intervention: A two-year longitudinal study of decision rules and procedures. *Journal of Educational Psychology, 98,* 394–409.

Connor, C., Craig, H., Raudenbush, S., Heavner, K., & Zwolan, T. (2006). The age at which young deaf children receive cochlear implants and their vocabulary and speech-production growth: Is there an added value for early implantation? *Ear & Hearing, 27*(6), 628–643.

Conyers, L. M., Reynolds, A. J., & Ou, S. (2003). The effect of early childhood intervention on subsequent special education services: Findings from the Chicago Child-Parent Centers. *Educational Evaluation and Policy Analysis, 25*(1), 75–95.

Cope, N., Harold, D., Hill, G., Moskvina, V., Stevenson, J., Holmans, P., et al. (2005). Strong evidence that KIAA0319 on chromosome 6p is a susceptibility gene for developmental dyslexia. *The American Journal of Human Genetics, 76*(4), 581–591.

Corn, A. L., & Lusk, K. E. (2010). Perspectives on low vision. In A. Corn & J. Erin (Eds.) *Foundations of low vision: Clinical and functional perspectives* (2nd ed., pp. 3–34). New York, NY: American Foundation for the Blind,.

Corso, R., Santos, R., & Roof, V. (2002). Honoring diversity in early childhood educational material. *Teaching Exceptional Children, 34*(3), 30–37.

Cortiella, C. (2009). *The State of Learning Disabilities*. New York, NY: National Center for Learning Disabilities.

Cortiella, C., & Burnette, J. (2009). *Challenging change: How schools and districts are improving the performance of special education students*. New York, NY: The National Center for Learning Disabilities.

Cosmos, C. (2001). Abuse of children with disabilities. In *Today* (pp. 1–15). Arlington, VA: Council for Exceptional Children.

Coufal, K. (Ed.). (2007). Letter from the editor. *Communication Disorders Quarterly, 28*(3), 133–134.

Council for Exceptional Children. (2003). *What every special educator must know: The international standards for the preparation and certification of special education teachers*. Arlington, VA: Author.

Council for Exceptional Children. (2006). *Council for Exceptional Children policy and advocacy services: Understanding IDEA 2004 regulations*. Arlington, VA: Author.

Council for Exceptional Children. (2007). *Understanding IDEA 2004: Frequently asked questions*. Arlington, VA: Author.

Council for Exceptional Children. (2010). *Positive behavior interventions & supports*. Arlington, VA: CEC.

Cowley, G. (2000). Understanding autism. *Newsweek*, July 23, 2000, 3.

Cox, M., & Paley, B. (1997). Families as systems. *Annual Review of Psychology, 48*, 243–267.

Coy, J. K., & Anderson, E. A. (2010). Instruction in the use of optical devices for children and youths. In A. Corn, & J. Erin (Eds.), *Foundations of low vision: Clinical and functional perspectives* (2nd ed.). New York, NY: American Foundation for the Blind, 527–588.

Craniofacial Journal, 45(1), 1–17.

Crews, S., Bender, H., Gresham, F.M., Kern, L., Vanderwood, M., & Cook, C.R. (2007). Risk and protective factors of emotional and/or behavioral disorders in children and adolescents: A "mega"-analytic synthesis. *Behavioral Disorders, 32*(2), 64–77.

Cross, T. (2008). Suicide. In J. Plucker & C. Callahan (Eds.), *Critical issues and practices in gifted education* (pp. 629–640). Waco, TX: Prufrock Press.

Cross, T., Cassady, J., & Miller, K. (2006). Suicide ideation and personality characteristics among gifted adolescents. *Gifted Child Quarterly, 50*, 295–306.

Cryer, D., & Clifford, R. (Eds.). (2003). *Early childhood education and care in the U.S.A.* Baltimore, MD: Brookes.

Cullinan, D. (2004). Classification and definition of emotional and behavioral disorders. In R. Rutherford, M. Quinn, & S. Mathur (Eds.), *Handbook of research in emotional and behavior disorders* (pp. 32–53). New York, NY: Guilford Press.

Cutting, L. E., & Denckla, M. B. (2003). Attention: Relationships between attention-deficit hyperactivity disorder and learning disabilities. In H. L. Swanson, K. R. Harris, & S. Graham (Eds.), *Handbook of learning disabilities* (pp. 125–139). New York, NY: Guilford Press.

DaDeppo, L. M. W. (2009). Integration factors related to the academic success and intent to persist of college students with learning disabilities. *Learning Disabilities Research & Practice, 24*(3), 122–131.

Dai, D. Y., & Sternberg, R.J. (2004). Beyond cognitivism: Toward an integrated understanding of intellectual functioning and development. In D. Dai & R. Sterberg (Eds) *Motivation, emotion and cognition.* (pp. 3–38). New Jersey/London: Lawrence Erlbaum Associates, Inc.

Dautenhahn, K., & Billard, A. (2002). Games children with autism can play with Robota, a humanoid robotic doll. In S. Keates, P. M. Langdon, P. J. Clarkson, & P. Robinson (Eds.) *Universal access and assistive technology* (pp. 179–190). London, England: Springer-Verlag.

Davis, A., Kruczek, T., & McIntosh, D. (2006). Understanding and treating psychopathology in schools: Introduction to the special issue. *Psychology in the Schools, 43*(4).

Davis, D. (1988). Nutrition in the prevention and reversal of mental retardation. In F. Menolascino & J. Stark (Eds.), *Preventive and curative intervention in mental retardation* (pp. 177–222). Baltimore, MD: Brookes.

Dawson, G. (2008). Early behavioral intervention, brain plasticity, and the prevention of autism spectrum disorder. *Development and psychopathology, 20*, 775–803.

de Jong, E. P., Lopriore, E., Vossen, A., Steggerda, S. J., Te Pas, A. B., Kroes, A., & Walther, F. J. (2010). Is routine TORCH screening warranted in neonates with lenticulostriate vasculopathy? *Neonatology, 97*, 274–278.

Deafness Research Foundation. (2000). *Research News, 1*(1).

Delgado, C. (2009). Fourth grade outcomes of children with a preschool history of developmental disability. *Education and Training in Developmental Disabilities, 44*(4), 573–579.

Dell, A., Newton, D., & Petroff, J. (2008). *Assistive technology in the classroom: Enhancing the school experiences of students with disabilities.* Columbus, OH: Pearson Merrill Prentice Hall.

Department of Health & Human Services. (2003). *Monitoring the future: National results on adolescent drug use.* Rockville, MD: U.S. Department of Health and Human Services.

Deshler, D. D., Robinson, S., & Mellard, D. F. (2009). Instructional principles for optimizing outcomes for adolescents with learning disabilities. In G. D. Siderides & T. A. Citro (Eds.), *Classroom strategies for struggling learners* (pp. 173–189). Weston, MA: Learning Disabilities Association Worldwide.

Deshler, D., Schumaker, J., Lenz, B., Bulgren, J., Hock, M., Knight, J., & Ehren, B. (2001). Ensuring content-area learning by secondary students with learning disabilities. *Learning Disabilities Research and Practice, 16*(2), 96–108.

DiCarlo, C., Banajee, M., & Buras-Stricklin, S. (2000). Embedding augmentative communication within early childhood classrooms. *Young Exceptional Children, 3*(3), 18–26.

DiCarlo, C., & Vagianos, L. (2009). Using child preferences to increase play across interest centers in inclusive early childhood classrooms. *Young Exceptional Children, 12*(4), 31–39.

Dickman, G. E. (1996). Learning disabilities and behavior. In S. C. Cramer & W. Ellis (Eds.), *Learning disabilities* (pp. 215–228). Baltimore, MD: Brookes.

Dionne, G., Dale, P., Boivin, M., & Plomin, R. (2003). Genetic evidence for bidirectional effects of early lexical and grammatical development. *Child Development, 74*(2), 394–412.

Division for Learning Disabilities. (2007). *Thinking about response to intervention and learning disabilities: A teacher's guide.* Arlington, VA: Author.

Dixon, F., & Moon, S. (2006). (Eds.). *The Handbook of Secondary Gifted Education.* Waco: TX. Prufrock Press, Inc.

Doig, K., & Werner, E. (2000). The marriage of a traditional lecture-based curriculum and problem-based learning: Are the offspring vigorous? *Medical Teacher, 22*, 173–178.

Dong, W. K., & Greenough, W. T. (2004) Plasticity of non-neuronal brain tissue: Roles in developmental disorders. *Mental Retardation and Developmental Disabilities Research Reviews, 10*(2), 85–90.

Donovan, M., & Cross, C. (2002) *Minority students in special and gifted education.* Washington, DC: National Academy Press.

Dorman, J. P., & Pellegrino, L. (1998). *Caring for children with cerebral palsy: A team approach.* Baltimore, MD: Brookes.

Downing, J., & Eichinger, J. (2003). Creating learning opportunities for students with severe disabilities in inclusive classrooms. *Teaching Exceptional Children, 36*(1), 26–31.

Duchan, J. F. (2008). *Getting here: A short history of speech pathology in America.* Retrieved from http:// www.acsu.buffalo.edu/~duchan/history.html

Duke Center for Human Genetics. (2010). *Disorders: Neural tube defects (NTDs).* Retrieved from http:// www.chg.duke.edu/diseases/ntd.html

Duncan, J. (2009). Parental readiness for cochlear implant decision-making. *Cochlear Implants International, 10*(S1), 38–42.

Dunlap, G., & Carr, E. (2007). Positive behavior support and developmental disabilities: A summary and analysis of research. In S. Odom, B. Horner, M. Snell, & J. Blacher (Eds.), *Handbook of developmental disabilities* (pp. 469–482). New York, NY: Guilford Press.

Dunlap, G., Strain, P., Fox, L., Carta, J., Conroy, M., Smith, B., Kern, L., Hemmeter, M. L., Timm, M., McCart, A., Sailor, W., Markey, U., Markey, D. J., Lardieri, S., & Sowell, C. (2006). Preventing and intervention with young children's challenging behavior: Perspectives regarding current knowledge. *Behavioral Disorders, 32*(1), 29–45.

Dunst, C. J. (2007). Early intervention for infants and toddlers with developmental disabilities. In S. L. Odom, R. H. Horner, M. E. Snell, & J. Blacher (Eds.), *Handbook of developmental disabilities* (pp. 161–180). New York, NY: Guilford Press.

Dweck, C. S. (2007). The perils and promises of praise. *Educational Leadership, 65*(2).

Dworzynski, K., Remington, A., Rijsdijk, F., Howell, P., and Plomin, R. (2007). Genetic etiology in cases of recovered and persistent stuttering in an unselected, longitudinal sample of young twins. *American Journal of Speech-Language Pathology, 16*, 169–178.

Early, D., Maxwell, K., Clifford, R., Pianta, R., Ritchie, S., Howes, C., et al. (2007). Teachers' education, classroom quality, and young children's academic skills: Results from seven studies of preschool programs. *Child Development, 78*(2), 558–580.

Easterbrooks, S. (1999). Improving practice for students with hearing impairments. *Exceptional Children, 65*(4), 537–554.

Eber, L., & Keenan, C. (2004). Collaboration with other agencies: Wraparound and systems of care for children and youth with EBD. In R. Rutherford, M. Quinn, & S. Mathur (Eds.), *Handbook of research in emotional and behavioral disorders* (p. 502). New York, NY: Guilford Press.

Eber, L., Sugai, G., Smith, C., & Scott, T. (2002). Wraparound and positive behavioral interventions and supports in the schools. *Journal of Emotional and Behavioral Disorders, 10*(3), 171.

Eckenrode, L., Fennell, P., & Hearsey, K. (2007). *Tasks galore for the real world.* Chapel Hill, NC: Tasks Galore.

Edens, R. M., Murdick, N. L., & Gartin, B. C. (2003). Preventing infection in the classroom: The use of universal precautions. *Teaching Exceptional Children, 35*(4), 62–66.

Education for all handicapped children act. (1975). (PL) 94–142. Washington, DC: U.S. House of Representatives.

Edwards, J., & Tyskiewicz, E. (1999). Cochlear implants. In J. Stokes (Ed.), *The hearing impaired infant: The first eighteen months* (pp. 129–162). London, England: Whurr. (Distributed by Paul H. Brookes)

Edyburn, D. L. (2006). Assistive technology and mild disabilities. *Special Education Technology Practice, 8*(4), 18–28.

Egger, H. L., & Angold, A. (2006). Common emotional and behavioral disorders in preschool children: presentation, nosology, and epidemiology. *Journal of Child Psychiatry, 47*(3/4), 313–337.

Eichenwald, E., & Stark, A. (2008). Management and outcomes of very low birth weight. *New England Journal of Medicine, 358*, 1700–1711.

Eikeseth, S., Smith, T., Jahr, E., & Eldevik, S. (2007). Outcome for children with autism who began intensive behavioral treatment between ages 4 and 7. *Behavior Modification, 31*(3), 264–278.

Elias, S. (2005). *Special needs trusts.* Berkeley, CA: Nolo Press.

Elliott, D. S., Hamburg, B. A., & Williams, K. R. (1998). *Violence in American schools.* New York, NY: Cambridge University Press.

Ellis, E., Farmer, T., & Newman, J. (2005). Big ideas about teaching big ideas. *Teaching Exceptional Children, 38*(1), 34–40.

Erickson, K., Hatton, D., Roy, V., Fox, D., & Renne, D. (2007). Literacy in early intervention for children with visual impairments: Insights from individual cases. *Journal of Visual Impairment and Blindness, 101*(2), 80–95.

Erickson, K. A., & Hatton, D. (2007a). Expanding understanding of emergent literacy: Empirical support for a new framework. *Journal of Visual Impairment and Blindness, 101*(5), 261–277.

Erickson, K. A., & Hatton, D. (2007b). Literacy and visual impairment. *Seminars in Speech and Language, 28*, 58–68.

Erin, J. N., & Topor, I. (2010a). Functional vision assessment of children with low vision, including those with multiple disabilities. In A. Corn & J. Erin (Eds.) *Foundations of low vision: Clinical and functional perspectives* (2nd ed., pp. 339–397). New York, NY: American Foundation for the Blind.

Erin, J. N., & Topor, I. (2010b). Instruction in visual techniques for students with low vision, including those with multiple disabilities. In A. Corn & J. Erin (Eds.), *Foundations of low vision: Clinical and functional perspectives* (2nd ed.). New York, NY: American Foundation for the Blind, 398–441.

Erwin, E., & Brown, F. (2003). A contextual framework for understanding self-determination in early childhood environment. *Infants and Young Children, 16*(4), 1.

Fagan, M. K., & Pisoni, D. B. (2010). Hearing experience and receptive vocabulary development in deaf children with cochlear implants. *Journal of Deaf Studies and Deaf Education, 15*(2), 149–161.

Faggella-Luby, M., & Deshler, D. D. (2008). Reading comprehension in adolescents with LD: What we know, what we need to know. *Learning Disability Research and Practice, 23*(2), 70–78.

Falvey, M. A., Coot, J., Bishop, K. D., & Grenot-Scheyer, M. (1989). Educational and curricular adaptations. In S. Stainback, W. Stainback, & M. Forest (Eds.), *Educating all students in the mainstream of regular education.* Baltimore, MD: Brookes.

Farmer, T., Farmer, E., Estell, D., & Hutchins, B. (2007). The developmental dynamics of aggression and the prevention of school violence. *Journal of Emotional and Behavioral Disorders, 15*(4), 197–208.

Fazzi, D. L., & Naimy, B. J. (2010). Orientation and mobility services for children and youths with low vision. In A. Corn & J. Erin (Eds.) *Foundations of low vision: Clinical and functional perspectives* (2nd ed., pp. 655–727). New York, NY: American Foundation for the Blind,.

Ferrell, K. (2007). Issues in the field of blindness and low-vision. Retrieved Jul, 2010, from http://www.unco.edu/ncssd/resources/issues_bvi.pdf.

Ferrell, K., Shaw, A., & Dietz, S. (1998). *Project PRISM: A longitudinal study of developmental patterns of children who are visually impaired.* Greeley: University of Northern Colorado, Division of Special Education.

Ferrell, K., & Suvak, P. (1995). *Educational outcomes for Colorado students with visual disabilities.* Greeley, CO: University of Northern Colorado.

Fey, M., Windsor, J., & Warren, S. (Eds.). (1995). *Language intervention: Preschool through elementary years.* Baltimore, MD: Brookes.

Field, G. (2009). The effects of the use of Renzulli learning on student achievement in reading comprehension, reading fluency, social studies, and science. *International Journal of Emerging Technologies, 4,* 29–39.

Field, S., & Hoffman, A. (2007). Self-determination in secondary transition assessment. *Assessment for Effective Intervention, 32*(3), 181–190.

Field, T. (1989). Interaction coaching for high risk infants and their parents. *Prevention in Human Services, 1,* 8–54.

Fields, E., Farmer, E., Apperson, J., Mustillo, S., & Simmers, D. (2006). Treatment and posttreatment effects of residential treatment using a re-education model. *Behavioral Disorders, 31*(3), 312–322.

Firth, N., Greaves, D., & Frydenberg, E. (2010). Coping styles and strategies: A comparison of adolescent students with and without learning disabilities. *Journal of Learning Disabilities, 43*(1), 77–85.

Flavell, J., & Miller, P. (1998). Social cognition. In W. Damon (Ed.), *Handbook of child psychology: Vol. 2. Cognition, perception and language* (5th ed., pp. 851–898). New York, NY: Wiley.

Flax, J., Realpe-Bonilla, T., Hirsch, L., Brzustowicz, L., Bartlett, C., & Tallal, P. (2003). Specific language impairment in families: Evidence for co-occurrence with reading impairments. *Journal of Speech, Language, and Hearing Research, 46,* 530–543.

Fletcher, J. M., Denton, C., & Francis, D. J. (2005). Validity of alternative approaches for the identification of learning disabilities: Operationalizing unexpected underachievement. *Journal of Learning Disabilities, 38,* 545–552.

Flynn, J. (1999). Searching for justice: The discovery of IQ gains over time. *American Psychologist, 54*(1), 5–20.

Fombonne, E. (2003). The prevalence of autism. *Journal of the American Medical Association, 289,* 97–89.

Ford, D. Y., & Grantham, T. C. (2003). Providing access for culturally diverse gifted students: From deficit to dynamic thinking. *Theory Into Practice, 42*(3), 217–225.

Ford, D. Y. (2002). Racial identity among gifted African American students. In M. Neihart, S. Reis, N. Robinson, & S. Moon (Eds.), *The social and emotional development of gifted children: What do we know?* (pp. 155–164). Waco, TX: Prufrock Press.

Ford, D. Y., & Grantham, T. C. (2003). Providing access for culturally diverse gifted students: From deficit to dynamic thinking. *Theory Into Practice, 42*(3), 217–225.

Ford, D. Y., & Harris, J. J., III. (1999). *Multicultural gifted education.* New York, NY: Teachers College Press.

Ford, D. Y., Moore, J. L. III., & Milner, H. R. (2005). Beyond colorblindness: A model of culture with implications for gifted education. *Roeper Review, 27*(2), 97–103.

Forgatch, M., Patterson, G., Degarmo, D., & Beldavs Z. (2009). Testing the Oregon delinquency model with 9-year follow-up of the Oregon divorce study. *Developmental Psychopathology, 21*(2): 637–660.

Foshay, J. D., & Ludlow, B. L. (2005). Implementing computer-mediated instructional supports. In M. Wehmeyer & M. Agran (Eds.), *Mental retardation and intellectual disabilities: Teaching students using innovative and research-based strategies.* Boston: Merrill/Prentice Hall.

Fossett, B., & Mirenda, P. (2007). Augmentative and alternative communication. In S. Odom, B. Horner, M. Snell, & J. Blacher (Eds.), *Handbook of developmental disabilities* (pp. 330–348). New York, NY: Guilford Press.

Fowler, A. (1998). Language in mental retardation: Associations with and dissociations from general cognition. In J. Burack, R. Hodapp, & E. Zigler (Eds.), *Handbook of mental retardation and development* (pp. 290–333). New York, NY: Cambridge University Press.

Fowler, S., & Ostrosky, M., & Yates, T. (2007). Teaching and Learning in the early years. In L. Florian (Ed.), *The Sage handbook of special education.* London, England: Sage Publications, Ltd.

Fowler, S. A., Ostrosky, M. M., & Yates, T. J. (2007). Teaching and learning in the early years. In L. Florian (Ed.), *The Sage handbook of special education* (pp. 349–359). Thousand Oaks, CA: Sage.

Fox, L., Carta, J., Strain, P., Dunlap, G., & Hemmeter, M. L. (2010). Response to intervention and the pyramid model. *Infants and Young Children, 23*(1), 3–13.

Fox, L., Dunlap, G., Hemmeter, M. L., Joseph, G., & Strain, P. (2003). The teaching pyramid: A model for supporting social competence and preventing challenging behavior in young children. *Young Children, 58*(4), 48–52.

Fox, J., & Gable, R. A. (2004). Functional behavioral assessment. In R. Rutherford, M. Quinn, & S. Mathur (Eds.), *Handbook of Research in Emotional and Behavioral Disorders* (pp. 143–162). New York: Guilford.

Fox, L., & Smith, B. (2007). *Policy brief: Promoting social, emotional and behavioral outcomes of young children served under IDEA.* Center on the Social and Emotional Foundations for Early Learning.

Frances, A. (2010, April, 23). DSM5 should not expand bipolar II disorder. *Psychology Today* (April 23, 2010)

Franks, B. A., Miller, M. D., Wolff, E. J., & Landry, K. (2004). HIV/AIDS and the teachers of young children. *Early Child Development and Care, 174*(3), 229–241.

Fraser, D. (2003). From the playful to the profound: What metaphors tell us about gifted children. *Roeper Review, 25,* 183.

Freberg, L. A. (2006). *Discovering biological psychology.* Boston, MA: Houghton Mifflin.

Friend, A. C., Summers, J. A., & Turnbull, A. P. (2009). Impacts of family support in early childhood intervention research. *Education and Training in Developmental Disabilities, 44*(4), 453–470.

Fuchs, D., & Fuchs, L. S. (2006). Introduction to response to intervention: What, why, and how valid is it? *Reading Research Quarterly, 41*(1), 93–98.

Fuchs D., Fuchs, L. S., Compton, D. L., Bouton, B., Caffrey, E., Hill, L. (2007). Dynamic assessment as responsive to intervention. *Teaching Exceptional Children, 39*(5), 58–63.

Fuchs, D., Fuchs, L. S., Mathes, P. G., Lipsey, M. L., & Roberts, P. H. (2002). Is "learning disabilities" just a fancy term for low achievement? A meta-analysis of reading differences between low achievers with and without the label. In R. Bradley, L. Danielson, & D. Hallahan (Eds.), *Identification of learning disabilities* (pp. 737–762). Mahwah, NJ: Erlbaum.

Fuchs, D., Fuchs, L., Mathes, P., & Simmons, D. (1997). Peer-assisted learning strategies: Making classrooms more responsive to diversity. *American Educational Research Journal, 34*(1), 174–206.

Fuchs, D., Mock, D., Morgan, P. L., & Young, C. L. (2003). Responsiveness-to-intervention: Definitions, evidence, and implications for the learning disabilities construct. *Learning Disabilities Research and Practice, 18*(3), 157–171.

Fuchs, L. S., & Fuchs, D. (2007). A model for implementing responsiveness to intervention. *Teaching Exceptional Children, 39*(5), 14–20.

Fuchs, L. S., Fuchs, D., Prentice, K., Hamlett, C. L., Finelli, R., Courey, S. J. (2004). Enhancing mathematical problem solving among third-grade students with schema-based instruction. *Journal of Educational Psychology, 96*, 635–647.

Galaburda, A. M. (2005). Neurology of learning disabilities: What will the future bring? The answer comes from the successes of the recent past. *Learning Disability Quarterly, 28*, 107–109.

Gallagher, D. (2007). Challenging orthodoxy in special education: on longstanding debates and philosophical divides. In L. Florian (Ed.), *The Sage handbook of special education*. London, England: Sage Publications, Ltd.

Gallagher, J. (1972). The special education contract for mildly handicapped children. *Exceptional Children, 38*, 527–535.

Gallagher, J. (2000). The beginnings of federal help for young children with disabilities. *Topics in Early Childhood Special Education* (pp. 3–6). Austin, TX: PRO-ED.

Gallagher, J. (2002). Interventions and children with special needs. In A. Cranston-Gingus & E. Taylor, *Rethinking professional issues in special education* (pp. 43–68). Westport, CT: Ablex.

Gallagher, J. (2006). *Driving change in special education*. Baltimore, MD: Brookes.

Gallagher, J. (2009). Teaching evaluation and judgment. *Gifted Educator Communicator*, Spring, 16–19.

Gallagher, J., & Clifford, R. (2000). The missing support infrastructure in early childhood. *Early Childhood Research and Practice, 2*(1), 1–24.

Gallagher, J., Danaher, J., & Clifford, R. (2009). The evolution of the National Early Childhood Technical Assistance Center. *Topics in Early Childhood Special Education, 29*, 7–23.

Gallagher, J., & Gallagher, S. (1994). *Teaching the gifted child* (4th ed.). Boston, MA: Allyn & Bacon.

Gallagher, J. J., & Bray, W. (2002). *Project insight: Program evaluation*. Chapel Hill, NC: Frank Porter Graham Child Development Institute.

Gallagher, J. J., Cook, E., & Shoffner, M. (2003). *Project insight II: Program evaluation*. Chapel Hill, NC: Frank Porter Graham Child Development Institute.

Gallagher, P., & Lambert, R. (2006). Classroom quality, concentration of children with special needs, and child outcomes in Head Start. *Exceptional Children, 73*(1), 31–52.

Gallagher, P., Powell, T., & Rhodes, C. (2006). *Brothers and sisters: A special part of exceptional families*. Baltimore, MD: Paul H. Brookes.

Gallagher, S., & Stepien, W. (1996). Content acquisition in problem based learning: Depth versus breadth in American studies. *Journal for the Education of the Gifted, 19*, 257–275.

Gannon, J. (1981). *Deaf heritage: A narrative history of deaf America*. Silver Spring, MD: National Association of the Deaf.

Garcia, C., & Magnuson, K. (2000). Cultural difference. In J. Shonkoff & S. Meisels (Eds.), *Handbook of early intervention* (pp. 94–114). New York, NY: Cambridge University Press.

Gardner, D. (1983). A nation at risk: The imperative for education reform. Washington, DC: United States Department of Education.

Gardner, H. (1993). *Multiple intelligences: The theory in practice*. New York, NY: Basic Books.

Gardner, H. (2006). *The development and education of the mind: The collected works of Howard Gardner*. London: Routledge.

Gallaudet Research Institute (November 2008). *Regional and national summary report of data from the 2007–2008 annual survey of deaf and hard of hearing children and youth*. Washington, DC: GRI, Gallaudet University.

Geers, A., Tobey, E., Moog, J., & Brenner, C. (2008). Long-term outcomes of cochlear implantation in the preschool years: From elementary grades to high school. *International Journal of Audiology, 47*, S21–S30.

Gene therapy. (2010). In *Wikipedia, the free encyclopedia*. Retrieved from en.wikipedia.org/wiki/Gene_therapy

Gerber, M. M., Jimenez, T., Leafstedt, J., Villaruz, J., Richards, C., & English, J. (2004). English reading effects of small-group intensive intervention in Spanish for K-1 English learners. *Learning Disabilities Research and Practice, 19*, 239–251.

Gersten, R., Compton, D., Connor, C. M., Dimino, J., Santoro, L., Linan-Thompson, S., & Tilly, W. D. (2008). *Assisting students struggling with reading: Response to Intervention and multi-tier intervention for reading in the primary grades. A practice guide*. (NCEE 2009-4045). Washington, DC: National Center for Education Evaluation and Regional Assistance, Institute of Education Sciences, U.S. Department of Education. Retrieved from http://ies.ed.gov/ncee/wwc/publications/practiceguides/.

Getzels, J., & Jackson, P. (1962). *Creativity and intelligence*. New York, NY: Wiley.

Gillis, M., West, T., & Coleman, M. R. (2010). *Early learning observation & rating scale: Development manual*. New York: National Center for Learning Disabilities.

Gillis, M., West, T., & Coleman, M. R. (2010). *Early learning observation & rating scale: Teacher's guide*. New York: National Center for Learning Disabilities.

Gildroy, P., & Deshler, D. D. (2008). Effective learning strategy instruction. In R. Morris & N. Mather (Eds.), *Evidence-based practices for students with learning and behavioral challenges* (pp. 288–301). London, England: Routledge.

Girolametto, L., & Weitzman, E. (2007). Promoting peer interaction skills: Professional development for early childhood educators and preschool teachers. *Topics in Language Disorders, 27*(2), 93–110.

Given, B. (2002). *Teaching to the brain's natural learning systems*. Alexandria, VA: Association for Supervision and Curriculum Development.

Gladwell, M. (2008). *Outliers*. Boston, MA: Little Brown and Company.

Glago, K., Mastropieri, M., & Scruggs, T. (2008). Improving problem solving of elementary students with mild disabilities. *Remedial and Special Education, 20*(10), 1–9.

Gleason, J. B. (Ed.). (2005). *The development of language*, 6th ed. Boston, MA: Pearson.

Glidden, L. M., & Jobe, B. (2007). Measuring parental daily rewards and worries in the transition to adulthood. *American Journal on Mental Retardation, 112*(4), 275–288.

Goldin-Meadow, S. (1998). The resilience of language in humans. In C. Snowden & M. Hanberger (Eds.), *Social influence on vocal development* (pp. 293–311). New York, NY: Cambridge University Press.

Goldstein, B., & Iglesias, A. (2001). The effect on phonological analysis: Evidence from Spanish-speaking children. *American Journal of Speech-Language Pathology, 10*(1), 394–406.

Goldstein, H., Schneider, N., & Thiemann, K. (2007). Peer-mediated social communication intervention: When clinical expertise informs treatment development and evaluation. *Topics in Language Disorders, 27*(2), 182–199.

Goodman, S., & Wittenstein, S. (Eds.). (2002). *Collaborative assessment.* New York, NY: American Foundation for the Blind.

Goodrich, G., & Sowell, V. (1996). Low vision: A history in progress. In A. Corn & A. Koenig (Eds.), *Foundations of low vision: Clinical and functional perspectives* (pp. 397–414). New York, NY: American Foundation for the Blind.

Gottfriedson, D. (1997). School based crime prevention. In Sherman, L. et al. (Eds.), *Preventing crime: What works, what doesn't, what's promising: A report to the United States Congress,* (pp. 1–74). Washington, DC: U. S. Department of Justice.

Gottlieb, G. (1997). *Synthesizing nature-nurture: Prenatal roots of instinctive behavior.* Mahwah, NJ: Erlbaum.

Grandin, T. (1988). Teaching tips from a recovered autistic. *Focus on Autistic Behavior, 5,* 1–15.

Grandin, T. (1995). The learning style of people with autism: An autobiography. In K. Quill (Ed.), *Teaching children with autism: Methods to enhance communication and socialization* (pp. 33–52). Albany, NY: Delmar.

Graham, S., & Harris, K.R. (2009). Almost 30 years of writing research: Making sense of it all with *The Wrath of Khan. Learning Disabilities Research & Practice, 24*(2), 58–68.

Greenberg, M., & Kusche, C. (1998). Preventive intervention for school-age deaf children: The PATHS curriculum. *Journal of Deaf Studies and Deaf Education, 3*(1), 49–63.

Greenspan, S. (1999). A contextual perspective on adaptive behavior. In R. Schalock (Ed.), *Adaptive behavior and its measurements: Implications for the field of mental retardation* (pp. 15–42). Washington, DC: American Association on Mental Retardation.

Greenspan, S., & Switzky, H. (2006). *Forty-four years of AAMR Manuals.* Washington, DC: American Association on Mental Retardation.

Greenspan, S., & Wieder, S. (2006). *Engaging autism: Using the floor-time approach to help.* Cambridge, MA: DaCapo Press.

Grenot-Scheyer, M. (1994). The nature of interactions between students with severe disabilities and their friends and acquaintances without disabilities. *Journal of the Association for Persons with Severe Handicaps, 19,* 253–262.

Gresham, F. (1998). Social skills training: Should we raze, remodel or rebuild? *Behavior Disorders, 24*(1), 19–25.

Gresham, F. (2007). Response to intervention and emotional and behavioral disorders. *Assessment for Effective Intervention, 32*(4), 214–222.

Gresham, F., Beebe-Frankenberger, M., & Macmillan, D. (1999). A selective review of treatments for children with autism: Description and methodological considerations. *School Psychology Review, 28*(44), 559–575.

Gresham, F., Van, M., & Cook, C. (2006). Social skills training for teaching replacement behaviors: Remediating acquisition deficits in at-risk students. *Behavioral Disorders, 31*(4), 363–377.

Gresham, F. M., & Kern, L. (2004). Internalizing behavior problems in children and adolescents. In R. Rutherford, M. Quinn, & S. Mathur (Eds.), *Handbook of research in emotional and behavioral disorders.* New York, NY: Guilford Press.

Grier, E. C., & Hodges, H. F. (1998). HIV/AIDS: A challenge in the classroom. *Public Health Nursing, 15*(4), 257–262.

Grisham-Brown, J., Hemmeter, M. L., & Pretti-Frontczak, K. (2005). *Blended practices for teaching young children in inclusive settings.* Baltimore, MD: Brookes.

Gross, M., & Van Vliet, V. (2003). *Radical acceleration of highly gifted students.* Sydney, Australia: University of South Wales.

Grzywacz, P. (Ed.). (2001). *Students with disabilities and special education* (18th ed.). Birmingham, AL: Oakstone.

Guiberson, M. M., Barrett, K. C., Jancosek, E. G., & Itano, C. Y. (2006). Language maintenance and loss in preschool-age children of Mexican immigrants: Longitudinal study. *Communication Disorders Quarterly, 28*(1), 4–17.

Guralnick, M. (1997). *The effectiveness of early intervention.* Baltimore, MD: Brookes.

Guralnick, M. (1998). Effectiveness of early intervention: A developmental perspective. *American Journal of Mental Retardation, 102*(4), 319–345.

Guralnick, M. (2001). A framework for change in early childhood inclusion. In M. Guralnick (Ed.), *Early childhood inclusion: Focus on change* (pp. 3–38). Baltimore, MD: Brookes.

Guralnick, M., Hammond, M., Connor, R., & Neville, B. (2006). Stability, change, and correlates of the peer relationships of young children with mild developmental delays. *Child Development, 77*(2), 312–324.

Guralnick, M. J. (Ed.). (2005). *The developmental systems approach to early intervention.* Baltimore, MD: Brookes.

Guralnick, M. J., Conner, R. T., & Johnson, L. C. (2009). Home-based peer social networks of young children with Down syndrome: A developmental perspective. *American Journal on Intellectual and Developmental Disabilities, 114*(5), 340–355.

Hall, L. J. (2009). *Autism spectrum disorders: From theory to practice.* Columbus, OH: Merrill Publishing Co.

Hallahan, D. P., & Mock, D. R. (2003). A brief history of the field of learning disabilities. In H. L. Swanson, K. R. Harris, & S. Graham (Eds.), *Handbook of learning disabilities* (pp. 16–29). New York, NY: Guilford Press.

Hallahan, D., & Mercer, C. (2002). Learning disabilities: Historical perspective. In R. Bradley, L. Danielson, & D. Hallahan (Eds.), *Identification of learning disabilities: Research to practice* (pp. 1–67). Mahwah, NJ: Erlbaum.

Halpern, R. (2000). Early childhood intervention. In J. Shonkoff & S. Meisels (Eds.), *Handbook of early intervention* (pp. 361–386). New York, NY: Cambridge University Press.

Hammil, D. (2004). What we know about correlates of reading. *Exceptional Children, 70*(4), 453–468.

Hanks, J., & Velaski, A. (2003). A cooperative collaboration between speech-language pathology and deaf education. *Teaching Exceptional Children, 36*(4), 58–63.

Harms, T., & Clifford, R. (1980). *Infant/toddler environmental rating scales.* New York, NY: Teachers College Press.

Harms, T., Cryer, D., & Clifford, R. M. (1990). *Infant/toddler environment rating scale.* New York, NY: Teachers College Press.

Harrison, A., & Coleman, M. R. (2004). *Do you teach some who . . . : An observational reporting procedure to identify gifted behaviors in children.* Chapel Hill, NC: University of North Carolina, Frank Porter Graham Child Development Institute, Project U-STARS PLUS.

Harry, B. (1997). Application and misapplications of ecological principles in working with families from diverse cultural backgrounds. In J. Paul, M. Churton, W. Morse, A. Duchnowski, B. Epanchin, P. Osnes, & R. Smith (Eds.), *Special education practice: Applying the knowledge, affirming the values and creating the future* (pp. 156–170). Pacific Grove, CA: Brooks/Cole.

Harry, B. (2007). The disproportionate placement of ethnic minorities in special education. In L. Florian (Ed.), *The Sage handbook of special education* (pp. 67–84). New York, NY: Sage Publications.

Harry, B., & Klingner, J. (2006). *Why are so many minority students in special education? Understanding race and disability in schools.* New York, NY: Teachers College Press.

Harry, B., Rueda, R., & Kalyanpur, M. (1999). Cultural reciprocity in sociocultural perspective: Adapting the normalization principle for family collaboration. *Exceptional Children, 66*(1), 123–136.

Hart, J. (2009). Strategies for culturally and linguistically diverse students with special needs. *Preventing School Failure, 53*(3), 197–208.

Hary, B. (2007). The disproportionate placement of ethnic minorities in special education. In L. Florian (Ed.), *The Sage Handbook of Special Education*. London, England: Sage Publications, Ltd.

Hasazi, S., Gordon, L., & Roe, C. (1985). Factors associated with the employment status of handicapped youth exiting high school from 1979 to 1983. *Exceptional Children, 51*, 455–465.

Haskins, R. (2007). Fighting poverty through incentives and work mandates for young men. *The Future of Children* [Policy brief] (pp. 1–7). Princeton, NJ: Brookings Institution Press.

Hasselbring, T. (1997). The future of special education and the role of technology. In J. Paul, M. Churton, W. Morse, A. Duchnowski, B. Epanchin, P. Osnes, & R. Smith (Eds.), *Special education practice: Applying the knowledge, affirming the values and creating the future* (pp. 118–135). Pacific Grove, CA: Brooks/Cole.

Hasselbring, T. (2001). A possible future of special education technology. *Journal of Special Education Technology, 16*(4), 19–26.

Hatlen, P. (1998). Foreword. In S. Z. Sacks & R. K. Silberman (Eds.), *Educating students who have visual impairments with other disabilities* (pp. xv–xvi). Baltimore, MD: Brookes.

Hatlen, P. (2000a). The core curriculum for blind and visually impaired students, including those with additional disabilities. In A. J. Koenig & M. C. Holbrook (Eds.), *Foundations of education: Vol. 2. Instructional strategies for teaching children and youths with visual impairments* (2nd ed., p. 781). New York, NY: AFB Press.

Hatlen, P. (2000b). Historical perspectives. In A. Koenig & M. Holbrook (Eds.), *Foundations of education: Vol. I. History and theory of teaching children and youths with visual impairments* (2nd ed., pp. 1–54). New York, NY: AFB Press.

Hatlen, P. (2003). *Impact of literacy on the expanded curriculum.* Paper presented at the Getting in Touch with Literacy Conference, December 4. Retrieved from http://www.tsvbi. edu/agenda/literacy.htm

Hatton, D. D., Bailey, D. B., Burchinal, M. R., & Ferrell, K. A. (1997). Developmental growth curves of preschool children with vision impairments. *Child Development, 68*(5), 788–806.

Hatton, D. D., Bailey, D. B., Roberts, J. P., Skinner, M., Mayhew, L., Clark, R. D., et al. (2000). Early intervention services for young boys with fragile X syndrome. *Journal of Early Intervention, 23*, 235–251.

Hayes, H., Geers, A. E., Treiman, R., & Moog, J. S. (2009). Receptive vocabulary development in deaf children with cochlear implants: Achievement in an intensive auditory-oral education setting. *Ear & Hearing, 30*(1), 128–135.

Haywood, H. (2006). Broader perspectives on mental retardation. In H. Switzky & S. Greenspan (Eds.), *What is mental retardation?* (pp. xv–xx). Washington, DC: American Association for Mental Retardation.

Hebbler, K., Spiker, D., Bailey, D., Scarborough, A., Mallik, S., Simeonsson, R., Singer, M., & Nelson, L. (2007). *Early intervention for infants and toddlers with disabilities and their families: Participants, services and outcomes: Final report of the National Early Intervention Longitudinal Study (NEILS).* Menlo Park, CA: Stanford Research Institute. Retrieved from http://www.sri .com/neils/

Heinemann, A., & Shontz, F. (1984). Adjustment following disability: Representative case studies. *Rehabilitation Counseling Bulletin, 28*(1), 3–14.

Heller, K. W., Alberto, P. A., Forney, P. E., & Schwartzman, M. N. (Eds.). (2007). *Understanding physical, sensory, and health impairments: Characteristics and educational implications.* Belmont, CA: Wadsworth.

Helmstetter, E., Peck, C., & Giangreco, M. (1994). Outcomes of interaction with peers of moderate and severe disabilities: A statewide survey of high school students. *Journal of the Association for Persons with Severe Handicaps, 19*(4), 260–276.

Hemmeter, M. L., Fox, L., Jack, S., & Broyles, L. (2007). A program-wide model of positive behavior support in early childhood settings. *Journal of Early Intervention, 29*(4), 337–355.

Hennessey, B., & Annabele, T. (2010). Creativity. *Annual Review of Psychology, 61*, 569–597.

Henningsson, G., Kuehn, D. P., Sell, D., Sweeney, T., Trost-Cardamone, J. E., Whitehill, T. L., & Speech Parameters Group. (2008). Universal parameters for reporting speech outcomes in individuals with cleft palate. *Cleft Palate 45*(1), 1–17.

Henry Ford Health System. (2008). *Spinal curvatures and deformities.* Retrieved from http://www. henryford.com/body.cfm?id=39075

Herr, C. M., & Bateman, B. D. (2003). Learning disabilities and the law. In H. L. Swanson, K. R. Harris, & S. Graham (Eds.), *Handbook of learning disabilities* (pp. 57–75). New York, NY: Guilford Press.

Herter, G., Knightly, C., & Steinberg, A. (2002). Hearing: Sound and silences. In M. Batshaw (Ed.), *Children with disabilities* (5th ed., pp. 193–228). Baltimore, MD: Brookes.

Herzberg-Davis, H. & Callahan, C. (2008). Advanced placement and international baccalaureate programs. In J. Plucker & C. Callahan (Eds.). *Critical Issues and Practices in Gifted Education: What the Research Says* (31–34). Waco, TX: Prufrock Press.

Hidi, S., & Ainley, M. (2008). Interest and self-regulation: Relationships between two variables that influence learning. In D. Schunk & B. J. Zimmerman (Eds) *Motivation and self-regulated learning: theory, research, and applications* (p. 77–109). New York/London: Lawrence Erlbaum Associates, Inc.

Hill, J., & Coufal, K. (2005). A retrospective examination of social skills, linguistics, and student outcomes. *Communication Disorders Quarterly, 27*(1), 33–46.

Hill, J. L., & Davis, A. C. (1999). *Meeting the needs of students with special physical and health needs.* Upper Saddle River, NJ: Prentice-Hall.

Hitchcock, C., Meyer, A., Rose, D., & Jackson, R. (2002). Providing new access to the general curriculum: Universal design for learning. *Teaching Exceptional Children, 32*, 8–17.

Hoeft, F., Hernandez, A., McMillon, G., Taylor-Hill, H., Martindale, J., Meyler, A., Keller, T., Siok, W. T., Deutsch, G. K., Just, M. A., Whitfield-Gabrieli, S., & Gabrieli, J. D. (2006). Neural basis of dyslexia: A comparison between dyslexic and nondyslexic children equated for reading ability. *The Journal of Neuroscience, 26*(42), 10700–10708.

Hoff, E. (2004). Progress, but not a full solution to the logical problem of language acquisition. *Journal of Child Language, 31*, 923–926.

Hoff, E. (2009). *Language development* (4th ed.). Belmont, CA: Wadsworth Cengage Learning.

Hoff, E., and Elledge, C. (2005). Bilingualism as one of many environmental variables that affect language development. In J. Cohen, K. T. McAlister, K. (Eds.), *Proceedings of the 4th International Symposium on Bilingualism* (pp. 1034–1040). Sommerville, MD: Cascadilla Press.

Hoglund, T. (1999). Time magazine covers gene therapy. Retrieved from www.mdsupport.org/library/jgenether.html

Hojnoski, R., Caskie, G., Gischlar, K., Key, J., Barry, A., & Hughes, C. (2009). Data display preference, acceptability, and accuracy among urban Head Start teachers. *Journal of Early Intervention, 32*(1), 38–53.

Hojnoski, R., Gischlar, K., & Missall, K. (2009). Improving child outcomes with data-based decision making graphing data. *Young Exceptional Children, 12*(4) 15–30.

Holahan, C., & Sears, R. (1995). *The gifted group in later maturity*. Stanford, CA: Stanford University Press.

Holbrook, A. J., Koenig, M. C., & Rex, E. J. (2010). Instruction of literacy skills to children and youths with low vision. In A. Corn & J. Erin (Ed.), *Foundations of low vision: Clinical and functional perspectives* (2nd ed., pp. 484–526). New York, NY: American Foundation for the Blind.

Holbrook, M. C., & Koenig, A. J. (2000). *Foundations of education*. New York, NY: AFB Press.

Hollingworth, L. (1942). *Children above 180 IQ*. New York, NY: World Book.

Horner, R., Sugai, G., Swolenski, K., Eber, L., Nakasoto, J., Todd, A., & Zsperanzay, J. (2009). A randomized, wait-list controlled effectiveness trial assessing school-wide positive behavior support in elementary schools. *Journal of Positive Behavior Interventions. 11*, 133–145.

Horowitz, S., Kaloi, L., & Petroff, S. (2007). *Transition to kindergarten: policy implications for struggling learners and those who may be at risk for learning disabilities*. New York, NY: National Center for Learning Disabilities.

Hua, C. B., & Coleman, M. R. (2002). Preparing twice exceptional students for adult lives: A critical need. *Understanding Our Gifted 14*(2), 17–19.

Huebner, K. (2000). Visual impairment. In M. Holbrook & A. Koenig (Eds.), *Foundations of education: History and theory of teaching children and youth with visual impairments* (pp. 55–76). New York, NY: AFB Press.

Hughes, M., Dote-Kwan, J., & Dolendo, J. (1998). A close look at the cognitive play of preschoolers with visual impairments in the home. *Exceptional Children, 64*(4), 451–462.

Human Genome Project (n.d.). Retrieved from http://www.ornl.gov/sci/techresources/Human_Genome/home.shtml#index

Hunt, J. M. (1961). *Intelligence and experience*. New York, NY: Ronald Press.

Hunt, P., & McDonnell, J. (2007). Inclusive education. In S. Odom, B. Horner, M. Snell, & J. Blacher (Eds.), *Handbook of developmental disabilities* (pp. 269–291). New York, NY: Guilford Press.

Hunt, P., Soto, G., Maier, J., & Doering, K. (2003). Collaborative teaming to support students at risk and students with severe disabilities in general education classrooms. *Exceptional Children, 69*(3), 315–332.

Hwa-Froelich, D., Kasambira, D. C., & Moleski, A. M. (2007). Communicative functions of African American Head Start children. *Communication Disorders Q*uarterly, 28(2), 77–91.

Hynd, G. (1992). Neurological aspects of dyslexia. *Journal of Learning Disabilities, 25*, 100–113.

Hyter, Y. D. (2007). Pragmatic language assessment: A pragmatics-as-social-practice model. *Topics in Language Disorders, 27*(2), 128–145.

Immordino-Yang, M.H., & Damasio, A. (2007). We feel, therefore we learn: The relevance of affective and social neuroscience to education. *Mind, Brain, and Education, 1*(1), 3–10.

Individuals with Disabilities Education Improvement Act of 2004, PL 108–446, U. S. Department of Education, Washington, DC.

Jackson, L., Ryndak, D. L., & Billingsley, F. (2000). Useful practices in inclusive education: A preliminary view of what experts in moderate to severe disabilities are saying. *Journal of the Association for Persons with Severe Handicaps, 25*(3), 129–141.

Jenkins, J., & O'Connor, R. (2002). Identification and intervention for young children with reading/learning disabilities. In R. Bradley, L. Danielson, & D. Hallahan (Eds.), *Identification of learning disabilities: Research to practice* (pp. 99–172). Mahwah, NJ: Erlbaum.

Jenkins, J., Speltz, M., & Odom, S. (1985). Integrating normal and handicapped preschoolers: Effects on child development and social interaction. *Exceptional Children, 52*(1), 7–17.

Jensen, E. (1998). *Teaching with the brain in mind*. Alexandria, VA: Association for Supervision and Curriculum Development.

Jensen, E. (2000). *Different brains, different learners: How to reach the hard to reach*. San Diego, CA: The Brain Store.

Jensen, E. P. (2008). A fresh look at brain-based education. *Phi Delta Kappan, 89*(6), 408–417.

Johnsen, S. K. (Ed.). (2004). *Identifying gifted students: A practical guide*. Waco, TX: Prufrock Press and Texas Association for the Gifted and Talented.

Johnson, J. R., & McIntosh, A. S. (2009). Toward a cultural perspective and understanding of the disability and deaf experience in special and multicultural education. *Remedial and Special Education, 30*(2), 67–83.

Johnson, K. L., Dudgeon, B., Kuehn, C., & Walker, W. (2007). Assistive technology use among adolescents and young adults with spina bifida. *American Journal of Public health, 97*(2), 330–336.

Joint Committee on Infant Hearing. (2007). *Year 2007 position statement: Principles and guidelines for early hearing detection and intervention*. Available from www.asha.org/policy

Jones, M. (2009). A study of novice special educators' views of evidence-based practices. *Teacher Education and Special Education, 32*(1), 101–120.

Jones, T. W, Jones, J. K., & Ewing, K. M. (2006). Students with multiple disabilities. In D. F. Moore and D. S. Martin (Eds.), *Deaf learners: Developments in curriculum and instruction*. (pp. 127–143). Washington, DC: Gallaudet University Press.

Jung, L. (2003). National learning opportunities for young exceptional children. *Exceptional Children, 6*(3), 21–26.

Jusczyk, E. W. (1997). *The discovery of spoken language*. Cambridge, MA: MIT Press.

Just, M., & Varma, S. (2007). The organization of thinking: What functional brain imaging reveals about the neuroarchitecture of complex cognition. *Cognitive, Affective, and Behavioral Neuroscience, 1*(3), 153–191.

Justice, L., Mashburn, A. J., Hamre, B. K., and Pianta, R. C. (2008). Quality of language and literacy instruction in preschool classrooms serving at-risk pupils. *Early Childhood Research Quarterly, 23*, 51–68.

Kagan, S. (1989). The structural approach to cooperative learning. *Educational Leadership, 47*(4), 12–15.

Kahn, L., Hurth, J., Kasperzak, C. M., Diefendorf, M. J., Goode, S. E., & Ringwalt, S. S. (2009). The National Early Childhood Technical Assistance Center Model for long-term systems change. *Topics in Early Childhood Special Education, 29*, 24–40.

Kaiser, A. (2000). Teaching functional communication skills. In M. Snell & F. Brown (Eds.), *Instruction of students with severe disabilities* (5th ed., pp. 453–492). Upper Saddle River, NJ: Merrill.

Kaiser, A., & Gray, D. (1993). *Enhancing children's research foundation for intervention: Vol. 2. Communication and language series.* Baltimore, MD: Brookes.

Kaiser, A., & Hancock, T. (2003). Teaching parents new skills to support their young children's development. *Infants and Young Children, 26*(1), 9–21.

Kaiser, J., & Voss, S. (2009). Gene therapy in a new light. *Smithsonian, 39* (10), 54–61.

Kam, C. M., Greenberg, M., & Kusche, C. (2004). Sustained effects of the PATHS curriculum on the social and psychological adjustment of children in social and psychological adjustment of children in special education. *Journal of Emotional & Behavioral Disorders, 12*(2), 66–78.

Kame'enui, E. J. (2007). A new paradigm: Responsiveness to intervention. *Teaching Exceptional Children, 39*(5), 6–7.

Kana, R., Keller, T., Chertassky, V., Minshew, N., & Just, M. (2008). Atypical frontal-posterior synchronization of Theory of Mind regions in autism during mental state attribution. *Social Neuroscience, 4*(2), 135–152.

Kanner, L. (1943). Autistic disturbance of affective contact. *Nervous Child, 2*, 217–250.

Kapperman, G., Heinze, T., & Sticken, J. (2000). Mathematics. In A. J. Koenig & M. C. Holbrook (Eds.), *Foundations of education: Vol. 2. Instructional strategies for teaching children and youths with visual impairments* (2nd ed., pp. 370–399). New York, NY: American Foundation for the Blind.

Kasari, C., & Bauminger, N. (1998). Social and emotional development in children with mental retardation. In J. Burack, R. Hodapp, & E. Zigler (Eds.), *Handbook of mental retardation and development* (pp. 411–433). New York, NY: Cambridge University Press.

Katsiyannis, A., Landrum, T., & Reid, R. (2002, Winter). Rights and responsibilities under Section 504. *Beyond Behavior*, 9–15.

Kauffman, J., Brigham, F., & Mock, D. (2004). Historical to contemporary perspectives of the field of behavior disorders. In R. Rutherford, M. Quinn, & S. Mathur (Eds.), *Handbook of research in emotional and behavioral disorders* (pp. 15–31). New York, NY: Guilford Press.

Kauffman, J. M. (2002). *Education reform: Bright people sometimes say stupid things about education.* Lanham, MD: Scarecrow Education.

Kavale, K. (2007). Quantitative research synthesis: meta-analysis of research on meeting special educational needs. In L. Florian (Ed.), *The Sage Handbook of Special Education.* London, England: Sage Publications, Ltd.

Kavale, K., Mathur, S., & Mostert, M. (2004). Social skills training and teaching social behavior to students with emotional and behavioral disorders. In R. Rutherford, M. Quinn, & S. Mathur (Eds.), *Handbook of research in emotional and behavioral disorders* (pp. 446–461). New York, NY: Guilford Press.

Kavale, K. A., & Forness, S. R. (1999). Interference, inhibition, and learning disability: A commentary on Dempster and Corkill. *Educational Psychology Review, 11*(2), 97–104.

Kavale, K. A., Holdnack, J. A., & Mostert, M. P. (2005). Responsiveness to intervention and the identification of specific learning disability: A critique and alternative proposal. *Learning Disability Quarterly, 28*(1), 2–16.

Kearney, K. (1999). Gifted children and homeschooling: Historical and contemporary perspectives. In S. Cline & K. Hegeman (Eds.), *Gifted education in the twenty-first century* (pp. 175–194). Delray Beach, FL: Winslow Press.

Kerr, B. A., & Cohn, S. J. (2001). *Smart boys: Talent, manhood, and the search for meaning.* Scottsdale, AZ: Great Potential.

Kerr, M., & Nelson, C. (2002). *Addressing behavior problems* (4th ed.). Upper Saddle River, NJ: Prentice Hall.

Key, J. D., Brown, R. T., Marsh, L. D., Spratt, E. G., & Recknor, J. C. (2001). Depressive symptoms in adolescents with a chronic illness. *Children's Health Care, 30*(4), 283–292.

Keyser-Marcus, L., Briel, L., Sherron-Targett, P., Yasuda, S., Johnson, S., & Wehman, P. (2002). Enhancing the schooling of students with traumatic brain injury. *Teaching Exceptional Children, 34*(4), 62–67.

KidsHealth. (2009, April). Cerebral Palsy. Retrieved from kidshealth.org

KidsHealth. (2010, June). Your brain & nervous system. Retrieved from kidshealth.org

Kim, A., Vaughn, S., Elbaum, B., Hughes, M., Sloan, C., & Sridhar, D. (2003). Effect of toys on group composition for children with disabilities: A synthesis. *Journal of Early Intervention, 25*(3), 189–205.

King-Sears, M., & Carpenter, C. (2005). Teaching self-management to elementary students with developmental disabilities. In M. Wehmeyer & M. Agran (Eds.), *Mental retardation and intellectual disabilities: Teaching students using innovative and research-based strategies.* Boston, MA: Merrill/Prentice Hall.

Kirby, J. R., Silvestri, R., Allingham, B. H., Parrila, R., & LaFave, C. B. (2008). Learning strategies and study approaches of postsecondary students with dyslexia. *Journal of Learning Disabilities, 41*(1), 85–96.

Kirk, S. (1950). A project for pre-school mentally handicapped children. *American Journal of Mental Deficiency, 55*, 305–310.

Kitano, M. (2007). Gifted girls. In J. Plucker & C. Callahan (Eds.) *Critical issues and practices in gifted education* (pp. 225–240). Waco, TX: Prufrock Press.

Klingner, J. & Harry, B. (2006). The special education referral and decision-making process for English language learners. *Teachers College Record, 108*, 1–20.

Klingner, J., Blanchett, W., & Harry, B. (2007). Race, culture, and developmental disabilities. In S. Odom, B. Horner, M. Snell, & J. Blacher (Eds.), *Handbook of developmental disabilities* (pp. 55–76). New York, NY: Guilford Press.

Klingner, J., & Harry, B. (2006). The special education referral and decision-making process for English language learners. *Teachers College Record, 108*, 1–20.

Knight, M. (2003). A natural history of language. *Contemporary Psychology, 48*(3), 306–308.

Kochhar-Bryant, C. A. (2007). The summary of performance as transition "passport" to employment and independent living. *Assessment for Effective Intervention, 32*(3), 160–170.

Koegel, R., & Koegel, L. (1995). *Teaching children with autism: Strategies for initiating positive interactions and improving learning opportunities.* Baltimore, MD: Brookes.

Koegel, R. L., & Koegel, L. K. (2007). *Pivotal response treatments for autism: communication, social & academic development*. Baltimore MD: Paul H. Brookes.

Koenig, A., & Holbrook, M. (2000). Literacy skills. In A. Koenig & M. Holbrook (Eds.), *Foundations of education: Vol. II. Instructional strategies for teaching children and youths with visual impairments* (2nd ed., pp. 264–329). New York, NY: Foundation for the Blind Press.

Koenig, A., & Rex, E. (1996). Instruction of literacy skills to children and youths with low vision. In A. Corn & A. Koenig (Eds.), *Foundations of low vision: Clinical and functional perspectives* (pp. 280–305). New York, NY: American Foundation for the Blind.

Koenig, A. J., & Holbrook, M. C. (2010). Selection and assessment of learning and literacy media for children and youths with low vision. In A. Corn & J. Erin (Eds.), *Foundations of low vision: Clinical and functional perspectives* (2nd ed., pp. 442–483). New York, NY: American Foundation for the Blind.

Koester, L. S., Karkowski, A., & Traci, M. (1998). How do deaf and hearing mothers regain eye contact when their infants look away? *American Annals of the Deaf, 143*(1), 5–13.

Kolloff, P. (2003). State supported residential high schools. In N. Colangelo & C. Davis (Eds.), *Handbook of gifted education* (pp. 219–228). Boston, MA: Allyn & Bacon.

Kolvin, I., Miller, F.J., Scott, D.M., Gatzanis, S.R., & Fleeting, M. (1990). *Continuities of depravation. The Newcastle 1,000 family study*. (1990) Aldershot, England.

Konidaris, J. (1997). A sibling's perspective on autism. In D. Cohen & F. Volkman (Eds.), *Handbook of autism and pervasive developmental disorders* (2nd ed., pp. 1021–1031). New York, NY: Wiley.

Kortering, L. J., Braziel, P. M., & Tomkins, J. R. (2002). The challenge of school completion among youths with behavioral disorders: Another side of the story. *Behavioral Disorders, 27*, 142–154.

Kosine, N. R. (2007). Preparing students with learning disabilities for postsecondary education: What the research literature tells us about transition programs. *Journal of Special Education Leadership, 20*(2), 93–104.

Krajicek, M., Steinke, T., Hertzden, D., Anastasiow, N., & Skandel, S. (2003a). *Handbook for the care of infants and toddlers with disabilities and chronic conditions*. Austin, TX: PRO-ED.

Krajicek, M., Steinke, T., Hertzdeng, D., Anastasiow, N., & Skandel, S. (Eds.). (2003b). *Instructor's guide for the handbook for the care of infants and toddlers with disabilities and chronic conditions*. Austin, TX: PRO-ED.

Krauss, M. W., Seltzer, M. M., Gordon, R., & Friedman, D. H. (1996). Binding ties: The roles of adult siblings of persons with mental retardation. *Mental Retardation, 34*, 83–93.

Krauss, R., Thurman, K., Brodsky, W., Betancourt, L., Giannetta, J., & Hart, H. (2000). Caregivers' interaction behavior with prenatally cocaine-exposed and non-exposed preschoolers. *Journal of Early Intervention, 23*(1), 62–73.

Kravets, M. (2006). Hidden disabilities: Another diverse population [Electronic version]. *Journal of College Admission, 190*, 18–25.

Kuehn, B. M. (2007). CDC: Autism spectrum disorders common. *JAMA: Journal of the American Medical Association, 297*, 940.

Kumar, R., & Christian, S. (2009). Genetics of autism spectrum disorders. *Current Neurological Neuroscience Reports, 9*(3), 188–197.

Kunzman, R. (2008). Homeschooling. In J. Plucker & C. Callahan (Eds.). *Critical Issues and Practices in Gifted Education: What the Research Says* (155–166). Waco, TX: Prufrock Press.

Kurima, K., Peters, L., Yang, Y., Riazuddin, S., Ahmet, Z., Naz, S., Arnaud, D., Drury, S., Mo, J., Makishima, T., Ghosh, M.,

Menon, P., Deshmukh, D., Oddoux, C., Ostrer, H., Khan, S., Riazuddin, S., Deininger, P., Hamton, L., Sullivan, S., Batty, J., Keats, B., Wilcox, E., Friedman, T., & Griffith, A. (2002). Dominant and recessive deafness caused by mutations of a novel gene, TMC1, required for cochlear hair-cell function. *Nature Genetics, 30*, 277–284.

Lacava, P. G., Golan, O., Baron-Cohen, S., & Myles, B. S. (2007). Using assistive technology to teach emotion recognition to students with Asperger syndrome. *Remedial and Special Education, 28*(3), 174–181.

Lahey, M., & Bloom, L. (1988). *Language disorders and language development*. Columbus, OH: Merrill.

Lahm, E. L., & Nichels, B. L. (1999). What do you know? Assistive technology competencies for special educators. *Teaching Exceptional Children, 32*, 56–63.

Lansing, A. E., Max, J. E., Delis, D. C., Fox, P. T., Lancaster, J., Manes, F. F., & Schatz, A. (2004). Verbal learning and memory after childhood stroke. *Journal of the International Neuropsychological Society, 10*, 742–752.

Lazarus, S., Thurlow, M., Lail, K., & Christensen, L. (2009). A longitudinal analysis of state accommodation policies. *Journal of Special Education, 43*(2), 67–80.

Leber's congenital amaurosis. (2010, July). In *Wikipedia, The Free Encyclopedia*. Retrieved July, 2010, from http://en.wikipedia.org/w/index.php?title=Leber%27s_congenital_amaurosis&oldid=383286527.

Lee, A. S. Y., Law, J., & Gibbon, F. E. (2009). Electropalatography for articulation disorders associated with cleft palate (review). *The Cochrane Library, 4*, 1–23.

Lee, V., & Burkam, D. (2002). *Inequality at the starting gate: Social background differences in achievement as children begin school*. Washington, DC: Economic Policy Institute.

Leet, A., Dormans, J., & Tosi, L. (2002). Muscles, bones, and nerves: The body's framework. In M. Batshaw (Ed.), *Children with disabilities* (5th ed., pp. 263–286). Baltimore, MD: Brookes.

Leffert, J., Siperstein, G., & Millikan, E. (2000). Understanding social adaptation in children with mental retardation. *Exceptional Children, 66*(4), 530–545.

Leong, S. (1996). Preschool orientation and mobility: A review of the literature. *Journal of Visual Impairment and Blindness, 90*, 145–153.

Lerner, J., & Johns, B. (2009). *Learning disabilities and related mild disabilities*. Boston, MA: Houghton Mifflin.

Lerner, R. M. (1986). *The nature of human plasticity*. New York, NY: Cambridge University Press.

LeRoy, M. (Director). (1956). The bad seed [Motion Picture]. United States: Warner Bros. Pictures.

Levine, M. (2003). *The myth of laziness*. New York, NY: Simon & Schuster.

Levine, M. (2005). *Ready or not, here life comes*. New York, NY: Simon & Schuster.

Levine, M. (2006, Summer). The NBO promotes family-centered care in early intervention. *Ab Initio*. Retrieved from www.brazelton-institute.com/abinitio2006summer/art3.html

Lewis, T., Hudson, S., Richter, M., & Johnson, N. (2004). Scientifically supported practices in emotional and behavioral disorders: A proposed approach and brief review of current practices. *Behavioral Disorders, 29*(3), 247–259.

Lewis, T., Lewis-Palmer, T., Newcomer, L., & Stichter, J. (2004). Applied behavior analysis and the education and treatment of students with emotional and behavioral disorders. In R. Rutherford, M. Quinn, & S. Mathur (Eds.), *Handbook of research in emotional and behavior disorders* (pp. 523–545). New York, NY: The Guilford Press.

Lewis, T., & Russo, R. (1998). Educational assessment for students who have visual impairments with other disabilities. In S. Sacks & R. Silberman (Eds.), *Educating students who have visual impairments with other disabilities* (pp. 39–72). Baltimore, MD: Brookes.

Lewis, M. D., & Stieben, J. (2004). Emotion regulation in the brain: conceptual issues and directions for developmental research. *Child Development, 75*(2), 371–376.

Liefert, F. (2003). Introduction to visual impairment. In S. Goodman & S. Wittenstein (Eds.), *Collaborative assessment* (pp. 1–22). New York, NY: American Foundation for the Blind.

Light, S., Beukelman, D., & Reichle, B. (2003). *Communicative competence: Who uses AAC.* Baltimore, MD: Brookes.

Lillo-Martin, D. (1997). In support of the language acquisition device. In M. Marschark, P. Simple, D. Lillo-Martin, R. Campbell, & V. Everhart (Eds.), *Relations of language and thought.* New York, NY: Oxford University Press.

Linder, T. (1993). *Transitional play-based assessment.* Baltimore, MD: Brookes.

Linn, B., & Shore, B. (2008). Critical thinking. In J. Plucker & C. Callahan (Eds.), *Critical issues and practices in gifted education* (pp. 155–165). Waco, TX: Prufrock Press.

Linnenbrink, E. A., & Pintrich, P. R. (2004). Role of affect in cognitive processing in academic contexts. In D. Dai & R.J. Sterberg (Eds) *Motivation, emotion, and cognition.* (pp. 57–87). New Jersey/London: Lawrence Erlbaum Associates, Inc.

Liptak, G. (2002). Neural tube defects. In M. Batshaw (Ed.), *Children with disabilities* (5th ed., pp. 467–492). Baltimore, MD: Brookes.

Loeber, R., & Farrington, D. (Eds.). (1998). *Serious and violent juvenile offenders: Risk factors and successful interventions.* London, England: Sage.

Lord, C. (1995). Follow-up of two-year-olds referred for possible autism. *Journal of Child Psychology and Psychiatry, 36,* 1365–1382.

Lord, C. (2001). *Children with autism.* Washington, DC: National Academy of Sciences.

Lord, C., & Risi, S. (2000). Diagnosis of autism spectrum disorders in young children. In A. Wetherby, & B. Prizant (Eds.), *Autism spectrum disorders* (pp. 11–30). Baltimore, MD: Brookes.

Lovaas, O., & Buch, G. (1997). Intensive behavioral intervention with young children with autism. In N. Singh, *Prevention and treatment of severe behavior problems.* Pacific Grove, CA: Brooks/Cole.

Lovaas, O. J. (1993). The development of a treatment project for developmentally disabled and autistic children. *Journal of Applied Behavior Analyses, 26*(4), 617–630.

Love, J., Harrison, L., Sagi-Schwartz, A., van IJzendoorn, M., Ross, C., Ungerer, J., et al. (2003). Child care quality matters. *Child Development, 74*(4), 1021–1033.

Loveland, K., & Tunali-Kotoski, B. (1998). Development of adaptive behavior in persons with mental retardation. In J. Burack, R. Hodapp, & E. Zigler (Eds.), *Handbook of mental retardation and development* (pp. 521–541). New York, NY: Cambridge University Press.

Lowenfeld, B. (Ed.). (1973). *The visually handicapped child in school.* New York, NY: Day.

Lubinski, D. (2009). Cognitive epidemiology: With emphasis on untangling cognitive ability and socioeconomic status. *Intelligence, 37,* 625–633.

Lubinski, D., & Benbow, C. P. (2006). Study of mathematically precocious youth after 35 years: Uncovering antecedents for the development of math-science expertise. *Perspectives in Psychological Science, 1,* 316–345.

Lubinski, D., Benbow, C. P., Webb, R. M., & Bleske-Rechek, A. (2006). Tracking exceptional human capital over two decades. *Psychological Science, 27,* 194–199.

Lubinski, D., Webb, R. M., Morelock, M. J., & Benbow, C. P. (2001). Top 1 in 10,000: A 10-year follow-up of the profoundly gifted. *Journal of Applied Psychology, 86,* 718–729.

Luby, J. L., Heffelfinger, A., Mrakotsky, C., Brown, K., Hessler, M., Wallis, J., & Spitznagel, E. (2003). The Clinical Picture of Depression in Preschool Children. *Journal of the American Academy of Child Adolescent Psychiatry, 42*(3): 340–348.

Luckner, J., & Handley, C. M. (2008). A summary of the reading comprehension research undertaken with students who are deaf or hard of hearing. *American Annals of the Deaf, 153*(1), 6–36.

Luckner, J. L. (2006). Evidence-based practices with students who are deaf. *Communication Disorders Quarterly, 28*(1), 49–52.

Luckner, J. L., & Muir, S. (2001). Successful students who are deaf in general education settings [Electronic version]. *American Annals of the Deaf, 146*(5), 435–446.

Luckner, J. L., Sebald, A. M., Cooney, J., Young, J., & Muir, S. G. (2005/2006). An examination of the evidence-based literacy research in deaf education [Electronic version]. *American Annals of the Deaf, 150*(5), 443–456.

Lundy, B. (2003). Father and mother-infant face-to-face interactions: Differences in mind-related comments and infant attachment? *Infant Behavior and Development, 26,* 200–212.

Luze, G., & Hughes, K. (2008). Using individual growth and development indicators to assess child and program outcomes. *Young Exceptional Children, 12*(1), 31–41.

Lynas, W. (2000). Communication options. In J. Stokes (Ed.), *The hearing impaired infant: The first eighteen months* (pp. 98–128). London, England: Whurr. (Distributed by Paul H. Brookes)

Lyon, G. R. (1995). Toward a definition of dyslexia. *Annals of Dyslexia, 45,* 3–27.

Lytle, R., & Rovins, N. (1997). Reforming deaf education. *American Annals of the Deaf, 142*(1), 7–15.

MA: Pearson. pp. 516.

Maag, J. (2007). Behavioral theory and practice: current and future issues. In L. Florian (Ed.). *The Sage Handbook of Special Education.* London, England: Sage Publications, Ltd.

Maccini, P., Mulcahy, C. A., & Wilson, M. G. (2007). A follow-up of mathematics interventions for secondary students with learning disabilities. *Learning Disabilities Practice, 22*(1), 58–75.

MacMillan, D., Siperstein, G., & Heffert, J. (2006). *Children with mild mental retardation: A challenge for classification practices—Revised.* Washington, DC: American Association on Mental Retardation.

MacMillan, D. L., & Siperstein, G. N. (2002). Learning disabilities as operationally defined by schools. In R. Bradley, L. Danielson, & D. P. Hallahan (Eds.), *Identification of learning disabilities: Research to practice* (pp. 287–333). Mahwah, NJ: Erlbaum.

Maguire, M. J., Hirsh-Pasek, K., Golinkoff, R. M., Imai, M., Haryu, E., Vanegas, S., Okada, H., Pulverman, R., & Sanchez-Davis, B. (2010). A developmental shift from similar to language-specific strategies in verb acquisition: A comparison of English, Spanish, and Japanese. *Cognition, 114,* 299–319.

Mahoney, G., & Perales, F. (2003). Using relationship-focused intervention to enhance the social-emotional functioning of young children with autism spectrum disorders. *TECSE, 23,* 74–86.

Mainzer, R. W., Deschler, D., Coleman, M. R., Kozleski, E., & Rodriguez-Walling, M. (2003). To ensure the learning of every child with a disability: Report to the Council of Exceptional Children. *Exceptional Children, 35,* 1–12.

Maisog, J. M., Einbinder, E. R., Flowers, D. L., Turkeltaub, P.E., & Eden, G.F. (2008). A meta-analysis of functional neuroimaging studies of dyslexia. *Annals of the New York Academy of Sciences, 1145,* 237–259.

Maller, S. J. (2003). Intellectual assessment of deaf people: A critical review of core concepts and issues. In M. Marschark & P. Spencer (Eds.). *Oxford handbook of deaf studies, language and education.* (pp. 451–463). New York: Oxford University Press.

Malloy, P. (2009). Who are children who are deaf-blind? *Division on Visual Impairments Quarterly, 54*(3), 5–7.

March of Dimes. (2010). *Birth defects and genetic conditions.* Retrieved from www.marchofdimes. com/pnhec/4439.asp

Marland, S. (1972). *Education of the gifted and talented.* Report to the Congress of the United States by the U.S. Commissioner of Education Washington, DC: U.S. Government Printing Office.

Marschark, M., Lang, H., & Albertini, J. (2002). *Educating deaf students.* New York, NY: Oxford University Press.

Marschark, M., Rhoten, C., & Fabich, M. (2007). Effects of cochlear implants on children's reading and academic achievement. *Journal of Deaf Studies and Deaf Education, 12*(3), 269–282.

Marshall, J. K., & Mirenda, P. (2002). Parent-professional collaboration for positive behavior support in the home. *Focus on Autism and Developmental Disabilities, 17*, 216–228.

Martindale, M. (2007). Children with significant hearing loss: Learning to listen, talk, and read: Evidence-based best practices. *Communication Disorders Quarterly, 28*(2), 73–76.

Mason, R., Williams, D., Kana, R., Minshew, N., & Just, M. (2008). Theory of Mind disruption and recruitment of the right hemisphere during narrative comprehension in autism. *Neuropsychologia, 46*, 269–280.

Mattison, R. (2004). Psychiatric and psychological assessment of emotional and behavior disorders during school mental health consultation. In R. Rutherford, M. Quinn, & D. Mathur (Eds.) *Handbook of research in emotional and behavior disorders.* New York, NY: The Guilford Press, 163–180.

Mauk, G., & White, K. (1995). Giving children a sound beginning: The promise of universal hearing screening. *Volta Review, 97*(1), 5–32.

Maxwell, N. L., Bellisimo, Y., & Mergendoller, J. (2001). Problem-based learning: Modifying the medical school model for teaching high school economics. *Social Studies, 92*, 73–78.

Mayer, C., & Akamatsu, C. T. (1999). Bilingual-bicultural models of literacy education for deaf students: Considering the claims. *Australian Journal of Education of the Deaf, 2*, 5–9.

McCabe, A., & Champion, T. B. (2010). A matter of vocabulary II: Low-income African American children's performance on the Expressive Vocabulary Test. *Communication Disorders Quarterly, 31*(3), 162–169.

McCandliss, B., & Noble, K. (2003). The development of reading impairment: A cognitive neuroscience model. *Mental Retardation and Developmental Disabilities Research Reviews, 9*, 196–205.

McCarthy, M. (1994). Inclusion and the law: Recent judicial decisions. *Phi Delta Kappa Research Bulletin*, No. 13.

McCartney, K., Burchinal, M., Clarke-Stewart, A., Bub, K., Owen, M., Belsky, J., & NICHD Early Child Care Research Network. (2010). Testing a series of causal propositions relating time in child care to children's externalizing behavior. *Developmental Psychology, 46*(1), 1–17.

McCathren, R., Yoder, P., & Warren, S. (1995). The role of directives in early language intervention. *Journal of Early Intervention, 19*(2), 91–101.

McCoach, D. B., & Siegle, D. (2003). Factors that differentiate underachieving gifted students from high-achieving gifted students. *Gifted Child Quarterly, 47*, 144–154.

McCombs, K., & Moore, D. (2002). Substance abuse prevention and intervention for students with disabilities: A call to educators. *ERIC Digest, E627*.

McConnell, S. (2000). *Interventions to facilitate social interaction for young children with autism: Review of available research and recommendations for educational intervention* [Paper prepared for National Research Council of the National Academy of Sciences]. Minneapolis, MN: University of Minnesota.

McCormick, L., Loeb, D. F., & Schiefelbusch, R. L. (2003). *Supporting children with communication difficulties in inclusive settings: School-based language intervention* (2nd ed.). Needham Heights, MA: Allyn & Bacon.

McGee, G., Feldman, R., & Morrier, M. (1997). Benchmarks of social treatment for children with autism. *Journal of Autism and Developmental Disorders, 27*, 353–364.

McGough, S. M., & Schirmer, B. R. (2005). Teaching reading to children who are deaf: Do the conclusions of the National Reading Panel apply? [Electronic version]. *Review of Educational Research, 75*(1), 83–117.

McGregor, D., & Farrenkopf, C. (2000). Recreation and leisure skills. In A. Koenig & M. Holbrook (Eds.), *Foundations of education: Vol. II. Instructional strategies for teaching children and youths with visual impairments* (2nd ed., pp. 653–678). New York, NY: Foundation for the Blind Press.

McGuffin, P., Riley, B., & Plomin, R. (2001). Toward behavioral genomics. *Science, 291*, 1232–1249.

McLaughlin, A. E., Campbell, F. C., Pungello, E. P., & Skinner, M. (2007). Depressive symptoms in young adults: The influences of the early home environment and early educational childcare. *Child Development, 78*, 746–756.

McLaughlin, J., & Lewis, R. (2001). *Assessing students with special needs* (5th ed.). Upper Saddle River, NJ: Prentice-Hall.

McNamara, J.K., & Willoughby, T. (2010). A longitudinal study of risk-taking behavior in adolescents with learning disabilities. *Learning Disabilities: Research & Practice, 25*(1), 11–24.

McWilliam, R. A., & Bailey, D. B. (1992). Promoting engagement and mastery. In D. B. Bailey & M. Wolery (Eds.), *Teaching infants and preschoolers with disabilities* (2nd ed., pp. 230–255). New York, NY: Macmillan.

McWilliam, R. A., & Casey, A. M. (2008). *Engagement of every child in the preschool classroom.* Baltimore, MD: Brookes.

Mesibov, G. (2006). A tribute to Eric Schopler. Journal of Autism and Developmental Disorders. 36(8), 967–970.

Mesibov, G., Schopler, E., & Hearsey, K. (1994). Structured teaching. In E. Schopler & G. Mesibov (Eds.), *Behavioral issues in autism* (pp. 195–207). New York, NY: Plenum.

Mesibov, G. B. (1999). Are children with autism better off in an autism classroom or multidisability classroom? *Journal of Autism and Developmental Disorders, 29*, 429.

Mesibov, G. B., Shea, V., & Schopler, E. et al. (2005). *The TEACCH approach to autism spectrum disorders.* New York, NY: Kluwer Academic/Plenum.

Metz, I. (1991). Albuquerque, New Mexico. In M. Anderson & P. Goldberg (Eds.), *Cultural competence in screening and assessment* (pp. 8–10). (Available from PACER Center, 4826 Chicago Avenue South, Minneapolis, MN 55417-1095).

Meyer, D., & Vadasy, P., (2007). *Sibshops: Workshops for siblings of children with special needs.* Baltimore, MD: Paul H. Brookes.

Meyer, L. H., Peck, C. A., & Brown, L. (1991). *Critical issues in the lives of people with severe disabilities.* Baltimore, MD: Brookes.

Michaud, L., Semel-Concepcíon, J., Duhaime, A., & Lazar, M. (2002). Traumatic brain injury. In M. Batshaw (Ed.), *Children with disabilities* (5th ed., pp. 525–546). Baltimore, MD: Brookes.

Miles, B., & Riggio, M. (1999). *Remarkable conversations: A guide to developing meaningful communication with children and young adults who are deafblind.* Watertown, MA: Perkins School for the Blind.

Milian, M. (2000). Multicultural issues. In A. Koenig & M. Holbrook (Eds.), *Foundations of education: Vol. I. History and theory of teaching children and youths with visual impairments* (2nd ed., pp. 197–217). New York, NY: American Foundation for the Blind Press.

Milian, M., & Ferrell, D. (1998). *Preparing special educators to meet the needs of students who are learning English as a second language and are visually impaired: A monograph.* (ERIC Document Reproduction Service No. ED426545).

Miller, C. J., Sanchez, J., & Hynd, G. W. (2003). Neurological correlates of reading disabilities. In H. L. Swanson, K. R. Harris, & S. Graham (Eds.), *Handbook of learning disabilities* (pp. 242–255). New York, NY: Guilford Press.

Mistrett, S., Ruffino, A., Lane, S., Robinson, L., Reed, P., & Milbourne, S. (2006). *Technology supports for young children* [TAM Technology Fan]. Arlington, VA: Technology and Media Division (TAM).

Moeller, M. P. (2000). Early intervention and language development in children who are deaf and hard of hearing [Electronic version]. *Pediatrics, 106*(3), e43. Retrieved from http://www.pediatrics.org/cgi/content/full/106/3/e43

Montague, M., Enders, C., & Castor, M. (2005). *A longitudinal study of students at risk for learning behavior and emotional disorders.* Paper presented at the American Educational Researchers Association. Montreal, Canada.

Montessori, M. (1912). *The Montessori method.* New York, NY: Frederick A. Stokes.

Montgomery, J. K. (2006). Your competitive edge: The art of interpersonal communication. *Communication Disorders Quarterly, 28*(1), 56–58.

Moore, D., Cheng, Y., McGrath, P., & Powell, N. (2005). Collaborative virtual environment technology for people with autism. *Focus on Autism and Other Developmental Disabilities, 20*(4), 231–243.

Moores, D. (1996). *Educating the deaf: Psychology, principles, and practices* (4th ed.). Boston, MA: Houghton Mifflin.

Moores, D. (2000). *Educating the deaf: Psychology, principles, and practices* (5th ed.). Boston, MA: Houghton Mifflin.

Morrison, R., Sainato, D., Benchaaban, D., & Endo, S. (2002). Increasing play skills of children with autism using activity schedules and correspondence training. *Journal of Early Intervention, 25*, 58–72.

MSM Productions (2008). What is deaf culture? Retrieved from http://www.deafculture.com/.

Mukherjee, S., Lightfoot, J., & Sloper, P. (2000). The inclusion of pupils with a chronic health condition in mainstream school: What does it mean for teachers? *Educational Research, 42*(1), 59–72.

Muratori, M., Stanley, J., Ng, L., Ng, J., Gross, M., Tao, T. & Tao B. (2006). Insights from SMPY's greatest child prodigies: Drs. Terrence (Terry) Tao and Lenhard (Lenny) Ng reflect on their talent development. *Gifted Child Quarterly, 50*(4), 307–324.

National Academies of Sciences. (2006). *Rising Above the Gathering Storm.* Washington, DC: National Academies Press.

National Association for the Deaf. (2000). *Position statement on cochlear implants.* Retrieved from www.nad.org/issues/health-care/cochlear-implants

National Association for the Deaf. (2008). *Position statement on mental health series for deaf children.* Retrieved from www.nad.org/issues/health-care/mental-health-services/for-deaf-children

National Association for the Deaf. (2010). *Position statement on early hearing detection and intervention.* Retrieved from www.nad.org/issues/early-intervention/position-statement-early-hearing-detection-and-intervention

National Association for the Education of Young Children. (2009). *Developmentally appropriate practice in early childhood programs serving children from birth through age 8* [Position statement]. Washington, DC: Author.

National Association of State Directors of Special Education. (2005). *Response to intervention: Policy considerations and implementations.* Alexandria, VA: Author.

National Information Center on Children and Youth with Disabilities. (2000). *Severe and/or multiple disabilities.* (Available from NICHCY, P.O. Box 1492, Washington, DC, 20013).

National Information Center on Deafness. (1999). Deafness: A fact sheet. (Available from NICD, Gallaudet University, 800 Florida Ave., N.E., Washington, DC 20002-3695.)

National Institute of Child Health and Human Development. (2000). *Report of the National Reading Panel. Teaching children to read: An evidence-based assessment of the scientific research literature on reading and its implications for reading instruction* (NIH Publication No. 00–4769). Washington, DC: U.S. Government Printing Office.

National Institute on Deafness and Other Communication Disorders. (2010). *Hearing loss in children: Delayed speech and language.* (Available from NIDCD Information Clearinghouse, National Institute of Health, One Communication Avenue, Bethesda, MD 20892-3456.)

National Institute of Mental Health. (2001). *Blueprint for change: Research on child and adolescent mental health.* Rockville, MD: Author.

National Institute of Mental Health. (2010). Treatment of children with mental illness. U.S. Dept of Health and Human Services. Retrieved from www.nimh.nih.gov/health

National Organization on Fetal Alcohol Syndrome. (2004). What teachers need to know about FASD. Washington, DC: National Organization on Fetal Alcohol Syndrome.

National Research Council. (2002). *Minority students in special and gifted education.* Washington, DC: National Academy Press.

National Standards Project. (2009). Randolph, MA: National Autism Center.

National Suicide Prevention Lifeline. 1-800-273-8255. Washington, DC: U.S. Department of Health and Human Services.

Neece, C., Blacher, J., & Baker, B. (2010). Impact on siblings of children with intellectual disability: The role of child behavior problems. *American Journal on Intellectual and Developmental Disabilities, 115*(4), 291–306.

Nehring, W. M. (2007). Cultural considerations for children with intellectual and developmental disabilities. *Journal of Pediatric Nursing, 22*(2), 93–102.

Neihart, M. (2000). Gifted children with Asperger's syndrome. *Gifted Child Quarterly, 44*, 222–230.

Neihart, M., Reis, S., Robinson, N., & Moon, S. (Eds.). (2002). *The social and emotional development of gifted children: What do we know?* Waco, TX: Prufrock Press.

Nelson, C., & Huefner, D. (2003). Young children with autism: Judicial responses to the Lovaas and discrete trial training debates. *Journal of Early Intervention, 26*, 1–19.

Nelson, J., Crabtree, M., Marchand-Martella, N., & Martella, R. (1998). Teaching good behavior in the whole school. *Teaching Exceptional Children, 30*(4), 4–9.

Newman, S. (2008). Neural bases of giftedness. In J. Plucker & C. Callahan (Eds.). *Critical Issues and Practices in Gifted Education: What the Research Says* (469–478). Waco, TX: Prufrock Press.

Newschaffer, C. J., Croen, L. A., Daniels, J., Giarelli, E., Grether, J. K., Levy, S., et al. (2007). The epidemiology of autism spectrum disorders. *Annual Review of Public Health, 28*, 235–258.

Newton, J., Horner, R., Ard, W., LeBaron, N., & Sapperton, G. (1994). Social aspects and social relationship of individuals with disability. *Mental Retardation, 32*(5), 393–402.

Niu, W. & Sternberg, R.J. (2003). Societal and school influences on student creativity: The case of China. *Psychology in the Schools, 40*(1), 103–114.

Noonan, M. J., & McCormick, L. (2006). *Young children with disabilities in natural environments: Methods and procedures.* Baltimore, MD: Brookes.

Nugent, J. K., & Blanchard, Y. (2006). Newborn behavior and development: Implications for health care professionals. In J. F. Travers & K. Theis (Eds.), *The handbook of human development for health care professionals* (pp. 79–94). Boston, MA: Jones & Bartlett.

Nugent, J. K., Blanchard, Y., & Stewart, J. S. (2007). Supporting parents of premature infants: An infant focused family-centered approach. In D. Brodsky & M. A. Ouellette (Eds.), *Primary care of the premature infant.* New York, NY: Elsevier.

Nugent, J. K., Keefer, C. H., Minear, S., Johnson, L. C., & Blanchard, Y. (2007). *Understanding newborn behavior and early relationships: The Newborn Behavioral Observations (NBO) system handbook.* Baltimore, MD: Brookes.

O'Neill, J., Gothelf, C., Cohen, S., Lehman, L., & Woolf, S. (1991). *A curricular approach to support the transition to adulthood of adolescents with visual or dual sensory impairments and cognitive disabilities.* Albany, NY: New York State Education Department, Office of Special Education and Rehabilitation Services.

Odom, S., Horner, R., Snell, & Blacher, J. (2007). Postschool and adult issues. *Handbook of developmental disabilities.* New York, NY: Guilford Press.

Odom, S. L. (2009). The tie that binds: Evidence-based practice, implementation science, and child outcomes. *Topics in Early Childhood Special Education, 29*, 53–61.

Odom, S. L., Boyd, B. A., Hall, L. J., & Hume, K. (2008). Evaluation of comprehensive treatment models for individuals with autism spectrum disorders. *Journal of Autism and Developmental Disorders, 40*, 425–436.

Odom, S. L., Horner, R. H., Snell, M. E., & Blacher, J. (Eds.). (2007). *Handbook of developmental disabilities.* New York NY: Guilford Press.

Odom, S. L., Rogers, S., McDougle, C. J., Hume, K., & McGee, G. (2007). Early intervention for children with autism spectrum disorder. In S. L. Odom, R. H. Horner, M. E. Snell, & J. Blacher (Eds.), *Handbook of developmental disabilities* (pp. 199–223). New York, NY: Guilford Press.

Office of Special Education Programs. (2003). *Twenty-fourth annual report to Congress.* Washington, DC: Author.

Okolo, C. M. (2006). Content-area applications. *Journal of Special Education Technology, 21*(4), 58–61.

Olley, J. (1999). Curriculum for students with autism. *School Psychology Review, 28*(4), 595–604.

Olmstead, J. E. (1991). *Itinerant teaching: Tricks of the trade for teachers of blind and visually impaired students.* New York, NY: American Foundation for the Blind.

Olswang, L. B., Coggins, T. E., & Svensson, L. (2007). Assessing social communication in the classroom: Observing manner and duration of performance. *Topics in Language Disorders, 27*(2), 111–127.

Olszewski-Kubilius, P. (2010). Two perspectives on statistics in gifted education. In B. Thompson & R. Subotnik (Eds.). *Methodologies for Conducting Research on Giftedness.* Washington, DC: American Psychological Association.

Ornstein, P., Schaaf, J., Hooper, S., Hatton, D., Mirrett, P., & Bailey, D. B. (2008). Memory skills of boys with Fragile X syndrome. *American Journal on Mental Retardation, 113*(6), 453–465.

Oritz, A. (2001). English language learners with special needs: Effective instructional strategies. *LD Online.* Retrieved 4/17/10 from www.ldonline.org/article/English_language_learners_with_special_needs.htm

Orton Dyslexia Research Committee. (1994). Operational definition of dyslexia. *Perspectives, 20*(5), 4.

Osher, D., Cartledge, G., Oswald, D., Sutherland, K., Artiles, A., & Coutinho, M. (2004). Issues of cultural and linguistic competency and disproportionate representation. In R. Rutherford, M. Quinn, & S. Mather (Eds.), *Handbook of research in behavioral disorders.* New York, NY: Guilford Press.

Osofsky, J. D., & Thompson, D. (2000). Adaptive and mal-adaptive parenting: Perspectives on risk and protective factors. In J. P. Shonkoff & S. J. Meisels (Eds.), *Handbook of early childhood intervention* (2nd ed., pp. 54–75). Cambridge, UK: Cambridge University Press.

Packer, L. (2004). *Overview of sensory integration.* Retrieved from http://www.shcoolbehavior.com/conditions_sensoryoverview.htm

Page, T. (2007, August 20). Parallel play. *The New Yorker,* 36–41.

Pandey, J., Verbalis, A., Robins, D., Boorstein, H., Klin, A., Babitz, T., et al. (2008). Screening for autism in older and younger toddlers with the modified checklist for autism in toddlers. *Autism: The International Journal of Research and Practice, 12*, 513.

Parette, H., & Petch-Hogan, B. (2000). Approaching families. *Teaching Exceptional Children, 33*(2), 4–10.

Paracchini, S., Scerri, T., & Monaco, A.P. (2007). The genetic lexicon of dyslexia. *Annual Review of Genomics and Human Genetics, 8,* 57–79.

Paul, P., & Quigley, S. (1994). *Education and deafness.* White Plains, NY: Longman.

Paul, R. (1995). *Language disorders from infancy through adolescence: Assessment and intervention.* St. Louis, MO: Mosby.

Pellegrino, L. (2002). Cerebral palsy. In M. Batshaw (Ed.), *Children with disabilities* (5th ed., pp. 443–466). Baltimore, MD: Brookes.

Pennington, B. F. (2009). How neuropsychology informs our understanding of developmental disorders. *Journal of Child Psychology and Psychiatry, 50*(1–2), 72–78.

Perry, D., & Kaufmann, R. (2009). *Policy brief: Integrating early childhood mental health consultation with the pyramid model.* National Center for Effective Mental Health Consultation, University of South Florida.

Pershelli, A. (2007). Memory strategies to use with students following traumatic brain injury. *Physical Disabilities: Education and Related Services, 26*(1), 31–46.

Petitto, L., & Marentette, P. (1991). Babbling in the manual mode: Evidence for the ontogeny of language. *Science, 251,* 1493–1495.

Pianta, P., Howes, C., Burchinal, M., Bryant, D., Clifford, R., Early, D., & Barbarin, O. (2005). Features of pre-kindergarten programs, classrooms, and teachers: Do they predict observed classroom quality and child-teacher interactions? *Applied Developmental Science, 9*(3), 144–159.

Pianta, R. C. (2007). Early education in transition. In R. C. Pianta, M. J. Cox, & K. L. Snow (Eds.), *School readiness and the transition to kindergarten in the era of accountability.* Baltimore, MD: Brookes.

Pianta, R. C., & Cox, M. J. (2002). *The transition to kindergarten: Research, policy, training and practice.* Baltimore, MD: Brookes.

Pianta, R. C., Cox, M. J., Early, D., & Taylor, L. (1999). Kindergarten teachers' practices related to the transition to school: Results of a national survey. *Elementary School Journal, 100,* 71–86.

Pianta, R. C., Cox, M. J., & Snow, K. L. (2007). *School readiness and the transition to kindergarten in the era of accountability.* Baltimore, MD: Brookes.

Pianta, R. C., & Kraft-Sayre, M. (2003). *Successful kindergarten transition.* Baltimore, MD: Brookes.

Pierangelo, R., & Giuliani, G. (2006). *Learning disabilities: A practical approach to foundations, assessment, diagnosis, and teaching.* Boston, MA: Pearson Education.

Plomin, R., Defries, J., Craig I., & McGuffin, P. (2003). *Behavioral genetics in the postgenomic era.* Washington, DC: American Psychological Association.

Plomin, R., & Petrill, S. (1997). Genetics and intelligence: What's new? *Intelligence, 24*(1), 53–77.

Plucker, J., & Callahan, C. (Eds.). (2008). *Critical issues and practices in gifted education.* Waco, TX: Prufrock Publishers.

Pogrund, R., & Fazzi, D. (Eds.). (2002). *Early focus: Working with young blind and visually impaired children and their families* (2nd ed.). New York, NY: American Foundation for the Blind.

Polsgrove, L., & Smith, S. (2004). Informal practice in teaching self-control to children with emotional and behavior disorders. In R. Rutherford, M. Quinn, & S. Mathur (Eds.), *Handbook of research in emotional and behavior disorders* (pp. 399–425). New York, NY: Guilford Press.

Porter, R. S. (Ed.). (2008). *The Merck manual online.* Whitehouse Station, NJ: Merck Research Laboratories.

Povenmire-Kirk, T.C., Lindstrom, L., & Bullis, M. (2010). De escuela a la vida adulta/from school to adult life: Transition needs for Latino youth with disabilities and their families. *Career Development for Exceptional Individuals, 33*(1), 41–51.

Powls, A., Botting, N.,Cooke, R.W.I.,Stephenson, G. & Marlow, N. (1997). Visual impairment in low birthweight children. *Arch Dis Child, 76,* 82–87.

Prabhala (2007). *Intellectual and Developmental Disabilities, 45*(1), 1–3.

President's Commission on Excellence in Special Education. (2002). *A new era: Revitalizing special education for children and their families.* Retrieved from www.ed.gov/inits/commissionsboards/whspecialeducation/index.html

Presley, I. (2010). The impact of assistive technology: Assessment and instruction for children and youths with low vision. In A. Corn & J. Erin, *Foundations of low vision: Clinical and functional perspectives* (2nd ed., pp. 589–654). New York, NY: American Foundation for the Blind.

Prevalence and incidence of hearing loss in children. (n.d.). Retrieved from http://www.asha.org/ public/hearing/disorders/types.htm

Prevatt, F. A., Heffer, R. W., & Lowe, T. A. (2000). A review of school reintegration programs for children with pediatric cancers. *Journal of School Psychology, 38*(5), 447–467.

Priester, G. H., & Goorhuis-Brouwer, S. M. (2008). Speech and language development in toddlers with and without cleft palate. *International Journal of Pediatric Otorhinolaryngology, 72,* 801–806.

Pueschel, S., Scala, P., Weidenman, L., & Bernier, J. (Eds.). (1995). *The special child* (2nd ed.). Baltimore, MD: Brookes.

Quesenberry, A., Ostrosky, M. M., & Corso, R. (2007). Skilled and knowledgeable caregivers: The role of fathers in supporting young children's development. *Young Exceptional Children, 10*(4), 11–19.

Rainnie, D. G., Bergeron, R., Sajdyk, T., Patil, M., Gehlert, D., & Shekar, A. (2004). Corticotrophin releasing factor-induced synaptic plasticity in the amygdala translates stress into emotional disorders. *The Journal of Neuroscience, 24*(14), 3471–3479.

Ramos, V., & Gardner, H. (2003). Multiple intelligences: A perspective on gifted. In N. Colangelo & G. Davis (Eds.), *Handbook of gifted education* (pp. 100–112).Boston, MA: Allyn & Bacon.

Rattner, E. (2008, April 8). New bionic eye could restore site. *The Future of Things.* Retrieved from thefutureofthings.com/print.php?itemTypeId=2&itemid=1152

Raus-Bahrami, K., Short, B., & Batshaw, M. (2002). Premature and small-for-date babies. In M. Batshaw (Ed.), *Children with disabilities* (5th ed., pp. 85–106). Baltimore, MD: Brookes.

Reed, S., Anita, S. D., & Kreimeyer, K. H. (2008). Academic status of deaf and hard-of-hearing students in public schools: Student, home, and service facilitators and detractors. *Journal of Deaf Studies and Deaf Education, 13*(4), 485–502.

Reis, D. (2003). Child effects in family systems. In A. C. Crocker & A. Booth (Eds.), *Child influence on family dynamics* (pp. 1–23). Mahwah, NJ: Erlbaum.

Reis, S. (2008). Talented readers. In J. Plucker & C. Callahan (Eds.), *Critical issues and practices in gifted education* (pp. 655–668). Waco, TX: Prufrock Press.

Reis, S., & McCoach, D. (2000). The underachievement of gifted students: What do we know and where do we go? *Gifted Child Quarterly, 44,* 152–170.

Reis, S., & Renzulli, J. (2009). Is there still a need for gifted education? An examination of current research. *Learning and Individual Differences, 10,* 1–10.

Reis, S. M. (2003). Gifted girls, twenty-five years later: Hopes realized and new challenges found. *Roeper Review, 25,* 154–157.

Renzulli, J. S. (2002). Expanding the conception of giftedness to include co-cognitive traits and to promote social capital. *Phi Delta Kappan, 84*(1), 33–58.

Renzulli, J. S. & Reed, R. E. (2008). Intelligences outside the normal curve: Co-cognitive traits that contribute to giftedness. In J. Plucker & C. Callahan (Eds.). *Critical Issues and Practices in Gifted Education: What the Research Says* (303–319). Waco, TX: Prufrock Press.

Renzulli, J. S. & Reis, S. M. (1997). *The schoolwide enrichment model: A how-to guide for educational excellence* (2nd ed.). Mansfield Center, CT: Creative Learning Press, Inc.

Riggio, M. (2009). Deafblindness: Educational service guidelines. *DVI Quarterly, 54*(3), 13–14.

Ritchie, S., Maxwell, K. L., & Clifford, R. M. (2007). First-School: A new vision for education. In B. Pianta, M. Cox, & K. Snow (Eds.), *School readiness and the transition to kindergarten in the era of accountability* (pp. 85–96). Baltimore, MD: Brookes.

Ritzman, M. J., Sanger, D., & Coufal, K. L. (2006). A case study of a collaborative speech-language pathologist. *Communication Disorders Quarterly, 27*(4), 221–231.

Roberts, J., Burchinal, M., & Bailey, D. (1994). Communication among preschoolers with and without disabilities in same-age and mixed-age classes. *American Journal of Mental Retardation, 99*(3), 231–249.

Robinson, A., Shore, B., & Enersen, D. (2007). *Best practices in gifted education.* Waco, TX: Prufrock Press.

Robinson, N., Zigler, E., & Gallagher, J. (2000). Two tails of the normal curve: Similarities and differences in the study of mental retardation and differences in the study of mental retardation and giftedness. *American Psychologist, 55*(112), 1413–1424.

Roeper, A. (2003). The young gifted girl: A contemporary view. *Roeper Review, 25,* 151–153.

Rogers, S. J., & Vismara, L. A. (2008). Evidence-based comprehensive treatments for early autism. *Journal of Clinical Child and Adolescent Psychology, 37,* 8.

Rolstad, & J. MacSwan, 1034–1040. Sommerville, MA: Cascadilla Press.

Rose, D., & Meyer, A. (2002). *Teaching every student in the digital age.* Alexandria, VA: Association for Curriculum Development.

Rose, R. (2007). Curriculum considerations in meeting special educational needs. In L. Florian (Ed.). *The Sage Handbook of Special Education.* London, England: Sage Publications, Ltd.

Rosenkoetter, S. E., Hains, A. H., & Fowler, S. A. (1994). *Bridging early services for children with special needs and their families: A practical guide for transition planning.* Baltimore, MD: Brookes.

Rosenkoetter, S. E., Whaley, K. T., Hains, A. H., & Pierce, L. (2001). The evolution of transition policy for young children with special needs and their families. *Topics in Early Childhood Special Education, 21*(1), 3–15.

Ross, P. (Ed.). (1993). *National excellence.* Washington, DC: U.S. Department of Education.

Roth, F., Troia, G., Worthington, C., & Handy, D. (2006). Promoting awareness of sounds in speech: A follow-up report of an early intervention program for children with speech and language impairments. *Learning Disabilities Quarterly, 29*, 67–88.

Rourke, B. P. (1994). Neuropsychological assessment of children with learning disabilities. In G. Lyon (Ed.), *Frames of reference for the assessment of learning disabilities* (pp. 475–514). Baltimore, MD: Brookes.

Rourke, B. P. (Ed.). (1991). *Neuropsychological validation of learning disability subtypes.* New York, NY: Guilford Press.

Rous, B., Myers, C. T., & Stricklin, S. B. (2007). Strategies for supporting transitions of young children with special needs and their families. *Journal of Early Intervention, 30*(1), 1–18.

Rous, B. S., & Hallam, R. A. (2006). *Tools for transition in early childhood: A step by step guide for agencies, teachers and families.* Baltimore, MD: Brookes.

Rouse, M., & McLaughlin, M. (2007). Changing perspectives of special education in the evolving context of educational reform. In L. Florian (Ed.), *The Sage Handbook of Special Education.* London, England: Sage Publications, Ltd.

Russell, M., Hoffman, T., & Higgins, J. (2009). NimbleTools: A universally designed test delivery system. *Teaching Exceptional Children, 42*(2), 6–12.

Rutstein, R., Conlon, C., & Batshaw, M. L. (1997). HIV and AIDS. In M. L. Batshaw (Ed.), *Children with disabilities* (pp. 163–181). Baltimore, MD: Brookes.

Rutter, M. (1996). Autism research: Prospects and priorities. *Journal of Autism and Developmental Disorders, 26*, 257–275.

Rutter, M. (1997). Nature-nurture integration: The example of antisocial behavior. *American Psychologist, 52*, 390–398.

Rutter, M. (2000). Resilience reconsidered: Conceptual considerations, empirical findings,and policy implications. In J. P. Shonkoff & S. J. Meisels (Eds.), *Handbook of early childhood intervention* (2nd ed., pp. 651–682). NewYork: Cambridge University Press.

Rutter, M. (2003). Commentary: Causal processes leading to antisocial behavior. *Developmental Psychology, 39*, 372–378.

Rutter, M., (2007). *Genes and behaviors: Nature and nurture interplay explained.* Malden, MA: Blackwell Publishing.

Rutter, M., Galler, H., & Hagell, A. (1998). *Antisocial behavior by young people.* New York, NY: Cambridge University Press.

Rylance, B. J. (1997). Predictors of high school graduation or dropping out for youths with severe emotional disturbance. *Behavioral Disorders, 23*, 5–18.

Ryndak, D., & Alper, S. (2003). *Curriculum and instruction for students with significant disabilities in inclusive settings* (2nd ed.). Boston, MA: Allyn & Bacon.

Sacks, S. (1992). The social development of visually impaired children: A theoretical perspective. In S. Sacks, L. Kekelis, & R. Gaylord-Ross (Eds.), *The development of social skills by blind and visually impaired students* (pp. 3–12). New York, NY: American Foundation for the Blind.

Sacks, S., & Silberman, R. (1998). *Educating students who have visual impairments with other disabilities* (pp. 3–38). Baltimore, MD: Brookes.

Sacks, S., Wolffe, K., & Tierney, D. (1998). Lifestyles of students with visual impairments: Preliminary studies of social networks. *Exceptional Children, 64*(4), 463–478.

Saenz, T. I., & Felix, D. M. (2006). English-speaking Latino parents' literacy practices in Southern California. *Communication Disorders Quarterly, 28*(2), 93–106.

Sakai, K. L. (2005). Language acquisition and brain development. *Science, 310*, 815–819.

Salend, S., & Salinas, A. (2003). Language differences or learning difficulties. *Teaching Exceptional Children, 35*(4), 36–43.

Sallows, G. O., & Graupner, T. D. (2005). Intensive behavioral treatment for children with autism: Four-year outcome and predictors. *American Journal on Mental Retardation, 110*(6), 417–438.

Salvia, J., Ysseldyke, J. E., & Bolt, S. (2007). *Assessment in special and inclusive education* (10th ed.). Boston, MA: Houghton Mifflin.

Salvia, J., Ysseldyke, J., & Bolt, S. (2010). Assessment in special and inclusive education (11th ed.). Boston, MA: Wadsworth Publishing.

Sameroff, A. (1990). Neo-environmental perspectives on developmental theory. In R. Hodapp, J. Burack, & E. Zigler (Eds.), *Issues in the developmental approach to mental retardation.* New York, NY: Cambridge University Press.

Sameroff, A., & Fiese, B. (2000). Transactional regulation. In J. Shonkoff & S. Meisels (Eds.), *Handbook of early intervention* (pp. 135–159). New York, NY: Cambridge University Press.

Sandall, S., Hemmeter, M. L., Smith, B. J., & McLean, M. E. (2005). *DEC recommended practices: A comprehensive guide for practical application in early intervention/early childhood special education.* Missoula, MT: Division for Early Childhood.

Sandall, S., & Ostrosky, M. (Eds.). (2000). *Natural environments and inclusion* [Monograph Series 2]. Denver, CO: Council for Exceptional Children, Division for Early Childhood.

Sandman, C. A., & Kemp, A. S. (2007). Neuroscience of developmental disabilities. In S. L. Odom, R. H. Horner, M. E. Snell, & J. Blacher (Eds.), *Handbook of developmental disabilities* (pp. 129–157). New York, NY: Guilford Press.

Schaeffer, C., Petras, H., Ialongo, N., Poduska, J., & Kellam, S. (2003). Modeling growth in boys' aggressive behavior across elementary school: Links to later criminal involvement, conduct disorder, and antisocial personality disorder. *Developmental Psychology, 39*, 1020–1035.

Schalock, R., (Chair). (2010) *Intellectual disability: Definition, classification, and systems of support* (11th edition). Washington, DC: American Association on Intellectual and Developmental Disabilities.

Scherer, N. J., D'Antonio, L. L., & McGahey, H. (2008). Early intervention for speech impairment in children with cleft palate. *Cleft Palate-Craniofacial Journal, 45*(1), 1–31.

Scherer, N. J., Williams, A. L., & Proctor-Williams, K. (2008). Early and later vocalization skills in children with and without cleft palate. *International Journal of Pediatric Otorhinolaryngology, 72*, 827–840.

Scheuermann, A. M., Deshler, D. D., & Schumaker, J. B. (2009). The effects of the explicit inquiry routine on the performance of students with learning disabilities on one-variable equations. *Learning Disability Quarterly, 32*, 103–120.

Schirmer, B. R., & Schaffer, L. (2010). Guiding reading approach: Teaching reading to students who are deaf and others who struggle. *Teaching Exceptional Children, 42*(5), 52–58.

Schonberg, R., & Tifft, C. (2002). Birth defects, prenatal diagnoses and fetal therapy. In M. Batshaw (Ed.), *Children with disabilities* (5th ed., pp. 27–42). Baltimore, MD: Brookes.

Schopler, E., Mesibov, G., & Hearsey, K. (1995). Structured teaching in the TEACCH system. In E. Schopler & G. Mesibov (Eds.), *Learning and cognition in autism* (pp. 243–268). New York, NY: Plenum Press.

Schroth, S. T. (2008). Levels of service. In J. Plucker & C. Callahan (Eds.). *Critical Issues and Practices in Gifted Education: What the Research Says* (321–339). Waco, TX: Prufrock Press.

Schumaker, J. B., & Deshler, D. D. (2010). Using a tiered intervention model in secondary schools to improve academic outcomes in subject-area courses. In M. R. Shinn & H. M. Walker (Eds.), *Intervention for achievement and behavior problems in a three-tier model including RTI*. Bethesda, MD: National Association of School Psychologists.

Schwartz, I. (2000). Standing on the shoulders of giants: Looking ahead to facilitating membership and relationships for children with disabilities. *Topics in Early Childhood Special Education, 20*(2), 123–128.

Schwartz, I. S., & Sandall, S. R. (2010). Is autism the disability that breaks Part C? A commentary on "Infants and toddlers with Autism Spectrum Disorder: early identification and early intervention," by Boyd, Odom, Humphreys, and Sam. *Journal of Early Intervention, 32*(2) 105–109.

Schwartz, T. L. (2010). Causes of visual impairments: Pathology and its implications. In A. Corn & J. Erin (Eds.), *Foundations of low vision: Clinical and functional perspectives* (2nd ed., pp. 137–191). New York, NY: American Foundation for the Blind.

Schweinhart, L. J., Montie, J., Xiang, Z., Barnett, W. S., Belfield, C. R., & Nores, M. (2005). *Lifetime effects: The High/Scope Perry Preschool study through age 40* [Monograph of the High/Scope Educational Research Foundation, No. 14]. Ypsilanti, MI: High/Scope Press.

Seida, J., Ospona, M., Karkhaneh, M., Hartling, L., Smith, V., & Clark, B. (2009). Systematic reviews of psychosocial interventions for autism: An umbrella review. *Developmental Medicine & Child Neurology, 51*, 95–104.

Serry, T., & Blaney, P. (1999). A four-year investigation into phonetic inventory development in young cochlear implant users. *Journal of Speech, Language, and Hearing Research, 42*(1), 887–899.

Shattell, M. M., Bartlett, R., & Rowe, T. (2008). "I have always felt different": The experience of attention-deficit/hyperactivity disorder in childhood. *Journal of Pediatric Nursing, 23*(1), 49–57.

Shaywitz, S. E., & Shaywitz, B. A. (2008). Paying attention to reading: The neurobiology of reading and dyslexia. *Development and Psychopathology, 20*, 1329–1349.

Shea, V. (2005). A perspective on the research literature related to early intensive behavioral intervention for young children with autism. *Communication Disorders Quarterly, 26*(2), 102–111.

Shiu, S. (2001). Issues in the education of students with chronic illness. *International Journal of Disability, Development and Education, 48*(3), 269–281.

Shonkoff, J. P., & Phillips, D. A. (2000). *From neurons to neighborhoods: The science of early childhood development.* Washington, DC: National Academies Press.

Sibling Support Project. (2010). Bellevue, WA: A Kindering Center Program.

Silberman, R. (2000). Children and youths with visual impairments and other exceptionalities. In A. Koenig & M. Holbrook (Eds.), *Foundations of education: Vol. I. History and theory of teaching children and youths with visual impairments* (2nd ed., pp. 173–198). New York, NY: American Foundation for the Blind Press.

Silberman, R., & Brown, F. (1998). Alternative approaches to assessing students who have visual impairments with other disabilities in classroom and community environments. In S. Sacks & R. Silberman (Eds.), *Educating students who have visual impairments with other disabilities* (pp. 73–98). Baltimore, MD: Brookes.

Silver, L. B., (2010). Is your child's learning disability the only problem? You should know about other related disorders. Learning Disabilities Association of America. Retrieved April 15, 2010, from http://www.ldanatl.org/aboutld/parents/ld_basics/comorbidity.asp.

Silverman, L. (1997). Family counseling with the gifted. In N. Colangelo & G. Davis (Eds.), *Handbook of gifted education* (2nd ed., pp. 382–397). Boston, MA: Allyn & Bacon.

Silverman, L. (1998). The highly gifted. In J. VanTassel-Baska (Ed.), *Excellence in educating gifted and talented learners* (pp. 115–128). Denver, CO: Love.

Silverman, L. K. (2002). Asynchronous development. In M. Neihart, S. Reis, N. Robinson, & S. Moon (Eds.), *The social and emotional development of gifted children: What do we know?* (pp. 31–40). Waco, TX: Prufrock Press.

Simms, L., & Thumann, H. (2007). In search of a new, linguistically and culturally sensitive paradigm in deaf education. *American Annals of the Deaf, 152*(3), 302–311.

Simonoff, E., Bolton, P., & Rutter, M. (1998). Genetic perspectives on mental retardation. In J. Burack, R. Hodapp, & E. Zigler (Eds.), *Handbook of mental retardation and development* (pp. 41–79). New York, NY: Cambridge University Press.

Simonsen, B., Shaw, S., Faggella-Luby, M., Sugai, G., Coyne, M. D., Rhein, B., Madaus, J. W., Alfano, M. (2008). A schoolwide model for service delivery. *Remedial and Special Education, 31*(1).

Sisk, D. (2009). Myth 13: The regular classroom teacher can "go it alone." *Gifted Child Quarterly, 53*(4), 269–271.

Skeels, H. M. (1966). Adult status of children with contrasting early life experiences. *Monographs of the Society for Research in Child Development, 31*(Serial No. 105).

Skeels, H. M., & Dye, H. (1939). A study of the effects of differential stimulation on mentally retarded children. *Proceedings and Addresses of the American Association on Mental Deficiency 44*, 114–136.

Slobin, D. (2006). Imitation and grammatical development in children. In A. Bundura (Ed.), *Psychological modeling: Conflicting theories* (p. 166). New Brunswick, NJ: Transaction Publishers.

Smith, A. (2005). *The brain's behind it: New knowledge about the brain and learning.* Norwalk, CT: Crown House.

Smith, A. J., Bainbridge, J. W. & Ali, R. R. (2009). Prospects for retinal gene replacement therapy. *Trends in Genetics, 25*(4), 156–165.

Smith, K. (2010). RTI/NTID's center on access technology: Helping deaf students succeed in college. Retrieved from http://nysstlc.syr.edu/Newsletter/researchspotlight/NTIDCAT/default.aspx.

Smith, T., Groen, A., & Wynn, J. W. (2000). Randomized trial of intensive early intervention for children with pervasive developmental disorder. *American Journal of Mental Retardation, 105*(4), 269–295.

Snell, M., & Voorhees, M. (2006). On being labeled with mental retardation. In H. Switzky & S. Greenspan (Eds.), *What is mental retardation?* Washington, DC: American Association on Mental Retardation.

Solish, A., Perry, A., & Minnes, P. (2010). Participation of children with and without disabilities in social, recreational, and leisure activities. *Journal of Applied Research in Intellectual Disabilities, 23*, 226–236.

Sopko, K., & Reder, N. (2007). *Public and parent reporting requirements: NCLB and IDEA regulations.* Alexandria, VA: National Association of State Directors of Special Education.

Sopko, K. M. (2009). Early childhood mental health services: Four case studies. *inForum In Depth Policy Analysis.* Alexandria, VA: NASDSE.

Sousa, D. (2001). *How the brain learns: A classroom teacher's guide* (2nd ed.). Thousand Oaks, CA: Corwin Press, Inc.

Southern California Comprehensive Assistance Center. (2005). Six research based guiding principles serving the needs of English learners in preschool "school readiness" programs. Paper developed by a Working Group from Eight County Offices of Education.

Sparling, J. (2007). *Creative curriculum learning games: 12–24 months.* St. Paul, MN: Red Leaf Press.

Sparrow, R. (2010). Implants and ethnocide: Learning from the cochlear implant controversy. *Disability & Society, 25*(4), 455–466.

Sparrow, S., Cichetti, D., & Balla, D. (2006). Vineland adaptive behavior scales (2nd ed.) (Vineland-II). San Antonio, TX: Pearson.

Spear-Swerling, L. (2006). Learning disabilities in English language learners. *LD Online.* Retrieved 4/17/10 from www.ldonline.org/article/learning_disabilities_in_English_language_learners.htm

Spencer, P., Ertling, C., & Marschark, M. (2000). *The deaf child in the family and at school.* Mahwah, NJ: Erlbaum.

Spiegel, H., & Bonwit, A. (2002). HIV infection in children. In M. Batshaw (Ed.), *Children with disabilities* (5th ed., pp. 123–139). Baltimore, MD: Brookes.

Spinath, F., Harlaar, N., Ronald, A., & Plomin, R. (2004). Substantial genetic influence on mild mental impairment in early childhood. *American Journal of Mental Retardation, 109,* 34–43.

Spitz, H. (2006). How we eradicated familial (hereditary) mental retardation-updated. In H. Switzky & S. Greenspan (Eds.), *What is mental retardation?* (pp. 81–92). Washington, DC: American Association for Mental Retardation.

Sprague, J., & Walker, H. (2000). Early identification and invention for youth with antisocial and violent behavior. *Exceptional Children, 66*(3), 367–379.

Spungin, S. (Ed.). (2002). *When you have a visually impaired child in your classroom: A guide for teachers.* New York, NY: American Foundation for the Blind.

Squires, J., & Bricker, D. (2007). *An activity-based approach to developing young children's social emotional competence.* Baltimore, MD: Brookes.

Stancliffe, R., & Lakin, C. (2007). Independent living. In S. Odom, R. Horner, M. Snell, & J. Blacher. Handbook of Developmental Disabilities. New York, NY: The Guilford Press, p. 429–448.

Stang, K., Carter, K., Lane, K. L., & Pierson, M. (2009). Perspectives of general and special educators on fostering self-determination in elementary and middle school. *Journal of Special Education, 43*(4), 94–106.

Stanley, J. (1997). In the beginning: The study of mathematically precocious youth. In C. Benbow & D. Lubinski (Eds.), *Intellectual talents psychometric and social issues.* Baltimore, MD: Johns Hopkins Press.

Steinberg, A., & Knightly, C. (1997). Hearing: Sounds and silences. In M. L. Batshaw (Ed.), *Children with disabilities* (pp. 241–274). Baltimore, MD: Brookes.

Stenhoff, D. M., & Lignugaris-Kraft, B. (2007). A review of the effects of peer tutoring on students with mild disabilities in secondary settings. *Exceptional Children, 74*(1), 8–30.

Stephens, K. (2008). Applicable Federal and State policy, law and legal considerations gifted education. In S. Pfeiffer (Ed.), *Handbook of Giftedness in Children* (pp. 387–408). New York, NY: Springer.

Stephens, T., Blackhurst, A., & Magliocca, L. (1982). *Teaching mainstreamed students.* New York, NY: Wiley.

Sternberg, R. (1997). *Successful intelligence.* New York, NY: Plume.

Sternberg, R. J. (2008). The answer depends on the question: A reply to Eric Jensen. *Phi Delta Kappan, 89*(6), 418–420.

Sternberg, R. J., & Grigorenko, E. L. (2002). The theory of successful intelligence as a basis for gifted education. *Gifted Child Quarterly, 46*(4), 265–277.

Stinson, M., & Foster, S. (2000). Socialization of deaf children and youths in school. In P. Spencer, C. Ertling, & M. Marschark (Eds.), *The deaf child in the family and at school* (pp. 191–209). Mahwah, NJ: Erlbaum.

Stokes, J. (Ed.). (1999). *Hearing impaired infants: Support in the first eighteen months.* London, England: Whurr. (Distributed by Paul H. Brookes).

Stone, W., Lee, E., Ashford, L., Brissie, J., Hepburn, S., Coonrod, E., & Bahr, H. (1999). Can autism be diagnosed accurately in children under 3 years? *Journal of Child Psychology and Psychiatry, 40,* 219–226.

Stone, W., Ousley, O., & Littleford, C. (1997). Motor imitation in young children with autism: What's the object? *Journal of Abnormal Child Psychology, 25*(6), 475–483.

Strain, P., Kohler, F., & Goldstein, H. (1996). Learning experiences, an alternative program: Peer-mediated interventions for young children with autism. In E. Hibbs & P. Jensen (Eds.), *Psychosocial treatments for child and adolescent disorders: Empirically based strategies for clinical practice* (pp. 573–586). Washington, DC: American Psychological Association.

Strand, S., Drury, I., & Smith, P. (2006). Sex differences in cognitive abilities test scores: A UK national picture. *British Journal of Educational Psychology, 76,* 463–480.

Strauss, M. (1999). Hearing loss and CMV. *Volta Review, 99*(5), 71–77.

Stremel, K. (2009). Cochlear implants for children with blindness or visual impairments. *DVI Quarterly, 54*(3), 23–25.

Stremel, K., & Campbell, P. H. (2007). Implementation of early intervention within natural environments. *Early Childhood Services, 1*(2), 83–105.

Subotnick, R. (Director) (2010). *The other three r's: Reasoning, resilience and responsibility.* Washington, DC: American Psychological Association.

Subotnik, R., Kassan, L., Summers, E., & Wasser, A. (1993). *Genius revisited: High IQ children grown up.* Norwood, NJ: Ablex.

Sugai, G., & Horner, R. (2006). A promising approach for expanding and sustaining the implementation of schoolwide positive behavior support. *School Psychology Review, 35,* 245–259.

Surgeon General. (2001). *Youth violence: A report of the surgeon general.* Retrieved from http://www. surgeongeneral.gov/library/youthviolence/default.htm

Swanson, H. L., Harris, K. R., & Graham, S. (2003). Overview of foundations, causes, instruction, and methodology in the field of learning disabilities. In H. L. Swanson, K. R. Harris, & S. Graham (Eds.), *Handbook of learning disabilities* (pp. 3–15). New York, NY: Guilford Press.

Swanson, H. L., & Sáez, L. (2003). Memory difficulties in children and adults with learning disabilities. In H. L. Swanson, K. R. Harris, & S. Graham (Eds.), *Handbook of learning disabilities* (pp. 182–198). New York, NY: Guilford Press.

Swanson, H. L, Zheng, X., & Jerman, O. (2009). Working memory, short-term memory, and reading disabilities: A selective meta-analysis of the literature. *Journal of Learning Disabilities, 42*(3), 260–287.

Switzky, H., & Greenspan, S. (2006). Lessons from the Atkins Decision for the next *AAMR Manual.* In H. Switzky & S. Greenspan (Eds.), *What is mental retardation?* Washington, DC: American Association on Mental Retardation.

Sze, S. (2009). The effects of assistive technology on students with disabilities. *Journal of Educational Technology Systems, 37*(4), 419–429.

Tannenbaum, A. (2000). A history of giftedness in school and society. In K. Heller, R. Subotnik, & R. Sternberg (Eds.), *International handbook on gifted.* New York, NY: Elsever.

Tartaglia, N. R., Hansen, R. L., & Hagerman, R. J. (2007). Advances in genetics. In S. L. Odom, R. H. Horner, M. E. Snell, & J. Blacher (Eds.), *Handbook of developmental disabilities* (pp. 98–128). New York, NY: Guilford Press.

Taylor, B., Miller, E., Lingam, R., Andrews, N., Simmons, A., & Stowe, J. (2002). Measles, mumps, and rubella vaccination and bowel problems or developmental regression in children with autism: Population study. *British Medical Journal, 324,* 393–396.

Telecommunications for the Deaf and Hard of Hearing, Inc. (TDI). (2010). *TDI national directory & resource guide.* Silver Spring, MD: Author.

Tellefson, M. (2009). Using the teaching cane strategy with children who are deaf-blind. *Division on Visual Impairments Quarterly, 54*(3), 28–31.

Terman, L., & Oden, M. (1947). *The gifted child grows up: Twenty-five-year follow-up of a superior group* (Vol. 4). Stanford, CA: Stanford University Press.

Tharpe, A. M. (2008). Unilateral and mild bilateral hearing loss in children: Past and current perspectives. *Trends in Amplification, 12*(1), 7–15.

Third International Mathematics and Science Study. (1998). Washington, DC: U.S. Department of Education.

Thompson, R. A., & Raikes, H. A. (2007). Early socioemotional development and the roots of school readiness. In J. Knitzer, R. Kaufmann, & D. Perry (Eds.), *Early childhood mental health.* Baltimore, MD: Paul H. Brookes Publishing Co, pp. 13–35.

Thompson, T. (2005). Paul E. Meehl and B. F. Skinner: Autotaxia, autotype and autism. *Behavioral Philosophy, 33,* 101–131.

Thompson, T., Moore, T., & Symons, F. (2007). In S. Odom, B. Horner, M. Snell, & J. Blacher (Eds.), *Handbook of developmental disabilities* (pp. 501–528). New York, NY: Guilford Press.

Thornton, C., & Karjewski, J. (1993). Death education for teachers: A refocused concern relative to medically fragile children. *Intervention in School and Clinic, 29*(1), 31–35.

Timler, G. R., Vogler-Elias, D., & McGill, K. F. (2007). Strategies for promoting generalization of social communication skills in preschoolers and school-aged children. *Topics in Language Disorders, 27*(2), 167–181.

Tomlinson, C. (2008). Differentiated instruction. In J. Plucker & C. Callahan (Eds.), *Critical issues and practices in gifted education* (pp. 167–178). Waco, TX: Prufrock Press.

Torrance, E. (1969). *Creativity.* Belmont, CA: Dimensions.

Townes, T. M. (2008). Gene replacement therapy for sickle cell disease and other blood disorders. In *Hematology.* Retrieved from asheducationbook.hematologylibrary.org

Treffinger, D., Young, G., Selby, E., & Shepardson, C. (2002). *Assessing creativity: A guide for educators.* Storrs, CT: National Research Center on the Gifted and Talented.

Trends in International Math and Science Study – (TIMSS) (1998). Washington, DC: National Center for Educational Statistics.

Trezek, B. J., & Wang, Y. (2006). Implications of utilizing a phonics-based reading curriculum with children who are deaf or hard of hearing. *Journal of Deaf Studies and Deaf Education, 11*(2), 202–213.

Trezek, B. J., Wang, Y., Woods, D. G., Gampp, T. L. & Paul, P. V. (2007). Using visual phonics to supplement beginning reading instruction for students who are deaf or hard of hearing. *Journal of Deaf Studies and Deaf Education, 12*(3), 373–384.

Trief, E. (1998c). *Working with visually impaired young students : A curriculum guide for 3 to 5 year olds.* Springfield, IL: Charles C. Thomas.

Trivette, C. M., & Dunst, C. (2010). Evaluating family-based practices: Parenting experiences scale. *Young Exceptional Children, 7*(3), 12–19.

Tsatsanis, K. (2004). Heterogeneity in learning style in Asperger syndrome and high-functioning autism. *Topics in Language Disorders, 24*(4), 260–270.

Turnbull, A., Brown, I., Turnbull, H. R., & Braddock, D. (Eds.). (2004). *Mental retardation and quality of life: International perspectives.* Washington, DC: American Association of Mental Retardation.

Turnbull, A., & Turnbull, H. (2002). From the old to the new paradigm of disabilities and families. In J. Paul, C. Lavely, A. Cranston-Gingras, & E. Taylor (Eds.), *Rethinking professional issues in special education* (pp. 83–118). Westbrook, CT: Ablex.

Turnbull, A., Turnbull, H., Shank, M., & Leal, D. (1995). *Exceptional lives: Special education in today's schools.* Upper Saddle River, NJ: Prentice-Hall.

Turnbull, A., Zuna, N., Turnbull, H., Poston, D., & Summers, J. (2007). Families as partners in educational decision making: Current implementation and future directions. In S. Odom, B. Horner, M. Snell, & J. Blacher (Eds.), *Handbook of developmental disabilities* (pp. 570–590). New York, NY: Guilford Press.

Turnbull, A. P., Turbiville, V. & Turnbull, H. R. (2000). Evolution of family-professional partnership models: Collective empowerment as the model for the early 21st century. In S. J. Meisels & J. P. Shonkoff (Eds.), *Handbook of Early Intervention* (pp. 630–650). New York: Cambridge University Press.

Turnbull, A. P., & Turnbull, H. R. (1990). *Families, professionals, and exceptionality: A special partnership* (2nd ed.). Upper Saddle River, NJ: Pearson.

Turnbull, A. P., & Turnbull, H. R. (1997). *Families, professionals, and exceptionality: A special partnership* (3rd ed.). Upper Saddle River, NJ: Merrill.

Turnbull, A. P., & Turnbull, H. R. (2004). *Individuals with Disabilities Education Act: Resources for Educators.* Paper presented at the Conference on Equity, Community, and Social Justice for Urban Students. New York, NY.

Turnbull, A. P., & Turnbull, H. R. (2006). *Families, professionals and exceptionality: A special partnership.* Upper Saddle River, NJ: Pearson/Merrill-Prentice Hall.

Turnbull, H., Stowe, M., Turnbull, A., & Schrandt, M. (2007). Public policy and developmental disabilities: A 35-year retrospective and a 5-year prospective based on the core concepts of disability policy. In S. Odom, B. Horner, M. Snell, & J. Blacher (Eds.), *Handbook of developmental disabilities* (pp. 15–34). New York, NY: Guilford Press.

Tuttle, D., & Tuttle, N. (1996). *Self-esteem and adjusting with blindness* (2nd ed.). Springfield, IL: Thomas.

Tuttle, D., & Tuttle, N. (2000). Psychosocial needs of children and youths. In M. C. Holbrook & A. J. Koenig (Eds.), *Foundations of education: Vol. 1. History and theory of teaching children and youths with visual impairments* (2nd ed., p. 167). New York, NY: AFB Press.

Tuttle, D., & Tuttle, N. (2004). *Self-esteem and adjusting with blindness: The process of responding to life's demands* (3rd ed.). Springfield, IL: Charles C. Thomas.

Twachtman-Cullen, D. (2000). Moveable children with autism spectrum disorders. In A. Wetherby & B. Prizant (Eds.), *Autism spectrum disorders: A transactional developmental perspective* (pp. 225–250). Baltimore, MD: Brookes.

Type, degree, and configuration of hearing loss. (n.d.). Retrieved from http://www.asha.org/public/ hearing/disorders/types.htm

Unger, D., Tressell, P., Jones, C. W., & Park, E. (2004). Involvement of low-income single caregivers in child-focused early intervention services: Implications for caregiver-child interaction. *Family Relations, 53*(2), 210–218.

University of Melbourne. (2010, April 12). Bionic eye in sight: Wide-view neurostimulator concept unveiled. *ScienceDaily*. Retrieved from www.sciencedaily.com/releases/2010/03/100330092815.htm

University of Sheffield. (2010, June 10). Novel gene replacement therapy holds promise for Spinal Muscular Atrophy. Retrieved from http://www.news-medical.net/news/20100610/Novel-gene-replacement-therapy-holds-promise-for-Spinal-Muscular-Atrophy.aspx.

U.S. Bureau of the Census. (2005). *Mothers in the work force*. Washington, DC: National Network of Child Care Resources and Referral.

U.S. Department of Education (2002). *Elementary and secondary school civil rights compliance report*. Washington, DC: Office of Civil Rights.

U.S. Department of Education. (2003). *Twenty-fourth annual report to Congress: Individuals with Disabilities Education Act*. Washington, DC: Office of Special Education Programs.

U.S. Department of Education. (2005). *Twenty-sixth annual report to Congress: Implementation of the Individuals with Disabilities Act*. Washington, DC: Office of Special Education Programs.

U.S. Department of Education. (2006). *Twenty-seventh annual report to Congress on the implementation of the Individuals with Disabilities Act*. Washington, DC: U.S. Department of Education.

U.S. Department of Education. (2008). *Twenty-eighth annual report to Congress*. Washington, DC: Office of Special Education Programs.

U.S. Department of Education, National Center for Education Statistics. (2009). *Indicators of school crime and safety: 2009*. Washington, DC: U.S. Government Printing Office.

U.S. Department of Education, National Center for Education Statistics. (2009). *The condition of education 2004* (NCES 2004-077). Washington, DC: U.S. Government Printing Office.

U.S. Department of Education, Office of Special Education Programs (2004). *Individuals with Disabilities Education Improvement Act of 2004*. Washington, DC

U.S. Department of Education, Office of Special Education Programs. (n.d.). *Child find*. Retrieved from http://www.childfindidea.org/

Valdez, K., Williamson, C., & Wagner, M. (1990). *The national longitudinal study of special education students. Statistical almanac: Vol. 3. Youth categorized as emotionally disturbed*. Menlo Park, CA: SRI International.

VanDerHeyden, A. M., & Snyder, P. (2006). Integrating frameworks from early childhood intervention and school psychology to accelerate growth for all young children. *School Psychology Review, 35*, 519–534.

Van Tassel-Baska, J. (2003). What matters in curriculum for gifted learners: Reflections on theory, research and productive giftedness. In N. Colangelo & G. Davis (Eds.), *Handbook on gifted education* (pp. 174–183). Boston, MA: Allyn & Bacon.

Van Tassel-Baska, J. (Ed.). (2004). *Curriculum of gifted and talented students*. Thousand Oaks, CA: Corwin Press.

Van Tassel-Baska, J. & Stamburgh, T. (2006). *Overlooked gems*. Washington, DC: National Association for Gifted Children.

Vaughn, S., & Fuchs, L. (2003). Redefining learning disabilities as inadequate response to instruction: The promise and potential problem. *Learning Disabilities Research and Practice, 18*(3), 137–146.

Vaughn, S., & Wanzek, J., & Denton, C. (2007). Teaching elementary students who experience difficulties in learning. In L. Florian (Ed.). *The Sage Handbook of Special Education*. London, England: Sage Publications, Ltd.

Vellutino, F. R., Scanlon, D. M., Sipay, E. R., Small, S. G., Pratt, A., Chen, R., et al. (1996). Cognitive profiles of difficult-to-remediate and readily remediated poor readers: Early intervention as a vehicle for distinguishing between cognitive and experiential deficits as basic cause of specific reading disability. *Journal of Educational Psychology, 88*(4), 601–638.

Villa, R. & Thousand, J. (1995). *Creating an inclusive school*. Alexandria, VA: Association for Society for Curriculum Development

Villegas, A. M., & Lucas, T. (2002). Preparing culturally responsive teachers: Rethinking the curriculum. *Journal of Teacher Education, 53*, 20–32.

Visual cortex. (2010, June 29). In Wikipedia, the free encyclopedia. Retrieved from en.wikipedia.org/wiki/visual_cortex

Voeltz, L. (1980). Children's attitudes toward handicapped peers. *American Journal of Mental Deficiency, 84*, 455–464.

Volkmar, F., Paul, R., Klin, A., & Cohen, D. (2007). *Handbook of autism and pervasive developmental disabilities* (3rd ed). New York, NY: Wiley.

Wachs, T. (2000). *Necessary but not sufficient*. Washington, DC: American Pyschological Association.

Wai, J., Lubinski, D., & Benbow, C. (2009). Spatial ability for STEM domains: Aligning over 50 years of cumulative psychological knowledge solidifies its importance. *Journal of Educational Psychology, 101*(4), 817–835.

Walker, H. M., Calvin, G., & Ramsey, E. (1995). *Antisocial behavior in school: Strategies and best practices*. Pacific Grove, CA: Brooks/Cole.

Wallace, T., Anderson A., Bartholomay, T., & Hupp, S. (2002). An ecobehavioral examination of high school classrooms that include students with disabilities. *Exceptional Children, 68*, 345–360.

Ward, D. (2008). The aetiology and treatment of developmental stammering in childhood. *Archives of Disease in Childhood, 93*, 68–71.

Ward, L., & McCune, S. (2002). The first weeks of life. In M. Batshaw (Ed.), *Children with disabilities* (5th ed., pp. 69–84). Baltimore, MD: Brookes.

Warren, F. (1985). Call them liars who would say all is well. In H. Turnbull & A. Turnbull (Eds.), *Parents speak out: Then and now*. Columbus, OH: Merrill.

Watson, A. H., Ito, M., Smith, R. O., & Anderson, L. T. (2010). Effort of assistive technology in a public school setting. *American Journal of Occupational Therapy, 64*(1), 18–29.

Watt, N., Wetherby, A. M., Barber, A., & Morgan, L. (2008). Repetitive and stereotyped behaviors in children with autism spectrum disorders in the second year of life. *Journal of Autism and Developmental Disorders, 38*, 15–18.

Waxman, R., Spencer, P., & Poisson, S. (1996). Interactions between mothers and deaf and hearing children. *Journal of Early Intervention, 20*(4), 341–355.

Webb, J., Gore, J., Amend, E., & DeVries, A. (2007). *A parent's guide to gifted children*. Scottsdale, AZ: Great Potential Press.

Wehmeyer, M. (2006). Self-determination and individuals with severe disabilities: Reexamining meanings and interpretations. *Research and Practice in Severe Disabilities, 30*, 113–120.

Wehmeyer, M., & Schwartz, M. (1998). The relationship between self-determination and quality of life. *Education and Training in Mental Retardation and Developmental Disabilities, 33*, 3–12.

Wehmeyer, M. L., Agran, M., & Hughes, C. (1998). *Teaching self-determination skills to students with disabilities*. Baltimore, MD: Brookes.

Weisz, J. (1999). Cognitive performance and learned helplessness in mentally retarded persons. In E. Zigler & D. Bennett-Gates (Eds.), *Personality development in individuals with mental retardation* (pp. 17–46). New York, NY: Cambridge University Press.

Werner, E. E. (2000). Protective factors and individual resilience. In J. P. Shonkoff & S. J. Meisels (Eds.), *Handbook of early childhood intervention* (2nd ed., pp. 115–132). New York, NY: Cambridge University Press.

Werner, E. E., & Smith, R. S. (1992). *Overcoming the odds: High risk children from birth to adulthood*. Ithaca, NY: Cornell University Press.

Werner, E. E., & Smith, R. S. (2001). *Journeys from childhood to midlife: Risk, resilience, and recovery*. Ithaca, NY: Cornell University Press.

Wery, J., & Nietfeld, J. (2010). Supporting self-regulated learning with exceptional children. *Teaching Exceptional Children, 42*(4), 70–78.

Westmaas, M. (2009). A mom's view on vision. *Division on Visual Impairments Quarterly, 54*(3), 9–11.

White, W., & Renzulli, J. (1987). A forty-year follow-up of students who attended Leta Hollingworth's school for gifted children. *Roeper Review, 10*(2), 89–94.

Whitten, E., Esteves, K., & Woodrow, A. (2009). *RTI success: Proven tools and strategies for schools and classrooms*. Minneapolis, MN: Free Spirit Book Publishing.

Wiener, N. (1953). *Exprodigy: My childhood and youth*. New York, NY: Simon and Schuster.

Williams, J. P. (2003). Teaching text structure to improve reading comprehension. In H. L. Swanson, K. R. Harris, & S. Graham (Eds.), *Handbook of learning disabilities* (pp. 293–305). New York, NY: Guilford Press.

Willingham, D. (2008). When and how neuroscience applies to education. *Phi Delta Kappan, 89*(6), 421–423.

Willis, J. (2008). Building a bridge from neuroscience to the classroom. *Phi Delta Kappan, 89*(6), 424–427.

Wilson, V., Little, J., Coleman, M., & Gallagher, J. (1997). Distance learning: One school's experience on the information highway. *The Journal for Secondary Gifted Education, IX*(2), 89–100.

Winerman, L. (2005). The mind's mirror. *Monitor on Psychology, 36*(9), 1–5.

Winton, P., & Buysse, V. (Eds.). (2004). Program evaluation. *Early Developments, 8*(3).

Winton, P., Buysse, V., & Hamrick, C. (Eds.). (2006). How FPG got its groove. *Early Developments, 10*(1).

Winton, P. J., McCollum, J. A., & Catlett, C. (2008). A framework and recommendation for a cross-agency professional development system. In P. J. Winton, J. A. McCollum, & C. Catlett (Eds.), *Practical approaches to early childhood professional development* (pp. 263–272). Washington, DC: Zero to Three National Center for Infants, Toddlers, and Families.

Wirt, J., Rooney, P., Choy, S., Provasnik, S., et al. (2004). *The condition of education 2004*. Washington, DC: National Center for Education Statistics.

Wolfe, P., & Brandt, R. (1998). What do we know from brain research? *Educational Leadership, 56*(3), 8–13.

Wolgemuth, J. R., Cobb, R. B., & Alwell, M. (2008). The effects of mnemonic interventions on academic outcomes for youth with disabilities: A systematic review. *Learning Disabilities Research & Practice, 23*(1), 1–10.

Wong, B. (Ed.). (2004). *Learning about learning disabilities* (3rd ed.). New York, NY: Academic Press.

Wong, B. Y. L., Harris, K. R., Graham, S., & Butler, D. L. (2003). Cognitive strategies instruction research in learning disabilities. In H. L. Swanson, K. R. Harris, & S. Graham (Eds.), *Handbook of learning disabilities* (pp. 383–402). New York, NY: Guilford Press.

Wood, L., Lasker, J., Siegel-Causey, E., Beukelman, D., & Ball, L. (1998). An input framework for augmentative and alternative communication. *Augmentative and Alternative Communication, 14*, 261–267.

Wunsch, M., Conlon, C., & Scheidt, L. (2002). Substance abuse: A preventable threat to child development. In M. Batshaw (Ed.), *Children with disabilities* (5th ed., pp. 107–122). Baltimore, MD: Brookes.

Wyner, J. S., Bridgeland, J. M., & Diiulio, J. J. (2009). *Achievementrap: How America is failing millions of high-achieving students from lower-income families*. A report from the Jack Kent Cooke Foundation. Retrieved from www.jkcf.org/assets/files/0000/0084/Achievement_Trap.pdf.

Yamaki, K., & Fugiura, G. (2002). Employment and income status of adults with developmental disabilities living in the community. *Mental Retardation, 40*(2), 132–144.

Yirmiya, N., Erel, O., Shaked, M., & Solomonica-Levi, D. (1998). Meta-analysis comparing theory of mind abilities of individuals with autism, individuals with mental retardation, and normally developing individuals. *Psychological Bulletin, 124*, 283–307.

Yoder, P., & Stone, W. (2006). Randomized comparison of two communication interventions for preschoolers with autism spectrum disorders. *Journal of Consulting and Clinical Psychology, 74*, 426–435.

Yoder, P., & Warren, S. (2004). Early predictors of language in children with and without Down syndrome. *American Journal of Mental Retardation, 109*, 285–300.

Yore, L. D., Anderson, J. O., & Shymansky, J. A. (2005). Sensing the impact of elementary school science reform: A study of stakeholder perceptions of implementation, constructivist strategies, and school-home collaboration. *Journal of Science Teacher Education, 16*, 65–88.

Yoshinaga-Itano, C., Sedey, A. L., Coulter, D. K., & Mehl, A. L. (1998). Language of early- and later-identified children with hearing loss. *Pediatrics, 102*(5), 1161–1171.

Zang, D., Katsiyannis, A., & Kortering, L. J. (2007). Performance on exit exams by students with disabilities: A four-year analysis. *Career Development for Exceptional Individuals, 30*(1), 48–57.

Zeitlin, S., & Williamson, G. (1994). *Coping in young children*. Baltimore, MD: Brookes.

Zero to Three. (2009). *Early Childhood Mental Health*. Retrieved from www.zerotothree.org/site/PageServer?pagename=key_mental_health

Zhao, Y. (2007). Speech technology and its potential for special education. *Journal of Special Education Technology, 22*(3), 35–41.

Zigler, E., Finn-Stevenson, M., & Hall, N. (2003). *The first three years and beyond: Brain development and social policy*. New Haven, CT: Yale University Press.

Zigler, E., & Styfco, S. (1993). Using research and theory to justify and inform Head Start expansion. *Society for Research in Child Development, 7*(2), 11–19.

Zigler, E., & Styfco, S. (2004). Head Start's national reporting system: A work in progress. *Pediatrics, 114*, 858–859.

Zimmerman, B. J., & Schunk, D. H. (2008). Motivation: An essential dimension of self-regulated learning. In D. Schunk & B. J. Zimmerman (Eds) *Motivation and self-regulated learning: Theory, research, and applications* (p. 1–30). New York/London: Lawrence Erlbaum Associates.

Zimmerman, G. J., Zebehazy, K. T., & Moon, M. L. (2010). Optics and low vision devices. In A. Corn & J. Erin (Eds.), *Foundations of low vision: Clinical and functional perspectives* (2nd ed., pp. 192–237). New York, NY: American Foundation for the Blind.

Zwaigenbaum, L., Thurm, A., Stone, W., Baranek, G., Bryson, S., Iverson, J., et al. (2007). Studying the emergence of autism spectrum disorders in high-risk infants: Methodological and practical issues. *Journal of Autism and Developmental Disorders, 37*, 466–480.

Subject Index

Name Index

What Every Special Educator Must Know and Be Able to Do: The CEC Core Standards

The standards for our field define the knowledge and skills needed to practice professionally. We present here a shortened form of the CEC core standards. On the textbook website we give the full standard and the set of knowledge and skills that accompany each of these standards. You may wish to go to the website and print a full set of the knowledge and skills so that you can reflect on these as you monitor your learning and experiences.

Standard #1: Foundations of Special Education	Special educators understand the field as an evolving and changing discipline based on philosophies, evidence-based principles and theories, relevant laws and policies, and historical points of view. Special educators understand how issues of human diversity can impact families, cultures, and schools, and how these complex human issues can interact with the delivery of special education services. Special educators use this knowledge as a ground upon which to construct their own personal understandings and philosophies of special education.
Standard #2: Development and Characteristics of Learners	Special educators know and demonstrate respect for their students first as unique human beings; understanding the similarities and differences in human development and the characteristics between and among individuals with and without exceptional learning needs. Special educators understand how the experiences of individuals with exceptional learning needs can impact families, as well as the individual's ability to learn, interact socially, and live as fulfilled contributing members of the community.
Standard #3: Individual Learning Differences	Special educators understand the effects that an exceptional condition can have on an individual's learning in school and throughout life. Special educators understand that the beliefs, traditions, and values across and within cultures can affect relationships among and between students, their families, and the school community. The understanding of these learning differences and their possible interactions provides the foundation upon which special educators individualize instruction to provide meaningful and challenging learning for individuals with exceptional learning needs.
Standard #4: Instructional Strategies	Special educators possess a repertoire of evidence-based instructional strategies to individualize instruction for persons with exceptional learning needs. Special educators select, adapt, and use these instructional strategies to promote positive learning results in general and special curricula and to appropriately modify learning environments for individuals with exceptional learning needs. They enhance the learning of critical thinking, problem-solving, and performance skills of individuals with exceptional learning needs, and increase their self-awareness, self-management, self-control, self-reliance, and self–esteem. Moreover, special educators emphasize the development, maintenance, and generalization of knowledge and skills across environments, settings, and the lifespan.
Standard #5: Learning Environments and Social Interactions	Special educators actively create learning environments for individuals with exceptional learning needs that foster cultural understanding, safety and emotional well-being, positive social interactions, and active engagement of individuals with exceptional learning needs. Special educators shape environments to encourage the independence, self-motivation, self-direction, personal empowerment, and self-advocacy of individuals with exceptional learning needs.

CEC Code of Ethics for Educators of Individuals with Exceptionalities

The following principles form the Code of Ethics for educators who serve individuals with exceptionalities. Special education professionals are responsible for upholding and advancing these principles. Members of the Council for Exceptional Children agree to judge and be judged by them in accordance with the spirit and provisions of this Code.

A. Special education professionals are committed to developing the highest educational for and quality of life potential of individuals with exceptionalities.

B. Special education professionals promote and maintain a high level of competence and integrity in practicing their profession.

C. Special education professionals engage in professional activities which benefit individuals with exceptionalities, their families, other colleagues, students, or research subjects.

D. Special education professionals exercise objective professional judgment in the practice of their profession.

E. Special education professionals strive to advance their knowledge and skills regarding the education of individuals with exceptionalities.

F. Special education professionals work within the standards and policies of their profession.

G. Special education professionals seek to uphold and improve where necessary the laws, regulations, and policies governing the delivery of special education and related services and the practice of their profession.

H. Special education professionals do not condone or participate in unethical or illegal acts, nor violate professional standards adopted by the Delegate Assembly of CEC.